The Work of Empire

JUSTIN F. JACKSON

The Work of Empire

War, Occupation, and the
Making of American Colonialism
in Cuba and the Philippines

The University of North Carolina Press *Chapel Hill*

© 2025 The University of North Carolina Press
All rights reserved
Set in Arno Pro by Westchester Publishing Services
Manufactured in the United States of America

Library of Congress Cataloging-in-Publication Data
Names: Jackson, Justin F., author.
Title: The work of empire : war, occupation, and the making of American colonialism in Cuba and the Philippines / Justin F. Jackson.
Description: Chapel Hill : The University of North Carolina Press, [2025] | Includes bibliographical references and index.
Identifiers: LCCN 2024045134 | ISBN 9781469660318 (cloth) | ISBN 9781469660325 (paperback) | ISBN 9781469660332 (epub) | ISBN 9781469680279 (pdf)
Subjects: LCSH: United States. Army—Management. | United States. Army—Officials and employees. | Local officials and employees—Political aspects. | Foreign workers, Chinese—Political aspects. | United States—Insular possessions—Administration—History—19th century. | United States—Insular possessions—Administration—History—20th century. | Cuba—History—1895– | Cuba—History—1899-1906. | Philippines—History—1898-1946. | BISAC: HISTORY / Military / General | SOCIAL SCIENCE / Ethnic Studies / Caribbean & Latin American Studies
Classification: LCC F970 .J33 2025 | DDC 973.8/91—dc23/eng/20241206
LC record available at https://lccn.loc.gov/2024045134

Cover art: *Giving Directions to Major Howard at Calumpit*, General Lawton in the Philippines, May –December 1899, Box 20, William Dinwiddie Papers, US Army Heritage and Education Center; lined paper, 1902, Wilbur Wright and Orville Wright papers, 1809–1979, Library of Congress, Manuscript Division.

This book will be made open access within three years of publication thanks to Path to Open, a program developed in partnership between JSTOR, the American Council of Learned Societies (ACLS), University of Michigan Press, and The University of North Carolina Press to bring about equitable access and impact for the entire scholarly community, including authors, researchers, libraries, and university presses around the world. Learn more at https://about.jstor.org/path-to-open/

For product safety concerns under the European Union's General Product Safety Regulation (EU GPSR), please contact gpsr@mare-nostrum.co.uk or write to the University of North Carolina Press and Mare Nostrum Group B.V., Mauritskade 21D, 1091 GC Amsterdam, The Netherlands.

*This book is dedicated to my mother, and the
the memory of my father, and my godfather, Paul Daiute,
who knew the costs of empire.*

Sovereignty is not synonymous with freedom, autonomy, and self-determination. On the contrary, sovereignty is always a mechanism for one class to rule over others; it always carries a colonial relation at its heart.

—Hardt and Negri, *Assembly*

Freedom begins with sovereignty, and sovereignty has to do with bodies.

—Snyder, *On Freedom*

Contents

List of Illustrations ix

INTRODUCTION
Questions of Labor: Making War, Colonialism, and Sovereignty in the US Empire of 1898 1

Part I
Knowledge

CHAPTER ONE
Occupied Constantly and Worked to Death: Military-Colonial Intermediaries and the Political Economy of Counterinsurgency 23

CHAPTER TWO
Bearing Soldiers' Burdens: The Scientific Management of Sovereignty and Subaltern Labor 63

Part II
Infrastructure

CHAPTER THREE
An Army of Workmen: The *Polista* Politics of Military-Colonial Public Works 109

CHAPTER FOUR
Always through the Datto: Building Roads and Subcontracted Sovereignty in Mindanao and Pinar del Río 152

Part III
Bodies

CHAPTER FIVE
The Chinese Experiment: Race, Labor, and Migration in the Army's Empire of Exclusion 193

CHAPTER SIX
Military Necessities: Reproducing Sovereignty in the Colonial Sexual Economy of War 233

EPILOGUE
The Days of the Empire: Forgetting the Legacies of War's Work in the 1898 Era 271

Acknowledgments 281

Notes 285

Bibliography 339

Index 381

Illustrations

FIGURES

A Scout Hiding under Palm Leaves 31

Municipal Home Rule for the Filipinos 47

Moro Cargadores, Malabang, P.I., Feb. 1905 98

Moro Cargadores Packed for the March 99

Pigeon Dick, a Perfect Cargadore Type 103

Santiago, Cuba. Building Road to San Juan Battlefield 116

General Wood and Other Officials at the Review of the Street Cleaning Department on the Alameda 124

A Roadman and His Tools 151

A Conference of State with Moro Chiefs 166

Moros Working with Americans upon the Road 168

Road Work by Capt. Smith, Corps of Engineers, U.S.A. 185

Malolos. Chinese Litter Bearers Used by Medical Department Accompanying the Expedition. March 1899 208

Statement of Coal Handled by Contracts, Chinese Labor, and Filipino Laborers, July 1, 1901, to June 30, 1902, Army Transport Service, Manila, P.I. 222

"Quanto Valo" Scene in Camp of the 16th Infantry, P.I. 255

MAPS

I.1 Cuba, 1898 6

I.2 Philippines, 1898 7

1.1 Santiago Province, Cuba, 1898 29

1.2 Central and Southern Luzon, Philippines, 1898 37

1.3 Northern Luzon, Philippines, 1898 52

2.1 Mindanao and the Sulu Archipelago, Philippines, 1899 86

4.1 The Lanao Country, Mindanao, Philippines, 1902 155

4.2 Pinar del Río Province, Cuba, 1906 180

The Work of Empire

INTRODUCTION

Questions of Labor
Making War, Colonialism, and Sovereignty in the US Empire of 1898

General Hugh Lenox Scott, an intelligent man, knew empire building was hard work, but he was not always clear about who did it. Born in 1853, the Kentucky native cultivated a curiosity, rare in his army, about the foreigners he fought and ruled at his nation's shifting frontiers. Managing Native American scouts, he learned indigenous sign languages; occupying Cuba after the 1898 war with Spain, he collected curios of colonial war and repression; and by 1903, he enriched his knowledge of "inferior races," as he described them, among Islamic Moros in the southern Philippines. In 1906, he returned to the states to teach a modernizing Progressive Era army as the new superintendent of his alma mater, West Point. Scott promoted enlightened military paternalism wherever and whenever possible. Addressing graduates of Harvard's military training program in 1909, he enthused that some would "go almost at once to the tropics to assist in carrying the 'white man's burden.'" Yet Scott warned they would succeed in this task only if they approached "the native with a sympathetic attitude of liberality endeavoring to put yourself in his place." Whether undertaking "command of armies or the governorship of peoples," these young men, he advised, were expected to honor gentlemanly virtues and dispense "unfailing justice," "especially to weaker and dependent peoples."[1]

For all Scott's erudition and empathy, however, he never entertained the possibility that "weaker" and "dependent" peoples themselves may have contributed to the United States' recent record in warfare and rule abroad. During speeches to alumni associations and the patrician Society of Colonial Wars in 1908 and 1909, the general mystified the agents of his military's civilizing mission. Boasting that Cuba and the Philippines had received "peace and a strong uplift to education, commerce, agriculture, and good government," Scott attributed this triumph solely to his troops' "years of incessant labor." Such beneficence, he suggested, made their nation exceptional, distinguishing it from Europe's extractive empires in Asia and Africa. Americans neither exploited Cuba nor retained it as a colony. Instead, declared Scott, Yankee soldiers handed the island back to its people, "with new roads, light and school houses," its "first public library," "300,000 children in school," "one million of dollars in the Treasury, and a government national, provincial, and municipal constructed by Cubans." The general believed an equally benign occupation had elevated Moros, whom most Americans regarded as savages. In the southern Philippines, he related, "slavery has been put down," "schools are established in many places," and "agriculture and commerce have multiplied many times." Across the archipelago, cheered Scott, US troops left new "schools, roads, and railroads," ensured that "epidemics [would] no longer run their course," and kept its people "at peace with one another."[2]

Scott's old boss at Havana, Gen. Leonard Wood, shared his roseate view of their army's accomplishments in the tropics, but at least he recognized that its soldiers had often relied on others to achieve them. Wood presided over his nation's ascent to great-power status in late July 1898 at Santiago de Cuba, when a victorious campaign to seize the city, made jointly with separatist insurgents, culminated in his appointment as Santiago's military governor. Imposing an occupation over Cuban nationalists' objections, Yankee generals had already angered Liberation Army counterparts by insisting they furnish men for manual labor and excluding them from surrender talks. Now, in a region devastated by a three-year-long war that had killed some 200,000 Cubans and ravaged the island's agricultural economy, Wood added insult to injury by tying humanitarian relief to work. To sanitize Santiago as yellow fever and other diseases sickened and killed Cuban civilians, Spanish prisoners, and American troops, the general leveraged his army's monopoly over food, declaring he would ration able-bodied men only if they helped its soldiers clean the city.[3]

Santiago's new alcalde, Emilio Bacardí y Moreau, recognized this militarized coercion's imperial dimensions. Heir to the region's rum dynasty and an ardent patriot, Bacardí, like many Cubans of his generation, tried to reconcile the bitterness of national independence deferred with US domination's economic opportunities. In his inaugural speech, Bacardí took credit for ending the Yankees' "forced labor." At the same time, he endorsed their plans to "encourage the material development of the population" through public works that he welcomed as a means to give "employment to those who need it most." In Wood's opinion, these were thousands of unpaid and starving insurgents outside the city, ready to contest what *independentistas* feared and many Americans hoped would be annexation. Bacardí watched Wood neutralize the Liberation Army by tying survival to sweat. He offered the rebels jobs on streets and roads—if they abandoned their regiments. Pacification, Wood understood, was "a question of labor."[4]

Two years later, Filipinos used American soldiers' draconian labor demands against them, dealing a stunning blow to their counterinsurgency efforts. On the Visayan island of Samar in August 1901, a Ninth US Infantry company occupied Balangiga, a coastal municipality of some 2,000 souls. Making their livelihoods impossible by confiscating crops, livestock, and fishing supplies without compensation, the Americans ordered seventy men to make the town orderly, sanitary, and defensible by cleaning streets and homes, but did not feed or pay them. At night, soldiers packed them into two sweltering conical tents designed to accommodate no more than thirty-two people, making sleep impossible. When US troops sought more workers by invoking a moribund corvée, Eugenio Daza, a thirty-year-old schoolteacher-turned-guerrilla captain, made it a Trojan horse. Sending dozens of *voluntarios* feigning as pliant laborers, Daza years later marveled that his enemies had never suspected their loyalties. How, he asked, could they have thought the "only object" of such a "large number of men" was to cut "weeds and herbs"?[5]

Forced labor proved fatal. On September 28, as the Americans breakfasted in Balangiga's plaza, children rang church bells to signal some 200 pretend laborers gathered nearby. Suddenly, armed with bolos they had used to beautify the town, they attacked. Of some seventy-four US troops, only twenty-six escaped the lopsided melee; most of them succumbed to mortal injuries, inflicted as they ran and swam for their lives. By contrast, only twenty-eight of Daza's several hundred assailants perished. Generals at Manila, deeming it a "massacre," retaliated harshly. Sending in the marines, they burned Balangiga to the ground; only the church bells, seized as trophies, were spared. Daza surrendered, but a few years later he recruited men, including Balangiga veterans, to repress a new rebellion against US rule. Americans rewarded Daza with a seat in a new Filipino legislature.[6]

Scott's oratorical obfuscation, Wood's disciplinary pacification, Bacardí's protest, and Daza's revenge each evoke this book's central claim. American soldiers' attempts to utilize Cuban and Filipino labor during their war with Spain in 1898, and subsequent wars and occupations, produced an imperial politics of sovereignty that determined Americans' colonialism in these islands and US military reform itself. Whether they guided or translated for American troops, cleaned or built city streets and rural highways, or carried supplies and sold sex, ordinary Cubans and Filipinos enabled the martial activity that made the United States a world power by the dawn of the twentieth century. In turn, this work of empire decisively shaped Americans' colonial project in the Philippines and neocolonial relations with Cuba, leaving lasting imprints on insular societies and states. Cuban and Filipino labor for US armies reshaped these islands' politics and influenced their transitions to new capitalist economies. As an expression of Americans' military colonialism, this work of empire creatively fused and transformed metropolitan and colonial cultures, including hierarchies, discourses, and identities of race and ethnicity, gender, and nation. Yet the myriad tensions that accompanied this work also constrained the United States' sovereignty and contributed to its undoing. The politics of the labor its military needed to wage wars and govern foreigners in the 1898 era made and unmade Americans' imperial power.

IF SCHOLARS KNOW THAT empire and sovereignty are intertwined, what these essentially political ideas and phenomena have to do with work, or workers, is less certain. Originating in ancient Rome, *imperium* initially referred to the legal right of kings and republican consuls to punish and execute citizens and conscript and command them for war; only later did empire mean a ruler's right to govern other lands and their inhabitants. Modernity, at least in Europe, both expressed and obscured this imperial genealogy of sovereignty by transferring its locus to a new kind of state: the nation-state. During the seventeenth century, European elites made the formal recognition of each state's right to make its own internal policy, free from other states' interference, into a new basis of diplomatic relations: "territorial" sovereignty. By locating the authority for this territorially sacrosanct state in the newly imagined nation itself, Europeans birthed the concept of "popular" sovereignty. That they simultaneously these same rights to Americans, Asians, and Africans while seizing their lands and labor surely reveals the coterminous historical career of imperial and national sovereignties. Yet revolutions in North America, France, and Haiti transformed nationalism from a mode of imperial ambition into a powerful new force fueling challenges to empire. This world-historical event has prompted scholars to distinguish empires from nations. Whereas the former imposed and accepted rigidly unequal political hierarchies across culturally differentiated spaces and subjects, the latter seek political uniformity by extending equal citizenship to a culturally homogenized people across a single territory. In these two kinds of states, sovereignty itself seems discrepant. Whereas empires involve "asymmetries," "degrees," or "gradations" of sovereignty between a dominant metropole and subordinate peripheries, nations aspire to undivided sovereignty in their territory while making that principle the basis for world order.[7]

If such categorical distinctions help historians recognize the United States' relations with Cuba and the Philippines beginning in 1898 as imperial in nature, their familiar narratives of American empire tend to associate sovereignty exclusively with "national" polities and nation-state elites. This approach has the merit of acknowledging that US interventions in anticolonial revolutions ended with more than just victory over Spain; they imposed Americans' control on islands already claimed by Cuban and Filipino nationalists. Colonized in the sixteenth century, both Cuba and the Philippines during the late nineteenth century were rocked by vibrant movements demanding reforms and autonomy from Spain, which, by the 1860s, inspired separatist insurrection in Cuba. Yet most Americans seemed ambivalent about Madrid's aging empire and its colonial critics. Indeed, as sugar plantations in Cuba—fueled by the labor of enslaved Africans and indentured Chinese—generated extraordinary wealth, some fantasized about annexing the island. After the United States abolished slavery in 1865, many Cubans idolized the country as a model for the prosperous, progressive, and free republic that Spain denied them. In turn, some Americans supported Cubans three years later when they rebelled. Though separatists would eventually lose what became known as the Ten Years' War, revolution pushed Spain to alter imperial policy; colonial authorities, among other changes, emancipated Cuba's slaves by 1886. These events inspired parallel protests in the Philippines. Here by the 1880s, educated *indio* and mestizo elites, styling themselves as "enlightened ones," or *ilustrados*, fashioned their own national identity while advocating liberal reforms. More revolts ensued, first in Cuba in 1895, then in the Philippines the following year. Before José Martí and José Rizal became national icons as martyrs who perished while heroically resisting Spain, however, these activist intellectuals fretted about the intentions of the United States, an industrializing expansionist behemoth. Yet surviving Cuban and Filipino leaders, both soldiers and civilians, still craved Americans' support.[8]

By the end of 1898, much to these revolutionaries' dismay, US invaders who had just helped them defeat a common Spanish enemy now refused to recognize their nation-states. Americans both disclaimed and declared imperial intents. With the passage of the Teller Amendment in April 1898, President William McKinley (a Republican) and a Republican-dominated Congress repudiated annexing Cuba to gain Democratic support and financing for war against Spain. As US navies and armies attacked Spanish fleets and soldiers overseas, McKinley's administration, deeming Cubans and Filipinos not sufficiently civilized to rule themselves, ignored nationalists' putative regimes. It refused to recognize Cuban separatists' provisional government, backed by exiles' revolutionary junta in New York. It also disregarded the regime that Gen. Emilio Aguinaldo declared at Cavite, near Manila, in June 1898, two years after the Katipunan, a nationalist secret society, rose up against Spain. By December,

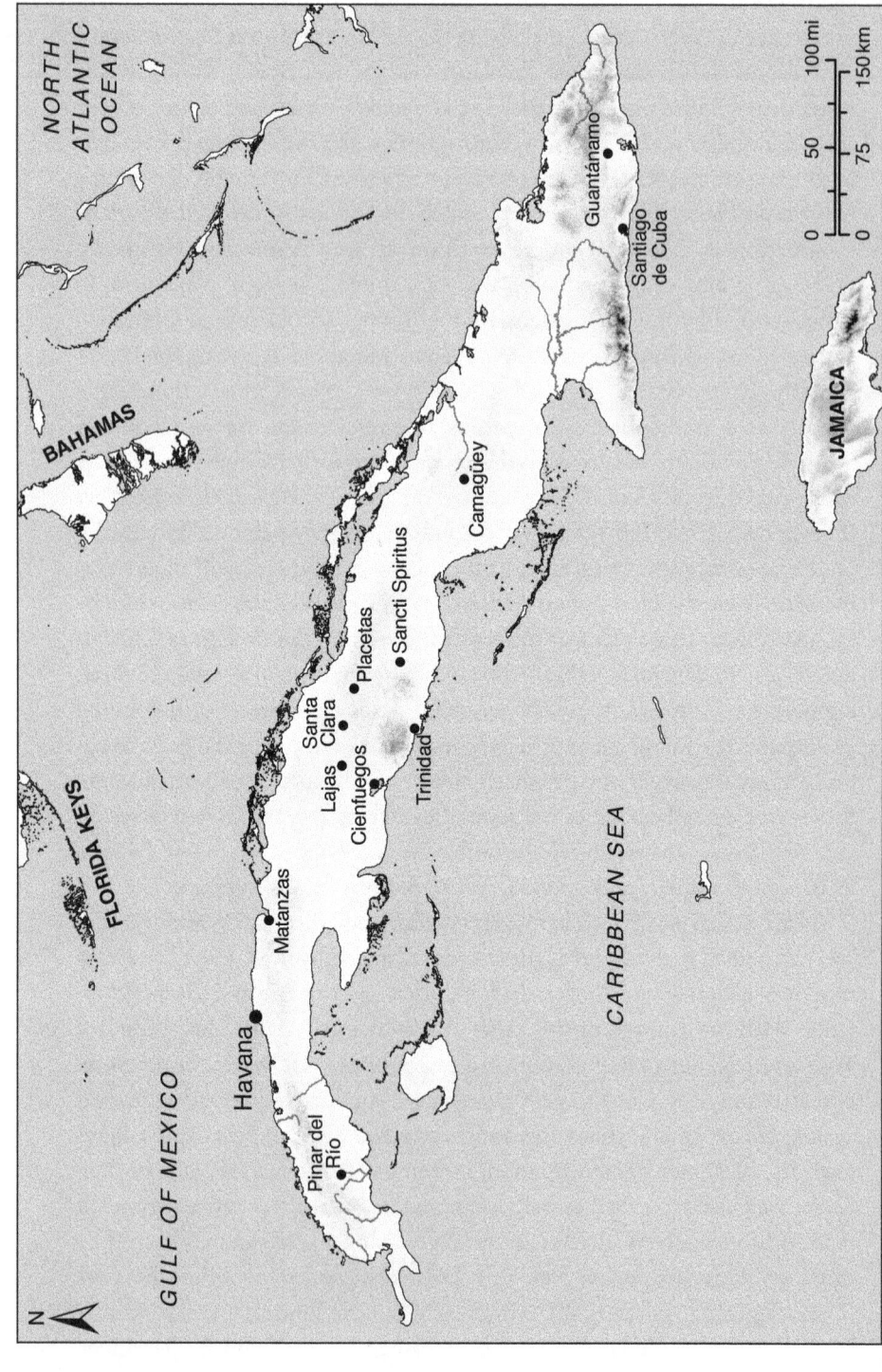

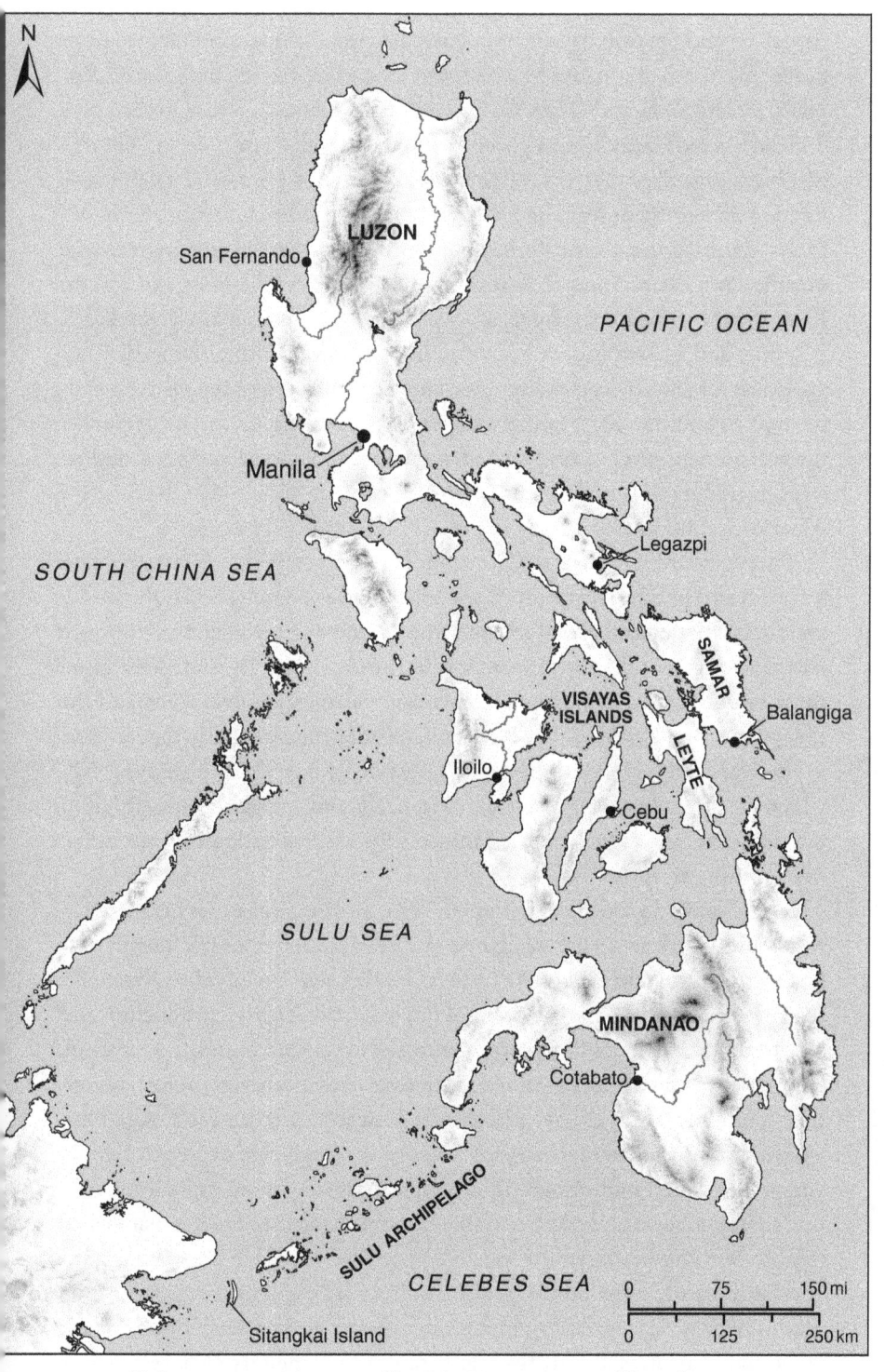

MAP I.2 Philippines, 1898. Map created by Gabe Moss, courtesy of the author.

American and Spanish diplomats at Paris, barring Cubans and Filipinos from peace talks, signed a treaty in which the United States acquired the Philippines, Puerto Rico, and Guam for $20 million. Americans also agreed to govern Cuba temporarily, until a government able to safeguard "life and liberty" had been organized. Yet US officials who regarded Cubans and Filipinos as inferior denied them legal or political equality within an expanded United States, granting them only limited and localized sovereignty. Congressional organic laws establishing civil governments in the Philippines and Puerto Rico, and the so-called Insular Cases decided by the Supreme Court, excluded Filipinos and Puerto Ricans from statehood and citizenship. By 1902, Congress also forced Cuba's constitutional convention to accept the Platt Amendment as a condition of its formal independence. Making Cuba a protectorate, the amendment severely constrained the new republic's sovereignty in several ways, including by authorizing the US government to invade in the future if Americans thought it necessary to protect their lives and properties.[9]

This standard narrative of US empire, and its emphasis on national and international political institutions and elites, leaves unaddressed how society and social relations may have affected empire's layered sovereignties—or been affected by them. Like Hugh Scott, it veils the ideas, activity, and identities of those whose work also facilitated Americans' sovereignty over Cuba and the Philippines, and challenged it. It fails to consider the possibility that empire, in the words of historian Julie Greene, has often been "a modality through which class was lived, experienced, organized, and struggled through." Empire building, she argues, "placed the control and regulation of labor at the heart of the enterprise."[10]

In this spirit, a growing literature on labor and empire invites historians to revisit how work and workers figured in this conjuncture of US foreign relations and Cuban and Philippine history. Yet this scholarship often overlooks the labor that occurred at the point of imperial sovereignty's production and reproduction itself: military power, expressed in war and occupation. Instead, labor's ties to empire are examined in contests over "domestic" political economy and diplomacy; clashes between American capital and non-American workers abroad; or border-crossing flows of working-class migrants, culture, and politics. Such studies address venerable questions about capitalism's relation to imperialism and transcend them, scrutinizing how empire manifested in labor relations beyond those touched by territorialized US state sovereignty. Yet this literature often misses how the militarized elaboration and operation of sovereignty so central to empire's expansion and contraction was itself work. Even histories of early twentieth-century US military enclaves, such as the Panama Canal Zone or the Guantánamo naval base, unintentionally abstract the labor of empire from the violence of imperial formation, leaving underinvestigated the material underpinnings of warfare and its politics. Labor was essential to US empire not for producing commodities or trade unionism but for generating the coercive state capacity that imperial and national elites required to assert and maintain sovereignty. The only fetish involved in this labor was force, or the fiction that military action alone ensured peoples' assent to authority. Emperors may dream of having empires, settlers may prepare them, and capitalists may exploit them, yet armies and navies—and today, air forces—establish, defend, and lose them through a kind of "violence work" roughly comparable to policing.[11]

Nevertheless, as Leonard Wood and Emilio Bacardí appreciated, soldiers rarely build empires by themselves. In the 1898 era, the US military's dependence on local labor and other resources to wage war and occupation insinuated especially martial imperatives into Americans' civilizing mission in Cuba and the Philippines, part of a historical phenomenon best described as "military colonialism." By emphasizing how wars and occupations affected the changing relations between colonizers and colonized that determined imperial formation, a concept of military colonialism enables scholars to make US empire legible as a labor process. The extraordinary amount of work that American troops exacted from thousands of Cubans and Filipinos over more than a decade could not have failed to shape their nation's colonial projects and their effects on these islands' societies, polities, and cultures. Yankee troops invaded Cuba twice before governing it over extended durations, with the Military Government from late 1898 to early 1902, and with the Provisional Government from late 1906 to early 1909. In the Philippines, US troops backed a military regime and fought insurgents in Luzon and the Visayas until mid-1902, when Theodore Roosevelt, president after McKinley's assassination, declared victory. A permanent US garrison clashed with rebels on Samar and Moros in the south, where American generals ruled until 1913. At every step, war and occupation hinged on US soldiers' exploitation of Cubans and Filipinos. Their labor power, that most fundamental element of everyday life, acted as an engine for colonizing by martial means.[12]

Studying military colonialism in the 1898 era revises a historiography that often narrates the Spanish-American War and its outcomes from metropolitan-centered questions about how a weak federal state became strong by new trade, diplomacy, and wars beyond North America. A social and political history of war and occupation rooted in colonial histories, by contrast, asks how work and workers at the kinetic boundaries of US expansion influenced this military-institutional transformation. In 1898, the "old army," woefully unprepared and under-resourced for its new global missions, had to exploit colonial labor to execute them. Early that year, the regular army seemed little more than a frontier constabulary, scattered in garrisons throughout the US West. Reformers attempting to modernize both it and the War Department considered them disorganized and sclerotic institutions hobbled by an antiquated republican citizen-soldier tradition. War with Spain seemed to confirm their criticism. Confused planning, a chaotic mobilization of 275,000 wartime volunteers, and jumbled overland and overseas transport disrupted the war, and neglect of supply and sanitation sickened troops, scandalizing the public and sparking congressional investigations. Army commands in Cuba and the Philippines never exceeded 70,000 troops in either place. A minimalist and hidebound military acquiring and running empire on the cheap thus had to exploit colonial labor in order to vanquish Spanish enemies, subdue insurgents, govern 9 million people, and rebuild shattered economies. Of course, military historians have long recognized how these conflicts spurred progressive reforms. By 1899, Secretary of War Elihu Root, inspired by European militaries and industrializing America's managerial revolution, increased the regular army's size, established service colleges and a general staff, and tightened federal control over state militias. American soldiers also made a "new army" capable of garrisoning Cuba and the Philippines as well as Puerto Rico, Hawai'i, and the Panama Canal, however, by exploiting their labor.[13]

If historians now recognize how the US Army had a crucial "multi-purpose" role in nineteenth-century settler and capitalist expansion at the United States' territorial boundaries in North America, this study suggests that war and occupation extended that function to new frontiers on others' backs. The labor of 1898 therefore marked both continuity and rupture in a longer history of US empire. To be sure, men who waged "irregular" warfare against Native Americans in the trans-Mississippi West brought "Indian fighting" to the Philippines, as well as a racialized knowledge of indigenous and Latin peoples which they transposed on Cubans and Filipinos. Still, few regular officers, most of them superannuated, had any experience in civil government, acquired in the US South during the Civil War and Reconstruction. Commanders such as Hugh Scott and Leonard Wood never ruled Native Americans directly but only "policed" them on behalf of a civilian Interior Department and its Indian Bureau. The army's metamorphosis thus crystallized in its soldiers' encounters with colonial labor, as empire welded Americans' ways of war and work.[14]

Military colonizing in Cuba and the Philippines also left martial imprints on insular capitalist economies and political economies. By the 1890s to varying degrees, liberalizing Spanish reforms had integrated these colonies into world markets, encouraging the agricultural-export and extractive industries on which these islands had already become dependent. Spain's empire further stunted dynamic economic development by investing little in public goods and promoting tax and trade policies that enriched few beyond planters, merchants, and Madrid (and, in the Philippines, the church). Scholars have amply documented the ambiguity of US occupations' economic policies, which reinforced this economic path dependency in some ways and disrupted it in others. Anti-monopolists and anti-imperialists in the US Congress barred generals in Cuba from leasing public franchises to foreigners; in the Philippines, they limited the amount of land Americans and other investors could purchase and mandated a silver currency. Military governors claiming to respect the rights and interests of occupied peoples and seeking to avoid appearances of corruption rarely acted at the behest of particular American firms.[15]

Despite tensions in US military regimes' policy, however, their exploitation of tropical labor ultimately consolidated colonial trends in insular capitalist economies that favored wealthier landowners and foreign businessmen at the expense of poorer peasants and workers. To be sure, American troops, often celebrating a national mission to emancipate colonized peoples and civilize them through capital accumulation, appropriated their labor not to secure profits but to win wars, pacify insurgents, and alleviate humanitarian crises. Yet the coercive methods by which these soldiers frequently mobilized Cuban and Filipino workers reflected not just martial imperatives but the weight of colonial and global imperial pasts in which Europeans and Americans often forced economic change on others. Soldiers' compulsion of poor Cuban men, including separatist veterans, became the postwar precondition for an agricultural-industrial recovery, shifting land and other property into American hands. In the Philippines, militarized labor conscription expanded markets in wage labor and agricultural commodities, reinforcing the socio-economic dominance of Filipino landlords and Moro elites. In both colonies, a US Army serving as the employer of last resort pushed workers to rehabilitate colonial capitalisms in ways that ultimately benefited elites much more than the poor.[16]

THIS HISTORY OF MILITARY COLONIALISM recognizes the labor of the Cubans and Filipinos who toiled for American soldiers as a human crucible of imperial formation by adopting what sociologist Julian Go defines as the "subaltern standpoint." By studying change from the relational "geopolitical and social position" of subordinated "peripheral groups ... within global imperial hierarchies," in Go's formulation, this bottom-up and outside-in perspective helps illuminate how empire and society constituted each other over time. A subaltern history of US empire also invites scholars to provincialize class, at least as it is usually theorized in the Global North. Labor relations particular to colonial war and occupation rarely resembled those between workers and employers in industrial-capitalist metropoles. If "class consciousness" remains the lodestar of working-class politics among some labor historians, the subjectivity of subalterns working for US troops, this book contends, cohered in a politics of sovereignty. Exploring why and how militarized work configured Americans' colonialism and neocolonialism in these islands thus offers a necessary counterpoint to narratives that tend to locate empire exclusively or essentially in the top-down decision-making and discourse of various state elites. It treats a subaltern multitude—including American enlisted men who performed "military labor"—as historical subjects and objects relative to imperial and colonial elites who tried to control them and contested colonial workspaces. It also challenges a dualist epistemology in social and national histories that poses a false dichotomy between "collaboration" and "resistance." Instead, this book recognizes empire as a shifting set of relations constituted by dynamic processes of cooperation and conflict.[17]

This method stages several interventions in historiography. The first stresses the subaltern quality of military-colonial labor as a gesture meant to challenge normative categories of "the worker" or the "working class." As Hugh Scott's speeches suggest, his army's exploitation of Cubans and Filipinos rested on a sense shared by European, American, and colonial elites that the tropical poor were sociocultural inferiors not to be trusted with self-rule, much less economic freedom or resources. In the fin de siècle epoch of monopoly capital, high imperialism, and scientific racism, ordinary Cubans and Filipinos emerging from slavery and peonage seemed to exist at the margins of civilizing global currents of bourgeois modernity. American soldiers' concepts of race and ethnicity, gender, religious beliefs, and industrial technology joined class as forces that primed them to see these laborers as exotic others. Americans constructed the Cuban and Filipino subaltern by juxtaposing them against the "modern" worker idealized in a metropolitan mold: the free white male breadwinner, earning wages to support himself and female and child dependents in urban manufacturing. Often former slaves or indebted peasants in rural areas, Cubans and Filipinos toiling for the US military were more like sailors, convicts, or soldiers, existing in a liminal state between the presumably antithetical archetypes of "free" laborer and unfree chattel slave. As Eugenio Daza appreciated, Americans' perception that such men and women passively tolerated not only colonization but unwaged labor and the social domination of rural landowning elites increased their vulnerability to militarized coercion. Cubans and Filipinos working for US troops thus joined the many other kinds of unfree labor that pervaded economic life beyond industrializing metropoles in the late nineteenth century, as an imperial world moved tectonically toward work exchanged voluntarily for wages. Indeed, as some American laborers gained more legal freedoms via state regulation of industrial workplaces in this era, military colonization allowed US soldiers to turn tropical islands into laboratories for experiments in labor coercion that many workers no longer tolerated at home.[18]

A second intervention applies alternative theories of sovereignty, the problem at the center of US military colonialism's peculiar labor politics. Scholarship that would conceive sovereignty as an essentially statist phenomenon, involving elites' capacity to determine conduct within a polity's territory without external legal constraint, cannot explain the total social history of imperial formation in the 1898 era. The subterranean history of military colonizing reconstructed here suggests that claims to effective sovereignty proliferated beyond the formal legal and institutional parameters of states and the elites who decided their official acts. Thus, political scientists' concept of "social sovereignty" best captures how struggles over the right to rule labor in war-torn and occupied Cuba and the Philippines often transpired in the absence of substantive US, Cuban, and Filipino state sovereignties. Amid the turmoil of imperial transition, colonial elites excluded from imperial and nationalist governments, or marginalized within them, often asserted an informal but meaningful effective sovereignty over subalterns. Even relatively powerless Cuban and Filipino workers and American enlisted men themselves pursued what might be described as a "subaltern sovereignty" over their own lives and labor in self-activity not always recognizably nationalist in origin or character. Subalterns' attempts to control their work, and that of others, often revealed not a logic of the nation-state but rather a mélange of quotidian personal motives, from survival and security to status and profit. Indeed, various state elites frequently asserted authority over labor in response to subaltern claims to "sovereignty from below."[19]

Attending to the alternative sovereignties surfacing in empire's work sheds new light on social tensions inside elite-led anticolonial nationalist projects, which often tended to idealize sovereignty in Eurocentric statist terms. By the

1890s, leading Cuban and Filipino separatists, absorbing liberal and republican politics and adapting them to anticolonial ends, premised the fulfillment of popular sovereignty on states that would unify nations by making them relatively autonomous from colonial society's class hierarchies. In this vision, new nation-states were to remake Cubans and Filipinos into national citizenries enjoying equal rights and representation through governments expressing a general will. By 1898, however, the social strains of recession, revolt, and war started to fracture nationalist movements and this idealized sovereignty along elite and popular lines. In Cuba, a new ideology of *cubanidad*, articulated best by José Martí, united all Cubans into a single nation regardless of race, class, or gender. Yet intersecting political and economic crises during the tumultuous 1890s, and postwar competition for power among revolutionary, popular, and pro-imperialist nationalists, under the pressure of US influence and intervention, fragmented imagined nations and sovereignties. Wealthier and educated creole planters and professionals who dominated nationalist politics often accommodated occupying Yankees as they jockeyed for civil jobs, elected offices, and economic security. Such behavior outraged nationalist militants harboring more egalitarian aspirations.[20]

Social fissures similarly disrupted nationalist politics in the Philippines. Before 1898, Spain delegated its sovereignty to a complex hierarchy of local legatees, from governors and Catholic clergy down to the local *indio* elite from which *ilustrados* and their anticolonial Propaganda movement emerged. Filipino nationalists—above all Apolinario Mabini, theoretician and adviser to Gen. Emilio Aguinaldo—wished to integrate the archipelago's diverse peoples by forging a modern state modeled on Enlightenment and revolutionary ideals of popular and national sovereignty. Yet the Katipuneros' 1896 revolt, Spanish repression, and US invasion exacerbated tensions between poor and elite Filipinos. Evasive peasants and millenarian rebels evoked an alternative national sovereignty expressed in traditional religious and communal values of sacrifice and mutualism. By early 1899, however, US occupation and war, and civilian American commissioners' promises of liberal reforms, started to split Filipino elites into militant and accommodationist factions, further weakening Gen. Aguinaldo's fledgling republic at Malolos.[21]

Though analysis of sovereignty's social dimension reveals shared features in the labor politics of US wars and occupations in Cuba and the Philippines, this comparative study also identifies and seeks to explain significant differences in empire's work between them. Avoiding a methodological nationalism that would artificially segregate two parts of an imperial whole, this study uses labor to ask how and why wars and occupations in two roughly comparable colonies experiencing transition between the same empires generated varied effects. Unlike other islands seized from Spain by the United States in 1898, Cuba and the Philippines between 1895 and 1913 simultaneously and sequentially endured Spanish and US imperial rule and warfare. Their common but distinctive pasts as Spanish colonies, punctuated by contingencies of revolution and US intervention, greatly determined military colonialism's convergent and divergent features and outcomes. Comparison reveals that shifting institutional and legal divisions and distributions of state authority among Americans, Cubans, and Filipinos especially determined elites' and subalterns' relative power to control colonial labor and the conditions of its exploitation. If nonstate or quasi-state elites often exercised effective sovereignty over workers, the coercive authority of state elites—and subalterns' ability to make claims on it—decisively influenced the social relations of imperial formation. Comparative analysis of Cuban and Filipino work for the US military thus affirms observations that sovereignty is never absolute and fixed but always aspirational and fluid, and "continually negotiated on the ground." Labor struggles between colonizer and colonized limited Americans' sovereignty abroad, ensuring it was never fully realized but staggered, partial, and porous.[22]

Comparison also indicates that empire developed through a world-spanning field of militarized cross-cultural interaction in which the labor techniques of war and occupation became one of many imperial processes driving globalization. Narratives of US empire and colonialism examining mutual flows of people, ideas, and objects between a metropolitan "core" and a single "peripheral" site often miss cognate exchange between peripheral sites themselves. Yet the late nineteenth-century transportation and communication revolutions that enabled American soldiers to mount interventions and maintain occupations across the globe also forged a *histoire croisée* of colonial labor practices that knitted together spaces of war and empire. Soldiers transiting from Cuba to the Philippines, and sometimes back to Cuba, gained vital experience in exploiting tropical workforces in one colony that they later translated and adapted in the next. Empire's work thus entailed more than just a transimperial mimesis by which US soldiers and colonial elites imitated other imperial states' techniques for mobilizing and managing tropical labor. It also involved an intraimperial circulation of military-colonial culture evident in discrete work practices. This book explores this global itinerary within and across multiple scales by reconstructing military colonizing's history at microlevels of region and locale often bypassed in studies of elites in Washington, Havana, and Manila. It focuses on the local history of Luzon, Samar, and

Mindanao, in the Philippines, and the provinces of Oriente, Pinar del Río, and Cienfuegos in Cuba. This permits a thicker description of the politics of sovereignty that emerged throughout the United States' imperial archipelago in the 1898 era.[23]

THIS BOOK'S THREE THEMATIC PARTS each contain two internally chronological and comparative chapters that reconstruct types of military-colonial labor; the politics of sovereignty they created; and their impact on the histories of Cuba, the Philippines, and the US Army. The chapters in part 1, "Knowledge," show how Cubans' and Filipinos' cognitive labor, and American soldiers' struggle to understand and control it, structured US imperial warfare, colonial state formation, and military reform. Before American and colonial civilians made these islands legible to an imperial US state through anthropology, geography, and history or censuses, museums, and maps, American troops conquered and governed them by exploiting subaltern mental labor. In turn, these soldiers' coercive attempts to know colonized workers formed a military-imperial analogue to capitalist missionaries' efforts to prepare subaltern peoples for rote labor elsewhere in the post-emancipation tropics. Empire's intellectual work, often brokered by colonial elites, produced a militarized knowledge of the exoticized island laborer that shaped Americans' empire and cosmopolitan culture in a globalizing age.[24]

Chapter 1 demonstrates that the coerced and voluntary work of military intermediaries both facilitated and constrained the exploitation of colonized peoples' geographic and linguistic intelligence, as subalterns bent local knowledge to their own ends. Not unlike translators and other cultural brokers mediating colonial encounters and labor diasporas elsewhere in this era, interpreters and guides vital to US warfare and occupation navigated a fraught physical and mental middle ground.[25] Yet Americans' appropriation of Cubans' and Filipinos' knowledge determined the outcomes of these wars and occupations, and shaped the colonial states and cultures they left in their wake. Chapter 2 examines the politics of US Army officers' attempts to study and manage manual colonial laborers according to metropolitan and colonial sciences of race, climate, and industry, among others. Progressive Era American commanders, professionalizing in part by controlling and improving Cuban and Filipino workers, tried to project and perfect industrial modernity through subaltern labor. In turn, their civilizing ideal of efficiency, expressed in a militarized science of colonial warfare, shaped highly racialized imperial and national discourses regarding Cuban and Filipino capacities for sovereignty. Yet subaltern self-activity confounded Americans' attempts to scientifically know and exploit them.

The chapters in part 2, "Infrastructure," outline a military-colonial political economy of public works, traveling its global circuits as war and occupation hinged on apparently mundane matters of overland transport. In both Cuba and the Philippines, US soldiers made roadbuilding a colonial technology of state building and socio-spatial transformation, projecting metropolitan modernism through tropical landscapes and laborers. In colonies not yet integrated by rail, better and more roads compressed space through time by facilitating the movement of people, goods, and information, and redirecting them to serve imperial and colonial political and economic elites. Cuban and Filipino toil on city streets and rural highways forged infrastructural states that made public works just as crucial to colonialism and its culture as other reforms inspired by Americans' encounter with the tropics. In the *longue durée*, military-colonial mobility regimes merely extended a much older imperial practice by which armies, from ancient Rome and early modern Britain to nineteenth-century North America, built roads to project power. In 1898, however, soldiers steeped in the civilizing rationality of a "technological sublime" found they had to depend on uncivilized subalterns to create and maintain infrastructure.[26]

Part 2's chapters examine the imperial technopolitics of the army engineer by mapping how roadwork created an unstable architecture of sovereignty, forcing US soldiers to struggle with Cubans and Filipinos over public works and their intended and unintended consequences. Chapter 3 originates 1898-era infrastructure in American warriors' response to Spanish colonialism's legacies in island geographies and political economies, and in contingencies of war and postwar economic and humanitarian crisis. Cubans and Filipinos used US occupiers' partial concessions of state authority to civilian elites to exert sovereignty over the labor and taxes Americans needed to build highways. Chapter 4 explores colonized elites' remarkable ability to constrain and confound the US military's control of infrastructural work as an example of imperial sovereignty's subcontractual structure. Despite US troops' claims that they subdued and civilized tropical environments and labor with roadbuilding, infrastructure actually delineated the boundaries of Americans' ability to transform colonial space and subjects.

The book's final part, "Bodies," explores how the work of war and occupation married metropolitan and colonial ideologies and hierarchies of race and gender in a militarized corporeal politics of sovereignty. Paradoxically, the bodies of the most mobile and immobilized colonial workers became nodes of sovereignty through which American soldiers struggled to enhance their power to regulate colonial societies. Yet subaltern self-activity also exposed the boundaries of US occupiers' disciplinary power in the tropics. Hierarchy in the army even made subalterns of American enlisted men who invoked their whiteness and masculinity while clashing with officers over who would enjoy sovereignty over military-colonial labor, and under what terms.[27]

Part 3 studies the bodily politics surrounding those workers perhaps most stigmatized in Americans' new colonial empire: Chinese men and prostitutes. Chapter 5 narrates the politics of Chinese migrant laborers in the 1898 era, showing how US military regimes eventually imposed mainland-style exclusion rules barring their entry, even as soldiers exploited Chinese workforces. Though Chinese laborers and brokers sought to restore diminished sovereignty over their migration and work, they failed to prevent US occupiers from reinforcing preexisting and persistent nativisms and ethnonationalisms, in metropole and colonies. Chapter 6 addresses military-colonialism's fraught sexual terrain. Empire's sexual economies made US troops' relations with island women and laborers, including sex workers, a delicate and dangerous question. A politics of sex and sovereignty that cohered in the martial regulation of commodified sex and reproductive labor redounded on American enlisted men, subjecting them to the same bio-discipline their officers imposed on colonized women.[28]

This book's archive presented challenges of limited and fragmentary evidence well-known to social and colonial historians. Cuban and Filipino laborers were typically illiterate, unlike most Americans invading their islands. As a rule, they left few paper traces through which one may discern their experiences or perceptions of US war or occupation from their own perspective; indeed, this condition was virtually a prerequisite of their subaltern status. If read against the proverbial grain, however, voluminous American military records, reports, and correspondence, personal manuscripts, and journalism offer filtered insight into these workers' lives, labor, and mentalités. Spanish-language texts about Cuban and Filipino labor, written mostly by elite Cuban and Filipino men, also tend to refract the perceptions and experience of colonial and national elites.[29] Yet evidence hiding in crumbling sheaves of colonial records, revolutionaries' scattered papers, and insect-eaten tri-folded army correspondence suggest that not all who made the modern world's imperial history need remain forever invisible.

A BRIEF NOTE ABOUT LANGUAGE: terms used here to refer to historical individuals in and from the United States, Cuba, and the Philippines follow traditional conventions in the United States on the assumption that most readers will encounter this book from this nation's cultural and linguistic context. This choice implies no particular authorial perspective on today's fraught politics of language but only an aspiration to a narrative style of simplicity and consistency. Thus Cubans are distinguished from "Americans," here signifying persons originally from the United States, and ethnic Filipinos are differentiated from Chinese, Moro, Igorot, and Lumad persons. The author recognizes that a desire to critique colonialism's imprint on vernaculars, past and present, may lead some to prefer other terms.

Part I
Knowledge

CHAPTER ONE

Occupied Constantly and Worked to Death
Military-Colonial Intermediaries and the Political Economy of Counterinsurgency

By 1905, Harry S. Howland believed he had finally accomplished a military feat of imperial mastery worth narrating to fellow army officers. That year, this ambitious twenty-eight-year-old army lieutenant detailed for the US Infantry Association's journal his Twenty-Third Infantry Provisional Company's pursuit of Ali, a Moro datu on the island of Mindanao who had defied US rule. Though they failed to capture Ali, he felt their four-months-long expedition through the vast 9,000 square-mile basin of central Mindanao's Rio Grande (today the Pulangi River) seemed victory enough. In its first six weeks out, Howland's 100-man column crossed 400 miles of what he described as "the most difficult country in the Philippines in which to conduct military operations." Yet his account implied the company had moved through hilly forests and lowland jungle, sun-baked fields of high cogon grass, impenetrable swamps, and a watery labyrinth of lakes and river deltas all without the aid of any Moros living there. Carrying a map showing towns but not trails in a region lacking roads, Howland oriented by compass, woodcraft, the sun, and stars. Traversing the Rio Grande without guides, he conceded, was "certain to be difficult" and "entail much delay." As white men racialized their ability to explore and conquer the tropics, however, Howland attributed his troops' mobility solely to their superior skill.[1]

Contrary to Howland's narrative, army records show American troops frequently depended on Moros to navigate the Rio Grande successfully. Especially helpful had been Datu Piang, most prominent of the region's Moros, and also Ali's father-in-law. After US forces first arrived in Mindanao in December 1899, Piang and Ali furnished them with laborers for operations targeting other Moros near Lake Lanao, to the north. When Ali decided to resist the Americans' new antislavery and tax policies, Piang stood with the occupiers. He offered them intelligence on Ali as well as Moro porters and guides.[2]

In his article, however, Howland barely acknowledged Moros' contributions to his mobility. Piang's guides, he griped, rarely knew the countryside beyond a twenty-mile radius from their homes. Howland blamed Moros' allegedly localized geographical knowledge not on their race or conflicted loyalties but on what he perceived was their organic connection to their environment. Over time, he speculated, the verdant jungle's incessant and luxuriant floral growth and erosion from rains obscured and destroyed distinctive landscape features stored in Moros' spatial memories. Yet the lieutenant's solution to this problem actually underscored the degree to which his army relied on indigenous intellects. Whenever Howland sensed he had exhausted a Moro guide's familiarity with a particular area, he released him, but then tried to conscript the next Moro man he met. This practice came with its own complications, including bloodshed. Moros, the lieutenant related, became "scarce" as his unit moved deeper into Mindanao's interior. The "occasional natives" it stumbled upon, he noted, "fled and never stopped until they had made good their escape"—or had been "brought down by a bullet." Reflecting on untrustworthy captives, one of whom absconded with arms, Howland advised readers that "natives taken prisoner make the best guides," even if "too strict a watch cannot be kept upon" those showing "friendliness."[3]

Howland did recognize the linguistic assistance of fellow Euro-American colonizers. Between two Spaniards of "inestimable value" whom his army on Mindanao employed regularly as interpreters, Howland thought Tomas Torres especially talented. Excelling in Spanish and Moro dialects, Torres, he alleged, had a gift for detecting dissimulation in Moros whom most Americans found absolutely inscrutable. If Nicodemus Lambier lacked Torres's intuition and formal education, Howland praised him for combining linguistic and geographical acuity with brutality. A veteran of Spanish army campaigns against the Moros, Lambier thoroughly knew the Rio Grande and English, Spanish, Moro, and aboriginal dialects. He also had few scruples about torture. Lambier, hinted Howland, took "no half measures in dealing with the natives." Indeed, US officers frequently had translators warn Moro captives that they would kill them if they did not lead them to Ali. American counterinsurgents thus grasped that they could not subdue Moros unless they could speak with them. In Mindanao, Howland admitted, the interpreter, "indispensable" to field operations, "plays a part almost next in importance to the commanding officer." Such an "intermediary," he argued, facilitated crucial interactions between officers and others, whether "friends or enemies, allies, prisoners or cargadores." "A command accompanied by a good interpreter," the lieutenant insisted, was "more likely to accomplish its object than not." Without one, Howland wrote, "many opportunities are lost."[4]

Howland's field notes distilled much of his army's experience exploiting subalterns' local knowledge in the 1898 era. Historians have documented how

US warfare and colonialism in Cuba and the Philippines hinged on information that Americans accessed through various indigenous intermediaries, from police and doctors to census takers and social workers.[5] Yet the guides and interpreters who enabled US soldiers to navigate alien environments and foreign cultures provided the cognitive labor on which the most protean phase of empire building often turned. Their work became a precarious middle ground in sovereignty's imperial politics. As Americans and their enemies realized that Cubans' and Filipinos' geographic and linguistic capacities might decide the outcomes of occupation and war, guides and translators walked and talked at the kinetic intersection of clashing claims to rule. Amid insurgency and counterinsurgency in the Philippines, these military-colonial intermediaries especially met distrust, hostility, and violence. Yet Cuban and Filipino guides and interpreters were never ciphers of omnipotent imperial wills; they made history in their own right. At first almost monopolizing local knowledge, these in-between individuals used Americans' demands on them as a means to pursue self-interests, whether or not these aligned with imperial or nationalist aims. Equally decisive were colonial elites who brokered intelligence, guides, and other labor for US soldiers from motives that ranged from profit and power to survival and revenge.

Howland's account also captured how trust between colonizers and the colonized configured the political economy of counterinsurgency. As fungible qualities exchanged between Americans, Cubans, and Filipinos, trust and distrust became a kind of social currency essential to the militarized mobilization and management of subaltern cognitive labor. Americans and colonial intermediaries earned, exploited, and liquidated trust with each other over time, as conditions required, and in response to often volatile contingencies.[6] Military-colonial intermediaries thus became an intercultural terrain over which Americans struggled to control the benefits, and betrayals, of empire.

BY 1898, MILITARY INTERMEDIARIES were hardly novel in Cuba and the Philippines. Earlier that century, Spanish officials organized Cubans in segregated militias to suppress internal dangers, such as slave revolts, and external threats, including filibusterers. During the Ten Years' War and the 1895 war, thousands of Cubans, some of them ex-insurgents, joined paramilitary units that helped peninsular forces combat separatist *insurrectos* that were difficult to find without *prácticos*, or guides who knew interior landscapes. In the Philippines beginning in 1868, colonial authorities recruited *indio* men for a similar body, the Guardia Civil, and used them to suppress growing dissent; they also enlisted Guardia veterans to police

Manila. After the Katipuneros' revolt in 1896, Spanish-led *guardias* fought Gen. Emilio Aguinaldo's rebels.[7]

American soldiers invading and occupying these islands, however, also forged an inter-imperial culture of the militarized intermediary as they translated encounters with Cuban and Filipino guides and interpreters through prior experience with Native American scouts. Army reformers such as Arthur Wagner greatly valued Indians' utility in imparting the geographic and linguistic knowledge his army needed to access in order to wage frontier warfare. Other officers, including Robert Bullard and Henry Lawton, claimed to appropriate Native American tactics of stealth and surprise. In the 1870s, the US Army began to organize regular "Indian Scout" companies, in part as a strategy to assimilate indigenous men resisting reservation life by appealing to warrior culture. Yet some scouts' poor discipline, opportunistic attacks on tribal enemies, and, on rare occasions, mutiny troubled the experiment. If enlightened officers like Hugh Scott and John Pershing endorsed the Indian Scouts, most peers, among them Leonard Wood, disparaged and distrusted them. By the late 1890s, the War Department, deeming the scouts an abject failure, dissolved them. Yet they became templates for the "native" auxiliaries that US Army commanders in the Philippines soon deployed effectively against insurgents there. Lt. Matthew Batson's late 1899 recruitment of Macabebe men in Pampanga province, among them former Spanish loyalists, inspired peers to form their own companies, which later became the germ of Philippine Scout and Constabulary units.[8]

Macabebes were not the first colonial peoples to assist Batson in the tropics, however. Even before US expeditionary forces started landing near Santiago in late June 1898, Cubans who facilitated Yankee military reconnaissance and communications preceded imminent joint operations against a common Spanish enemy. By the end of that month, Cuban insurgents who guided Batson to enemy lines at El Caney permitted him to survey ground, across which Gen. Lawton attacked a few days later, with success. Though Cuban scouts practically enabled Yankee field operations, Batson, like his racist white comrades, dismissed the martial abilities of the Afro-Cuban men who constituted most of the Cuban Liberation Army's ranks. By marginalizing Cuban rebels' role in the victorious campaign to seize Santiago, Americans legitimized their own unwillingness to recognize Cuba's sovereignty.[9] Yet these intermediaries' knowledgeable labor for Yankee soldiers during the 1898 war also forged a fruitful if fraught neocolonial culture of cooperation between Cubans and Americans that persisted into the postwar.

An imperial mystique of myth and metaphor shrouded what Americans knew about Cuba before they invaded in 1898, obscuring Cuban realities. This fog of constructed perception rose up during the nineteenth century from Yankees' and Cubans' ever-increasing economic and cultural ties, and convergent and conflicting national dreams. Starting in the 1820s, Americans profited handsomely by investing capital and technical expertise in Cuban sugar and tobacco and exporting most of the goods that Cuba imported. Yankees built and operated much of the island's industrial infrastructure, from *ingenios* and *centrales* processing cane sugar to the railroads and oceanic vessels that transported it. In turn, more and more Cubans shuttled north for business, education, and employment. In the United States, members of a small but growing creole Cuban middle class attended universities and colleges, forged transnational commercial partnerships, and naturalized, while poorer migrants made cigars in New York City and Florida. Beginning in the 1820s, Cuban reformers and revolutionaries fleeing Spanish repression also took refuge in the north. Separatists' military defeats by the early 1880s significantly expanded this exile population. Early in the next decade, the émigré leadership of the Partido Revolucionario Cubano(PRC), led by José Martí, sought Yankee elites' support for revolt by downplaying their movement's popular, agrarian, and multiracial dimensions. Yet this strategy strengthened rationales by which Americans came to justify intervention, occupation, and neocolonial hegemony. Still, by May 1898, once the Teller Amendment appeared to foreclose annexation, separatists believed US invaders shared their commitment to "Cuba Libre."[10]

Cubans offered a great deal of the intelligence that Americans used to plan their campaign. Since the war had started in Oriente three years earlier, Cuban exiles joined Yankee entrepreneurs and volunteers in showering the War Department with data. Most of this flowed to the department's new Military Information Division (MID), established in 1891, tasked with collecting geographic, economic, and military intelligence on foreign lands for future operations. By 1897, MID staffers, now focused on Cuba, started gathering data on subjects ranging from Spanish arms and troop locations to road conditions and tropical disease. Early the next year, anticipating war, they distributed reports and maps to senior US Army commanders.[11]

This preliminary knowledge's limited value became clear to Yankee officers who found themselves having to rely on Cubans for any level of detailed insight into their enemy and Oriente's landscape, as well as English-Spanish communication. This dynamic developed imperial qualities even before

Gen. William Shafter and his Fifth Corps departed from Florida. At Tampa in early June, Shafter discreetly followed White House orders that he not recognize Cuban revolutionaries' authority in any way. He assiduously avoided separatist representatives, even when they might have secured Cuban pilots he needed to shepherd army transports safely along Cuba's coastline. In the expedition, Shafter's only informants regarding Oriente's "topographical and climatic" conditions were two Cuban exiles; one, Dr. Joaquín Castillo, was the brother of a Liberation Army general. Beyond them, Shafter knew little about eastern Cuba. Only slightly less knowledgeable about Oriente than Spanish predecessors who had struggled to wage war in a mostly uncharted wilderness, the general later admitted that he disembarked in Cuba carrying only large-scale maps of the island, not eastern Cuba itself.[12]

The Fifth Corps' situational ignorance compelled it to enlist the cooperation of Cuba's insurgent army. Only after landing at Daiquirí, some eighteen miles east of Santiago, on June 22 did Shafter and subordinates realize they needed Cubans to guide their advance west toward Spanish forces concentrated at Santiago. Martial mobility became linked to language, as Shafter and his generals had to communicate with rebel commanders to coordinate movements and procure the scouts they required. Given that only a few invading US soldiers were fluent in Spanish, Shafter was lucky that many high-ranking insurgents already spoke English. He knew this would be the case thanks to Fredrick Funston, a Kansan who served as an artillerist for generals Máximo Gómez and Calixto García in Oriente before he returned to the states and fed Shafter intelligence. Funston learned that the planters, cattlemen, and urban professionals who commanded the Liberation Army—among "the best men of the native Cuban population," in his opinion—spoke English. García, commanding insurgents in the east, had learned English while exiled in New York. Indeed, at a June 20 conference near Aserradero, on the coast twenty miles west of Santiago, García placed his army at Shafter's disposal and made plans to shield the landing at Daiquirí, without the need for any translator. García later claimed that Shafter violated a promise he made there to allow insurgents to occupy Santiago after the city fell. (Given García's fluency, mistranslation seems unlikely.) In reports, Shafter elided that detail but thanked García for accurate pointers on Spanish troop locations. Months later, Shafter admitted that he had relied on García for ascertaining "the character of the country" beyond a "pencil-sketch of the ground and roads east of Santiago." If Cuban officers' social background as educated and expatriate men facilitated such communication in English, white Yankee officers believed race impeded it in Spanish. Capt. Richard Wilson, his regiment's only Spanish speaker,

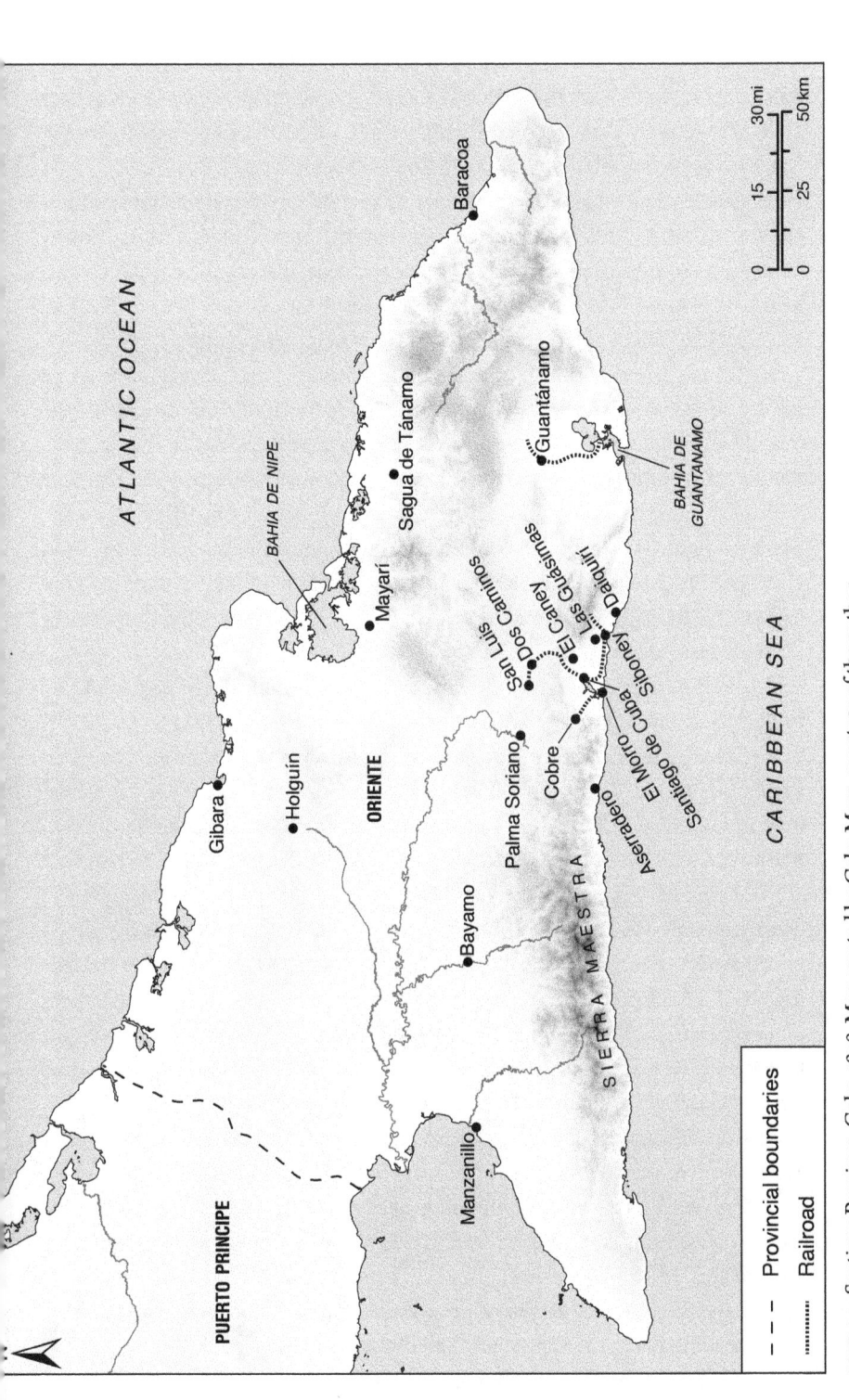

MAP 1.1 Santiago Province, Cuba, 1898. Map created by Gabe Moss, courtesy of the author.

confessed inability to comprehend Afro-Cuban rebels. He believed the linguistic legacy of enslaved Haitians' forced migration to Oriente a century earlier, following slave revolt in that former French colony, explained the "barbarous patois" of its "ignorant . . . lower classes."[13]

Yankee invaders' perception of Cubans as subaltern by virtue of their race, class, and culture both legitimated their repudiation of Cuba's national sovereignty and soured their armies' cautious wartime alliance. The Fifth Corps' nearly all-white ranks often displayed contempt for García's bedraggled and mostly Afro-Cuban army, accusing its men of being poor soldiers, effeminate cowards, and shirking thieves. Such insinuations ignored the pragmatism of a poorly supplied and exhausted separatist rank and file that rationally preferred fresh and better-equipped Americans to bear the brunt of the fighting. Shafter and subordinates only reinforced their own disregard for Cubans' mettle by aggressively excluding them from combat and insisting that they perform manual labor. As his columns pushed toward El Caney, Shafter asked García to furnish Cuban soldiers to carry US Army supplies on roads proving impassable by wagons. Offended, García declined, grumbling that he "did not wish his men to become pack-mules."[14]

By crafting a postwar public consensus that Cubans never provided any military assistance, however, American commanders officially erased a record of knowledgeable insurgent labor that Cubans might have rightfully invoked to claim national sovereignty. Their imperial amnesia was perhaps most salient in the memoir Theodore Roosevelt wrote to consolidate the heroic reputation he won by organizing the Rough Riders and leading them to triumph at San Juan Hill. Like other Yankees, Roosevelt noted that he initially believed insurgents might be "useful as guides and scouts," but not "serious fighting"; in retrospect, he insisted they "turned out to be nearly useless, even for this purpose." If officers' private memoirs more readily acknowledged Cuban guides' martial utility and agency, they also recorded perceptions that legitimized empire. Capt. Richard Wilson actually empathized with a Cuban scout who he claimed had justifiably disappeared before battle at El Caney after an American officer verbally abused him without cause. Yet Wilson, like other Yankees, attributed other guides' reluctance to aid them to their radical alterity as Cubans. Noting a "vast difference between them and us in everything—language, customs, appearance, and methods"—Wilson believed each army's culture and "ideas of government" were "irreconcilable."[15]

Cuban veterans and historians proudly maintained that insurgents contributed substantially to the campaign. The division led by Gen. Demetrio Castillo Duany, Joaquín Castillo's brother, covered the Fifth Corps' disembarkations,

A Scout Hiding under Palm Leaves. Conveying Cuban insurgents' difference from most American troops, by race and accoutrement, during the Santiago campaign, this photograph also suggests Cubans' skill as guides experienced in guerrilla warfare. Hemment, *Cannon and Camera.*

first at Daiquirí and then at Siboney, where Yankee vessels deposited some of Gen. García's troops. García's men also made coordinated attacks on Spanish troops and diversionary feints, and stood in reserve at several clashes, including El Caney. Yet US War Department records and reports also refute Yankees' imperial revisionism, amply documenting how Shafter and his generals relied extensively on Liberation Army scouts and guides to navigate Oriente's countryside. On June 22, immediately after American forces landed at Daiquirí, Maj. Gen. Joseph Wheeler's cavalry division marched west to Siboney behind Gen. Castillo's troops; these men, the former Confederate noted, knew "the country thoroughly." At Siboney, Castillo sketched Wheeler a rough map of the area marking enemy positions that allowed Gen. Samuel B. M. Young's cavalry brigade—including Roosevelt's volunteers—to tramp north. Leading them were Col. Carlos Gonzalo Clavell and his regiment, whom Castillo assigned to the Yankees as scouts, flankers, and skirmishers. Roosevelt later blamed Spaniards' ambush of the column at Las Guásimas on one of Clavell's Cubans. At least one Rough Rider, however, alleged that their Cuban guides detected Spaniards there and notified the Yankees prior to the fight; Richard Harding Davis, an embedded journalist, found no fault with them. Following Santiago's capitulation on July 17, García's men guided US soldiers to interior destinations to accept surrenders from Spanish troops at other posts.[16]

Americans' perceptions of Cuban military intermediaries varied partly by rank as enlisted men, compared to imperious officers, more frequently recorded and appreciated insurgents' provision of local knowledge. A few rank and filers, some communicating with rebels by hand signals, lauded their Cuban guides, showing not just sympathy for their cause but sincere gratitude for their aid. Pvt. Charles Gauvreau, a young New York volunteer, praised Cuban scouts who climbed trees to retrieve green coconuts for thirsty Americans as they marched from Daiquirí to Siboney. Cpl. Herbert Kohr remembered how insurgents led his brigade as it rushed north from Siboney to relieve embattled troops at Las Guásimas. Over the next few days, he recalled, Cuban guides who "understood the lay of the country" acted as a pioneer vanguard, hacking paths in the jungle and slashing small trees and brush to fill swampy terrain. Just before San Juan Hill, journalist and novelist Stephen Crane, joining the expedition as a war correspondent, observed that the average Yankee "does not regard his ally as a good man for the fighting line." Yet Crane described the average rebel as a "vigilant" soldier whose "knowledge of the country" and "woodcraft" seemed far "superior to that of the American." In fiction, Crane portrayed *prácticos* as stealthy warriors possessing "the skill of cats." A newspaper headline reflected his countrymen's ambivalence about Cubans: "They Are Good Scouts, but American Troops Do Not Look with Favor on Them and They Do Not Understand Us."[17]

In fact, Cubans often *did* understand Yankee troops because they supplied the labor of translation. Not only did many senior Cuban officers speak English; Cubans enlisted in the US Army also served as linguists, enabling the communications with insurgents, civilians, and Spaniards which made operations and diplomacy possible. As guns fell silent, these Cubans allowed the Americans to install the civil-administrative machinery of occupation. Joining Gen. Henry Lawton's staff at Tampa, Ramón G. Mendoza, born in Cuba but naturalized in the states, served throughout the campaign. When Shafter ordered Lt. Col. Arthur Wagner to reconnoiter Spanish lines by trailing squads of Cuban insurgents who did not speak English, Mendoza translated for him. Later serving as chief interpreter for Lawton and Leonard Wood as they established military governments over Oriente and Santiago, respectively, Mendoza served as their interlocutor with Gen. Demetrio Castillo Duany. With these two Cubans' help, Lawton and Wood neutralized *independentistas*' provisional government in Camagüey, the Santa Cruz de la Sur Assembly; organized new Cuban-run municipalities; and demobilized the Liberation Army. By translating Spanish judicial codes, Mendoza enabled Wood's earliest criminal justice reforms.[18]

Equally indispensable as a linguistic go-between was Aurelius E. Mestre, a Havana-born lawyer who left during the Ten Years' War. Ending up in New York, Mestre graduated from City College, then returned to Cuba and managed his family's sugar estate. He again left for the North just before the final independence war, and in 1898 he enlisted there. During the Santiago campaign, Mestre served as aide and interpreter to Gen. Wheeler, who credited him with bravery at Las Guásimas; among other tasks, Mestre interrogated Spaniards captured at San Juan Hill. Both Mendoza and Mestre translated for Shafter during surrender negotiations with Spain's Gen. José Toral. After the war, Wood, politically ambitious, trusted Mestre enough to send him to Washington for an audience with President William McKinley. Even Wood admitted that his ability to rule the city and province hinged partly on Cuban interpreters, as he had learned only a "smattering" of Spanish in the 1880s, during the Apache Wars. Wood's staff, eager to boost their boss's reputation, claimed he knew Spanish well enough to startle Cubans by interrupting translated conversations, in response to talk "not intended for his ears." At Santiago, army quartermasters, courts, hospitals, and sanitary and relief offices all hired Cuban interpreters.[19]

Occupation policy ensured that language infused Cuba's neocolonial state formation, as militarized translation signified a sovereignty divided between US soldiers and the Cubans they incorporated into administration. At Santiago in late July and early August 1898, Shafter, having already outraged separatists by excluding them from postwar governance, further angered nationalists by sustaining pro-Spanish loyalists in municipal offices. After Shafter departed in mid-August, Leonard Wood tried to mollify separatist militants by appointing Cubans to replace these officials. Yet an order that Wood promulgated in early October, stipulating that Cubans fluent in English would have preference in hiring, virtually guaranteed that Cubans entering the subordinate civil bureaucracy would be creole elites most inclined to accommodate US rule. Often former Liberals and Autonomists who favored reconciliation with Spain prior to the 1895 war (or during it), these men possessed more wealth and education, and lighter skins, than most insurgents and Cubans at large. Often selected among 50,000 expatriates who returned to Cuba from the states during the war and after it, many learned English either in the North or in Cuba while doing business. Admiring much about American culture, ideals, and technologies, these pragmatic elites temporarily tolerated US rule, even as Wood and some subordinates publicly entertained annexation.[20]

Like other Cubans working for the occupiers, interpreters worked at the nexus of competing national claims to sovereign authority over the island. By facilitating everyday exchange between US soldiers and Cuban officials and civilians, however, these intermediaries accrued an insiders' knowledge of administration that gave them a degree of control over it. This made them vulnerable to Yankee criticisms that they served only for private gain, not in the interest of the public or "clean government," as mainland American progressives understood it. As politics became a profession for Cubans who had lost property and wealth to decades of intermittent war and recession, Americans increasingly scorned translators as symbols of pervasive corruption. Not unlike civil servants in the states, a few Cuban linguists did indulge in graft, including by exploiting US occupiers' ignorance of Spanish-era laws. Yankees, however, fixated on such peculation as another reason to doubt Cubans' capacities for self-rule. Deriding them as an "Army of Expectation," correspondent Herbert P. Williams insisted that interpreters were like other Cubans scheming to wring "all the money possible out of the United States." They "browbeat Cubans who favor permanent American control," he sneered, just "to hasten our removal from the island" and "get office under the Cuban republic."[21]

The occupation's need for intermediaries and their local knowledge receded gradually. A dwindling US garrison's growing familiarity with the island, its people, and its language, in conjunction with the spread of Yankee capital and culture, made postwar Cuba more legible to Americans and vulnerable to their influence. The organization of all-Cuban police forces greatly reduced US soldiers' need to directly interact with the occupied. In the summer of 1899, after Leonard Wood tried to pacify insurgents by recruiting them into new Rural Guard units, Maj.-Gen. John R. Brooke, the new military governor at Havana, made them the template for a new island-wide paramilitary force. The army's externalization of policing manpower needs allowed the War Department to reduce expenses by decreasing US Army personnel on the island to 11,000 by the end of that year. Simultaneously, Wood made language central to the imperial program of progressive state building he was promoting to Washington as part of his personal campaign to take Brooke's job. Appealing to President McKinley's interest in a "colonial army," Wood proposed that the US government form Cuban regiments, commanded by white American officers, and assimilate them into the regular US Army. Imitating other colonial states' use of "native" soldiers in Africa and Asia, Wood's idea appealed to reformers such as Elihu Root, the new secretary of war, who admired Great Britain's exploitation of "martial races" as an example of enlightened imperial administration.[22]

Notably, Wood made the labor of linguistic knowledge central to his rationale for recruiting Cuban forces. The subaltern soldier would not only enhance military efficiency by minimizing the expense of a US garrison susceptible to yellow fever; he would also mitigate cultural gaps and tensions that Wood believed had bedeviled Yankee soldiers. That occupiers remained "ignorant of the language" and "customs of the people," Wood wrote McKinley, had regrettably incited "many small misunderstandings with the natives." Wood's recommendation languished, however, as Cubans, under US sanction, organized their own army. Some American soldiers also undermined Wood's logic by learning Spanish. The War Department, anticipating future operations on the island, similarly tried to reduce its dependence on Cubans' geographical knowledge and haphazard maps inherited from Spaniards. In 1899, US Army engineers sought to make the island legible to future interventionists by systematically surveying it, yet they failed to finish mapping the island before evacuating in May 1902. By displacing Cubans' geographical knowledge, military cartography was to remake Cuba into an Americanized colonial space suited for lasting subordination.[23]

Cuba's linguistic colonization by Americanized English during the United States' first two interventions partly eroded the communicative gulf that separated most Yankees from Cubans in 1898. As the occupiers' tongue became the neocolonial lingua franca of government, business, education, and culture, thousands of Cubans, from Gen. Máximo Gómez down to Havana bootblacks, studied English. Seeking economic opportunity and pleasurable consumption through encounters and business with Americans' growing colony in Cuba, cosmopolitans learned English by attending classes and studying textbooks. Cuban elites seeking financial security in managerial positions for foreign-owned sugar estates and other firms also took jobs as translators. Yet English's ascent in Cuba contributed to the wholesale transformation of the island's civic and commercial culture as Yankees rushed to remake Cuba in their own image. Cubans who desired the trappings˚ of a capitalist modernity they associated with the United States more greatly influenced early republican everyday life, as they adopted American technologies, techniques, and consumer tastes and adapted them to insular conditions.[24] The knowledge work of war and occupation enabled this imperial metamorphosis.

IF MILITARY INTERMEDIARIES SMOOTHED US empire building in Cuba, they proved absolutely essential to imperial formation in the Philippines. In late June 1898, as Cubans pointed Shafter's Fifth Corps toward Santiago, a sister US Army expedition dispatched from San Francisco landed at Cavite on Manila Bay some ten miles southwest of the city. As with Yankees' simultaneous campaign in Oriente, Americans coordinated their siege of a Spanish-garrisoned city with an anticolonial army. Despite this striking parallel, intermediaries in the Philippines, who insurgency soon made even more crucial to US Army operations had a greater power to determine their outcome. If joint victory at Santiago produced a relatively peaceful postwar occupation in Cuba, counterparts' triumph at Manila in early August 1898, by contrast, precipitated a tense and tenuous standoff with Filipino nationalists that exploded after little more than five months. Thus, compared to Cuba, insurgency and counterinsurgency in the Philippines imparted volatility and violence to an imperial politics of sovereignty that coalesced in part through American soldiers' struggles to exploit subalterns' local knowledge.

If US soldiers arrived in Cuba with a preconceived image of that island, counterparts in Asia invaded a virtual tabula rasa. No more than a dozen Americans, mostly merchants at Manila, lived in the Philippines in April 1898, when MID staff at the War Department, considering operations there for the first time, resorted to consulting entries from the *Encyclopaedia Britannica*. Gen. Arthur MacArthur Jr. later testified that a "distinctive characteristic of the command" that disembarked at Cavite in June 1898 was an "absolute ignorance" of the Philippines "in respect to geography, climate, people, and the general aspects of nature."[25]

Very few Americans, military or civilian, ever became fluent in any language spoken in the archipelago other than Spanish. Still, neither prior to the 1898 invasion nor afterward did the War Department or any senior commanders in the Philippines make it policy to teach officers or enlisted men Castilian, much less Tagalog or any of the islands' dozens of other dialects. Expeditionary forces landing at Manila in 1898, composed partly of volunteers from western US states and territories, included men who learned Spanish while living or serving in the Southwest. In 1899, personnel who had acquired an idiomatic facility with Spanish in Cuba arrived with some ability in the language. To pass the time during the transpacific transit, some officers convened impromptu Spanish classes for comrades of rank. In the summer of

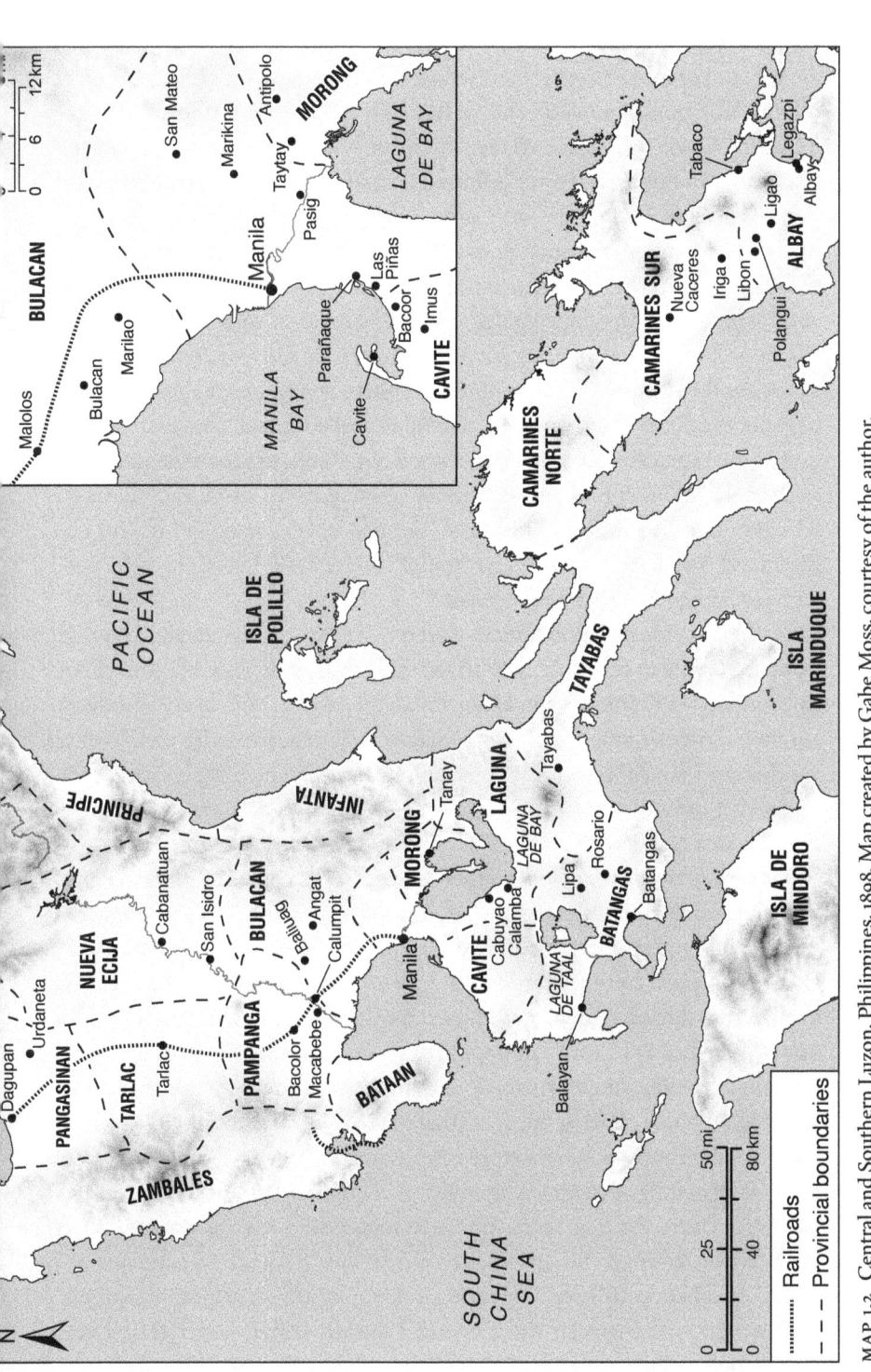

MAP 1.2 Central and Southern Luzon, Philippines, 1898. Map created by Gabe Moss, courtesy of the author.

1898, on the leg between Honolulu and Manila, Evaristo de Montalvo, a Cuban émigré and volunteer, instructed fellow Utah Artillery officers; generals at Manila, noticing Montalvo's ability, had him interrogate Spanish prisoners, including Guam's governor. Many American soldiers tried to pick up everyday words and phrases. Fewer acquired and studied English-Spanish phrase books, or "catechisms," on their own initiative; a few scholastic company commanders purchased such booklets in quantity and distributed them to enlisted men. Yet formal instruction seemed less necessary as Americans and Filipinos each developed pidgins; deriding them as "carabao Spanish" and "bamboo English," Americans perceived this crude form of communication as yet another sign of the Philippines' primitive conditions. As soldiers here, like those in Cuba, often resorted to facial expressions and hand gestures, the exceptional Spanish-speaking soldier stood out. Reminiscing about his service as a veteran, Wilmer Blackett—a western cowboy, circus hand, and railroader who patriotically volunteered in 1898—recalled how he initially felt "lost" on the island. Yet Blackett claimed he "found" himself and "got along very well" with civilians after he learned Spanish.[26]

Naturally, given such linguistic poverty, US Army commanders landing troops at Cavite in early July 1898 prized the few persons available and willing to translate for them. Among other tasks, the logistics of an expeditionary landing and besieging Manila immediately required men who could act as conduits to Spanish-speaking Filipino and Chinese foremen supervising workforces that did not know or use it. Yet rising tensions over sovereignty with Filipino insurgents joined linguistic misunderstanding as forces thwarting Americans' power over colonial labor. Of course, as historian Vicente Rafael notes regarding the politics of translation in the colonial Philippines, language's inherently slippery and playful nature never allowed those who interpreted for US soldiers to convey or understand the exact meanings of words precisely as all parties intended them, at all times. Yet the logistical difficulties involved in this parochial US Army's attempt to wage war overseas clearly made imperial labor relations another source of confusion. Army quartermasters who directed Filipinos piloting the boats that ferried troops and supplies to shore, and the Filipino and Chinese stevedores unloading them, complained about their "foreign tongue and peculiar training." These workers, observed journalist Oscar Davis, did not seem "quick to understand what is wanted." Only gradually, he reported, did Americans realize it was "no good to get excited and swear," and better to "keep calm and sit down until you get an interpreter." Before relations between the US and Filipino armies soured, however, even rebels helped Americans exploit local labor by translating for them.

Gen. Aguinaldo's brother-in-law briefly organized carabao carts to haul supplies because he could transmit US soldiers' instructions, issued in Spanish, to Tagalog-speaking drivers. The Americans also occupied Manila in early August without an adequate force of linguists. The few Europeans in the city able to translate ignored the invaders' entreaties for help as they resumed business. Davis's late June observation that "interpreters were very few and hard to get" described a persistent problem. The army's few American translators, he noted, "were occupied constantly and worked to death."[27]

American interpreters became even more critical to army operations in February 1899, when a new war, provoked by US annexation, shifted them into a counterinsurgency mode. The career of one translingual volunteer, Jack Ganzhorn, suggested their continued significance in military operations. Ganzhorn, an Arizona ranch hand who joined the US Navy in 1898, had enlisted by August 1899 in one of twenty-five new US volunteer infantry regiments organized to fight Aguinaldo's nationalists. By October 1899, his talent in Spanish caught the attention of Gen. Henry Lawton, who made Ganzhorn an interpreter for his division's elite scout unit, led by fellow westerners who styled themselves as "Indian fighters," then his headquarters staff. After Lawton's December 1899 death, Ganzhorn returned to his regiment as it garrisoned San Isidro, Nueva Ecija's capital. There, Frederick Funston, then a general after leading a Kansas volunteer regiment, made him translator for his "Headquarters Scouts" as it hunted Filipino guerrillas.[28]

Such English-Spanish interpreters, however, were of limited value in a polyglot linguistic terrain in which a tiny minority of Filipinos spoke or read Spanish. Though Castilian long functioned as the Philippines' colonial lingua franca of government, religion, and commerce, few in the islands beyond several thousand Spaniards and mestizo officials, clergy, soldiers, and their families ever gained fluency or literacy in it before 1898. Spanish-speaking *indios* were largely limited to *principales*, members of the local elite families who served the colonial state and Catholic Church as subordinate municipal officials. Initially holding office by virtue of claims of lineal descent from precontact nobility, the *principalía* by the late eighteenth century took advantage of agricultural commercialization to amass lands. Increasingly able to acquire formal educations at Catholic schools and universities at Manila, indio and mestizo professionals, planters, and businessmen learning Spanish acquired a superior status relative to poor peasants who typically knew only local dialects. Catholic friars also ignored perennial royal mandates that they impart indios Spanish well until the 1860s, when reforms established parish elementary schools designed, in part, to impart it to indio and mestizo children. Such efforts were doomed by friars' obstinacy, popular disinterest, and anticolonial unrest; by 1870, an estimated 3 percent of 385,000 students had mastered Spanish. Spaniards' intermarriage with principales reinforced Castilian's use in elite families but failed to penetrate indio society at large. By 1898, colonial authorities estimated that no more than 5 percent to 7 percent of the population was fluent.[29]

The Philippines' pre-1898 history thus shaped the imperial politics of counterinsurgency and the linguistic labor it required largely along colonial class lines, at least early in the war. In occupied Manila, and smaller cities and towns that the Americans gradually garrisoned, their limited knowledge of Spanish and absolute ignorance of indigenous dialects usually restricted US soldiers' communication with Filipinos to elite Spanish-speaking men. The 1903 census reported that only 2 percent of Filipinos and less than 1 percent of Filipinas enjoyed a "superior education"—a category suggesting fluency and literacy in Castilian—and estimated that no more than 10 percent of Filipinos knew Spanish to any degree. The vast majority of Hispanicized and Christianized Filipinos thus spoke only Tagalog, Ilocano, Bikol, or Visayan; being poor peasants in rural areas, most of this population was also illiterate in their own vernacular. This social fact effectively confined American troops' substantive dialogue with Filipinos to the principales who continued to monopolize local political authority and socioeconomic power under nationalist and US military regimes. It also granted these elite Filipinos extraordinary influence over flows of information that both Americans and revolutionaries realized were absolutely essential to contesting each other's claims to sovereignty. By filtering intelligence and the social relations of trust needed to produce and share good intelligence reliably through the principales this linguistic landscape also enabled Filipino elites to use language according to their own self-interests and cultural assumptions. William H. Taft, first arriving in the islands in February 1900 as the second Philippine Commission's secretary, recapitulated the army's experience. Nearly all Filipinos, he observed, communicated "with the government, the courts," and "people of other provinces" through Spanish-fluent elites. Though Pvt. Peter Konrad realized that "Spanish was the Legal [sic] language" when he garrisoned Bucay, in northern Luzon's Abra Province, he also noted that "only the educated learned that," not "natives livin[g] in small Barrios."[30]

The nascent US colonial state's inability to impart English to Filipinos only deepened American troops' linguistic dependency on elite Spanish-speakers. By endorsing English instruction, the US military regime prefigured the civilian Philippine Commission's educational and language policies. Beginning in August 1898 at Manila, American commanders sought to showcase US sovereignty's enlightened civilizing mission by reviving old primary schools and establishing new ones. Often utilizing American soldiers as teachers, some army schools promoted benevolent assimilation by teaching not only Spanish and English but subjects familiar to elementary education at home, such as arithmetic, geography, and US history, occasionally with new English textbooks. By late 1900, the military government's new Department of Public Instruction had organized some 1,000 such schools, serving roughly 100,000 students across the archipelago. Hastily organized and poorly resourced, however, army schools usually lacked decent buildings, much less new books and other supplies. Absent taxes on landed property, most towns did not have enough funds to support them or hire private teachers. Many soldiers, using old Catholic parochial texts, found them "better than nothing."[31]

The occupation's educational efforts thus failed to propagate Filipinos' linguistic "amalgamation," as one soldier described their aims. Department director Capt. Albert Todd admitted that a pedagogy based on "the old Spanish system" had "small intrinsic utility" in schools, which, in his view, seemed most valuable for demonstrating Americans' "good will." Todd himself believed that "no public work" was "so important" (except for roadbuilding, which he considered even more vital for "good communications"). Filipinos' acquisition of English, he insisted, would prevent "distrusts and misunderstandings" endemic wherever "rulers and the ruled have diverse speech." Others argued that English instruction would aid counterinsurgency by empowering exploited peasants. Brig. Gen. James F. Smith, governor of the island of Negros, thought teaching the language could be "a potent factor in bringing the lower classes . . . into more cordial relations with Americans." "The advancement of the Filipino race," he believed, required educating "the laboring classes and the poor," who could not afford private schooling. By late 1900, Gen. Arthur McArthur, endorsing this logic, urged the War Department and the Philippine Commission to match a recent $1 million roads appropriation with $2 million for schools, as measures designed equally "to pacify the people." Taft, however, later criticized the army's "chaotic" policy for its pedagogy's "poor" results. Despite some Filipino youths' enthusiasm for "Americano," and some soldiers' sincere desire to impart a new "mother-tongue," commissioners alleged that few Filipinos beyond Manila seemed to learn English.[32]

The commission barely improved on the army's efforts, even as its officials dreamt of unifying a polyglot archipelago under a single imperial lexicon. By early 1901, its new Bureau of Education replaced soldier-teachers with educational missionaries recruited from the United States, so-called Thomasites (after their army transport), and mandated that civilians instruct in English exclusively. Carrying schoolbooks instead of Krags, Thomasites evoked a peaceful and paternal Protestant ethic of social uplift. Yet American rhetoric describing these civilian teachers as an "army" of educators suggested a lingering militarized ethos to US colonial education. Some veterans, including former soldier-teachers, stayed in the islands and their classrooms, becoming members of what one American hailed as a "second army of occupation." Compared to Cubans, though, Filipinos seemed less interested in studying the occupiers' language; most stuck with vernaculars. By 1901, commissioners estimated that no more than 10,000 people in the archipelago, not including US troops, had English fluency; presumably, most if not all were American and European civilians. Thus Spanish, through the Filipino elites speaking and reading it, remained Americans' "medium of communication" to all other Filipinos, in Taft's words.[33]

The war's shift during late 1899 and early 1900 from conventional warfare, concentrated in central Luzon, to guerrilla warfare and counterinsurgency across the archipelago intensified Americans' need for intelligence and thus English-Spanish interpreters. Such intermediaries enabled not just field operations but also civil administration as US officers sought to enlist Spanish-speaking notables in organizing municipal governments and police forces to deploy against insurgents. Americans' dependence on local elites for doing business with ordinary Filipinos, however, often required an attenuated chain of translation that demanded time—and Herculean patience—from all parties. One American veteran recalled serving on a "circus" of a court-martial at Malolos that adjudicated a soldier's alleged pig theft. The captain claimed that an English-Spanish translator spoke with a second Spanish-speaking translator who, in turn, interrogated Tagalog-speaking witnesses before transmitting their testimony back to the first interpreter, who then addressed Americans. The military's dual-language judicial procedure persisted under the Philippine Commission, which initially required that courts use English first, if possible, before Spanish if needed. In 1906, commissioners who believed that Spanish would remain the islands' elite language made English the exclusive legal vernacular. The convoluted nature of wartime army courts, in which "the justice of decisions" turned "on the truthfulness of interpretation," as one provost marshal put it, had cried out for standardization.[34]

American soldiers' inability to communicate directly with most Filipinos risked more than mistranslation. This incapacity threatened US sovereignty and its legitimacy by increasing the likelihood of incidents that could harm and alienate civilians whose loyalty American authorities craved. A few conscientious army officers tried to mitigate this risk by learning basic phrases in

Tagalog or other dialects. Capt. Perry Miles, recalling the invasion of northern Cavite province in June and July 1899, noted that "the language difficulty was always a factor in our dealings, official and social"; in Las Piñas, he claimed, no more than a dozen residents had known Spanish. Miles mastered a few words and phrases in Tagalog, including morning and afternoon greetings, and inquiries into road conditions. To prevent sentries from firing on Filipinos who were not likely to know English or Spanish commands to "halt" or "advance," he memorized them in Tagalog and taught them to enlisted men. Remembering that the few Americans with any aptitude for native dialects "gained the most intimacy and confidence of the population," Miles noted they were often assigned to translate or do other intelligence work. Still, the archipelago's balkanized culture restricted local knowledge's spatial range. Translators conversant in one tongue, Americans griped, often did not know another spoken just ten or twenty miles away. This "tower of Babel," one veteran recalled, became a source of "agony" to the army's guides.[35]

In such an environment, US Army commanders naturally valued the few trustworthy individuals who spoke English, Spanish, and native archipelagic dialects. They also competed to monopolize such intermediaries' services, even at the expense of fellow officers' operations. In the summer of 1898, however, perhaps only two Americans qualified for such a trilingual status. One of them, Maj. Frank S. Bourns, a thirty-two-year-old wartime volunteer, first visited the islands eleven years earlier as a University of Michigan undergraduate and novice ornithologist on an expedition to collect museum specimens led by Joseph B. Steere, a faculty zoologist and paleontologist. Bourns returned with fellow Steere student Dean Worcester for a second trip that lasted from 1890 to 1893. Visiting most major islands, Bourns developed an impressive knowledge of Tagalog as well as Spanish. Arriving at Cavite in July 1898 as a surgeon, Bourns overnight became a translator for Gen. Francis V. Greene and Gen. Thomas Anderson. Gen. Arthur MacArthur, also part of the invasion, described him as "one of the best interpreters that I ever saw."[36]

Crucially, Bourns's linguistic versatility and labor forged an American intelligence apparatus capable of enlisting Filipinos of all classes in the consolidation of US sovereignty. Over the next two months, as his army confronted Spanish troops and sidelined erstwhile Filipino allies, Bourns translated documents that passed between their commanders. Interrogating Spanish deserters, he mediated surrender negotiations with Spanish generals from which US generals excluded Gen. Aguinaldo and his staff. As postwar tensions between their armies mounted, however, Bourns pumped Filipino civilians for information. In September 1898, when Gen. Elwell S. Otis, new army commander and military governor, named Bourns president of Manila's Board of Health, he befriended several Filipino doctors, including Trinidad H. Pardo de Tavera, whom Otis also named to the board. By early 1899, Bourns was handling Pardo de Tavera and other *ilustrados* as intelligence assets. Easing their retreat from the Malolos republic, the major helped Taft turn these *americanistas* into the nucleus of the pro-peace Partido Federal by December 1900. Yet Bourns also told members of President McKinley's First Philippine Commission, led by Cornell University president Jacob Schurman, that his Tagalog enabled him to gather equally vital intelligence from non-elites. After Schurman arrived in February 1899, Bourns told him that his "personal acquaintances with many of the people," especially "in the lower and middle classes," granted him access to "information not otherwise obtainable."[37]

Bourns's linguistic labor involved a politics of translation pivoting on trust. Between late 1898 and January 1899, his small corps of Filipino informants in and around Manila allowed US occupiers to manage rising tensions with Aguinaldo's republic and army. Yet Bourns believed he only established and maintained this network because his Tagalog obviated the need for a second Filipino interpreter, whom informants would never have trusted given revolutionaries' intrigue in the city. "As a rule," Bourns told Schurman's commissioners, Filipinos seemed "very willing to talk whenever they found anyone who could speak their language." Yet they also showed a "great disinclination to talk through an interpreter," he said, if "they lacked confidence" in him.[38]

The suspect translator to whom Bourns alluded here was almost certainly Teodoro Sandico. Born at Manila in 1860, Sandico studied law there and in Spain before he joined the Freemasons, a locus of indio and mestizo dissent in a colony run by friars. By 1889, Sandico was helping run *La Solidaridad*, the Propagandists' newspaper, in Madrid. In 1897, he joined Aguinaldo and his exiled coterie at Hong Kong. Fluent in English, Sandico translated during talks with US diplomats and negotiated Adm. George Dewey's arms shipments to the islands following victory at Manila Bay. In August 1898, however, immediately after the Americans occupied Manila, Sandico, one of Aguinaldo's few English-speaking interpreters, cleverly exploited his role as a linguistic interlocutor to subvert US sovereignty. While serving as the Malolos republic's chief diplomat, Sandico secured a job translating for the American provost marshal's office in Manila as it policed and monitored revolutionaries. A double agent, Sandico gathered intelligence on the occupiers and conducted counterintelligence by surveilling pro-annexationist Filipino informants. By September, under the occupiers' noses, he also started covertly organizing a nationalist militia inside the city. According to Gen. Otis, the scheme eluded detection because insurgents pretended the groups were nothing more than fraternal "popular clubs" meant "to give the poorer classes amusement and education." Otis, outraged when the ruse was discovered, alleged that Sandico even convened "public entertainments in athletics to which our officers were invited, and in which our soldiers were asked to participate." By December, Manila's provost marshal, Gen. Robert Hughes, exposed Sandico's plot, fired him, and warned him to cease all clandestine activity. Yet at least one other Filipino interpreter working for the Americans continued to feed Aguinaldo information. War in early February primed Sandico to detonate his urban guerrillas, but their desultory attacks did little more than destroy Tondo. In July 1899, when Bourns quit the army for the states, Otis handed his Filipino network to Dean Worcester, his fellow Steere student, Philippine Commission member, and only other American with equal agility in native languages. After Bourns returned to the islands in 1900, he helped Worcester turn their friends into Federalistas.[39]

Bourns and Worcester were exceptions to a rule of linguistic incapacity that weakened US counterinsurgency. In central Luzon, as US operations against Aguinaldo's forces expanded in geographic reach, logistical complexity, and civil-administrative responsibility throughout 1899, senior army officers grew desperate for linguists. In extremis, Gen. Henry Lawton's tribulations illustrated both their army's dependence on translators and transimperial currents of militarized knowledge. In late April 1899, Lawton pushed his division north from Manila through Bulacan and Pampanga provinces, pressing insurgents led by Gen. Antonio Luna without any Spanish-Tagalog interpreter. From Angat, Lawton complained to Gen. Otis that he had resorted to using the Filipino manservant of Henry A. Ramsden, Great Britain's vice-consul in the islands, after they visited Lawton's camp. Ramsden, born in Cuba, was the son of the British consul at Santiago; in fact, his father had been posted there in July 1898 when Lawton's army occupied the city. Though Lawton found the junior Ramsden's Filipino aide "invaluable," the man soon returned to his regular duties at Manila. Lawton telegraphed Otis that he "must communicate with citizens" and pleaded with Otis to lobby Ramsden to return the Filipino. Austere to a fault, Otis refused. Ramsden compensated by finding at Baliuag two "intelligent" men to assist Lawton as guides and interpreters: a Spaniard, freed from insurgent captivity, and the town's Spanish-era presidente. Approved by Otis, they lasted eight days. When Lawton implored Manila to send him a Spaniard fluent in English, Otis's headquarters replied such a person would be "difficult to find."[40]

Bourns's intelligence work hinted that ilustrados were more accessible and reliable as linguistic adjuncts. These Filipino elites soon proved to be the linchpins of Americans' earliest attempts to establish the local administrative superstructure of US occupation beyond Manila. In early July 1899, after peace negotiations faltered, Lawton's division pushed south into Cavite province, pressing insurgents led by Lt. Gen. Mariano Trías. As Lawton's troops seized and garrisoned Las Piñas, Parañaque, Bacoor, and Imus, the general ordered his subordinates to organize new municipal governments run by Filipino officials, some of whom they claimed welcomed the Americans. Yet Lawton and his brigadiers, eager to promote US sovereignty and its benefits, but lacking the interpreters they needed to communicate with Tagalog speakers, looked to Dean Worcester and his Filipino associates for help. Visiting Lawton's lines, Worcester himself attributed various "difficulties" between occupiers and occupied to the "inability of the two parties concerned to understand each other."[41]

Worcester's ilustrado associate, Felipe Calderon, resolved this crisis for Lawton, and embodied Filipino intermediaries' linguistic labor as a counterrevolutionary force. A forty-one-year-old lawyer who owned large plantations in Cavite and Batangas, Calderon in late 1898 drafted the Malolos constitution, aided by Cayetano Arellano, an ilustrado jurist and Calderon's former boss. Fearing that Aguinaldo and his allies wished to impose populist-military dictatorship, however, Calderon, expressing a preference for an "oligarchy of intelligence," soon turned *americanista*. By April 1899, he was encouraging Schurman's civil commissioners to "attract" Filipinos to US sovereignty with promises of reforms. In June 1899, with Arellano's assistance, Calderon also helped the Americans organize new district civil courts with Filipino justices in and about Manila. That same month, after Worcester and Calderon told Lawton and Otis that Caviteños desired local government, Otis authorized Worcester to have Calderon and Arellano draft a "simple scheme." Their plan blended municipal reforms of the 1893 Maura Law with American-style democracy, making local officials subject to popular elections. After Otis approved the new system, Lawton enlisted Worcester and Calderon for the translation he needed to implement it. Meeting with Caviteño principales at Parañaque, Las Piñas, Bacoor, and Imus, Worcester transmitted Lawton's words in Spanish to Calderon, who translated them into Tagalog, which Worcester claimed he spoke "perfectly." Worcester also related that assembled elites, initially terrified, quickly warmed to pledges that they could retain all taxes and elect their presidente and cabezas, the chiefs of barrios. As Otis adopted Calderon's municipal plan, one civilian American observer

Municipal Home Rule for the Filipinos. This sketch portrays *ilustrado* Felipe Calderon translating for Maj. Gen. Henry Lawton, Dean Worcester, and Brig. Gen. Frederick D. Grant (*seated, right to left*) as they organize a Filipino-run municipal government at Las Piñas in Cavite Province in late June 1899. The artist both acknowledged Calderon's role in intercultural communication and obscured his agency in colonial counterinsurgency, failing to identify him by name. From Wilcox, *Harper's History of the War in the Philippines*, 215.

gushed that the mestizo's "energetic eloquence" made locals enthusiastic for Lawton's "home rule" of "fraternity, equality, and liberty."[42]

If ensuing guerrilla warfare eroded such imperial optimism, the Ramsden episode and Cavite conferences prefigured a spatial politics of linguistic intermediacy that shaped Lawton's operational capabilities. The farther his division moved from Manila and its cooperative multilingual elites, the more the general struggled to access Spanish-Tagalog translators. By late summer, as newly arrived American army wives at Manila fumed that Chinese and Filipino servants did not understand English, Lawton groused that he needed an interpreter just to talk with his chef. The army's need for interpreters became clear in the lengths to which Lawton went to procure them. By September

1899, Lawton had imported from Texas one M. K. Nelson, known to San Antonio's army post there, to act as his new English-Spanish translator. Yet Lawton went without a Spanish-Tagalog interpreter until early December, when Manila sent one to his division, halted at Cabanatuan. Two weeks later, Lawton was killed at San Mateo.[43]

The US Army's resort to British consular aides, ilustrados, and interpreters from the Southwest all showed how linguistic labor in the Philippines, as in Cuba, rested on preexisting imperial histories and infrastructures of intercultural communication. Army records and American soldiers' narratives indicate that Spaniards and mestizos constituted the largest demographic of intermediaries aiding US troops early in the Philippine War. Between late 1899 and early 1900, columns dispersing into central and later northern and southern Luzon progressively defeated insurgent forces before breaking into small detachments to garrison towns and patrol barrios. This introduced them to hundreds of Spaniards, many of whom left Filipino captivity by release, escape, or liberation. Dozens served US troops as guides and interpreters. Many were veterans of Spain's army or the Guardia Civil; a few had served with the insurgents.[44]

Available sources rarely convey Spaniards' motives for working with the Americans, but protection and pay ranked high. In counterinsurgency's political economy, cultural affinities between colonizers fostered familiarity and trust. The enmities of the 1898 war behind them, Americans recognized Spanish intermediaries as fellow white men who shared hostility toward Filipino revolutionaries. Army officers' reports often acknowledged Spaniards' role in helping US soldiers track and locate guerrillas, arms caches, and Spanish and American prisoners. Not all Spaniards proved trustworthy. American officers, accusing some of malfeasance and abuse, learned that old colonial habits die hard. Spanish intermediaries also manipulated their new allies. In early 1900 at Batangas province, one clever army captain persuaded Col. Robert Bullard to help him chase phantom American prisoners from Lipa to Rosario as a ruse to rescue fellow Spaniards held by Gen. Miguel Malvar.[45] Spanish guides and interpreters, symbolizing the continuity of local knowledge in imperial transition, transferred the spatial memory and cant of colonialism to a new sovereignty.

Chinese and Chinese mestizo men also frequently guided the Americans. Katipuneros' 1896 revolt, renewed warfare with Spain in 1898, and ensuing US war and occupation exacerbated longstanding tensions between Filipinos and Chinese. Filipinos' resentment toward Chinese merchants' and craftsmen's economic power in Spain's colony figured prominently in nationalist discourse. Though Aguinaldo's revolutionary government and the Malolos republic maintained some discriminatory Spanish policies in taxation and other areas, he officially discouraged anti-Chinese violence and sought to enlist Chinese elites as allies. Still, during the Philippine War, many Chinese—seeking safety for their lives and property—allied with US occupiers, even after the Americans banned Chinese migration to the islands. Revolutionaries anticipated this danger. In February 1899, only a few days into the conflict, Felipe Buencamino, the interior secretary, warned Filipinos to be vigilant for Chinese "spies." In Batangas, Albay, and other Luzon provinces, "Chinos" who guided US forces to insurgent troops, camps, and arms often faced intimidation and suffered violent reprisals.[46]

By early 1900, however, as US occupiers throughout Luzon confronted guerrilla warfare, Filipinos increasingly provided crucial knowledgeable labor. Their social networks and geographic consciousness became especially critical to American soldiers' capacity to identify and locate insurgents and sympathetic civilians aiding them. During the conventional warfare of 1899, US troops rarely needed guides to locate Aguinaldo's army. Americans aggressively pursuing insurgents across central Luzon's thickly settled plains easily detected and attacked massed Filipino formations by staying as close to them as possible. Relying on field observation, Spanish maps (which they often complained were inaccurate), army engineers' surveys and route maps, and civilian intelligence, US soldiers usually found the Liberation Army easily and fixed it in combat. American commanders used Filipinos guides infrequently and spontaneously in response to tactical contingencies. Fighting between Lawton's and Trías's troops in northern Cavite in June 1899 illustrated the dynamic. Pushing south from Manila, Lawton initially hesitated to assault roughly 1,000 entrenched insurgents guarding several strategic bridges over the Zapote River, near its mouth on Manila Bay. The general and aides searched in vain for a route around Filipino defenses until a local man, Tomas Torres, volunteered to guide them. Lacking a Tagalog-fluent interpreter, Lawton and his staff communicated with Torres only by hand signals, yet he revealed a path along the beach and through salt marshes that let the Americans maneuver behind the insurgents' left, undetected. Frontal and flank assaults routed the Filipinos, who inflicted few casualties—including Torres, whom Lawton and aides found killed by a bullet. Meeting the man's wife on the beach, baby in her arms, searching for him, they asked Manila to issue her a consolation payment. Ten months later, the garrison at Bacoor was still giving rice to Torres's bereaved mother amid food scarcity exacerbated by the occupation.[47]

In his report, Lawton ennobled Torres's role in victory at Zapote Bridge by suggesting that it proved Filipinos were willing to voluntarily sacrifice themselves for US sovereignty. Yet as Howland's Mindanao expedition suggested, American counterinsurgents often forcibly expropriated subaltern local knowledge and knowledgeable labor. Problems of coercion and trust thus troubled the political economy of counterinsurgency even during the war's conventional phase, in 1899 and early 1900, when Filipinos often seemed to guide US soldiers by their own volition. Indeed, army officers' reports from this period originated a trope ubiquitous in the war's American literature: the "amigo" guide. Seemingly friendly at first, when these amigos offered to guide Americans' columns, such Filipinos, they alleged, suddenly and inexplicably became unhelpful or even hostile. Officers began recording suspicions that these strangers intentionally diverted them from objectives over lengthy, exhausting, and time-consuming routes. Americans thus added the amigo guide to torrid tropical heat, torrential rains, and poor roads as factors frustrating their mobility. Gen. Samuel B. M. Young, a veteran of the Civil War and Cuba, where he led a cavalry brigade for Lawton, documented the phenomenon. In late November 1899, Young's troopers raced north through Pangasinan province in pursuit of Gen. Aguinaldo and followers shielding his retreat. At Binalonan, Young asked a Filipino to point him northwest, to Pozorrubio. Instead, the man sent his cavalry on a road leading west to Manaoag, thus buying Aguinaldo's retinue time to flee. "The guide," growled Young, "was not shot because he could not be found."[48]

Young's amigo guide heralded a kinetic dialectic of enticement and exploitation suffusing military intermediaries' labor during the war's guerrilla phase and future Pulahan and Moro conflicts. American troops penetrating rural areas far from Manila broke into detachments to occupy small cities and towns. Tasked with imposing and enforcing civil order, however, US garrisons lacked both good maps of remote regions and linguists able to translate between Spanish and vernaculars. Identifying and finding insurgents who seemed to melt into the civilian population or impenetrable jungles and mountains placed a premium on tapping local knowledge. Americans organizing municipalities in late 1899 and early 1900 initially assumed officials' loyalty, and regularly employed these Filipinos and police as guides and interpreters. Easing their collaboration, US commanders placed these men on army or civil payrolls and paid them cash from "secret service" funds. Some intermediaries even bargained with US handlers for higher salaries.[49]

By early 1900, however, escalating guerilla warfare incentivized coercive means for eliciting Filipinos' cognitive labor. As American commanders, struggling to find and suppress insurgents, gradually realized that some overtly friendly civilians were actually aiding armed nationalists covertly, they devised various techniques for forcibly extracting Filipinos' knowledge. The ambiguities of Civil War–era law of war and its permissive doctrine of "military necessity" empowered US soldiers to exploit their thin protections for civilians and captives. Drafted by Columbia University professor Francis Lieber and adopted in 1863 by Union armies as General Orders No. 100 (GO 100), this code served as the default legal framework for US military operations in the Philippines. Though Civil War veterans and regular officers trained at West Point were more familiar with GO 100 than were volunteers, commanders of all kinds took advantage of the code's conflicting licenses and limits. The Lieber Code, as it was known, authorized occupying troops to harshly punish irregular warriors. It also allowed American soldiers to conscript civilian guides whenever they could not "obtain them otherwise" and to kill them if they "misled intentionally," as well as any civilian who guided the enemy voluntarily. At the same time, GO 100 seemed to restrain Americans' coercive power over guides by proscribing torture. Army officers conscripting Filipino guides often selectively exploited GO 100's authorities and ignored its constraints as needed; using techniques such as water torture and mock executions, some outsourced torture to colonial auxiliaries. By late 1900, both Young and McArthur explicitly invoked the Lieber Code as they sought legal cover for draconian counterinsurgency.[50]

Events in northwestern Luzon demonstrated how dueling assertions of state sovereignty ensnared intermediaries and their cognitive labor in a perverse dialectic of militarized coercion only loosely regulated by law. Led by Gen. Young's cavalry, the first US troops to enter the Ilocos region, in December 1899, met a geographical and cultural environment quite different from that which they encountered in central Luzon. The Ilocos, inhabited at this time by some 531,000 people, may be divided roughly into two zones. The first—western lowlands along the South China Sea serrated by river valleys, chiefly the Abra—was populated by Hispanized and Catholicized Ilocano speakers. Some 3,600 square miles in area, this coastal region had been organized by Spanish officials into four provinces, running some 200 miles from south to north: La Union, Ilocos Sur, Ilocos Norte, and Abra, with Abra to the east of Ilocos Sur. The other zone—an interior area composed of the rugged Cordillera mountains—was inhabited mostly by animist aborigines, known as Igorots, who long resisted Spain's Catholic colonialism. Following Spanish-era precedent, the Philippine Commission later organized its provinces of Benguet, Lepanto, and Bontoc into a special administration: the Mountain Province. In late 1899, however, Young's pursuit of Aguinaldo brought a new war to the Ilocos.

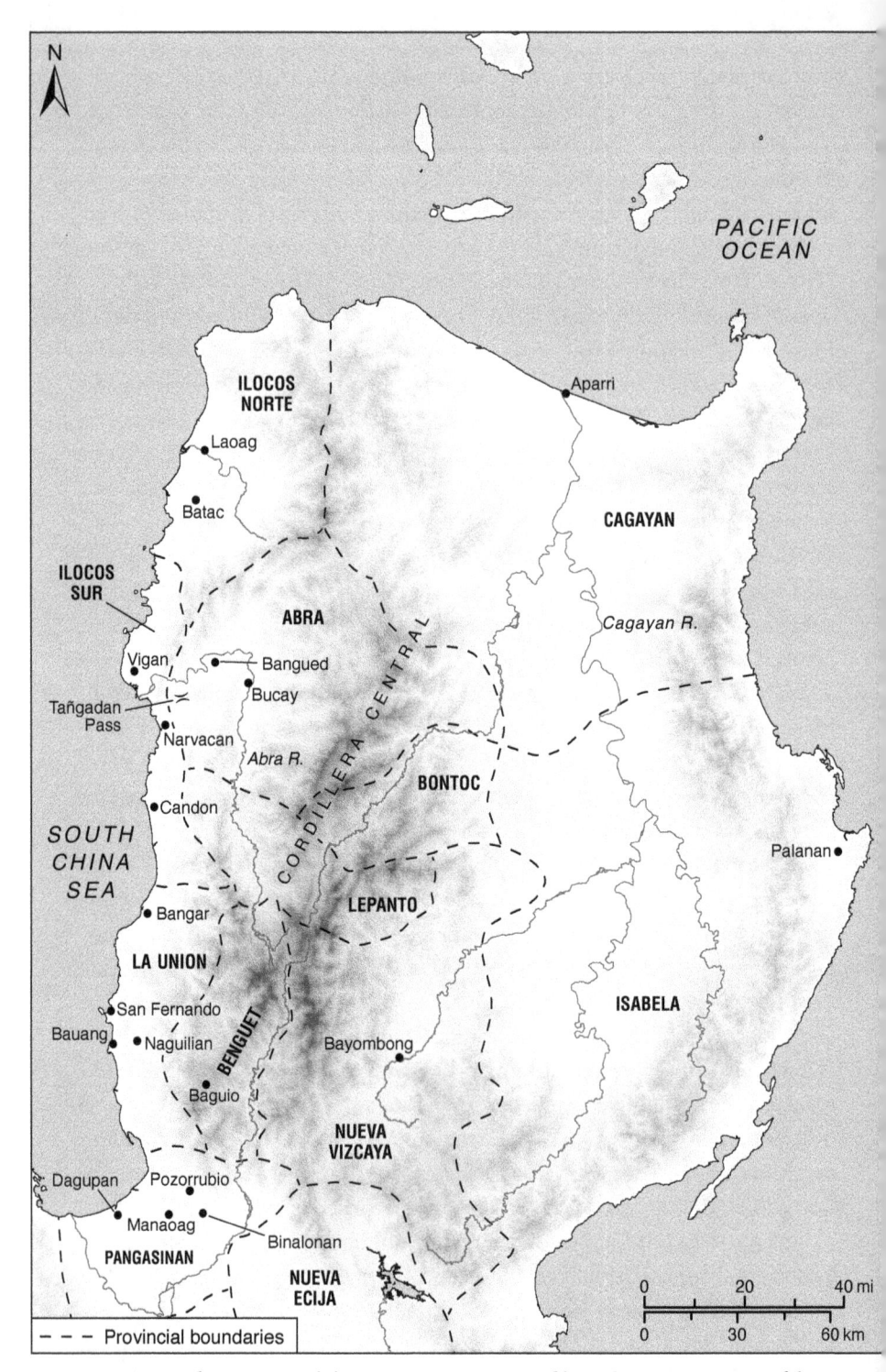

MAP 1.3 Northern Luzon, Philippines, 1898. Map created by Gabe Moss, courtesy of the author.

Squeezing civilians between rival armies and states, US invaders forced Ilocanos and Igorots to choose whether or not they would cooperate with them.[51]

Ilocanos and Igorots were hardly new to labor coercion. In 1898 and 1899, Tagalog revolutionaries and their Ilocano allies impressed Ilocano and Igorot men for various tasks, from carrying supplies to constructing fortifications. While Americans claimed that Ilocanos and Igorots served willingly as guides, couriers, and cargadores (from the Spanish *cargar*, "to carry"), Young's reports hinted at omnipresent violence. Reaching Narvacan in Ilocos Sur in early December 1899, his troopers met three Ilocano men who claimed they had escaped from Gen. Manuel Tinio's camp at Tañgadan Pass, guarding a route into Abra province, where insurgents forced them to build trenches. The Ilocanos led Young's 250 troops there. Backed by reinforcements, they dislodged 700 Filipinos commanded by Lt. Col. Blas Villamor and Maj. Juan Villamor, cousins from Abra. Young's praise for his Ilocano guides' "loyal service" underscored their peril. If "caught by the insurgents they would be put to death," he admitted, but "if they attempted treachery with my people, they would be shot."[52]

Increasingly, insurgency and counterinsurgency here turned on Ilocanos' and Igorots' local geographic and linguistic knowledge and the colonial social relations in which it was embedded. Following defeat at Tañgadan, Maj. Juan Villamor shifted his men into what his cousin Blas described as "a war of the small against the big." Gen. Young, following Gen. Otis's orders, imposed a defensive occupation by installing garrisons, organizing municipal governments, and protecting officials, all on the flawed assumption that Ilocanos did not support a Tagalog-led revolution. Young and subordinates also began to recruit, or compel, local Filipino officials, police, and other civilians for translating and guiding. A few Ilocanos acted in dual capacities. Individuals noted in US Army records as "interpreters" often served as guides or identified place names for towns and other details on maps; Ilocanos classified as "guides" sometimes translated between Spanish and Ilocano. Such language work became key in a region where few knew Spanish. A 1900 survey of Vigan, Ilocos Sur's capital, estimated that 1 percent of its adult men could read, write, or speak any language other than Ilocano. Indeed, Lt. Harold P. Howard noted that in this same year, Young administered loyalty oaths to 2,000 surrendered insurgents, aided by a priest translating from Spanish to Ilocano. Eventually, Howard tried to reduce Americans' need for local linguists by crafting Ilocano primers that allowed US soldiers themselves to say "I want a guide," "I want twelve cargadores," and "Is the road good?"[53]

Ilocano and Igorot knowledge paid dividends. Guides warned carefree US Army officers not to cross open ground and thus unwittingly expose their patrols to insurgent spotters watching from distant hills and mountaintops. They estimated accurately the time it would take for troops to travel from one point to another on foot or horseback—information essential for successfully coordinating separate detachments' tactical movements. If some commanders applauded guides and interpreters for enabling small victories, the obverse was also true. Army officers who lacked guides often complained of useless maps with markings that did not actually correspond to terrain, or an inability to plan and execute movements. Without interpreters, they struggled to gather intelligence. They also blamed mistakes, losses, and defeats on intermediaries. In April 1901, when Capt. George A. Dodd and two Ilocano police failed to find insurgents reported to be near Batac, he blamed guides, though he detected "no duplicity" in their "conduct."[54]

American army officers' various methods for mobilizing and managing Filipino intermediaries tended to reflect their improvisational pragmatism. If they lacked voluntary guides, commanders typically conscripted substitutes, either immediately before field operations or during them. Given that captured insurgents usually had the most recent and thus more accurate and actionable information, some Americans developed a preference for capturing guerrillas in the field, just so they could compel them to lead their captors to comrades. (On at least one occasion, Americans forced US deserters they had just nabbed to guide them.) Inevitably, captive insurgents' greater intelligence value but opposing loyalties made them vulnerable to threats and torture; some prisoners complied when promised money or freedom. The militarized colonial qualities of intermediaries' labor, however, blurred tidy lines between willing and unwilling cooperation. They even caused some US commanders to question the benefits, if any, to which guides might be entitled. A few officers debated whether guides wounded in action should receive the same medical care as troops.[55]

With time, however, Americans saw advantages to formalizing the work of "voluntary" Filipino intermediaries. In February 1900, as Lt. Col. Robert Lee Howze took command of Ilocos Norte from his headquarters at Laoag, he telegraphed Gen. Young requesting permission to "enlist" two "natives of good character" for each garrison to act as guides, couriers, and interpreters. Howze, a Texan and West Pointer who served in the Indian Wars and Cuba, argued that such persons would be crucial to the success of local governments and schools, which, in his view, tended "to cement interests common to natives" and Americans. Young concurred and persuaded Gen. Otis to authorize each post on Luzon with one or more companies to hire one interpreter, "scout," or guide, and pay them up to 65 pesos a month. Manila soon required that any guide not already on army payrolls receive compensation after each operation in sums up to 30 pesos. Bounties for captured guns made it profitable for Filipinos to aid Americans, especially in regions where specie was scarce. Money's efficacy in securing and regularizing occupiers' access to local knowledge was evident in nationalists' attempts to discredit it. By March 1900, insurgents tried to reinforce flagging morale by alleging that Chinese and "wicked Filipinos" guiding enemies on Luzon had fallen for their "trickery," believing the invaders would "keep their promises." "Many have been deceived" and "received no pay," one rebel claimed, "after delivering themselves body and soul."[56]

In the Ilocos, as elsewhere on Luzon, Filipino elites who previously served the Spanish preserved their status and income by parlaying their knowledge for the new colonizers. When Gen. Young found that Mariano Acosta— Vigan's alcalde under the Spanish, later elected to that position under Aguinaldo's republic—seemed "very friendly," he gave him a job translating for $25 US gold a month. To justify such expenses, commanders regularly evaluated interpreters' ability for superiors, describing their educational credentials as well as particular "capability and expression" in various languages. Yet the military's institutionalization of elite Filipino knowledge had its drawbacks. Using these men to access subaltern knowledge risked activating the rural social hierarchy that many Americans claimed to abhor as a vestige of Spain's exploitative colonialism. Describing these class relations as "feudalism" or as "patron-client" relations, Americans then and scholars since recognized that principales' participation in cognitive coercion reinforced their local socioeconomic and political power.[57]

Americans' alliances of convenience with intermediaries could appear to revive colonial-style cruelties that soldiers claimed their enlightened occupation had abolished. At Laoag in early 1900, Howze made Aguedo Agbayani, an Ilocano politico, his chief interpreter and "civil adjutant." In 1896, as Laoag's mayor, Agbayani defied local Katipuneros; two years later, he welcomed the Ilocos' Spanish governor when he retreated from a rout at Candon. Agbayani's methods yielded captured insurgents and arms, and the gratitude of Gen. Young, who rewarded him with a $150 monthly salary. Yet Agbayani's brutal treatment of prisoners sparked accusations of fatal torture from credible sources, including a conscientious US Army provost judge. The allegations reached Manila and upset Taft, given his program to convince Filipinos of US sovereignty's benevolence. Even Gen. Manuel Tinio himself wrote Howze, protesting acts "unworthy" of US soldiers "who profess the principles of liberty." Pressured by Taft, Young told Howze to strip Agbayani of his office, high salary, and secret service funds, but Howze resisted, and insisted that Ilocos Norte should remain "exclusively under military control." Hailing Agbayani's effectiveness in counterinsurgency, Howze dismissed the allegations against him as false rumors, manufactured by "enemies of Good Government and enemies of Americans." Even after he stripped Agbayani of pay and power, however, Howze's endorsement of the man haunted him. Whenever Howze was up for promotion, the abuses at Laoag resurfaced as stains on his record.[58]

For some Filipino intermediaries, the regularization of their labor also facilitated upward social mobility. In this regard, few contributed more to Americans' victory in Luzon—and gained more from it—than Crispulo Patajo. Originally from Bauang, in La Union, this tenant farmer and probable schoolteacher joined a brother and brother-in-law in 1897 as founding members of La Guardia de Honor, a millenarian Catholic sect with Dominican origins, in Pangasinan province. Promoting a militant Catholic agrarianism in defiance of friars and Filipino landlords, the group claimed empty lands at Cabaruan, a barrio of Urdaneta. Cabaruan quickly attracted as many as 40,000 adherents, mostly peasants drawn to its egalitarian ideals and communal life and disaffected by principales' persistent and corrupt rule. Guardia leaders initially allied with the Katipunan, yet mounting tensions between the sect and nationalists reflected larger social divisions, which by late 1898 began bleeding into the revolution itself. In areas of central and northern Luzon, preexisting class tensions exacerbated by anticolonial revolt, recession, and ecological and epidemiological disaster frayed peasants' deference to Filipino elites and sparked open and popular resistance. Between late 1898 and late 1899, as the Guardia's message spread to Tarlac, Zambales, Nueva Ecija, and Ilocos Sur, alarmed Filipino and US authorities increasingly feared that the group threatened their sovereignty. By November 1899, however, after US soldiers raided Cabaruan and arrested Guardia leaders, Patajo sided with them.[59]

Patajo's career demonstrated that even the most loyal Filipino intermediaries served the Americans from self-interested and quotidian motives, including exacting revenge against insurgents for transgressions as petty as theft. After Patajo briefly helped US troops hunt insurgents in Pangasinan, he returned to Bauang carrying Americans' endorsement. When he started recruiting for his old sect but required that new Guardia members swear allegiance to the United States, Bauang's presidente arrested him. From jail, Patajo denounced the official as a revolutionary, then offered to expose the entire guerrilla infrastructure in the province. Liberating Patajo, Col. William

Duvall, La Union's military governor, made use of him and an estimated 300 followers, most armed only with clubs and bolos before Duvall gave them captured arms. In March 1900 at Naguilian, on the trail from Bauang into Benguet province, Patajo ferreted out guerrillas and sympathizers and forced others to join him. Deemed "absolutely reliable" by Naguilian's garrison, Patajo ingratiated himself with Lt. William T. Johnston, Duvall's intelligence aide. As their new "Chief Detective," he led up to 500 Guardia loyalists on a crusade, or rampage, to eradicate insurgency in the region.[60]

Patajo's entrepreneurial warfare undermined occupiers' civilizing agenda. Scouring La Union, Benguet, and Ilocos Sur, Patajo and Guardia adherents terrorized insurgents and civilians alike, denouncing, assaulting, robbing, and killing regardless of victims' apparent political leanings. Duvall and Johnston incentivized such tactics by refusing to pay them anything but cash for rifles. Patajo's militia even cajoled, or threatened, US Army quartermaster employees into handing over food, forage, and labor. Patajo shifted several towns into the Americans' column, but his appointment of fellow Guardias and relatives to salaried posts in new municipal governments smacked of sectarian nepotism. Despite such tactics, or because of them, the Americans credited great progress in the Ilocos to Patajo and his gang. Revolutionaries agreed; as early as April 1900 they promised to kill all Guardia supporters and burn down their homes. Frustrated, Gen. Manuel Tinio later added conciliation to intimidation. Declaring his desire to "disappear" Patajo, the "traitor and terrible *americanista*," the general promised to pay 150 pesos for "his severed head." Patajo survived and went on to aid counterinsurgents in Abra and Batangas. Accepting a regular commission in the Philippine Scouts, he climbed US Army ranks higher than any other Filipino at the time. Winning a major's clover leaf, Patajo retired at Fort Leavenworth in 1905.[61]

Tinio's proclamation confirmed both the effectiveness of US-allied intermediaries and insurgents' willingness to counter it with equally coercive measures. In the Ilocos and other parts of Luzon, guerrillas not only promised but inflicted reprisals against Filipinos who guided US troops, voluntarily or not. Despite Americans' attempts to shield them from retaliation by obscuring their identities, these individuals' safety could never be entirely guaranteed.[62] As the Ilocos showed, Filipinos who aided US troops tacked between the Scylla of GO 100 and the Charybdis of insurgents' revenge, risking violent coercion and retaliation from both sides.

Early in the Ilocos' occupation, rebels there began systematically targeting civilians who they believed had guided the Americans or interpreted for them. In February 1900, Col. Juan Villamor informed *abreños* that they were now "forbidden to act as guides to the American soldiers or columns in their marches from town to town or from barrio to barrio." Any person caught violating the order, he warned, could expect instant death. The zeal with which Villamor enforced this decree, however, suggested the extent to which *abreño* intermediaries had already damaged the revolution. A week after it appeared, Maj. Thomas Ashburn, commander at Bangued, reported two guides assassinated. At nearby San Jose, insurgents struck again. Abducting a man who had guided the Americans "faithfully," they shot him and the town's presidente and vice presidente. Then, at a barrio five miles up the Abra River from Bangued, twenty insurgents kidnapped a police officer who had recently led Ashburn's patrols; never found, the major presumed him dead. By late March, Gen. Tinio, impressed by Villamor's example, mandated instant death for anyone "who voluntarily offers to serve as guides for the enemy, unless it be for the purpose of misleading them from the true path." Notified of Tinio's order, Col. Duvall ordered subordinates in Ilocos Sur to warn the presidentes that Americans would inflict "the same punishment" on any official complying with it. Although Young made Duvall's retaliatory threat official policy in June 1900 by invoking GO 100, insurgents throughout the archipelago issued similar warnings that year and into the next. Americans and Filipinos thus trapped Ilocanos in a vice of mutual coercion, promising fatal consequences for anyone caught guiding the enemy. To dissuade Filipinos, some insurgents started killing the relatives of guides and interpreters.[63]

Guerillas' threats, facilitated and strengthened by ties of kinship, economic interest, and ideology, increasingly prompted Americans to question the loyalties of former insurgents turned intermediaries. The story of Maj. Joaquin Natividad fed such fears. From Nueva Ecija province, Natividad established his patriotic bona fides in 1896 when he backed the Katipuneros; he later joined Aguinaldo in exile at Hong Kong. In early December 1899, after Natividad surrendered to Howze at Laoag, he won the colonel's trust by feeding him reliable intelligence on Gen. Tinio and his troops. When Young paroled him, Natividad spent months translating for him. Yet Young began to wonder about Natividad when he sought permission to visit a town not yet garrisoned, allegedly to visit his wife; Young, investigating, discovered that Natividad had never married. Perhaps sensing Young's suspicion, Natividad defected and resumed command of Ilocos Norte's insurgents. In early 1901, though, he surrendered again, this time to Gen. Frederick Funston, in Nueva Ecija. Funston briefly considered including him in his scheme to capture Emilio Aguinaldo, which hinged on a Filipino posing as commander of a fake guerrilla column. Wisely, given Natividad's record and Young's threats to shoot him on sight,

Funston decided against it. Some distrustful Americans used guiding itself as a stratagem, requesting guides from local officials to deceive insurgents about imminent operations or to test their fealty. Gen. Young even tried arresting a "bad man" by asking him to guide troops "as a pretext."[64]

Such incidents revealed the making of a political economy of counterinsurgency based increasingly on Americans' and Filipinos' perceptions of each other's trustworthiness. In a tense, plastic, and nebulous market of trust and distrust, militarized colonial knowledge work pushed Americans and intermediaries to constantly reevaluate each other's intentions, and the costs and benefits of satisfying or defying them. In the proverbial house of mirrors that made up this contest over sovereignty, the false Filipino guide loomed large as an especially enigmatic and troubling figure.

As early as May 1900, when Duvall and Johnston discovered the insurgency's underground existence in Ilocos Sur, Americans in the region regularly doubted the fidelity of guides and other auxiliaries, including Ilocano officials supplying them. As Pvt. Richard Johnson, posted at Naguilian, recalled, Americans frequently wondered if such guides had played a "double-game" and "purposely led us astray." Fears of false guides only enhanced Americans' willingness to employ violence, or threats, to elicit faithful service and good intelligence. Given GO 100's prohibition of torture, however, occupiers rarely admitted they practiced it. Reports and memoirs often alluded to torture, and cloaked its use in allusion and euphemism. Domestic controversy over war atrocities, culminating in early 1902 Senate hearings, reinforced Americans' circumspection.[65]

When enlisted men and veterans were not writing for publication, or musing in their old age, however, they were more transparent about having tortured or killed Filipino guides. To superiors, relatives, or posterity, they recounted harming Filipinos and threatening them with death to extract information and service. William Oliver Trafton, a Texan volunteer who served in Abra from 1900 to 1901, recalled in his memoir how his unit of mounted scouts often hanged prisoners who pled ignorance of insurgents' whereabouts. According to Trafton, this frontier technique usually secured captives' assent to guide the Americans. Yet torture, he conceded, had not necessarily elicited honesty or loyalty. "Many times I think he talked too much," Trafton later remembered, "for he would send us into a death trap and get the Devil shot out of us." Army records, regimental histories, and personal narratives documenting such events affirmed Trafton's wisdom. His unit often made tortured guides "go in front and lead us to where the insurgents were." Yet the false guide invariably led them into ambushes "in thick brush," where he "would only have to make a few yards" before he was "out of sight." "At the first crack of a gun," explained Trafton, the guide "would duck and be gone if we did not shoot him on the spot."[66]

Trafton's memoir evoked the false Filipino guide's ubiquity in war literature. Haunting American soldiers' consciousness and imagination, this mysterious figure, a modern iteration of the trickster character in Filipino folklore, even populated war novels penned by US veterans. Strikingly, Americans' accounts betrayed a feeling that the false guide had victimized them, not the reverse.[67] False guides thus became palimpsests for Americans' response to a strange and terrifying guerrilla conflict that often seemed more like shadow-boxing than war.

Of course, false guides were never purely the invention of fatigued counterinsurgent psyches. In the Ilocos and beyond, Americans discovered correspondence documenting their existence and duplicity; revolutionaries' memoirs also confirmed they intentionally used false guides. Such persons had vital military functions: at minimum, they further exhausted, distracted, and demoralized US soldiers already suffering the physical and mental toll of "hikes" after insurgents, the tropical climate and diseases, and a hostile or indifferent people in a faraway land. Americans imputed various nefarious acts to false guides. Alleging they functioned as human alarms, soldiers claimed that guides who they had notified of imminent operations tipped off guerillas nearby, allowing them to escape or organize attacks and ambushes taking advantage of Americans' vulnerabilities. Guides' alleged techniques for undermining US operations ranged from coughing as they approached a suspicious village to killing the officer they just volunteered to lead. Unsurprisingly, some Americans, increasingly leery, dispensed with guides altogether as soon as they acquired knowledge of the countryside. A few clever officers devised countermeasures. When a "friendly native" volunteered to take troops to camps or arms, these commanders brought a second trustworthy guide to check the first. One American believed this technique allowed him to "anticipate treachery."[68]

These fears indicated the extent to which the minefields of trust and distrust that accompanied the work of military intermediaries also extended into US headquarters. Most American officers, relying necessarily on a shifting roster of guides and interpreters, rarely trusted them all fully or equally. Army commanders managed Filipino intermediaries in a dangerous minuet of intelligence and counterintelligence. Requiring their local knowledge, US military authorities still sought to deny these individuals access to valuable information, which, if it fell into the wrong hands, might disrupt operations and harm American soldiers. Funston's famous 1901 capture of Gen. Emilio Aguinaldo rested on such a fragile foundation of intercultural trust. At Nueva Ecija in late 1900, when Funston nearly captured Brig. Gen. Urbano Lacuna, he discovered blank and stamped insurgent letterhead that became key to his plans to march unopposed into Aguinaldo's camp. The ploy revolved around the pretense that Funston would appear to be the prisoner of an insurgent column, which, in fact, were Macabebe scouts posing as insurgents. The charade hinged on forwarding Aguinaldo forged correspondence using Lacuna's blank paper, notifying the general of Lacuna's intent to send the fake column.[69]

Such deception called for discretion. To forge Lacuna's signature, Funston relied on the expert penmanship of Roman Roque, an ex-insurgent officer who had surrendered to Funston and then worked as his interpreter. Roque, fluent and literate in both English and Tagalog, also spoke Pangasinan and Ilocano. After several days of practice, he produced an authentic-appearing script. Yet Funston never actually told Roque its purpose. The general, however, did trust another aide, Lazaro Segovia, enough to include him in the ruse. A Spaniard who claimed to have been in the islands since 1891, Segovia had been a sergeant in a Spanish regiment in the Ilocos when US forces invaded. Perhaps an adventurer and opportunist, Segovia in late 1898 joined the insurgent army following Manila's capitulation, serving as a lieutenant. In May 1900, however, he too surrendered to Funston, at San Isidro. Despite this record, Funston clearly felt that Segovia had proved his trustworthiness and talents as a "secret service man," guide, and interpreter fluent in English and Tagalog, as he kept Segovia fully abreast of the plot to snatch Aguinaldo. Funston had Segovia translate from Tagalog into Spanish a coded letter from the fugitive general that finally revealed his camp's location, at Palanan, in Isabela province. Describing Segovia as a "versatile and courageous Spaniard," the general even brought him on the risky but successful expedition.[70] Americans managing intermediaries thus constantly scrutinized their trustworthiness— never a fixed quantity but a moving and elusive target.

Roque's career showed how imperial transition made military intermediaries' labor, and the trust it accumulated, into capital by which these persons secured postwar political and social status. Elites who migrated from Spanish and republican offices to public posts in the new US colonial state often used their cognitive labor to secure lasting power. Even after the torture scandal cost Aguedo Agbayani his authority and salary at Laoag, he secured a position as Ilocos Norte's first US-era civil governor. (Agbayani enjoyed it only a few months before dying in a cholera epidemic.) Despite Gen. Young's threats to kill him, Joaquin Natividad boosted his credit with Taft's commission by organizing the Federalistas in Nueva Ecija and persuading others to surrender. Natividad studied law, became an accomplished attorney, and clerked for the islands' new Supreme Court. Remarkably, less-than-trustworthy men also ascended the civilian-run colonial hierarchy. At Nueva Ecija by 1901, Roman Roque leveraged his service for Funston into an appointment as provincial secretary. Incredibly, only eight years after Americans discovered Teodoro Sandico's machinations at Manila, he won gubernatorial election in Bulacan province. Some liberal army officers accepted the Philippine Commission's conciliatory approach. In March 1901, Col. William McCaskey, replacing Robert Howze as Laoag's commander, warned superiors that if they and Filipino allies prosecuted every insurgent guilty of war crimes who had since turned *americanista*, "there would be none left to assist us."[71]

The new civilian US colonial regime's administrative needs, not military necessity, ultimately settled the political economy of intermediaries in the Philippines. The army's formal employment of "native" interpreters on Luzon declined significantly after mid-1901 when American troops and their Filipino partners suppressed insurgents in most of the island, and generals started transferring civil authority to Taft's commission and local elites. By July that year, the army received just over half of the $17.4 million it requested from Manila's new civilian government to pay translators. To Taft, Gen. Adna Chaffee's headquarters complained that his troops' overworked linguists were "almost constantly employed in securing military information" in the twelve Luzon provinces which his army still ruled. Chaffee's aides even appealed to commissioners' stated interest in economic recovery and expansion. Slashing the ranks of military interpreters, they warned, would "seriously retard commercial transactions." Their case for Manila's financing of colonial-military translation fell on deaf ears, even as US troops came to rely heavily on translators and other auxiliaries during the Pulahan and Moro wars.[72] Yet intermediaries' imprint on US imperial formation endured. Like Cubans, Filipinos used their knowledge to secure a beachhead of postwar and post-occupation privilege and power, even at the cost of continued submission to US sovereignty. In a globalizing age of industry, however, American soldiers' desire for tropical knowledge extended to a science of subaltern manual labor equally essential to the making of US empire abroad.

CHAPTER TWO

Bearing Soldiers' Burdens
The Scientific Management of Sovereignty and Subaltern Labor

Major Littleton W. T. Waller did not need to know the subaltern to slaughter them. Landing at Samar in late September 1901, Waller seemed to share the view of his commander and fellow Cuba veteran, Brig. Gen. Jacob Hurd Smith, that force alone would avenge comrades ambushed at Balangiga earlier that month. Born in 1856 into a patrician family of slave-owning Virginia planters, Waller had an impressive imperial career. Going ashore in Egypt in 1882 while the British suppressed an uprising which, once crushed, established their protectorate there, Waller saw naval action at Santiago in 1898, then two years later suppressed Boxers at Beijing. Now, ordered by Smith to make Samar "a howling wilderness," Waller razed Balangiga and commenced a classic colonial-style punitive campaign. If some Orientalist American soldiers thought they could subdue Filipinos by studying them, Waller betrayed no such curiosity. The colonized registered in his consciousness as either implacable enemies to be destroyed or dispensable instruments to be exploited.[1]

Waller's disinterest in knowing the Filipinos he killed was most evident in his notorious extrajudicial execution of eleven Visayan porters. Their murder illustrated the profound effect that US military knowledge of tropical labor, or lack of it, often had on the work of empire and its politics. For professionalizing Progressive Era army officers committed to making war scientific, the incident at best signified a catastrophic failure of military leadership and ethics. Yet the violent ignorance fueling Waller's brutality also reflected many white imperialists' belief in their racial fitness for colonial exploration and conquest. Indeed, Waller and his Marines embodied the Anglo-Saxon hubris that Englishman Rudyard Kipling recently hailed ironically in a poem inviting Americans to "take up the White Man's burden."[2] Loyal Filipinos bore its weight.

In late December 1901, Waller, against the advice of army colleagues, attempted an audacious expedition across southern Samar which his poor planning and faulty logistics doomed to failure. From Lanang (today Llorente) on its east coast, Waller's column of fifty-seven Marines, two Visayan scouts, and thirty-three cargadores, armed with bolos for cutting trails, cut west inland by a route that no American had used before. Plodding up a river valley, they quickly consumed their four days' supply of rations. Fatigued and faltering, the Marine column started disintegrating, physically and mentally. Splitting up the command, Waller pressed on, barely surviving the two-week trek it took to reach Basey, northwest of Balangiga. The thirty-three Americans and nearly twenty Visayans who remained, led by Lt. Alexander Williams, fared much worse. Trying to return to Lanang, Williams's detachment left behind eleven Marines who were never seen again. A relief party found his group "in a wretched condition," near death. Williams, delirious, arrested ten cargadores and telephoned Waller, alleging they had committed "mutiny and treachery" and "deserved to be shot." The Marines later claimed the porters hoarded food, hid matches and bolos, and refused to make trails and camps or carry messages. "Surly," "overbearing," "selfish," and "plotting," the cargadores, they insisted, "had to be driven" to "do anything." Williams claimed one attacked him with a bolo, bit him, and escaped with two others.[3]

Illness and fatigue, so often causing psychological instability in imperialists who regarded themselves as the rational conquerors of irrational peoples, warped Waller's judgment. Though his expedition never spotted a single insurgent, a Basey official's confession that he had aided the enemy prompted paranoid Marines to imagine a cargador fifth column. Prostrated by fever, Waller now claimed that a Visayan scout had tried to bolo him; designating him a spy, Waller had him tortured and shot, and his corpse dumped in the street. The next day, after a two-hour "investigation," the major ordered the execution of Williams's ten cargadores by firing squad. Waller never interrogated them or granted them the trial to which division commander Gen. Adna Chaffee believed they were entitled. The major merely sent Smith a curt telegram: "It became necessary," he wrote, "to expend eleven native prisoners"—a number equal to his lost Marines that suggests a "grim arithmetic" of revenge, in one historian's view.[4]

A counterinsurgent cult of brutality, not just magical thinking or draconian readings of military necessity, contributed to these cargadores' demise. Testimony at courts-martial for Waller and Smith held at Manila a few months later illuminated a militarized colonial-style labor coercion on Samar that preceded the Marines and primed their callousness. Waller deflected culpability by insisting that Smith told him to "kill and burn" and "take no prisoners." As they reoccupied Balangiga, the major advised his men they could place "no trust" in "treacherous, brave and savage" natives, and he urged them to "punish treachery immediately with death." Yet occupiers' perception that *samareños* were uncivilized, and thus unfree, also made them vulnerable to violence. Even before Waller ordered Marines at Balangiga to "impress native labor," a naval blockade and reconcentration disrupted the island's agricultural and fishing economy and food supplies. As rice prices skyrocketed and specie disappeared, refugees from destroyed villages in US-garrisoned towns, now depending on the occupiers for sustenance, became a captive workforce. Waller's cargadores included both "hired packers"—a term implying voluntary service—and prisoners, some of whom he "released" during the expedition and promised to pay. Porters' liminal status between martial conscripts and civilian employees thus made it easier for Waller to eliminate them. Recruited mostly from Basey's "lower classes," whom the Marines saw as "almost savages," samareño porters, they believed, required surveillance and intimidation, not study or investigation. Lt. Williams claimed he had taken precautions by spreading out cargadores, denying them access to firearms, and collecting their bolos at night. Still, he felt that only their "inherent fear of a superior race" allowed him to survive the ordeal.[5]

Despite Marines' racialization of their porters, their fatal assertions of sovereignty over these subalterns ultimately rested on ignorance of them as individuals. At trial, Marines who did not speak or understand Visayan, much less Spanish, admitted they never learned the bearers' names. Instead, they assigned them mocking noms de guerre like "Buckshy," "Big Joe," "Rummy," and "Locust"—not an uncommon practice. Waller was thus indicted for murdering "eleven men, names unknown, natives of the Philippine Islands." Acquitted, Waller went on to train counterinsurgents in the Caribbean. Smith, found guilty of "conduct prejudicial to good order," was nudged into retirement. Chaffee endorsed the judge advocate opinion's condemnation of Waller for tarnishing a sovereignty bound by law, and he criticized the verdicts as a "miscarriage of justice." Samar's "real condition of affairs," he feared, would "never be ascertained."[6]

Five years later, US Army officers on Samar repudiated Marines' blunt approach to managing cargadores in favor of knowledge-based techniques. In 1898, American soldiers in Cuba and the Philippines began elaborating a militarized science of subaltern labor arguably more aligned with what they perceived as their exceptional nation's enlightened civilizing mission in the tropics. Soldiers who observed colonial manual laborers and recorded, analyzed, and disseminated their findings about them exhibited a pragmatic empiricism amenable to empire. Channeling cultures of the machine and steam engine in modern military thought, their martial scientism befitted an imperial age energized by new theories and technologies, from evolution and electricity to machine guns. Expressing a cosmopolitan urge to master nature and naturalized peoples also evident in Europeans' contemporary colonial warfare, US troops likewise sought to rationalize warfare by perfecting their exploitation of subalterns. If Progressive Era military culture only partly embraced reason, many officers shared domestic reformers' faith that capitalist reason would civilize tropical labor in a post-slavery age.[7]

War and occupation in the 1898 era hinged on remaking Cubans and Filipinos into workforces capable of projecting imperial sovereignty and yielding the knowledge necessary to perfect its projection. In turn, the US military's attempts to reengineer colonial labor rested on and reshaped a politics of Cuban and Filipino ethnicity, nationality, and industry that both legitimated and challenged imperial and anticolonial assertions of sovereignty. Americans in arms thus walked a proverbial tightrope. They touted an ability to know racialized subalterns and manage and improve their labor, but not so well as to imply that colonial subjects' enhanced industriousness signaled an equally mature capacity for self-rule. The militarized imperial workspace thus became a proto-Taylorist factory in the tropical battlefield.[8] It promised to produce new peoples who would be more permeable to Americans' civilizing standards yet still subordinate.

Soldiers' knowledge of Cuban and Filipino labor was never as scientific or secular as they advertised, in method or findings. Inevitably, their studies reflected a faith in the social power of technology, rooted in metropolitan pieties and cultural bias. Channeling conventions of biology, geography, and climate through racialized explanations for different cultures' variable social and historical development, American troops valorized efficiency as a prerequisite for progress. The militarized science of the subaltern also involved other empire's histories, especially those of Spain and its former colonies. As they reconstructed discourses of the colonized laborer as a subject impervious to efficiency, US soldiers' knowledge of subalterns conveyed fin de siècle ideology, not objective truths or falsifiable theories about Cubans' or Filipinos' industrial abilities.[9]

The military-colonial science of the subaltern both celebrated and obscured Americans' deferral of Cuban and Philippine national sovereignty. Army officers trying to "improve" tropical workforces through techniques ranging from physical violence to vocational education rarely grappled with the totality of colonial and global social relations that made the work of empire possible. They exuded confidence that scrutinizing subaltern labor revealed universal laws by which cosmopolitan capital might promote open and free markets and wage labor among benighted tropical peoples. Studying and calibrating the colonized worker, they hoped, would liberate them from oppressive social hierarchies and atavistic customs inherited from precontact and colonial pasts. Yet US soldiers' increasingly self-aware management never delivered the mastery it promised. Even as a militarized science of industry informed Americans' deliberations about these islands' futures, their encounters with stubborn Cuban and Philippine histories and subjects also revealed and fueled subbalterns' claims to sovereignty over their labor and lives.[10]

BY 1898, A NEW CULT of efficiency in the United States, emanating from Americans' impulse to bring order to rapid and chaotic industrialization after the Civil War, sparked and sanctified technological and organizational revolution and cultural transformation. For Americans in the 1890s, "efficiency" meant multiple things. It was a personal attribute, an icon of the machine, a celebration of savings and profit realized by rationalized production, and a vision of social harmony latent in professional experts' use of scientific methods. By the end of the decade, efficiency's high temple already rested on a foundation of "scientific management," invented by industrial engineer Frederick Winslow Taylor and his disciples. Taylorism transformed manufacturing by combining new machines and accounting methods with close scrutiny and redesign of work processes as means to reduce labor costs and workers' control.[11]

No institution, not even the US military, was left untouched by Americans' quixotic crusade to make everything efficient. A scientific way of war imparted to cadets at West Point, with its curricular emphasis on civil and military engineering, predisposed regular army officers to partake of this reform. Since the 1820s, the Army Corps of Engineers played an outsized role in North America's economic development. Building roads, harbors, and canals key to commercial, settler, and territorial expansion, regular officers at arsenals joined civilian artisans, mechanics, and laborers in devising new mass production techniques. Postbellum army reformers, inspired by Europe, pressed managerial revolution in the military as they sought to centralize and streamline the War Department. They came to see their profession, according to one historian, as a "body of expert knowledge that could be codified, imparted, and regulated."[12]

Before 1898, this efficiency craze had already spilled across US borders, carried on globalizing circuits of influence energized by American investors, educators, and missionaries. In nineteenth-century Cuba, Yankees' observations of its laborers, mostly sugar plantation workforces, remained impressionistic and anecdotal. By the 1880s, however, American capitalists who bought up old sugar plantations and established new ones, and the managers they brought with them, had greater incentives to know Cuban labor. Edwin Atkins, an entrepreneur eager to perfect island workers as they transitioned from slavery to freedom, exemplified this class. In the late 1870s, this Boston Brahmin and banker milked family business ties to acquire estates in and around Cienfuegos. Atkins's paternal management of his mostly Afro-Cuban workforce evoked a romantic nostalgia for the plantation life he experienced briefly before slavery's abolition. By reifying the relative efficiency of Latin, Afro-Cuban, and Chinese into racial traits, Atkins sought an "economy of labor, saving of waste, and increase of yield" that could make Soledad run "like clockwork." By 1900, Atkins shared his racial knowledge of different Cuban workers' industry with US occupiers as planters clamored for cheap labor.[13]

Naturally, US troops never made it their mission to run Cuban industry, even after they started organizing Rural Guards to defend planters and colonists from social banditry. Yankee soldiers' laboratory for experimenting with Cuban labor was not the sugar plantation but the occupied city. At Oriente in 1898, problems of sanitation, long a concern for stationary armies in the United States and Cuba, metastasized into a mortal threat.[14] Following the victorious joint Cuban-US campaign to seize Santiago, Yankee troops there responded to cascading military, political, and biological crises by attempting to scientifically subdue the subaltern. Yet Cubans ensured that their sanitary civilizing mission involved a politics of sovereignty.

American troops occupying Santiago on July 17 confronted grave questions of human survival and social peace that threatened to undo their rule even as they imposed it. President William McKinley had already ordered Gen. William Shafter to establish a military government and reject Cubans' claims to authority over the island. At the same time, Shafter's Fifth Corps stumbled toward physical collapse. Dysfunctional supply lines and troops' exposure to torrid tropical weather alternating between scorching sun, cold nights, and drenching downpours exacerbated their fatigue. As a result, by late July mosquito-borne yellow fever and malaria spread rapidly through the ranks. With this weakened army, Shafter contemplated occupying a vast region still hosting 24,000 surrendered Spanish troops. Tens of thousands of Cuban civilians languishing in the city, many sick and starving or near starvation, required care, as did pro-Spanish loyalists and Spanish prisoners of war, until they could be repatriated. Eager to prevent clashes between Cuban insurgents and Spanish troops, Shafter also faced rising tensions with the Liberation Army after his government barred it from governing the city.[15] Biological emergency and rival sovereignties together forged a new militarized science of subaltern labor.

Americans who lacked the martial manpower they needed to adequately address these crises instead appropriated civilian Cuban labor. To make tropical space safe for occupation, Yankee commanders compelled Cubans to clean their own cities. Yet US soldiers also believed that compulsory sanitization might discipline and redeem Cubans whom they considered uncivilized and unfit to govern their own bodies, much less an independent nation. Occupiers thus strived to align Cuban subjects and socio-spatial relationships with metropolitan ideals of health, order, and industry. At Oriente, Yankee soldiers' neocolonial sanitary conscription merged postwar relief with global ambition, moral uplift with racist paternalism, and the armed expropriation of subaltern labor with urban science.

The militarized American sanitation of Cuba thus reflected not a preexisting design to inculcate biomedical citizenship in colonial subjects so much as a contingent conjuncture of colonial history and flawed scientific knowledge. Only in 1900 did US Army medical officers' experiments at Havana confirm the theory, first posited by Cuban doctor Carlos J. Finlay, that mosquitoes transmitted yellow fever and malaria. Until then, Americans, accepting "contagionist" concepts of disease, believed that "miasmatic" air and water caused these deadly illnesses and that human contact spread them. In late 1897, a yellow fever epidemic in the states that many Americans attributed to Cuba paralyzed southern US coastal cities, inspiring panic and quarantines. Some called for intervening in the island's independence war not to aid nationalists or ameliorate civilian suffering but to protect the nation's health. In early 1898, Shafter and staff, worried that yellow fever might destroy their army, sought to minimize its exposure with a speedy campaign.[16]

Even before US troops seized Santiago, events confirmed their commanders' worst fears. While yellow fever each day sickened hundreds and killed dozens of American soldiers, others contracted and succumbed to malaria, dysentery, and typhoid. By early August, more than 4,000 men, or a quarter of the Fifth Corps, had fallen sick; in some units, more than half of the ranks became incapacitated. Shafter, typically dilatory, responded to terrified subordinates' protests by removing camps from lowland sites to higher elevations. The War Department rushed to recall his army and replace it with a garrison of "immunes," or white and African American volunteers from the US South. Following popular conventions that exposure or racial makeup made denizens of tropical climates invulnerable to such diseases, President McKinley had authorized ten new immune regiments for Cuban service. Transports landing them at Santiago in early August returned with Shafter's army, who quarantined at Long Island, but more than 500 troops died from disease—twice the number of US dead from combat. A patriotic American public that previously sympathized with Cuban civilians now fixated on ailing volunteers rather than the estimated 150,000 Cubans who perished due to Gen. Valeriano Weyler's *reconcentracion* policy—roughly 10 percent of the island's prewar population.[17]

Given such dire conditions, it was no coincidence that Shafter handed control of Santiago to an army doctor obsessed with hygiene. On July 20, only three days after Spanish troops surrendered, Shafter ordered Brig. Gen. Leonard Wood to start "feeding the people, finding means to give them employment, and reestablishing civil government." Born in 1860, this Massachusetts native, fired from Harvard Medical School, joined the army as a contract surgeon. In 1886, Wood joined Henry Lawton in the cross-border pursuit of Goyahkla, known as Geronimo, and his Apache warriors that finally captured them. Now, in July 1898, after Wood left a plum post as President McKinley's physician for the colonelship of the First US Volunteer Cavalry (the Rough Riders), Lawton again supervised him after Shafter named him Oriente's new governor. Just before the fight at San Juan Hill, Wood handed the Rough Riders to its lieutenant colonel and his close friend, Theodore Roosevelt. Both Republicans committed to physical fitness, Wood and Roosevelt promoted the masculine cult of the "strenuous life" so central to Americans' 1890s gendered political culture and pro-imperial discourse. If Wood's background made him more likely than Roosevelt to speak through science, he also carried a big stick against Cuban labor.[18]

Characterized by historians as an "armed progressive," Wood crystallized his reformism through attempts to sanitize Santiago using Cuban labor. The general embodied a professionalizing officer corps whose overseas careers in the 1898 era invigorated efforts to make their army mirror the rationalized society that progressives idealized at home. Like activists who tamed monopoly, purified partisan corruption, rescued children, and assimilated foreigners, armed progressives believed that bureaucracies guided by science should supplant the anarchy of laissez-faire. Progressives also sought to discipline poor, working-class, and immigrant Americans who seemed to threaten a social order dominated by the white, Anglo-Saxon, and Protestant bourgeois families in which many progressives had been raised. Wood's scientific management of Cuban labor thus reoriented progressivism's dual logic of social reform and control according to a new imperial compass. On July 18, McKinley told Shafter to establish an occupation "as free from severity as possible" and reassure civilians that Americans came to Cuba not to "make war upon [them]" but to "protect them in their homes," "employment," and "personal and religious rights." To many Cubans, however, Wood's labor coercion vitiated this enlightened mandate, no matter how much he insisted he abjured "militarism" and "military pedantry."[19]

Wood maintained that his army's conscription of Cuban labor for public health expressed only the United States' benevolent desire to alleviate human suffering. By late July, the city, inhabited prewar by some 50,000 residents, now hosted approximately 136,000 people, most of them civilians, including refugees from a denuded countryside. Santiago and its suburbs contained 12,000 Spanish prisoners, nearly a third of whom were crippled by yellow fever, malaria, or other illness. Of approximately 15,000 ill civilians, roughly 200 were dying each day, mostly from disease aggravated by starvation. Food became scarce as early as April due to the US blockade. Troops heard rumors that Spaniards' hoarding had forced civilians to eat horses.[20]

Occupiers' perceptions of Cuban urbanity legitimated labor coercion. Wood's private letters to his wife almost read like prewar tourist advertisements as he romanticized Santiago as an artifact of premodern Hispanic culture. In letters written in August 1898, Wood described its oldest quarter, perched high above the harbor, as "old Europe." "Exactly like a picture of Toledo," "little two-wheeled carts," he told his wife, "struggle up and down the steep and narrow lanes over the rough paved streets." Yet his publications and fawning Yankee journalists represented the city as a tropical cesspool that required stringent sanitization. Like his counterparts in the Philippines, Wood translated his initial experience of the postwar tropical city through the senses. In public writings, the general narrated Santiago as the putrid antithesis of the antiseptic American cityscape that progressives now valorized. Santiago's streets, Wood informed readers in the states, were cluttered with "decomposing heaps of refuse of all kinds," including uninterred animal carcasses. Residents, he claimed, had been discovered inside homes "half-buried in pestilential filth," including unburied corpses. "The very air," he wrote with literary flair, seemed "laden with death." By attributing the city's uncivilized state to Cubans themselves, and racializing uncleanliness as a trait justifying US sovereignty, Wood and his comrades ignored how three years of war had created such conditions. In fact, over the previous twenty years, municipal authorities and Spanish and Cuban doctors in Santiago, reflecting a modernizing colonial state, attempted to improve its public health. War in 1895 ended such efforts and further delegitimized Spain's sovereignty in the city as services collapsed. Now, in July 1898, Yankees claimed that twenty demoralized street sweepers were Santiago's only sanitary resource. While Wood wrote his mother that "people here are quiet and orderly," he also condemned them as "lazy" for not "keeping themselves or their houses and grounds in first class condition."[21]

Americans' juxtaposition of their presumably scientific sensibility against dirty Cuban subjects and spaces legitimated both US sovereignty and the labor coercion consolidating it. Though technically a civilian, George M. Barbour, whom Wood immediately entrusted with the task of sanitizing Santiago, ensured that the city's cleansing energized militarist postbellum metropolitan cultures of urban public health. An intemperate veteran of the Civil and Indian Wars who worked in Buffalo Bill Cody's Wild West circus, Barbour joined a rough military and frontier spirit to theatrical spectacle, one honed in labor-intensive performances that primed American audiences for new imperial endeavors. In the 1880s, during Chicago's rapid and tumultuous industrialization, he served as the city's street-cleaning commissioner. Barbour's real education began the next decade in New York City as apprentice to George E. Waring Jr., the father of Gilded Age urban sanitation. Waring's applied science had civilian origins; trained in agriculture and engineering, he helped Frederick Law Olmstead design Central Park's drainage. Yet Union Army service imparted to Waring the honorific "Colonel" and a martial mentality he carried into postwar life.[22]

Waring and Barbour embodied the masculinist civic identity of Gilded Age reformers, many of them veterans, who invoked martial patriotism as they battled immigrant-run urban political machines in pursuit of disinterested public policy. In 1895, after New York's reformist Republican mayor William Strong made Waring the city's street-cleaning commissioner, the colonel angered Tammany Hall by firing politically connected supervisors and replacing them with army engineers. Waring imposed a progressive military ethos on his mostly Italian street-cleaning employees. To garner public support, he dressed them in new uniforms of spotless white linen now associated with the medical profession and marched his so-called White Wings in parades. Waring softened this regimented culture, and sought to detach his workforce from Democrats and enhance their efficiency, by nearly doubling their pay and granting them an eight-hour day. In 1898, Waring joined Barbour in volunteering for the war, but his service proved tragically brief. In October, after President McKinley asked him to stay in Havana to help modernize sewers and streets, the colonel expired from yellow fever. Yet Waring's Hippocratic faith in "pure air, pure water, and a pure soil" gained a new lease on life in Cuba as an imperial index of civilization. At a time when germ theory and bacteriology was not yet universally accepted, Cuban doctors and engineers praised Waring's ideas and endorsed them for Havana and other cities. Waring's system first took root at Santiago in July 1898, however, after he dispatched Barbour there.[23]

Occupiers' sanitation of Santiago resembled a scientific war against subaltern labor. Yankee soldiers' coercion of civilians to clean the city reinforced their racialized assumptions that Cubans worked only in response to force, or threats. Wood ordered Barbour to divide the city into sanitary districts, survey them, and begin cleaning them. Lacking personnel, they tried recruiting volunteers. When this failed, Barbour resorted to martial compulsion. Addressed as "major" only in recognition of past service, Barbour projected military authority by purchasing a uniform. Then, in the middle of night, he dispatched squads of Yankee soldiers into Santiago's residential neighborhoods, from which they dragooned some 600 to 1,000 adult men. Organizing these Cubans into gangs of 100, troops worked them in three consecutive shifts, day and night, for weeks. Wood touted this disciplinary rhythm, and his workforce's demography, as proof of his progressivism. Heedless of social rank which egalitarian Yankees associated with Spanish aristocracy, his soldiers disregarded Cuban men's claims to wealth or status; Wood and Barbour crowed that their gangs included lawyers, doctors, merchants, and professors. Hierarchy and distinction also surrendered to neocolonial scientific racism, as Barbour described conscripts as a "stupid, ignorant mob of wildly excited but eager specimens of humanity."[24]

Yankee occupiers objectifying Cubans through the language of science took pride in making their labor more efficient. Initially, white US Army officers, noncommissioned white and Black officers, and enlisted "immunes" cajoled Cubans to clean streets and homes using only tree branches, oil can scraps, or hoop iron. Riding on horseback, Wood tried to perfect cleaning techniques that he believed were just as primitive as their tools. A micromanaging military Taylorist, the general dismounted regularly to personally redirect workers' bodily movements. Modeling reform for his soldiers, he ordered Cubans to deposit piles of trash closer to carts and sweep streets by pushing dirt and refuse downhill toward Santiago's harbor. Wood and Barbour thus legitimated US sovereignty by essentializing Cubans' work methods into signs of racialized cultural difference. George Kennan, a journalist chronicling these officers' careers, channeled their imperial condescension. "In one of our cities a street-cleaning commissioner may fairly count on a certain amount of intelligence in his laboring force," wrote Kennan. Yet "in a Cuban city," he observed, "street-cleaners are not only inexperienced but often stupid."[25]

A Yankee discourse of Cubans' uncleanliness, mental poverty, and physical torpor became a neocolonial brief for impressment. Wood's letters clarified a tautological logic that Cubans' lackluster compliance with labor coercion itself justified compulsion. In early August, he grumbled to his wife that "the people are almost impossible and simply will not work under any condition if they can help it." His soldiers, he claimed, had to "drive them to keep them at work." Rarely, the general conceded that the war had "entirely brutalized" Cubans. More often, Wood and his comrades in Santiago interpreted their reluctance as a pathetic void of civic spirit that represented both a cultural condition and an imperial invitation. Indeed, Wood revealed forced labor's neocolonial character by hinting that his army employed violence no longer permitted to compel industry at home following emancipation. Early in the occupation, he explained to *Scribner's*, Cubans "did not want to work." Yet "men who refused and held back," Wood insisted, elliptically, "soon learned that there were things far more unpleasant than cheerful obedience." "All who could work," he wrote, had been "compelled to do so."[26]

Soldiers further justified sanitary imperialism by suggesting that forced labor transformed "gangs of timid, suspicious and superstitious laborers," as Barbour described them, into pliable units of hygienic productivity. Success fed ambition. While Barbour's and Wood's sanitary workforce at Santiago never exceeded 1,200 men, by early August they considered drafting 4,000 Cubans for the effort. By early September, the major claimed his gangs had scoured the city's main plazas and most major thoroughfares and disinfected stagnant pools and drains with iron sulphate and lime chloride. By late October, he alleged they had removed from streets and houses up to 1,400 corpses, both human and animal. Conscripted cart drivers hauled the dead and tons of trash to the suburbs, deposited them in a heap, and incinerated them with kerosene.[27] Phoenix-like, this funereal pyre monumentalized Americans' resolve to make Cuba safe for empire.

Though Wood eventually used cash wages to elicit voluntary labor, he weaponized his regime's near-absolute control over regional food supplies into a biological instrument for continuously expropriating work from Cubans. For weeks, Yankee troops, Red Cross volunteers, and Cubans pressed into relief efforts distributed rations to between 18,000 and 20,000 households daily. As local foodstuffs slowly increased, however, Wood ordered that all able-bodied Cuban men applying for rations would get them only if they did sanitary work. The general seemed to soften coercion by promising to pay cash for labor whenever quartermaster funds became available; by mid-August, at least one officer was paying forced street cleaners a dollar per day. Unsurprisingly, Yankees reported that Cubans relished opportunities to work for money whenever possible. Even Wood later acknowledged that Cubans seemed "anxious" to work when they realized they would "receive a regular salary for the work which they performed."[28]

Wood's ability, or decision, to pay laborers cash—occurring probably in October, when he gained access to provincial customs—had unintended consequences. On its face, monetized wages superficially made conscripts seem more like the free labor that Cubans and Yankees normalized in postslavery societies. Yet open labor markets' fitful revival actually reinforced Americans' perceptions that Cubans' particular racial-cultural character made them industrial inferiors. Some alleged that Barbour's new Cuban foremen pocketed workers' paychecks; others bemoaned street cleaners' "slovenly ways." Most distressing to the Americans, militarized Cuban wage workers behaved as if they were not subaltern at all but rational actors pursuing self-interest, even collectively. In early November, Barbour's workers walked out, demanding a fifty-cent increase in daily wages. Strikers turned Wood's food monopoly against him, amassing a war chest of a month's worth of US-issued rations to outlast the occupiers. Their protest rankled arriviste Yankee entrepreneurs who complained that Wood's one-dollar daily wage for street cleaners exceeded prevailing rates and was depriving them of workers.[29] Unlike US troops, private employers could not use guns to expropriate labor.

Wood rejected strikers' demands and retaliated by threatening to enforce indirect labor coercion still legal in Cuba and some US states: an antivagrancy law. In the late 1880s, Cuban elites suddenly faced a footloose proletarian population that included not only 200,000 emancipated Afro-Cubans but tens of thousands of *gallego* immigrants from Spain. To control them, colonial authorities found various ways to punish mobility without proof of employment, including sentencing vagrants to public works labor without pay. Wood invoked that measure, warning he would arrest "idle" men and have municipal courts he controlled sentence them to thirty days cleaning streets, without pay. Denying mine owners' requests that they be allowed to import labor, Wood himself threatened to import strikebreakers. The display of force finally made street cleaners fold.[30]

Militarized labor coercion strengthened US sovereignty over Cubans' everyday life in public health and beyond. At Santiago, where Wood eventually made Barbour sanitary commissioner, the major endeavored to permanently alter santiagueros *santiagueros'* behavior. Prohibiting residents from dumping trash on thoroughfares, Barbour distributed pails to facilitate compliance with a new collection system. Occupiers also strictly enforced new health codes. Yankee soldiers who spotted "respectable" Cuban men urinating on walls or in public streets forced them to clean up after themselves. In five months, they killed some 6,000 wild dogs. Barbour enforced bio-discipline with corporal punishment. Carrying a heavy riding crop, he celebrated using it on malefactors—a symbolically potent gesture in a society that abolished slavery in most Cubans' lifetimes. To address postwar shortages and inflation, Wood regulated the local economy. When retailers charged extortionate prices, he imposed price controls on bakers, butchers, and supplies needed for sanitation. If Cuban officials did not rush to execute his orders, he had soldiers drag them to his office and threatened them with jail. Comparing his rule to that of "the Pasha," or Ottoman imperial governors, Wood gushed that "forcing the dirty and shiftless to work" and promising "prison for every failure to obey open to every man, rich or poor," brought Cubans "to terms" and permitted "the starving to live."[31]

A shift to paying Cuban sanitizers cash comported with incremental steps Wood's regime took in late 1898 toward relaxing martial law. In late October, a few weeks after he replaced Gen. Henry Lawton as Oriente's governor, Wood issued a lofty declaration, serving "the temporary purpose of a Constitution," that guaranteed "personal rights and privileges" not protected by Spanish-era codes. To make law "conform to the beneficient [sic] principles of an enlightened civilization," his civil charter adapted the Bill of Rights. Among other things, it granted a right to peaceful assembly, freedom of religion, and open and accountable courts, and prohibited seizing property "for public use without compensation."[32] If Cubans read this last clause as a retreat from labor coercion, compulsion under the occupation merely took new forms.

At Santiago, the imperial labor politics of science and sovereignty persisted most visibly in its Sanitary Department, which Barbour ran for three years as his personal fiefdom. Imitating Waring, Barbour militarized his Cuban street cleaners. He compelled them to wear spotless white caps, jackets, and pants with military-style blue trim, and to salute him and his Yankee assistants; he also paraded them for sightseeing US congressional delegations. By May 1899, Barbour boasted that his army had made Santiago "as clean and as healthy as any city in the world." According to Barbour, "American ideas," "constant attention, unremitting energy, and a good heavy Spanish riding whip frequently used" effected the transformation—not, apparently, the 200 Cuban street cleaners or the 35 Cuban-driven wagon teams removing at least 200 loads of waste every day. Barbour hardly tolerated the Afro-Cuban population from which he recruited employees; such persons, he told journalists, he found "extremely ignorant, careless, superstitious and filthy." Nor did cleanliness necessarily earn self-rule. Invoking tropes that infantilized Cubans as children who required Yankees' stern but paternal tutelage, Barbour prefigured the Platt Amendment's logic by hinting that Cuba's unhygienic state might require lasting US rule. Foisted by Americans on Cuba's constitutional convention as a precondition for evacuation, the amendment required that their new republic uphold the occupation's sanitary measures.[33]

Barbour's post-Cuba career charted militarized sanitary labor's intraimperial evolution. Departing Cuba, he expanded his scientific-colonial résumé to the Philippines, where by 1903 he ran Manila's "pail conservancy system" for its Board of Health. Responsible for the human waste of a city five times greater in population than Santiago, Barbour joined soldiers in the archipelago who targeted colonized bodies as mortal threats to empire, even as he resented civilian bureaucrats' constraints on his authority. To a fellow Cuba veteran, Barbour complained that he could "effect very radical results here and very rapidly" if only he were "given a free hand" and "surely sustained as I was elsewhere"; Manila, he blustered, would become the "place that Sherman referred to about war." Barbour's brusque and alcoholic personality likely sealed his marginalization. In 1904, Wood, now the Moro Province's governor, named Barbour secretary of police and sanitation at Zamboanga, a Mindanao port, the provincial capital, and site of the army's regional headquarters. While there, he aided the army's first urban beautification in the Muslim south, transforming that port into a well-ordered space suitable for healthful bourgeois Anglo-Saxon habitation—partly by coercing Moro labor. After two years, however, Barbour resigned and accepted virtual exile as a customs agent at Sitangkai, the Philippines' southernmost island, so remote that American tourists visited it to view "pristine" Moro culture.[34]

Yankee soldiers' science of subaltern labor cohered in other encounters. Whether stevedoring cargo or repairing public buildings, Cubans' work informed occupiers' amorphous and shifting knowledge of their industrial and political capacities. Not all Americans were pessimistic, nor did they always essentialize Cuban laborers by attributing their perceived traits to culture, history, or biology, according to Lamarckian or Darwinian doctrines. Like Yankee and Cuban ideas about race, ethnicity, and nationality, ideas about labor were fluid, divergent, and often contradictory, contingent on shifting relations. Still, even Americans' optimistic views about Cubans as workers tended to legitimate US sovereignty over their island.[35]

Occupiers' sense that Cubans knew they were being judged on their ability to discipline themselves, and thus their civility, imparted to soldiers' pseudo-science an everyday politics of performance. In 1898, notes historian Ada Ferrer, revolutionary Cuban elites knew that white US audiences doubted their capacity for self-rule and felt the need to prove their modernity and eligibility for sovereign nationhood. Analogously, US soldiers often believed that Cubans seemed eager to show their worth as workers. Watching stevedores unload his transport at Santiago harbor, one private in the Eighth Illinois, an African American volunteer regiment, somewhat self-reflexively believed that the "sight of their new benefactors made them feel grateful." Toiling like "little Turks," the Cubans, he felt, "wanted to show what adepts they were at handling dockage or freight." Exoticizing Cuban labor in this way, however, also exposed qualities that might hinder cultural assimilation and social progress. One Iowa volunteer, interpreting stevedores' accidents and arguments as evidence that Cubans were "a very excitable people," invoked common stereotypes of Latins as anarchic and irrational. Such perceptions solidified Americans' imperial intuition that Cubans were too inefficient to be trusted with substantive sovereignty over themselves in workplaces or the halls of government.[36]

Even sympathetic Yankee troops who attributed Cubans' productivity to external influences tended to construct their labor as a proxy for ethnonational character. Historicist and environmentalist theories of Cuban labor rarely escaped racist and nationalist presumptions that Cubans required occupiers' paternal industrial guidance. Maj. George Brown, touring Cuba in late 1899 and early 1900, considered the sight of campesinos working hard at agricultural "reconstruction" a reason to reject comrades' dour wisdom that "Cuban character" seemed "irredeemably bad." Cubans, he realized, were "industrious by nature." Any apparent defect he blamed on their having "been subject to a system of government and industrial serfdom that naturally has modified and warped" their "good qualities." Repudiating planters' belief that Cubans only cut cane if they were starving, Brown insisted they would rationally pursue their self-interest if given "patient handling," medicine, "more wholesome food," and "wages." Even such positive judgments, however, usually reinforced the scientific racism invigorating metropolitan theories of social evolution. If staff represented his views, Pedro Betancourt—a University of Pennsylvania–trained doctor and insurgent general who governed Matanzas for the US occupation—believed that Cubans were destined to poverty. His secretary, discussing joblessness in February 1900, knew that "in every community there is always a certain number of individuals adverse [sic] to 'the struggle for life.'" A "social detritus [his emphasis]" that "swims and ferments," such persons he deemed the "natural morbid offspring of the race and the species."[37]

Contemporary scientific theory informed a comparative racialism by which US officials and elite Cubans devised a convoluted taxonomy ascribing Cuban laborers' varied productivity to race, ethnicity, and nationality, even as they conflated these categories. As in other aspects of the Yankee occupation, Leonard Wood as Oriente's governor from late 1898 to late 1899 articulated discourses that other American commanders and civilians later imitated. Especially telling was his favorable estimation of Spaniards relative to Cubans, whom he found deficient. Wood's perception shaped his support for white labor migration from Europe and his opposition to Chinese and African-descended migrants. In January 1899, Wood told US senators that *peninsulares* in his road gangs seemed like virtual machines. "Industrious, temperate, frugal, and quiet," these Spaniards, he alleged, were "almost without animation or spirit." Native Cubans he dismissed as slackers at best; at worst, they seemed predisposed to crime, everyday resistance, and collective action. Wood's subordinates concurred. Lt. Robert Hamilton, supervising public works in Oriente, endorsed schemes to import Spanish labor as a way to weaken Cubans, who he claimed "learn early the power of combinations."[38]

Yankee soldiers often argued that American workers were more efficient than Cubans in part because they almost always racialized the former as white. Such assumptions influenced more sophisticated civilian studies. In 1902, Victor Clark, a US Bureau of Labor economist, published a report that relied on army officers' statements on the relative abilities of Cuban and Yankee skilled tradesmen. A progressive social scientist attentive to externalities, Clark contended that Cuba's climate, regardless of race, did not "encourage long-continued physical labor." "The American, the Spaniard, the white native, and the Negro," he insisted, were "all subject to this influence."[39] Yet Clark's extensive empirical proof of Cubans' relative inefficiency buttressed an imperial discourse of labor that legitimated US hegemony over Cuba.

Clark's martial predecessors shaped his explanations for Cubans' deficiency deficits. Cubans' productivity, he argued, reflected their disorderly, even violent nature. By contrast, Spaniards, observed Clark, were "not quarrelsome, and do not usually carry concealed weapons." Like soldiers, Clark also deemed Cubans incapable of skilled labor. For roadbuilding and other work requiring engineers, foremen, and clerks, US commanders hired or imported white technicians from the mainland or British Jamaica, forging transimperial labor flows that soon fed the Panama Canal. Only slowly did Wood or Cuban bureaucrats under him at Santiago, and later Havana, hire Cubans for such positions. Yankees' presumably superior expertise hardly kept Cubans from criticizing them. In March 1900, the alcalde of Palma Soriano, near Santiago, claimed that "incompetent management" left shoddy highways that would not survive seasonal rains.[40]

American soldiers also sought to rationalize Cubans' work according to metropolitan industrial norms and fair labor practices. They frequently decried a culture of patronage and clientage which they believed disincentivized hard work by robbing Cubans of the fruits of their toil. Pervasive allegations that Cuban foremen and contractors peculated in employees' wages implied that islanders were not ready for ethical self-governance. In 1899, Wood told US senators that he surprised Oriente's cynical road laborers by mandating that army officers pay them individually using vouchers requiring their signatures. By 1901, Yankee paymasters in the region, distributing $68,000 monthly to 1,400 highway workers, counted out their wages in front of them, foremen, and timekeepers. Commanders and quartermasters at Havana and elsewhere, claiming to discover "frauds of all kinds," instituted similar policies. Wood, governing Cuba by December 1899, extended Oriente's clean procedures to the entire agricultural sector. In 1900, he promulgated a civil order that prohibited employers from paying laborers in vouchers or tokens—a post-slavery custom by which planters slashed labor costs and maintained wage earners' dependence on them. (Nine years later, Cuba's congress proscribed the practice.) Wood and fellow Yankees saw such corruption as another baleful legacy of Spanish rule. Cubans, the general told New York's Union League, had been "perverted by a system which has compelled deceit, dishonesty, and subterfuge in every department of life." Yet soldiers who ignored graft in Northern industry found in such reports another rationale for US rule in Cuba.[41]

AT THE SAME TIME that American troops scrutinized Cuban labor, counterparts in the Philippines strained to make archipelagic subalterns more efficient for empire. Yet different histories, contexts, and contingencies distinguished the Philippines' militarized colonial knowledge from its Cuban cousin. As Waller's expedition suggested, violent struggles over sovereignty in these islands elevated the political and cultural stakes involved in studying and reforming tropical labor. In Cuba, with its brief US war in 1898 and temporary and mostly peaceful occupations, a military science of subaltern labor refracted the logic of civil government more than combat. In the Philippines, however, the reverse was true. American officers there considered efficiency far more essential to the day-to-day outcomes of military operations.

Discourses differentiating colonizers from the colonized also inflected American soldiers' knowledge of the tropical subaltern with greater intensity and complexity in the Philippines. The longer duration of the US military's presence, and sustained contact with local workforces, accounted partly for this greater salience. Cuban workers' more thoroughly Hispanized and Catholicized culture, despite syncretic creole and African influences, also made them more legible to Yankee troops than archipelagic peoples only partly acculturated to Spanish colonization. Thus, Americans in the Philippines tended to see its extremely diverse peoples as less civilized than Cubans and thus less amenable to the culture of science they considered so fundamental to progress and order. As in Cuba, however, US troops frequently ascribed "native" industry to innate racial qualities and turned evaluations of subalterns' industrial capacity into judgments of their capacity for sovereignty.[42] Compared to Cuba, where Yankee occupiers prepared to transfer nominal national sovereignty to local elites, comrades building a colonial state in the Philippines only gradually granted limited self-government to Filipinos. Accordingly, these Americans enjoyed greater power to reform subalterns. Still, coercive colonial customs and US troops' dependence on colonial brokers limited soldiers' ability to scientifically transform Filipinos and the social relations in which they were embedded.

Lastly, in the Philippines, where capitalist wage labor developed unevenly by 1898, subaltern science reflected and portended a more intrusive US military role in reforming colonial economic culture. Compared to occupied Cuba, then, militarized knowledge of tropical workers figured more prominently in Americans' efforts to promote a civilizing capitalism founded on voluntary labor markets. Nonetheless, as Waller's expedition illustrated, insurgency and counterinsurgency infused US Army officers' mission to remold subaltern labor with kinetic violence, real or threatened. Indeed, the cargador, so essential to US field operations in the Philippines, came to embody both the promise and the pitfalls of the militarized science of industry. More than any other manual laborer in Americans' empire of 1898, porters bore the physical and ideological burdens of a martial and industrial rationality guiding US Army officers' experiments with colonial labor.[43]

If the cargador had not existed before Americans invaded the Philippines, they would have had to invent him. Used in the siege of Manila, porters became critical to US military mobility on Luzon in 1899 during campaigns against Gen. Emilio Aguinaldo's insurgents. Handicapped by paltry transportation resources, army quartermasters resorted to Filipino and Chinese carts and livestock, often carabao, to pull them. Luzon lacked modern highways except for three dilapidated roads radiating out from Manila that monsoons made virtually impassable; a single railroad ran north from the city to Dagupan. Hobbled by Gen. Elwell Otis's austerity, US troops' mobility was not aided by some commanders' heroics. Influenced by the frontier myth of the white American warrior who vanquished enemies by sheer force and willpower or by imitating "Indian fighting," senior officers, especially Gen. Henry Lawton, ignored physical limits on logistics to the point of self-sabotage. Soldiers who attributed their fatigue to a racial unfitness for labor in the tropics also hailed Asians' relative ability for porterage. By early 1900, troops installing garrisons and pursuing guerrillas in remote and rugged areas of Luzon, far from rivers and coastlines, needed cargadores to resupply overland.[44]

Americans' exploitation of archipelagic porters proceeded by imperial transition as colonial history offered expedient coercive labor customs damaged by revolution but not yet dead. Army officers could justify impressing cargadores and thus violating metropolitan norms of liberty of contract as a "military necessity" under GO 100, which authorized "appropriation of whatever an enemy's country affords necessary for the subsistence and safety of the army." Yet Spanish-era laws mostly sustained by US-organized municipalities limited Americans' effective sovereignty over cargadores and bolstered a countersovereignty rooted in social hierarchy and subalterns themselves. To secure porters, US Army officers often relied on local Filipino officials to invoke the Spanish-era corvée, the *polo y servicio*, which by 1884 required all adult indio men to provide public authorities fifteen days' labor annually or pay for exemption. The corrupt administration of the corvée itself—principales pocketed exemption fees and failed to pay forced laborers rice or wages—partly explained the parlous state of Luzon's roads. In turn, this incentivized Spanish and Republican Filipino officials' habitual cargador conscription. American soldiers usually respected legal regulations on the *polo* meant to protect peasants. They used porters briefly, for a single operation, then discharged them. This satisfied Spanish laws that barred officials from taking conscripts from fields during planting and harvesting, thus ensuring the labor needed to pay tribute. When an operation ended, US troops typically let cargadores decamp for home.[45]

Americans' practices imparted a spatial and performative politics to porterage that reflected competing claims to sovereignty over labor. Especially illuminating was US commanders' preference to discharge cargadores mid-operation and replace them with a fresh cohort, obtained by conscripting men from a new location. This practice both recognized porters' physical limits and accommodated Filipinos' expectations that Americans would obey the rules of the system. It also allowed US columns to continuously carry their own food and thus avoid requisitions that risked alienating civilians, especially in areas where food was scarce (sometimes by American design). Shifting military conditions and contingencies that affected cargadores' behavior, and thus US soldiers' perception of their labor, also induced subaltern performances of loyalty. Where guerrillas made civilians afraid to aid the occupiers or leave garrisons' relative safety, conscription gave cargadores and brokers political cover to cooperate.[46] The *americanos*, they might tell *insurrectos*, made them do it.

Still, if Americans on Luzon during the Philippine War generally experienced little difficulty mobilizing cargador labor, porterage rarely advanced a capitalist civilizing mission. Army commanders' reliance on local officials to broker burden bearers and other aid often made them instruments of elite Filipinos' purposes. In Nueva Vizcaya province in late 1899 and early 1900, Col. Lyman W. V. Kennon and Gen. Frederick Funston found indispensable one Francisco Madrid, a former insurgent captain, as he organized some 1,000 "loyal" and "industrious" Ilocanos for porterage, public works, and scouting. Some soldiers, however, objected to the violent intimidation and fraudulent spiritualism by which Madrid pressured its inhabitants to satisfy Americans' labor demands. Madrid's methods backfired when peasants ran to the mountains. In lowland areas of the Ilocos, where the US Army regularly coerced and hired cargador labor for expeditions into the hills, Ilocanos who came to expect timely payment protested late wages. Moreover, compensated but coerced cargador service did not always seem conducive to Filipina-managed household economies. Ilocano women sometimes petitioned Americans to either return male relatives they impressed as bearers or inform them of their whereabouts. In areas of Luzon where specie and wage labor were rare, such as the Cordillera, US troops drafting Igorot men for porterage claimed these aborigines showed little interest in money. Officers' anecdotal commentary on different ethnicities' efficiency as porters also never reached the level of ethnography, much less the militarized Taylorism on display in occupied Cuba.[47] Blurring divides between freedom and force, and civility and savagery, coerced and waged burden-bearing during the war never generated the scientific culture needed to rationalize militarized manual colonial labor.

A science of militarized cargador service materialized only later, in the southern Philippines, as American soldiers fought Moro and Visayan rebels. Invading Mindanao and the Sulu Archipelago in the spring of 1899, US commanders pragmatically followed imperial precedent by conceding substantial autonomy to the region's Muslim majority. In 1878, the sultan of Sulu formally acknowledged Spain's authority without ceding control over Moros' everyday life. In December 1899, his Tausūg successor at Jolo, Jamalul Kiram II, signed a treaty with Gen. John Bates that extended this modus vivendi under US sovereignty. In effect, the Kiram-Bates Treaty made the region a protectorate in which American troops managed Mindanao-Sulu's external relations and governed its small Filipino and Christian population but left Moros' local sovereignty intact. Bates promised not to interfere with their Islamic faith or customs and recognized the titles of the Sulu sultanate and lesser datus. He also pledged to honor their rights to tax Moros, enforce religious law, and trade freely with Luzon and the Visayas. In return for monthly sums, the sultan permitted Americans to suppress piracy, regulate foreign trade (including a ban on importing firearms), and control legal matters involving non-Moros. Yet US officials never inked a similar pact with Mindanao datus who did not recognize Sulu's suzerainty.[48]

Gen. Bates's proviso that his government would only temporarily respect Moro slavery, however, virtually guaranteed conflict over the institution. It also placed labor at the center of the so-called Moro problem by which European colonists, and now Americans, puzzled over how to rule Southeast Asian Muslims given their fierce desire for local autonomy, which Westerners often attributed to their religion and race. The Kiram-Bates Treaty's single explicit mention of slavery recognized slaves' rights to purchase their freedom. Yet President McKinley, reluctant to openly violate the Thirteenth Amendment, had Bates notify Kiram that the United States could not authorize or consent to slavery, and reserved the issue for future deliberation. By late 1903, this fragile status quo of divided sovereignty began to unravel when Mindanao-Sulu's military governors asserted direct rule over Moros. Ensuing conflict catalyzed American military efforts to study and rationalize Moro cargadores, a vital resource on islands mostly lacking roads.[49]

This scientific conjuncture emerged from operations on Mindanao, the second-largest island in the Philippines, located in its southwest, a region that Spaniards and Americans designated as Cotabato, after its chief port. This small entrepôt sat in the delta of the sprawling 300-mile-long Pulangi River, aptly named the Rio Grande de Mindanao. By 1903, its vast basin, nearly 10,000 square miles in area, was inhabited by some 125,000 people, nearly all Maguindanao, one of thirteen linguistic groups then making up the province's estimated 300,000 Moros; a handful of Christian Filipinos and Chinese lived in Cotabato proper. Named after their dialect's infinitive "to be inundated," the Maguindanao dominated lowlands crossed by tributaries that flowed into two giant marshlands before their waters emptied via the Pulangi into the Cotabato delta and Illana Bay. In 1899, the Maguindanao had long since shifted their livelihoods from piracy and maritime slave raiding to agricultural subsistence and commerce. Their datus derived political authority from claims of blood lineage and relation by marriage to ancestors who had introduced Islam to the region in the fourteenth century, and the honor attached to hereditary rank. Yet Moro elites' effective sovereignty over subalterns rested less on aristocratic criteria and more on a practical calculus: the number of dependent male followers whom they ruled and exploited. Datus won and kept adherents' loyalty through their personal charisma and by providing protection and credit and resolving disputes while enforcing Islamic and customary law. Although a "myth of sanctified inequality" legitimated datus' politico-religious status, these elites' social power, according to one scholar, rested on force, or their ability to "command fear and respect." Datus who failed to do so or abused their authority might lose followers to other datus, yet these elites' competitive and collective interests tended to constrain even that marginal freedom.[50]

Datus' social power also rested on control over agricultural resources and the spoils of war and trade in a tributary political economy. Peasants who occupied this class hierarchy's middle stratum enjoyed a nominal legal freedom relative to a lower stratum of enslaved Moros and non-Moros. Though Quranic doctrine favored communal ownership of land, datus decided its use. Yet their power rested more on controlling labor. Growing staples, peasants paid tribute in crops or other goods and military and labor service; in turn, datus used surplus wealth to support themselves and followers and to finance trade and war. By 1898, Cotabato's leading datus enjoyed different but linked economic bases of power shaped by valley geography. Upriver Maguindanao datus, most powerful among them Datu Ali, accrued wealth from rice cultivated mostly by slaves, including upland pagans, known today as the Lumad, whom these Moros enslaved. By contrast, datus downriver, especially Datu Piang, accumulated riches from controlling commodity trade and setting terms with Chinese merchants at Cotabato to facilitate exports and imports. Piang's loyalties and interests as a regional strongman lay more with trading networks throughout Southeast Asia than with colonial or Filipino elites at Manila.[51]

American soldiers asserting sovereignty over Moros and their labor necessarily navigated Moro politics, social hierarchy, and economic culture, even as they sought to transform them. They started by exploiting fissures between various datus and between datus and their followers, already exacerbated by Spanish predecessors. While a single sultanate historically ruled the Maguindanao, that ethnoreligious polity, like Sulu, was a "segmentary" state in which the sultan enjoyed little authority over other Moros, whose datus only ever briefly united for war or trade while competing for adherents. American soldiers, viewing Moros through a metrocentric lens, thus considered their

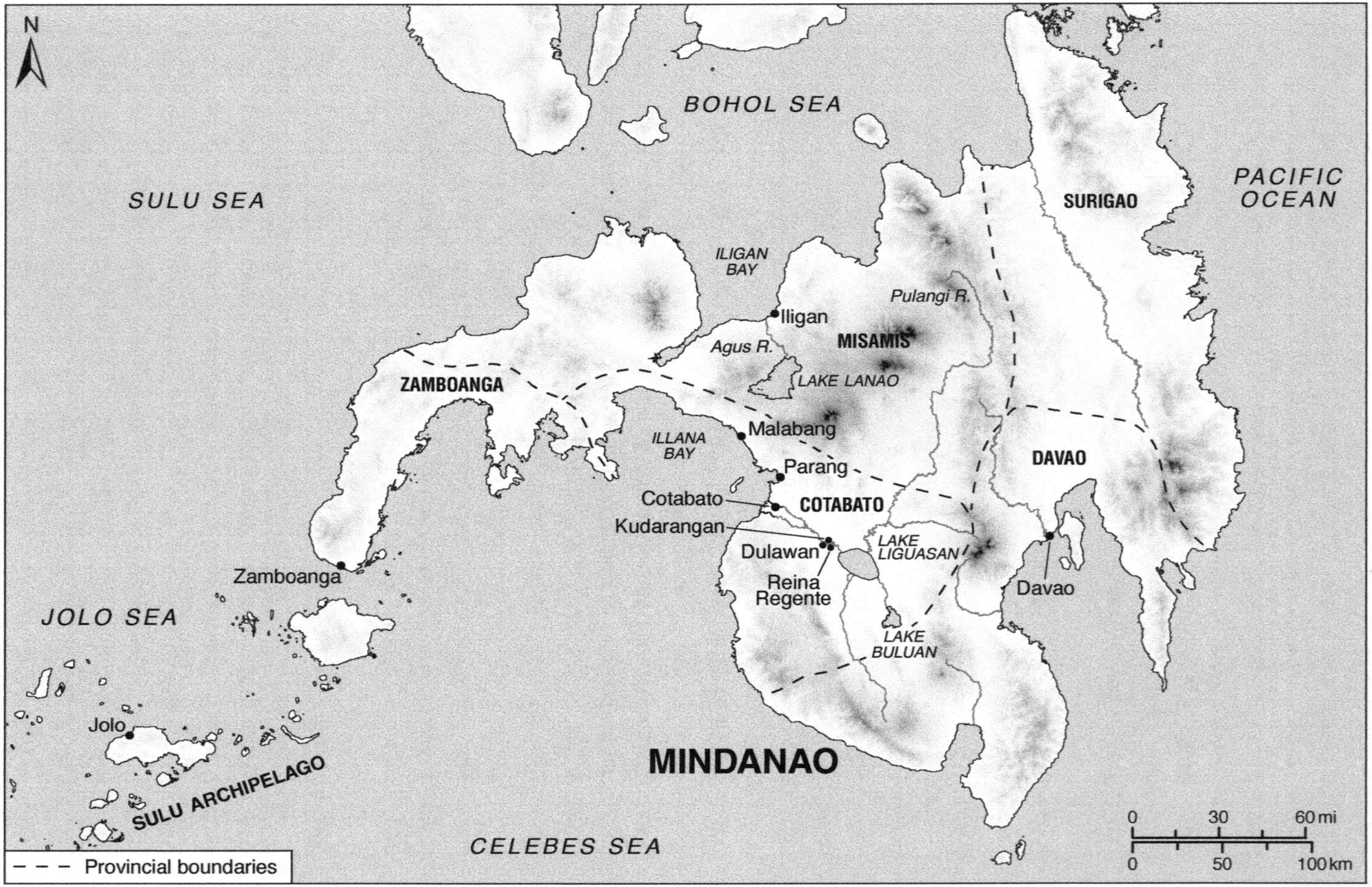
N
BOHOL SEA
SULU SEA
PACIFIC OCEAN
SURIGAO
ILIGAN BAY
Pulangi R.
Iligan
Agus R.
MISAMIS
LAKE LANAO
ZAMBOANGA
Malabang
ILLANA BAY
DAVAO
Parang
Cotabato
COTABATO
Kudarangan
LAKE LIGUASAN
Dulawan
Reina Regente
Davao
Zamboanga
JOLO SEA
LAKE BULUAN
Jolo
MINDANAO
SULU ARCHIPELAGO
CELEBES SEA
Provincial boundaries
0 30 60 mi
0 50 100 km

culture as primitive, patriarchal, and anarchic. Plagued by datus' incessant struggle for followers, slaves, and resources, Moro society to them seemed based on fluid, byzantine, and impenetrable sets of personal, kinship, military, and financial ties.[52]

Occupiers who compared these features of Moro culture to feudalism saw their mission to promote wage labor in Mindanao-Sulu as part of a larger colonial project to modernize Moros through capitalism. As historian Michael Hawkins argues, white bourgeois American officers governing the region constructed the Moro as a colonial subaltern through an ideology of imperial historicism. To them, Moros made savage by their Islamic faith, primitive technology, communalism, debt slavery, and polygamy represented a precapitalist phase in a universal linear and stagist process of sociohistorical evolution. Racializing Moros' economic behavior, Americans hoped to harness their evident hunger for wealth and their work ethic to advance free markets, waged labor, and industrial technology. Despite their fears that a tropical habitus invited torpor, Americans often perceived Moros as more promising industrial subjects than Filipinos, whom they frequently criticized for being "lazy" and disinterested in savings.[53]

Occupiers determined they could move Moros' culture forward in time only by freeing peasants and slaves from datus' tyranny and bringing their labor under a civilizing sovereignty. By rationalizing Moros' work, American soldiers hoped to replace Moro elites' zero-sum competition and exploitation with the idealized equality of liberal capitalism. Yet US troops could access porters only through the datus that brokered their labor. Suspending Moro subalterns between metropolitan modernity and colonial elites' claims to autonomy and custom, the military science of the cargador necessarily negotiated class hierarchy in Maguindanao society itself. One of many "scientifically validated managerial structures" meant to remake Moros into sedentary workforces, as historian Oli Charbonneau argues, porterage would help Moros "escape the twin despotisms of the local datu" and a "primitive labor system."[54]

Occupiers' shifting ties with Datu Piang illustrated how the work of empire reflected and influenced Americans' and Moro elites' struggle for sovereignty over Moro labor. Spanish penetration of the Pulangi valley in 1861 damaged the prestige of its sultan, Datu Uto, and enabled Piang, his subaltern, to succeed him by the early 1890s. Piang was born in 1846 to a Chinese trader and a Moro mother. From his home at Dulawan, twenty-five miles upriver from Cotabato, Piang developed a paternalist reputation that belied ruthless ambition. Aiding the Spaniards even after Jesuit missionaries began redeeming Moro slaves, he earned cash and political capital by selling food to Spanish troops and constructing their garrisons. When the Spanish withdrew from the region in 1899, Piang moved quickly to fill the power vacuum.[55]

Amid Filipino revolution and imperial transition, however, Piang enjoyed a tenuous effective sovereignty over Cotabato, as his common birth forced him to ally with datu nobility, especially Ali, Uto's son. In September 1899, after the two men's followers raided Cotabato and terrorized and killed Filipino revolutionaries there, Piang made himself its "supreme authority." In January 1901, he consolidated his alliance with Ali by marrying his daughter to him. Yet Najeeb Saleeby, a Protestant Lebanese American army physician and Cuba veteran, and the US colonial state's resident expert on Moro culture and history, noted that Piang was "looked down upon and hated" by "Moros of the blood." Piang therefore sought to strengthen his position vis-à-vis Maguindanao datus by allying himself with US invaders, just as he had with their Spanish predecessors. In December 1899, Piang wrote Datu Mandi at Zamboanga, Gen. Bates's new ally, conveying his desire "to be subject to the North American Nation." Indeed, that month Piang rolled out the red carpet for US sovereignty and science. Welcoming US troops to Cotabato, he did not object to their commander's attempt to remedy what the American described as the port town's "vast accumulation of filth." Maj. Lloyd M. Brett, an Indian War veteran who had served at Santiago, valued Leonard Wood's sanitary example. Brett imposed strict public health rules, regulated prices and wages, and hired Moros to clean streets. Still, according to Bates, Piang received him at Cotabato flying a US flag, and cordially offered the general "troops for any purpose."[56]

If Piang hoped business with a new empire might solidify his sovereignty over the Maguindanao, American soldiers often objected to his near-absolute power over followers. Though army officers fretted that Ali's and Piang's "factions" persecuted other datus, Piang rapidly made himself vital as a labor broker. From some 15,000 adherents, he rented hundreds of cargadores to the US Army for operations against Maranao to the north, as well as guides and boats. Yet occupiers' liberal ethics quickly clashed with Moro values. During an April 1902 raid that culminated at the battle of Bayan, near Lake Lanao, American officers angered several hundred of Piang's porters by barring them from joining the assault. Dejected, they dropped their packs and walked back to Cotabato, much to the chagrin of the bewildered Americans. Their sense that Piang's men irrationally honored a warrior ethos over their contractual obligations anticipated future tensions between a subaltern mentalité and militarized science.[57]

Compared to Cuba, however, US occupiers' scientific capitalism clashed more deeply and continuously with a local colonial political economy rooted in Moro elites' social power. American commanders who paid Piang and other datu brokers in lump sums, which they expected them to distribute to laborers, believed this would promote liberating markets in wage work. Yet the past retained its grip. Army engineers who saw their Maguindanao road gangs quit after they tried to pay them wages directly, not through their headmen, suspected that these datus recalled them. Datus' claims that their peasants would earn more growing rice suggested a tributary mindset. Piang himself translated business with Americans through a patron-client frame, as William H. Taft discovered when meeting him in April 1901. Reporting to Elihu Root, Taft gloated that Piang had "acknowledged the sovereignty of the American government" and pledged "that his followers . . . would willingly obey" it. Yet when Taft asked Piang if he would sell gutta-percha for a new telegraphic cable to link San Francisco and Manila, the datu replied deferentially that the Americans might "have it without paying for it." Taft, shocked, said this was not how his government "deals with anybody that is loyal to it." Americans were "not in the habit of taking things without paying for them from any persons whether subject to their sovereignty or not"; they paid "money," he responded, "and what the thing is worth." Piang replied that Taft's army had "received and treated" Moros "as brothers," and he craved political capital with the Americans by supplying them with labor and other assets, even if it cost him.[58]

Escalating tensions over slavery catalyzed a politics of sovereignty inherent to the US military's drive to liberalize and rationalize Moro cargador labor. By 1899, most Maguindanao slaves were fellow Maguindanao peasants bonded to datus by debt, usually credit extended to farm, support family, and pay tribute. A quarter of Maguindanao were freemen sold by datus, or freemen who had sold themselves, to settle debts amounting to no more than $50 Mexican. Most Americans found this "mild slavery" less troubling, if more puzzling, than African chattel slavery abolished in the Western Hemisphere by the late 1880s. Reducing enslavement to racial difference, occupiers imbibing social-evolutionary theory and romantic myths about paternalist Southern plantations often saw slavery as an organic social step toward industrial modernity. Moro slaves and enslavers, they believed, would inevitably adopt liberal labor markets.[59]

Over time, however, occupiers found certain features of Moro slavery disturbing, especially the passing of enslaved status from debtor to children. Given the Kiram-Bates Treaty's open door to abolition, a few junior army officers entertained gradual and compensated emancipation. Some, like the commander at Malabang—a coastal port some forty miles north of Cotabato—proposed a transitional indenture system, comparable to the transitional *patronato* system in Cuba during the early 1880s, in which his army and other employers would purchase slaves' labor for six-month terms "to gradually divorce them from their Datohs." By July 1901, Cotabato's new commander, Maj. Lea Febiger, effectively proscribed the institution. Refusing to return runaways, he declined to recognize "a man's body as collateral" for any debt incurred after "American conquest." Yet Febiger's antislavery writ, like that of Spaniards before him, extended only to the port and its immediate environs. Piang and upriver datus retained most of their slaves and sought to punish and recapture fugitives, including those fleeing to US troops.[60]

Indeed, Febiger represented a new iteration of an older imperial paradox at Cotabato, in which colonizers who abhorred datus' exploitation still depended on it. Jesuits' redemption of Moros' slaves especially reflected Spain's awkward relationship to the institution. As early as the 1850s, Spaniards in the Pulangi delta, promoting their Catholic empire's opposition to secular slavery, proposed subduing Maguindanao datus by "attracting" their slaves. Though Spanish authorities never pressed systematic abolition, by the late 1880s their interference with Maguindanao slavery provoked the warfare that ended Datu Uto's rule. Febiger, however, articulated a new imperial critique of Moro slavery through an American egalitarianism which regarded the institution as only one facet of datus' abuse of dependent labor. Febiger distinguished Moro slaves from chattel in legal terms, conceding that debt bondsmen seemed "more like peons of the soil, vassals or serfs of feudal times." Yet he found it intolerable that "hardly a single follower of any dato" seemed "not in his debt for money, supplies, or material advanced." Such "vassalage," he believed, granted datus a "power of life and death over all their followers" that no principled American could permit under the "broad base of the Constitution." Nonetheless, even as Febiger saw Piang as a "savage" whose "shrewd" business talents came from "Chinese blood," he recognized him as the only "prominent" datu to grasp what "American invasion means," particularly its "business opportunities." Piang, realized Febiger, was "the fulcrum on which our lever should work" for "uplifting" Cotabato.[61]

Still, American occupiers' faith that they could modernize Moros and weaken slavery by commodifying their labor rested on flawed Orientalist assumptions that Maguindanao never before received cash for work. While true for upper valley Moros, some Maguindanao at Cotabato and garrisoned coastal towns had already worked for wages paid by Chinese merchants and US troops. By representing Moro labor as unwaged, American soldiers could conceive of their exploitation of brokered Maguindanao cargadores as a blow against datu tyranny. In June 1903, Lt. H. M. Cooper, escorting British geographer and journalist Arnold Henry Savage-Landor on a trip upriver, regarded the Moro guide and six cargadores whom he hired from Piang as regrettably subaltern. "Poor, ignorant, and superstitious," his burden bearers, claimed Cooper, did "not know the use of money." Giving Piang "nearly all their products—cocoanuts, corn, rice, potatoes, [and] cane," he marveled that they received "but little (in trade) in return," yet "greatly admire their Datto [sic], who can easily command all [of] them."[62] American occupiers therefore exaggerated datus' sovereignty over Moro labor to construct a parallel illusion of imperial sovereignty as a revolutionary and emancipatory force.

By the summer of 1902, however, a newly aggressive US antislavery policy linked the promise of waged Moro cargador labor with a direct American assault on datus' sovereignty. In August, Gen. George W. Davis, Mindanao-Sulu's commander, ordered officers to shield runaway slaves. Their nation, Davis reminded subordinates, had come "to teach and convince these people that all men are born free and equal" and that there was "no such thing as inherited caste or privilege." Yet Davis also knew that implementing this vision would upset Moros' "whole system of tribal and patriarchal government." It would, he admitted, create a new society "not held together by the dicta of a Sultan, Datto, or Priest."[63]

Events tempered Davis's imperial ambitions, as American soldiers' attempts to insinuate their sovereign power between Moro elites and Moro commoners precipitated warfare that tested their liberalizing and scientific industrial ideals against colonial realities. In July 1903, Taft's Philippine Commission ratified its dual mandate over the islands by organizing Mindanao-Sulu as a new "Moro Province," distinct from provinces in Luzon and the Visayas dominated by Hispanized and Christianized Filipinos. In the latter areas, first US military governors and then Taft's commission gradually entrusted local elites with municipal and later provincial government; Taft also offered them representation in the commission itself and a legislative assembly at Manila. Rule over Muslims in the South, however, was handed over to American generals. The new Moro Province's governor was to be the region's senior army officer, who would make policy with a five-member Legislative Council composed of fellow commanders. In September 1903, this body reorganized the Moro Province into civil districts, each entrusted to a governor and board (also initially army officers and veterans). Early the next year, the council subdivided these districts into municipalities to be administered by "civilized" American, Filipino, and Chinese residents, and "tribal wards" for

Muslims and the Lumad, to be run by datu headmen expected to enforce secular law.[64]

This administrative reform reflected US Army commanders' desire to radically diminish datus' local autonomy, despite a minority opinion articulated by Najeeb Saleeby that it would be wiser to preserve Moro elites' titular power. Direct military rule also advanced occupiers' desire to use liberal labor schemes to interpose US sovereignty between datus and subalterns. Taft's commission signaled its support for military-colonial reform by making Gen. Leonard Wood the Moro Province's first governor. Wood sought to subjugate Moros through transimperial knowledge and science. Visiting British Egypt, British India, and Dutch Borneo, he amassed a small library on Islam and Muslim history, culture, and politics. Yet Wood, compared to Europeans, endorsed a more aggressive assertion of sovereignty over Asia's Muslims, even as he initially entertained gradual emancipation. In January 1904, he stated that his policy would be "to develop individualism" among Moros by teaching them "to stand upon their own feet independent of petty chieftains."[65]

Measures that Wood implemented in September 1903 abrogated the Kiram-Bates Treaty and projected his liberal reason from Cuba into new imperial zones. Outlawing slave owning, trading, and raiding, they authorized provincial courts to sentence any Moro found guilty of violating the new laws to up to twenty years in prison. Simultaneously, Wood's regime imposed an annual one-peso-per-capita "cedula" tax on all Moro men between the ages of eighteen and fifty-five. Transposing onto Moros the same punishments Wood applied against Cuban laborers at Santiago, the new cedula law recommended prosecuting tax delinquents as vagrants; if convicted, they were to toil on public works to pay their fine, at a rate valued at fifty cents daily. Wood tried conciliating datus by exempting Moros at Cotabato and Zamboanga from paying cedulas for the rest of 1903; he granted the same dispensation to all other Moros until 1905. These policies' immediate significance, however, lay in their visceral assault on Mindanao's distribution of effective sovereignty. While datus might resent paying tribute to Christians, new rules restricting their right to fine followers—long a means of debt enslavement—further attenuated their power over Moro subalterns.[66]

Unsurprisingly, upriver datus in Cotabato, controlling thousands of slaves, saw Wood's new regime as a dagger aimed at the social base of their power. With characteristic hubris, Wood in early 1904 prematurely seized on reports of declining slave trading and hunting in the region as evidence that his progressive mandate was already emancipating Moro subalterns. "All former slaves," he cheered, now understood they could "not be compelled to remain with their former masters." Moro freemen who learned they had "a right to their own property and their own labor," predicted Wood, would inspire other Moros to demand "protection against the exactions of the dato." Yet the general succeeded only in destabilizing the fragile balance of sovereignty that had kept Maguindanao country relatively peaceful. Wood's strident abolitionism, as historian Michael Salman notes, "destroyed the political and economic system of indirect rule over the whole valley" that his army had been cautiously exercising through Piang.[67]

Unlike in Cuba, however, Wood's labor policy in Mindanao evolved as part of American counterinsurgency. In February 1904, Wood responded preemptively to rumors that Datu Ali planned to revolt by organizing and leading an expedition upriver to intimidate him. En route, he consulted with Piang, who he reported "fears and hates" Ali, and vowed "to use his utmost influence and endeavor to bring about [Ali's] capture." After Wood's column destroyed Ali's *kota*, or fortified village, near Kudarangan, the historic center of Maguindanao resistance to Spanish rule, Ali eluded the Americans. Escaping with a retinue of sixty armed Moros and conscripting men to carry supplies, the renegade datu commenced guerrilla warfare against the occupiers and allies, including Piang. Authorized by Wood to capture or kill Ali himself, Piang supplied his troops with porters, vintas, and other aid and collected the cedula from his followers. As American troops destroyed upriver villages presumed to support Ali and their rice surpluses, they forced 20,000 Maguindanao into garrisoned towns.[68] Yet the war against Ali spawned another conflict over labor. As both Ali and Piang sought to preserve their power over their followers, Wood assailed Piang's control of Moro cargadores almost as much as he attacked Ali.

To be sure, Wood's cargador policy expressed a larger "developmentalist fantasy" for Mindanao similar to that which he previously envisioned for eastern Cuba. Refracting an idealized history of settler expansion in North America, Wood at Oriente, and now Mindanao, hoped that white American colonists would modernize tropical frontiers by establishing plantations producing agricultural commodities for export. Yet the relative absence of a free waged labor market in the southern Philippines led Wood to prioritize commodifying colonial labor—an unnecessary step in Cuba's more evenly developed capitalist economy. If Wood's coercion of Cuban labor diminished over time, however, counterinsurgency prompted Wood at Cotabato to embrace force as a means to civilize subalterns, continuously and scientifically. In this sense, Wood's cargador policy neatly reinforced his military regime's broader efforts to remake Moros into self-disciplining and profit-maximizing economic subjects. Army officers in Mindanao-Sulu also organized marketplaces, agricultural fairs, and new secular schools imparting industrial education.[69] Yet Wood's response to Piang's brokerage stood out as an attempt to rationalize colonized labor at the militarized point of imperial sovereignty's production: field operations.

More than just cost cutting, Wood's cargador policy advanced a counterinsurgency strategy by which his army sought to assert effective sovereignty over Piang by threatening his social power. From Zamboanga in July 1904, Wood ordered subordinates on Mindanao to decrease "the supply of troops in the field down to the most economic basis consistent with efficiency." The general made it clear that this directive targeted Piang, as he specifically required Cotabato's commander to reduce "to the lowest possible point" his various contracts with datus. Wood disapproved a fifty-cent US per diem rate that Piang, and perhaps others, had been charging for each cargador (with seventy-five cents for Moro foremen). Henceforth, officers were authorized to hire cargadores exclusively at thirty cents a day plus rations. Wood also capped the number of Moros they could employ. To prevent overspending on "idle" cargadores, in the general's phrasing, he set a maximum cargador and boat quota for each roughly 100-man company at no more than ten porters and six vintas. Wood justified the orders by claiming they would cut army labor expenses in Mindanao by half. Yet stipulations that subordinates were to start paying all cargadores "direct and not through dattos [sic]" revealed Wood's true purpose.[70] Even if subordinates still accessed laborers only through Piang or other datus, he expected them to deny these brokers their customary wage packets and ensure that Moro men received their wages directly, in full.

Wood's cargador order did more than extend the empire of fair labor practices he promoted in Cuba. It also integrated counterinsurgency imperatives with his overall crusade to remake Mindanao into a paradise for settler capital. Eager to improve on his progressive record at Santiago, Wood justified unmediated military-labor markets and slashing Moros' wages as judicious boosts to private employers. Not unlike Yankee merchants at Oriente, American pioneers starting hemp plantations on Mindanao complained that US Army wages were robbing them of Moro workforces by distorting labor markets. Already worried that absent and confused land titles and laws limiting the acreage foreigners could buy were stymying foreign investment, Wood resolved not to further discourage business with "foolishly high prices paid by army officials for labor." He feared premium wages had fueled inflation without increasing agricultural productivity, especially among Moros whose datus discouraged industry by seizing peasant surpluses. The cargador order, the general affirmed, would "adjust matters."[71]

Instead of readjustment, however, Wood's labor policy generated a volatile politics of sovereignty that disrupted his army's counterinsurgency nearly as much as it strengthened it. By July 1904, subordinates shared suspicions that Piang had been covertly helping his rebel son-in-law. They speculated that Piang was passing information to Ali and intentionally supplying them with stale or inaccurate intelligence. Army officers even started wondering if their requests to Piang for cargadores was allowing him to alert Ali in advance about operations. When Wood promulgated his new cargador policy, then, he notified Piang that his army would no longer continue to pay contracts with him on a monthly basis—"good round sums," as one private recalled. Now Wood's army would compensate Piang only when Ali had been captured or killed. The Americans pressured Cotabato's leading datu in other ways. In October 1904, they prohibited most river traffic and capped the amount of food Chinese merchants sold at markets taxed by Piang. Meant to starve Ali of food and income, these steps also hurt Piang's profits.[72]

Ironically, Wood's attempt to intensify counterinsurgency by rationalizing labor policy triggered a host of unintended effects, ultimately truncating his army's power over Moro subalterns. While Piang barely lost his grip on dependents, Americans' attempts to individuate them as colonial subjects encouraged Moro workers to assert sovereignty over themselves, in defiance of both Americans and datus. As in Cuba, occupiers' shift from coerced to nominally free waged labor nurtured collectivism among militarized workers. In September and October 1904, dozens of Moro employees at Malabang rejected Wood's wage cuts in two consecutive walkouts. As soldiers replaced strikers, even Malabang's commander and quartermaster sympathized with the Moros.[73] Wood's passion for efficiency thus strained the culture of mutual reciprocity that had evolved between US commanders and Moro brokers and followers. By weakening Piang's ability to earn and distribute cash income to peasants, Wood's economism crippled martial mobility precisely when his troops needed it most.

Indeed, US Army records suggest that Wood's policy unleashed a volitional spirit among Moro subalterns. Their self-activity militated against militarized employment requiring relatively sedentist labor and reflected peasant traditions of protest by avoidance across agrarian Southeast Asia. By late 1904, American commanders throughout the Pulangi valley began reporting that it had become harder to hire Maguindanao porters, either through Piang or themselves. Ali's attacks near Piang's home at Dulawan partly explained

Moros' evasion. Yet Wood's reduced wages and halted payments to Piang also ignited labor refusal. Moros declining army officers' offers of work said that Piang stopped paying his cargadores. By December, commanders were desperate. Some begged Wood's headquarters at Zamboanga to hire cargadores there and ship them to Cotabato; others asked for authority to impress aboriginal Tirurays as substitutes. At Reina Regente, where Moros, "scared to death," refused to carry messages beyond its garrison's line of sight, one officer griped he could find only seventeen carriers, a number sufficient only for "short trips," and he asked comrades downriver to forward more. Moros "have no inducement to work," the commander wrote, as Piang "does not pay them"; they "run away" at "every chance." "Only cargadores from distant points and in direct employ of government," he pleaded, "can be depended on."[74]

Wood's strenuous imperial economy encouraged subordinates to take their own steps to rationalize their sovereignty over Moro labor. If Lt. Harry S. Howland's journal article on lessons learned during his anti-Ali expedition in late 1904 and early 1905 discussed cargadores, his narrative exposed the contradictions of a military-colonial science of the subaltern. Boasting that he had "whipped" cargadores "into systematic shape," Howland exuded a technocratic managerial confidence that observing tropical labor would necessarily yield best practices that imparted mastery over it. Yet his admission that operations in the Rio Grande had been impossible without porters also revealed his army's dependency on Moro labor.[75]

Howland reduced cargador exploitation to a series of universal natural laws. The supply of porters and their physiques, he argued, constituted the greatest factors determining US military mobility on Mindanao. Yet the lieutenant believed the greatest challenge to exploiting cargadores involved calculating the total volume and weight of supplies an army column and its carriers would require, given a particular operation's planned route and duration, and the need to distribute it among porters to ensure their maximum efficiency. Naturally, as a West Pointer, Howland crafted a mathematical formula accounting for all the variables figuring into porters' average pack weight—the key to their productivity. Admitting that Moros' efficiency differed by individual, he warned against "overloading" as "false economy," and identified forty pounds as ideal. Howland also challenged Wood's austerity by recommending a 1:1 cargador-soldier ratio as that most likely to guarantee success. Some officers, he noted, preferred even more laborers.[76]

Most striking, however, Howland unwittingly revealed hidden transcripts of Moro porters' assertions of sovereignty over their labor. By insisting that commanders must always be the ultimate arbiter of pack weights, Howland implicitly recognized that Moro porters tried to alter them. Even his racist Orientalist humor recognized assertions of autonomy, though the lieutenant dismissed them as infantile anti-imperialism. Moros who "object, and swear by Allah," that they could not carry forty pounds, advised Howland, "would raise the same rumpus" over twenty. The Moro protesting his pack, he reassured readers, "will eventually shoulder his burden and jog along, laughing and talking like a child, twitting any of his fellows that show fatigue before he does." Apparently this sociability in cargador culture did not extend to pole carrying. Moros, argued the lieutenant, preferred "to jog along alone, each with his own load, independent of any of his fellows." More important, given the vital question of pack weights, Howland urged officers to allow Moros to arrange their packs. Racializing Moros' skill, he believed they had "a method of their own that cannot be improved upon." "To attempt to change it," he counseled, was a "waste of time." Moros had "their own way with a load," he reported, "and their own way is best."[77]

Howland made more concessions to Moro labor. Essentializing cargadores' attachment to home and family as ethnic traits, he warned that they inevitably became "homesick and discontented" if in the field longer than a month. For operations of greater duration, he recommended that Moros be paid frequently and in person, preferably weekly when camped near settlements, to allow for "amusement and diversion" and to satisfy their "inherent" cravings for tobacco, betel nut, and games of chance. Most alarming for US imperial sovereignty, though, Howland reminded fellow officers that they could never trust Moro cargadores. Trafficking in colonial discourse of the Moro as a fierce warrior—symbolized by the fanatic juramentado, who, inspired by Islamic faith, assailed Christians spontaneously with a kris—Howland advised comrades to surveil carriers constantly, especially given Moros' "mania" for firearms. Most intriguing, Howland urged officers to recruit Moros from locales other than their area of operation. Noting that this technique prevented them from deserting to nearby kin and communities, he acknowledged that some carriers had abandoned his army.[78]

Howland also confirmed fears of cargador disloyalty when he recommended, contrary to Wood's orders, that commanders would better exploit them by using Moro foremen. He advised brother officers to make the most intelligent or respected man among their porters a "cargador boss." This intercultural managerial intermediary, explained Howland, received "jurisdiction" over fellow burden bearers analogous to that "exercised by a company commander over his company." Representing Moro cargadores to officers, "if they have any complaints to make," this foreman was to "see that they all do

Moro Cargadores, Malabang, P.I., Feb. 1905. Identified by Col. Philip Reade as cargadores for the Twenty-Third Infantry, these five Moro men appear to represent the type of burden bearers whom Lt. Harry Howland recruited from Malabang in late 1904 and early 1905 for operations against Datu Ali; see Reade, "The Cargadore in Mindanao," 114. From box 4, Marvin Hepler Photograph Collection, US Army Heritage and Education Center.

their work," "report or himself discipline any delinquents," assign jobs in camp, and assemble them when summoned. Supervised by quartermaster sergeants, Moro foremen were to help them discipline porters by recording their names and assigning each a number, marked on tags of canvas or cloth affixed to clothing, designating their organization. Rank had its privileges. The boss, Howland instructed, should carry a lighter pack or none at all. Having him "carry as large a load as the ordinary tao," he contended, "lowers him in the eyes of his fellows" and "weakens his influence over them." Indulging Moros' warrior culture, the lieutenant also recommended that the boss be one of the few cargadores permitted to keep a bolo, as a "sign of personal authority and power." If others needed bolos to cut trails or make camp, the foreman was to collect them at night to prevent insider attacks and desertions.[79]

Howland's research only illustrated how little junior officers' applied science translated into policy, even when armed progressives like Wood were in charge. If Col. Philip Reade, Howland's commander at Malabang, cribbed the lieutenant's insights in his own publication on "The Cargador in Mindanao,"

Moro Cargadores Packed for the March. Appearing in an article in which Lt. Harry Howland's commanding officer, Col. Philip Reade, cribbed his findings on field operations in Mindanao, this photograph offers a rear view of the same Moro bearers depicted in Figure 2.1A. This image also unintentionally conveyed American soldiers' accommodation of colonial labor. Dated August 12, 1904, and depicting "five (5) Moros employed as cargadores at Malabang" for Howland's Twenty-Third Infantry provisional company, the group portrait, according to Reade's caption, shows how "each cargador has packed his cargo as best suited him." From Reade, "The Cargador in Mindanao," 119.

neither Wood nor other generals adopted their recommendations. Yet American officers continued to experiment. Some issued Moro bearers certificates of service that recognized their names and loyalty. Others kept payrolls that required marks from typically illiterate Moros as a means to ensure honest remuneration. Yet liberal scientific rationality never solved the army's labor needs on Mindanao or beyond. As late as November 1905, Howland grumbled that Piang still struggled to supply cargadores on time. He also claimed they showed a "lack of experience"—possibly evidence that Piang's inability, or refusal, to pay followers made it harder for him to impose upon those who hauled in the past. Such pressures relaxed in October 1905, when US troops and Philippine Scouts, possibly tipped off by Piang, crossed over from Davao and surprised Ali at his refuge near Simpetan and killed him, ending the rebellion.[80]

Ali's death allowed Piang to consolidate his power over Cotabato. When military rule ended in 1913, Piang, having declared himself sultan, survived by trading sovereignty for subordinate political status and immense wealth. As Cotabato's tribal ward leader, he managed Maguindanao relations with foreign colonizers and capital, and a Filipinized government at Manila. Alliance with the Americans, however, did not radically transform Cotabato Moros' social hierarchy. Piang and fellow datus continued to enslave peasants, as colonial officials who selectively enforced antislavery laws usually targeted Ali's former allies. Not even land commodification changed the balance of social power between datus and followers.[81]

Nor did victory against Ali solidify any army consensus on how to manage Moro cargadores. Debate fixated on cargador-soldier ratios as officers routinely criticized and violated Gen. Wood's quota of ten bearers per company. Such dissent may have prompted policy revision. In late 1905, amid the Pulahan rebellion on Samar, Wood, now commanding the Philippine Division, authorized sixty native porters to every 100 US troops for a ten-day hike. Earlier that year, Wood channeled Howland's hubris in reports on the Moro Province, gloating that Moro cargadores "go anywhere the troops go, are easily handled, and give the minimum of trouble." Yet antislavery laws and new plantations barely fostered open markets in Moro wage labor. Throughout Mindanao-Sulu, American garrisons continued to rely on datu brokers and impressment to secure cargadores. Nor were all Moro bearers so easily handled, as Lt. Edward C. Bolton, Davao's governor and a former mechanical engineer, learned in June 1906. Backing planters who were pushing datus to supply Moro and Lumad labor, Bolton encountered a Moro leader rumored to be planning revolt; offering to carry Bolton's things, the man and a companion killed him in his sleep. Such events, if rare, kept panicky Americans from recognizing the risks that Moros ran working for them, as injured cargadores receiving care in army hospitals could testify.[82]

Insider attacks epitomized the subaltern irrationality that Americans associated with the Pulahan revolt on Samar, where their militarized science of colonial labor reached its apogee. Paradoxically, this conflict yielded the clearest proof of US troops' utter inability to rationalize imperial labor relations. In their civilizing mentalité, Pulahanes competed for space with Moros as symbols of a primitive unreason that made archipelagic peoples resistant to enlightenment. In fact, revolutionary nationalism and opportunistic social banditry inspired Pulahan insurgency as much as animist spiritualism and a history of millenarian revolts on Samar going back to the Dios-Dios movement of the 1880s. Above all, Pulahanes reflected mountain-dwelling peasants' resentment toward coastal urban elites who taxed them, controlled their trade, and conscripted their labor. Yet Americans reduced the rebels, named after their red (*pula*) uniforms, to religious zealots. For them, Pulahanes' belief in the protective power of *anting-anting*, or magical talismans, marked them as artifacts of a peasant spiritualism destined to retreat before bourgeois and secular reason. By February 1904, as US officials introduced schools and sanitation to Samar's interior, Pulahanes began attacking police, Americans' Visayan allies, and Catholic churches. Their concentration in upland areas lacking roads unsuited for pack animals forced US troops and Philippine auxiliaries to use cargadores extensively for operations.[83]

Given the Philippine Commission's ban on the corvée, US Army officers on Samar tried to distance themselves from the brutality of Waller's Marines. In July 1905, Brig. Gen. William H. Carter, commanding the Visayas, proscribed cargador conscription, alleging that the practice involved "many elements of injustice." Carter ordered subordinates to offer "a small but fixed rate of wages" and pay "each laborer in person to prevent a percentage being demanded by village officials." Carter's policy also had a counterinsurgent logic. Voluntary and fairly compensated porterage, he believed, would enhance the "contentment" of civilians living near US garrisons. In June 1906, Gen. Leonard Wood applied Carter's mandate to the entire Philippines. Ignoring lessons from Mindanao, however, Wood reverted to his prior parsimony, even as he took steps to regularize cargador service. Ordering each garrison on Samar to organize a permanent "Corps of Cargadores" recruited "from the best material available," he permitted each company only twenty-five porters, paid the same rate as Philippine Scouts. In February 1907, Wood expanded this policy to the entire archipelago. Subordinates were to "build up a willing and reliable service," in his words, by ensuring that bearers were "thoroughly trained" and "treated with kindness."[84]

Officers executing Wood's new Corps of Cargadore policy showed how far military management had progressed since Waller's dark days. Maj. Hugh D. Wise, a Virginian and West Pointer, led Philippine Scouts in Samar's northeastern Catubig valley before he published his own field notes, in the same journal that disseminated Howland's findings. Wise endorsed Wood's new measures. Selective recruitment, and paternal management of a permanent force, he concurred, enhanced porters' efficiency. Yet Wise, more than Howland, wrestled with the gap between colonial realities and Americans' aspirations to military-technical mastery over subaltern labor.[85]

Wise's catalog of desirable traits for cargador candidates suggested a protoethnographic strategy for institutionalizing liberalized labor. Like any decent Cartesian, Wise started with intellect. Noting that samareños' "process of reasoning" was "often very different from ours," he warned readers that the most "salient features" of their "mental and moral composition" seemed to be "ignorance, superstition, self-reliance and independence." Peasants filling Pulahan ranks, he noted, were "almost inconceivably ignorant." Yet officers necessarily approaching the cargador as a "pack animal," in Wise's view, first needed to scrutinize their physiques. Stressing the imperative of choosing "healthy" men, he preferred those from the mountainous interior conditioned by hauling goods to market. Tall men "apt to have some weak spot in their mechanism," and small men "handicapped" by large packs, he urged, should be avoided, along with men made "slow and awkward" by "big lumpy muscles." Wise's ideal carrier was "a man of average size of his tribe, stockily built, deep of chest with short back and neck." A photographic profile of "Pigeon Dick," capturing the major's "Perfect Cargadore Type," conveyed this archetype, even as its subject's name echoed the dehumanization of Waller's Marines. Still, improving on that expedition's disastrous logistics, Wise recommended liberal rations for cargadores despite pack weights and Orientalist wisdom that Filipinos needed "only a little dried fish and a handful of rice." If the Visayan "rarely does such work as is exacted of him as a cargadore," he insisted, "plenty of good nourishment" equaled "better service, heavier packs and faster marches." Wise's empiricism reflected a new appreciation for expertise as a means to resolve the archipelago's labor question. "The peculiarities and prejudices of the race," he wrote, could be "a powerful instrument in the hands of an officer who understands them."[86]

By contrast with Howland, however, Wise revealed an almost cynical knowledge of colonial elite and subaltern capacities to subvert imperial sovereignty. To be sure, Wise, like Howland, understood that "haphazard" impressment increased the likelihood of cargador malingering and mutiny, and counterintelligence failures. Wise shared Howland's paternalism, urging readers to issue porters light uniforms, to make them "more comfortable" and "prevent their being killed by mistake in a fight." Yet his discussion of surveillance techniques suggested a more panoptical attitude. Advising brother officers to assign guards to watch for "signs of treachery," he urged them to mark cargadores' clothing with badges to better "compel their loyalty" and "prevent their escape."[87]

If Wise's techniques seemed to recapitulate Waller's post-Balangiga paranoia, he recognized more than Howland that cargador loyalties were contingent and fluid. Wise insisted that if treated "kindly" and "without compulsion," samareños recruited from garrisoned areas, where their families stayed behind, might serve as "a valuable adjunct" in combat. Yet he also warned that men impressed from a contested area, or who seemed "uneasy or doubtful" about a fight's outcome, might "join the enemy"—a frightening scenario for

Pigeon Dick, a Perfect Cargadore Type. Accompanying Hugh Wise's field notes on Samar, this profile, emphasizing the Visayan cargador's size relative to his bulky pack, conveyed both US Army officers' confidence that they could scientifically select racialized Filipino labor and maximize their military efficiency, and American soldiers' dehumanization of disposable colonial labor. From Wise, "Notes on Field Service in Samar," 31.

American soldiers contemplating Pulahanes' legendary bolo rushes en masse. Unintentionally, Wise thus exposed commanders' inability to truly know subalterns' interiority; only an inner racial nature, revealed by overt behavior, might be studied. Yet this insight also recognized cargadores' capacity to influence operations. If "failing to disarm suspicious cargadores" might "turn out to be a disaster," admitted Wise, "disarming friendly or loyal cargadores may, by its evident lack of confidence, make them treacherous or induce them to desert."[88] The scientific military management of colonial labor, it seemed, never guaranteed an absolutely reliable cargador workforce.

In reality, Wise's superficial science rested on an overall counterinsurgency strategy almost as brutal as that of Waller's era. Glossing over the larger social context of the anti-Pulahan campaign, Wise's field notes failed to acknowledge how reconcentration on Samar again manufactured a captive surplus of civilian labor in garrisoned towns vulnerable to martial exploitation. Samar during the Pulahan war thus spawned not a free market of waged workers so much as a reserve army of coercible colonial labor. Despite US commanders' anti-impressment policy, junior army officers who complained that they could not find willing volunteers to fill cargador quotas simply impressed men, often aided by local Visayan officials. The army's failure to pay drafted workers on time, as promised, also discouraged voluntary cooperation. By May 1906, Carter's successor, Brig. Gen. James Buchanan, endorsed his ban on cargador conscription as good politics. Yet Buchanan's replacement, Col. Charles A. Williams, lamented that subordinates routinely violated it.[89]

Williams's career marked the tragic denouement of armed American progressives' efforts to scientifically promote liberal capitalist colonial labor relations. Though this West Virginian and West Pointer initially maintained the anti-coercion policy, by early 1906, Williams's inability to recruit voluntary porters led him to condemn a free market approach as hopelessly impractical. The colonel capitulated in April when the few men he had been able to hire on Leyte who had not held out for higher wages demanded to be discharged the moment they stepped into the field on Samar. Subordinates' reassurance that their cargadores were "voluntary attendants" meant, in Williams's view, that Americans seemed politically "to-day as far from the masses as we were six years ago." Wood's constant economizing did not help. The general's decision later that year to slash wages for all army civilian employees in the archipelago paralyzed Samar operations. As an already receding pool of willing men refused to carry for less pay, soldiers had to haul their own equipage; remote garrisons in the interior went weeks without resupply. As officers criticized Wood's reduced cap on the cargador corps, Hugh Wise lamented that late paymasters forced him to pay burden bearers from his own pocket.[90]

Army officers' ambition to rationalize subaltern tropical labor was destined to founder on the same colonial reefs of class hierarchy and coercion that fueled popular rebellions like that of the Pulahanes. Brig. Gen. Albert L. Mills, Williams's successor as the Visayas' commander, wrestled with this imperial conundrum. A West Pointer awarded the Medal of Honor for action at San Juan Hill, Mills in 1907 regretted that cargador conscription imposed "a great burden upon the people of the peaceful coastal towns and interfered very materially with their domestic and agricultural pursuits." Yet he also argued that Visayan elites not only tolerated militarized conscription but facilitated it because they never suffered its burdens. If compulsion "brought home to the people as nothing else would the undesirableness of lawlessness," its "hardships," Mills argued, should not have been "confined to the ignorant and friendless tao." If "more evenly imposed upon his protected brother" and "citizens superior in wealth and position to both," the general contended, Pulahanes' rebellion would have ended much sooner.[91] If such equalitarian zeal evoked Leonard Wood's idealism at Santiago, his infrastructural ambitions at Oriente similarly constructed an imperial politics of sovereignty that defied Americans' intentions.

Part II
Infrastructure

CHAPTER THREE

An Army of Workmen
The Polista *Politics of Military-Colonial Public Works*

The Rough Riders took San Juan Hill, but they never conquered Cuba's rough roads. Landing at Daiquirí on June 22, 1898, Americans in the First US Volunteer Cavalry quickly discovered that highways marked on War Department maps were only rock-strewn trails, hewn deep into the earth by decades of traffic, erosion, and disrepair. Narrow and muddy, they barely accommodated men and mules in single file, much less wagons. As Oriente's hilly terrain, thick vegetation, and deep ravines made off-road movement even worse, soldiers realized they could only enhance mobility and resupply by repairing roads. Fifth Corps commander Gen. William Shafter drafted state volunteers, but they fatigued after two days in the heat and rain, leaving roadways "all but impassable." Shafter learned his army would have to approach Santiago via a six-foot-wide path across San Juan Hill, encumbered by large rocks—"one of the worst pieces of highway" Gen. Joseph Wheeler had ever seen—or an equally bad road via El Caney. To postwar critics, Shafter blamed slow progress on roads that seemed more like "bridle paths" and "natural obstacles."[1]

His army struggled to secure labor to fix them. Shafter, a highly decorated Civil War veteran, knew volunteers craved battlefield glory, not "digging and smoothing," which, as correspondent Stephen Crane noted, "gains no encrusted medals." Shafter had no luck with Gen. Calixto García, who rebuffed his request for troops as an insult. While desperate quartermasters considered importing 400 laborers from faraway Washington, DC, Shafter hired 200 Cubans to repair the "mule track" between Las Guásimas and El Caney. Yet his government's refusal to recognize García and other separatist leaders as representatives of a sovereign nation-state also alienated civilians. By early July, Shafter's generals, besieging Santiago, found few Cubans willing to work the roads. Perhaps they knew it would not win them medals, either.[2]

The US armies that invaded and occupied Cuba and the Philippines in 1898 quickly came to depend on colonial labor to improve infrastructure essential to their missions. For Americans from an industrializing and urbanizing metropole latticed by railroads and electric trolleys, highways seemed mundane, almost anachronistic, the fixation of bicyclists and rural farmers lobbying for "good roads." Yet highways were hardly quotidian matters in the making and unmaking of sovereignty in the colonized tropics. Soldiers who considered roads crucial not just for war and pacification but for economic development embraced public works as an imperial technology of colonial rule. Constructed with the assistance of Cuban and Filipino elites and subalterns, highways and other projects were intended to enhance martial mobility, state building, and capital accumulation. In addition to reforms in taxation, policing, and communications, new and improved highways promised to strengthen central states at Havana and Manila and boost agricultural exports. As globalizing empires' steam engines and grand canals accelerated and multiplied connections between continents and cultures, remaking space and time, military roadbuilding crudely integrated the local and global through a technopolitics of labor control and engineering that transformed war-torn and occupied island colonies.[3]

If better and more roads fueled mobility and trade, however, they never delivered the mastery over tropical spaces and subjects that American troops expected they would. In the hothouse conjuncture of 1898, the political economy of public works generated an unanticipated politics of sovereignty in which colonized subalterns reengineered infrastructure to their own ends. In Cuba and the Philippines, poorly resourced US armies confronted intersecting military, humanitarian, and economic crises by forcing the occupied to toil on roads and streets. Generals tried to placate insular elites' unmet desires for modernity and national sovereignty by incorporating them in local administration. Yet just as militarized labor exploitation ultimately enabled subalterns to subvert Americans' aspirations, colonial elites' inclusion in occupation regimes granted them influence over infrastructure, and the labor and money it required. The tense politics this created allowed the colonized to mediate the militarized remaking of island landscapes and co-determine its effects.

ORIENTE, CUBA'S EASTERNMOST PROVINCE, proved fertile soil for infrastructural imaginaries in 1898. Less populated and farmed than central Cuba, where sugar estates spreading out from Havana produced vast riches, Oriente has a rough geography that shaped its unique socioeconomic development. A jagged peninsula some 16,573 square miles in area, the province, bounded by ocean on the north, east, and south, and Puerto Principe province to the west, resembles an anvil with its top bent westward. Its topography impressed US military observers as "extremely broken and precipitous." The Sierra Maestra, Cuba's tallest mountains, hugs Oriente's southern coast, carving valleys around Santiago de Cuba and Guantánamo; like lesser mountains to the north and east, they project hills and ridges forming lush interior valleys. Relative to other provinces, Oriente's terrain thwarted industrial sugar and nurtured smallholding, especially among enslaved Afro-Cubans and free descendants who used it, and legal customs, to flee slave owners and authorities. The cockpit of separatist insurrection, Oriente after the Ten Years' War received a wave of migrants. Poor whites escaping sugar planters' tightening grip on land and labor, and emancipated Cubans of color, joined Spaniards in seeking autonomy by settling abundant unclaimed lands. In 1899, despite low fertility, high mortality, and war, some 327,000 people lived in Oriente, nearly half of them Afro-Cubans—the highest rate of any province. Even as sugar increased as a percentage of landholdings and exports, fruits, vegetables, and coffee predominated, raised mostly by small farmers on communal lands.[4]

The same environment that stunted Oriente's industrial development preserved the region's status as a refuge for runaway slaves, campesinos, and insurgents, frustrating colonial elites who knew that better and more roads would help them police the region. The province's nearly sixty miles of railroad, built by planters to move commodities to ports, lacked arteries and charged high rates. They did little to help small farmers, who often moved surpluses to market by pack mule. Envying the modern highways of "civilized nations," planters lobbied Havana to improve "limited and imperfect" roads which they regarded as "a terrible menace" in all seasons. Yet officials did little more than compel slaves and convicts to repair tracks near Santiago. Americans invading Oriente in June 1898 plausibly believed it lacked a single highway able to resist rains or traffic.[5]

The US troops who occupied Santiago in late July that year quickly came to understand that the east's infrastructure affected their ability to address economic emergency as well as humanitarian and public health disasters. The 1895 war, launched nearby, inflicted more damage on Oriente than any other part of the island. Sugar estates already battered by the Ten Years' War and recession, utilizing only a third of regional farmland, were smaller, less efficient, and less profitable than their competitors. Spanish and insurgent requisitions, *reconcentración*, and rebels' destruction of plantations had ravaged a nascent sugar industry in the east that historically offered poor peasants seasonal income. In late 1898, however, large planters lacked the capital and credit necessary to resume production. They were in no position to hire thousands of impoverished civilians huddled at Santiago, nor could poor Cubans easily restart cultivation for themselves after the war dispersed labor and livestock and laid waste to farmlands. Reviving them and starting new plots required seed, implements, and animals, but few had the financial means to procure them. The 1899 census indicated eastern agriculturists' precarity. While more than one in five *orientales* that year worked in farming, nearly 70 percent of them, some 69,000 people, neither owned nor rented land. Cultivated acreage, down a third from prewar levels, as farms that used to raise crops on eighty acres now used only ten, suggested a bleak future. Sugar estates that year, hiring a fraction of prewar workforces, harvested a tenth to a third of prewar crops.[6]

Such conditions explain why Gen. Leonard Wood successfully used starvation to compel thousands of Cuban men to sanitize Santiago between late July and early September 1898. By July that year, recession, insurgency, *reconcentratión*, and a US naval blockade had devastated subsistence farming as well as the agricultural commodity exports that paid for imported rice and other staples in the past. Other than Yankee occupiers, only retailers, vegetable gardeners, and scattered plots tended by *pacificos* offered comestibles, yet few Cubans had money with which to buy them, at inflated prices, nor had goods to barter. Initially rationing as many as 50,000 people a day, Wood, sometime between late August and early September, turned his army's monopoly over food into a cudgel for coercing labor. Restricting gratis rations to women and children, the general declared that his occupation would feed able-bodied Cuban men only if they cleaned the city. The new policy coincided with, and likely implemented, explicit orders from President McKinley that US generals should feed only the disabled or those "in immediate danger of perishing." "The people," his White House enjoined, "should be encouraged to go to work and earn a living."[7]

McKinley's mandate projected into new imperial space a bourgeois metropolitan distaste for welfare embedded in late Gilded Age's Americans' laissez-faire ethos. Calls for government aid for the unemployed earlier in the 1890s, amid severe recession, ossified elite and middle-class qualms about public assistance. Influenced by classical liberalism, Protestant moralism, and social Darwinism, many Americans feared that relief debased recipients by making them dependent wards of the state rather than the self-reliant individuals required by free markets, God, and evolution. Wood, tapping racist-environmentalist stereotypes about tropical labor as he dismissed Cubans as "naturally indolent," quickly determined that rationing was "pauperising [sic]" them. Embracing scientific charity principles current in the states, army officers at Santiago joined Red Cross volunteers who started inspecting households to verify the "worthy poor." Arriviste Yankee retailers, described by one journalist as a "new army" of "commercial occupation," may have prompted this scrutiny after complaining that rivals and wealthier Cubans sent proxies to accumulate food to hoard or sell. Even American humanitarians tempered their altruism with the market's disciplinary logic. Clara Barton, extending her postbellum international relief work to Cuba, defended her organization's intent not to "interfere with business nor encourage vagrancy" but to "encourage suffering humanity to get up and be doing." Before US Army doctors at Havana adopted similar measures, which their Cuban partners would later adopt as best practice for the early republic, Wood's subordinates praised him for curing charity's "tendency to create an army of beggars."[8]

The recalibration of postwar relief reinforced infrastructural reform, as occupiers coerced Cuban labor to cement sanitary science to the neocolonial reconstruction of urban space. Months before US Army engineers at Havana hired Cubans to renovate its streets and install modern sewers, Wood started similar projects at Santiago. Horrified to discover that residents dumped human waste onto its byways because they lacked underground sewerage, he noted that streets' deeply rutted state prevented drainage. Dusting off old public works plans, Wood redirected conscripts to start rebuilding Santiago's 116 miles of thoroughfares. Prioritizing high-traffic streets, they replaced corroded dirt and cobblestone surfaces, resting on limestone bases, with new rock bottoms topped by concrete. Laying new sewer and water pipes beneath them for future use, they crested and guttered streets to protect new surfaces and harness rainfall that could push waste down into Santiago harbor. To pave them, Wood inked a $30,000-per-month contract with the Barber Asphalt Company, a monopolized firm co-owned by Gen. Francis V. Greene, a retired army engineer and Republican loyalist who had joined the Manila expedition. The next year, Congress, with the Foraker Act, barred the occupation from leasing franchises to foreigners. Yet Wood's deal anticipated the fusion of force and business evident in President Theodore Roosevelt's aggressive defense of foreign capital in the region. In 1903, when Barber's "asphalt trust" disputed tar pit concessions in Venezuela, and funded revolt, Roosevelt sent gunboats.[9]

An odor of coercion lingered over Yankee soldiers' urban sanitation, even as rising food supplies and tax revenues incrementally allowed new US garrisons across Cuba to replace conscripted labor, paid only rations, with voluntary workforces compensated in cash. By early 1899, commanders around the island, imitating Wood's practices at Oriente, employed Cubans to rebuild streets, install sewers, and dredge ports, all to ensure public health. By July that year, the US regime had spent more than $1.7 million in civil revenues to clean municipalities according to stringent standards first set at Santiago. Each day thousands of Cuban men swept hundreds of miles of city streets and sprayed them with "electrozone," a disinfectant made of electrolyzed seawater. Vital statistics suggest this activity reduced mortality but did not eliminate yellow fever; a summer 1899 outbreak petrified US officers who responded by imposing quarantines and relocating camps. Army experiments at Havana in 1900 that confirmed mosquitoes were disease vectors seemed to justify strict measures. After the Americans spent $9.7 million on sanitation, or a fifth of the occupation's total spending, the Platt Amendment forced Cuba's republic to maintain their efforts.[10]

Just as rationales for coercing labor at Santiago shifted from biological imperative to social discipline, Wood's reasons for ever-more ambitious public works plans evolved from sanitation to economic recovery. By early October 1898, he began articulating a political-economic logic for infrastructural improvement that exceeded purely military concerns about policing the region. Highway repairs and construction funded by customs revenues, he now argued, could function as a countercyclical engine for capitalist revitalization and transformation, benefiting Cubans and occupiers alike. More modern highways, the general claimed, would spur agricultural recovery and expansion, especially among campesinos, by reducing transport costs and opening the wilderness. Rising commodity exports paying for necessary imports would then generate customs receipts, funding more public works. Deluged by poor farmers' pleas for assistance, Wood believed that paying road laborers cash would garner savings they could invest in farms and spend in a region lacking specie and credit. If Wood thought that only his regime had the resources to fix infrastructure, he obscured its coercive origins by promoting roadbuilding as a benevolent and progressive machine for economic development.[11]

Bureaucratic barriers to this infrastructural political economy signified tensions inside the occupation over the colonial-style compulsion that Wood's public works required. Cubans' anger at "forced labor" expressed resentment toward Yankee occupiers who denied not just their national independence but the dignity of fair wages earned freely in a postslavery society. This manifested in protests against Gen. Henry Lawton, commander of US troops in Oriente, acting as its provincial governor, when he seemed unable or unwilling to aid workers. By early August, 1,000 disgruntled men, assembling daily at his quartermaster's office to demand money for work done during the campaign, marched on Lawton's headquarters "on verge of riot." Worse still, given Yankees' self-image as paternal saviors of a feminized Cuba, the army's failure to pay thirty *lavenderas* at Santiago's military hospital, mostly widows with children, became a "matter of notoriety," Lawton told Washington, much to its "discredit." Controlling all municipal budgets and Oriente's treasury, however, Lawton rejected Wood's requests for US monies and local revenues for public works. Peeved, Wood asked Secretary of War Russell Alger to intervene against this "obstructionist," to no avail. Lawton tried mollifying his subordinate by offering him the provincial governorship, but Wood declined, and they nearly came to blows. Self-destruction resolved the standoff. In early October, Lawton, enraged at being passed over for promotion, went on an alcoholic binge; after trashing a bar, he bit Santiago's police chief. Alger rushed him home on leave and assigned Wood to take his place. Now in control of the province, Wood won access to its $100,000 surplus, a sum that soon grew by 150 percent.[12]

Now able to pay wages in cash, not just food, Wood raced to implement his public works plans. Supervised by Lt. Matthew Hanna, an Ohioan whom Wood later made director of Cuba's schools, army officers soon had 2,000 Cuban men repairing Santiago's streets. As work shifted from sanitation to beautification, municipal councilors appointed by Wood, pleased by an elegant new boulevard popular with pedestrians and horse, carriage, and bicycle riders, named it after him. Outside the city, gangs crowned, guttered, and metaled roadways to Cobre, Caney, and El Morro, the fortress at the bay's entrance. Garrisons at Manzanillo, Holguín, Mayarí, and Guantánamo started similar projects. Yet Yankees hoping to reform cramped urban colonial space according to late Gilded Age "city beautiful" aesthetics ignored this work's compulsory nature in a region lacking food and specie. That occupiers continued to give laborers a choice to be paid in rations or money implied that scarcity still made food more valuable than cash. A US-imposed exchange rate of fifty centavos Spanish silver to the US gold dollar also placed roadworkers' daily wage of seventy-five US cents, or fifty cents and a ration, below prewar wage rates.[13]

Wood and Yankee admirers advertised wage labor on public works as proof of their altruistic nation's modernizing civilizing mission. High turnover on road gangs, they claimed, showed that infrastructure transformed slothful Cuban welfare recipients into neo-Jeffersonian yeomen. Highway jobs churning laborers into the rural interior armed with savings, they argued, fueled agricultural revival and slashed relief. Correlation is not causation, but the number of rations issued at Santiago decreased from a high of 935,000 in September 1898 to zero by February. Wood and fawning journalists transmuted survival into sovereignty. "Profitable labor" on roads, one writer alleged, increased support for annexation or another "form of permanent American control" among Cuba's "working, self-supporting class." Infrastructure, they

Santiago, Cuba. Building Road to San Juan Battlefield. Depicting workers repairing a highway to make it less vulnerable to erosion in late 1898 or early 1899, this War Department photograph linked US troops' access to sites of victory against Spain to postwar infrastructural reform of neocolonial space meant to pacify insurgents, spur economic recovery, and discipline labor. Photo from volume 1, box 17, RG 111-RB, NARA.

argued, detached Cubans from nationalists who sought only the spoils of office.[14]

Such hyperbole papered over a tense politics of sovereignty troubling relations between Americans and Cuban nationalists at Oriente in late 1898. Given that US troops occupied Santiago over insurgents' objections, some 11,000 rebels camped nearby posed a serious threat. Even as Gen. Calixto García tried to resign in protest of Yankees' governance of Santiago, his Liberation Army remained the only force on the island able to contest it. As Wood and others openly entertained annexation, many Cubans feared US designs on the island. Rebels' dependence on American rations thus injected grave questions of pacification into the labor politics of public works. Especially problematic was García's insistence on maintaining his army in the field to secure back pay which the Partido Revolucionario Cubano junta promised its soldiers during the war. Amid contretemps between civilian and military separatist leadership, however, the provisional Council of Government and its successor, the assembly at Santa Cruz del Sur, struggled to finance insurgents' pay. García and other generals, maintaining their army as a final guarantee of independence, also insisted it would disband only when paid.[15]

In response, Wood's occupation again leveraged its food monopoly to wrest labor from Cubans, this time to demobilize the Liberation Army and divert its manpower to public works. American generals quickly realized they could exploit Cubans' dependence on US Army foodstuffs. In early September, Lawton received a request from Gen. Agustín Cebreco, one of Oriente's legendary jefes of color, to forward rations to his camps at Dos Caminos and El Cobre. In telegrams to Washington, Lawton channeled local planters' fears that a leveling popular army might continue to "pilfer" crops by depicting insurgents as a barrier to economic recovery. Simultaneously, he hinted slyly that only his government was in a position to give them jobs. Ordered by McKinley to stop feeding García's men, Lawton told Cebreco he would ration his troops one last time. Emphasizing his wish for their "early disbanding," Lawton told Cebreco his men could eat "individually," as civilians, until they could "secure employment or mature a crop on their plantations." Then he ignored Liberation Army commanders' additional pleas for help.[16]

Lawton's food-for-peace and labor policy strained insurgents' bonds with their officers and injured their patriotic pride. As Cebreco and other commanders reported they would be unable to maintain their ranks without food, they released them to find work. Yet employment by occupiers did not necessarily yield submission. In early September, 200 of Cebreco's soldiers entering Santiago, looking for rations, were told by Lawton they could have them if they unloaded food and other supplies at the docks. Two weeks later, fifty veterans who accepted this offer went on strike, demanding payment in cash, not food. Yankee moralists condemned this protest as ingratitude, yet Cuban patriots defended their dignity. Gen. Enrique Collazo, a Santiago native, admonished the Americans. At least Spain after the Ten Years' War (in which he fought) had "common-sense," Collazo declared; it had "paid the insurgents enough money to allow them to return to their homes and begin work." His troops, insisted Collazo, desired merely "an opportunity to work for themselves," not "charity." By early October, Lt. Col. Henry B. Osgood, supervising relief efforts, warned Washington that the "situation here will soon be dangerous." It asked "too much of human nature," he wrote, "to deny aid to armed men who "want to work, but have neither food, money nor tools to begin anew," and expect them to stay peaceful "while their families are naked and starving." Though Wood dismissed Osgood as hysterical, he later conceded the situation's explosiveness. By mid-1899, after the Liberation Army demobilized, Wood alleged that Gen. García had stormed into his office the previous October demanding work and food. Wood claimed that he responded, "they would have neither while they remained under arms," blustered that war "might be the best way out," and got García to release his troops.[17]

Wood could insinuate that he single-handedly disarmed eastern insurgents with roadwork because he outlived alternative narratives. In December 1898, García died in the states, where he had been pressing federal policymakers to fund his army's pay. In fact, Cuban generals' posturing and diplomacy did more than Wood to push Washington into neutralizing the Liberation Army with cash. By the summer of 1899, US Army paymasters, using leftover congressional war appropriations, distributed a seventy-five-dollar bounty to each Cuban soldier in exchange for guns deposited at arsenals. Wood's boasts that he pacified Oriente's rebels with public works thus glossed over the many factors driving the insurgent army's dissolution between late 1898 and early 1899. Most important, Cuban civilian leaders forced it. The Santa Cruz Assembly dismissed García in late August, and by the end of September it ordered commanders near Santiago to release their troops. In fact, well into 1899, officers in Oriente freed their men to work several days a week or more but mustered them biweekly for drill and review. Such activity likely did not cease until March 1899, when Gen. Máximo Gómez, having secured money from Washington, urged his soldiers to cooperate with the Yankees, including by working for them.[18]

In fact, Wood contemplated various schemes for pacifying the Liberation Army before he finally settled on public works. In September 1898, he floated giving each insurgent twenty-five dollars in cash and twenty-five dollars in farm implements, but Cubans considered the sums insufficient to start farms. Then Wood considered land reform of a conservative kind. As Gen. Collazo implied, Spain after the Ten Years' War rewarded *peninsular* officers, loyalists, and pardoned insurgents with grants of public lands and livestock in Oriente, partly to develop the wild region, including by building roads. In late October 1898, Wood considered deeding thirty-three acres of public estate to each Cuban veteran who served up to April that year, before US entry into the war flooded insurgent ranks with volunteers. Public lands were bountiful in the east; by late 1898, one-fifth of Oriente's land was in private hands, and only 11 percent was cultivated. Yet Wood's idea evoked social policies in the states that had encouraged soldiers to settle frontiers much more than popular Cuban dreams. In 1896, Gen. Gómez had sought plebian support, and recruits, by pledging to give them confiscated loyalist properties. Like his strategy targeting sugar estates, Gómez's declaration reflected his ambition to remake Cuba into a republic of small farmers. Planters, fearing such redistribution, favored Wood's liberal alternative, but like his bounties, it never took root.[19]

Still, Cuban veterans bristled at the notion of trading guns for brooms or shovels. Rising food supplies allowed them to spurn the occupiers' rations-for-labor tradeoff, maintained by some US commanders even as others started to pay workers in cash. At St. Jago and Gibara, patriots rejected American commanders' demands that they work or starve. Beyond Oriente, at Sancti Spiritus, fifty outraged veterans declared they were "soldiers," "not street-cleaners." At San Luis, one irate officer threatened to "take to the mountains"—invoking Oriente's insurrectionist tradition—rather than suffer Yankees' "discourtesy" and "despotic" "tyranny." Still, Wood insisted that highway jobs immunized Cubans from anti-American radicalism. Nationalists failed to "stir up the people," he crowed, because his army gave them "something to do." "All that is wanted in Cuba to ensure good order," Wood affirmed, was "an army of workmen."[20]

Paltry sources do not reveal the demography of road laborers in Oriente or the immediate impact of highway projects on regional economic recovery. Wood's utilitarian rationales for roadbuilding, however, multiplied along with its spatial progress. By early 1899, as US garrisons throughout the east used rations to conscript Cubans into sanitizing towns and rebuilding streets and highways, Wood argued that public works made the region safe for the foreign capital and migrants he considered essential for its development. The general and aides even appealed to antimonopoly politics as they built a road linking Santiago to San Luis, parallel to the region's single major rail line, to allow farmers to avoid its "practically prohibitive" rates. Critics condemned the expensive project as "Wood's Folly," but he defended it as a boon to campesinos. Infrastructure even took on carceral qualities as Wood argued that he rehabilitated prisoners by forcing them to craft brooms for street sweeping and crush rock for roadbeds.[21] Roads' tangible materiality fed Americans' faith in their modernizing impact.

The occupation's public works transformed eastern landscapes. By the end of 1899 and Wood's tenure as Oriente's governor, Cuban workers built fifteen miles of new macadamized and crowned highway. They repaired at least 200 miles of country roadway, installing new bridges and culverts and making them passable for wagons by ditching, filling holes, and clearing vegetation. Yet infrastructure's greatest achievement was ideological. Roadbuilding seemed to validate an imperial philosophy that public goods benefited Cubans without exploiting them, securing practical annexation by Americanization. Wood's liberal vision of highways as an egalitarian technology of economic growth thus imposed on a new colonial space the same settler impulse of social mobility through frontier expansion that American historian Frederick Jackson Turner had recently hailed as the germ of democracy. Indeed, at Oriente, Wood articulated the developmentalist fantasy that he could remake the colonial tropics into an industrial paradise which he later applied on Mindanao, in the southern Philippines. Facts rarely punctured this vision. By late 1899, Wood attributed rising farm outputs in Oriente to roadwork. Yet Cuban farmers' continued pleas for direct aid both suggested these gains were limited to sugar estates and justified more roadbuilding.[22]

Not all US military authorities shared Wood's zeal for public works. As the occupation's administrative structure changed, so did infrastructure's politics. Between early October and late December 1898, Wood ruled Oriente virtually as his personal policy fiefdom, in public works and other areas. With little guidance from Washington, he experimented in wholesale policy reform, from criminal justice to schooling. On January 1, 1899, however, at Havana, Maj. Gen. John R. Brooke installed the new Military Government, taking control of the army and civil bureaucracy. Wood became one of four generals running various provinces; with Oriente, he now took control of Puerto Príncipe. Public works thus became only one of several strategies for economic recovery that generals advocated, ranging from farmers' banks to direct aid.[23]

Patchwork militarized state formation fostered policy divergence as Brooke and Wood articulated clashing political-economic approaches. Reluctant to take action without explicit orders from a White House disinterested in the details of governing Cuba, Brooke limited himself to straightening out finances, demobilizing the Liberation Army, and organizing departments headed by Cuban elites whom he appointed. His traditionalism ensured bureaucratic dispute over the island's reconstruction. A sixty-year-old Union veteran, Brooke had commanded US troops invading Puerto Rico and was acting as its military governor when McKinley moved him to Havana. His austerity reflected Gilded Age Republicans' laissez-faire mentalité. Brooke embraced Wood's disciplinary moralism but not his progressive state building as he slashed internal taxes and spending while adopting Wood's food-for-work policy. Only "economy," he believed, would put Cuba "on the highway of progress." Lower taxes enabled by lower spending, he argued, would reduce burdens on business in a credit-poor economy and allow "idle" capital to accumulate in private banks that would eventually lend to poor farmers.[24]

If Brooke's Spartan liberalism seemed poised to undo Wood's infrastructural ambitions, public works' most powerful lobby proved to be Cubans themselves. Never simply a technocratic imposition of empire, the politics of roadwork turned on Cubans' skillful negotiation of US occupation. At Oriente by early 1899, Wood, unlike his fellow generals, had already organized municipalities and a provisional provincial government, staffed by Cuban officials whom he had appointed and now supervised. Brooke thus awkwardly overlaid a new administrative structure onto a preexisting regime at Oriente in which many Cubans were already invested, personally and politically. By selecting separatist leaders to run localities, Wood meant to win over nationalist Cuban elites and enlist them in diverting Cuba's poor majority, including veterans, from anti-American populism. Ironically, given Wood's progressive disapproval of partisan policy, his Cuban civil substate fueled patronage and clientage through which *orientales* forged their own political networks. Seizing civil salaries and public works as paths to security and prosperity in a precarious postwar economy, Cubans in Oriente overwhelmingly endorsed Wood's infrastructure, even as they waited patiently for independence.[25]

Less like Moro datus and more like Filipino elites whom the Philippine Commission hoped to educate in self-government, the Cubans who accepted posts in Wood's occupation welcomed state-driven economic growth. Most were wealthy and educated planters or professionals who had spent time in the states and absorbed its culture, including a politics and technology they valorized as modern. Typically senior separatists, they begrudgingly helped Yankees run Cuba as a temporary expedient on the road to full sovereignty.[26]

Two Cubans cooperating with Wood at Oriente personified such elites, even as they bent Yankees' public works to their own purposes. Demetrio Castillo Duany became the linchpin of Wood's late 1898 efforts to create a civil state in the shadow of nationalists' dual regime. Born at Santiago in 1856, Castillo owned a controlling interest in iron mines at Jaragua as well as coconut plantations. Fleeing Cuba after the Guerra Chiquita, he landed in New York, where, like other Cuban expatriates, he naturalized and opened his own school, in business. Entering the *manigua* in July 1895, Castillo served as aide to Gen. Antonio Maceo. Later commanding his own regiment, by June 1898 he led a brigade aiding US invaders. No cipher, Castillo had objected to Yankees' earliest claims to sovereignty over Cuba in July when they retained Spanish-era officials, first at El Caney and then Santiago, even after insurgents voted to make him that city's new alcalde. Castillo also endorsed García's protest against US rule of Santiago.[27]

A pragmatist, Castillo soon elected to cooperate. By mid-August, Gen. Lawton told Washington that this "intelligent and influential Cuban" had become critical to his attempts to dissolve rebels' provisional government and army. After Lawton departed, Castillo became Wood's "civil advisor." On Wood's behalf, he toured the province, organizing each municipality's "most prominent and reliable men" into committees that nominated candidates for appointive office. Castillo's prestige and contacts made him Wood's natural pick for civil governor. In that position, he rewarded friends and allies, including fellow veterans, with civil jobs. Income and loyalty made these "Castillistas" Oriente's first postwar political network.[28]

Emilio Bacardí exemplified how infrastructure both legitimated and challenged US sovereignty in Cuba's new urban politics. Son of the peninsular who founded the rum company that later made their name famous, Bacardí, born in 1844, became Oriente's wealthiest man after he inherited his father's distillery. An ardent separatist, Bacardí clandestinely supported revolutionaries during the Ten Years' War. Following their defeat in 1878, however, he distanced himself from diehards like Antonio Maceo. Organizing the local Liberal Party and endorsing its campaign for autonomy, Bacardí in 1879 won a city council seat in Santiago's first free election. After Maceo's failed insurrection, however, authorities arrested him and sentenced him to four years in prison, spent mostly on the Chafarinas Islands, off Morocco's coast. By 1894, Bacardí returned to the revolutionary fold. Backing the PRC's insurrection, he used business trips to New York City to facilitate communications with José Martí. At Santiago, while directing Santiago's chamber of commerce, Bacardí led the underground Club Moncada, named for the martyred general who triggered the 1895 uprising, and taxed planters and smuggled arms. In 1896, Spanish officials again arrested him and exiled him to the Chafarinas. Two years later, as the war ended, Bacardí, having been released, took refuge with family in Jamaica.[29]

Like Demetrio Castillo, Bacardí oscillated between criticizing the Americans and cooperating with them. In August 1898, when he learned that Yankees at Santiago were threatening to jail residents who did not report a death in their home, he penned an open letter denouncing draconian military rule. "The obligation of those in authority," he protested, was to serve the suffering; it was "not for those who suffer to be at the disposition of those who command." Returning to Santiago by October, Bacardí learned that the occupiers had dissolved his old city council. While separatists recognized Club Moncada leaders as the city's ruling junta, Wood by late November sought to placate these nationalists, and neuter their dual state, by making Bacardí the city's new alcalde. Authorizing him to organize a new assembly, Wood gave it little power. Yet Bacardí was no puppet. When he entered city hall to accept the resignation of the acting mayor, Maj. James H. McLeary, Bacardí persuaded soldiers on his staff to quit, then replaced McLeary's men with rebel allies. Though he resigned in July 1899, following a dispute with Castillo over regulatory authority in the city, Bacardí won back the mayoralty in 1901 by popular election.[30]

If Bacardí and Castillo embodied the early republican state's top-down neocolonial origins, they also illustrated how patronage networks coalescing under the US occupation conveyed bottom-up Cuban support for infrastructure through Cuban elites. Brooke's policies thus exposed how Wood's public works had created their own cross-class labor politics. On his second day in office, Brooke issued orders that granted the governor absolute control over provincial customs and discretion to allocate them. His dictate threatened to destroy the regional fiscal autonomy on which Wood's infrastructural improvements, and Cuban clients and patrons, had come to depend. Nationalists were already angered by Brooke's exclusion of insurgents from ceremonies marking the transfer of sovereignty to the United States. In December at Santiago, Wood himself barred *veteranos*, mostly Afro-Cubans, from memorializing Gen. Antonio Maceo under arms.[31]

Brooke's power and money grab sparked a furious backlash, partly nationalist but also localist in nature, as Cubans joined Wood in insisting that Brooke reinstate their authority to collect and spend provincial customs as they wished. *Orientales'* fierce regionalism reflected a history of eastern separatism that included demands for autonomy from both Spain and Havana. At the end of the Ten Years' War, as historian Adriana Chira notes, Antonio Maceo, channeling the abolitionism of Oriente's large population of free and enslaved Cubans of color, proposed that it break away from Cuba to form an anti-slavery bloc with Haiti and Jamaica. Wood wedded this fierce regionalism to his stolid defense of bureaucratic autonomy. As Wood told Brooke he had endangered US rule by idling some 1,700 roadworkers, Castillo and Bacardí organized rallies at Santiago's main plaza, attended by thousands and endorsed by the Club Moncada as well as the city's veteran, business, and professional associations. Delegations from Bayamo, Sagua de Tánamo, and Mayarí signaled wider disquiet. Santiago newspapers agitated Brooke by hinting that he might provoke another insurrection. Rebels editing *El Cubano*, decrying his fiat as a "boa-constrictor tightening its coils," hinted it should be "resisted in the mountains." *La Independencia* described the policy as "a matter of life and death."[32]

General Wood and Other Officials at the Review of the Street Cleaning Department on the Alameda. A late 1898 or early 1899 portrait of senior US and Cuban authorities in Santiago, overlooking its harbor, this photograph documents a neocolonial coalition for public works in addition to Oriente's formidable geography; the Sierra Maestra looms in the background. Sitting, from left to right, are Gen. Leonard Wood, Maj. George Barbour, Emilio Bacardí, and most likely Gen. Joaquín Castillo Duany. Standing, from left, are Gen. Ezra P. Ewers (following Wood, Santiago's military governor) and almost certainly Gen. Demetrio Castillo Duany. From Wood, "Santiago since the Surrender," 526.

The only revolution in the offing, however, was a gradual intraimperial reorganization of military administration, provoked by Wood but rooted in Cubans' savvy appeal to Yankees' venerated federalism and zeal for social uplift. Under pressure, Brooke temporarily suspended his order only three days after issuing it. Yet Wood sought to appeal to Washington directly, circumventing the chain of command, just as he had with Lawton. Telling Brooke that his Cuban laborers seemed "pacified," he won Alger's permission to travel north to make his case. Embarking from Santiago to cheers from 6,000 Cubans, Wood led a delegation that included Lt. Matthew Hanna, who attributed

Oriente's "Americanization" to public works, and Gen. Joaquín Castillo Duany, Demetrio's brother, Maceo's former doctor, and the city hospital's director. Representing Santiago entrepreneurs, Castillo sounded like a Populist as he denounced Havana as a "corrupt center of speculators, business schemes," and "office seekers."[33]

In the states, Wood adroitly used Hanna and Castillo as proxies, refraining from criticizing Brooke in public. Yet he defended colonial public works and free speech to audiences, including New York's Union League, US senators, and President McKinley himself. Privately, Wood urged the White House to curb Brooke's authority by investing decision-making power in a federal council of regional military governors. To War Department officials, he argued that infrastructure gave US commanders "real authority and influence among the people." "They know he has the money," explained Wood, and the "means of subsistence for themselves and their families." He also seized on reports that more protests had erupted at Santiago after rumors circulated that Brooke would permit more roadbuilding only if Wood paid laborers in rations. The news reinforced his claims that public works pacified. Forcing rebels to give "good honest labor," the general insisted, was "an educational process in ... civilization."[34]

Wood harnessed Oriente's crusade for regional sovereignty to his political ambitions, as he made public works the centerpiece of a campaign to take Brooke's job. Empowered by metropolitan support, Wood went to Havana to negotiate an agreement that would permit him to keep the $230,000 the province possessed prior to January 1 for roads. Yet bureaucratic infighting over customs receipts and mass protest persisted. In March, when Brooke disapproved a works-heavy monthly budget, Wood catalyzed more unrest by halting projects employing some 4,000 men. Not subtly, Bacardí echoed Santiago merchants' dire warnings. "Though we are perfectly friendly," he telegrammed Brooke, the "policy seems suicidal." "Public improvements," Bacardí elaborated, were "greatly needed," and men were "greatly in need of work." Santiago's *El Porvenir* discerned "only one course" for those "without work and food": "namely—to become banditti." Brooke again backtracked and rescinded his hold on spending.[35]

As Brooke's rivalry with Wood devolved into petty acrimony, the latter's bureaucratic ascendancy rested on mobilizing Cubans and Americans. Wood solicited voters' support in the states with publications and interviews while lobbying McKinley and Theodore Roosevelt, his old friend and rising Republican star. Though Wood insisted that road jobs inoculated Cubans from nationalism, the political economy of public works in fact split protean republican politics. As the general toured Oriente and Puerto Principe with Maj. George Barbour and Gov. Demetrio Castillo, and promised more public spending to campesinos and workers' circles, Joaquín Castillo organized his brother's appointees into the Partido Republicano Federal Democrático. The PRFD tempered its nationalism with a regionalist fiscalism tacitly endorsing Wood's infrastructural agenda. By contrast, the Partido Nacional Cubano, led locally by Gen. Quintín Bandera and nationally by Gen. Máximo Gómez, hewed closer to Brooke's centralism, denouncing provincial autonomy as a prologue to "anarchy, misery, and barbarism." Even as Wood loathed the idea of enfranchising poor, working-class, and Black Cubans, he used popular regional support for infrastructure to win over Gen. William Ludlow, army engineer and Havana's governor, as well as Alger, the secretary of war. Then Wood won the backing of Alger's replacement, Elihu Root, who recognized him as a fellow progressive reformer. Wood sent Gov. Castillo to Washington to lobby the new secretary, who accepted their opinion that Brooke's interference was crippling the occupation by paralyzing local governments. By December, Root and McKinley replaced Brooke with Wood. Roosevelt cheered, styling Wood as a modern "Rajah Brook"—exactly the "English type of colonial administrator" that America needed "at this time."[36]

Ironically, as Cuba's new governor, Wood maintained Brooke's fiscal centralization to fund a massive infrastructural effort across the island. In 1900, while preparing Cubans for self-government by organizing a census, preliminary to elections for delegates to a constitutional convention, he drastically hiked the scale and tempo of public works. Money and labor poured into streets and highways as well as government buildings, bridges, sewer, water, trolleys, and wharves and harbors. Taking special interest in Oriente, where he made sure US Army engineers retained control of sanitation, Wood repudiated his old decentralism. As politicos like Demetrio Castillo continued to argue that local governments should control taxes and public works, Wood countered that municipalities were too incompetent, inefficient, and penurious for the job. Still, his generous spending on highways garnered acclaim across Cuban society. Even the weighty sugar planters of the Círculo de Hacendados y Agricultores welcomed it.[37]

Validated by popular support, the occupation physically altered the island. By the time troops evacuated in May 1902, the Military Government had spent $22 million on public works—nearly half its total expenditures. The result was infrastructural development at a scale and speed unprecedented in Cuba's history. Wood's regime created 100 kilometers of metaled highway—almost a third of the 256 kilometers built under Spain—and repaired 300 more kilometers. Records do not reveal the total number of Cubans who found jobs on them. Given the high turnover, however, one estimate that 20,000 toiled on the roads at any one time meant that a substantial portion of Cuba's 800,000-person labor force had worked on them.[38]

These impressive numbers veiled weaknesses in Wood's rule by infrastructure, not least of which was the gap between accomplishments and Yankees' perception of Cuba's actual needs. In early 1900, Wood believed that the island required at least 1,500 miles of new first-class "turnpike," at a minimum cost of $15 million. Despite modern engineering techniques, highways constructed beyond Oriente, where mountain quarries furnished hard stone, often used limestone beds that melted under tropical rains. Insufficient supplies of steamrollers and culverts similarly reduced roads' longevity. Wood tried preserving them by imposing weight limits and requiring rubber tires for poor farmers' two-wheeled *carreton*, but Cuban officials hesitated to enforce them.[39]

The neocolonial politics of personnel and policy also caused headaches. As Cubans clamored for government jobs, Wood established a public works department at Havana responsible for all projects outside Oriente. He handed it to José Ramón Villalón, a separatist with a Lehigh University engineering degree. Like other Cuban secretaries, Villalón received army supervision—in this case, Maj. William M. Black, an engineer. Black pushed Villalón to replace Spanish-era public works rules with those of his army's Corps of Engineers, then hired Yankees instead of Cubans. Villalón only slowly hired Cuban staff, irking nationalists, among them Salvador Cisneros Betancourt, the provisional republic's president at the end of the Ten Years' War. Villalón also signed lucrative cost-plus contracts with American-owned construction firms, incorporated in Cuba to elude the Foraker Act. Some Cubans criticized his department for concentrating work near Havana and its sugar zones, as had the Spanish. Wood's agriculture secretary, Perfecto Lacosta—a *hacendado*, University of Pennsylvania graduate, former Havana mayor, and sugar planters' association president—contended that Wood's highways would offer little help to farmers unless rail was also expanded. Wood agreed. Cleverly avoiding the Foraker Act, he granted railroad magnate William C. Van Horne "revocable licenses" to build an east–west railway on public lands. Employers blamed wage inflation on public works, but Cubans' preference for payment in US gold, rather than depreciated Spanish silver, fueled higher labor costs. Critics also claimed that occupiers' eight-hour workday for civil servants, aligned with new laws covering federal government employees in the states, created unnecessary jobs.[40]

Such economism failed to appreciate infrastructure's extramilitary function and intended and unintended consequences, especially in Oriente. Roadbuilding there may have marginally enhanced agricultural productivity by reducing small farmers' transport costs, opening new lands to cultivation, and linking interior valleys to ports. Yet a quadrupling of Oriente's agricultural exports between 1899 and 1907 rested on a rapid expansion of large-scale sugar latifundia that ultimately spelled the demise of the small-scale independent agriculture that historically dominated the region. Between 1899 and 1904, Oriente's sugar harvest more than tripled, even as its total number of farms fell by half—a rate faster than other regions. Foreign sugar corporations' amassing of real estate denied the East's rising population access to land, and autonomy, by displacing squatters and encroaching on the public estate. More than roads, Oriente's expanding rail network catalyzed this dramatic transformation. Large and highly capitalized Yankee-owned sugar estates used their control of rail to squeeze peasants and *colonos* who needed access to mills and ports. Oriente thus heralded a Cuban agricultural economy falling under Yankees' control. By 1902, American-owned *centrales* were already producing 40 percent of Cuban sugar.[41] In the long run, transportation revolution did not revitalize Oriente's peasantry so much as ensure its proletarianization, making the East more like the rest of Cuba.

Other occupation policies conspired with economic trends to thwart roadbuilding's benefit to eastern smallholders. In Cuba at large, prewar patterns in wealth and land distribution, scarce credit, and high capital investment costs frustrated an equitable division of public lands, much less a redistribution of existing properties. By 1902, Wood also took measures that strongly favored large landowners, creditors, and foreign investors. Though Gen. Brooke rejected public loans for farmers, he also paused collection of real estate debts. As governor, however, Wood lifted Brooke's stay order. By clarifying land titles and imposing regressive taxes based on farm income, not falling property values, Wood hastened Cubans' sales of farmland to foreigners. His support for a trade treaty that would create a preferred US market for Cuban sugar, ratified by 1903, also intensified Yankee investments, especially in Oriente. For more and more *orientales*, sugar's empire made smallholding less and less attainable and sustainable. Many became *colonos*, leasing or renting small plots from foreign-owned plantations; others became permanent wage laborers. To survive, some became bandits.[42]

Militarized infrastructure thus affected Cuba's political culture more than its economy. Born as an emergency response to postwar crisis, public works mutated into a countercyclical means of social relief propping up neocolonial capitalism. In roadbuilding, the Cuban republic hoped to blunt seasonal joblessness afflicting a growing agro-proletariat dependent on Yankee sugar firms for income. As early as 1900, Cubans observed, laborers came to rely on highway work in *el tiempo muerto*, or the "dead time" between planting and harvests. Adopted by Cuban politicians as a means to shore up electoral support among poorer Cubans after Gen. Wood failed to restrict male suffrage, jobs on roads reflected the political logic of an economy passing under the control of foreign shareholders, banks, and consumers. As patronage, it mirrored and reinforced the coercive paternalism characterizing laborers' dependence on Cuban-managed Yankee-owned sugar plantations. As policy, it created a political-economic feedback loop, creating its own constituency for more public spending. Tomás Estrada Palma, the republic's new president, made this clear in June 1902 when he slashed highway work. In Oriente, Bayamo's alcalde, and owners of *ingenios* (sugar mills) at Palma Soriano, objected that the decision would ruin countless families. When Lt. Matthew Hanna returned to Santiago that September, he attributed "labor conditions" there—"as bad [as] at any time since the war"—to layoffs at mines, at sugar estates, and on roads. Writing George Barbour, one Yankee merchant reported that 14,000 idled men were wondering why the republic was broke "when the Yankees always had money to burn."[43]

AS IN CUBA, war and occupation in the Philippines created a politics of imperial infrastructure involving questions of coercion, taxation, and capitalist transformation. Yet different contexts of nationalist insurgency and counterinsurgency, colonial state formation, and economic culture in the archipelago particularized its politics of public works. As with Cuba, US soldiers in the Philippines used force to expropriate labor; indeed, some applied the same methods they had just devised in the Caribbean. In the archipelago, however, warfare against insurgents imparted a kinetic quality to Americans' infrastructural efforts. Violence also enhanced the effective sovereignty US soldiers and their opponents wielded over labor. Compared to Cuba, then, in the Philippines colonial elites facing rival claims on their loyalty and labor brokerage exercised less social power over infrastructure, and subaltern activity took subtler forms.

Divergent processes of state formation also distinguished the politics of militarized infrastructure in the Philippines. Occupiers there, as in Cuba, eventually granted elite Filipinos nominal local state authority. Yet political-institutional continuity and change amid imperial transition differentiated the archipelago's infrastructural state from its neocolonial Caribbean cousin.

While Yankee troops in 1902 and 1909 handed power over public works to Cuban elites, Filipino notables' gradual incorporation in a tutelary civilian-run US colonial government granted them less control over infrastructure. Enduring labor coercion in the Philippines evoked the legacy of a militarized US sovereignty over workers that existed only briefly in Cuba.

Lastly, the Philippines' uneven capitalist development, compared to Cuba, ensured that American soldiers there embraced infrastructure as a means to promote wage labor itself as a civilizing agent. Limited wage labor markets in the archipelago allowed Americans to believe that militarized public works would emancipate peasants from oppressive landowning elites by commodifying their labor. Yet roadbuilding's potential to transform the Philippines continued to be blunted by inherited social hierarchy and custom. As highways transitioned from being military necessities to lessons in modernity, American civilians' incorporation of Filipinos into the colonial state obscured infrastructure's coercive colonial and military origins and operation.

Cascading local and global interactions greatly influenced the historical context in which Americans' infrastructural efforts unfolded in the Philippines. By 1898, despite agricultural commercialization, most Filipinos did not work for wages. The labor of poor peasants, who that year constituted roughly 40 percent of the islands' Christian Filipino population, existed mostly outside the cash nexus, even as landlords, creditors, and state authorities negotiated exchanges of labor, goods, and taxes in monetary values. Voluntary and contractual labor for cash was highly localized, limited to Manila and other ports, and plantation zones sending them crops, principally sugar, in Pampanga, in Luzon, and on Negros, in the Visayan islands; tobacco, in northern Luzon's Cagayan Valley; and abaca, or hemp, in the Bicol region and Samar. In a few areas, wage workers harvested timber. Beyond these regions, specie was rare. Even where it circulated, shortages of small-denomination copper and silver coin forced employers to pay labor in credit and in-kind exchange. Peasants and landlords who measured credits and debits in money values rarely settled with them cash. Extra-household labor usually transpired by mutual custom in kinship and communal networks regulated by corporate indigenous and Christian norms.[44]

Since the late sixteenth century, a colonial administrative hierarchy run by Spanish bureaucrats and Catholic friars rested on *indio* elites and their domination of an impoverished rural majority. Classified as the *principalía*, these notables held municipal office by virtue of lineal descent from pre-Spanish nobility, passing this heritable status to children. Under Spain's sovereignty, *principales*' kinship networks became local oligarchies extracting taxes and agricultural labor from neighbors. By the mid-nineteenth century, as Spanish officials promoted agricultural commercialization, friars and principales who seized and privatized communal lands forced peasants to become tenants growing cash crops instead of staples, especially rice. Principales, invoking reciprocal indigenous values of debt and gratitude, bound the *tao* in chains of dependency, regularly extending them credit, often at high interest, so they could pay rent and taxes and buy food, seeds, cattle, and implements. Colonial authorities tried to limit local elites' private power over labor by outlawing debts and imprisonment for debts in sums greater than five pesos. Still, by the 1890s, most colonial wealth flowed from exploited rural agriculturists.[45]

Perhaps nothing signaled indio elites' power over the tao more than the *polo y servicio*, the labor corvée for public works by which principales annually collected labor from adult indio men. Often conflated with "personal services" that indios owed Catholic friars, the polo originally required that all indio taxpayers between the ages of sixteen and sixty work forty days a year under *cabezas de barangay*, the indio heads of barrios. Alternatively, they might secure exemption by paying the *gobernadorcillo*, their indio municipal mayor, a three-peso fine, the *falla*. Spanish policy distinguished this activity from slavery by regulating it. Rules required that officials pay *polistas* a small wage of four pesos' worth of rice and a quarter real, from funds generated by fallas, for each day of work. That peninsulares, mestizos, and principales, and their kin and descendants, were exempt from tribute of any kind indicated the *polo*'s administrative locus in a local indio elite mediating ties between Spanish colonizers and peasants.[46]

The corvée spawned corruption and abuse, especially as agricultural commercialization by the 1820s incentivized labor coercion for infrastructural improvement. Few tao could ever afford to pay fallas outright, and among principales who had an interest in enforcing this fine, some imposed it on sick, elderly, and disabled men customarily exempted from the tax. Some eluded service by bribing officials or borrowing more from landowners to pay for exemption. Principales pocketed fallas meant to fund polistas' wages, often by shifting costs to public coffers reserved for other uses. They also made money by catering to polistas' needs while away from home. Though laws barred principales from using polistas for nonmilitary purposes or removing them from fields during planting and harvests, the allure of lucrative cash crops vitiated such protections. Planters drafted polistas to build and repair roads to ports so they could move more crops to market faster. Poor censuses and municipal records made collection uneven. Yet the corvée incited popular resentment and episodic revolt; in 1872, polistas mutinying at

Cavite's navy yard sparked repression that catalyzed the Propaganda movement. By 1893, Spanish officials reduced the polo's term from forty to fifteen days per year and made the tribute a simple poll tax. These changes, and wage labor that allowed more indios to pay for exemption, drastically reduced the supply of labor available for public works. The fruits of tributary infrastructure were poor and limited roads that frustrated the movement of peoples, goods, and information, just as they did in eastern Cuba. Though Spain built three "royal highways" on Luzon that led outward from Manila, these tracks and arterial roads were barely maintained and unusable in monsoons.[47]

If nationalist revolution in 1896 weakened colonial forced labor customs, competitive state building by US invaders and Filipino insurgents in the summer of 1898 placed work and its coercion at the center of clashing sovereignties. Orders issued by President McKinley in May 1898 granting Gen. Wesley Merritt, commanding the expedition to Manila, "absolute and supreme" authority in the islands seemed to impose restraints. Filipinos who "perform their duties," McKinley stipulated, would be "entitled to security in their persons and property." The president also instructed Merritt to enforce existing municipal laws, "such as [those that] affect private rights of persons and property." Merritt's August 14 proclamation established a military government along McKinley's liberal lines. Yet his caveat that soldiers would not disturb Filipinos except when "necessary for the good of the service" legalized military coercion already underway. As they landed troops at Cavite in late June, US Army quartermasters' attempts to impress Filipino carts incited tensions with nationalists. Frustrated, Gen. Thomas Anderson wrote Gen. Emilio Aguinaldo, insisting that civilians "must supply us with labor."[48]

Filipino revolutionaries considered controlling labor a core attribute of their state's sovereignty. Their ability to regulate work and workers signified the claims of an organic and unified political nation transcending social class. Yet that power also expressed the economic interests of Filipino elites like Aguinaldo, himself a mestizo landowner and local official from Cavite. By late June 1898, Aguinaldo had ordered local Filipino officials to convene elections for new municipalities; in turn, these bodies were to elect provincial governors and delegates to a congress tasked with crafting a constitution. By granting suffrage exclusively to adult men of "social position," however, Aguinaldo's regime empowered elites who enjoyed local political office and socioeconomic power under the Spanish to reproduce that authority and status through a new national state. Assembling at Malolos, north of Manila, in mid-September 1898, congressional delegates, most of whom Aguinaldo appointed, came from such elite backgrounds, as did most of Aguinaldo's army officers and cabinet members. While many were landowners or professionals in small towns and rural areas who already occupied local public posts at the municipal or provincial level, others hailed from the urban elite of civil servants, clerks, and university-educated *ilustrados*, concentrated in Manila, that forged the Propaganda movement and Katipunan. If such men condemned Spain's exploitative tributary rule, they also expected that the republic would preserve their wealth and status. The Malolos constitution, ratified in January 1899, protected private property, permitting its confiscation only by legal process for public necessity. Republican officials also opposed militant Filipino labor; in late 1898, they criticized striking artisans and railroad workers. As the "civilized world" wondered if Filipinos were ready "for self-government," such protests, they claimed, impugned the "national character."[49]

While most elite Filipino nationalists assumed that their government would allow them to continue exploiting rural and urban labor, the Malolos republic also conceded popular opposition to coercive colonial customs. In late October 1898, Felipe Buencamino, Aguinaldo's public works secretary, encouraged Luzon's provincial governors to improve highways by voluntary means. Invoking an imperial politics of recognition, Buencamino hailed "the maintenance and construction of means of communication" as "among the most important obligations of civilized nations." Acknowledging rural elites' "clamor" for roadwork, however, he urged local officials to abstain from compelling labor to do it. Denouncing the polo as an "infamous service" that "degraded our dignity," Buencamino insisted that the institution created "immoral speculation" rather than the "arteries of social life" required for economic and national development. Authorities, he advised, should elicit peasants' labor by appealing to their civic spirit. On January 5, 1899, Aguinaldo affirmed Buencamino's stance by abolishing the corvée, condemning it as "oppressive to the citizens and especially the poor who live by daily labor." The republic, he declared, would not "gratuitously utilize the services of citizens or oblige anyone to work for private benefit." If it required "the services of its sons," he declared, "all of them for love and patriotism must render them." Instructions for disseminating the order spoke to its populism. Interior secretary Teodoro Sandico told municipalities to have flag-bearing police read it aloud in local dialects before crying three times: "Long live Democracy!" and "Long live the Poor!"[50]

This patriotic voluntarist ethic quickly unraveled under the pressure of armed hostilities with the Americans and rising social tensions between elites and peasants. Erupting outside Manila in the first week of February 1899, the new war negated peacetime constraints on expropriation and exposed rival armies' relative will and capacity to compel Filipino resources, including labor. Both US and Filipino officials authorized soldiers to override civilian authorities, if necessary, to procure material aid. As fighting spread in central Luzon, logistical needs pushed both armies to impress two-wheeled carts and draft animals, usually carabao, as well as drivers (some of whom tried to hide their vehicles and livestock). Disparate finances greatly shaped the politics of wartime coercion. American soldiers who paid cash on the spot or credibly promised future reimbursement more easily elicited Filipinos' willful cooperation, compared to revolutionaries lacking specie and an ample treasury. Straining to generate tax revenues and control the currency needed for it, republican authorities increasingly resorted to requisitions that risked popular support. By April 1899, when Aguinaldo mandated that citizens comply with his army's seizure of food, carts, or other materiel, many Filipinos doubted his government's ability to redeem receipts.[51]

As in Cuba, where nationalists' penury intensified internal divisions and weakened their claims to sovereignty relative to US occupiers, Filipino revolutionaries' poverty exacerbated civil-military and class tensions. By early 1899, the Malolos republic tried generating revenue by issuing bonds; selling confiscated properties; and imposing tariffs and taxes on the church, merchants, manufacturers, and friar estates' tenants. Yet war escalated fiscal crisis. Aguinaldo's government balanced fears that higher taxes would alienate the wealthier Filipinos most able to fund it with desires to retain popular support. In February 1899, the Malolos congress imposed a voluntary progressive war tax on landed property, issuing those paying it a "certificate of citizenship." After the tax failed to generate much revenue, however, congressmen the next month made it mandatory. The results damaged the republic's legitimacy. Officials caught peculating or helping well-connected wealthy men evade payment symbolized persistent colonial-style corruption. Then Filipino authorities seemed to revive class-based coercion when they encouraged landowners to comply by exempting payees from "patriotic labor" on public works and threatened to arrest men found without certificates outside their hometowns.[52] War and taxes thus signaled to peasants that elites still escaped tribute.

If Americans' cash acted as the proverbial carrot by which they enticed Filipino labor, food scarcity became their stick. Like their predecessors in Cuba, soldiers on Luzon in 1899 conditioned civilians' survival on infrastructural work. Yet the archipelago's history of forced labor, and the violence of counterinsurgency, made subaltern stomachs and bodies there more susceptible to compulsion, and for a longer duration. Wartime food shortages in central and southwestern Luzon had deep roots in agricultural commercialization and its biological consequences, as tenant farmers and wage laborers abandoned subsistence for cash crops. By 1898, many Filipinos depended on less nutritious imported milled rice, conducive to beriberi. Industrial farming caused deforestation and aridification that magnified floods' destructiveness. By the 1880s and 1890s, a rinderpest epidemic killed carabao needed for plowing and milk, and locusts ravaged corn and sugar fields. Invasive plant species resistant to native pests further reduced harvests, as did intermittent drought between 1896 and 1903. Filipinos suffered more after the 1896 revolt drained southcentral Luzon of labor, livestock, and metal tools. As imported rice prices increased and refugees fled, starvation stalked Cavite and Batangas. Peace in August 1898 revived farming briefly, but war in early 1899 left peasants little time to plant and harvest.[53]

Counterinsurgency intensified food scarcity. In February, two weeks into the war, Gen. Elwell S. Otis began restricting the transport of rice across US lines to starve Aguinaldo's army. New garrisons expanding outward from Manila that year imposed similar restrictions as they confiscated and destroyed foodstuffs, cattle, and farming and fishing equipment. By mid-1899, a blockade targeting insurgents' ability to import food and other materiel also affected civilians. American garrisons' insatiable appetites inflated food prices and emptied markets. These events' cumulative effect on civilian mortality is difficult to know precisely, given imperfect demographic data. Yet thousands of "excess" deaths above prewar rates in southcentral Luzon by 1903, mostly from malaria, dysentery, and cholera, suggest a malnourished colonized people, one of many in this era vulnerable to coercion by colonizers' control of food.[54]

Compared to Cuba, however, where US occupiers used rations to compel labor while seeking to rapidly expand the food supply, Americans on Luzon intentionally sought to limit and regulate food to crush insurgency. Colonial warfare thus created and sustained conditions by which US commanders sought to perfect the militarized food-for-work practices they implemented earlier in Cuba. In March 1899, Gen. Henry W. Lawton, recovered from service at Oriente, arrived at Manila to command the Eighth Army Corps' First Division. As noted, Lawton ended a push into northern Cavite and Laguna provinces in June that year by garrisoning towns. As in Cuba, US troops at Bacoor, Paranaque, Las Piñas, and Calamba fed civilians by confiscating rice, distributing it to starving civilians, and supplementing it with army rations. Lawton's orders to brigadiers, one of whom served with Lawton at Santiago, emphasized food policy's military function. To keep civilians from resupplying insurgents, he stipulated that rations be issued, and food be sold by licensed merchants at regulated prices, strictly on a day-to-day basis, in "small lots." His army was to feed civilians until they harvested the next rice crop, under close supervision. A petition from Las Piñas residents asking for permission to travel to Manila to procure food suggests that civilians now depended on Lawton's army to survive.[55]

Though Lawton revised his food-for-work policy according to the same disciplinary logic his army had articulated in Cuba, counterinsurgency sharpened its coercive edge. After generals complained that eating by "idle natives" was giving "encouragement to laziness while there are means of work," Lawton applied scientific charity principles, ordering them to scrutinize relief applicants' finances. Rationing's "whole idea," he clarified, had been "to alleviate distress," not "promote poverty." Henceforth, Lawton mandated, subordinates were to issue food gratis to women, children, and "invalids," and sell rations to households with means. Able-bodied male Filipino relief applicants, however, would eat only if they agreed to "give value in work on roads" or clean streets. Officers' reports that they immediately assembled large gangs of workers for such tasks suggested compliance. As at Santiago, Lawton's generals started paying coerced Filipinos a small cash wage; some garrisons sold rice surpluses to fund them. Yet subalterns skewered Americans' fantasies that working for food yielded sovereignty over them. In mid-June, Lawton's paymaster, Robert D. Carter, wrote home that he had recently distributed wages to sixty Filipinos at Las Piñas for labor, "the greater part of which," he griped, "was never performed." The money, he speculated, had gone to the revolution, as the "very men we paid were later found among the insurgent dead." Quartermasters who discovered canned beef in insurgent trenches, and officers who discovered that rebels planned to kill Bacoor's president as he organized roadwork, learned that Filipinos also found ways to exploit forced labor for food.[56]

More than just food scarcity ensured Filipinos' cooperation with the US Army's labor demands. Lawton's simulacrum of sovereignty rested partly on the inertia of colonial custom. During summer 1899 operations in northern Cavite and Laguna, neither Lawton nor his generals explicitly invoked the polo. Their authority for compulsion seemed to rest on military rather than civil law. To some degree, Filipinos' compliance involved a performance of assent to US authority. As historians note, local Filipino officials, especially early in the war, tried to satisfy insurgents and Americans simultaneously—a delicate and increasingly dangerous balancing act. The same dynamic held for US occupiers' requests for labor; indeed, some American Army officers used Filipinos' response to gauge their loyalty. Nevertheless, obliging municipal officials, Lawton's provision of food and wages, and laborers' conscription for one- to two-week terms all implied that his army and Filipino authorities casually rehabilitated the corvée. To be sure, local elites' willingness to enforce labor did not necessarily explain subaltern acquiescence. Spanish-era records, if accurate, show that peasants in these northern Cavite and Laguna towns paid the polo in work earlier that decade. Such evidence might be interpreted as indicating that the tao in 1899 still accepted coercion as the prerogative of local elites acting on behalf of an alien sovereignty. Yet popular opposition to the polo, evident in the Malolos republic's policy, also suggests that some peasants may have complied reluctantly.[57]

Narrating Filipinos' forced labor through sources written almost exclusively by the Americans who compelled it, however, risks reproducing colonizers' gaze and the ideologies behind it. Such an approach reduces Filipinos to passive vessels who validated the counterinsurgent logic of occupiers' civilizing infrastructure by operationalizing it, thus implying they assented to US sovereignty. Polistas, in such a narrative, become palimpsests for American soldiers' conviction that public works and wage labor were destined to detach Filipino peasants from the local elites who led nationalist resistance and reattach them to US military modernizers. Like economic-reductionist theories of peasant revolt, or political scientists' patron-client model for political behavior, however, this approach fails to explain subaltern sovereignty.[58]

Filipino narratives present their own interpretive hazards. Folk knowledge and oral memory collected in local histories from the 1950s document lingering anger at compulsory labor for Spanish and Japanese authorities but rarely acknowledged that done for Americans. Instead, Filipinos' memories tended to recycle the US colonial state's official rhetoric that its rule was modern, progressive, and emancipatory. Residents of Calamba, in Laguna province, praised Americans' "liberal policies," from education and participatory government to "good roads." In this useful past for a postcolonial Philippines, even coercion became redemptive. At Bangar, in La Union, older Filipinos recalled the early US colonial era as a time of "new liberty" that ended tribute and forced labor. Though they admitted "there were [public] works" under the Americans, compulsion to complete them no longer seemed intolerable because laborers "were already given compensation." Local historians' frequent description of labor on public works as "communal" also implied that Filipinos experienced them, or at least memorialized them, as a civic responsibility based in reciprocity between kin and neighbors.[59]

On the one hand, such memories reflected what historian Reynaldo Ileto characterizes as postwar Filipinos' "selective remembering" of US colonialism. Filipinization, Commonwealth-era autonomy, and shared victory against Japanese occupiers made forced labor for American troops a "nonevent" just as much as the war with Americans itself. On the other hand, local histories recorded Filipinos' accurate perceptions that the US Army's practices for conscripting their labor for roads had often diverged substantially from those of Spain and, later, Japan. This difference was most visible in Americans' tendency to pay polistas cash wages. Their army's wages for forced labor may have enhanced peasants' acquiescence in the short term. In the long run, however, as in Cuba, wages eroded peasants' willingness to submit to coercion. As American soldiers paid conscripts in specie, and rice harvests increased food supplies, their power to use rations to wrest labor from peasants diminished. Indeed, by late 1899 and throughout 1900, army officers' requests for money for road repairs in Luzon reported that Filipinos were refusing to work for rice alone; even when forced, they demanded cash. Such obstinacy likely prompted Gen. Otis in March 1900 to order his army to pay Filipinos' wages exclusively in coin, if at a miserly rate.[60] Here, as in Cuba, subalterns' search for sovereignty pushed occupiers to use money to elicit labor.

The US military government's reorganization of municipalities soon made forced labor a legal obligation that implicated Filipino officials in the assertion of imperial sovereignty. As noted, Lawton's occupation of northern Cavite and Laguna in June 1899 involved his army's earliest attempts to establish local Filipino-run governments beyond Manila. By codifying generals' administrative experiments, Gen. Otis's municipal civil orders grafted Spanish-era law, including the polo, onto an embryonic US colonial state superstructure that rested largely on preexisting and overlapping social and political hierarchies. Issued in August 1899, GO 43 authorized popular viva voce elections for a president and cabezas. Charged with policing, sanitation, taxation, and education, these municipal officials were permitted to draft new local laws and enforce them at American army officers' discretion. Subsequent US military government policy, however, suppressed GO 43's populist democracy in favor of preserving the principalia's domination of the peasantry. GO 40, promulgated by Gen. Otis in March 1900, closely followed Spanish and republican policy by sharply restricting the franchise. Leaving the election of presidents and vice presidents to cabezas, GO 40 limited voting for cabezas to men of education and wealth, thus imposing class-based exclusions of the kind that Wood sought but failed to secure in Cuba. This new order enfranchised men at least twenty-three years in age who met at least one of three qualifications: prior status as a principale, fluency and literacy in Spanish or English, or annual tax payments worth thirty pesos or more. Given that a tiny fraction of Filipinos beyond Manila fit such criteria, GO 40 allowed the *principalía* to reassert its oligarchic grip on public authority and socioeconomic status. Simultaneously, GO 40 required them to enforce municipal code derived from the 1893 Maura Law, including the corvée. If local elites worried that peasants resented being compelled to work the roads, they did not have to fear being punished at the polls.[61]

Most US Army officers during the war focused pragmatically on the military aspects of counterinsurgency. Little interested in the minutiae of local administration, they rarely recorded thoughts about the polo, its legality, or related procedures. Treating forced labor as an expediency, they usually emphasized its results more than its history or methods, when they mentioned it at all. Officiously, American commanders tabulated thousands of laborers and bull carts mobilized, and thousands of dollars in exemption fees collected and wages paid. Filipinos' record-keeping listed laborers' names, number of days served, and wages paid, making the work seem mundane. These documents' formatting itself implied unremarkable imperial continuity; Filipino officials drafted them using the same style, grids, and letterhead as they had under Spain. Sometimes, however, these papers became transcripts of subaltern sovereignty. A few officials cited them when they protested to US commanders that taxpayers had still not received the wages that the Americans had promised them.[62]

Paradoxically, US Army officers who promoted their new municipalities as a pedagogical exercise in civilizing liberal governance often interpreted Filipino elites' cooperation with forced labor as proof of enduring colonial exploitation. Presidentes' and cabezas' pocketing of conscripts' wages, they argued, represented a persistent cacique class that risked peasants' support for US sovereignty. Such observations challenged a conventional American wisdom, expressed by the likes of Gen. Samuel B. M. Young, the Ilocos' governor, that coerced labor on public works pacified peasants because the wages they received alleviated the poverty that motivated popular support for insurgents. Yet even Young, an irascible Indian Wars and Cuba veteran dripping with racist contempt for Filipinos, conceded that the corvée involved corruption and inflicted "great difficulty among the people." Still, Young accepted its involuntary nature as the cost of doing colonial business, and he deferred to subordinates and Ilocano officials on procedural details. Fielding an inquiry from Col. William Duvall on how to mobilize road labor at San Fernando, Young noted only that some officers felt it had been "better to simply direct the presidents to have certain work done on the road," "without mentioning the fact that it was to be done under the old road tax law." He advised

Duvall to act cautiously, not "permit the presidents to be oppressive," and force all men to pay it—even Spaniards and Chinese exempted in the past.[63]

As in Cuba, compulsory infrastructural labor on Luzon catalyzed claims to sovereignty that crossed divides of nation, ethnicity, and class. Opposition to the Americans' polo partly exhibited the cumulative impacts of colonial capitalism and anticolonial revolution. Firms employing Filipino wage laborers, such as the Manila-Dagupan railroad, demanded that soldiers stop drafting them. In the southern Camarines, an agent for the Philippine Lumber and Development Company—Luzon's largest employer after the US Army—proposed half-jokingly that the firm could just deduct workers' pay and forward it to Manila. Conceding the polo's unpopularity, some Filipino officials shamed "clerks, merchants, and servants" into paying it.[64]

Compared to Cubans, however, few Filipinos openly criticized forced labor for the Americans. As US counterinsurgents subjected local authorities to increasingly harsh military courts, municipal elites were relatively less free than Cubans to question occupiers' policies or practices. The few who did, however, cleverly appealed to liberal American principles of free labor, sanctified by the Civil War and abolition. Echoing revolutionaries' propaganda that Americans planned to enslave Filipinos, just as they had persons of African descent, such criticism reflected a remarkable transimperial knowledge of the United States and its history. The most eloquent of these rare protests issued from the pen of Vigan's alcalde, Jose Rivero, who likely enforced the polo while serving as that town's Spanish-era mayor. In November 1900, Rivero, now elected, refused to obey Gen. Young's orders to mobilize labor for nearby roads, insisting that "times have changed." Appealing to the Philippine Commission's reformist rhetoric, Rivero prodded Young to admit the moral equivalency of bondage and the corvée. "A slave cannot exist," he insisted, in "a nation noble and free as America." "Slavery in the islands," wrote Rivero, had "disapered [sic] with the Spanish government." Ignoring his pleas, Young told the mayor to send men for the roads.[65]

If some American soldiers similarly regarded forced labor as anachronistic, they tended to regard it as evidence of Filipinos' lower status on a temporal scale of social evolution. Tautologically, labor conscription, from Orientalists' viewpoint, became a symbol of colonial alterity that itself justified impressment. At Bicolandia in early 1901, Lt. Col. James Parker, a forty-seven-year-old West Pointer and, like Young, an Indian Wars and Cuba veteran, worried that disruptions to the regional hemp trade were damaging popular support. To enhance the "prosperity" of Albay province by facilitating the "free exchange of commodities," he pressured the alcaldes of Libon and Polangui to find men to repair an old twelve-mile highway linking the two towns. For one week under an army engineer's supervision, 1,500 polistas paid only rice cleared brush and roots with bolos, broke clods of earth with sharpened sticks, and shoveled with wooden spades. In his memoir, however, Parker narrated this event not as imperial coercion but a sign of an antique rural social hierarchy that industrial reason had made anomalous. Conscripts suffered "under a sort of military discipline," he wrote, a "revival of the forced labor of the Middle Ages." "The mayor or alcalde," related Parker, "would order certain work on a public road or street, specifying the number of laborers from each barrio or ward." Then "the order would be published by the town crier," after which "lieutenants of each barrio would select their men and march them at the appointed time to the work." Claiming Bicols played "rough instruments made in the forest" to encourage workers with "weird and barbaric strains," Parker familiarized the unfamiliar for American readers. Europe's barons, he reminded them, had "animated and cheered their laborers with rude music" to build cathedrals and castles. The rural Philippines, he implied, was likewise ruled by venal landlords who exploited malleable and superstitious masses. Yet Parker never acknowledged that his army's destruction of subsistence rice crops in the region had given these Bicol men cause to work for food.[66]

A few US Army officers decried such scenes as colonial class oppression that demanded amelioration. Yet their efforts floundered in a military bureaucracy increasingly at odds with the Philippine Commission's dual civilian authority. From Dagupan in December 1900, Maj. Charles A. Williams expressed dismay after investigating the corvée. Claiming that one in four taxpayers preferred to pay for exemption but were too poor to do so, Williams thought missing municipal records suggested pervasive corruption. That cabezas "turn out men at any time of the year to work on the roads," he wrote, meant only that "some are imposed on or that the full tax is not systematically met." "At best," he protested to superiors, the custom signified "shocking discrimination in favor of the richer." Yet Williams's criticisms generated rebuke, not reform. In January 1901, when Maj. Robert S. Abernathy intercepted a letter Williams had sent William H. Taft's office seeking legal guidance, he dismissed its concerns by decontextualizing them. Comparing the corvée to road taxes in the states, Abernathy insisted that American citizens never found labor or money for highways "an arbitrary or unjust tax." The major thus glossed over more than just Filipinos' lack of sovereignty; he also ignored Good Roads activists' success in convincing northern states to replace "statute" labor with taxpayer-funded contract and convict workforces. The very same month, Taft's commission prohibited newly reorganized municipalities from invoking the corvée. Yet Gen. Arthur MacArthur's headquarters told Williams that the 1893 law mandating the polo was still in force. Only in April 1901, after complaints reached MacArthur, and possibly Taft, that US troops were conscripting Ilocanos for the Benguet Road, did the general proscribe subordinates' use of the corvée. Yet MacArthur's order applied only to the Ilocos region, and not all officers there consistently enforced it.[67]

The passage of legislative and later executive authority from MacArthur's military regime to Taft's civilian government between September 1900 and July 1901 boosted commissioners' rhetoric that peaceful colonial tutelage was replacing armed autocracy. Yet just as public works' political-economic logic survived in Cuba after occupation, the militarized logic of road labor and its coercive colonial nature lived on in the Philippines, even after fighting on Luzon ended by mid-1902. In 1900, as Taft curried Filipino elites' support by promising representation and economic development, military infrastructural efforts proceeded apace. As US garrisons in northern Luzon alone repaired some 1,000 miles of roadway by mid-1900, Gen. Otis and his successor, Gen. MacArthur, each justified highway construction by appealing to the Philippine Commission's civilizing agenda. Downplaying roadbuilding's draconian methods, they argued that public works raised Filipinos' income and agricultural exports. No other policy, affirmed Otis, convinced Filipinos of his nation's "kindly intentions" than "highway repairs." MacArthur, sharing Otis's boosterism, ensured that their military regime by September 1900 spent at least $508,000 on roads, mostly on wages. As in Cuba, though, much of this "emergency" work, done by officers without engineering training and workers without modern tools, did not last long.[68]

If politically adept generals appealed to roadbuilding's economic utility, civilian American bureaucrats, and the Filipino elites they sought as partners, recognized its essentially martial function. That said, pacifying insurgents with road jobs, as Leonard Wood purported to do in Cuba, never figured much in official US plans for the Philippines. The idea surfaced in early 1899 diplomacy between Jacob Schurman's commission and Aguinaldo's government that broached limited autonomy for Filipinos under a US protectorate. In early April, Schurman issued a proclamation that promised various reforms long sought by anticolonial activists, including "public works of manifest advantage," and printed 25,000 copies in Spanish and Tagalog. As the document circulated behind rebel lines, Col. Manuel Arguelles, who failed to negotiate peace with the Americans back in January, now shuttled back and forth to Manila. His tepid support for an armistice angered Gen. Antonio Luna—the firebrand leading Aguinaldo's army—and Luna accused Arguelles of treason and arrested him. Yet *ilustrados*' support for peace pushed Aguinaldo to replace his revolutionary cabinet, led by Apolinario Mabini, with a new pro-peace faction led by Felipe Buencamino and Pedro Paterno. On May 19, they sent delegates to Schurman. Cognizant of tensions within the republican state, one Filipino entertained imperial patronage as a means to appease Luna and fellow militants, and asked if the US Army would assimilate insurgents into its ranks. Demurring, commissioners said only a few Filipino regiments "could be so employed." One of the Americans—probably Dean Worcester, who had already wondered if jobs on roads might be arranged for Filipinos "not otherwise engaged"—asked if Aguinaldo's soldiers might be set to "building roads or in other public works" to "enable them to support themselves."[69]

The Filipino delegation's response to this particular proposal is unknown, but events hint that Gen. Luna and other diehard nationalists would have rejected it, not unlike counterparts in Cuba. Luna arrested Paterno, Buencamino, and other pro-peace cabinet members; in June, Luna, accused of dictatorial abuses, died at the hands of troops loyal to Aguinaldo. As insurgents on Luzon were killed, captured, or capitulated, some veterans hailed roadwork's benefits. Gen. Mariano Trías, an old Paterno ally, justified surrendering to the Americans' in March 1901 in part by praising their commitment to infrastructural development. By early 1902, after he had joined pro-peace Federalistas and became Cavite's new *americanista* governor, Trías reassured Taft that roadbuilding served "good order and progress" because it quieted "recalcitrants."[70]

Trías's conversion validated the Philippine Commission's strategy to "attract" Filipinos to US sovereignty by downplaying roadbuilding's counterinsurgent purpose and instead stressing its economic potential. In September 1900, when commissioners inherited legislative authority, their very first law allocated $1 million for new highways. Taft advertised the investment as an Americanizing act of benevolent assimilation and racial uplift. Spatializing US sovereignty, modernized public design was to distinguish Americans' progressive colonialism from Spain's retrograde and neglectful exploitation. Infrastructural improvement, argued Taft, would ensure the social evolution of a people whom Spaniards' intentional policy of "isolation" had made "ignorant and credulous." Dismissing the islands' "so-called highways" as "merely rude trails," Taft affirmed that "a people without roads" was "necessarily savage." Joining education as a civilizing agent, modern highways, he envisioned, would abate regional and ethnic parochialisms, rectify uneven development, and stimulate commerce, profiting wealthy and poor alike. Though Taft occasionally acknowledged roadbuilding's "value from a military standpoint," he obscured infrastructure's martial function in the rhetoric of progressive colonialism. As Thomasites replaced soldiers, Taft cheered that highways were "second to primary schools as an educator of the people." Nationalists saw through such rhetoric. Isabelo de los Reyes, Ilocano anarchist and labor organizer, criticized commissioners' road to their resort at Baguio, in Benguet, as an unnecessary expense that veiled ulterior motives. "The imperialists," he wrote in November 1900, "need to open new railroads, bridges and highways for their military plans."[71]

Such commentary apprehended how the new civilian regime's infrastructure depended transitionally on the US Army and its institutional capacities. In fact, the Philippine Commission's September 1900 roadbuilding program merely implemented plans for systematic work that the army's Corps of Engineers had already drawn up, but which Gen. MacArthur had not been able to persuade the War Department to fund. Once financed, these projects, spanning almost the entire length of Luzon, from Dagupan to Camarines Sur, were immediately started by army engineer detachments using Filipino labor. Contrary to Taft's rhetoric, however, American engineer officers specifically designed these roads as means to spatially rationalize counterinsurgency. Prioritizing work on "trunk lines" that extended radially from strategically located garrisons to secondary posts linked by telegraph, the new roads were meant to allow mounted troops to reach these peripheral installations in less than twenty-four hours, in any season. The thousand miles of modern highway they left were also accompanied by new Signal Corps telephone and telegram lines; together, these communications enhanced Manila's ability to police criminalized dissidence. If commissioners' roads had an "incidental benefit" for Filipinos, MacArthur told US senators in April 1902, their "primary purpose," he confirmed, had been "military advantage."[72]

American civilians further sublimated commission roadbuilding's coercive martial and colonial qualities by insisting that the wages it dispensed to Filipino peasants freed them from cacique domination. In May 1905, Victor Clark, the US Bureau of Labor economist, published a report on labor in the Philippines that elevated this ideological claim to the status of empirical social science. As with Cubans, Clark tended to reject racist discourses about Filipino labor as he attributed their poverty and industrial inefficiency to historical, environmental, and sociocultural factors. His belief in Filipinos' permeability to external influence, however, inspired optimism that merely paying them wages was liberating them from the "primitive" serfdom of debt peonage. By commodifying peasants' labor, Clark affirmed, roadbuilding taught the tao the dignity of work and its real value; such lessons could only hasten the demise of their exploitation by landowning elites. Roadwork penetrating Luzon's "remoter provinces," in his view, promised to accelerate the reform most urgently needed in the islands: a "speedy and ready transition from a social state where many workers are in quasi-servitude, to one where they are industrially independent." Clark advanced his thesis by racializing Filipinos' cooperation with compulsion. In his mind, Filipinos' "Malay" heritage, imparting a "gregarious work instinct," primed them to accept forced labor. Still, waged labor, even if coerced, would free Filipinos. By "crystallizing labor" in "public works," colonizers who might not be able to "enforce individual accumulation," Clark believed, could "encourage communal" lessons in modernity.[73]

American civilians thus accepted US Army commanders' faith that wages for roadbuilding operated as a civilizing vanguard of economic liberty, despite their origins in coercion. Technocratic army engineers conveyed this attitude in data-heavy reports conveying a panoptical certitude that infrastructure could be abstracted from colonial politics and reduced to quantitative criteria of physics, time, and money. Yet engineers' reports also suggested that most Filipinos worked on their roads between late 1900 and 1902 only because cooperative local Filipino officials compelled them to do so. Even after January 1901, when Taft's commission proscribed the polo, army engineers described workforces as "enforced" or "impressed." Yet they claimed wages induced compliance from peasants, some of whom took jobs directly from contractors or US troops.[74]

Nevertheless, cash wages hardly ensured Filipino cooperation with army engineers on their terms. Corps of Engineers personnel documented pervasive subaltern assertions of sovereignty over their own labor. Depending on Filipino laborers and municipal officials to build highways, these Americans often found both lackluster. Criticizing elite brokers as corrupt, they accused them of graft, abuse, and waste, and devised various techniques to correct them. In early 1902, Lt. William Caples struggled to complete repairs to a road between Bay, in Laguna province, and Batangas City which local officials said they wanted. Requiring Filipino *capatazes* to pay men their wages in front of him, Caples gradually replaced foremen with hard workers. Then he tried improving gangs' efficiency by abandoning piece rates for higher daily wages. When this incentive failed, Caples fired both foremen and their gangs; he did the same when laborers did not return tools on payday. Invoking classic Orientalist tropes, Caples argued that Filipinos did not understand "kindness and mercy" but only "force and justice." If soldiers failed to rule road workers "with a just but iron hand," Caples counseled comrades, "no work can be obtained from them."[75]

Indeed, peasant self-activity on highways defied colonial perceptions of their alterity. Some laborers seemed to confirm Clark's theories challenging Americans' racist claims that Filipinos could not grasp their wages' value in a new monetary system or learn to save. Realizing their pay's comparative worth, given new silver–gold exchange rates, some Filipinos refused to work on roads unless engineers paid them more. Sympathetic army officers, and even a visiting American Federation of Labor agent, welcomed such willfulness as a sign of progress. Yet recognizing subalterns as rational, volitional, and self-interested invited an unsettling specter of comparison. Filipinos no longer seen as irrational, passive, or inefficient might seem more like men eligible for national sovereignty.[76]

The Philippine Commission's delegation of political authority to local Filipino elites also reflected imperial infrastructure's militarized pedigree. By entrusting new provincial governments in "pacified" areas of Luzon and the Visayas in February 1901 to his new Filipino partners, Taft conceived of local administrations as tutelary experiments in self-rule. Yet Manila still reserved bureaucratic control of public works to US military personnel. Three-member boards running each province, all initially appointed by Taft, included a governor, a treasurer, and a "provincial supervisor" whose main responsibility would be public works. By requiring engineering credentials for supervisors, however, Taft's commission virtually ensured these posts went to the only persons on the islands with professional training: American soldiers and veterans. The commission fully centralized its control over local public works in 1905 when it replaced provincial supervisors with "district engineers" employed by a new Bureau of Public Works at Manila.[77] Thus commissioners did for Luzon and the Visayas what Wood had already done for Oriente. Handing infrastructure to US military experts, they denied colonial elites' access to the state machinery of spatial-cultural reform.

Military-colonial compulsion survived in civilian-era public works in other ways. As the US colonial state struggled to secure labor for roadbuilding without coercion, army engineers' postwar recommendations to commissioners framed roadbuilding's imperial politics. The top engineer on the islands by the end of the Philippine War, Capt. William Wright Harts, anticipated subsequent policy. Born in Springfield, Illinois, a year after Abraham Lincoln's assassination, Harts pursued a storied military career after graduating from West Point, in 1889. As an aide to President Woodrow Wilson, Harts supervised the Lincoln Memorial's construction.[78] Yet this son of Lincoln's adopted hometown signaled how colonial imperatives often trumped this first Republican president's cherished free labor ideals.

Having managed some 1,000 miles of highway work throughout Luzon by 1903, Capt. Harts that year believed these results accomplished roadbuilding's primary mission: "repression of the insurrection." Like civilian commissioners, however, he viewed insufficient tax revenues as a serious barrier to much-needed infrastructural development. Manila assumed that a new property tax levied by provincial boards would allow local Filipino-run governments to replace proscribed labor conscription with voluntary waged labor. Yet the real estate tax failed to generate adequate funds. In 1903, American commissioners who saw this deficit as evidence of lax enforcement and corruption decided to fund local public works straight from Manila. Yet customs and reduced internal taxation, including a new one-peso per capita cedula, also failed to garner enough monies. Even when Luzon's provincial supervisors offered wages, they complained that cash itself failed to attract workers, especially during planting and harvesting. In the breach, some provincial officials, including Americans, violated the ban on the polo or tolerated Filipino municipal authorities who did. Other Americans lamented coercion's persistence as a sign that a landed oligarchy was still undermining liberal colonial reform.[79]

Harts urged Manila to resolve infrastructural crisis by resorting to compulsion. Commissioners, he advised, should simply resurrect the Spanish-era labor corvée. If local Filipino officials facing elections found this "impolitic," Harts urged them to consider Filipino convicts a suitable alternative. Strangely, Harts' proposal acknowledged neither Spanish army engineers' extensive use of prisoners for roadbuilding nor his own army's utilization of convicts for street and road work throughout Luzon and the Visayas. Like many American progressives in the colonies, Harts drew inspiration from metropolitan practice. If he acknowledged trade unionists' opposition to penal labor in the states, Harts argued that the primitive labor markets in the Philippines negated such concerns there. He also embraced carceral reformers' disciplinary logic that convict labor deterred crime and enhanced productivity. (Americans directing colonial prisons in the Philippines, including US Army officers, made the same claims). The "severest punishment" for Filipino "vagrants"—men who Harts believed were just "as much opposed to work as the same classes found elsewhere"—would be "to compel them to work hard." Toil on highways was an "object lesson" that gave a "strong incentive to the criminal to reform."[80]

Harts's coercive military-colonial labor schemes prefigured the entire panoply of public works policymaking that emerged under the Philippine

Commission. Historians usually attribute Americans' systematic improvement of archipelagic infrastructure to its civilian administrators, above all William Cameron Forbes. Yet this archetypal colonial bureaucrat merely walked paths already blazed by martial predecessors. A Boston Brahmin and New York banker with a transportation portfolio, Forbes made roadbuilding the keystone of his early Philippine career. Serving as secretary of commerce and police beginning in 1904, Forbes started a four-year stint as governor in 1909, until Woodrow Wilson's election ended Republican patronage. When he first arrived in the islands, Forbes was horrified to discover that their highways were often impassible during monsoons, and he became obsessed with fixing them. Frequently touring the archipelago, he concluded that the $3 million that Americans had invested in roads since 1899 had been wasted, leaving none capable of withstanding traffic or tropical rains. Provincial governors pleaded for help, as did planters who complained that bad or nonexistent roads forced them to hike export prices by a third, hurting their competitiveness.[81]

Forbes's resort to convict labor, however, reflected a military-colonial imprint. In 1905, he partnered with Gen. Henry Corbin, the Philippine Division's commander, to "experiment" in using prisoners from Manila's Bilibid prison to build roads, under American soldiers' supervision. Severely overcrowded, Bilibid's inmates suffered high mortality rates; in December 1904, when several hundred rioted, guards killed nineteen and injured forty others. That month, Forbes sent 500 of Bilibid's most "well-behaved" convicts to Albay to build an eighteen-mile highway between Tabaco and Ligao meant to facilitate hemp exports. Underfed, and suffering death rates higher than those at Manila, fifty-seven men seized guns and escaped in March 1905; troops killed thirteen and captured all but two, whom they returned to Bilibid. Undeterred, Forbes and the army expanded convict road labor, including on Mindanao. He even forced inmates to help preserve new highways by having them build wider wheels for carts which he then promised to give to any Filipino who worked thirty days on the roads.[82]

Just as Cubans' inclusion in civil administration weakened US soldiers' power to conscript labor there, the Philippine Commission's incorporation of Filipino elites in a new colonial legislature restrained Manila's ability to coerce labor. By 1906, commissioners prepared to make good on promises to create a lower legislative body, the Philippine Assembly, as a next step in Filipinos' political tutelage. Elected by a miniscule elite Christian electorate on Luzon and in the Visayas representing 1.4 percent of the colony's population, assembly members were to draft and approve bills for consideration by the Philippine Commission. Commissioners, a majority of whom remained

American appointees, could amend or veto them. In July of that year, Forbes proposed they could finally resolve insufficient resources for public works by requiring all adult Filipino men who paid the cedula to also provide municipal authorities five days of work annually on local highways, or an equivalent fee.[83]

Appearing to revive colonial and military-style labor coercion, the bill succumbed to the contradictions of colonial democratization. Filipino members of the commission, led by *ilustrado* Trinidad H. Pardo de Tavera, a founder of the new nationalist Partido Nacional Progresista, amended Forbes's bill by mandating that every provincial governor, and a majority of provincial board members in each province, would need to ratify it before the law could take effect in any one province. Joined by fellow commissioner Benito Legarda, a former revolutionary and cofounder of the Federalistas, Pardo de Tavera also tried to sabotage Forbes's tax by requiring that municipalities furnish each laborer ten centavos' worth of food, knowing they could never afford such an expense. Manuel Quezon, Tayabas's former governor, also seeking an assembly seat, and Juan Cailles, Laguna's ex-insurgent governor, reassured Forbes that his bill would pass muster in the provinces. By October, however, "overwhelming" majorities in provincial boards, the members of which also aspired for assembly seats, rejected Forbes's road tax with "pronounced" hostility, in his words. The polo "had been so obnoxious," he realized, that Filipinos "rebelled against anything" like "a law requiring forced labor." Forbes noted that Cailles faced "a great deal of political abuse" after endorsing his bill, and nearly lost reelection.[84]

If Wood as Cuba's governor expanded infrastructure efforts by centralizing revenues, Forbes expanded them by increasing taxes and dividing revenues between Manila and the provinces. By May 1907, Forbes convinced commissioners to generate more funding for public works by authorizing each province to independently double their cedula. He incentivized this option by preemptively appropriating 1.2 million pesos for roads but offered them only to provinces that adopted the higher cedula. Then Forbes pledged to reserve 10 percent of all future insular revenues for roads and other public projects and distribute them equitably among provinces according to their population. This new measure won commissioners' approval, and within three years every provincial board raised the cedula. Together, Forbes' reforms unleashed infrastructure. Each year between 1908 and 1913, provinces spent more than 2 million pesos in local taxes on roads and bridges, for which Manila advanced an extra 1.5 million to 2.2 million pesos. To rationalize the work, Forbes and civil engineers at its public works bureau classified highways by traffic volume and type, and paved priority roads with stone or asphalt.[85]

Like Leonard Wood, Forbes publicized his policies as sui generis genius. Yet his strategy for preserving new roads betrayed martial and intraimperial roots. Forbes's new highway maintenance program borrowed explicitly from the *"caminero"* system that Wood developed first in Cuba and later instituted in the Moro Province using "native" stewards. In fact, in 1903, army engineers including Harts urged Manila to organize camineros, but inadequate funds had limited their experiments with them to a few corners of Luzon. By 1907, however, Forbes's cedulas supplied the necessary funding. Functioning as infrastructural sentinels, Filipino camineros, like Maj. Barbour's Santiago street sweepers, embodied the militarized assertion of US sovereignty over everyday colonial life. Manila's public works bureau—soon directed by Warwick Greene, Gen. Francis V. Greene's son—paid each caminero to continuously monitor and repair two kilometers of road in the dry season and one in the monsoon season, at an annual cost of $175 per kilometer. Evoking martial origins and state authority, and American progressives' crusade to conserve natural resources by exploiting them efficiently, poorly compensated camineros wore regular red uniforms with service stripes as they filled ruts, dug ditches, and cleared vegetation. Following Wood's Cuban example in other ways, Forbes pushed camineros to enforce new laws prohibiting sleds and other "engines of destruction." Bicycle-riding American inspectors ensured that camineros employed techniques current in the states, and plied them with didactic English-Tagalog guidebooks illustrating best practices. Cedulas and camineros improved archipelagic roads—and Forbes's career. As "first-class" highways in Luzon and the Visayas grew from 300 miles in 1907 to more than 1,300 miles by 1913, Forbes boasted that his roads were better than most in the states.[86]

The polo's official persistence in special administrative zones that the Philippine Commission created to govern non-Christians reflected a dual mandate by which Americans extended indirect local rule to Hispanized Christian Filipinos but imposed direct rule on others. In northern Luzon's Mountain Province, organized in 1905 and ruled initially by US Army veterans, commissioners required Igorot men to annually pay a two-peso tax for roads or provide ten days' labor on them, or a substitute. American authorities mobilized thousands of Igorot men to improve roads and trails even as they paid them wages—none more famously than the Philippine Constabulary's Lt. Jefferson Davis Gallman (named for his uncle, a former Confederate president). In Luzon and the Visayas, however, the polo endured casually, by force of habit, tolerated begrudgingly by Filipino peasants and Manila Americans. Forbes's constant pressure on local officials to maintain

A Roadman and His Tools. The caption for this photograph of a Filipino caminero on Leyte, maintaining its coastal road between Tacloban and Palo, circa 1913, recorded US colonial officials' sense that this quasi-military workforce required close surveillance. As an American Bureau of Public Works engineer explained, "The caminero in a red uniform is not as apt to lay down and idle or go to his near-by house, or into a tienda, if dressed in red. His excuse, that the inspector had passed him but probably did not see him will be more improbable than if he wore ordinary clothes and could run the risk of being passed unobserved when doing wrong"; see Schmeling, "Maintenance of First-Class Roads in the Philippines," 18. Photo from box 17, Photographs of the Philippine Islands, 1898, RG 350-P, NARA, College Park, Maryland.

and improve roads and streets, manifest in regular tours, encouraged such coercion. In his diary, Forbes treated this custom as a colonial curiosity. Luzon's municipal presidents, he noted with pleasurable sarcasm, often prepared for his inspections by making "volunteer labor" repair highways.[87] His observation alluded to a parallel history, in the Moro Province and western Cuba, suggesting that colonial elites' sovereignty over tropical landscapes and labor often constrained US soldiers' imperial capacity to transform them.

CHAPTER FOUR

Always through the Datto
Building Roads and Subcontracted Sovereignty in Mindanao and Pinar del Río

Few Americans organized the work of their new empire with more gusto than the US Army's Maj. Robert Lee Bullard. His prodigious confidence as colonizer conveyed a regionalized racial identity befitting the high-imperial age's globalizing color line. Born to slave-owning Alabamans in 1861 as William Robert, Bullard changed his name to honor the Confederacy's most beloved general before he attended West Point. Reared in New South racial paternalism, Bullard regarded his command of African American volunteers in 1898, and pacification of Filipino nationalists and Cuban laborers, as sequential episodes in a martial career spent managing subaltern peoples. In his cosmopolitan imaginary, militarized infrastructure uplifted and pacified unruly races, transforming them into quiescent industrial moderns. Moro roadbuilding in Mindanao, he told *Atlantic Monthly* readers in 1903, had been "a great stride for savages," making them "peaceful workers" who "opened the way to their own civilization." Yet Bullard insisted that only sensitive white men like himself could rule Moros through labor. Those who "only talked to Moros of friendship and our benevolent institutions" but never "worked, paid, and fed them," the major wrote, had "not even scratched the surface of Moro character."[1]

Bullard's abundant self-encomiums contained clues that he never actually exercised much sovereignty over colonial laborers, much less the colonial elites on whom he relied to broker them. Bullard's admission that he "employed, worked, and paid" Moros "always through the datto" reflected the paradox that Americans could conquer Mindanao and its Muslims only by acknowledging and exploiting datus' sovereignty over Moro peasants and slaves. To be sure, Bullard implied that he cleverly co-opted Moro elites by lavishing datus with bonuses and making foremen of laborers. The major claimed he perfected such techniques in Cuba during its second US occupation. At Oriente in 1907, Bullard alleged, he quelled a walkout among road workers by replacing Yankee and Cuban supervisors with strike leaders and increasing their pay. Contrary to Bullard's published accounts of imperial mastery, however, internal army records showed that Cubans turned militarized infrastructure to their own ends. The next year, Bullard reacted to unemployed Cubans' protests for public relief by urging superiors to rush $100,000 to make work for them on highways.[2] Such events expressed not Yankee soldiers' absolute power or technical genius so much as the divided nature of imperial sovereignty, as tropical peoples forced Americans to cede control over labor and landscapes.

Hardly omnipotent or omniscient, US troops in the Philippines and Cuba rarely admitted that the peoples they occupied constrained their ability to build island infrastructure. Yet Americans' dependence on colonial brokers reflected and helped produce imperial formations in which US military and civilian authorities shared both formal and effective sovereignty with local elites. Evident in roadbuilding, this "subcontracted" sovereignty, in the lexicon of industrial organization, frustrated Americans' aims as much as it facilitated them.[3] Colonial elites and institutions therefore co-created infrastructural states in Cuba and the Philippines. On Mindanao, US Army officers like Bullard found themselves forced to concede Moro datus' social sovereignty over subalterns in order to access Moro labor, even as they designed roadbuilding as a means for eroding Moros' political autonomy. In Cuba, by contrast, ambitious politicians, corrupt bureaucrats, savvy contractors, and rebellious workers dashed Yankee soldiers' expectations that their authority would grant them control over public works. Adapting labor practices as they moved from one colony to the next, American troops met resistant peoples and resilient social hierarchies that split the sovereignty they believed infrastructure would secure.

AMERICAN SOLDIERS, FIRST ATTEMPTING to project effective US sovereignty into northern-central Mindanao in 1902, knew its Moro inhabitants as fierce warriors who had successfully repelled foreign intruders for centuries. Known as Maranao, or "people of the lake," these Moros used the geography of this region, centered around Lake Lanao, to preserve their independence. The laguna, resting on the Lanao-Bukidnon plateau some 2,200 feet above sea level and covering 100 square miles in area, is cradled by deeply forested hills and mountains reaching 3,000 to 6,000 feet in altitude. Lanao's waters empty northward via the Agus River, running roughly 20 miles and descending roughly 100 feet per mile, until they reach the Bohol Sea. These features, making the Lanao basin a virtual fortress, confined Spanish colonization to a few coastal settlements including Iligan, located near the Agus's mouth. The Maranao, residing in lowlands surrounding the lake and along the Agus River, subsisted mostly on fish and rice, and raised cattle and chicken while also growing coffee, sweet potatoes, tapioca, sugar, cacao, abaca, cotton, and coconuts.

Talented artisans, they wove cloth and baskets, carved wood, and crafted brass, iron, silver, and gold works, which they traded along with rice surpluses and hemp at Iligan and towns south of the lake. By 1902, according to Americans' estimates, some 80,000 to 100,000 Maranao lived in 450 villages ruled by roughly 150 datus.[4]

Just as US troops at Cotabato mobilized Maguindanao cargadores through datus, counterparts who sought to use infrastructure to occupy the Lanao country necessarily had to tap Maranao elites' sovereignty over Moro men to build it. Maranao society, highly stratified by status, power, and wealth, was cemented by structures of kinship and mutual obligation, in addition to economic interdependence, military need, and religious law, all solidified by values of honor, duty, and shame. Datus who ruled by virtue of claims of lineal descent from Muslim missionaries, or intermarriage into this hereditary aristocracy, invoked political and ecclesiastical authority to govern slaves and "free" peasants. Familial ties often linked the latter class of *sakops* to datus. Serving these elites as a warrior and agricultural laborer, the sakop paid tribute in taxes, fees, and tithes according to Islamic law and custom, often with portions of crops raised on nominally communal lands. Yet the sakop's only real agency, according to one scholar, lay in his "right to attach himself to a leader and to abandon him if he chose." Below this peasant stratum were datus' slaves, typically sakops who owed them debts incurred in food or money. As with the Maguindanao, debt bondage differed from chattel slavery; Maranao could emancipate themselves by repaying what they owed. For tribute and labor, slaves and sakops expected datus' protection and support. On Mindanao, the datu nobility constituted perhaps 1 to 2 percent of the Moro population, slaves roughly 10 percent, and the rest commoners.[5]

Maranao political organization rested on diffuse claims of sovereignty. Though authority among datus practically resembled that of the Tausūg and Maguindanao, the Maranao, by contrast, had no single sultanate claiming a formal right to rule subordinate Moro polities. The Maranao were confederated in four principalities, each ruled by a sultan. In turn, these datus' power rested on shifting pyramidal relations in which subordinate datus ruled sections, towns, and villages. Political community at the village level, organized by kinship and ancestral claims to land, was dominated by a datu headman and an elders' council enforcing customary and Islamic law. Some Lanao datus countered Spanish and US claims to sovereignty with a religious countersovereignty resting on a global Islamic community centered on the Ottoman sultanate at Istanbul. Maranao politics thus led Americans to perceive their culture as essentially feudal and anarchic. In 1903, Lt. John Pershing believed

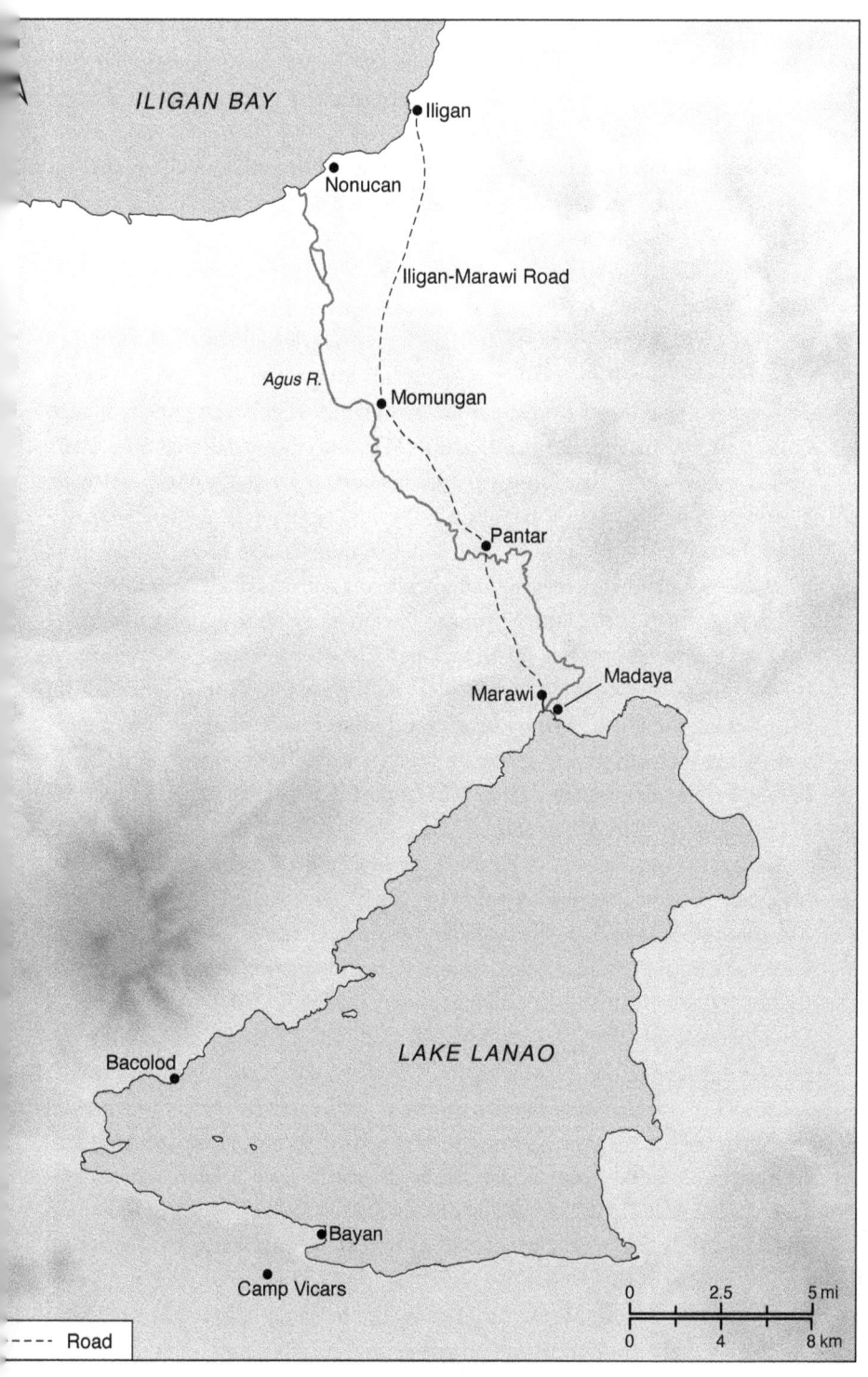

MAP 4.1 The Lanao Country, Mindanao, Philippines, 1902. Map created by Gabe Moss, courtesy of the author.

each rancheria was "practically independent of every other," governed by "its own sultan or dato" who denied "the right of every other sultan or dato to dictate to him."[6]

Intestine divisions did not prevent Maranao from thwarting Spaniards' efforts to impose what they detested as *gobirno a sawrang tao*, or foreign rule, until the late nineteenth century. After Spanish troops in 1891 garrisoned coastlines north and southwest of Lanao, the Philippines' governor, Gen. Valeriano Weyler, made the first of several attempts to invade it. Disease, supply problems, and Moros' guerrilla warfare forced Weyler's troops to retreat, but his successor, Gen. Ramón Blanco, found advantage in infrastructure. In 1895, Blanco used 3,000 soldiers and hundreds of Chinese and Visayan civilians to build a wagon road south from Iligan to Marawi, a village located on Lanao's northwestern shore. By August they constructed a twenty-one-mile track, clearing the jungle some 100 feet on both sides to prevent surprise Moro attacks. Blanco installed an outpost at Marawi, then used the road to transport by sections four small steel gunboats, originally fabricated at Hong Kong. Reassembling them at the lake, Spaniards used the vessels to bombard lakeside rancherias into submission. Insurrection in Cuba the next year diverted Spanish military resources, including Weyler and Blanco, and kept colonizers from maintaining the Iligan–Marawi road. Katipuneros' revolt in 1896, and the US war two years later, prompted Spain's troops to withdraw again; by December 1898, they had evacuated from Mindanao. Filipino rebels ruled Iligan until US troops arrived in April 1900.[7]

Compared to comrades at Zamboanga and Cotabato, who found Moro datus ready partners, American soldiers gingerly established contact with the Maranao. Mindanao-Sulu's first US commander, Gen. William A. Kobbé, preferred a policy of commercial attraction rather than armed invasion. Maranao trade at US-garrisoned ports such as Iligan, Kobbé hoped, would encourage friendly relations. Though Lanao Moros spurned wage labor for Spanish employers at Iligan and other towns, Kobbé believed exchange would persuade Moros who "suffered from the depredations and exactions of the more powerful dattos" to settle nearby. Given the Kiram-Bates Treaty, Kobbé and his subordinates refrained from aggressively interfering with Maranao slavery. Commanders at Iligan forbade Moro men from selling Moro women and children to Visayan men and refused to return escaped slaves to Moro masters. Kobbé, like other Indian War veterans, viewed Moros through a prism of prior encounters with Native Americans, and he thought Maranao showed a greater capacity for industrial progress. Rejecting colonial stereotypes of

Moros as naturally "lazy," he insisted that the Maranao suffered merely from a "warrior's contempt for labor."[8]

Kobbé's optimism encouraged US occupiers to predicate their imperial assertion of sovereignty in Lanao on remaking Maranao society and its social relations through liberal capitalist labor. American soldiers, perceiving Moros as premodern primitives, assumed they could civilize and pacify them by exposing them to wage work. Enlightened and paternal US troops were to invite Moro subalterns to liberate themselves by experiencing the magic of profits in a colonial marketplace. No longer paying tribute to datus, Maranao peasants and slaves earning cash for themselves were to become a vanguard of progress, remaking Mindanao into a tropical paradise of capital accumulation. By assimilating the culture of private property, Maranao laborers, or so American soldiers believed, would gradually acquire associated individual social and political freedoms, undermining datus' exploitative rule.[9]

As a strategy for promoting US sovereignty in Lanao, military-colonial labor missionizing also developed organically within the army's hierarchy, from the bottom up. Capt. Charles B. Hagadorn, commander at Malabang, a port some twenty miles south of Lake Lanao, exemplified this process. By early 1901, Hagadorn claimed that Maranao who visited the port were eager to trade, and he tried learning their language and ingratiating himself with a few datus. Traveling to the lake's south shore and back, accompanied only by a sergeant and eight datus and their retinues, Hagadorn reported that Moros there were "a dignified race, of fine physique, cultivating large farms with industry and skill." To be sure, he racialized the Maranao in ways that merited caution. Though the captain considered Islam no obstacle to their industrialization, he identified troubling traits in lake Moros. Finding them "totally lacking in foresight," "not shrewd," and unable to "handle merchandise," such attributes did not exactly lend themselves to entrepreneurialism. Yet Hagadorn confirmed Kobbé's sense that the Maranao man seemed "very willing to work." His Orientalist observation that "firm, kind handling" quickly made the Moro "the most loyal of followers" lent the captain confidence that waged labor could "gradually divorce them from their Datohs [sic]," thus offering a "final solution of the Moro problem."[10]

If most American officers embraced an economic strategy for pacifying the Maranao, Gen. George W. Davis, a West Pointer and army engineer who replaced Kobbé as Mindanao-Sulu's commander in August 1901, fixated on infrastructural development as its main tactic. A technocrat by inclination, Davis made roadbuilding central to his administration of western Cuba and

Puerto Rico between late 1898 and 1900 before he deployed to the Philippines; he went on to become the Panama Canal Zone's first governor in 1904. Exuding an almost evangelical faith in infrastructure's potential to transform society, Davis affirmed its greatest beneficiaries in Mindanao would be Moros themselves. Mindanao-Sulu's later US military governors, above all Leonard Wood, believed American settlers could create open markets in Moro wage labor. Davis, on the other hand, trafficking in climatic theories of race, thought Anglo-Saxons would never tolerate the region's tropical conditions. (Davis did entertain colonizing Mindanao with African Americans from the US South.) The Maranao's "ingenuity and industry," evident in their agriculture and crafts, and "eagerness to obtain money," gave Davis reason to think his army could remake them into "agricultural and mechanical laborers" abandoning "their life of idleness and savagery." Unlike Kobbé and Hagadorn, however, Davis explicitly invoked transimperial knowledge as he affirmed that Islam would not prevent Moros' capitalist assimilation. The Ottoman Empire, British India and Brunei, and Dutch Java, the general opined, proved that Muslims could be "useful members of the[ir] communities," if "handled properly." Occupation, he prophesied, would soon turn "fanatical Moro and pagan savages" into "industrious laborers," as "peaceable and contented as the subjects of Raja Brooke in Borneo."[11]

Such fantasies inevitably clashed with the US government's diplomatic recognition of Moro elites' autonomy. Though the Kiram-Bates Treaty of 1899 technically did not apply to the Maranao, American troops in the Lanao country, like those in Sulu, initially accommodated datus' effective sovereignty over Moro adherents. Gen. Davis's labor missionizing thus pivoted on an apparent contradiction: his army could undermine datus' social power over Moros only by formally respecting that power and accessing it to procure their workers. As at Cotabato, the politics of Moro slavery crystallized this dilemma. In October 1901, Davis admitted that "the worst misfortune that could befall a Moro community, and the nation responsible for good order among the Moros, would be to upset and destroy the patriarchal despotism of their chiefs." Yet Davis soon thereafter risked just that. Orders he issued in early March 1902, instructing subordinates to use "peaceful means" to "overcome" Lanao Moros' "desire" to "remain isolated and to exclude Americans" by purchasing their products and hiring their labor, seemed to extend Kobbé's hesitant policy. Later that month, however, Davis suddenly required officers to notify Moros that US law officially prohibited enslavement. Subordinates, fearing his order would provoke violence, pushed Davis to clarify that they were to prevent masters from reclaiming runaway slaves.

Yet his antislavery mandate's aggressive interposition of sovereignty between datus and slaves inflamed tensions, as small Moro parties attacked US troops south of the lake.[12]

Gen. Davis responded to these hostilities by resolving to conquer the Maranao with infrastructure. If his attempt to build roads to Lake Lanao seemed to reproduce recent colonial history, however, it rested on military experiments in recruiting Moro workers that the Spaniards never tried. The labor diplomacy of John J. Pershing, at the time a forty-one-year-old cavalry lieutenant, demonstrated the promise and pitfalls of a pacification strategy hinging on obstinate Moro datus. A Missourian and West Pointer, Pershing, like Bullard, approached his encounters with Moros through prior encounters with Native Americans, whom he fought and managed as scouts, and African Americans, whom he commanded as cavalrymen. Seeing combat at San Juan Hill, Pershing served briefly at Washington, DC, as chief of the War Department's new Division of Customs and Insular Affairs, before he wrangled a Philippine assignment more likely to offer promotion in December 1899. Serving at Zamboanga as adjutant general, Pershing in November 1901 persuaded Davis to make him Iligan's commander after he enthusiastically endorsed the general's objective of "opening up the Lanao country."[13]

Navigating the imperial politics of divided sovereignty, Pershing's overtures to northern Lanao's datus rested on a faith that his army could enlist them to build infrastructure as labor brokers. At Iligan, Pershing regularly entered its market to talk with Lanao Moros and collect intelligence. His outreach won a visit from Amai Manabilang, the eminent former sultan of Madaya, a village near Marawi. One of the few Maranao datus to have sued for peace with Gen. Ramón Blanco, Manabilang resumed that intermediary role. Pershing sought to make Manabilang his emissary to Lanao datus by acknowledging his local sovereignty. Avoiding discussion of slavery or polygamy and noting that Washington had diplomatic relations with Istanbul, Pershing pledged to "permit the dattos to govern their own people in their own way." He also emphasized the benefit of "new roads to facilitate the transport of Moro products to market."[14]

Pershing's performative recognition of Maranao sovereignty failed to secure Moro labor. In late December 1901, after he surveyed the section of the old road to Marawi closest to Iligan, the lieutenant reported to Davis that the sultan of Momungan, a rancheria just a few miles upriver, seemed "anxious to have his Moros employed" in rebuilding it. Yet this datu's offer of fifty men, at a rate of fifty cents each in Mexican silver and rice a day, generated no breakthrough. In February, Pershing, investigating rumors that lake datus were "interested in the matter," traveled there unarmed, accompanied only by a Visayan interpreter and the sultans of Bacolod and Madaya. Meeting datus assembled at Madaya, Pershing had Manabilang endorse his promise not to interfere with Moros' faith or customs and convey his army's plans for rehabilitating the Iligan–Marawi road. At this juncture, however, lake datus declined to furnish men for construction. Indeed, Manabilang told Pershing that Moros "could make more money by working in the fields." Disappointed, the captain informed Davis the Maranao could "probably be induced to work on the Marawi end." Yet Pershing also noted the datus had said they would "assist us" only "if we could get no other labor."[15]

Moro elites' ambivalence reflected their awareness, gleaned from bitter recent experience, that militarized infrastructure only advanced foreign sovereignty at the expense of Maranao autonomy. It also influenced Pershing's skepticism regarding Moros' racial capacity for capitalist civility. On the one hand, Pershing racialized Maranao culture, making it a barrier to industrial assimilation and imperial sovereignty. He represented the Moro as subaltern by underlining his "peculiar ... character": "first, that he is a savage; second, that he is a Malay, and, third, that he is a Mohammedan." This admixture, in his view, instilled in the Moro an "almost infinite combination of superstitions, prejudices, and suspicions," and made him "a difficult person to handle until fully understood." To control such a colonial subject without "brute force," contended Pershing, one had to first "win his implicit confidence." Only "by patience and continuous effort" could a non-Moro come to "guide and direct his thoughts and actions." On the other hand, Pershing, like Davis, discerned in the Maranao's "desire for riches" their possible susceptibility to liberal-capitalist "reason." Thus, the lieutenant realized that his army's procurement of Moro labor—"a great step towards the settlement of the Moro question"—would depend on datus' coercive power over dependent slaves and peasants. "In peace or in war," realized Pershing, "the supremacy of the datto over his followers" and their "unflinching obedience" constituted "the force that makes accomplishment possible."[16]

Events in southern Lanao in 1902 seemed to affirm Pershing's strategy, as rising tensions between Americans and Maranao there seemed to doom his army's efforts to win datus' cooperation for roadbuilding. In early 1902, after a new spate of Moro attacks on US soldiers which they attributed to men from Bayan, on the lake's south shore, Malabang's commander sent its datu an olive branch. His army, he professed, wished only to "explore the country, build roads, and secure trade routes to the coast." When Bayan Moros spurned this peace offering, however, Gen. Davis, determined to "continue to occupy the country and maintain United States sovereignty," dispatched in early May more than 1,000 US soldiers. Storming Bayan's two forts, or kotas, they killed as many as 400 Maranao, including the sultans of Bayan and Pandapatan, and captured nearly 100 other Moros. Suffering only ten soldiers dead and several dozen wounded, the Americans' assault on Bayan anticipated the asymmetric nature of intermittent Moro-US warfare over the next ten years. In the battle's aftermath, the Americans installed a nearby garrison, Camp Vicars, positioned strategically between Malabang and Lake Lanao. To ensure its resupply, troops began constructing a twenty-two-mile-long road from Malabang. Directing the work with 600 regulars, army engineers recruited a number of Moro workers, but they soon departed. Another detachment, building a road between garrisons at Parang and Cotabato, likewise struggled to secure and retain Moro manpower.[17]

Maj. Robert Bullard, whom Gen. Davis assigned later that year to rebuild the old Iligan–Marawi road, had greater success with Maranao datus and their brokered labor. Bullard boasted that his ability to pacify Moros with infrastructure derived from extensive experience managing subalterns. An 1885 West Point graduate, Bullard hunted Geronimo in Arizona before languishing on various frontier posts. In 1898 he jumped at an opportunity for wartime service by accepting the colonelcy of the Third Alabama Infantry, a regiment of African American volunteers. Yet Jim Crow mobilization dashed his hopes for combat, as the state's Democratic governor and War Department officials refused to let Black volunteers join the invasion of Cuba. Still, Bullard believed he redeemed this stateside command by making it a New South exercise in developing undisciplined Black military labor. Bullard, like most fellow officers, regarded African American soldiers as inferior compared to white counterparts. Still, he prided himself on his genteel and racial paternalist approach to command. Bullard defended his men by confronting abusive white streetcar conductors; on one occasion, he shielded them from a murderous mob of white Tennessee troops. Bullard also claimed that his leadership of the Thirty-Ninth Infantry Volunteers in counterinsurgency during the Philippine War enhanced his knowledge of the subaltern. Operating in Luzon's Laguna and Batangas provinces, the regiment styled itself as "Bullard's Indians," when its colonel claimed they practiced Apache stealth and deception. Unsurprisingly, Bullard readied for his Mindanao assignment at Manila in mid-1902 by studying the Koran and Moro culture and dialects. "Living among the simple negroes of the South" and "the Tagalogs in Luzon," he later maintained, taught him that "to speak the language of the people in their way was the very best means of approaching them."[18]

Bullard's failure to fully exploit white troops for the Iligan–Marawi road, however, reinforced his strategic mandate to recruit Moro labor. In early November 1902, after Gen. Davis left for Manila to take over the Philippine Division and Gen. Samuel S. Sumner took his place, Bullard started work on the road outside Iligan. The 350 Americans of his Twenty-Eighth Infantry made slow progress, as slashing brush, blasting trees and boulders, and shoveling earth battered their health and morale. By the end of the month, Gen. Nelson Miles, returning from a tour of Mindanao-Sulu, reported to Davis that Bullard's men did not seem "zealous." In response, Davis urged Sumner to find "Filipinos or Moros for the hardest manual labor." Several hundred reinforcements who arrived in January 1903, led by Maj. Lyman W. V. Kennon (soon managing the Benguet Road's construction), quickly succumbed to fatigue, thus seeming to confirm the logic of Davis's directive and his theory that white men could not toil in the tropics.[19]

Neither Filipinos nor Moros appeared anxious to prove their industrial mettle. Bullard tried to entice Maranao men passing his camps to enter his tent for conversation, in their own tongue, during which he claimed he had liberally quoted the Koran. Like Pershing, Bullard also tried to reassure skeptical Moros by distinguishing his nation's colonialism from that of Spain. The US Army, he pleaded, sought capital accumulation, not conquest. Soldiers wished "to open roads" only to help Maranao "buy, sell, trade," and "work with the Americans and grow rich." An improved road to Iligan, he insisted, would "bring the Moros all the valuable and useful things which they saw we had." Echoing Pershing's Orientalism, Bullard explained his preliminary failure to persuade datus to furnish labor as a function of their alterity. Moros' disinterest in industry, he maintained, expressed the norms of a patriarchal warrior culture that repudiated free labor and relegated manual work to women and slaves. Lanao datus, he later wrote, could not fathom why foreigners "who could drive many to work in slavery" offered Moros "pay for their labor."[20]

By making the Maranao subaltern, Bullard mystified the process by which datus eventually satisfied his labor demands. Contrary to self-aggrandizing published narratives in which Bullard portrayed Moros as pliable primitives yielding to capable colonizers, US Army records suggest that Lanao datus were savvy brokers who manipulated divided sovereignty. Before Bullard started the work, Davis authorized him to spend up to $20,000 for Moro labor. Sumner also told Bullard he could pay each Moro worker, or datu brokers, a daily wage or a per capita rate of fifty centavos Mexican silver and a pound and a half of rice. Recognizing datus' sovereignty, Bullard offered them a contractor's bonus for delivering labor. Yet fighting in southern Lanao may have reinforced their predisposition to reject Bullard's overtures. In early November, Amai Manabilang politely declined the major's invitations to furnish labor, even as he pledged deferentially to circulate Bullard's offer to fellow datus. "We do not object to construction of the road or the building of the forts," he explained by letter, "providing nothing bad is done."[21]

Maranao datus' motives or reasoning behind their eventual decision to send Bullard workers is unknowable, as few sources exist that directly express their perspective on the road in their own words. Some may have favorably reviewed his hiring of Moros near Iligan for porterage, early in the construction, as an incentive. Equally plausible may have been the trust Americans earned after they ameliorated disease. By December 1902, a cholera epidemic that had ravaged Luzon and the Visayas reached northern Mindanao. According to Pershing's estimates, it killed roughly 1,500 Maranao and sickened many more. Compounded by rinderpest that decimated Moros' carabao livestock, the cholera outbreak almost certainly disrupted agriculture in the region. Bullard and a subordinate officer later maintained that they finally befriended northern Lanao datus, and secured their labor, after they advised them to boil water and shared quinine. Indulging the classic trope of the white colonizer who pacifies primitive peoples by exposing them to scientific rationality, their stories strain credulity. Obviating Moros' agency by reducing them to inert recipients of American altruism, this sanitized tale of benevolent conquest and medical conversion erased Moros' subjectivity and decision-making within the context of their own communities, culture, and sense of sovereignty. That Moros stole tools from Bullard's camps and fired shots into them at night suggests that Maranao both suspected Americans' intentions and acted on their own perceived self-interests.[22]

Contemporaneous correspondence shows that Maranao elites in fact compelled Bullard to engage in delicate and arduous labor negotiations, even after they started providing him with men. Alandug of Nonucan, near Iligan, became the first Maranao datu to supply Bullard with workers, in late January 1903. In a folksy narrative Bullard published in the *Atlantic Monthly* that year, he portrayed his recruitment and handling of Alandug's laborers as a triumph of sensitive imperial mastery, demonstrating his prowess at securing subalterns' assent to US sovereignty. Yet army records from the time reveal that Bullard bargained with Alandug over wages for several days before the datu finally sent him twenty men, at a per capita cost of fifty cents and rice, paid at the end of each day. Describing them to *Atlantic* readers as a "scabby lot of boys and slaves," Bullard underscored his civilizing skill. Yet laborers' unfree status suggested that Alandug did not actually attach much significance to Bullard or his road. Expending little social capital for the Americans, Alandug mobilized younger and bonded men whom he could more easily coerce. Bullard also obscured datus' agency as brokers by claiming that his managerial paternalism elicited even more cooperation. By carefully treating Alandug's first batch of men "like kings," Bullard claimed he quickly attracted twenty more Moros, armed with daggers and krises, who expected the same pay. These "free" followers, and their voluntary labor, the major implied, represented the first sign that his army would be able to pacify Maranao with public works. Yet Bullard never clarified for readers that these free peasants' arrival coincided with the dry months of Lanao's agricultural cycle. Even if rinderpest and cholera had not paralyzed farming, the season freed these men from fields through which they paid tribute.[23] By presenting his army's exploitation of Moro social hierarchy as a sign of imperial sovereignty, Bullard concealed colonial coercion's vital role in militarized infrastructure.

Indeed, Bullard's publicity obscured how Alandug shrewdly leveraged ongoing labor policy deliberations inside the army hierarchy. A few days after Bullard first reported receiving Moro workers, Gen. Sumner urged him to get more Moros "interested in the road for political effect." Alandug, perhaps sensing Bullard's desperation, suddenly withdrew his men. His *Atlantic Monthly* article papered over this evidence of divided sovereignty by turning intercultural bargaining into a humorous anecdote cultivating American readers' sense of Moros' radical difference. In his typically folkloric style, Bullard narrated Alandug's retraction of his workers as the absurd act of a Muslim patriarch protecting his polygamous privileges, rather than a colonial elite's rational effort to maximize income. Alleging that a "low-bred, common" Moro at the jobsite eloped with two of Alandug's wives, Bullard claimed that the datu rallied his men to pursue the malefactor. Unlike bourgeois metropolitans who honored liberal capitalist norms of contractual obligation, Moros, implied the major, violated modern secular reason. Yet Bullard's yarn, as always, made himself and his nation's sovereignty its victors, as he insinuated that wage labor's charms strained Moro elites' power over their adherents. "In a day or two," he wrote, Alandug's men "sneaked back to work without him" to get "the sure pay and regular food" that made them "forget their datto's anger."[24]

To the contrary, Alandug had been as deliberately calculating as any American subcontractor, demonstrating an uncanny ability to read Bullard and manipulate his army's drive to enlist Moro labor. In fact, US Army records show that the datu recalled his men only after the major rejected his demand that he more than double their daily wage, to $1.20 Mexican and rations.

Sumner telegraphed Bullard that Alandug had made it known at Iligan that he understood its quartermaster was already paying Moro employees $1.00 to $1.25 per day. The datu, warned Sumner, might be "holding out" for higher wages. Bullard's response revealed Alandug's upper hand. Anxious to retain this datu's men as a basis for attracting more Moro workers, Bullard begged Sumner to increase their pay to at least $1.00 Mexican. "If we do not get them now," he pleaded, "we may not get them at all." Sumner approved the raise but Davis balked, and Alandug's men trickled back to the road to work at the original rate. Only now did northern Lanao datus' aversion begin to dissipate. Within the next few weeks, Bullard reported, several hundred more Moros joined the road at his fifty-cent per diem wage. He retired US soldiers, a third of whom had fallen ill from malaria or other ailments.[25]

By describing Alandug's action to American readers as a "strike," Bullard exposed a contradictory narrative that simultaneously denied and conceded datus' effective sovereignty. On the one hand, Bullard exaggerated his influence over Maranao elites, claiming that he exploited their feudalistic rivalries to wrest more labor from them. The irresistible allure of lucrative wage packets and contractors' bonuses, he suggested, exacerbated datus' competition for wealth, prestige, and male followers. Bullard thus insinuated that his labor policy's efficacy rested on a classic imperial technique of *divide et impera*. Bullard also maintained that datus' brokerage integrated northern Lanao's otherwise decentralized Moro polities. Mixing men from disparate villages in work gangs, he alleged, smoothed animosities that had festered, in his words, under the ancient law of "an eye for an eye, conduct for conduct to all generations."[26]

On the other hand, Bullard unintentionally revealed his army's fecklessness as he provided evidence that its infrastructural progress necessarily depended on acknowledging Moro elites' sovereignty, including over Moro labor. In a late March 1903 meeting with twenty-four datus at his camp at Pantar, roughly two-thirds up the Agus River valley, Bullard tried to elicit workers from them by pledging that his army's power and presence in Lanao would remain remote, superficial, and indirect. Though the sultan of Bacolod, a village just south of Marawi, voiced opposition, most datus at Pantar declared they would not contest the final leg of road construction. While Bullard that month reported that tool shortages forced him to turn away Moros, he also claimed that seventeen sultans and datus sent labor. These brokers, the major insinuated, formally acknowledged US sovereignty by accepting army storm flags from him as gifts. Bullard portrayed their desire for the tiny banners comically as naive primitivism. Yet datus plausibly saw these flags as symbols of the subcontracted nature of sovereignty in Lanao.[27]

A Conference of State with Moro Chiefs. Though Maj. Robert Bullard celebrated his prowess at securing Maranao workers for building the Iligan–Marawi road on Mindanao in 1903, northern Lanao's datus forced him to engage in several months of complex and continuous diplomacy and bargaining before they sent him laborers. From box 9, Robert L. Bullard Papers, Manuscripts Division, Library of Congress, Washington, DC.

Bullard's mockery of Maranao elites missed how they used their brokerage to maintain their own sovereignty over Moro labor. Publicly, Bullard argued that he convinced some datus to furnish workers by manipulating their eagerness to preserve their own reputation and influence vis-à-vis headmen who were already boosting their own prestige with followers by furnishing men. Ignoring a metropolitan legal logic of contracts, these datu latecomers, Bullard suggested, demanded that he grant them the same terms he offered other datus, regardless of their ability to actually deliver the number of workers or complete the task he required. Bullard also claimed he incentivized competitive brokerage by starting a new gang and then paying them a full day's wage for only a half day's work. He painted the results as further proof of Moros' alterity, portraying datus as irrational Asian chiefs who valued display more than profit. Datus who supplied men under the original terms, alleged Bullard, now insisted on the same advantage; a few, he wrote, even offered men gratis for several days, just to curry Bullard's favor. Datus' "jealous" insistence on equal contracts, he intimated, merely reflected their anachronistic feudal-patriarchal values. In this view, labor contracting became just another means by which Moro elites competed for male followers.[28] Yet this solipsistic narrative elided how Lanao datus supplied labor to consolidate their own paternal rule. By generating wages and earning bonuses, they enhanced the patronage they could deliver to the peasant sakop.

Bullard downplayed these contradictions by promoting roadwork's counterinsurgent effects. Ambitious for higher rank typically earned from combat leadership, he envied Pershing and other peers who fought Maranao south and east of Lake Lanao. Bullard compensated by exaggerating the dangerousness of his workforce and his ability to pacify them with public works. In November 1902, only days after starting the road, Bullard boasted to superiors that "dynamiting trees and stumps makes [an] impressive object lesson to the Moros." For the *Atlantic Monthly*, the major, typically hyperbolic, depicted Maranao he employed as "the most impulsive, violent, and dangerous people" with whom "the US government had ever dealt." Racializing Moro men as inherently violent and volatile, Bullard represented his roadworkers as more bombs than men: inscrutable and incendiary, they were like "infernal machines," he wrote, "ready to go off at any time." Bullard thus constructed the Moro laborer as cousin of the juramentado, or the Islamic holy warrior who accepted ritual suicide by "running amuck," attacking Americans or other Christians, seemingly at random, usually with a kris. Of course, given regional tensions, Bullard's perception was not pure imagination. In March 1903, when a lieutenant arrived at his camp in hot pursuit of Moros from Bacolod, Bullard, knowing its sultan opposed the road, begged superiors to stop him, to prevent "disaster to all."[29] Yet no Americans on the road were attacked after their army finally hired Moros to build it.

Bullard suggested he exercised effective sovereignty over Maranao workers by devising managerial techniques that exacted greater compliance and efficiency. He claimed that his sensitive supervision ensured their tractability, as he barred US enlisted men from issuing them orders without first receiving his authorization. Bullard also maintained that he took pains to make eye contact with Moros whenever he addressed them directly, preferably in their own tongue, without an interpreter. Yet the major littered narratives with hints that Maranao datus and their male followers enjoyed a degree of control over the work process. He deflected Moros' defiance of American norms of liberty of contract and industrial time-discipline by painting it as proof of their alterity. Maranao men, "in apparent good faith," observed

Moros Working with Americans upon the Road. While Bullard claimed he successfully enlisted Maranao datus in his army's infrastructural conquest of northern Lanao, these elites' relative disinterest in the Iligan–Marawi road seems evident here in these workers' relative youth. Datus, this photograph suggests, sent Americans their most vulnerable and least valuable labor. From box 9, Robert L. Bullard Papers, Manuscripts Division, Library of Congress, Washington, DC.

Bullard, believed his "order to go to work now" meant "*any time to-day*," because "*now* and *to-day*" in their language, he explained, were "the same word" (his emphasis). Some, he noted, demanded a day's pay at the end of a few hours' work.[30] Yet such activity, if true, merely signified resilient Moro notions of time, exchange, and mutuality which US occupiers had to accommodate to finish construction.

Bullard contended that he displaced Lanao datus' effective sovereignty over peasants by establishing unmediated relations with sakops working the road. By paying Maranao laborers directly and making some foremen who then transmitted his orders to fellow subalterns, Bullard argued that militarized employment detached them from datus. Suggesting that he encouraged Maranao men to recognize their property rights in their own labor, the major contended that he successfully inculcated industrial rationality. Bullard also invested his co-optative management with intraimperial racial meaning. Just as he pacified Black volunteers by promoting some to a noncommissioned officer's rank, Bullard averred that he appeased Moros by elevating them to a foreman's role.[31]

Bullard's narratives granted his army and its infrastructure a power to transform the Maranao that neither ever enjoyed. Though Lanao's governor in 1905 insisted the Moro "will work if he sees pay ahead," the Iligan–Marawi road's reconstruction only marginally stimulated a local market in wage labor, if at all. Bullard crowed that the male adherents of those datus who spurned his entreaties eventually came to work for him independently, on their own volition. Some datus may have sought to maintain peasants' loyalty by releasing them to earn wages on the road. Local historians claim Maranao men later toiled for wages in American-owned logging and sawmill operations and plantations, but few foreigners settled the Lanao country during the era of US military rule. Some Maranao received wages when they joined Philippine Scouts and Constabulary units manned by Moro enlisted men. That Lt. John McAuley Palmer, Lanao's governor from 1906 to 1907, attributed its substantial population of footloose young and unmarried Moro men to "a slackening of traditional authority," in one historian's words, suggests that wage labor may have attenuated datus' social sovereignty. If the Iligan–Marawi road's immediate socioeconomic effects in the Lanao country were opaque, however, its completion in June 1903 represented an infrastructural feat in the Philippines, rivaled in scale only by the Benguet Road—at least in expense and workers employed. By then, Bullard claimed the road's construction involved 3,000 Moro laborers and cost more than 58,000 Mexican silver pesos, or $29,000 US in wage payments and datu bonuses.[32]

The Iligan–Marawi road enabled the US Army to project deeper into Mindanao an imperial sovereignty strengthened by colonial political reform. While Bullard finished the road, the Philippine Commission organized the new Moro Province and entrusted its administration to generals. As noted, the province's creation paved the way for US military governors to abrogate the Kiram-Bates Treaty, thus ending its modus vivendi of indirect rule. Political order in northern Lanao, as elsewhere in Mindanao-Sulu, soon bifurcated between coastal self-governing municipalities and districts, designated for Christians and foreigners, and direct American military rule of Moro tribal wards in the interior, run by datus.[33]

Appointed as the new Lanao district's first American civil governor, Bullard claimed he governed the Maranao by the same techniques he used to build the Iligan–Marawi road. From Camp Keithley at Marawi, he administered Maranao affairs from November 1903 to June 1904, when deteriorating health prompted him to return to the states. Affirming the Orientalist dictum that "one-man power without formality, backed by force and a knowledge of the conditions, and exercised upon the people through their dattos," seemed to be the "only way" to govern Moros, the major fused attraction and force. He encouraged Maranao compliance with the new cedula by reminding datus that they already paid duties on imported cotton cloth and other luxuries they bought at Iligan with monies earned on the road. Continuing to hire Moro labor, though in fewer numbers, for porterage and other tasks, Bullard, like Davis, never shared Leonard Wood's enthusiasm for attracting white agricultural settlers to Mindanao. Though he led several punitive expeditions against the Maranao, Bullard repudiated the collective-style punishments that Pershing and Wood inflicted. The road, he subsequently wrote, taught him that "Moros could be managed in two ways only": "by putting them at work and keeping them at work, or by putting them in fear and keeping them in fear." The major "preferred the method of work."[34]

Lust for combat and rank that Bullard recorded in his Mindanao diary, however, suggested that labor and warfare were not the antipodes of empire he purported them to be. If Pershing and Bullard each forged alliances with Maranao datus that prevented bloodshed in northern Lanao, Pershing never believed infrastructure and violence were incompatible. In 1903, he took the lead chastising villages whose men were serially attacking his troops. Yet Pershing also urged Lanao datus to embrace roadbuilding, through which his army intended to "give employment to many" at "good wages." Bubbling tensions led to bloodshed. In April, Pershing's troops stormed Bacolod, killing 9 datus and 111 other Moros. Then, in an impressive tour de force, Pershing marched a column around the lake and killed hundreds more defiant Maranao, suffering only a handful of casualties. Still, garrisons at Keithley and Vicars, reinforced by fresh troops and supplied via new roads from Iligan and Malabang, only temporarily silenced Moro resistance. Maranao datus' localized claims to sovereignty in the Lanao country persisted. Colonial security forces were fighting Moro rebels in the region well into the 1930s.[35]

If American soldiers' highways never settled the "Moro question," they contributed to an imperial infrastructure state in the Moro Province built largely on the labor of colonized Muslims. Leonard Wood and Tasker Bliss, ruling the province for most of its first six years, carried with them to Mindanao from occupied Cuba a modernizer's faith that public works could catalyze colonial socioeconomic transformation. Spending nearly half of all provincial revenues on highways and other public works, these generals used brokered Moro labor to open 200 miles of roadway. Though American planters complained that army wages unfairly exceeded prevailing rates for agricultural work, this nascent labor market forced them to raise their pay. To maintain highways, Wood introduced the caminero system he developed in Cuba, using Moro men. As in Luzon and Visayas, roadwork on Mindanao implicated the colonial carceral state. In 1905, Wood joined with William Cameron Forbes to rehabilitate the Iligan–Marawi road using the labor of several hundred convicts, imported from Manila's infamous Bilibid prison.[36]

Militarized roadbuilding's long-term impact on Mindanao's economy is nearly as difficult to measure as its short-term political-military and sociocultural effects. New and improved highways, as well as additional ones, may have magnified the influence of other colonial infrastructure, such as "Moro Exchanges," which US soldiers established in garrisoned towns. If advocates such as Maj. John Finley claimed these markets increased Moros' support for roads and other public works, transport improvements also facilitated flows of foreign migrants and capital into Mindanao. This was especially the case in Davao, where American emigrants, joined by entrepreneurial US Army and Philippine Constabulary veterans and former American civil officials, established plantations and ranches. While US troops initially built roads in the region, American planters eventually used voluntary and coerced Moros and Lumad laborers to grow crops, mostly hemp, and build and repair roads that would move those crops to market. Davao contributed most to the growth in value of Mindanao's farm exports, from ₱746,771 in 1905 to more than ₱6.4 million by 1913. Yet the fact that less than half of one percent of exports that year shipped from Iligan suggested that roads mostly failed to induce capitalist industry in northern Lanao.[37]

Infrastructure's greater significance in the Moro Province resided in its military function, consolidating a US colonial state that gradually diminished Moro elites' effective sovereignty. As noted, beginning in late 1903, on Jolo and Mindanao, Gen. Leonard Wood repeatedly resorted to arms to impose and defend new antislavery and taxation policies. Like Davis's roadbuilding, these measures, Wood believed, would erode datus' control of peasants and slaves and enhance American sovereignty by tying Moro subalterns directly to US authority. Yet Wood preferred to conjure an agricultural workforce for Mindanao planters by indirect means. Provincial officials elicited labor from Filipino Christians by passing vagrancy laws and putting convicts to work. They also established compulsory primary schools that adopted industrial education.[38]

Wood's successor as governor, Gen. Tasker Bliss, had fewer qualms about coercing labor. In 1906, the provincial legislature approved his recommendation that it impose the same levy that Forbes proposed that year to the Philippine Commission, forcing all adult taxpaying men to work two weeks on roads or pay a small fine. Though Wood and fellow officers thought Bliss was too soft on Moros, he abjured the democratic process that allowed Filipinos to scuttle Forbes's highway tax for Luzon and the Visayas. Bliss acknowledged American officials' "reluctance to enact laws of this character in view of the known opposition of the natives." As a martial autocrat, though, he accepted his regime's direct authority over Moros. No official in the province, believed Bliss, could "deny that he is part of a despotic machine" and was himself "in greater or lesser degree a despot"—even if he aspired nobly to join "that class of despots who have left a part of the world better than they found it."[39]

John J. Pershing sought to be such an enlightened despot in 1909 when, now a general, he became the Moro Province's last military governor. Even as Pershing ruthlessly suppressed Moro resistance, he presided over an imperial infrastructure state in decline. As the Philippine Commission insisted that the province pay for public works exclusively by internal revenues, not bonds or loans issued by Manila, funds dried up. By 1910, Pershing halted all new work, scrapped plans for 50 kilometers of modern highway, and restricted efforts to repairing and maintaining the province's existing 164 kilometers of roads. Deeming Wood's camineros too costly a method for preserving them, Pershing replaced them with gang labor secured by the corvée. By 1913, after rising customs receipts and direct loans from Manila improved finances, coercion no longer seemed necessary. By then, Pershing extinguished the last embers of Moro rebellion on Jolo Island, provoked by his move to confiscate all Moro firearms and swords. In 1911 at Bud Dajo, his army besieged resistant Moros, five years after it had killed at least 600 men, women, and children there; in 1913, at Bud Bagsak, Pershing killed 500 more. In 1911 at Taglibi, US troops crushed Moros who violently resisted labor conscription. Yet desultory Moro resistance and violent American retribution persisted after US military rule ended. Not even 1,500 miles of new trails and roads built in the region since 1899 could stop it.[40]

THE SECOND AMERICAN INTERVENTION in Cuba both reinvigorated and frustrated roadbuilding as a military-colonial technology of state building and labor relations. Planned by US Army officers and civilian bureaucrats but executed through Cuban officials, contractors, and laborers, the Provisional Government's extensive public works program had dramatic physical results.

It built more road mileage in less time than had either the Military Government or the Cuban republic. Yet its political and economic effects were mixed. Better and more highways enhanced central state capacities to police remote rural areas that historically hosted challenges to its rule. In some areas, they may have expanded agricultural commerce by reducing transport costs for *colonos* and campesinos. Roadbuilding undoubtedly strengthened an infrastructural state, instantiated during the first occupation, in which public works reinforced the island's neocolonial political economy, dispensing patronage and relief to ameliorate structural inequalities.

Compared to the southern Philippines, however, where a military-colonial regime bolstered American soldiers' authority at the expense of Moro autonomy, the politics of divided sovereignty in occupied Cuba drastically limited occupiers' power over public works. By 1906, Cubans who had ruled themselves for four years claimed a nominally independent nation-state even as US hegemony, fastened on them by the Platt Amendment, still constrained their freedom of action. Relative to Moros, then, Cubans enjoying a subordinate sovereignty under the Provisional Government had more capacity to manipulate infrastructure for their own ends. Thus, compared to predecessors in Cuba and counterparts in the Moro Province, Yankee soldiers and civilian officials in Cuba during the second occupation faced a relatively more resilient and defiant society and civil state. Cuba's political elites and parties, professionals and planters, and popular classes of small farmers and urban and rural wage workers all exerted greater control over the island's politics and economy than they had in 1898. They forced Yankees to accept a subcontracted sovereignty over infrastructure as well as other spheres of Cuban life.

Americans often failed to appreciate how the neocolonial transformation of the island's capitalist economy since the war of 1898 had impelled Cubans to wrest private gain from public policy. Early republican politics reflected an increasingly precarious existence for Cubans trying to survive a changing economic system that still distributed its spoils inequitably, but now as a result of growing Yankee influence. By the end of the first occupation in 1902, Americans and Europeans investing in a credit-poor postwar Cuba had already started to monopolize the island's mining, banking, utilities, and transportation industries, as well as ranching, tobacco, and cigar making. Most Cubans' opportunities to acquire, own, and retain land continued to recede, due largely to their inability to access loans and capital (reinforced by US occupation policies, as noted earlier). American speculators and railroads gobbled up real estate often marketed at discounts by indebted owners. By 1906, American investors owned an estimated 15 percent of all Cuban land. That year, foreigners of all nationalities owned fully 60 percent of all rural farm properties (not including *peninsulares*, owning an additional 15 percent), while Cubans themselves controlled only a quarter of the island's arable land. Amid rapid postwar inflation, Cubans suffered not just fewer opportunities to work for themselves but a decline in purchasing power and living standards. In sugar and tobacco, wage laborers often lacked reliable income for three to four months a year. By 1907, joblessness stalked at least a half-million Cubans, as tens of thousands of migrants arriving annually, mostly poor Spanish gallegos, competed with native-born men for jobs, housing, and other resources.[41]

Unsurprisingly, such conditions encouraged patron-client politics, as public officials used state resources to reward friends and partisan allies. As in the United States, where middle-class reformers assailed the graft sustaining party machines, government jobs in Cuba spawned and reinforced party formation. By raising the personal stakes of politics, however, early republican patronage intensified partisanship. Congressional elections in 1904 catalyzed the formation of the Liberal Party, a coalition united mostly by opposition to President Tomás Estrada Palma's grip on civil offices. An *oriental* planter with separatist credentials, Estrada Palma served as the rebels' provisional president during the Ten Years' War; in the 1890s, he acted as the Cuban Revolutionary Party's minister and jefe. Estrada Palma personified a class of wealthy, educated, and white creole elites who accommodated Yankees' expanding influence in Cuba. In 1898, he lobbied for US intervention; in 1901, he endorsed the Platt Amendment; and in 1902, he supported the trade reciprocity framework that produced the sugar treaty. While Estrada Palma initially refused to affiliate with any party, by 1904 he had aligned with Cuba's Republicans. Led by fellow former civilian separatist leaders, the Republicans backed the president's laissez-faire free trade policies, friendship with foreign interests, and equitable allocation of appointments to men of various political stripes. By 1905, however, electoral pressures pushed Estrada Palma to join a new party, the Moderates, dominated by prominent fellow white civilian separatists. Liberals led by Gen. José Miguel Gómez, representing separatist military chieftains, enjoyed a somewhat broader popular base among veterans, professionals, urban and rural industrial laborers, and campesinos. Though both parties articulated a nonracial nationalism, Liberals found more support from Cubans of color, disproportionately poorer due to employment discrimination, land inaccessibility, and unfunded veteran's pensions. As strident nationalists, Liberals criticized Estrada Palma's regime and party for tacitly accepting Yankees' expanding economic power in Cuba.[42]

The new republic's infrastructural efforts reinforced a political culture of patronage. Building on the first US occupation's policies, Estrada Palma's public works signaled Cuban elites' awareness that roadbuilding curried voters' support, especially among a growing class of agricultural wage earners. By the end of 1903, his administration constructed 79 kilometers of metaled highway—almost as much as the 107 kilometers built under the Military Government—and by 1906, it built another 225 kilometers. Yet history and politics ensured these efforts' uneven effects. Estrada Palma's regime, like his Spanish colonial predecessors, focused highway improvements on the sugar provinces of Havana, Matanzas, and Santa Clara, but neglected Pinar del Río and Oriente, where small farmers and *colonos* needed them more. After his Moderate Party hoarded public works allocations as a political slush fund, then rigged elections, these two regions became staging grounds for Liberal revolt.[43]

General ballots scheduled for late 1905 raised partisan patronage politics to the boiling point of civil war. Before polls slated for December, Estrada Palma's Moderates purged Liberals from national, provincial, and municipal offices; this included veterans who first secured jobs under the occupation. Using police and Rural Guards to intimidate Liberal supporters, Moderates packed electoral boards. Liberal Party leaders condemned the election as fraudulent and boycotted it; Moderates claimed triumph in every office, at every level, across the island. Estrada Palma's administration only further infuriated Liberals as they celebrated a $20 million surplus but refused to spend it on veterans or workers demanding pensions and relief.[44]

By manipulating the Platt Amendment's promise to protect American properties, Liberals sought to leverage empire against Estrada Palma. By August 1906, rumored coup plots involving Liberal notables, among them generals José Miguel Gómez and Demetrio Castillo Duany, roiled Havana. In Pinar del Río, rebels forming a "Constitutional Army" quickly overwhelmed government forces. They also sought to provoke US invasion by threatening to torch foreign-owned plantations. Estrada Palma's arrests of prominent Liberals only fanned the flames of civil strife. By early September, after insurgents seized much of Pinar del Río, Havana, and Santa Clara provinces, Estrada Palma asked President Theodore Roosevelt for military assistance. As Roosevelt dispatched warships and marines to Havana, he also sent two envoys to mediate the dispute, including William H. Taft, now the secretary of war. After they failed to persuade Estrada Palma to accept Liberals' demands that he annul the 1905 elections and dismiss his cabinet, the president and cabinet resigned. Roosevelt installed the new Provisional Government and named

Charles E. Magoon as its governor. A Republican lawyer from Nebraska and friend of John J. Pershing, Magoon had recently ruled the Panama Canal Zone. Roosevelt sent a new "Army of Cuban Pacification" of 6,000 troops under the command of Gen. J. Franklin Bell, who only a few years before had suppressed Filipino insurgents in northern Luzon.[45]

Magoon's nominally civilian regime depended on US Army officers and their recent experience in colonial rule, including infrastructural development. Appointing cabinet-level Cuban secretaries to head five bureaus, including a new Bureau of Public Works, he selected senior Yankee officers to act as their advisors. Unsurprisingly, given this administrative structure, Magoon quickly embraced roadbuilding as a means to resolve economic threats to pacification. First was high seasonal agricultural unemployment between harvests, lasting from May to December and overlapping with the rainy season. During this *tiempo muerto*, roadwork, Magoon argued, could provide farm laborers with much-needed income. Second, Magoon concluded that poor overland and water transportation systems inhibited small-scale agriculture by keeping farmers from marketing crops. Public works, he contended, could reduce high transportation costs. Third, Magoon asserted that jobs on roads and other improvements could help Cuban urbanites afford rising living costs, including exorbitant rents, compounded by falling profits for sugar cultivators, high interest rates, and low wages.[46] Public works, it seemed, would smooth Cuba's rocky transition from colonial to neocolonial capitalism.

Magoon's contribution to the Cuban infrastructure state reflected more than just military-colonial precedent, however. His passion for highways and other investments reflected his genuine Progressive Era commitment to efficiency and conservation in public administration, and fair competition in private enterprise. Cuba, lamented Magoon, had been "annually subjected to a great economic waste" by uneven overland transportation facilities. Enamored like many Americans with British colonialism, he frequently noted that Jamaica, only one-fifth the area of Cuba, enjoyed nearly twenty times as many miles of metaled roads. Magoon also echoed Cuban antimonopoly reformers, such as Ramiro Guerra y Sánchez, when he regretted that *colonos* who lacked good roads were forced to move cane to *centrales* along rail lines owned by the same firms. Still, Magoon's chief concern was cyclical agricultural joblessness—in his view, the greatest danger to political stability. Nearly three-fourths of all farm laborers, the governor noted, regularly went without income. Few workers in these industries, he realized, earned enough to support themselves and their families in the off-season. Cuba's "most important economic question," declared Magoon, was how to "secure employment for this larger number of men during the six months intervening between the harvest periods."[47]

Magoon's answer was an ambitious roadbuilding program of unprecedented scale. Yet his regime devised it from within the historical-institutional parameters of an infrastructural state already forged by the first US occupation and Cuba's republic. Yankee army officers influencing Magoon's policy included Military Government veterans, many with engineering backgrounds, predisposed to pacify occupied peoples with roads and other improvements. Lt. Col. William Murray Black, Magoon's public works supervisor, was an 1877 West Point graduate and Corps of Engineers officer who had served as Havana's chief engineer during the first intervention. Black's new plans entailed constructing a total 2,304 kilometers of modern roads over three years at an estimated cost of $13 million. Designed to cross the entire island, they would leave a grid of highways centered on a main track running from La Fe in the west to Santiago de Cuba in the east. From this central stem, new arterial roads were to lead north and south to at least one harbor, on both coasts, in each of Cuba's six provinces.[48]

Black's public works program confronted the legacy of a republican state that mostly paid lip service to infrastructural improvement. The last Cuban Congress to meet before the August revolt of 1906 appropriated more than $5.6 million for 232 different roads and bridges throughout the island, in sums for each project ranging from $1,000 to $100,000. In practice, however, Estrada Palma and Moderate allies had used these "phantom" projects as largesse to garner votes for the 1905 elections. Late the next year, Yankee officials seizing Cuba's treasury learned that the administration had spent little more than $100,000 of this allocation for only seventy-three projects, meant to leave 590 kilometers of new roadway. Magoon sought to remedy this shortfall by securing a $4.8 million US congressional appropriation for more than 100 roads and bridges. Yet this money, secured by early 1907, represented less than a quarter of the $20 million which Magoon and Black estimated was needed just to modernize Cuba's existing 380 kilometers of highways. Beyond maintenance, they recommended spending at least $5 million annually, for seven years, on new roads and bridges.[49]

By 1908, nationalists competing for votes in new elections would criticize Magoon's highways as a wasteful extravagance. Yet most Cubans welcomed them as an economic stimulus. Since 1902, American investors and engineers had joined a chorus of Cubans calling for roadbuilding. Sounding like Leonard Wood, they argued that more modern highways would only increase the exports that generated customs revenues, which in turn could be used to fund more public works. Cuban bureaucrats embraced this argument, and the patronage it offered, even as they reiterated Yankees' criticisms of Estrada Palma's corrupt administration. In 1908, Diego Lombillo Clark, Magoon's public works secretary and a civil engineer, complained that Cuba's first congressmen never adopted any "definite programme for road construction, and only appropriated amounts irregularly," in paltry sums, without a "definite system." This, he claimed, unnecessarily raised costs, as contracts that rarely justified the expense in plant generated "uneconomical methods of work." "Short portions of roads constructed" after 1902, he believed, were "of limited value" and "expensive to maintain." Lombillo Clark also recognized how public works created their own politics. Estrada Palma's few improvements, he feared, became "a pretext for popular clamor for further appropriations."[50]

If Cuban officials grasped how infrastructure created its own cross-class constituency, their subordinate position in the occupation bureaucracy signified the subcontracted sovereignty of an intervention splitting control of public works between Yankees and Cubans. Despite Progressive Era Americans' desire to divorce policy from partisanship, US Army officers crafting Magoon's road program at Havana implemented it in the provinces almost entirely through a mélange of public and private Cuban intermediaries. This included municipal and provincial public works officials and the construction firms and laborers whom they hired. Americans' dependence on Cubans inevitably aggravated tensions between the two groups. While Cubans tended to see top-down foreign control of infrastructure as an imperial infringement of their national sovereignty, Yankees tended to see Cubans as subalterns who corruptly warped roads to their own personal and partisan interests.[51]

Americans' perception that politics influenced public works more than the public interest was especially strong in Pinar del Río, the one province where US soldiers directly supervised roadbuilding. Magoon's regime paid special attention to this region, due to its severe industrial crisis and the fact that the August Revolt had started there. Known as the "Vuelta Abajo," Pinar del Río had been Cuban tobacco cultivation's fecund heart since the eighteenth century, yet its population and economy suffered greatly as a result of the 1895 war. In 1896, after Gen. Antonio Maceo's insurgent army invaded the province and burned half its towns, Gen. Valeriano Weyler punished separatist cigar manufacturers in Havana and Florida by halting all tobacco exports to the United States, *tabacaleras*' biggest market. Weyler's policy pushed even more *pinareños* into the rebels' camp as he occupied the region, built *trochas*, and fought insurgents led by Maceo and Gen. Quintín Bandera. Reconcentration removed an estimated 21 percent of all pinareños to Spanish-garrisoned towns, where more than 24,000, or nearly half of the region's *reconcentrados*, perished. Magoon and advisers believed that Pinar del Río's minimal and languishing transport infrastructure hampered postwar recovery and sowed the seeds of revolution. In 1898, the province, with only a single rail line to Havana and few roads passable by wagon year round, suffered freight costs that often exceeded the value of goods.[52]

Industrial and ecological disruption hampered Pinar del Río's postwar economy. Small tenant farmers growing most of the province's tobacco prior to the 1895 war only slowly recovered from its damages. They exerted less and less control over the industry as more land and market power flowed to foreign firms, most of them American. These companies, already dominating cigar and cigarette manufacturing at Havana, sought vertical control over production. Campesinos selling farms to Yankee investors became agricultural wage laborers or emigrated, many to Oriente, to start over. The August Revolt, and a poor growing season extended into the next year, deepened the plight of *tabacaleras* and a growing class of proletarians who relied on them—and foreign tobacco corporations—for income. In 1907, drought and a destructive cyclone reduced the harvest. Then excessive moisture, necessitating a longer drying period, delayed the crop's marketing until October. At the same time, financial panic rocking the United States and global economies cut demand. The 1908 crop fared badly after an unusually dry year complicated curing and prevented its marketing for ten months at very low prices. Census data suggested pinareños' plight. In 1907, among the 80 percent of the provincial population living in rural areas, more than 62,000 men, or a quarter of its inhabitants, reported employment in agriculture, mostly tobacco. That year, however, more than 49,000 men claimed they had no work at all.[53]

By March 1907, Magoon and Yankee military aides feared the political and social fallout of Pinar del Río's economic crisis. They made roadbuilding their panacea. That month, US Army intelligence officers in the province sent Havana alarming reports that mayors were covertly organizing party-based militias under the pretext of being guards for tobacco estates. Magoon, fearing recession might revive disorder, ordered Col. Black to immediately start highway projects in Pinar del Río, using "emergency methods to whatever extent that may be required." To remedy a lack of surveys and the region's difficult terrain, Black's public works bureau signed "cost-plus" contracts with Cuban construction firms covering all expenses—and guaranteeing tidy profits. In Pinar del Río, however, unlike elsewhere in Cuba, Black dispatched US

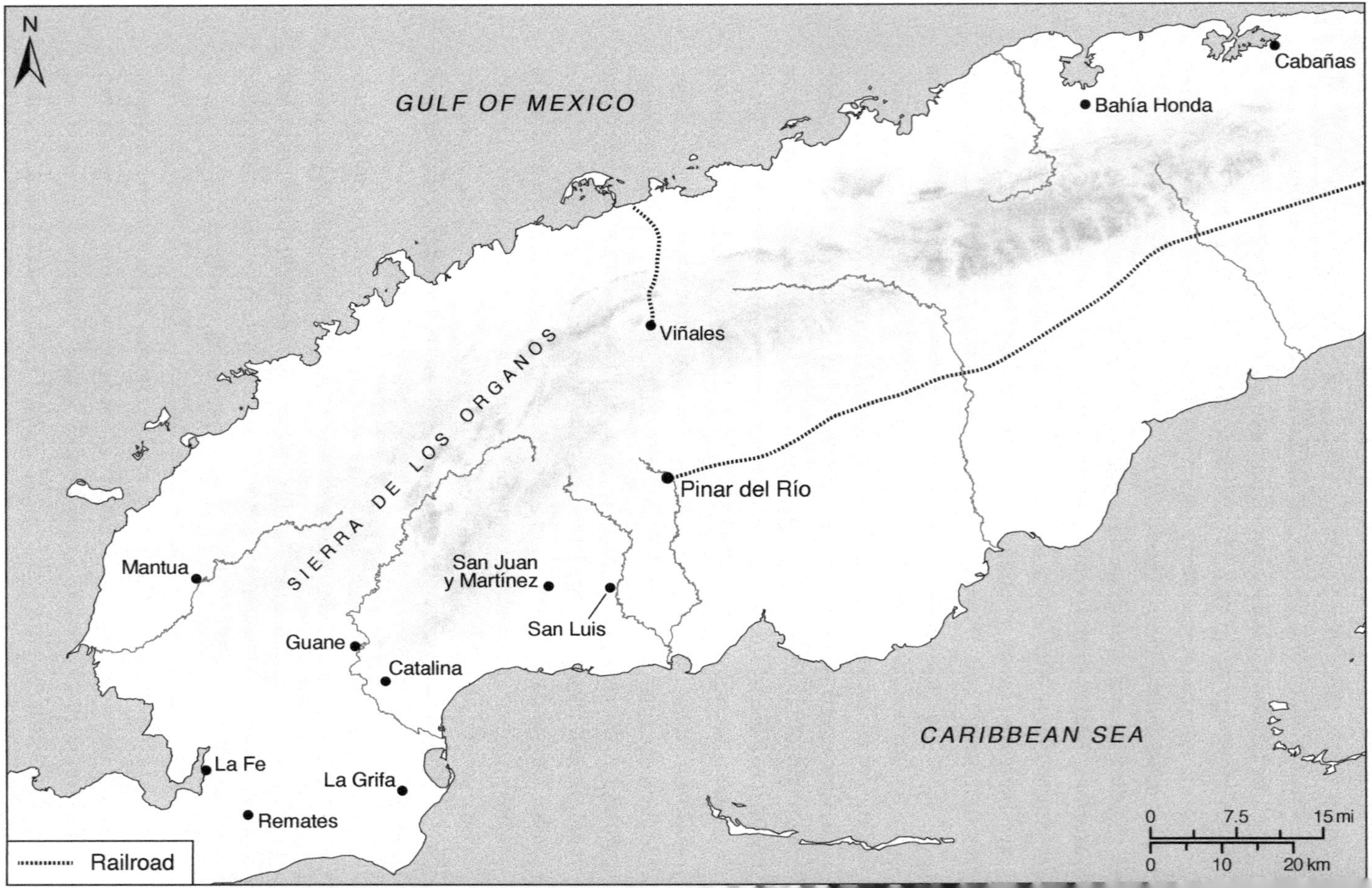
N
GULF OF MEXICO
Cabañas
Bahía Honda
Viñales
SIERRA DE LOS ORGANOS
Pinar del Río
Mantua
San Juan
y Martínez
San Luis
Guane
Catalina
CARIBBEAN SEA
La Fe
La Grifa
Remates
Railroad
0
7.5
15 mi
0
10
20 km

Army engineers to supervise the work. Maj. Mason M. Patrick, tasked with directing it, grasped its rationale as preemptive counterinsurgency. "The building of roads" in the province, he recognized, had been meant to "give employment to local labor" and "probably relieve" the "suffering, and consequent unrest," before it could "grow menacing."[54]

US Army engineers executing this work were confident in their political authority and technical expertise. They never anticipated the bureaucratic obstruction, managerial conflict, and labor troubles that subdivided sovereignty came to inflict on their endeavors. Perhaps the most vital of them was constructing a macadamized twenty-six-kilometer highway linking Pinar del Río city to Viñales, a small town to the north nestled in a lush valley formed by majestic limestone mountains shaped like gumdrops. Engineers led by Capt. Edward M. Markham started the work in May, supervising laborers, foremen, and equipment supplied by a Cuban contractor from Havana, E. A. Giberga, who received a cost plus 10.5 percent contract. Markham seemed competent to handle it. Graduating from West Point in 1899, he served twenty-five months in the Philippines, where he directed various projects on Luzon, including roads, under Capt. William W. Harts. He segmented the Viñales highway into three sections and placed each under a sergeant's control. Each sergeant commanded enlisted engineers acting as clerks, timekeepers, and surveyors who managed Giberga's laborers and supplies. This contractor himself personified Cubans' subordinate role in Yankees' militarized infrastructure. A civil engineer, Giberga during the first US occupation worked for US Army engineers at Havana, making professional connections that likely won him the contract from Black. Yet Giberga's use of his own Cuban foremen and timekeepers, and hiring of local men for road, quarry, and freight work, signified a fraught subcontracted sovereignty over the road that spelled trouble.[55]

A strike on the Viñales road exposed Americans' limited control over infrastructure and fueled their perception that Cubans treated public works as private spoils. On May 6, 150 of Giberga's *jornaleros* walked off the job and forced all other workers to join them. Their action's timing and demands suggests it may have been part of a wave of labor protest sweeping the island, inspired by Havana cigar workers demanding payment in US gold dollars. Strikers told Markham he would have to increase their compensation for ten hours' work to $1.40 US for them to return. Double the seventy cents US wage paid to tobacco hands in the province in 1902, the request seemed modest given inflation and their needs for off-season income; during the recent harvest, some tobacco workers earned as much as $4 US a day. When Markham counteroffered $1.25 for a ten-hour day, two-thirds of the strikers seemed amenable—until the militant minority, according to the captain, intimidated them into holding out. Peeved, Markham griped to Maj. Patrick that the Cubans considered their jobs a public "beneficia" and thought they should "have a large and prompt one." As Markham considered calling in Rural Guards or US cavalry to protect men willing to work, Giberga prepared to import strikebreakers from Havana. Intervention by Jose Antonio Caiñas, a local Liberal lawyer who claimed he had been authorized to negotiate for strikers, staved off drastic measures. Yet Caiñas's hints that Markham could defuse the crisis by hiring local foremen and drivers stirred the captain's suspicions. He balked, rejecting parochial "dictation." By the next day, Caiñas persuaded strikers to accept Markham's $1.25 offer. The officer grumbled that the strike had merely been a "theft backed by a few grafters," "disgruntled that the plums" were not "as ripe and juicy" as they initially expected.[56]

Markham's inability to believe that Cubans might have spontaneously organized a legitimate strike converged with Yankees' mounting fears of political disorder. American army engineers' contempt for militant roadworkers likely reflected racism. Census data suggests road workforces' possible ethnic demography in Pinar del Río. In 1907, its 240,000 residents included some 60,000 Afro-Cubans. In turn, one in four of all male agricultural workers, and just over 20 percent of all unemployed men in the region, were men of color. Tensions between US soldiers and Cubans may have also informed Americans' perceptions that nationalist interference and personal intrigue incited the walkout. In April 1907, just before the Viñales work started, a fight between US cavalrymen and Cuban Rural Guards in downtown Pinar del Río, sparked by a clash over prostitutes, provoked a riot. During the fracas, Gonzalez Molina, a provincial public works official, rode his horse into a crowd of Cubans while firing a revolver in the air, urging them to attack the Yankees. Maj. Patrick, ordering Markham to identify strike ringleaders and determine "if there is any one 'higher up' behind them," speculated that the Cuban chief engineer in the province's public works department masterminded the walkout as an opportunity for graft; Patrick may have been thinking of Molina or someone in his circle. Army intelligence officers, later identifying Molina as a Liberal Constitutional Army veteran, heard from informants that a relative had been extorting tobacco planters to pressure Magoon into giving the "turbulent element . . . profitable employment." Tensions mounted again in November following another raucous Yankee-Cuban fight in downtown Pinar del Río. The death of a US engineer, found on a roadside with a gunshot wound, did not help, though Markham deemed it a suicide.[57]

For army engineers obsessed with efficiency, Cuban contractors were just as problematic. Exercising a veto over public works, they embodied both Cubans' alterity and subcontracted sovereignty. To Yankee officers, Cuban construction firms and managers represented a neocolonial society they found hopelessly irrational, incompetent, and wasteful, if not also corrupt. Only gradually did the Americans realize that cost-plus agreements incentivized obstruction by encouraging Cubans to prolong construction. On the Viñales road, and despite the strike, Markham initially reported friendly relations with Giberga. In July, Patrick claimed that Giberga had gathered adequate resources, "displayed much energy," and wanted "to do the work well and economically." Yet Markham's ire grew as army engineers tried and failed to get Giberga to fire Cuban foremen who they alleged had refused to follow instructions, thus warranting the Americans' constant surveillance to ensure compliance. Patrick tried smoothing relations by replacing Markham. Yet his successor alleged that Giberga's foremen "openly or covertly resort to methods" that defeated "any improvement" in them, "while protesting that they are willing to do everything in their power to reduce costs." One army officer even speculated that Cuban contractors incited strikes when US engineers tried decreasing unit costs or directly hiring day labor. Yankees on the Viñales project alleged that workers colluded with Giberga to extend it. "Even if the contractor is honest and means to do economical work," reported Patrick, it was proving "difficult to get the best results from his subordinates," "foremen," and "ordinary laborers." "Generally more devoted to the interests of the contractor" than "the Government," the Cuban road worker, he felt, knew that he "profits more if their work is done inefficiently."[58]

Army officers complained that Magoon undercut them by responding weakly to Cuban labor unrest. Yet they failed to fully grasp how subdivided sovereignty circumscribed their power. Magoon's conciliation of organized workers, they argued, unduly enhanced Cubans' influence over economic policy. By early 1907, Magoon adopted the progressive neutralism of Roosevelt's labor policy in the states. Acknowledging Havana cigar makers' right to strike, he also vowed to protect strikebreakers' right to work free from violence. Army commanders condemned the governor's stance as misguided; such tolerance for collective action, they sensed, only invited more defiance. They may have been correct, as the cigar strike, and Magoon's judiciousness, inspired more strikes by stevedores and other laborers at Havana and beyond.[59]

Army officers' criticism of Magoon also reflected their perception that Cuban contractors and workers manipulated Yankee officials' desperation to pacify through infrastructure. An early September strike at Pinar del Río, on a highway between Bahía Honda and Cabañas, stoked such opinions. Workers demanded that the Cuban firm employing them reinstate Jaime Mir, a fired timekeeper and paymaster; raise wages by ten cents; provide medical care; and stop storing explosives in their barracks. Lt. Ernest Graves, sent to investigate, demurred on the first two requests. Workers' $1.20 daily wage, he claimed, already exceeded prevailing rates, and he argued that Mir had been justly discharged for embezzling workers' pay. After Graves brought Mir before a local court but covered his back pay, a magistrate dropped all charges. Yet Mir, the lieutenant alleged, kept the "strike alive by intimidation and agitation," as the aggrieved foreman and adherents paraded armed in Bahía Honda's streets, declaring "peaceful" intentions. Knowing Magoon's policy, Mir and strikers gained 100 signatures from local residents for a petition they forwarded to the governor. Magoon's reply, praising the Cubans for their nonviolence, confounded Graves, as did the contractor's accession to all demands except reinstating Mir. Rumors that Constitutional Army veterans were planning another rebellion in Pinar del Río strained Magoon's nerves and engineers' resolve. In October, when strikers on a highway project near San Juan y Martínez asked Magoon to pressure Yankee army engineers to accede to their demands, Maj. Patrick ordered them to fire all the laborers.[60]

Cubans' critique of Magoon's infrastructural state revealed other ways in which subcontracted sovereignty characterized the neocolonial politics of public works. Some Cubans turned Yankee allegations of incompetency and abuse on their head. Nationalist politicians condemned Magoon's spending for draining Cuba's treasury and producing few lasting results, as rains denuded new highways. Yet events at Pinar del Río and beyond suggest that most Cubans welcomed roadbuilding for distributing real benefits to poor and elite Cubans who rationally sought more spending. Infrastructural empire worked all too well, generating durable political coalitions for sustained public investment. Not only Cuban farmers and laborers stood to gain. Highway construction increased land values and stimulated more commerce for merchants and entrepreneurs, reducing transport costs for all kinds of goods. Many Cubans saw roadbuilding as a legitimate and vital source of patronage dispensed in budgets, salaries, contracts, and wages.

Events in southwestern Pinar del Río during 1908 illustrated how Magoon's ambitious roadbuilding unintentionally reinforced path development in Cuba's infrastructural state. Roads built their own politics, spurring calls for more jobs. In late February, Indalecio Sobrado, a former Liberation Army colonel, now Pinar del Río's Conservative governor, sent an alarming telegram to Magoon. At Guane, he reported, 3,000 men and women of all ages—a

Road Work by Capt. Smith, Corps of Engineers, U.S.A. This photograph of road work near Guane, in Cuba's Pinar del Rio province, in early June 1907, accompanied a report submitted by Capt. Clark S. Smith. Though US Army engineers like Smith initially supervised all roadwork in the province during the second intervention, their dependence on Cuban construction firms and contracted labor, depicted here, limited their power over public works. From box 1, E 993, RG 395, NARA, Washington, DC.

number equal to one-tenth of its population—gathered in mass meetings demanding "bread and work." Citing the drought, demonstrators asked Havana to immediately furnish relief by starting new roads in the area, just as occupiers had the year before with "emergency" work. In two days' time, at Las Martinas, near Remates, some 1,500 people—nearly half of that town's inhabitants—assembled to make similar demands. Skeptical US Army engineers, noting tobacco planters' complaints of labor shortages, dismissed the protests as a "bluff" to extort Havana.[61]

Magoon, however, believed the situation serious enough to warrant sober investigation, and he tapped intraimperial experience in infrastructural pacification by ordering Maj. Robert Bullard to investigate. After taking five days to survey conditions at Guane and Remates, Bullard confirmed that the prolonged dry spell indeed reduced the local tobacco harvest to less than half its average volume. Many small farmers, he reported, had produced only a quarter of their typical crop. The major neglected to mention that the immense purchasing power and control of local credit exercised by foreign monopolies, such as the Cuban Land and Leaf Tobacco Company, exacerbated the crisis. Bullard did note that the firm, after discharging roughly 800 men making thirty dollars a month, planned to lay off more and hire less than half the workforce it usually used for leaf packing. If unemployed men at Remates, who he estimated made up 25 percent of its population, were not yet starving, Bullard warned that half of its residents would soon need assistance to survive.[62]

Bullard's lobbying bolstered Magoon's impulse to stave off civil unrest by rushing more roadbuilding. Though plans for this corner of Pinar del Río originally involved a $15,000 appropriation, in a few days Havana allocated $100,000 for highway work near Remates, to be supervised directly by local Cuban officials. This spending had cascading and self-reinforcing political-economic effects, as other Cubans sensed that they could wrest more jobs from the Yankees. After 1,000 men had been hired at Las Martinas and La Grifa, Magoon fielded new demands for work from 300 men at Cortes and 1,800 more from nearby barrios. Local elites underscored emergency infrastructure's political function. Gen. Faustino "Pino" Guerra, who spearheaded the August Revolt there two years earlier, traveled to Havana to personally press Magoon to start more highways. By April, Magoon, anxious to maintain Guerra's cooperation, named him chief of Cuba's regular army. Yet protests persisted. The same month, Mantua's alcalde implored Sobrado and Magoon to start road projects that could employ laborers and farmers who were marching in the streets, demanding relief. A workers' committee, pledging pacific intent, petitioned Lt. Col. Black at Havana "not for charity" but for wages that men could earn honorably, alleviating conditions they ominously described as "a danger to all."[63]

Cross-class political pressure for public works impinged continuously on Americans' desire to divorce infrastructure from private and partisan advantage, especially as elections approached. Throughout early 1908, pinareños organized for August polls to decide municipal mayoralties, provincial governorships and councils, and congressional seats at Havana. Liberals and Conservatives, vying for votes from the 51,000 adult men in Pinar del Río eligible for the franchise, waged intense political combat. Pino Guerra upset partisan alignments by endorsing the presidential candidacy of Liberal Party leader Alfredo de Zayas over the party's standard bearer, Gen. José Miguel Gómez. Regional Liberals split, as did the party island-wide. From Pinar del Río city, Jose Caiñas, the lawyer who helped settle the Viñales strike, formed his own party, the Partido Regionalista Vueltabajero, advocating higher tariffs on American and foreign tobacco. Pinareños' intense politicking raised incentives for local politicians to reward friends and punish enemies. On March 25, not long after the emergency road project at Guane commenced, Gov. Sobrado alerted Magoon about renewed disturbances there. Suddenly and inexplicably, a Mr. Soler, a Cuban engineer in the provincial public works office, halted $45,000 worth of construction on roads near Guane and Remates. Sobrado telegraphed Magoon that Soler's decision to cease all work, after hiring only 400 or 500 of some 5,000 applicants, invited peril. "The town," he wrote, "wants work for all." Simultaneously, while Sobrado reported that idled Cubans elsewhere also demanded road jobs, he stressed the event's military dimension by requesting Rural Guards.[64]

Magoon started to wonder if pinareños were playing him. Speculating that Soler "either misunderstands his orders or is intentionally causing embarrassment," Magoon ordered Lt. Col. Black to investigate. His report confirmed the governor's worst fears. Soler, he alleged, provoked the mass strike at Remates by hiring only men who promised to vote for Zayas. Magoon dismissed Black's claim as "rumor" but wrote William H. Taft that the affair cast "a side light on the Cuban situation." A progressive like Taft, Magoon insisted that most Cubans wanted merit and equity, not political affiliation, to decide who received public jobs. People at Remates had been "willing to forego a much needed public improvement and endure the pangs of hunger," he maintained, as soon as they saw it was "tainted with partisan politics."[65]

Contrary to Magoon's faith in Cubans' civic spirit, US Army engineers insisted that corruption riddled Pinar del Río's emergency infrastructure. Cubans, they implied, deftly manipulated public works and divided sovereignty for their own self-interest. Highway projects around Remates persisted until late 1908, when Havana augmented an initial $50,000 installment with an additional $280,000. Lt. Theodore H. Dillon, scrutinizing this work for Lt. Col. Black, claimed to discover various grifts among Cuban inspectors and foremen. These schemers, he reported, doled out jobs based solely on party affiliation, kept shoddy accounts, and delayed payments to local laborers and merchants. Most outrageous, from Dillon's technocratic perspective, he alleged the Cubans completed little of the work awarded them. The lieutenant even claimed that some who had not welcomed his inquiries took "considerable trouble" to dissuade him, including by brandishing machetes and revolvers. Black worried that cowed Cuban foremen at Remates capitulated to such intimidation. Noting that even unpaid merchants threatened violence, Black seemed resigned to pervasive malfeasance. The Cubans, he told Magoon, "regarded the money spent on the road more as a donation to themselves to relieve real or fancied sufferings" than as money for actual construction. Feeling no "obligation to make a full return in labor or materials for the money given to them," people "living along the road," wrote Black, hatched "a general conspiracy ... to defraud the Government."[66]

Army engineers' belief that Cubans perverted public works almost certainly reflected bourgeois metropolitan racist fears regarding Afro-Cubans' growing assertiveness. Challenging nationalists' repudiation of racial identity, Black Cubans that decade increasingly protested racial discrimination, including unequal access to civil service jobs and salaries. To be sure, Yankee officers' reports from the region suggested that pinareños of all colors demanded road jobs and other relief. Yet Afro-Cubans' protests against exclusion from public employment during the second US occupation, at Pinar del Río and beyond, created a movement that soon coalesced in the Partido Independiente de Color (PIC), Cuba's first and controversial race-based political party. In late July 1907, Evaristo Estenoz—an Afro-Cuban labor leader originally from Oriente, and a former member of the Comité de Veteranos de Color—traveled through Pinar del Río. Having launched a failed rebellion there two years earlier in protest of rigged elections, before he joined the Constitutional Army, Estenoz called on Black pinareños to demand equal representation in politics and employment. In August, after Afro-Cubans at San Juan y Martínez denounced the disproportionately low number of Black men hired for census work, a "Protest Committee" demanded a fair division of public works jobs. The next year, Afro-Cuban veterans, accusing Liberal Party leaders of passing over Black men for civil service positions, formed the PIC to contest congressional elections on a platform of racial equality. In 1912, some Afro-Cuban pinareños backed the PIC's armed revolt, centered in Oriente, during which Estenoz and thousands died.[67]

If Afro-Cubans' protests illuminated the infrastructure state's uneven spoils, American officials publicly defended roadbuilding as a net political-economic gain for Cubans of all races and classes. As early as January 1908, Secretary of War Taft cited Magoon's public works, above all other economic policies, as evidence of his regime's "conspicuous success." By September that year, only a few months before Magoon transferred executive power to Cuba's newly elected president, Gen. José Miguel Gómez, his regime spent more than $13 million on highways and bridges, or roughly 55 percent of all Provisional Government monies expended on public works. Magoon's administration nearly doubled Cuba's total highways to nearly 1,400 new kilometers of roads, leaving some 200 kilometers of unfinished work to be completed by successors. In addition, US Army engineers and Cuban public works officials maintained or repaired an additional 1,900 kilometers of roadway. In Pinar del Río, projects supervised by Yankee army engineers built nearly 90 kilometers of modern highway, transforming the region's economic landscape. The new road to Viñales reduced travel time between that town and Pinar del Río from three days by cart to less than three hours by automobile. Some Americans believed this work pacified the West. Journalist Irene Wright argued that Magoon's roads rendered "revolution impracticable" there, in part by facilitating crop diversification that mitigated the ripple effects of failed tobacco harvests. Magoon considered roadbuilding his regime's greatest achievement. If the Cubans erected a memorial to the Provisional Government, one army engineer observed ironically, they might do worse than "carving a traction train in bas-relief around a concrete pedestal bearing a road roller."[68]

In fact, the mixed results of the second intervention's infrastructure necessarily reflected the split sovereignty of a regime that Magoon soon ceded to a restored republic. Initially, at Pinar del Río, both Liberals and their opponents feared highway improvements might reduce the region's autonomy by permitting Havana to more easily project military power in it. Yet neocolonial politics suggested the degree to which popular expectations for public works became embedded in Cuba's political culture. Reaching across divides of class and party affiliation, infrastructural investment now operated as a countercyclical policy tool, promising a political salve for Cuba's structural socioeconomic inequalities. In late July 1908, when Magoon responded to Cuban congressmen's calls for austerity by announcing that he would stop appropriating funds for roads, Havana newspaper editors and the Liga Agraria organized island-wide protests. Reproducing the political dynamic first seen at Oriente in 1899 in support of Wood's public works, Cubans protested that continued highway projects would stimulate economic growth, restore credit and enhance profits, and relieve seasonal agricultural unemployment. By 1909, these arguments became pillars of republican politics. Pinar del Río's Liberal convention that year praised Magoon's roads and enthusiastically endorsed Miguel Gómez's pledge to maintain and expand highway construction as an "urgent and transcendental" matter. "Efficient" modern highways, it declared, helped "expedite and facilitate commercial transactions" by "encouraging the establishment of new industries and revealing new horizons to intelligent speculation" in both "agricultural and commercial enterprise."[69]

Cuba's neocolonial path development gave its restored republic little choice but to sustain the infrastructure state. After Miguel Gómez assumed presidential office in January 1909, this charismatic war hero spent so much money on roads and other projects for political effect that Cubans famously called him "Tiburón"—after the proverb that when a shark bathes, it splashes water around. Starting multimillion-dollar projects in roads and other works in Pinar del Río and other provinces, Miguel Gómez distributed vital social relief and valuable patronage that undoubtedly fostered corruption. Yet infrastructural investment furnished much-needed income to Cubans struggling in an increasingly precarious economy. Miguel Gómez's patronage of middle- and upper-class Liberal professionals also helped neutralize criticisms of excessive spending that some nationalists leveled at Magoon. From Pinar del Río, small tenant farmers, agricultural laborers, businessmen, public works bureaucrats, and municipal and provincial officials all urged the new president to maintain the Yankees' high level of spending. Several times between June and August 1909, in the dead season, provincial councilors begged Havana to resume its unfinished work.[70] Infamous for pervasive graft, Miguel Gómez and his administration were prisoners of history. They only perfected a political economy of public works that they inherited from Yankee and republican predecessors.

With only partial success, Americans during the second US intervention had tried to apply lessons learned during previous wars and occupations in both Cuba and the Philippines. Building on the foundations of an infrastructural state originally laid by the US Military Government and the first republic, Magoon tried to use his nation's sovereignty and army engineers to transform Cuba's landscape and economy. Aided by men like Robert Bullard, however, public works in the Philippines and Cuba virtually depended on subaltern elites, laborers, and institutions. If American generals initially forced Cubans, Filipinos, and Moros to build roads, Cubans by 1909 seemed to be coercing US soldiers to improve infrastructure for them. Highways thus signified not absolute imperial power in the tropics so much as a subdivided sovereignty by which subalterns exhibited a capacity to exploit empire for their own ends. American soldiers' struggles to manage migration and sex during the wars and occupations of the 1898 era generated a parallel and even more explosive intraimperial politics of sovereignty.

Part III
Bodies

CHAPTER FIVE

The Chinese Experiment
Race, Labor, and Migration in the Army's Empire of Exclusion

In June 1898, just after Commodore George Dewey's Asiatic Squadron smashed Spain's fleet at Manila Bay, American troops at San Francisco boarded a steamer, the *China*, bound for the site of his victory. Since the 1850s, the *China* and other vessels owned by the Pacific Mail Steamship Company had projected America's commerce and sovereignty in that vast ocean by transporting goods and passengers, including Chinese. Now, to the dismay of California's organized white seamen, Pacific Mail ships chartered by the US Army retained their Chinese crews. The Sailors' Union of the Pacific (SUP) denounced the War Department for its betrayal. For years, the SUP had pressed the government to adopt an extraterritorial interpretation of the 1882 Chinese Restriction Act by applying it to US-flagged vessels. This would remove Chinese workers, whom the SUP and other exclusionists stigmatized as unfree, to make jobs for white men eligible for citizenship. Union activists were already incensed that Dewey had asked the navy secretary to allow eighty-eight Chinese sailors to enter the US mainland as a reward for loyal service at Manila, even though some had served for fifteen years and were native-born citizens. "Those who think that the Chinese Exclusion and Contract Labor laws apply to the Government," cried SUP stalwart Walter MacArthur, "should wake up."[1]

MacArthur probably cheered when Treasury Department officials, responsible for enforcing immigration laws, rejected Dewey's plea. Yet this rabid xenophobe could not have imagined that his nation's military in the Philippines would soon be employing Chinese by the thousands. In fact, Chinese likely constituted most of the 132,000 men whom quartermasters hired between July 1898 and July 1899 to move materiel in and around Manila, at a cost of more than $1.1 million. By 1900, the US Army had used Chinese for nearly every task that war and occupation required, except bearing arms. Serving as porters, litter bearers, and cart drivers, they also worked as carpenters, cooks, and gravediggers.[2]

If US occupiers extended exclusion to their nation's new colonial periphery, Chinese labor prompted some American soldiers to question its premises.

Many, favorably comparing Chinese to Filipino laborers, also missed how their government's denial of the Philippines' sovereignty may have affected the latter's willingness to work for invaders. If Lt. Col. James Worden Pope, the 1898 expeditions' chief quartermaster, praised Filipino boatmen who ferried men and materiel to shore, one subordinate found them "terrified or hostile" and reluctant unless forced. In the islands, however, Pope thought it was "difficult to see what could be done without the Chinese." He regarded them as absolutely essential "for carrying and genuine hard work."[3]

In the 1898 era, the US military exploitation of Chinese men, and regulation of their mobility, generated an imperial politics in which American troops, Chinese elites and laborers, and Cubans and Filipinos all struggled for sovereignty over racialized tropical workers. Chinese labor both facilitated and troubled imperial expansion as US troops attempted to rule islands which had their own unique histories of Chinese migration. If metropolitan and colonial pasts predisposed American soldiers to view the Chinese as racial others, their work for empire imparted a remarkable fluidity to the politics of race, labor, and nation.

The US military's colonial encounter with Chinese in the tropics unfolded through an intraimperial politics of racialized labor that spanned from Manila to Havana. In Cuba and the Philippines, American armies and occupations diverged temporarily from mainland conventions, seeming to establish exceptions to dominant anti-Chinese politics. By the late 1890s, in anglophone societies, Chinese migrant workers had become designated colloquially as "coolies"—a term originally coined to refer to indentured Indian peasants whom British and other European planters in Africa and the Americas, beginning in the 1840s, imported to replace emancipated slaves. Chinese arriving in California and other anglophone settler states met intense racial backlash, as whites believed their indentured status undermined economic freedoms and equality that they wanted reserved for Euro-Americans eligible for citizenship. The Qing empire's ban on out-migration made these men vulnerable to foreign sovereignty. Chinese authorities eventually recognized these migrant laborers as subjects when they negotiated treaties with states trafficking and receiving them, such as the United States in 1868 and Spain in 1877. Without Chinese diplomatic protection, however, Chinese labor migrants remained "quasi-stateless" peoples, lacking rights vis-à-vis governments and brokers.[4]

As Chinese men in North America found jobs in railroad construction and shoe factories, and on sugar plantations and steamships, white nativists stereotyped them as unfree and unassimilable subalterns enthralled to Chinese migrant brokers. After the Civil War ended African American chattel slavery, xenophobes alleged that Chinese endangered both triumphant free labor ideals and white workers' high standards for wages and consumption. By 1898, an often violent campaign to end Chinese immigration and expel Chinese already in the United States generated congressional legislation, treaties, and court decisions targeting them, as well as new technologies and bureaucracies restricting their mobility and legal rights. Exclusion energized Sinophobia across the globe. Annexationist designs on Cuba, Hawai'i, and the Philippines thus intensified debates in the United States over whether and how exclusion would apply to its new overseas territories.[5]

Yet the wars and occupations of 1898, and the labor they demanded, briefly carved out within metropolitan anti-Chinese politics what one scholar describes as "imperial openings." In the Philippines, US volunteers, most from the United States' western epicenter of Sinophobia, not only employed Chinese men but lauded them for their work ethic, loyalty, and bravery.[6] This uneven empire of exclusion extended to occupied Cuba, where Yankee troops during its first US occupation permitted most Chinese migrants to land. Yet anti-Sinicism in Cuba and the Philippines was never simply an extension of preexisting American attitudes. Spanish colonialism's legacies, including ethnic nationalisms, also inflamed relations between native islanders and Asian migrants. Chinese themselves also shaped this politics as they cooperated with US soldiers, and challenged them. Subaltern self-activity, belying the plastic nature of cross-cultural racial formation, troubled ideologies of race, labor, and nation abetting anti-Chinese empire.

In the long run, US war and occupation reinvigorated old and instigated new interethnic tensions dividing colonial societies, their nationalist movements, and putative postcolonial states. In the Philippines, American generals' and civilian bureaucrats' attempts to garner Filipino support for US sovereignty by stemming Chinese migration solidified an emerging racial binary between "Chinese" and "Filipinos." Over time, an anti-Chinese politics reinforced by military-colonial labor practices exacerbated Filipinos' opposition to Chinese migrants. White American enlisted men also shaped their own racial identity in relation to the Chinese workforces they managed, styling themselves as colonial masters of a degraded caste of Asian labor. Gradually, US officers came to believe that Filipinos' new capacity for industry would allow them to supplant Chinese as the workforce best suited to aid the archipelago's economic development. In Cuba, American occupiers' anti-Chinese restrictions reinforced an impulse to whiten the new republic and its working class as the island's booming sugar economy demanded labor. Filipinos' and

Cubans' adoption of Sinophobic immigration policies thus led some Americans to believe they might be closer to responsibly exercising national sovereignty.

AMERICANS INVADING THE PHILIPPINES in 1898 encountered a colonial society that differentiated native-born ethnic Filipinos from Chinese inhabitants in various ways. The Chinese presence in the archipelago dated from late sixteenth-century commerce by which merchants shipped luxury goods to Manila to sell for Mexican silver fueling the galleon trade. In a Catholic-dominated state, Spaniards' anxieties that Chinese refused to assimilate fueled tensions between Spaniards, Chinese, Chinese mestizos, and *indios* that intermittently exploded in Chinese rebellions and anti-Chinese pogroms and expulsions. Spanish tax and regulatory policy separating Spaniards and indios from Chinese and Chinese mestizos—typically born of Chinese fathers and indio mothers—reinforced ethnonational identities. By the early nineteenth century, Chinese mercantile networks positioned Chinese entrepreneurs to take advantage of agricultural commercialization, and they quickly came to dominate the islands' burgeoning import-export trade. Spanish officials, seeking to boost agricultural exports, encouraged Chinese in-migration to inject capital and markets into rural areas. A rising class of Chinese and Chinese mestizo businessmen, mostly retailers and artisans, included planters who acquired indio lands for cash crops. Yet Spaniards failed to attract Chinese labor to agriculture or induce greater industry among indios as intended. Though some Chinese established stores and workshops in provincial towns, most settled at Manila and other ports, taking up mercantile, craft, or manufacturing work.[7]

Indentured Chinese who first entered the Philippines in large numbers during the 1850s and 1860s were pushed into migrating by population growth, economic turmoil, and diminished opportunities for landownership amid the opium crisis, opium wars, and internal rebellions. By 1864, a Qing treaty with Spain that granted Chinese traders favored status and legally recognized contract labor increased Chinese arrivals in the archipelago. A Chinese population in the islands standing at 5,700 in 1847 grew to some 93,000 by 1886. Roughly 90 percent of these immigrants were Hokkien speakers, mostly peasants from southeastern China's Fujian Province who departed from Amoy (today Xiàmén); a lesser number came from Canton and left via Hong Kong. Chinese recruiters in villages and ports typically used kinship ties, goods, and credit to solicit migrants; less frequently, they resorted to deceit and coercion, including kidnapping. Shippers paid recruiters for each "sojourner" delivered and then sold the "credit ticket" that paid each migrant's oceanic passage as a labor contract to Chinese merchants, or *cabecillas*, at Manila and other ports; by the 1890s, they were worth fifty pesos. As migrant labor brokers, cabecillas facilitated the islands' urban and agricultural industrialization. Linking regional economies, they organized imports and exports, finance, and Chinese artisan guilds, and farmed revenues from Chinese, cockfights, and gambling. Cabecillas also patronized migrants through native-place associations, or *huiguan*, that tied "overseas" Chinese to mainland communities. For poor men planning to return home with savings, they offered work, housing, and protection. Cabecillas profited from loaning money to migrants, at high interest, to pay for cedulas, entry and medical inspection fees, the Chinese tribunal, and exemption from the corvée.[8]

Under the Spanish crown, cabecillas at Manila and other ports exercised a subordinate sovereignty over Chinese migrant colonies that were largely illegible to colonial surveillance. As middlemen managing transimperial circuits of labor and capital, these Chinese elites, trafficking in credit tickets, secured temporary rights to migrants' work and wages. Cabecillas used these migrants for their own businesses, usually as porters and stevedores, or rented them to traders and shippers. Fed poorly and lodged in warehouses and stores that served as cramped dormitories at night, poor migrants' living conditions sparked Spanish sanitary investigations and regulation. Cabecillas controlled indentured laborers through Chinese secret societies that managed opium and gambling networks and kept order in a rapidly growing and diversifying migrant community. These societies also acted as mutual-aid networks, offering newly arrived Chinese men much-needed support and safety. Once released from contracts, most Chinese preferred to become traders themselves or small-scale retailers managing *tiendas*. Many former indentures remained manual laborers, now "independent," living a precarious existence as *jornaleros*, taking jobs by the day. These sojourners were highly mobile. Part of chain migration that made the islands' Chinese communities almost exclusively homosocial, they sent for male relatives and returned to the mainland to bring male kin to Manila. While some returned to China, many frequently shuttled back and forth between the archipelago and Fujian. Jornaleros often moved between ports, including Manila, Iloilo, and Cebu.[9]

Historians have recently questioned the validity of categorical binaries of "unfree" and "free" labor by which Euro-Americans distinguished Chinese migrants from white workers eligible for citizenship in settler states. If profit-seeking cabecillas exercised social power over Chinese subalterns, they argue, brokers offered poor Chinese men a viable means to pursue opportunities abroad unavailable at home. Even scholars who argue that coercion and deceit pervaded mainland migrant recruitment concede that "less than satisfactory" indenture terms were still "generally honored" by cabecillas in the Philippines. Chinese also did work that many indios preferred not to do. By the mid-1880s, Manila's government decided to hire Chinese for public works rather than continue to force indios to comply with the corvée.[10]

Chinese migrant laborers occupied an ambiguous position in archipelagic society on the eve of US invasion. During the 1880s and early 1890s, Sinophobia, exacerbated by economic recession, roiled elite Spanish and indio circles. Anti-Chinese politics in the United States and Australia inspired Spaniards and Filipinos at Manila to demand similar restrictions. At best, Propagandists promoting a new Filipino national identity were ambivalent toward Chinese; one historian argues that *ilustrados* regarded them as "parasitic aliens and colonial collaborators." These reformers criticized Spain, among other things, for an open-door policy that increased the islands' Chinese to roughly 100,000 by 1896, or about 1.4 percent of the Philippines' population. By this time, nearly all were young male bachelors between the ages of twenty and thirty-five; between 80 percent and 90 percent were laborers. Yet Katipuneros' revolt and ensuing warfare in Luzon drastically reduced that number, as Chinese in the provinces fled to Manila and then left the city in 1898, when Gen. Emilio Aguinaldo's army besieged it. When US soldiers landed at Cavite in July of that year, the islands' Chinese inhabitants had declined by one-half to two-thirds.[11]

Though Americans' expeditionary forces that summer immediately employed Chinese labor at Cavite's docks to unload supplies, their commanders dramatically asserted sovereignty over Chinese migration in early August, not long after US troops occupied Manila. That month, as commerce resumed, hundreds and then thousands of Chinese men disembarked at the city. On September 16, Maj. Gen. Elwell S. Otis, the islands' new governor, cabled Washington that he had imposed the same anti-Chinese immigration laws enforced on the US mainland; ten days later, US Army officers assigned as customs agents officially promulgated them. Designed to prohibit the entry of laborers, Otis's rules banned all Chinese except merchants, students, and travelers carrying legitimate consular credentials, or those able to prove prior residency with cedulas or consular certificates. Like rules in North America, the "Otis order" excluded Chinese on racial criteria, not national origin per se. Subsequent US congressional statutes and Supreme Court jurisprudence further stigmatized Chinese in the islands, denying them the right to enter the US mainland, which they extended to ethnic Filipinos after recognizing them as US "nationals."[12]

Though some historians admit that no evidence exists suggesting that Otis issued this order at the behest of Washington, the weight of scholarship implies that his policy somehow signified an organic extension of mainland US anti-Chinese racism and politics. Yet its origins are opaque. No contemporaneous sources document Otis's reasons for the policy, and the general himself only ever offered post hoc rationales, beginning in 1899, in response to inquiries from State Department officials as they scrambled to deflect Qing officials' protests. No extant documents show that any federal official or agency ever instructed Otis to impose exclusion. Nor did the general seem to act out of personal anti-Sinicism, which, by all accounts, seemed mild compared to that of American peers. In April 1899, State Department staff read Otis's opinion that Chinese "methods" seemed essential for "conducting trade and performing labor" at Manila as a "qualifying ... statement" that signaled his qualms about the restrictions.[13]

Otis's limited discussion of the order's origins invite competing theories. In September 1899, when Chinese diplomats lambasted his regime's plans at Manila to deport 800 Chinese men shipped from Amoy who claimed prior residency, Otis stated elliptically that "race enmity between native and Chinese" in September 1898 had required "radical action." Without the order, he claimed, "Chinese immigration would have been enormous" and "unsettling" to the city's "social condition." Later, to Gen. Arthur MacArthur, his pro-exclusion successor as military governor, Otis asserted that Chinese who arrived at Manila in early September 1898 included "large numbers" of first-time migrants who had rushed to the city fearing "that the ultimate policy of our Government would be one of exclusion." Given subsequent diplomatic contretemps over the controversial rule, however, Otis apologized to shift blame for it.[14]

The least plausible of Otis's mea culpas involved his attempt to fault Chinese elites themselves for the order. The general several times claimed he imposed exclusion in response to "warring factions" inside Manila's Chinese community. As historian Andrew Wilson notes, tensions at Manila between Hokkien and Cantonese merchants regarding a newly established Chinese consulate did erupt in late 1898. The next year, Otis maintained that Cantonese accused the temporary counsel, Manila cabecilla Chen Qianshan, of abusing his office by charging legal migrants unauthorized fees. In turn, the general maintained, Chen requested his permission "to discipline his refractory countrymen." Yet the consulate dispute flared up in late October 1898, after Otis issued the order.[15] Like his account of racial antagonism, the story of intra-Chinese conflict appeared to be a convenient foil.

Otis's alternative portrayal of exclusion as an attempt to defuse an explosive military situation in September 1898 also read events backward, in this case from the retrospective standpoint of open hostilities with Filipino nationalists that had not yet transpired. In early 1900, Otis informed Gen. MacArthur that Filipinos' "well pronounced hostility to the unrestricted immigration of Chinese" had made exclusion a "military necessity." Despite mounting tensions in September 1898 between Aguinaldo and US troops occupying Manila against his government's wishes, no direct evidence exists to suggest that Aguinaldo, or the republic he convened that month at Malolos, demanded exclusion. British journalist John Foreman later claimed that Aguinaldo in April that year secured the pledge of Singapore's American consul that his nation would take "precautionary measures . . . against the influx of Chinese" when US forces invaded. Yet no independent source confirms Foreman's account. Despite Filipinos' Sinophobia and scattered Filipino violence against Chinese during the 1896 revolution and 1898 war, Aguinaldo in late 1898 eagerly sought the support of Chinese, especially wealthy elites able to supply funds. Aguinaldo repeatedly ordered and urged soldiers and citizens to refrain from persecuting Chinese, even as his regime maintained mild Spanish policies that classified them as aliens, required licenses for business, and taxed them heavily. Filipino revolutionary elites' ambivalence toward the Chinese was clear in an October 1899 foreign affairs ministry decree that granted them freedom of movement. Criticizing Chinese migrants as "a grave danger to public health" and "the working classes," it recognized their "exceptional ability" as a reason to admit them for plantation work.[16]

Otis's claims that exclusion had been a military necessity also responded to a bureaucratic politics of diplomacy in which State Department officials tried to appease irate Chinese ministers by portraying his order as the unhappy consequence of constitutional design. In July 1899, Secretary of State John Hay and aides reassured ambassador Wu Tingfang that Otis's order was only a temporary military measure, not "settled" US policy. Its legal authority, they told Wu, derived not from any normal decision-making process or consensus in the White House or Congress, but from Otis's "administrative discretion" as governor of a US territory at war. State officials pledged to Wu that they would press the War and Treasury Departments to lobby Congress to craft a permanent and just policy for the Philippines. Wu rejected the military necessity argument out of hand. Chinese in the islands, he noted, never harmed US sovereignty. Aware that brokers like Chen Qianshan were providing Chinese labor to US military operations against Aguinaldo's insurgents, Wu insisted that his countrymen "welcomed the advent of American authority" and even "rendered valuable assistance in the military movements."[17]

Otis's rationale for exclusion as military necessity became more plausible, however, in relation to his claims that emissaries from Aguinaldo's government had pressured him to impose it. In 1901 testimony to the US Senate, Otis insisted that "excited" Filipinos had visited his office at Manila in August and September 1898 in "large numbers," demanding that he stem the "considerable Chinese influx." Their protests, he said, "obliged" him to act "as a matter of protection." Otis did not identify personally the Filipinos who he claimed had lobbied him. Perhaps Otis had not wanted to disclose the identities of elites such as Trinidad H. Pardo de Tavera and Benito Legarda, who indeed met with him at this time but later betrayed the revolution. These ilustrados' Sinophobia, however, was evident in laws they passed that fall at Malolos as members of Aguinaldo's republican congress. Banning citizens from contracting with foreigners without permission, and barring non-natives from unloading cargo, these measures clearly targeted Chinese merchants and labor aiding US Army quartermasters. As future *americanistas,* however, Pardo de Tavera and Legarda may have perceived Otis's exclusion order as the first sign that Americans would grant reforms they had long sought from Spain. At Malolos by early 1899, both men were advocating for a US protectorate. They also went on to organize the pro-peace Partido Federal and join the Philippine Commission. Otis downplayed his role in placating Filipino elites, however, by attributing their demands for exclusion to what he described as the "old hereditary race prejudice" between "Chinese and Filipinos."[18]

If local colonial history prompted Otis's order, the evolution of its enforcement closely tracked exclusion's administrative history in North America, as his army improvised various techniques to assert sovereignty over mobile Chinese. His military regime honored exemptions for Chinese merchants, students, and diplomats recently canceled by mainland authorities. (Chinese worldwide responded in 1905 by boycotting American-made goods.) Yet Otis's greatest enforcement challenge involved distinguishing between former Chinese residents, who enjoyed a right to return, and first-time labor migrants prohibited from entry. Chinese could not depend on cedulas as proof of prior residency because few Chinese had procured them. Spanish officials' relaxation of baptismal and naturalization requirements for Chinese migrants also meant that returnees could not rely on such records either. At Manila by June 1899, some 21,000 Chinese jumped at the opportunity to purchase new cedulas. Yet Otis's customs agents also attempted to ensure "legal" transit by adopting mainland techniques of migrant control. At ports, they began recording applicants' name, age, occupation, thumb marks, and "physical marks or peculiarities" for duplicate certificates authorizing future reentry.[19]

As with exclusion in North America, however, US military immigration officials in the Philippines struggled to enforce an imperfect anti-Chinese system, which brokers and migrants found ways to exploit. As an alternative to cedulas, certificates issued by US consulates in mainland Chinese ports were initially accepted at Manila. Yet American customs officers began to suspect that Anson Burlingame Johnson, the US consul at Amoy, was regularly issuing certificates to fraudulent applicants. That Johnson regarded "free admission and employment of Chinese laborers" in the Philippines as a "necessity" likely raised pro-exclusion eyebrows. By April 1900, American customs in the archipelago started accepting only cedulas or other documents issued exclusively in the Philippines. The technical challenge of verifying legitimate cedulas and certificates, however, frustrated agents. Like counterparts in the states, US Army personnel racialized Chinese migrants, complaining that their allegedly uniform physiognomy made it impossible to validate personal descriptions. As in North America, where so-called paper sons attempted entry using documents originally issued to nonrelatives, kin, brokers, and smugglers circulated cedulas and certificates. By 1901, army customs officers also began requiring that Chinese returnees show proof of "property or domestic interests" in the islands. That year, however, Lt. Col. Enoch Crowder, Otis's former judge advocate general, now Gen. MacArthur's secretary, admitted that "large numbers" of Chinese "annually evaded the officials." The 1901 census, tabulating more than 50,000 Chinese in Manila alone—more than double its Chinese population in early 1898—prefigured how merchant brokers found ways to import Chinese indentured laborers, including by claiming them as minor children.[20]

American soldiers attempted to enhance migrant surveillance by drawing on an intraimperial circulation of anti-Chinese knowledge inside the US military itself. By late 1901, customs agents increased deportations after mandating that all departing Chinese supply two duplicate photographs of themselves: one for certificates, the other for records. Brig. Gen. James F. Smith, former governor of Negros and the islands' new customs director, instituted this innovation. (In 1906, he became the Philippines' governor.) Smith embodied mainland US Sinophobia's militarized imperial migration. Born at San Francisco in 1859, he became a lawyer active in the city's rabidly anti-Chinese Democratic circles, as politicians worked hand-in-glove with federal

"Chinese Bureau" staff. In the Philippines, Smith denounced employers who called for renewed Chinese immigration using the sandlot rhetoric of California exclusionism. These exploiters, he sneered, waxed nostalgic for "the good old days when they could stroll down the rialto and hire a terra-cotta edition of a pocket Hercules to carry 6 tons of coal . . . for a peseta a day and 2 chupas of rice." Chinese diplomats' protests against Gen. Otis's "sudden and severe order" suggested that it did significantly disrupt labor migration. Yet Crowder's complaint that scrutinizing Chinese "involved an immense amount of labor" also acknowledged persistent efforts to bypass enforcement. Testing restrictions by manipulating loopholes, Chinese migrants and brokers continued to evade them.[21]

Ironically, exclusion staunched flows of new Chinese migrants to Luzon just as US occupiers found their labor indispensable. From the start, American soldiers racially juxtaposed Chinese and Filipino labor, and often found the latter wanting. Such comparisons overlooked how the United States' imperial suppression of national sovereignty impinged on Filipinos' willingness to cooperate. As early as July, Aguinaldo and allies, distrusting the Americans, sought to dissuade fellow Filipinos from working for them. Unsurprisingly, US Army quartermasters perceived Filipinos as less reliable and efficient than Chinese employed for the same tasks. To be sure, Chinese did not earn universal praise. At Cavite in late June and July, Lt. Col. James Worden Pope, having organized sister expeditions from Tampa and San Francisco, struggled to find Filipinos willing to help move troops and supplies overland toward Manila. Deeming the few Chinese he found outside Manila as neither "sufficient in number nor equal to those direct from China," Pope sought permission to import 5,000 men from Amoy or Hong Kong—in his mind, "the best labor by far in the Orient." Rebuffed, Pope hired cart owners and drivers, including Chinese, from brokers, and impressed Filipino carts and drivers. Still, Americans at this time tended to favor Chinese over Filipinos, whom they usually disparaged as improvident, slothful, or disinterested in wage labor. They recognized Chinese as more like their own idealized Protestant selves, working hard, living frugally, and saving earnings.[22]

Soldiers' comparative racialization of Chinese and Filipino labor, however, shifted in dynamic relation to changing military and political conditions. Before war in 1899 hardened Americans' racism against Filipinos, they sometimes found them decent workers. At Cavite in late July 1898, Brig. Gen. Thomas Anderson scolded his countrymen, believing they had "underrated the native," who had "a civilization of their own." "For a tropical people they are industrious," he reported. "A small detail of natives," observed Anderson, "will do more work in a given time than a regiment of volunteers." Of course, even paternalist admiration could betray prejudice. Pope marveled at "Malays" who skillfully piloted the "queer little canoes" shuttling troops and supplies in Manila Bay, as he compared "funny little insurgents" to a "race of pigmies," "ill-fed and scrawny" like "negro children of ten years old." By the end of 1898, Pope even developed "sympathy" for Filipinos. Discerning in them "a good degree of intelligence" and capacity for "very faithful" labor, he regretted that "everybody curses them and treats them as bruits [sic]." Yet the new war soured Pope. By late February 1899, he was exclusively hiring Chinese labor for nearly all manual and skilled "mechanical" tasks. Pope described Chinese as "a constant source of wonder," unlike "wretched little Filipinos" whom he felt wrongly saw themselves as "superior to these Chinese."[23]

Manila's cabecillas benefited from such perceptions by renting labor and other resources to Pope's army, overnight the city's largest employer. By late 1898, quartermasters signed multiple contracts with Chen Qianshan, Manila's richest and most politically powerful Chinese merchant. Known as Don Carlos Palanca, an honorific bestowed on him by a Spanish patron who converted him to Catholicism, Chen, born at Fujian in 1844, moved to Manila at twelve years of age and apprenticed to a relative in drapery. By the 1870s, this bilingual entrepreneur built a thriving business importing rice and luxury goods, exporting sugar, lending money, and managing Manila's cockfighting and gambling rings. Yet Chen's influence and patronage stemmed mostly from his brokerage of the migration and labor of thousands of Chinese men, one source of the estimated half-million US dollars he accumulated during his lifetime.[24]

American occupiers doing business with Chen relied on the social sovereignty he exerted over Chinese subalterns. Under Spain, colonial officials relied on Chinese cabecillas at Manila to govern their own community through a corporate body, the Gremio de Chinos, itself led by a "Gobernadorcillo de los Sangleyes," whom they elected. Chen won this post for the first time in 1875, then earned reelection two more times before 1898. As the preeminent civic leader of Manila's Chinese, Chen acted as patron and enforcer. Farming revenues for Spanish authorities, he dispensed charity, filed lawsuits, sponsored a newspaper, and helped establish a Chinese cemetery and hospital. Chen's repute and influence even won him literary immortality in José Rizal's 1891 novel, *El Filibusterismo*, as the study for Quiroga, a cunning businessman refracting anti-Chinese stereotypes. By the late 1880s, Chen's power, immense but inscrutable to non-Chinese, prompted Spanish and mestizo fears that the Gremio de Chinos and its *gobernadorcillo* had become a powerful *imperium in imperio*, operating beyond colonial authorities' purview.[25] Such concerns, if exaggerated, recognized how cabecillas exerted sovereignty over Chinese migrants.

Revolt and warfare between 1896 and 1898 anticipated the politics of Chen Qianshan's relations with the Americans. Facing competing Spanish and insurgent armies' demands for Chinese workforces following Katipuneros' insurrection, Chen sought diplomatic protection as he assiduously sought to maintain neutrality. In November 1896, however, after Filipino rebels looted Chinese tiendas and homes in the provinces, Chen petitioned the Zongli Yamen, the Qing's foreign affairs ministry, to establish a consulate that could deflect Spanish officials' requests for Chinese laborers threatening to drag him and other cabecillas into the conflict. Acceding to them, he explained, would anger insurgents, yet denying them would alienate Spaniards shielding Chinese refugees at Manila. In May and June 1898, insurgents besieging Intramuros looted Chinese properties beyond its walls, including Chen's home. Chen's business with the US military in late 1898 thus extended his strategy to mitigate the risks of revolution and war through imperial protection and patronage. "Chinese can not live along with the Filipinos," he bluntly told Jacob Schurman's commission in June 1899, because they "will kill them."[26]

The US occupation of Manila in late 1898 encouraged Chen Qianshan to racially differentiate Chinese and Filipinos as part of a strategy to profit from American logistical needs, even as Otis's order disrupted his lucrative migrant brokerage business. While Chen made money by importing rice at inflated wartime prices, his losses from central Luzon's disrupted trade gave him reasons to aid Gen. Otis's deep-pocketed army. Between July and November, Chen satisfied quartermasters' transport needs, furnishing carabao, carts, and "coolie" drivers and cargadores. He rented warehouses as temporary shelters for US soldiers and inked tidy contracts to build them nipa barracks. Encouraging Americans to value Chinese labor, Chen told Schurman in June 1899 that Filipinos "don't care for work." If they "get a certain amount of money to-day," he said, they "won't work tomorrow." Chinese, he affirmed, were "industrious" and "good workmen."[27]

Chen's contribution to imperial racial formation did not rescue his waning sovereignty over Chinese labor. Otis's exclusion order dovetailed with other measures that eroded Chen's power over Chinese migrant men, and the political authority and social status attached to it. The general financially hurt Chen and fellow cabecillas by criminalizing gambling and abolishing tax farming. As conflict over the Chinese consulate suggested, however, Chen's failure to defeat exclusion damaged his prestige as Manila's leading cabecilla. By July 1898, when Spanish authorities finally authorized a consulate, Chen sought to use it to benefit his labor brokerage by successfully lobbying Qing authorities to appoint his son, Chen Gang, as consul. Yet bureaucracy and the 1898 war delayed his arrival. Chen Gang was still absent from Manila in September when his father, whom Otis earlier that month recognized as acting consul, failed to satisfy Beijing's mandate to stop the Americans from imposing exclusion.[28]

Disputes within Manila's Chinese community over the consulate further degraded Chen Qianshan's waning grip. Indeed, by the end of 1898, rising tensions prompted the State Department to refuse to recognize Chen Gang as China's new consul. According to Otis, Chen Qianshan's Cantonese, British, and German merchant competitors alleged that he would use his son's office to extort migrants. Hokkien cabecillas, rallying to Chen's defense, claimed that Otis had conspired with the British consul and mercantile rivals to defame Chen. By early 1899, however, Chen's son, mourning his deceased mother, resigned and traded places with Havana's consul, Li Rongyao. In October 1899, Chen Qianshan, desperate to reassert his control, posted "derogatory" broadsheets in downtown Manila criticizing Li Rongyao and questioning his credentials. The posters, in which Chen claimed to represent a "Department for Protection of Merchants in the Philippines"—sanctioned by imperial Beijing and Amoy—stated that only he had the authority to supervise lawful and safe Chinese transit between Manila and mainland China. Li Rongyao accused Chen of false representation and extortion. Annoyed by the intrigue, Otis threatened to deport Chen if he persisted. Stripped of his political power, Chen nevertheless remained Manila's richest merchant until he died, in late 1901.[29]

Though Otis severely disrupted such brokers' ability to import Chinese migrants, his army still exploited their effective sovereignty over Chinese laborers already at Manila. Quartermasters claimed that Chinese contractors freed them from the hassle of recruiting labor in a foreign and even hostile environment. Some attributed Chinese workers' relative efficiency and discipline to brokers' control. Independent jornaleros, observed US officers, could seem just as unreliable as Filipinos. In late 1900 and early 1901, Capt. Frederick J. Herman, stationed at El Deposito, near Manila, tried hiring and managing Chinese men himself to repair a washed-out highway linking US garrisons at Antipolo and Taytay. Yet he found few Chinese willing to work for him. Some men whom Herman did hire confounded him by refusing to sign payrolls or quitting and leaving before they collected their wages. The situation only stabilized after the captain found a contractor who furnished hundreds of Chinese but paid them less. Herman's resort to brokers reflected US officials' adaptability to colonial customs that decade, especially when building infrastructure. The "padrone" system, argued Herman, "relieved constructing Quartermasters of much needless work and worry" and proved "more economical than our American methods," to "which these laboring people objected."[30]

Renewed warfare in 1899 that pushed US soldiers to their physical limits prompted their army to systematically use contracted Chinese workforces for field operations. Their exploitation proved so essential for American logistical capacities that two officers from Gen. Arthur MacArthur's Second Division vied for credit over who first incorporated "coolies" into the army. In early March, as fighting persisted and spread beyond Manila's suburbs, officers claimed that enlisted Hospital Corpsmen, detailed for litter bearing, collapsed under the strain of hauling wounded Americans. Capt. Charles G. Sawtelle Jr., MacArthur's chief quartermaster, claimed that the sight of Chinese cart drivers' "almost universal good behavior" under fire inspired him to seek authority to hire 150 Chinese for the litters. Knowing some 8,000 to 10,000 Chinese laborers were available at Manila, out of a total 23,000 Chinese in the city, Sawtelle did not think supply a problem. He won permission to hire fifty, at a monthly per capita price of a daily "coolie" ration and twenty Mexican silver dollars—roughly equal to the fifty- to seventy-five-cent per diem rate paid Chinese porters in the city. Sawtelle believed "trials" with litter bearers would show that Chinese could meet the army's transport needs in "the wet or dry season."[31]

A rival claim involved racial-environmental scrutiny of Americans' and Asians' relative industrial abilities in the tropics. Maj. Henry F. Hoyt, a colorful frontier doctor and wartime volunteer serving as MacArthur's chief surgeon, insisted that he discovered the Chinese litter bearer in early 1899. Invoking theories that white men from temperate areas could not work in equatorial zones, Hoyt, in a folksy memoir, claimed that fighting "demonstrated that even *six* white men could carry a man but a short distance in that hot, humid, tropical climate" [his emphasis]. Less convincingly, Hoyt also invoked transimperial inspiration. Stopped at Hong Kong in early 1899 while en route to Manila, Hoyt averred that he witnessed a scene also frequently recorded by newcomers to Manila: Chinese men carrying objects as heavy and awkward as pianos using rope and bamboo poles, with "little apparent exertion or fatigue." By mid-April, Hoyt reported that Chinese bearers ensured "very little delay ... in getting wounded to the dressing station." "Coolies

Malolos. Chinese Litter Bearers Used by Medical Department Accompanying the Expedition, March 1899. Profiling Chinese litter bearers and the Hospital Corps enlisted men who supervised them in the foreground, this photograph's inclusion of reclining injured or resting American soldiers in the background evoked commanders' rationale for hiring Chinese for field operations in Luzon. From box 2½, RG 111-RB, NARA, College Park, Maryland.

accustomed to that kind of labor," he told superiors, moved injured Americans "more gently than by any other method." Regardless of these dueling claims to discovery, MacArthur's division by the end of that month hired from Chen Qianshan, and possibly other brokers, several hundred Chinese for litter bearing and assigned four to every infantry company, cavalry troop, battery, and band. By early 1900, Col. Charles Greenleaf, chief army surgeon, felt that these "patient, tireless, brave" men had been "all that could be desired."[32]

Chinese litter bearers' purported efficiency was partly the product of compulsion. Americans' use of physical threats against them signified the militarization of a racialized colonial workforce that occupied an uncomfortable liminal status between soldiers and civilians. Lt. Franklin M. Kemp, a surgeon in Gen. Henry Lawton's First Division, acknowledged such coercion in an article he published for a professional journal that examined "coolies" pseudo-scientifically as a "genus of bearers." Kemp accompanied Lawton's April 1899 raid across Laguna de Bay to Santa Cruz, during which quartermasters hired seventy-two "transportation coolies" for each regiment. Kemp attempted humor but conceded violence as he narrated one private's attempt to direct Chinese litter bearers with "a huge navy revolver and a long stick." Hoyt's racial paternalism prompted him to abjure rough treatment. "While men should be firm with the Chinese," he urged, he did "not approve of force in case of exhibition of timidity." Yet more than one American veteran admitted they inflicted "a little punching and prodding" to make Chinese "perform an errand or duty." Charitably, some blamed hesitation on "over-indulgence of the pipe," not "ill-humor or unwillingness."[33]

Such narratives contained contradictory messages about Chinese workers and their implications for empire. Affirming that Americans aspired to exercise sovereignty over the Chinese, they also hinted that US troops responded to their inability to absolutely control these laborers by racializing them. The longer the "coolie" experiment continued, the more problems it made for army personnel who explained them in racial terms. By mid-1899, as Manila brokers delivered hundreds of Chinese men to field units without providing their names or any other information by which Americans might identify them, US Army commanders struggled to find ways to control them. Like customs agents confronting Chinese migrants, American officers began alleging that Chinese workers' common racial physiognomy made it impossible to monitor them effectively. As Chinese employment grew in scale, so did soldiers' desire to discipline them by individuating them.[34]

Lawton's response to this crisis of racialized labor revealed both innovation and continuity in colonizers' practices for managing Chinese workforces. In early May 1899, as his division pushed north from Manila to confront Gen. Antonio Luna's forces, muddy roads that paralyzed carabao cart-based supply lines forced Lawton to hire several hundred more Chinese as porters. Yet orders he issued from Baliuag revealed his struggle to handle them. The Chinese, alleged the general, caused "much annoyance" by "wandering from the organizations to which they were attached" and "committing many minor depredations," which he left unspecified. Lawton thus required that each laborer be marked with a tag, affixed to their clothing, that "legibly marked in English" their assigned unit.[35]

This crude technology of racial-labor surveillance must have proved inadequate, given that Lawton's staff attempted to perfect it. During his division's excursion into Cavite in July 1899, Lawton's chief quartermaster, Maj. Guy Howard—son of Oliver Otis Howard, the Union general and Freedmen's Bureau director—instituted reforms. He required officers to submit monthly returns noting the precise number of "coolies" they received, discharged, or otherwise "dropped" from rolls. Howard organized this accounting system by designating each Chinese a personalized identification number and stamping it on a brass medallion for them to wear. Perhaps intentionally, this imitated the methods by which Manila's Spanish authorities and cabecillas had surveilled Chinese porters. Requiring them to pay to join the *gremio de cargadores*, they issued each man a number, noted in registration books and appearing on a badge, or *chapa numerada*, they were to wear on their right arm, fastened by a strap. As historian Jely Galang argues, just as the Chinese cargador seemed to have "lost his identity" as state and capital referred to him by a number, not a name, Howard's brass tags represented the Chinese worker as a unit of martial productivity rather than a human personality. Indeed, Howard's tags may have been a colonial precursor to the so-called dog tag, which the US Army first officially adopted during the Philippine war. In 1901, Chaplain Charles C. Pierce, directing the Morgue and Office of Identification at Manila, advocated issuing soldiers circular disks bearing a name and number to better identify them in case of injury or death. The logic of Howard's system was strictly disciplinary, however. Hoping to separate laborers from camp followers whom officers associated with petty crime, Lawton ordered arrested any Chinese man found in or near camp without the tag.[36]

Unintentionally, Lawton's rules revealed managerial chaos in the army, rooted in an ongoing struggle for sovereignty over its Chinese workforce. Implying that soldiers were poaching each other's laborers, he stipulated that no Chinese could be made to work for an American or unit other than that to which they had been originally assigned. Lawton further hinted at administrative disorder by prohibiting soldiers who lacked authority to manage a particular unit's Chinese workers from interfering "with Chinese not in misconduct." Yet Lawton also registered subaltern self-activity by warning sternly that he would hold officers accountable for the conduct of Chinese under their command. Lt. Kemp, reviewing this policy, inferred a racial knowledge of Chinese labor from evidence that these subalterns manipulated the army's confusion. When "distributed indiscriminately among large bodies of troops, with a different master every day," the Chinese, he lamented, "become lazy, lose interest and seek every opportunity or pretext to neglect their work." Injecting paternalism into Lawton's new policy of managerial devolution, however, Kemp exuded racist false hopes that organizational reform might yield true sovereignty over Chinese. "If proper interest" was "taken in their welfare," he wrote, they "develop a spirit du corps [sic]" and "doglike affection" for "superiors, responding heartily to every call."[37]

American soldiers' narratives and US Army records documenting the 1899 campaigns in Luzon confirm the speciousness of such race-based managerial fantasies. Otherwise competent officers seemed unable to determine precisely how many Chinese had been assigned to which unit, how many remained with their original organizations, and whether they were "hospital" or "transportation coolies." Such mayhem could make Chinese workforces seem more like mobs than orderly martial labor. In mid-May at Calumpit, Pvt. John Bowe, a Minnesota volunteer in Lawton's division, received orders to "herd" several hundred Chinese hired to repair a railway. "The only way we could be sure we had them," Bowe moaned in a letter home, "was to count them once in a while." "If we came within a dozen or twenty," he confessed, "we were doing well." In August, Lt. Harold P. Howard, delivering thirty-six Chinese to a road worksite at Marikina, noted that they lacked "organization," as "all talk[ed] at once." He eventually had six troops "round them up with sticks and drive them out to work like cattle." Soldiers bestowing "grotesquely humorous" and "vulgar" nicknames on Chinese further reified them as subalterns.[38]

More than military Orientalism obscured Chinese workers' humanity, however. Some Americans emphasized proletarian qualities as the source of their radical difference. In their eyes, the army's Chinese displayed none of the signs of a sedentary or propertied life that symbolized civility. In his memoir, Frederick Herman distinguished the mass of Chinese men building his highway from the stereotypical American worker by detailing their depersonalizing poverty. His perception that most "had no names" and "no homes" intersected with his observation that most had "no clothing worthy of mention." Beyond the army-issued brass tags, he noted that their only possessions were "a leather pouch worn on a belt around the middle, containing a porcelain spoon, a bundle of red prayer papers, and occasionally a few coins." Writing that most "used discarded tin cans or cocoanut shells for mess equipment," Herman as sarcastic military ethnographer claimed that "a few swanky characters among them owned a crockery rice bowl."[39] Chinese workers' meager kit thus marked them as degraded colonial labor.

Americans occasionally acknowledged other features of Chinese contract labor as a check on their sovereignty over them. Unlike litter bearers, large groups of Chinese hired for specific tasks, like highway and railroad repairs, often came with Chinese foremen who directed their work, much like workforces in Manila. To American officers, such middlemen often appeared to be an impediment to efficiency. At San Fernando in late May 1899, Capt. Charles Sawtelle regretted that "Chinese cabos, the latter speaking neither Spanish nor English," seemed "difficult to control or to direct to intelligent results." Disorganized gangs and the "impossibility of conveying through any other media than personal force the idea of what was to be done," he alleged, fouled productivity. As fighting in Luzon intensified and expanded geographically, contracts' brief terms also seemed to inhibit exploitation. Until the summer of 1899, quartermasters supporting operations near Manila typically hired Chinese porters by the operation, then returned them to the city and contractors. Yet as US columns moved farther from Manila that fall, commanders began worrying that episodic time-limited agreements eroded Chinese discipline. The army would benefit, they argued, from permanently retaining and assigning Chinese laborers according to a standardized quota.[40]

Rationalization by militarization promised more pliable racialized labor. By mid-July 1899, Maj. Guy Howard convinced Gen. Lawton that each company should maintain a minimum cohort of four Chinese, which officers could expand to a set maximum as needed. "If all the Chinamen are attained at the start of an expedition," insisted Lawton, as he sought authorization for the idea, "they prove unsatisfactory as they are not known to the organizations, frequently desert," and "arrive too late to be of service." Otis, typically parsimonious, nixed the concept of expandable cohorts, yet he approved hiring four Chinese for each company. Soon Lawton claimed that the "organization and selection" of Chinese men "known to their masters" had been the key to their effective exploitation.[41]

Lawton's aspiration to imperial mastery over Chinese workforces conveyed the racist fantasy of white American officers that their own racial aptitudes for managing nonwhite peoples was the critical factor unlocking the value of Chinese as military-colonial labor. In mid-1899, after Capt. Sawtelle supervised litter bearers for three months, he cheered that his Chinese were "controlled easily even when under fire" and did "their work faithfully" if "supervised and directed intelligently." Col. Pope may have initially thought that Chinese on Luzon had an "inferior physique and habits of ease unknown among the stalwart coolies" obtainable in China. By 1899, however, Pope felt confident that austere paternalists could exploit men whom he compared to draft animals. "When properly cared for and used with discretion," he professed, there was "no more useful kind of transportation." "The coolie can carry about half the amount of supplies that can be carried by a pack mule," enthused Pope, but "by no means requires the same amount of care." In 1900, for the *North American Review*, Maj. Louis Livingston Seaman, a volunteer engineer, shared a transimperial knowledge of Chinese martial ability that he acquired while participating in crushing the Boxer Rebellion. Lauding Europeans' use of Asian and African colonial troops, Seaman felt that Chinese soldiers' "lack of training" and "bad generalship" had led some to conclude erroneously that they were racially unfit for war. Chinese at Beijing with the British, he felt, had proved that their "innate bravery" could be activated by Anglo-Saxon commanders. Equally gifted US Army officers, he warranted, could direct such troops against Filipinos. "Like the negro, the Egyptian or the Malay," he wrote, "all the Chinaman wants is the inspiration and leadership of resolute white officers."[42]

Battle exposed such gross generalizations as an ideological facade, rooted in Orientalist and colonial racial and gender stereotypes. On the one hand, US troops interpreted what they recorded as Chinese men's fear under fire as proof of racial inferiority, relative to white soldiers they idealized as superior martial men. Some officers, perhaps uneasy about the white American enlisted ranks' mettle, made the faltering of a few Chinese into a universal racial flaw. Drawing on long-standing anglophone discourses that feminized Chinese men, they construed Chinese litter bearers' perceived cowardice as race-specific evidence of an inadequate or absent masculinity, thus using familiar tropes to represent Chinese laborers as excessively timid and self-interested. Other military Orientalists reduced their battlefield behavior to culture. Henry Hoyt ascribed litter bearers' willingness to endure combat to their society's superficial valorization of status and wealth. In one racist comic yarn, Hoyt alleged that the first Chinese he hired conquered their fear of the firing line only after a Montanan shamed them by awarding the one bearer who advanced a "medal," contrived from a leather rosette adorning a saddle.[43] Such denigrating tales implied that Chinese responded only to external reward, and were incapable of self-initiative.

If Americans' recognition of Chinese workers' courage seemed to challenge negative racial essentialisms, their racialization of Chinese labor reinforced a sense that ethnicity and culture explained such martial heroism. Soldiers often narrated litter bearers' bravery through Western tropes that styled Chinese men as impervious to pain and suffering. Lt. Kemp, in his typical hyperbole, argued that Chinese litter carriers displayed "the usual Oriental stoicism and passive indifference to danger" as they went "unhesitatingly and unostentatiously wherever led," even "to certain death." As a veteran, Joseph McManus racialized this steadfastness by attributing it to the spiritual fatalism of Confucianism, which he claimed left "no place in the skirmish line, no part of the battlefield, that they are afraid to penetrate." Chinese, he alleged, "go forward in an orderly and unconcerned manner, just as if they were stacking rice or coaling a steamer," always "firm in their conviction that no bullet or bolo can sever the thread of existence until their final hour has come." Americans therefore turned some Chinese workers' courage into a universal capacity for self-abnegation. Maj. Seaman recalled one litter bearer at Malolos in March 1899, shot in the thigh, who deposited his charge at a dressing station "as though nothing had happened." He "endured it all with the patience and stoicism of his race," wrote Seaman, surprised "that attention should be bestowed upon him at all."[44]

Some soldiers, it must be noted, attributed Chinese laborers' activity in combat to sources other than race. Some even questioned presumed racial differences when they recognized that Chinese workers' legalistic awareness of contract terms may have influenced their decisions about risking life and limb. Such comments acknowledged tacitly that Chinese might be just as rational as persons of any other ethnicity, nationality, or culture. Given litter bearers' "class and small pay," argued Maj. Crosby P. Miller, he believed they "showed commendable courage." "While they would hug the ground and shake with fear during an action," Miller maintained, "when ordered forward for work which they recognized as theirs," Chinese laborers, "with rare exceptions," he insisted, "were up and off intent upon their duties," their "fear forgotten." Capt. Harry L. Wells, an Oregon volunteer who participated in Lawton's spring 1899 drive into Bulacan province, thought litter bearers displayed "as much courage and freedom from excitement as the Hospital Corps men who accompanied them." He compared their bravery to Chinese cart drivers who he claimed "always exhibited a great deal of timidity when under fire." Yet Wells ascribed this discrepancy to workers' awareness of job responsibility. "One set of Chinamen had hired out as litter bearers, and did the work they were paid for doing"; others, he noted, had "not put any bullets in their contract." Chinese themselves confirmed such perceptions. At Manila in November 1899, cart drivers complained to China's consul that the businessman renting their labor, vehicles, and animals to US quartermasters for $4.50 a day had cut their wage by two dollars. Protesting it was hardly "sufficient to keep body and soul together," they asked him to get the Americans to stop the "contractor's tricks."[45]

White American soldiers' racialization of Chinese workers' combat behavior emerged in tandem and in tension with the self-racialization of their own martial capacities. Eager to prove their own manhood as white American men representing a rising empire in a world dominated by Europeans, some made their bravery before Asian workers into an imperial badge of ethnonational supremacy. Given a metropolitan culture that equated honorable military service and citizenship with Anglo-Saxon Protestants, white ethnic and immigrant soldiers sought to prove their masculine honor—and loyalty to their adopted nation—by distinguishing themselves from Chinese. In his memoir, Iowa volunteer Joseph Markey attempted humor by relating a story in which two Chinese assistants hesitated to join their boss, an Irish American cook, in taking food to the firing line. Asked how he found the "nerve" to push forward alone, the cook, according to Markey, replied "in a rich Irish brogue": "Do you think I was going to show 'cold feet' in front of a couple of Chinese?" If a few soldiers empathized with Chinese laborers as fellow emigrants, however, they still racialized them. In his memoir, Jacob Isselhard, a Dutch volunteer, condemned Otis's exclusion order as "gross ingratitude on our part." Yet Isselhard's remark that one-fourth of his company's men "owe their lives to the good and voluntary efforts of a 'pig-tail,' rendered in the nick of time," still identified Chinese as the subaltern other.[46]

American soldiers sometimes sympathized with Chinese workers who suffered Filipino attacks. Yet their response seemed to defend US sovereignty more than the Chinese. Chinese laborers' visible alliance with occupiers made them easy targets for nationalist insurgents and sympathizers. That Americans who reported a Chinese worker's disappearance or death did not always investigate such incidents, however, suggested their disposability as militarized labor. Yet commanders correctly viewed such incidents as assaults on US sovereignty, and sometimes they retaliated harshly. Outside Marilao in Bulacan province in late April 1899, Capt. Harry Wells sent a young Chinese porter into a barrio to find stray carabao to slaughter. The boy did not return by nightfall, and Wells and a fellow officer found him dead the next morning, his throat slashed, just 500 yards from their tent. In retribution, Wells burned the village—not exceptional as an American reaction to insurgents' guerrilla tactics.[47]

Contrary to Orientalist and nationalist discourse, Chinese workers were neither simply passive victims of US or Filipino violence nor disloyal collaborators. If their toil for American troops reflected motives to find income and safety or just obedience to brokers, their assertions of personal autonomy, criminality, and collective action signified a search for sovereignty over themselves that defied both contractors and rival state authorities. Like Chinese cargadores under Spanish rule who refused to stay at registered residences or fled Manila to escape taxation, the army's Chinese often flouted colonial control. Most commonly, they quit. Though frustrated army officers categorized this as "desertion," many Chinese clearly refused to accept the martial discipline such terminology implied. Capt. Charles Sawtelle admitted that several among the first Chinese he hired in March 1899 soon disappeared. Believing that migrants' social networks in and around Manila facilitated their escape, he proposed importing laborers straight from Hong Kong; being "strangers" in the archipelago, new emigrants, he believed, would be less likely to abscond. (Sawtelle did not acknowledge that his proposal would have violated exclusion.) Chinese quitting only increased by late 1899 when US Army operations' greater distances from Manila and tardy wage payments gave them good reasons to abscond. By July of that year, in Lawton's division alone, nearly seventy men, or 10 percent of its Chinese workforce, were reported absent without leave.[48]

American soldiers' complaints about Chinese laborers' drug use likewise captured a subterranean struggle over sovereignty, even as they energized anti-Sinicist stereotypes. Before 1898, Chinese had imported opium from Amoy and sold it through one of several state monopolies. Gen. Aguinaldo's revolutionary government continued to tax it, and Chen Qianshan lobbied him, unsuccessfully, for the right to collect its revenues. After Gen. Otis abolished the monopoly, further weakening Chen and other cabecillas, his regime taxed it as a legal import, keeping with policy in North America. Under US sovereignty, however, the opium trade and consumption at Manila and beyond expanded rapidly. Troops racialized and feminized those among their Chinese laborers who smoked opium using the same discourse that prohibitionists in the US mainland used to justify antinarcotics laws that Congress passed there by 1905. Army officers claimed that Chinese workers were less efficient without the stuff. "As soon as their opium runs out," one alleged, "they are of no use."[49]

Commanders' allegations of Chinese laborers' criminality also revealed a subaltern will to use war to self-advantage. During the 1899 campaigns, as Lawton's orders implied, Americans alleged that Chinese laborers and camp followers robbed and burned abandoned Filipino homes, and they sometimes arrested them for it. Their censures reflected a typical Sinophobic stereotype of the Chinese as "the trickiest and most cunning traffickers in the world," in one soldier's words. Yet Americans who naturalized Chinese scavenging also found it redemptive when the activity served imperial purposes. One economizing officer, essentializing Chinese as "expert looters," believed that this skill saved his army the expense of feeding them. Petty theft did not always benefit US sovereignty, however. Early in the war, American commanders suspected that litter bearers, like Chinese trailing US columns, scoured battlefields for spent rifle cartridges and sold them to insurgents. Given Americans' fears that Chinese made bolos and melted lead for insurgents, scrounging scrap showed equal entrepreneurialism.[50]

Chinese workers' marginal crimes paled before the malfeasance of brokers who enriched themselves at US sovereignty's expense. Competition in the Chinese contracting business intensified as exclusion in 1898 increased laborers' value by reducing their supply, just before war with Aguinaldo's army spiked Americans' demand for them. As Gen. Otis's order cut into Chen Qianshan's profits, new operators pounced on his loosened grip over Manila's import-export infrastructure, including Chinese workers moving the majority of trade goods in the city. Most prominent among them was Dickerson M. Carman, an American arriviste who by 1899 cornered much of Manila's transport, warehouse, and dock labor industries. Carman led a colorful if checkered life in the states. A speculator in California real estate, he had been arrested for fraud in Illinois, then attempted to attract investors in an Alaska goldfield before making his way to the Philippines. With capital furnished by San Francisco firms and East Coast manufacturers, Carman bought up Spanish firms that hauled commodities along the Pasig River and through customs, then loaded and unloaded them on the docks; he also gobbled up warehouses. According to Otis, whom Carman befriended, this "shrewd trader" made himself "indispensable to the Army," wrangling quartermaster contracts for ferrying supplies in Manila Bay and furnishing carts and drivers for field campaigns. Claiming he employed some 2,000 Filipino and Chinese a day at Manila, Carman rented out hundreds of Chinese men to US field units campaigning across Luzon between mid-1899 and early 1900.[51]

Nevertheless, Carman's profiteering nearly finished him once Otis realized he was "a great schemer and man of great cunning." In February 1901, Manila's provost marshal arrested Carman and a Spanish partner on charges that they sold arms and other goods to insurgents in Laguna province. Having facilitated ilustrados' last-ditch overtures for peace to Otis in January 1899, Carman may have milked contacts with revolutionaries to make side deals. Yet Carman was a slippery survivor. Implicated by credible witnesses, his reputation tarnished, he managed to get his case dismissed—perhaps because he hinted that he could expose Americans who had taken his bribes.[52]

Chinese collective action also revealed US sovereignty's vulnerabilities. Sometimes quitting en masse or organizing strikes, Chinese laborers for the army most likely knew that exclusion's constriction of the islands' low-waged labor pool strengthened their ability to command high wages and improve conditions. In late 1899, American army engineers accompanying Lawton's division as it pushed north from Manila recruited hundreds of Filipino, Chinese, and Macabebe men for corduroying mud-mired roads, repairing bridges, and building ferries. By late November, Lt. James C. Oakes capitulated to Chinese who "struck work and started back for Manila," first at Calumpit, then near Cabanatuan, in Nueva Ecija. Where wage labor was scarce, farther from Manila, some Chinese jornaleros bargained for higher pay. In March 1900 at Aparri, in Cagayan province, Chinese rejected a quartermaster's twenty-five-cent US daily wage for stevedoring and demanded two dollars instead. According to the *Manila American*, when the American balked and offered his lower rate to Filipinos, they "disdainfully replied that they were farmers and not coolies" and needed rice more than gold. The "trade union went to smash" when the quartermaster found troops to do the work, and the Chinese accepted his original rate.[53]

Chinese laborers' subversion of military discipline joined collectivism as factors that prompted commanders to reconsider their utility. By late 1899, American officers increasingly bemoaned that enlisted men's habitual reliance on Chinese for all sorts of tasks made them unwilling to perform fatigue duty. This was an inevitable if unintended consequence of the original logic behind their adoption: to relieve white men of manual labor in the tropics. "Where Chinamen abound" and "carry everything—and wages are low," wrote Oregon volunteer Capt. George Telfer from Manila in late February 1899, "it seems absurd to punish soldiers by making them beasts of burden" and then expect "them to fight with energy in a hot sun."[54]

Commanders sensed that enlisted men felt their exploitation of a colonial caste of racialized labor granted them an imperial wage, one absolving them of the menial toil normally expected of the rank and file. Chinese labor thus had a "demoralizing" effect on military discipline as soldiers became "apt," in one officer's words, "to develop an inability to carry a bucket of water or clean a gun." Capt. William I. Sibert rued this threat to martial hierarchy and efficiency in the summer of 1899, when his engineer detachment employed 600 Chinese men to repair the Manila–Dagupan railway. According to Sibert's biographer, he discovered this arrangement "proved to be a mistake" when he found three privates "bossing one Chinaman hard at work." "A white man," realized Sibert, "will not work alongside a strange race of people whom he is likely to look upon as inferiors." "The result of the Chinese experiment," he reflected, "was that every American soldier became a boss." By 1900, Maj. Crosby P. Miller, the chief quartermaster in the islands, noted a "tendency in the companies to require these Chinos to do all of the dirty work" in "kitchen and camp," and "handle all supplies." A Chinese workforce, he fretted, made enlisted men "think they could be called upon to do nothing but march and fight." A 1903 Manila newspaper headline on the construction of the Iligan–Marawi road, in Mindanao, posed the question simply: "Why Should American Soldiers Do Coolies' Work?"[55]

By early 1900, frustrations with shirking soldiers and the army's diminished need for large mobile workforces in Luzon as the war shifted from overland campaigns to insurgency and counterinsurgency spelled the end of the army's Chinese experiment. Its timing also augured the ascendancy of the Filipino worker in American colonial discourse and policy, as the Philippine Commission's civilizing mission embraced Filipinos' tutelage in industry and other spheres. Forever thrifty, Gen. Otis in February 1900 ordered division commanders to discharge all remaining contracted Chinese litter bearers and cargadores. Commanders who only a few months before lauded Chinese for their endurance and stoicism now criticized Chinese for their alleged inefficiency, rapid exhaustion, and criminality.[56] Such negative reviews partly reflected top-down pressure to cultivate Filipino loyalties emanating from William H. Taft's civilian commission, arriving in the islands by February 1900.

Historians typically narrate the Philippine Commission as the prime mover in Americans' project to remake Filipinos into modern industrial wage laborers. Beginning later in 1900, Taft and Fred Atkinson, his new superintendent of education, did consider adopting the vocational approach originally promoted by Booker T. Washington for African Americans in the US South through the Hampton and Tuskegee Institutes. Teaching Filipinos industry suited a global empire of racial education in which white North American and European capitalist missionaries traveled to the postslavery tropics to develop nonwhite stoop labor. In fact, US soldiers' management of Filipino workforces for war and occupation constituted Americans' very first steps to train subaltern labor for industry under the islands' new colonial regime.[57]

In late 1899, months before Taft and fellow commissioners arrived in the city, Chinese workers' militancy at Manila spurred US Army officers' interest in developing Filipino labor. In September, 200 Chinese employees at the quartermaster's depot caused a minor logistical crisis when they refused to move rations but then rejected reassignment to Malate and Caloocan. The Americans fired the Chinese and replaced them mostly with Macabebes from Pampanga—a population that proved their loyalty earlier that year while serving Lt. Matthew Batson as scouts. Throughout 1899, however, army quartermasters typically described Filipino strikebreakers and other "native" labor according to conventional colonial discourse; such men, in Gen. Otis's words, were "more or less indolent in normal conditions." One officer who complained that Filipino strikebreakers at Manila's Ordnance Department were "not systematic, rapid, or trustworthy" as laborers reported it seemed "nearly impossible to teach them these qualities."[58]

As the Taft commission's tutelary colonialism soon reconfigured the racial politics of military-colonial work, quartermasters adjusted to shifting winds, none more so than Capt. Archibald W. Butt. Butt, born in Georgia in 1865, went on to serve as secretary to presidents Roosevelt and Taft, and he gained fame posthumously after perishing in the *Titanic* disaster. Celebrated for having helped women and children into lifeboats while other first-class male passengers saved themselves, Butt symbolized a genteel masculinity sinking under the feminizing assault of industrial capitalism. Yet he won his reputation within Republican circles as an imperial quartermaster extraordinaire, first at Manila and then at Havana during its second US occupation. Though contemporaries praised Butt for his innovations in equine care—some of which perfected techniques first used by the British in South Africa during the Boer War—Butt also gained notoriety by conducting pathbreaking trials with Chinese and Filipino labor.[59]

Historians have documented how Butt made Manila's quartermaster depot a virtual laboratory for testing what he considered were the racial capacities of white American, Chinese, and Filipino labor. Yet his pseudo-scientific discovery of Filipinos' innate capacity for skilled work hinged on quasi-Taylorist assertions of sovereignty over preexisting colonial labor institutions. In September 1900, Butt took charge of the army's land transportation department and corrals, plus its hundreds of employees, including Chinese skilled craftsmen, American mechanics, and Filipino manual laborers. In reports, Butt narrated his personal campaign to develop Filipinos' industrial capacity as a progressive quest in racial-technical uplift. Though Butt in late 1900 claimed Filipinos were still at their "infancy in expert work," he found them "anxious to learn the American methods" and started training them in various crafts. Discerning their "expert workmanship" as painters, saddlers, vehicle repairmen, farriers, veterinary assistants, grounds police, and teamsters, Butt made it standing policy to replace skilled Americans and Chinese with Filipinos. Undoubtedly, one motive was cost cutting. At Manila, Chinese, possibly due to greater productivity, often earned up to 20 percent more than Filipinos in hourly wages. By substituting Filipinos in some trades, Butt claimed to reduce labor expenses by 65 percent. The secret to his success, however, lay in aggressively assaulting Filipino labor contractors' and foremen's role in production. These intermediaries, Butt believed, had a "demoralizing effect" on Filipinos who relied on them for jobs and income, even as they siphoned workers' wages.[60]

To make Filipino laborers free agents in an upstart labor market, Butt used his military authority to forcibly interpose imperial sovereignty between them and brokers. He directed Spanish and Tagalog interpreters, in his words, to "tell them, as they were paid, not to give up any of their money to anyone, and that they could always get work here." Firing padrones, Butt ordered US troops to stop workers from handing them their pay, and even jailed a grafting American supervisor. His "continuous warfare," in Butt's words, paralyzed production. Yet he claimed his campaign gradually accomplished the "complete alienation of labor and patron." Paying Filipinos first daily, then weekly and monthly, Butt established direct relations with workers, which he used to develop some into skilled higher-paid tradesmen. The captain thus recorded the US colonial state's first evidence that Filipinos could be as industrious, obedient, and technically adept as foreigners. By May 1901, Butt concluded confidently that "any labor which can be performed by Chinese can be performed equally well by the Filipinos." Compared to Chinese carpenters, foragers, and saddlers, Filipinos, he declared, were "more amenable to discipline, more imitative in their methods, more enthusiastic in their work for the work itself, and more easily assimilated by American workmen." By September 1902, after replacing all Chinese workers, and many Americans, with 950 Filipinos, Butt confidently assured Gov. Taft that the Filipino as "shiftless laborer" could be transformed into "a constant worker."[61]

As Chinese brokers and European and American employers cried that exclusion robbed them of unskilled labor, other quartermasters tested Filipinos' efficiency in manual work beyond agriculture. By April 1901, Maj. James B. Aleshire, having served in occupied Cuba, took command of the Army Transport Service at Manila and its workforce. While there, he claimed to make a heady racial discovery with coal stevedores at wharves on the Pasig River and at Cavite's Sangley Point. American predecessors used Chinese contract labor to move coal exclusively, he noted, because they assumed "Filipinos could not do this class of work." Aleshire investigated this theory by hiring Filipinos and segregating them from the Chinese in order to observe their relative efficiency by specific contract. He collected and tabulated a small heap of data indicating the number of men employed, coal moved monthly, pay rate, days employed, average tons handled per diem and per capita, and cost per ton. Aleshire alleged the average Filipino moved more coal than their Chinese counterpart—who, he noted, expected to be paid

Statement of coal handled by contracts, Chinese labor, and Filipino laborers, July 1, 1901, to June 30, 1902, army transport service, Manila, P. I.

[Rate and cost in United States currency.]

	By contract.			Day work (average).			Night work (average).			By Chinese labor.				By Filipino labor.							
	Pounds.	Rate per ton.	Total cost.	Men.	Day.	Rate.	Men.	Day.	Rate.	Cost.	Pounds.	Cost per ton.	Average per man per day in tons.	Bosses (average).			Laborers (average).			Cost.	Pounds.	Cost per ton.	Average tons per man per day.
														Men.	Day.	Rate.	Men.	Day.	Rate.				
July, 1901	16,213,200	$0.70	$5,066.69	...	...	...	...	...	...	...	...	...	...	2	5	$1.00	71	5	$0.50	$187.50	1,012,286	0.4150	Tons.Lbs. 1 988
August, 1901	22,077,441	.58	5,516.48	98	4	$0.75	43	4	$1.50	$552.00	978,850	$1.26	0.81	4	12	1.00	100	12	.50	648.50	3,031,895	.4787	1 289
September, 1901	2,720,413	.69	835.30	151	7	.75	55	7	1.50	1,370.25	4,592,000	.664	1 $\frac{2310}{2340}$	4	41	1.00	68	41	.50	1,558.00	14,421,811	.2425	2 691
October, 1901	5,967,360	.64	1,704.96	48	4	.75	100	4	1.50	588.00	2,665,600	.49½	2 $\frac{2340}{2240}$	8	24	1.00	165	24	.50	2,172.00	21,710,875	.2250	2 1,004
November, 1901	7,250,240	.56	1,815.06	...	...	...	...	...	...	...	...	...	...	10	20	1.00	153	29	.50	1,730.00	14,309,029	.2708	2 2,150
December, 1901	9,034,400	.49	1,989.40	...	...	...	...	...	...	...	...	...	...	14	29	1.00	298	29	.50	4,727.60	39,040,901	.2712	2 2,060
January, 1902	...	...	...	...	...	...	...	...	...	...	...	...	...	14	26	1.00	285	26	.50	4,069.00	28,063,936	.3239	1 1,366
February, 1902	4,928,000	.51	1,122.00	...	...	...	...	...	...	...	...	...	...	15	27	1.00	229	27	.50	3,496.50	27,919,132	.2806	1 1,971
March, 1902	10,402,560	.41	1,904.04	...	...	...	...	...	...	...	...	...	...	12	28	1.00	385	28	.50	5,726.00	33,942,482	.3778	1 806
April, 1902	4,737,600	.41	867.15	...	...	...	...	...	...	...	...	...	...	10	24	1.00	290	24	.50	3,720.00	32,130,482	.2593	2 217
May, 1902	...	...	...	...	...	...	...	...	...	...	...	...	...	10	21	1.00	265	21	.50	2,992.50	32,090,996	.2088	2 1,075
June, 1902	...	...	...	...	...	...	...	...	...	...	...	...	...	8	25	1.00	160	25	.50	2,200.00	21,729,844	.2314	2 739

Statement of Coal Handled by Contracts, Chinese Labor, and Filipino Laborers, July 1, 1901, to June 30, 1902, Army Transport Service, Manila, P.I. From US House, 57 Cong, 2d Sess., Doc. No. 2, Annual Reports of the War Department for the Fiscal Year Ended June 30, 1902, vol. 10, Report of the Philippine Commission, pt. 1 (Washington, DC: GPO, 1903), 167.

twenty-five US cents more a day. Filipinos, he insisted, could do "as much and as hard work as any laborers in the Orient."[62]

Aleshire inspired subordinates to conduct their own experiments. With pleasure, they reported that Filipinos, unlike Chinese, rarely quit, accepted Americans' technical instruction, and did not take two-hour lunches and fifteen-minute smoke breaks, or refuse to work on Sundays and nights unless paid double. Capt. F. H. Grant cheered that Filipinos also ceased observing religious holidays—a frequent source of employer complaints. He reported that Filipinos during the 1902 cholera epidemic stayed "faithfully" on the docks during a weeks-long quarantine, apparently unaware of their families' condition. If Chinese had still been there, Grant maintained, they "would have taken advantage of the occasion to demand higher wages." By year's end, Aleshire, hiring and managing more than 1,200 Filipino day laborers through Filipino bosses and paying each fifty cents a day, swore that "no workers could have worked harder or been more loyal."[63]

Not all in the US military subscribed to the idea that racialized labor could be studied scientifically. While American one questioned quartermasters' racial categories, naval officers seemed skeptical that laborers' relative ethnic or national attributes could be determined objectively. By 1903, Capt. Albert R. Couden, commanding Cavite's navy yard, employed Chinese molders but otherwise hired Filipinos. Comparing their efficiency, Couden averred, seemed a truly "futile" endeavor, given the "many variable quantities that have different values according to one's point of view." Lt. Gustave Kaemmerling, head of steam engineering, adopted a historicist standpoint. Given that Americans were "an entirely different race," he reflected, "we may be as much at fault as they" when rendering "unfavorable judgment" of Filipino labor. "Each views conditions from an entirely different standpoint," cautioned Kaemmerling, "and a position which one believes as correct as the other." Unlike "subjugated" peoples, Americans, he argued, "enjoyed all the advantages which freedom and generations of training and development have given us."[64]

Taft's commission dispensed with such subtleties. Instead, as part of their campaign to attract Filipino elites to US sovereignty, commissioners unquestioningly adopted quartermasters' opinion that Filipinos could reliably replace Chinese labor. Gen. Arthur MacArthur's ascension to the governorship in May 1900 consolidated this transition. MacArthur portrayed Chinese workers as an existential threat to Filipinos and a paternal US colonial state now dedicated to protecting and teaching them. Sensitive to Taft's nation-building mandate, MacArthur recycled mainland "yellow peril" discourse as he denounced the Chinese as an army of ruthless merchants and cheap labor, poised to undermine America's colonial capitalism. A Chinese fifth column in the archipelago, he warned, not only thwarted foreign investment; it would overwhelm Filipino wards who needed Americans' patient industrial stewardship if they were to learn how to compete in a globalizing world economy.[65]

MacArthur's attitude reflected more than just the typical Sinophobia of the US West, in which he spent so much of his post–Civil War service. The general's anti-Chinese attitude in the Philippines also reflected a localized imperative to legitimate colonial counterinsurgency as an exercise in building up a Filipino nation, rather than just destroying it. MacArthur absorbed a pro-Filipino anti-Chinese message as early as July 1899, when, as a member of Jacob Schurman's commission, he had listened to US consul Oscar F. Williams denounce the "coolie system" for denying poor Filipino men work. The next year, Gen. MacArthur as governor deployed American and Spanish colonial-era anti-coolie discourse to appeal to Filipino nativists' perception of the Chinese as an intolerably alien industrial empire within an empire. The Chinese, he vented in a July 1901 report, were an "economical army, without allegiance or attachment" to the Philippines, and dangerously "beyond the reach of insular authority." MacArthur admonished employers who called for renewed Chinese labor migration, arguing they made pacification harder. "One of the greatest difficulties attending military efforts to tranquilize the people of the Archipelago," he explained, had been Filipinos' "dread of sudden and excessive exploitation." By confirming revolutionaries' anti-American propaganda, pro-Chinese platitudes, MacArthur insisted, only fed Filipino anxieties that occupiers meant to "defraud them of their natural patrimony" and "relegate them" to "social and political inferiority."[66]

MacArthur indulged both colonial ethnonationalism and quartermasters' managerial paternalism as he attributed Filipinos' apparent faults as workers not to race, as he did for Chinese, but to environment and history. In his view, Filipinos' lack of industry was merely a legacy of a Spanish colonial regime that never developed the capacities of the colonized. Like Gen. James Smith, his Sinophobic customs chief, MacArthur believed that talk of Filipinos' deficiency as labor issued "almost exclusively from Europeans" who he deemed "exploiters, pure and simple," with "absolutely no interest in the islands beyond the immediate realization of enormous profits." Under Spanish sovereignty, he argued, low wages made Filipinos "indifferent" about "constant" work, "as their own wishes or interests were never consulted." Yet quartermasters' findings and higher wages, contended MacArthur, negated all skepticism about Filipinos' potential. To be sure, the general hinted coercion might be necessary to cultivate it. As late as 1901, he vowed to uphold Chinese exclusion, even if this meant Filipinos would have to be "judiciously pushed into work." By early 1902, however, MacArthur cited his army's recent "experience" with "public employees" to US senators as proof that the Filipino, when "properly paid," was just "like any other man" who "sticks to his job for motives of self-interest."[67]

American soldiers' vacillating judgments of Chinese and Filipino labor framed civilian successors' approach to Chinese exclusion. By July 1901, army quartermasters' reports had pushed Taft, now the Philippines' governor, to make improving Filipinos' industrial ability a central pillar of his civilizing mission. Teaching Filipinos skilled labor and the merits of wage work would not only enable Filipino elites and foreigners to more fully exploit the islands' natural and human wealth. Like roadbuilding, industrial education would enable peasants to free themselves from landowning caciques ensnaring them in debt. Compared to MacArthur, however, Taft seemed more solicitous of island employers, as Manila's Chamber of Commerce incessantly lobbied him and the US Congress to weaken exclusion. Taft entertained a Chinese guest-worker policy, advocated by Benito Legarda and other planters, that would have imported limited numbers of Chinese for agricultural work on brief contracts. Col. Enoch Crowder, MacArthur's secretary, also urged Taft to admit Chinese "mechanics" and "artisans" for limited durations, until industrial schools could train an adequate supply of skilled Filipino craftsmen. Taft endorsed Crowder's idea as a strategy for depressing what he believed were excessively high wages extorted by Chinese artisans who virtually monopolized Manila trades.[68]

Privately, however, Taft and fellow Manila Americans devised their own personal Chinese labor policy. Like many elites who preferred Chinese men rather than Filipinos for servants, Taft and senior army officers, including Col. James W. Pope, sought to reproduce imperial households by employing Chinese for cooking, cleaning, and other domestic tasks. The governor also knowingly violated exclusion by hiring Chinese directly from Hong Kong and Shanghai. Yet Taft, aspiring to higher office in the metropole, always accepted opposing unskilled Chinese as a baseline political imperative. He consistently endorsed exclusion, for both the Philippines and the US mainland, even while distancing himself from generals' rabid Sinophobia. In April 1901, Taft dismissed MacArthur as hyperbolic. Such rhetoric, he reassured US senators, made the Chinese migrant labor question in the islands "somewhat more immediately serious than anything that we saw or that I have seen there would justify."[69]

Still, Taft hewed closely to militarized knowledge as he constructed an ethnonationalist colonial labor politics that promoted Filipinos' industrial potential at the expense of Chinese. The governor frequently cited reports by Butt and other pro-Filipino army officers, lifting their ideas and careers. Under Americans' "intelligent supervision," Taft warranted, Filipinos would eventually transcend "indifference" to industrial wage labor and do it "competently, regularly, and with little or no friction." Such sentiments satisfied pro-exclusion elite Filipino Federalists. Yet even Taft's most bitter nationalist critics supported his regime's ban on Chinese migrant labor, none more so than Ilocano anarchist Isabelo de los Reyes, founder of the Philippines' first trade union—exclusively for Filipinos. Still, Taft always saw the Filipino laborer as a racial work in progress. In a December 1903 speech at Manila's Union Reading College, he defended exclusion by reminding his audience that US soldiers had shown that the Filipino did "fairly satisfactory" work when "under the control of a master who understands him." If soldiers discovered that Filipinos did not perform "so well as American or Chinese labor" in certain trades, Taft still believed they could "be made to do the work that this country requires." This pro-Filipino position never became the consensus within the army. In 1907, Maj. Livingston Seaman, reflecting social Darwinist values, still believed that "natural selection" made Chinese labor superior and worthy of importation.[70] Yet such views seemed increasingly heretical to a US colonial state that racially improved Filipinos by marginalizing Chinese.

THE 1898 ERA'S EMPIRE OF CHINESE EXCLUSION unfolded not only in the Pacific, however, but at a global scale via intraimperial flows of militarized knowledge and practice. American soldiers' assertions of sovereignty over diasporic Asian labor also sparked policymaking, as well as bureaucratic and diplomatic tensions, in North America. In early 1902, both MacArthur and Taft invoked the US Army's positive encounters with Filipino labor as they successfully lobbied Congress to permanently impose anti-Chinese immigration restrictions in the Philippines. Barring Chinese workers from the islands, they insisted, would be crucial to winning Filipinos' support for a US sovereignty resting on Filipino labor. Even Albert Beveridge, Indiana's pro-imperialist Republican senator, waxed admiringly about Butt's research at Manila as he inquired about the quartermaster's "personal devotion" to perfecting Filipinos "efficiency."[71]

The 1902 exclusion debate in Washington also marked the culmination of a worldwide military-colonial politics of Chinese labor migration that connected global Sinophobia to multiple US occupations. Historians usually date the US government's promulgation of Chinese exclusion in Cuba to May 1902, when Gen. Leonard Wood decreed it as one of his final acts as governor, as troops readied to evacuate.[72] Yet Cuba's occupation actually involved a confused and evolving immigration policy in which Yankee military governors who initially attempted to bring Cuba inside an expanded anti-Chinese wall soon retreated from exclusion. These two island societies' divergent pre-1898 histories of Chinese migration and labor influenced this temporary difference in imperial practice. Yet ascendant Sinophobia among Americans and colonized peoples produced similar anti-Chinese outcomes in both places.

Unlike counterparts at Manila in 1898, US troops occupying Cuba that year found an economy in which contracted Chinese migrant labor had virtually disappeared. Chinese first came to the island in large numbers in 1847 as indentured laborers, imported for planters after Britain's suppression of the transatlantic slave trade made enslaved Africans prohibitively expensive. Of the nearly half million Chinese migrants who entered the Americas between the 1840s and early 1880s, roughly 150,000, mostly Cantonese from the Pearl River region of Guangdong Province, survived the perilous overseas transit to land in Cuba. Doubly bound by their racialized status as degraded labor in a slave society, these indentured Chinese experienced a precarious status between freedom and bondage. Utilized on sugar plantations as well as on tobacco estates and in cigar factories, mines, and construction, they were subject to laws strongly resembling Cuba's slave codes. Working long days, and often denied the pittance of wages promised them, they suffered physical deprivation and abuse. Finding these conditions attractive, sugar planters in the US South imported Chinese laborers from Cuba well into the late 1860s. Legal reforms instituted in the 1870s, meant to grant Chinese marginal civil rights, were rarely enforced, as employers used various stratagems, some illegal, to compel them to serve beyond required eight-year terms. Less than 50 percent of indentures lived to enjoy the end of their contracts. By the late 1870s, waning hemispheric support for slavery after the Civil War, and Chinese diplomatic and Christian humanitarian protests, spurred investigative commissions and international agreements that halted the traffic.[73]

Chinese laborers faced arduous and unfree conditions until the abolition of slavery in 1886. While some Chinese men left the island, others stayed, most remaining on sugar estates; some planters, including Edwin Atkins, hired them through Chinese labor contractors. Beginning in the 1880s, they were joined by 5,000 Chinese "californianos" fleeing anti-Chinese violence in the US West. These refugees reestablished themselves as merchants, bankers, retailers, and restaurateurs, among other trades. During the 1895 war, several hundred Chinese joined insurgent ranks. By 1899, some 15,000 Chinese, nearly all men, made up roughly 1 percent of Cuba's population, living mostly at Havana and other cities. That year, some 8,000 worked as day laborers, while nearly 2,000 reported occupations as merchants or domestic servants.[74]

If footloose Chinese migrants forced US military authorities in both Cuba and the Philippines to navigate mainland immigration restrictions, imperial administrative confusion soon prompted Cuba's occupiers to relax its new anti-Chinese rules. In mid-January 1899, War Department officials, following Treasury Department guidance, ordered Gen. John R. Brooke, Cuba's new governor, to enforce US exclusion laws. Brooke's customs chief, Lt. Col. Tasker H. Bliss, and army officers acting as customs agents at Havana and fifteen other island ports complied immediately. By mid-March, Treasury officials were advising Brooke and Bliss on how to issue certificates to Chinese merchants and other "privileged Chinese" allowing them to lawfully enter North America. In mid-April, the Bureau of Insular Affairs' Circular No. 13 notified Brooke and fellow generals in the Philippines and Puerto Rico that all US immigration laws and regulations applied to "territory under government by the military forces of the United States."[75]

The challenge of regulating Chinese transit between the US mainland and Cuba, however, precipitated bureaucratic chaos. In early May, when three Chinese men on a steamship from New Orleans disembarked at Havana without the US-issued residency certificates that should have permitted them to enter the mainland, Bliss asked Washington if he should deport them to their port of departure. By claiming they left Hong Kong and passed through San Francisco, the emigrants, he noted, seemed to exercise Chinese persons' legal right to transit US territory en route to foreign destinations. Deporting these men to New Orleans, Bliss realized, would simply return them to a US port where they would likely also be denied entry, thus trapping them in an imperial anti-Chinese purgatory of immobility. In response, George de Rue Meiklejohn, assistant secretary of war, recognized Circular No. 13 as standing policy, not Brooke's January orders. He instructed Bliss to admit the Chinese migrants on the faulty rationale that exclusion laws had not yet been enforced in Cuba when they left China. When Meiklejohn asked Treasury officials how exclusion should function in US-occupied islands, though, its acting secretary advised him not to enforce exclusion in Cuba at all. Deferring to Congress and its constitutional plenary power over federal territory, he noted that legislators had not yet imposed anti-Chinese laws on any territories seized in 1898. Exclusion, the acting secretary insisted, "should not be promulgated" by the executive branch in any of them.[76]

The War Department responded by excising Cuba from the United States' newly expanded anti-Chinese empire. In early May, Meiklejohn ordered Gen.

Brooke to stop excluding Chinese from entry. "People of that race," as Col. Bliss explained a few months later, began entering the island "without restriction." On June 6, 1899, the War Department issued new regulations for Cuba that explicitly barred contract laborers but not Chinese nationals per se. The new provisions thus seemed to rehabilitate in spirit the Spanish-era treaties and laws that outlawed the so-called coolie trade. They also seemed to superficially honor the 1882 Chinese Restriction Act's original rationale as a measure barring only Chinese arriving as unfree labor.[77]

Absent any blanket racial ban on Chinese entrants, Bliss's agents struggled to enforce the anti-contract labor rules, even as they subjected Chinese to greater surveillance and control than other migrants. At Havana, Yankee army officers screened all arrivals at Triscornia, a new immigration facility the Military Government built to emulate New York's Ellis Island. Agents typically segregated Chinese from other immigrants and confined them temporarily at Triscornia's "Detention Camp"—evoking the "detention shed" used by the Pacific Mail Steamship Company on San Francisco's waterfront. They usually released Chinese after securing the "personal guarantee of responsible business people" in Havana's Chinese community, themselves endorsed by the Chinese consul general, that these arrivals had "employment" and would not become "public charges." (Originally implemented by states in North America to bar emigrants, the public charge rule had been adopted by the federal government in 1882.) Most likely, Chinese guarantors were prominent Havana merchants, organized in the Chinese Chamber of Commerce, whose *huiguan*, the Casino Chung Wah, used kinship and commercial ties with mainland China to bring family members and broker migrant labor. Such arrangements imply that some Chinese men continued to enter Cuba covertly as indentures. Yet US Army customs agents found it virtually impossible to discern the terms under which Chinese traveled to Cuba. By August 1900, Bliss, consulting a Treasury Department "Chinese Inspector" for advice, complained that "laxity in alien manifests" on US-flagged vessels transporting Chinese to Havana stymied enforcement. If immigration agents on the mainland understood "how difficult it is to arrive at the truth in many of these cases," he wrote, Bliss knew of "no effective remedy" other than simply barring all Chinese. Complaining privately that he had been "put in charge of the most corrupt service in the most corrupt city in the most (politically) corrupt country in the world," Bliss realized that brokers found creative ways to elude the anti-contract labor rules.[78]

For nearly three years, Cuba's slightly open door remained a striking anomaly in the United States' new empire of militarized exclusion. Occupied Cuba's singular position in Americans' new anti-Chinese colonial periphery produced, as in the Philippines, a peculiar conjuncture of migrant mobility and immobility. Persistent transimperial and intraimperial flows of Chinese compelled US military and civilian officials to negotiate with each other as well as Cubans and Chinese migrants, brokers, and officials for effective sovereignty over Asian labor. Irate Chinese diplomats protested whenever overzealous army customs agents "disquieted" their nationals in Cuba by rejecting Chinese whom they claimed had not broken existing provisions. By pledging to discipline his agents, however, Bliss revealed Chinese merchant brokers' ability to influence imperial US immigration administration. Yankee nativists and mainland customs officers also feared that brokers "clandestinely" used transit into Cuba, and from it, to funnel Chinese into the United States through Mexico. Indeed, Treasury investigators sometimes confirmed such smuggling. Cuban nativists fed their paranoia, including one man who claimed that a Havana "commission house" sent laborers disguised as "business men" to New York via Key West and New Orleans. Unfazed, Bliss dismissed such reports by noting that Chinese migration to Cuba declined significantly from prewar rates; during the fiscal year ending in June 1901, only 392 Chinese entered. Bliss's open tolerance for Chinese migrants irritated mainland xenophobes. Given constant complaints of labor shortages among planters and other employers, he welcomed them as a positive factor in Cuba's economic reconstruction. "Chinese laborers," Bliss wrote home, seemed "very satisfactory to the people here."[79]

That Bliss's boss, Leonard Wood, had a less forgiving attitude reflected this ambitious general's political sensitivity to metropolitan politics. Indeed, Wood's deference to Washington policymaking, as he prepared Cuba for its neocolonial position in Americans' expanding sugar kingdom, likely explained his decision to foist anti-Chinese policy on the new republic. Order No. 155, which Wood decreed on May 15, 1902, dramatically reversed the occupation's open door for Chinese labor migrants. As angry Chinese diplomats observed, the measure was more restrictive than US mainland rules. Barring all first-time entry of Chinese except for diplomats and their employees, Wood's order lacked the exemptions for merchants, students, and travelers nominally available in the Philippines (but no longer honored in North America). Perhaps more important, Order No. 155 severely limited Cubans' sovereignty over immigration policy and inflamed the island's rising nativism. Though US troops evacuated only days after Wood issued it, the Platt Amendment required that Cuba maintain all military orders until its congress saw fit to change them. By disrupting transnational networks linking Chinese Cubans to mainland China and the diaspora, Wood's ban instantly elicited an outcry from Chinese diplomats already upset that the US Congress had just made exclusion perpetual in North America and the Philippines. They noted the absurdity that Cuban officials enforcing Wood's order in June 1902 deported emigrants who left Hong Kong before he released it.[80]

Wood's exclusion policy, however, succeeded in its real intent: placating Yankee economic nationalists who had pressed Washington to bar Chinese labor from all insular territories seized in 1898. This included western sugar beet growers, represented by nativist and anti-imperialist congressional Democrats, who feared that planters in Cuba, as well as Hawai'i and the Philippines, would import lower-waged Chinese to produce cheaper sugar inside newly expanded US tariff walls. Their voices grew louder in 1901 as US and Cuban diplomats deliberated on a trade reciprocity treaty, which, when ratified two years later, guaranteed Cuban sugar a protected market in the states. Democratic senators' demands that Cuba adopt Chinese exclusion before any vote could be taken on the sugar treaty likely catalyzed Wood's decision to cement Order No. 155. In early 1902, while Wood lobbied congressmen to approve the treaty, Elihu Root, feeding him news of their negotiations, warned that sugar beet Democrats were threatening to scuttle the deal. Wood carried this economic exclusionary impulse to the Philippines. As the Moro Province's first governor, he defended laws against large foreign landholdings in Mindanao by arguing that planters' inevitable demands for Chinese labor would, if satisfied, inhibit the development of Muslim wage labor necessary for its civilization.[81]

In Cuba, as in the Philippines, occupiers' anti-Chinese mandate reinforced insular nativism and the racist populist economic nationalism energizing it. After 1902, as the sugar industry expanded rapidly, especially in Oriente, estate owners perennially claimed that labor shortages crippled production. Yet the ethnic logic of Order No. 155 became the ideological predicate by which a growing number of Cubans opposed Black Caribbean contract labor. In the aftermath of slavery and emancipation, Cuba's census, and its constitution's citizenship and naturalization clauses, differentiated African and Asian-descended Cubans from white Cubans in ways that encouraged Cubans to conflate color with foreignness. Echoing nineteenth-century creole forebears and occupiers including Leonard Wood, republican elites expressed desires to maintain the island's white majority while endorsing white migrants as the solution to alleged labor crisis. In 1906, as Cuba's congress debated legislation to codify Wood's exclusion order, nationalists invoked Chinese coolies as the degraded antithesis of the free white bracero. Legislation did not explicitly bar Chinese or Black migrants but allocated

$1 million to subsidize "colonization" by white Europeans. Massive emigration from Europe, however, eventually alarmed nativists; by 1930, 800,000 *gallegos* had arrived from Spain and the Canaries. During these same years, by contrast, very few Chinese found their way into Cuba.[82]

Inevitably, early republican immigration politics evolved in the long shadow of American exclusionism. During the second US intervention, Chinese diplomats at Havana pressed Cuban and US military authorities to permit Chinese to transit the island and urged full rights for Chinese merchants to enter Cuba's ports, but to no avail. In 1909, when US troops evacuated, Cuban congressmen rejected Chinese officials' requests that they renounce restriction. Brokers and smugglers still found ways to import labor, often by bribing and deception. Yet an increasingly explosive racial politics of contract labor, exacerbated by planters' relentless push for low-waged labor and Yankee occupiers' anti-Chinese stance, engulfed African-descended Cubans and migrants. By 1912, sugar planters' lobbying for permission to import Haitians and West Indians converged with Afro-Cubans' growing demands for legal and political equality. White Cuban racial backlash culminated at Oriente in violent repression of the PIC—the only party in the early republic to condemn opposition to Afro-Caribbean migrant labor. Only after this anti-Black pogrom did eastern sugar planters persuade President José Miguel Gómez to lift occupation-era anti-contract labor provisions. Over the next two decades, 300,000 Haitian and West Indian braceros arrived, almost all working on eastern sugar plantations. Though employers differentiated this "guest worker" policy from the indentured Chinese of the past, nativist Cubans styled both peoples as unassimilable foreigners.[83]

By 1909, Americans' wars and occupations had decisively reconfigured the politics of Chinese migration, labor, and race across the new US empire. In some ways, if only briefly, their army's employment of Chinese labor since 1898, and their government's loose immigration policy in Cuba, seemed to challenge a rising tide of anti-Chinese politics in the mainland and Spain's former colonies. Yet Americans' desire to win Filipino and Cuban support for US sovereignty pushed military and civilian authorities to impose anti-Chinese policies that satisfied both metropolitan and colonial interests at Chinese migrants' expense. This politics' intraimperial currents found a curious parallel in questions of sex and work that entangled American soldiers, and Cuban and Filipino women and men, in struggles over the most intimate realms of everyday life.

CHAPTER SIX

Military Necessities
Reproducing Sovereignty in the Colonial Sexual Economy of War

Cuban women who unwittingly touched off a riot at Cienfuegos in late June 1899, when they barred Yankees from a house of prostitution, had little control over their labor or lives, much less their occupied island. Yet Cuban and American men's clashing claims on Cuba—and on its most marginalized and vulnerable women—almost made such an incident inevitable. Like comrades at Havana, insurgents at Cienfuegos, angered by the "indifference" of an "intervening power" that refused to feed them or fund their back pay, bristled when US troops excluded them from ceremonies marking Spain's transfer of sovereignty to the United States. Such men, observed sugar planter Edwin Atkins, included Afro-Cubans, among them his former slaves, radicalized by war and revolution. While landowners could not "get enough men to run the estates," he complained to US Army commanders, "insurgents and idlers" nightly filled Cienfuegos yelling "Cuban Liberty," "followed by a mob crying 'down' with everything." Horrified, Atkins noted that a "dignified" white Yankee officer had been spotted "with a negress on his arm" at a "mixed" insurgent parade welcoming Gen. Máximo Gómez to the city on the February anniversary of the Grito de Baire, the declaration that commenced Cuba's final war for independence. Such scenes, he wrote President William McKinley, signaled "a condition bordering upon anarchy."[1]

Anarchy indeed seemed imminent at Cienfuegos, a city of roughly 50,000 people, as masculine ideals of honor exacerbated workers' disputes with the occupiers. In mid-April, its US Army quartermaster inflamed local opinion when he hired men to break a strike among Cuban masons he employed. Then, in mid-May, the quartermaster's refusal, or inability, to pay Cuban dockworkers moving military supplies, also recently unionized, ignited unrest. After two American soldiers facing a crowd of 1,000 Cubans seized weapons from a police officer and two veterans, the Yankees alleged the police chief arrived and declared, in a "very loud and insulting" way, that he would not let foreigners arrest his men or confiscate their arms. He dispersed the throng, but the next morning US troops caught the emasculated Cuban cop trying to "assassinate" the American who had disarmed him. Gen. José Miguel

Gómez, Santa Clara's civil governor, warned US counterparts that "trouble between soldiers and the people" might occur "any day." A "spark," feared Atkins, could "start a blaze" that "might be hard to put out."[2]

That spark, sex, flashed on June 24, during the city's festival for its patron saint, San Juan, as thousands were "masquerading," playing sports, and "enjoying themselves, on foot, horseback, and in carriages with the greatest good nature," according to one observer. The trouble started downtown when women at one of several bordellos on Santa Clara Street, near the waterfront, refused entry to three inebriated white American civilian quartermaster employees. Enraged, the men kicked the door, bashed it with a club, and beat a Chinese man who tried to intervene. As the Americans resisted arrest by police and armed civilians who rushed to the scene, the Cubans hit them with the flats of machetes, yelling "*cabrones!*" and knocked one to the ground. At that moment, Capt. Eben B. Fenton rolled up in a carriage. Seeing two countrymen crying for help, Fenton had them climb aboard and then sped away, crashing through a crowd of 200 Cubans, many in "gala dress." Shots fired at the runaway vehicle alarmed Lt. George DeGrasse Catlin, commanding a detachment nearby, slated to pay off 250 Cuban veterans the next day. After Catlin disarmed a Cuban police officer firing at the carriage and ordered troops coming to his rescue to open fire, the alcalde arrived with Higinio Esquerra y Rodríguez, a Cuban general whom occupiers had made jefe of the local Rural Guards. Before Esquerra dispersed the mob, a policeman and a Spanish bystander were shot, the latter mortally. Gen. James Wilson tried appeasing incensed Cubans by remanding the three malefactors to local courts and court-martialing Fenton and Catlin. Officers judging Fenton recognized the event's imperial aspects and admonished Fenton that he would have never "presumed" to so "interfere" with police in the states.[3]

If Americans handled the riot as a legal liability, Cuban men perceived it as a contest between national patriarchs over sexual access to Cuban women. In the early 1960s, centenarian Esteban Montejo, speaking to an anthropologist, recalled the event for his role in having defended feminine honor against Yankee insults. Montejo, a former slave and plantation laborer who served with Esquerra during the war, remembered that he had joined other "mambíses" that day in patrolling downtown Cienfuegos. White American soldiers using anti-Black slurs, he explained, often irritated respectable citizens while they searched for sex. "Dressed in khaki, pressed and neat, but almost always drunk," such men, he said, would "approach the houses," "see a pretty woman in the window or in the doorway, go up to her, and say, 'Fucky, Fucky, Margarita,' and in they would go." Seeing them "fooling around with the women, patting their behinds and laughing," he confessed, made him "hot under the collar." Still smoldering with machismo, Montejo reminisced that his band "had to wave our machetes in the air at a few American soldiers, scoundrels who wanted to have all the *criollas* like they were meat in the market." The Yankees, boasted Montejo, "never bothered any" women "there again."[4]

Montejo accurately insinuated that belligerent Yankees started the affair. Yet he passed over the fact that the women who also precipitated the riot had been at a "disreputable house" of "ill-fame," as US soldiers described it.[5] Montejo thus downplayed Cuban prostitutes' contribution to anti-imperial resistance, even as he condemned occupiers for trying to monopolize their sexual labor. Cuban men, he implied, wanted *criollas*, too. Like his Yankee antagonists, therefore, Montejo made sex workers passive objects in male-centered struggles over national sovereignty. Both conceding and veiling the existence of a subterranean sex industry, Cuban memory and US military law alike obscured colonized women's place in the work of empire.

In the imperial conjuncture of 1898, Cuban and Filipino women and their work occupied a fraught subaltern position within a uniquely colonial iteration of what one historian has conceived as "the sexual economy of war." As the San Juan riot suggests, imperial conflict over sovereignty that turned partly on gendered ideals of nationality and race often invested tropical women's sex and labor with incendiary political significance. Yet this incident also showed how poor Cuban women and Filipinas themselves shaped the course of US warfare and colonial rule. In war-torn and occupied islands, gendered and militarized class relations became a field of imperial power. American soldiers' and Cuban and Filipino women's and men's attempts to control colonized women's sexual activity and work, and their debate over its economic value and political and social meaning, informed broader colonial cultures of race, family, and nation.[6]

American soldiers in 1898 intervened in island societies where bourgeois and Catholic colonial values prescribed that women had to perform most work needed to maintain families and households, and male labor—what feminist scholars theorize as "social reproduction." Cuban and Philippine women expected to do the work of childbearing, care, and producing homemade goods allowed men to toil outside the home, often for cash. Yet war and occupation implicated colonized women's sex and work in the production and reproduction of conflicting claims to sovereignty itself. The gendered labor of empire thus created tense sexual and economic ties between two kinds of subalterns, women and soldiers, both of whom US Army commanders strained to control. This difficulty became most evident in their efforts to ensure soldiers' health by adopting Spanish and nationalist men's techniques for regulating prostitution.[7]

Given late nineteenth-century gender and class norms, however, few in these islands or the United States recognized prostitution as labor. Anticolonial men, making their putative nations metonyms for the idealized and pure colonial woman meriting male protection, excluded prostitutes from a national community often imagined as a family. Constructing their masculinity through and against Spanish empire, Cuban and Filipino men expressed Iberian values in nationalist discourse that invoked traditional, Christian, and bourgeois sexual mores. Expected to protect older and weaker dependents, including women and children, male revolutionaries venerated chaste and loyal women who served their country in marital and maternal roles, not combat. Valorizing monogamous heterosexuality in the private sphere of patriarchal families, however, they saw women's sexual commodification in a male-dominated public sphere as a degrading and immoral sign of colonial corruption and exploitation. Legitimating but concealing women's domestic work at home, these norms assumed the moral depravity of *mujeres publicas* in part because prostitutes divorced women's sexuality from the reproduction of families. In 1898's aftermath, Progressive Era American women's activism in the US metropole influenced many Cuban and Filipino feminists. But even as these women demanded equality with men in public life, they still accepted that women's natural role in society rested in their reproductive functions as monogamous wives and mothers.[8]

Yet the wars and occupations that made Americans' new empire implicated female subalterns' sex and labor—and gendered relations surrounding them—in larger struggles for power. In both Cuba and the Philippines, male anticolonial activists hailed women as "the moral center of national sovereignty," in one historian's words, even as some women challenged received patriarchal ideals by taking active roles in revolt. In colonial societies riven by class as well as other forms of hierarchy and identity, however, nationalist men never monopolized women's sexual activity or sexual labor. Subaltern women asserted a sort of sovereignty over their own sexual and reproductive labor in ways that did not always signal nationalist consciousness, intent, or loyalty. In turn, Cuban and Filipino nationalist men endorsed disenfranchising women and prohibiting prostitution as markers of modernity. They condemned prostitutes as the antithesis of civilized nationhood, especially when US troops patronized them.[9]

Imperial sexual economies in Cuba and the Philippines generated divergent and convergent outcomes, as American commanders adopted colonial practices and adapted and internalized them as they moved from one occupied island to the next. As US military medicine laid the foundations of American colonial public health, chaotic and dangerous sexual encounters between US soldiers and colonized women prompted their officers to experiment with various techniques for regulating sex and disease. American commanders concerned more with the day-to-day need to reproduce the labor of their male military personnel than moral rectitude quickly revived Spanish-era regulations that targeted prostitutes for biological surveillance and discipline. When this failed to suppress venereal disease (VD) in the ranks, army doctors redirected sexual policing against their own troops. Eventually, a military intent on managing intercourse between occupied women and occupying men forced both to carry the imperial burdens of public health.[10]

THE US ARMY'S INTERNAL REGULATION of sex prior to 1898 ensured that imperial formation that year would integrate problems of military and sexual labor. Policies that differentiated soldiers' marital rights by rank practically compelled enlisted men to engage in illicit sex. While the army permitted officers and sergeants to be married, or marry during service, it required enlisted men to be single when they joined the army and prohibited them from marrying while in it. Those who did wed were barred from reenlisting and faced court-martial if found to have concealed marriage at the time of enlistment or reenlistment. While these rules relieved the army of dependents, they also made military service less desirable, as many civilians already felt enlisted men were not paid enough to be breadwinners. The anti-marriage policy thus forced sex-seeking soldiers to patronize prostitutes (on the US frontier, often vulnerable poor women of color), marry or form common-law marriages in secret, or marry openly and face the consequences. By 1903, even junior officers were discouraged from taking vows.[11]

Spanish authorities in Cuba prior to 1898, by contrast, only regulated soldiers' sex indirectly as they attempted to preserve their physical health by policing prostitutes. At Havana in 1873, during the Ten Years' War, Spanish officials and Cuban academics, inspired by practices recently devised in France, drafted "Special Hygiene" codes, requiring the medical inspection and disciplining of sex workers. Organized in the city government, the Special Hygiene agency received a mandate to register all prostitutes and brothel owners, usually madams, for fees funding its work. Physicians conducted biweekly pelvic exams of all registered women, recorded results, and compelled symptomatic women to enter public hospitals for treatment. Like the British Contagious Diseases Acts, then, Cuba's Special Hygiene rules fixated on female sex workers as the source and vector of sexual illness. Designed to protect men's health, they especially stigmatized brothel-employed women, even while they punished with fines those prostitutes who failed to register. Building on efforts at Havana during the 1850s to geographically confine the legal sex trade to a so-called tolerance zone, new regulations further stigmatized women by promoting bourgeois norms of social propriety in public life. Havana police were authorized to fine, arrest, incarcerate, or expel sex workers who gathered in brothel doorways, solicited clients on the street or through brothel windows, or rode in open carriages. By 1877, authorities responding to soaring VD rates among Spanish soldiers revised regulations to make sexual commerce more legible to surveillance. Reducing fees for brothels in less populated areas, they now forced women to carry a "sanitation card," indicating their health, and required them to show it to hygiene staff, police, and clients upon request.[12]

Colonial officials never consistently enforced Special Hygiene rules, nor did they institute them uniformly across the island before the 1895 war threw their operation into disarray. Though authorities in Spanish-garrisoned areas sometimes maintained hygiene protocols, the wartime policing of prostitutes, whose ranks expanded with *reconcentrado* women struggling to survive, inspired nationalist protest. At Cienfuegos in March 1898, Edelmira Guerra, leader of Esparanza del Valle, one of Cuba's many all-female separatist clubs providing relief for *reconcentrados*, petitioned Autonomist Party officials to stop disciplining women who took up the sex trade. Intrusive pelvic exams and punitive isolation and treatment, Guerra protested, unjustly slandered women who preferred a more "honorable" trade and plied it only by necessity.[13]

American troops who first encountered this colonial sexual economy's remnants at Oriente, however, experienced it as a void of regulation. Occupying Santiago in August 1898, state volunteers in Gen. William Shafter's Fifth Corps responded to victory against Spain with paroxysms of postwar drinking and sex—and associated sporadic violence. White Southern infantry in "immune" regiments, replacing Shafter's departing army, joined an army portrayed in the metropole as chivalrous patriarchs liberating a feminized Cuba. Yet these men seemed to suffer an imperial crisis of masculinity after they missed a chance to prove their patriotic manhood in combat. They compensated by trying to impose New South racial and sexual norms and hierarchies on a society relatively more tolerant of racial mixing. White immunes provoked fisticuffs, sometimes with insurgents already disarmed at US checkpoints, while trying to enforce a Jim Crow color line in bars and brothels. A few, breaking into Cubans' homes, were court-martialed for rape. Seeking to prevent further incidents and preserve his nation's benevolent self-image, Shafter urged Washington to remove and disband the white immune regiments. Anticipating the army's turn toward temperance in 1898 era, the general also strictly regulated alcohol sales, which officers believed had been fueling soldierly disorder.[14]

Yankee commanders' response to sexual chaos at Oriente in late 1898 also reflected racist metropolitan and colonial conventions. Shafter and subordinates typically attributed white immunes' unruliness to poor leadership and indiscipline as wartime citizen-soldiers. White officers blamed African American garrison troops' alleged sexual improprieties, based more on their racial and class backgrounds than on the military culture. Black immunes, also from the US South, commanded by white officers, and all-Black Illinois and Kansas volunteer regiments bore the heavy racial and sexual burdens of both cultures' histories of slavery and segregation. African American commanders and their supporters, eager to win equal citizenship by serving in a war that seemed to bury sectionalism, adhered strictly to middle-class values of respectability. To Americans and Cubans, they represented themselves as Christian patriarchs who protected vulnerable women and their virtue. Narratives emphasizing Black soldiers' polite courtship and marriage with Oriente's women, however, stood in stark contrast to evidence that some joined white soldiers in stimulating a booming market for sex.[15]

The US Army's commanders reacted to this sexual commerce and its biological threat to their ability to reproduce healthy military labor by recapitulating metropolitan and colonial spatial strategies for regulating prostitution. These included "red light districts" by which civil and military authorities in the late nineteenth-century United States limited the sex trade to discrete neighborhoods, not unlike Cuba's "tolerance zones." By late November 1898, Gen. Leonard Wood, partnering with Santiago's new municipal government, ordered Maj. George Barbour's sanitation department to identify all brothels in the city before forcing them into a single district. Yet such efforts simply displaced sexual exchange to other neighborhoods, as officers griped that bars and brothels serving soldier clienteles were mushrooming beyond city limits. Similar measures the next year, in other garrisoned towns, yielded similar results.[16]

Poor Cuban women's need for cash in a shattered postwar society and economy ensured that suppressing or zoning bars and brothels did little to reduce supply in markets bustling in response to US soldiers' insatiable demand. At Oriente in 1899, according to the census, only about 4 percent of its

164,000 female inhabitants earned wages; a slightly higher rate of women of color, about 8 percent, earned money outside the home. As Wood and other occupiers early that year halted food relief, women without male breadwinners were forced to find work to support themselves and their children. In Oriente, the war widowed roughly one in six women; in 1899, one widow existed for every two married women. Many such poor women made ends meet by joining the large number of Cubans engaged in domestic or "personal service" of some kind. According to the census, more than one in five of all wage-earners in Cuba that year, men and women, were domestics. (By 1907, this ratio declined slightly to one in six). Most Cuban women, married or not, who worked outside their own homes for money in this era thus toiled in others' homes. In Cuba at large by 1899, two-thirds of all women earning wages did so in domestic service, the majority of them unmarried; in Oriente that year, slightly fewer women, or half of all female wage-earners, performed reproductive labor, most as laundresses or servants. Domestic labor in Cuba was also deeply racialized; in Oriente, the majority of *lavenderas* were women of color. In the east, as elsewhere on the island, most wage-earning women of color worked in domestic service, often for white Cubans; by 1907, three of four women of color workers in Oriente were *domésticas*. Waged reproductive labor in the east was also strongly associated with Afro-Cuban women; by 1907, just over 80 percent of all domestics in the region were women of color. In 1898, their ranks included Gen. Antonio Maceo's mother and sisters, who eked out an existence on the deceased general's farm, near San Luis, by washing Black Kansas volunteers' uniforms.[17]

The racialized hierarchy of reproductive labor in occupied Cuba stoked intersecting national myths, rooted in American and Cuban histories of plantation-based slavery, that constructed the African-descended woman as the universal domestic worker. In fact, most domestics in Cuba in this era were men, and many *domésticas* were white; in 1899, 65 percent of all white emigrant women in Cuba then earning wages, most from Spain, worked in Cubans' homes. Yet the racial politics attached to reproductive labor's physical and emotional intimacies inside households in the United States and Cuba also sexualized Black wage-earning Cuban women and made them vulnerable to the sexual degradation with which many Cubans and Americans associated prostitution, if not also slavery. In fact, experiential links between women's commodified domestic and sexual labor was discernable in some female Cuban prostitutes' life cycles. In 1902, Cuban officials at Havana noted that more than a third of Cuban prostitutes surveyed there reported prior employment as domestics, usually earning the lowest wages available to women on the island. Yet a racial and sexual politics that both universalized the domestic Cuban worker as an Afro-Cuban woman and strongly associated them with the island's sexual economy implied to some Cuban and American men that Black women were more sexually available than other women on the island. It also connected Cuban households as sites of hygienic labor, performed by female domestics, with the militarized colonial medical regulation of prostitutes. By the end of the first US occupation, Cuban doctors even came to associate prostitution and VD in certain Havana neighborhoods with the presence of Chinese men, some of whom served as domestics in city households.[18]

Real and imagined links between domestic and sexual labor in North America and Cuba played out early in the US occupation, first at Oriente, in late 1898. Hired by American troops to clean barracks and military hospitals and wash laundry, Cuban women proved essential to the US Army's capacity to reproduce the martial labor it required to occupy the island. A few lavenderas even embodied imperial continuity in military-colonial social reproduction. Having survived the independence war by washing Spanish soldiers' uniforms, or seeking laundry work from planters including Edwin Atkins, some did the same for Yankee soldiers. Though lavenderas earned slightly more than women in tobacco manufacturing, match factories, or paper mills, a few augmented their income by selling sex to troops, not unlike laundresses on frontier posts in the US West before 1898. Blurring lines between public exchange and private sex, these lavenderas' sexual entrepreneurialism frustrated commanders who feared their effect on discipline and soldiers' health. Outside Santiago in October 1898, when Col. Herbert Sargent suspected that laundresses in his camp were engaging in "illicit" activity, he banned them from tents and ordered officers to escort them at all times.[19]

Fearful that sexual traffic was spiking VD rates in the ranks, US Army officers reinforced prohibitionist and spatial segregation strategies by resurrecting the colonial medical regulation of prostitutes. Army medical officers who discovered a moribund Special Hygiene agency at Havana in December 1898 at first abolished the office, criticizing it for inefficiency and corruption. By January 1899, however, the new Military Government, desperate to reduce VD rates, resurrected Havana's old Special Hygiene system, making only slight adjustments. To generate more revenue to fund inspections, the Americans raised registration fees. They also prohibited alcohol sales in brothels to curb recurrent disorder involving soldiers. Though the new US regime seemed to mandate these policies for the entire island, commanders throughout Cuba, like their predecessors, instituted them ad hoc. Lackluster municipal Cuban officials, with few resources, rarely enforced the Yankees' revised Special Hygiene rules. Appreciating their military rationale, American occupiers understood them as "a measure of hygiene" and not "reformation."[20]

The US Army's doctors refracted regulation's patriarchal and bourgeois logic as they sought to reproduce soldierly labor by policing Cuban women. Alarmed that red-light districts did not seem to reduce VD, some enthusiastically endorsed the hygiene rules. By July 1900, Maj. Lawrence C. Carr, a surgeon in Oriente, reported infection rates there much higher than those in the states. Adding empire to regulation's rationale, however, Carr attributed sexual disease to Cubans at large, both prostitutes and male clientele. Painting Yankee troops as innocent and naive, Carr suggested their "distance from home" and "novel and unusual surroundings" was exposing them to syphilis and other ailments rooted in a "laxity of morals" and "want of cleanliness" among Cuba's "lower classes." Failing to "check the growing evil," Carr ordered Santiago officials to reorganize its moribund Special Hygiene office. By October, its staff registered and examined some 209 women.[21]

Regulation at Santiago generated data that suggested demographic similarities and differences between its prostitute population and those in other cities. In age and ethnicity, registered women in Oriente closely followed counterparts at Havana. At Santiago, nearly all women were thirty years of age or younger; 65 percent were white, 27 percent mestiza, and 8 percent Afro-Cuban. Their geographic origins, however, reflected Oriente's uniquely magnetic pull on migrants. Just over half of registered women claimed to be from the east. Some 17 percent hailed from Puerto Rico, while lesser numbers came from Santa Clara, Havana, and Matanzas provinces, 5 percent from Spain, and a handful from Mexico and Jamaica. Records also hinted at ties between domestic and sexual labor, as five women reported dual employment as washerwomen, seamstresses, ironers, and household maids. Cuban officials proudly reduced their numbers. In November 1901, Mayor Emilio Bacardí recommitted the city to biological and spatial policing. Within a year, Special Hygiene staff claimed they had significantly reduced the city's prostitute numbers, if not VD rates.[22]

American commanders, however, only gradually realized that spatial and medical regulation that reached only those women who were most visible to surveillance was failing to suppress VD. Covert prostitution's rapid growth in occupied Cuba thus exposed the outer limits of their army's effective sovereignty over subaltern sex and labor. Costly, embarrassing, and punitive, Special Hygiene rules motivated some women to work as "independent" or "clandestine" prostitutes. They evaded state authority by operating alone, in private and unadvertised domiciles, for competitive prices. Discreet and decentralized, this underground sex market vexed Yankee and Cuban officials alike. In July 1899, Maj. Joseph H. Dorst, seeing that not a single licensed brothel existed at Trinidad, in Santa Clara province, blamed its garrison's rising VD rates on a flourishing but unregulated flesh trade. "Not strictly professional prostitutes," its *clandestinas*, he claimed, were "scattered about singly in respectable houses." If they "cohabit[ed] with men," Dorst reported, they did not seem to "depend" on it "for a living."[23]

Yankee occupiers registered their frustration at having to share sovereignty with Cuban officials whom they criticized for not doing enough to suppress casual sex markets. Dorst lamented that Trinidad seemed to be "full of loose women, leading apparently respectable lives," the "immorality" of whom could not be "legally proven," but "with whom a taxed house of prostitution cannot compete." Clandestinas, he believed, continued to risk US soldiers' health only because Cuban police failed to properly monitor and treat them. At Manzanillo, in Oriente, in early 1901, a US Army surgeon, believing that Cuban authorities there regularly inspected registered women, attributed its garrison's dangerously high VD rates to prostitutes "not under police surveillance." Cubans rebuffed the allegation, replying that an "insignificant number" of licensed women, who served only Cuban men, were infected. Challenging empire, if not patriarchy, they blamed disease on Yankee commanders, who they insisted could improve enlisted men's health if they prevented them from sleeping with *clandestinas* in nearby homes.[24]

Like their Spanish predecessors, US Army officers explained ineffective regulation as a function of pervasive corruption. Events at Cienfuegos illustrated occupiers' fears that they could not depend on Cuban bureaucrats to help them police Cuban women. In March 1899, its city council, now acting under US auspices, reorganized the Special Hygiene agency; by September, staff registered some 200 to 250 women. The imperial politics of prostitution continued to be explosive. That same month, an inebriated US soldier in Cienfuegos nearly triggered another riot when he reportedly made "indecent proposals" to a Cuban woman on the street.[25]

Labor struggles in Cienfuegos, intersecting with problems of sexual commerce, also exposed graft. In February 1900, when lightermen at the port took advantage of the sugar harvest to strike for higher wages, sparking sympathy walkouts, local merchants and planters refused to settle. Gen. Wood's decision to dispatch his aide, Lt. Col. Hugh Scott, to investigate, and Gen. James Wilson's threats to send more troops, spurred municipal officials into arbitrating an agreement that significantly raised workers' pay. Edwin Atkins's allegations that the alcalde and lightermen's union president had schemed to secure votes in upcoming local elections, however, prompted Wood to ouster them. That summer, following more labor unrest and politicking, one of the city's factions accused incumbents of being anti-Americans who "abused" prostitutes for financial gain. Wood sent Scott again, this time to audit the vote. Only the next year did army investigators shed light on the sexual accusations. Two-thirds of the city's Special Hygiene revenue, they discovered, traditionally went to the provincial government; the rest had gone to city charities and the civil hospital. Yankee officers' curiosity was piqued, however, when Cubans protested their warnings that the city hygiene agency was required to keep all fees. Finding discrepancies in accounts, the prying Americans reported that Santa Clara's governor, Gen. José Miguel Gómez, had been pocketing half of all hygiene receipts as a "perquisite of his office."[26]

Occupied Cuba's sexual-disciplinary state always maintained Cuban women as its primary target. Yankee officers rarely entertained the idea that soldiers, not just women, warranted medical surveillance. A few probative army doctors, learning that many troops arrived in Cuba already infected, conceded regulation's flawed double standard. Like Cuban prostitutes, many enlisted men were caught hiding infections to avoid personal embarrassment, painful treatments, and angry superiors. Some surreptitiously sought help from Cuban doctors and pharmacists—"a serious menace" to their health, according to a skeptical Yankee surgeon. More than anything, they feared medical discharges, documented in service records, that might disqualify them for reenlistment and pensions. In a pacified Cuba, however, where healthy personnel seemed less urgent, most commanders showed leniency. A few devised practices that the rank and file found harsh, intrusive, and humiliating. Some inspected troops' genitalia in parade. Others posted infected men's names in barracks and denied them passes if they did not identify the woman, or women, with whom they had slept.[27]

Occupiers' paternal regard for male health extended only to US soldiers, however, not Cuban men. Maj. Frank Ives, an army surgeon examining troops weekly in Matanzas and Santa Clara provinces, quarantined infected troops so they would not "contaminate a woman" and thus "indirectly be the means of infecting others"—namely, other enlisted men. Officers also tended to oppose dishonorable discharges for VD, believing it injured self-esteem and harmed soldiers' future reproductive prospects. Among white Progressive Era Americans reared on social Darwinism, a desire to ensure that young veterans had the capacity to reproduce families converged with fears of Anglo-Saxon "race suicide." Their gentle touch, however, also reflected the lingering grasp of an individualistic Protestant moral ethos that advocated voluntary abstinence as the best means to protect martial bodies. In September 1902, when Maj. Valery Havard traveled to Brussels to attend the Second International Conference for the Prevention of Venereal Disease, he conveyed the pragmatic spirit of most medical officers in Cuba. Havard reviewed statistics that showed Special Hygiene rules had reduced VD in the ranks, even as he acknowledged that regulations remained imperfect and controversial. The major thus endorsed "moral prophylaxis," rooted in troops' "conscience" and "Christian character," as his army's best weapon in the war on sexual illness.[28]

AS AMERICAN COMMANDERS IN CUBA endorsed both soldiers' voluntary abstinence and the medical regulation of prostitutes, contingencies of war and colonialism in the Philippines pushed counterparts there to shift the onus of sexual policing from subaltern women to their own troops. This divergence in imperial practice largely reflected the urgent physical demands of a counterinsurgency war that placed a premium on reproducing healthy manpower. Yet sexual policing in the US military also derived from the sociocultural and biological dynamics of soldiers' lasting presence in the archipelago as a permanent colonial garrison. The longer Americans negotiated sexual-labor relations with Filipinas, the more they linked the reproduction of healthy martial labor to questions of sex and sovereignty.

Like comrades in Oriente during late 1898, US troops at Manila initially ignored preexisting local regulatory precedents devised to protect Spanish troops from diseases circulating in its burgeoning urban sex industry. By the 1850s, as the city's trade and population boomed, the number of women selling sex there, and sexual disease across Luzon, also grew. Agricultural commercialization, disrupting rural society, pushed thousands of young women to migrate to Manila to secure work that could support them and their poor landless families at home. Yet with few opportunities to earn wages in a merciless market economy dominated by men who barred women from most occupations and formal education, some of these women turned to prostitution. Usually single, childless, and illiterate indios who lost one or both parents, young women becoming prostitutes at Manila struggled to earn adequate income as seamstresses, laundresses, cigar rollers, shopkeepers, or domestic servants, all less lucrative than sex. While some prostituted themselves voluntarily, in a nominal legal sense, most were victims lured into the profession by coercion and deception. Pimps who paid the costs of settling in Manila, and sometimes promised to employ these women as servants, entrapped them in debt and used violence, threats, and confinement to force them to sell themselves.[29]

Manila's late nineteenth-century sex trade took many forms and suggested the nature of the sexual economy within the city and Luzon at large during the US colony's first years of war and occupation. Filipinas, often indebted to male pimps or female "minders," usually started in their teens or twenties and sold sex, on average, for seven to eight years. Managers controlled and extended their labor by paying them little more than room and board. Most women operated in small brothels or private residences owned by pimps, clients, or themselves. Others, not "professional" prostitutes, solicited clients on the street when they needed cash. The industry was centered along the Pasig River, near mercantile businesses and garrisons. In Binondo, with its hotels and theaters, resident Chinese laborers sometimes patronized women in opium dens or other shops.[30]

As Spanish officials in the late nineteenth century modernized their colonial state partly by criminalizing more activities, Manila authorities gradually shifted from repressing prostitution to regulating it. Initially, city police arrested sex workers for vagrancy, public disturbances, and petty crimes. Courts, sentencing women to brief jail terms or returning them to their hometowns, sometimes exiled recidivists to penal colonies on Mindanao. By the 1870s, however, Manila officials, following the reform spirit evident in Europe and other colonies, including Cuba, turned to limiting men's exposure to syphilis, gonorrhea, and other ailments. Forcing pelvic exams, they sent infected women to city prisons for treatment before releasing them.[31]

As in Cuba, colonial authorities in the Philippines formalized medical regulation to suppress rising VD rates in Spain's garrison. In 1897, as Spanish troops repressed Katipuneros' revolt outside Manila, their government established inside its municipal public health board a new "Public Hygiene" agency, remarkably similar to Cuba's Special Hygiene system. Its rules required all "public women" to register, buy licenses, and be examined twice a week; brothel proprietors also registered, for a fee. Hygiene staff and police were authorized to force such women into treatment at local hospitals, rather than jails, until cured. Prostitutes who resisted hospitalization faced arrest and imprisonment. As in Cuba, hygiene codes gratified bourgeois morals by obscuring the sexual economy, making it illegal for women to solicit in public and brothels to advertise. They also did little to reduce disease. Unevenly enforced and vitiated by graft, the hygiene rules spurred clandestine prostitution. At Manila by early 1898, more than half of all registered women and, in some units, more than a quarter of soldiers were infected.[32]

Americans' invasion in the summer of 1898 forced their army and Filipinos to reconcile imperatives for reproducing military labor with sovereignty over sex. Though revolution and war disrupted Manila's Public Hygiene agency, US troops landing at Cavite in July 1898 both stimulated local sex markets and signaled a sexual politics of imperial transition. Even as US troops besieged Manila, Gen. Emilio Aguinaldo sought to demonstrate his nation's sovereign capacity to govern itself by regulating sexual public health. American troops must have patronized prostitutes at Cavite before mid-August, when they seized Manila. On August 7, Cavite's provincial governor, Emiliano Riego de Dios, promulgated rules closely following Spain's old Public Hygiene system. Citing "complaints made by the foreign element" regarding contagions of syphilis and other illness, Riego meant to impose sanitary and social order. He ordered a new health board and Filipino doctors to both limit US troops' exposure and "prevent all kinds of scandals" in Cavite's brothels. Given scientific discourse describing diseases as "foreign," however, Riego's order anticipated later nationalist Filipino rhetoric blaming the islands' "syphilization" on American soldiers. In fact, sexual infection was not new in Cavite; in 1895, Spaniards at its navy yard reported high VD rates. By confirming Riego's order, however, Gen. Aguinaldo signaled that male Filipino nationalists accepted a patriarchal logic of sexual discipline that targeted women as disease vectors.[33]

Much as in Cuba, the US military regime in the Philippines adapted a colonial culture of medical regulation only after it failed to suppress VD by first restricting soldiers' access to drink and sex. Denied a chance to prove their martial manhood following a sham battle with Spanish troops, 20,000 American troops occupying Manila, nearly all volunteers from the US West, compensated with a libidinal frenzy of alcohol and commodified sex. Like Shafter at Santiago, Gen. Merritt and his successor, Gen. Elwell S. Otis, attempted to quell liquor-fueled disorder by regulating soldiers' access to alcohol. Otis used municipal codes to restrict American and foreign-owned saloons to the Escolta, the downtown's main commercial street. By June 1900, after Otis banned the sale of "vino" and other native liquors that US officials considered especially pernicious, only 170 licensed bars operated in a city of 200,000 people. In August 1898, however, after emergency alcohol restrictions barely reduced VD rates, horrified army doctors found that as many as half of men in some units had VD; only later did they realize that up to a third of US troops arrived infected. Eager to restore martial efficiency, commanders who attributed the outbreak to prostitutes tried to prevent troops from patronizing them. On November 1, Gen. Thomas Anderson barred enlisted men from "places of ill fame," or anywhere they seemed "likely to contract contagious diseases of any kind," and denied passes to violators. Filipino nationalists and Americans alike associated drunken soldiers' search for sex with home invasions and sexual assaults, which magnified rising tensions between their armies.[34]

As in Cuba, however, Manila's fluid sexual economy, colonial entrepreneurialism, and US occupiers' carnal appetites made it virtually impossible for army officers to keep troops from the sex trade. Gen. Robert P. Hughes, the city's provost marshal, ordered military police to enforce Anderson's order by finding "native females of bad character" and posting guards outside their brothels and homes. Hughes quickly realized such a method would be ineffective and impractical, however, and he immediately abandoned it; within days, Anderson rescinded his ban. Contending later that prohibitionism "could only succeed by making prisoners of the females," Hughes claimed that Manila's "social conditions" made Anderson's policy "absolutely abortive." As at Santiago, suppressive strategies did not curb the industry so much as reorganize it, making it less visible and thus harder to interdict. A soldier, observed Hughes, merely had to pay a peseta to *cocheros* or *calesa* drivers, runners, watchmen, or tipsters, all of whom quickly learned English slang, to have a woman "conducted to any designated locality to meet him."[35]

Like peers in Cuba, US commanders at Manila quickly replaced prohibition with colonial-style medical regulation, which they now justified as a military necessity. In early November 1898, Maj. Frank Bourns, Manila's new public health director, proposed new municipal codes, meant to supersede Anderson's ban, that essentially revived Spain's old Public Hygiene rules, with a few minor adjustments. Gen. Hughes instituted them instantly. Physicians were to inspect registered women on a weekly basis and, if infected, send them for treatment to a new facility, the San Lazaro leper hospital. Police also received authority to close any brothel in which certificates were not current or did not indicate a clean bill of health and keep them closed until all women had been examined. Hughes considered the measure essential for ensuring the reproduction of US military labor. Given that army doctors had hospitalized 300 troops and performed 50 surgical operations for VD, he later maintained the rules had seemed necessary to prevent an epidemic that could "very seriously cripple" an army 7,000 miles "from any reserve."[36]

Subaltern claims of effective sovereignty over sex continued to confound the American military's capacity to medically police colonial women. The sex industry's expanding and increasingly international workforce made enforcement harder. Within a few years, some 700 women had registered in the city, mostly Filipinas but also immigrants from Japan, the United States, Russia, India, and Europe, some smuggled in by international rings. Entrepreneurs evaded policing by opening new brothels just outside city lines. Prostitutes resenting costly fees and forced hospitalization paid bribes to inspectors and circulated clean certificates. In 1900, Board of Health agents, seeking to check this illicit traffic, required registered women to pay for new documents containing their photographs—not unlike army customs agents who used the same technique to control Chinese. American health officials also tried to stem corruption by taking over inspections from Filipino police and increasing their frequency. Yet a small staff, which by 1904 could visit only twenty to thirty brothels each night, in a city with roughly sixty such establishments, only went so far.[37]

As medical policing of prostitutes failed to reduce VD in the ranks, US military authorities, like those in Cuba, tried sexual-spatial segregation. By May 1900, Maj. Ira Brown, Manila's new health board director, believed that only a red-light district could guarantee the surveillance of a contained population of women needed for effective regulation. By August, Brown closed all brothels in the city and limited legal prostitution to Sampaloc, a suburb also known for female laundering. By November 1901, some forty-six establishments there employed at least 233 women, more than half of them Japanese, a fourth Filipinas, and the rest of various nationalities. Justifying his order partly as an attempt to establish an atmosphere of civil order and bourgeois propriety in Manila, Brown sought to accommodate the mores of a growing American colony that included army officers' and civil officials' wives and children. The logic of regulation transcended morality. To be sure, Brown argued that regulated prostitution functioned as a social "safety-valve" by which "crime is lessened" and "virtue protected." Yet like any good progressive, Brown embedded state action in market reason. Prostitution's unique biological risks, he believed, made it necessary to "surround this business with such safe-guards as will protect both parties to the contract." Liberal and legalist rhetoric thus obscured coercion, as Brown ordered arrested any prostitute who dared to "mingle with outside society."[38]

American moral reformers rejected such pragmatism as a repulsive blot on their virtuous colonizing nation. By October 1900, Christian "social purity" activists, already pushing the army to internally adopt temperance values by abolishing on-post "canteens," started a new campaign to force the military regime to banish the legal sex trade at Manila. Inspired by the British Parliament's 1886 repeal of the Contagious Diseases Acts, which had introduced colonial-style regulation to England, American anti-vice reformers in the early 1890s exposed the British Army's regulation of prostitution in colonial India. Now the Women's Christian Temperance Union, Anti-Saloon League, and associated organizations sought to maintain the United States' exceptional morality by extending their crusade to the Philippines. Social Darwinist fears that drunk and diseased soldiers would worsen racial and social "degeneration" at home further motivated them to ban militarized markets in drink and sex abroad.[39]

Escalating protests in late 1900 and early 1901 forced US military and civilian colonial bureaucrats to defend regulation as a vital tool for reproducing the martial manpower they needed to defend US sovereignty against insurgents. As social purity activists adroitly used congressional debate over Elihu Root's army reorganization bill as leverage, the embattled secretary of war pressed Gen. Arthur MacArthur and William H. Taft at Manila to distance the government from regulation. In circumspect statements, both men clarified that American authorities prudently regulated prostitution to preserve soldiers' health. By January 1902, Taft—now civil governor, politically ambitious, and sensitive to metropolitan politics—seemed to blame the policy on the generals. Regulation, he told Root, had been "purely" an "army police measure outside our jurisdiction." Yet even Taft admitted that this "military necessity" had greatly reduced "disability from this cause" within the ranks.[40]

MacArthur and Taft tried to reassure anxious Republicans at home by implying that judicious regulation could reproduce martial labor and morality simultaneously. Manila police, they noted, frequently arrested prostitutes, pimps, and brothel owners for petty crimes and felonies, including selling sex outside Sampaloc, and even jailed parents and other kin for prostituting female minors. A few junior army officers even openly disputed reformers' assumption that it seemed possible, or wise, to perfect colonial morality by prohibition. Maj. Henry Hoyt, for one, told Jacob Schurman's commission that abolishing prostitution and other local customs would be a Sisyphean task. Repression, he believed, would only encourage Filipinos "to disobey the laws" and "scatter the evils (so-called by Americans) along the highways," thus robbing them "of a large source of revenue."[41]

As Hoyt sensed, the socio-spatial reach of Luzon's sexual economy, and an attendant military-colonial logic of regulation, expanded alongside the US occupation's geographic footprint. Compared to Cuba, however, insurgency and counterinsurgency made the archipelago's politics of sexual sovereignty much more volatile, and powerful as a source of internal army reform. By late February 1899, the war's first month, Spanish and insurgent correspondence, newspapers, declarations, and rumors alleged that American soldiers abused

Filipino civilians, including by sexually assaulting Filipinas. Throughout central Luzon that year, unruly US troops, typically state volunteers, fed such perceptions by bad behavior, usually limited to looting civilian homes, businesses, and churches. A calcifying racism toward Filipinos hardened by guerrilla warfare, however, increased the likelihood that American troops would commit sexual violence and other abuses, or tolerate native allies who did. Available records suggest that US soldiers rarely committed rape or related atrocities. For Filipino nationalists, though, even anecdotal evidence of sexual crime reinforced anticolonial revolution as a defense of gendered indigenous and Catholic values. Exploiting emotionally resonant images of American troops as sexual predators and criminals, insurgents styled themselves as national patriarchs protecting female honor, dignity, and virtue.[42]

Some disciplinarian US Army commanders invoked these same ideals of paternal patriarchy and masculine honor when they punished soldiers for violating Filipinas. Bourgeois Victorian norms of gentlemanly conduct could trump the colonial differences of race and culture that seemed to ease American troops' abuses. Reviewing court-martial verdicts acquitting them, Gen. Thomas Anderson and some fellow officers argued that men, and especially soldiers, had an obligation to defend all women anywhere, regardless of class or ethnicity. This code even justified anti-American violence. In February 1903 at Balayan, in Batangas Province, a US court-martial recognized a Filipino man's right to defend his partner, a prostitute, by killing an inebriated American trooper whom he alleged had tried to rape her.[43]

Most US Army officers, however, prized their commands and careers more than Filipinos' perception of their nation's legitimacy in the islands. They tended to show leniency toward soldiers, especially fellow officers, court-martialed for sex crimes. Thus few Filipinas ever won justice from the American military during the war. For reasons of reputation as well as internal organizational cohesion, US enlisted men and officers, when facing accusations of sexual abuse, tended to protect one another. This was particularly true in the less disciplined state regiments that served in the Philippines until late 1899. Volunteers from the same communities and prewar militias, expecting to return home together, had few incentives to punish comrades. An American army enforcing military and civil law in most of Luzon until 1902, via military commissions and provost courts, denied Filipinas access to independent courts with more sympathetic Filipino judges and juries. The US military regime only began organizing the latter bodies outside Manila in January 1900; even then, Filipino courts' jurisdiction extended only to civil cases involving Filipinos. Only gradually did poor Filipinas successfully use them to challenge US soldiers' sexual violence or claims on property and child custody.[44]

Unsurprisingly, given a wartime legal system skewed toward American troops, army officers held to higher ethical standards than rank and filers sometimes defended themselves against allegations of sexual crime by manipulating the presence of legalized prostitution. A US colonial state that tolerated commodified sex thus reinforced double standards, present in both metropole and colony, blaming prostitution and sexual violence on women, not men. Officers facing court-martial often exculpated themselves and impugned Filipina accusers by disparaging them as "dishonorable" women. Depending on the circumstance, Americans conveniently denied or admitted that they sought to purchase sex at the time of alleged incidents. If this strategy weaponized stigmas attached to prostitution, it also exploited the permeable line between formal and informal sex markets that made Filipinas vulnerable to such insinuations.[45]

The early 1900 US occupation of Albay province, in southern Luzon, demonstrated how soldiers exploited gray areas between poor Filipinas' reproductive and sexual labor. In January, an expedition led by Brig. Gen. William A. Kobbé occupied Legazpi, the region's principal port, partly to revive the region's hemp exports. Local history hints at how Filipinos experienced the invasion's sexual politics. In the 1950s, some Legazpi residents claimed that civilians fled to the Mayon volcano's slopes for refuge after "many American soldiers tried to abuse the ladies." The memory had some validity. In February 1900, Lt. Thomas Campbell faced court-martial after a young woman in Legazpi alleged that he entered her home around midnight and tried to rape her in front of her foster mother and two children. At trial, the mother insisted the two were lavenderas, who "only washed soldier's clothes." American witnesses for the defense, however, used hearsay and character assassination to damage the Filipinas' credibility. Appealing to soldiers' knowledge that some domestics sold sex, they trafficked in patriarchal assumptions, shared by Spanish and Filipino men, that prostitutes by virtue of profession either welcomed and tolerated rape or could not be raped, by definition, as "public" women. One sergeant, testifying that he met these Filipinas while hunting for laundresses, claimed they said, "Margarita" (slang for "prostitute") and "poco tiempo, vamos aqui" (little time, we are quick here) while "sitting on the porch in a very unlady-like position—with clothes up over their knees." Brother officers slapped Campbell on the wrist.[46]

American soldiers' legal manipulation of regulations thus reflected a perception that Filipinas took advantage of their femininity, sex, and sexual labor to challenge or advance US imperial sovereignty. Claims in early 1899 that women outside Manila used various schemes, including feigned pregnancies, to smuggle rice and bullets past checkpoints prefigured anxieties that Filipinas used their gender to aid insurgency. As nationalist intellectuals like Isabelo de los Reyes recovered folklore of female spiritual leaders who deceived their enemies in war, Hilaria Aguinaldo, the general's wife and director of the Red Cross, urged Filipinas to use their wiles to lure Americans into ambushes. A few soldiers claimed that women falsely accused them of rape to cover up assassination attempts. Some officers even alleged that Filipinas who accused local Filipino officials of forcing women to prostitute themselves for US soldiers were retaliating against them for assisting counterinsurgents. Of course, rebels and sympathizers sometimes coerced and violently targeted Filipinas sexually involved with Americans; in a few instances, they harassed and killed lavenderas who took the invaders' money. By contrast, some US Army officers saw Filipinas sexually engaged with their soldiers as assets, not liabilities, given their access to vital intelligence; a few warned of impending attacks. In late 1902 during a cholera epidemic, Lt. George Rodney credited his revelation that residents of Tanay, in Laguna, tried to have a strict quarantine lifted by secretly burying dead outside town at night to a tip originally furnished by a hospital steward's lavendera. "A pretty girl of about nineteen years," she occupied, quipped Rodney, "a position toward him not contemplated by Army regulations." In 1907, Maj. Hugh Wise, reflecting on the anti-Pulahan war on Samar, claimed "the native prostitute" made "a valuable spy"; "unfortunately," her income led her to side with US troops.[47]

Such observations acknowledged the existence of a militarized sexual economy of empire that pressured poor Filipinas to give their labor, if not their love, to occupiers. As in Cuba, poor and working-class women's profitable commerce with American soldiers prompted a few to sell them sex, especially as troops manipulated women's poverty to elicit it. Officers believed that enlisted men often negotiated sex with Filipinas they encountered in marketplaces, especially *tenderas* augmenting family income by selling food and other merchandise in small shops and stalls. They even suspected poorly paid teachers did the same. Through its colonizing gaze, the memoir of Pvt. Richard Johnson illustrated how such encounters transpired. Stationed at Caloocan for two months in late 1899, Johnson recalled that "mutual suspicion" gradually ceded to "a little mutual intimacy" after Filipinas visited his camp to sell fruits, "trinkets," eggs, and laundry service. Caloocan's "modest women," with their "very high standard of morals," he remembered, initially found soldiers' "rough bold manner" frightening. By giving pennies and food to their children and displaying a "liberalness in spending money," the Americans gradually won the women's trust. Army medical officers, aware that market exchange sometimes led to sexual exchange, feared such illicit relations exposed troops to disease. In a medical lecture delivered at Minneapolis in 1900, Capt. Gilbert Seaman dispensed his belief that "dhobie itch" and other skin ailments helpfully diverted enlisted men in the islands "from other troubles." This included "the dusky-hued senorita who sells him bananas, and engages his fancy by the shy way she accepts his compliments, and the bewitching manner in which her full rounded breast peeps out from beneath her pinna chemisa"—never suggesting, he said, the "troubles *she* might bring him."[48]

As in Cuba, in the Philippines the laundress became the female worker that American soldiers most associated with informal sexual commerce. Laundering's feminized domesticity and staged intimacy, as troops and Filipinas exchanged men's clothing and cash, seemed especially suited to casual but commodified sex. As a labor process, colonial laundry appeared to elicit soldiers' eroticizing porno-tropical gaze, as lavenderas often combined clothes washing with bathing themselves and children in public, sometimes near US barracks. Soldiers' sexualization of laundresses further refracted their perception of these women as "savage" due to their primitive techniques. One mocking soldier's song, "A Filipino Family," about "a Philippine hombre / Who ate rice, fish, and legombre," added more doggerel:

> Su mujer fue lavendera;
> Whacked clothes in fuerte manera,
>   On the banks of the stream
>   Where the carabao dream—
> Which gave them an odor lijera.[49]

Americans' perception of lavenderas as subaltern by dint of their technology, class, gender, and race enhanced their vulnerability to sexual exploitation. Soldiers sometimes leveraged these Filipinas' financial dependence on their wages to coerce them into sex. Troops who had accrued large credits with laundresses occasionally used their unit's reassignment to new and distant posts to make payment contingent on sex. Some negotiated liaisons with lavenderas on credit and settled accounts on monthly or bimonthly paydays. Others declined to sexualize Filipina laundresses, celebrating them instead for an entrepreneurial initiative that validated Americans' liberal and capitalist civilizing mission. From Zambales Province in January 1902, Pvt. Rienzi B. Lemus related that one family became the "most prosperous" in the town his unit garrisoned by washing soldiers' clothes. Now "out of debt," he cheered,

"Quanto Valo" Scene in Camp of the 16th Infantry, P.I. Portraying haggling over bananas on Luzon in 1900, this staged stereograph—emphasizing Filipina tenderas' physical proximity to American soldiers and intimacy symbolized by smoking—evoked US Army officers' fears that women-run markets facilitated casual sexual commerce, which, by its unregulated nature, exposed naive troops to venereal disease. B. W. Kilburn, stereograph, 1900, courtesy of Keystone-Mast Collection, California Museum of Photography, University of California, Riverside.

they were financially "far in advance of their former creditor," a member of that class who he believed kept poor Filipinos in a state of "involuntary servitude."[50]

Far more prominent than the lavendera in the Philippines' imperial politics of sex and social reproduction, however, was the *querida*, or "female lover," "girlfriend," or common-law wife. Comparable to colonized women sexually entangled with colonizing men in other empires, the querida became associated by many American soldiers with domesticity, mutuality, and intimacy. Though Victorian moralist American critics often conflated "the querida system" and prostitution as institutions of equal turpitude, soldiers tended to differentiate queridas from sex workers. Discerning in her sexual-reproductive labor the illusive patriarchal promise of monogamous sex and household economies, enlisted men coveted the querida as a wage of empire. Through such "regular women," as they called them, rank and filers denied the marital privileges that officers enjoyed reaped women's labor—paid and unpaid, sexual and domestic. In turn, many commanders valued queridas' role in an imperialism of "good housekeeping" that enhanced US sovereignty by reproducing their colonial garrison's male military labor.[51]

Such informal relations, rarely involving marriage, were hardly new to the Philippines in 1898. Queridas embodied preexisting colonial customs of gender, sex, and class in which men, often elites, forged sexual unions with indio women, often poor and young. Within a Catholicized culture in which divorce was illegal, foreign men, especially Spaniards and Chinese, frequently established common-law marriages with Filipinas. Some Filipino men also took advantage of patriarchal double standards to pursue extramarital exploits. By the 1880s and 1890s, nationalist Propagandists condemned such affairs, especially with Spanish friars, for exploiting indio women. Other Filipino elites, such as Felipe Calderon, the product of one such union, endorsed these relations as a practical route to upward social mobility for indios. Gen. Elwell S. Otis attributed the regrettable prevalence of such "concubinage" in the islands to marriage's high cost, and in 1900 he instituted reforms. For Americans, queridas also extended the sexual culture of nineteenth-century settler expansion in North America. Soldiers and volunteers who served or lived in the US West often perceived Filipina queridas as analogous to Native American women who entered common-law marriages with American men. Employing a racist vernacular, they referred to queridas as "squaws" and partners as "squawmen."[52]

Neither queridas nor their American companions left much evidence of their own views or experiences of these relations. Most commentary, written by elite white Europeans and Americans, reflected colonizers' various class, gender, and racial biases. Nor did all US Army commanders consider the querida an improvement over prostitutes. Romantics who lamented an absence of affective attachment in both types of sexual encounter found the cultural gulf between soldiers and queridas too vast to create more than soulless exchange. At Legazpi in June 1902, Capt. Arthur Thayer conceded that "every soldier's pay" seemed "sufficient for him to keep a mistress and still have enough left for other things." Yet he criticized such "alliances" as "very degrading" to his men. Complaining that soldiers and queridas had "nothing ... in common" other than being heterosexual members of the opposite sex, Thayer lamented that they communicated merely by "a few words of mixed English, Spanish, and the native tongue, eked out by signs."[53]

Even if queridas experienced sex with soldiers as "transactional labor," as one historian argues, these subaltern women and American men still sought to exact sovereignty from them. Though queridas entered these sexual relationships voluntarily, in a nominal legal sense, relative to most prostitutes, material deprivation and insecurity motivated them both. Yet queridas—often young and poor, like prostitutes—also sought to wrest from this status a modicum of economic stability, improved living standards, perhaps support for dependents, physical protection, and even autonomy from family and employers. Becoming an American's querida thus represented a rational decision for some women in a largely rural agricultural society disrupted by commercialization, war, and ecological and biological stress. Though queridas were sometimes ostracized by family and community, some of these women, and their kin, may have considered themselves as clever for extracting financial support from US troops. For their part, soldier-partners clearly treasured queridas as a colonial reserve of reproductive labor. Cleaning troops' clothes and cooking for them, these Filipinas often maintained a shared domicile—when commanders felt comfortable violating army policy by allowing enlisted men to live "off-post," usually with overnight passes. Soldiers also exploited queridas' kin and social networks, and their local knowledge of languages and markets, when using them to complete tasks they preferred to avoid, given their ignorance and insurgent threats.[54]

It must be noted, however, that very few Filipinas ever became the queridas of US military personnel, even after the war. Nationalist pride and revolutionary threats, if not also taboos reinforced by family and church, dissuaded nearly all women. Despite its narrative of patriarchal colonial conquest, Richard Johnson's memoir evoked some of the factors that led most Filipinas and their families to decide that the costs of imperial intercourse were greater than its benefits. Johnson, recalling his time at Naguilian in La Union province, in early 1900, remembered that comrades gave corned beef, salmon, and hardtack rations to hungry children accompanying female peddlers as a "lead to contact with the women." Such gestures, he claimed, "often led to an invitation to the beneficiary's home" and "introduction to her mother" or "elder sister." Yet Johnson acknowledged that most women had been "extremely timid, and easily frightened by any suggestion of familiarity." Priests, widely respected in most of Luzon despite revolutionaries' anti-clericalism, reinforced this reluctance. At Naguilian, reminisced Johnson, they had warned women it was "almost an unpardonable sin" to have "connubial relations" with "non-Catholics" and "heathens." Johnson also noted that Filipinas contemplated such relations not as individuals in a liberal marketplace but as members of extended family economies. Describing Naguilian's denizens as "extremely provincial people," he claimed that poor women and their families seemed "amazed" by soldiers' "apparent wealth and extravagance"; a private's $15.60 monthly pay, he noted, was greater than most municipal officials' salary. Where goods were "so cheap" and household "needs so meager," Filipinos, asserted Johnson, knew that half of a soldiers' wages could keep an "average family in good circumstances for a month." Still, few accepted this "monthly allowance to possess a woman"; only Filipinas "of weaker will," he clarified, "fell for the temptation." In Naguilian, inhabited in 1903 by 3,000 women above the age of seventeen, only twenty became soldiers' queridas.[55]

By emphasizing that his company commander procured a querida before he permitted enlisted men to do so, Johnson also alluded to how US military hierarchy shaped the sexual politics of imperial sovereignty. On the whole, the officer corps seemed ambivalent about such relations. Some favored queridas for rescuing enlisted men from the enervations of tropical service, including off-post brothels and prostitutes on which they blamed diseases and disorder, and "neurasthenia," or depression, to which they believed white men were especially susceptible. Others, less generous and permissive, restricted or prohibited soldiers' access to queridas altogether, threatening what some came to regard as a patriarchal right of military-colonial manhood. Posted at Camp McGrath, outside Batangas City, in 1910, Richard Johnson described the garrison as a "squaw man's Paradice [sic]," where nearly half of his detachment had queridas, some by formal marriage. When a newly arrived "sour natured" officer limited each soldier's night passes to one per week, they circumvented the chain of command, complaining to higher ranks. White officers retaliated by reassigning the aggrieved men to the US mainland. A few, desperate to stay with Filipina partners, asked for and received discharges. Others reunited with their queridas months later by wrangling new orders that returned them to the islands.[56]

As this incident demonstrates, soldier-querida relations were ultimately determined by local and global political and military forces over which subalterns had little to no control. First and foremost, from Filipinas' perspective, insurgents and their sympathizers regulated these women's sexual activity as a question of loyalty to a sovereign nation-state. Revolutionaries occasionally targeted queridas for sleeping with the enemy, intimidating, assaulting, and even murdering them. Filipino officials in US military–organized municipalities also tried to police these relations out of personal and communal self-interest. Subject to US military law, anxious Filipino authorities knew that American troops exposed themselves to guerrilla attack when they visited queridas off-post, often at night. In November 1901, the president of Cabuyao, in Laguna, pleaded with Calamba's commander to stop his men from passing "their nights in special houses where they have lodged their mistresses," knowing he would suffer "if any misfortune should happen" to them.[57]

Filipinos also appreciated that a shifting sexual geography of military occupation, determined ultimately by the decisions of distant American generals and policymakers, fostered localized economies of reproductive labor. This had profound but unequal consequences for Filipinas and soldier-partners who experienced greater mobility. By 1902, as the war in Luzon and the Visayas came to a close, the War Department's decisions to either close garrisons or reassign entire units to new posts in the islands or abroad revealed communities that had become dependent on soldiers' wages, including queridas and families. Between 1902 and 1912, regiments were assigned to two-year tours in the archipelago, but after 1912, a handful of regiments were posted there permanently, and personnel began rotating in and out of the islands on an individual basis. In either scenario, queridas who relied on departing troops confronted unenviable options. A few veterans, taking discharges in the islands, became colonial settlers, establishing saloons or other enterprises employing queridas and families. Yet most queridas losing soldier-partners had few financial options but to call on family or friends, enter a capricious and gender-segregated labor market, or find a new soldier to support them. Like Filipinas left behind by Spanish soldiers, some Filipinas left behind by American troops also turned to prostitution. Their dilemma elicited occupiers' sympathy and sarcasm. In 1910, Richard Johnson, watching cavalrymen arrive at Camp McGrath to replace a reassigned regiment, observed a "considerable colony of 'floating' women," who had made their "living on concubinage service to soldiers," enter a "competitive scramble to snare themselves a man." The scene, he recalled years later, had been "the subject of much cynical levity."⁵⁸

Johnson's anecdote illustrates how US empire inevitably exposed as a pretense soldiers' aspirations to paternal patriarchy, despite their best intentions. Such events, for both the querida's American critics and her apologists, raised the specter of male "abandonment." Americans' racism and Filipinas' attachment to dependents and sedentary kin and communities kept these women from joining evacuating soldiers. Christian moralists thus condemned soldiers for adopting a colonial custom by which Spanish and European men, some bigamous, jettisoned "native" wives and children in Asia's colonies. Penalties for troops varied by rank. While enlisted men were sometimes denied reenlistment, army officers, expected to be bourgeois gentlemen, might be denied promotion. John Pershing learned this lesson in 1906. Having just married the daughter of the US senator chairing the Military Affairs Committee, rumors that he fathered two children with a querida at Zamboanga nearly scuttled Pershing's chance to jump to brigadier general. Civilian American officials defended the colonial state from such aspersions by painting it as a responsible patriarch. William Taft claimed he forced civil employees found cohabiting with Filipinas to produce a marriage certificate, marry, or resign. This policy did not cover the army, however. Later, as secretary of war, Taft tacitly acknowledged American soldiers' persistent ties with Filipina queridas, contrary to official army policy, when he stated that he preferred troops would not marry at all.⁵⁹

American elites thus tacitly tolerated Filipinas' informal sexual and reproductive labor for soldiers as a sad but inescapable feature of a garrisoned colony. This approach encouraged US enlisted men's attitude that relations with queridas were situational, contingent, and disposable. Undoubtedly, some troops displayed genuine emotional and ethical anguish when they quit queridas. Yet others exuded contempt for their sexual partners, seeing them as just as uncivilized and inferior as any other colonial subject. African American troops were hardly exempt from such sentiments, despite white counterparts' racist expectation, as in Cuba, that Black troops as men of color would naturally feel an affinity with the colonized. Like comrades in Cuba, few soldiers in the Philippines, Black or white, returned to the states with queridas, whom they reasonably feared family and friends would reject as pariahs; in some states, such unions would have broken antimiscegenation laws. Perverse racial and imperial barriers to lasting unions could make soldiers cynical about their nation's enlightened colonialism. In a letter home, Pvt. Rienzi Lemus, a Black regular, excoriated white troops at

Manila whom he saw boarding a ship home, leaving behind weeping "mistresses" he claimed they had been "deluding." The pathetic scene, Lemus felt, illustrated how soldiers "pacify and civilize the Filipinos."[60]

Lemus's letter alluded to the formation of a racialized sexual politics of the querida within a larger US colonial state premised on white supremacist segregation. As in Cuba, white Americans in the Philippines invoked racist metropolitan tropes about sexually aggressive Black men; some even alleged that undisciplined African American troops stiffened Filipinos' armed resistance. In 1902, Gov. Taft appealed to such stereotypes as he justified barring African American regiments from archipelagic service. Given Black anti-imperialist and antiracist sentiments that seemed validated when African Americans deserted—none more famously than David Fegan, who rebel comrades claimed acquired a querida before both perished—such racism reflected anxiety about Black solidarity with Filipinos. Yet African American soldiers themselves clearly claimed queridas as a wage of empire, in part as a means to compensate for segregationist hierarchies that relegated them to a subordinate status as men. At Zambales in 1901, Theophilus G. Steward, the Twenty-Fifth Infantry's chaplain, believed occupation permitted the Black soldier to claim a respectable manhood denied at home. "The Negro," he insisted, was "a kind husband here, as elsewhere." Yet many white officers policed metropolitan racial mores that proscribed interracial sex, especially when it emerged from the colonial shadows in visibly mixed-race marriages and offspring. In his memoir, Col. James Parker recorded his revulsion at a Bicol official who repeatedly told him "a splendid race would come from a mixture of American and native blood." Relieved that 400 troops occupying Iriga for thirteen months produced only one such child, Parker, despite his racism, alluded to how soldiers became the first American colonists to wrestle with the presence of "American mestizos" in the islands. By 1913, according to one estimate, some 1,400 mixed-race children lived there, nearly all the progeny of US troops.[61]

The race of subaltern sex, however, paled before epidemiology as a problem for a US military hierarchy mostly concerned during the Philippine War with the health of American soldiers. As the medical regulation of prostitutes failed to suppress VD, commanders and doctors sought relief by redirecting the colonial bio-disciplinary gaze onto their own troops. By issuing General Orders No. 101 (GO 101) in May 1901 at Manila, Gen. Arthur MacArthur dramatically shifted the imperial politics of sexual sovereignty. Recognizing that surveilling colonial women was failing to protect his troops, MacArthur reset the relational reproduction of military and sexual labor.

Diverging from simultaneous army practice in occupied Cuba, GO 101 reflected army officers' growing realization in the Philippines that they could reduce VD in the ranks only by exercising effective sovereignty over the sexual health of soldiers and women simultaneously. MacArthur's order thus required that medical officers in the islands inspect the genitalia of all enlisted men twice a month for "constitutional and local evidence of venereal infection." Not unlike Manila's prostitutes, diseased soldiers were to be forced into treatment until cured (in their case, at military hospitals) before returning to duty. Yet GO 101 sustained the prevailing assumption that Filipinas, not troops, were the primary vectors of sexual disease. It mandated that Filipino municipal officials help US commanders track VD detected in garrisons to "its source" by placing local women "under such surveillance as will prevent the spread of the disease." While a few conscientious American army officers already regularly examined troops, GO 101 aspired to systematize the medical policing of US soldiers throughout the colony.[62]

Historians have argued that MacArthur promulgated GO 101 to deflect American social purity activists' crusade against regulated prostitution. Yet the general also issued it in response to a mounting consensus inside the US Army that a subaltern multitude was thwarting top-down antivenereal efforts. By early 1901, medical officers feared that weak to nonexistent medical policing of sex workers beyond Manila had raised VD rates so high that they threatened the occupation's physical viability. Reports from Laguna Province documented local symptoms driving policy change from the bottom up, and the colonial periphery inward. By February 1901, Calamba's post surgeon blamed its garrison's near 50 percent infection rate on nearly two dozen registered women in town. They evaded surveillance, he claimed, by illegally exchanging "clean" certificates and moving from one US-occupied town to the next, eluding bio-discipline predicated on a sedentary workforce. Maj. Louis Mervin Maus, the army's chief surgeon in the Philippines and a Cuba occupation veteran, investigated. A University of Maryland medical school graduate who entered the army in 1874 and spent a year at Paris studying under Louis Pasteur, Maus's expertise focused on sanitation and bacteriology. His findings at Calamba confirmed hygiene rules' failure. Though Maus attributed this "inefficiency" mostly to colonial women, he also blamed Filipino officials and US soldiers; among the latter, he claimed, many avoided and never received proper medical care. As in Cuba, enlisted men who feared a dishonorable discharge that made them ineligible for a veteran's pension tried treating themselves or avoided treatment altogether.[63]

Maus catalyzed GO 101 when he recommended to MacArthur that he expand the scope of sexual regulation from prostitutes to US troops. Minimal and fragmentary records do not indicate whether US Army medical officers beyond Manila implemented it, or to what degree. By June 1901, the post surgeon at Calamba, of all places, seemed unaware of the new policy; its commander declaimed that soldiers' health would be best served by making Filipino officials quarantine infected women. Yet local authorities' policing of sex workers continued to fall short. As war ceased in most of Luzon by mid-1902, few municipal governments, now accountable to Taft's civilian regime, had the will or resources to regulate prostitutes for American troops. Many local Filipino authorities simply ignored or resisted US Army officers' orders and requests that they surveil and treat women who were selling sex to soldiers.[64]

Even as GO 101 conceded the fecklessness of an antivenereal method resting on soldiers' voluntary abstinence, a moralistic discourse promoting sexual restraint persisted in metropolitan politics, if not military practice. Famously, in March 1902, President Theodore Roosevelt directly called on US troops to refrain from indulging in "vices" of drink and sex. Alleging that such behaviors impaired the strenuous masculine life required for martial efficiency, Roosevelt's order made individual soldiers' volition and progressive values central to official American military policy. Yet its sanctimonious rhetoric was election-year political theater, designed to palliate Christian reformers; it had no effect on actual army practice.[65]

In fact, Roosevelt's appeal represented the public face of a covert intraimperial campaign inside the US executive branch designed to make regulations at Manila much less visible to American civilians' scrutiny. Pressured by Elihu Root at the War Department, Gen. MacArthur by March 1902 ordered city police to force brothel owners to remove all US flags, or flag-like symbols, from their buildings. Displayed to attract soldier clienteles, the patriotic emblems had unintentionally marked dens of iniquity for prying American anti-vice investigators. The day before Gov. Taft was slated to testify to senators at Washington about the regulation controversy, Root also ordered Manila's health board to stop collecting exam fees from prostitutes. He further instructed its agents to stop issuing women photographic inspection booklets—highly visible tokens of regulation, which savvy social-purity activists circulated among congressmen while lobbying at Washington. Henceforth, Root ordered, health inspectors in the city were to internally keep "their own records of names, descriptions, residences, and dates of examination." This would avoid "the liability of a misunderstanding" that they ran "a system of licensed prostitution."[66]

Coinciding with the early 1902 end of fighting in Luzon, Root's obfuscation of medical regulation at Manila shifted the imperial politics of sexual labor from the realm of wartime emergency to routine colonial public health. Lt. Col. Clarence Edwards, directing the War Department's Bureau of Insular Affairs, apologized to Christian reformers that policing sex workers in the Philippines had been an existential "military necessity." The army's VD crisis, he reassured, had "resolved itself into one of sanitation and the application of sanitary law." In reality, Taft's civilian regime sustained the sexual-disciplinary state it inherited from its martial predecessors. On the supply side of colonial sex markets, the commission encouraged the continued medical surveillance and discipline of prostitutes in areas with US garrisons. Indeed, in Mindanao-Sulu, army officers sought to avoid antagonizing Muslim Moros by proscribing soldier sex with Moro women. Instead, they tried to ensure troops' access to brothels with "professional" non-Moro prostitutes, including Japanese and other foreigners. Enlisted men, however, still found ways to arrange illicit relations with Moro women.[67]

Civilian bureaucrats also developed new techniques for suppressing the unregulated sex trade, some quite punitive. On the same day in March 1902 that Roosevelt called for soldierly self-denial, Manila's municipal board moved to morally cleanse the city by enacting a new vagrancy ordinance. Criminalizing any person "who habitually idly loiters about" in streets or public establishments, the law targeted prostitutes and pimps to incentivize their self-confinement to Sampaloc. Violators could be sentenced with fines as high as $100 for each offense, and jail terms up to six months entailing hard labor on streets. Commissioners the next year also authorized fines and arrests for any "lewd and dissolute person who lives in and about houses of ill-fame" and "every common prostitute and common drunkard" found in public, anywhere in the islands. The law authorized the incarceration and deportation of "dissolute, drunken, and lawless Americans," many of whom the commission claimed were veterans, who "associate with low Filipino women and live upon the proceeds of their labor." In 1903, commissioners further restricted soldiers' access to commodified sex by prohibiting liquor licenses for any business within two miles of US camps. Two years later, public health commissioner Maj. Edward C. Carter believed these measures made Manila as orderly and polite as Boston, New York, or London. "No woman of doubtful character," he cheered, was "permitted to appear" or solicit "in any public park or place."[68]

Simultaneously, American officers intensified colonial-style sexual surveillance inside the army, none with more fervor than GO 101's progenitor,

Maj. L. Mervin Maus. As the Philippines' public health commissioner in early 1902, Maus regretted having to implement Root's orders to dismantle Manila's medical-regulatory infrastructure. Prostitutes' photographic exam books, he felt, had been "essential" to keeping young US soldiers healthy and preserving their reproductive prospects. This support for regulation haunted Maus's career, as moralists dredged up his record whenever he sought promotion.[69]

A progressive par excellence, however, Maus embraced McArthur's inspections for enlisted men as a pragmatic step toward reproducing efficient military labor. He urged reluctant colleagues to consider VD in the ranks from the perspective of reducing costs and increasing benefits for their employer—the US Army. Maus never openly criticized Roosevelt's strategy of "lectures and moral talks." Deferentially, he even speculated it might cure ignorance about sexual disease among enlisted men, which he attributed to their working-class backgrounds. Yet bourgeois paternalism took second place to Maus's interest in exploiting the labor of recruits who he insisted had surrendered their bodily autonomy and personal freedom to the state, knowingly and willingly. At times, the major sounded like a modern humanist, encouraging commanders to stop treating soldiers as if they were "machines, or automatons, to be moved by a system of wires." Yet he dismissed criticisms that genital exams were excessively "humiliating" because they shamed "good" abstinent men. Given that "the government has some rights in the matter," as "it pays for the services of the men sick or well," Maus emphasized that diseased troops were "of no use" and even "an impediment and menace to the health of the other men." Soldiers, he felt, never objected to any "sensible or rational measures to preserve their health."[70]

Some medical officers in the Philippines, including the army's chief surgeon, celebrated medical surveillance for enlisted men. Others dismissed punitive measures as counterproductive, believing they encouraged soldiers to avoid treatment. Senior commanders embraced a sterner spirit. In February 1905, Gen. Henry Corbin, commanding the Philippine Division, noted that a third of all hospitalized soldiers in the archipelago were being treated for VD. Signaling abstinence's enduring appeal, he reissued Roosevelt's 1902 order and threatened to fire any civilian employee found infected. By November, Gen. Adna Chaffee, the acting secretary of war, extended Corbin's impulse to all enlisted men, telling officers he expected them to dishonorably discharge any soldier showing evidence of disease. Yet even Chaffee appreciated the need to retain "good soldiers," and he advised medical officers not to expel men who diligently tried to cure their infections. In 1909, when army doctors saw that VD rates among all enlistees had jumped from nearly 161 per thousand men in 1902 to nearly 197 per thousand, they believed the increase was the result of better testing and care. Army surgeons continued to attribute high VD rates in the islands to prostitutes and their lack of modern medical knowledge.[71]

BY 1907, THE SECOND US OCCUPATION of Cuba suggested that Americans' army had Pacification fully internalized colonial-style medical regulation. Its commander, Gen. James Franklin Bell, had in 1900 served briefly as provost marshal at Manila, where he vigilantly enforced a rehabilitated Public Hygiene system. Now, at Havana, Bell, like his predecessors in Cuba, initially tried to suppress VD rates in his garrison by banning prostitutes from spaces easily accessed by troops—namely Marianao, the bustling Havana suburb in which he located his headquarters, Camp Columbia. Bell and subordinates also tried to distinguish regulated from clandestine women. When these efforts failed, Bell, inspired by Maus's innovations, concentrated bio-discipline on soldiers. By January 1907, he ordered commanders throughout Cuba to inspect all troops weekly. Some surgeons protested that the policy actually harmed efficiency. Infected men completing enlistments, they alleged, were trying to reenlist in the states, where recruiters did not always administer VD exams, rather than in Cuba, where they were most needed.[72]

In a reoccupied Plattist republic riven by civil strife, however, the imperial politics of sexual labor seemed more toxic and perilous than ever. American soldiers, now enjoying less effective sovereignty over both Cubans and themselves, compensated by lashing out at Cuban women and men. Prostitutes and their workspaces became nodes of tension and violence as women suffered men's struggles over sex and military labor. A few Yankee troops, now facing punishment for their infections, attacked the women they held responsible. An incident in Camagüey's red-light district in May 1908 typified such events. A private who tracked down a prostitute at a licensed brothel handed his rifle to another soldier and commenced beating her, yelling she "gave me a dose of VD," according to a Cuban witness.[73]

As with road strikes, however, clashes at Pinar del Río in 1907 revealed the volcanic potential of rival national claims over Cuban workers—in this case, prostitutes—and Americans' waning power over them. On the evening of March 22, a US trooper entering a room at a brothel in the eponymous city's red-light district found a Cuban man inside who promptly ejected him. As their fight spilled out into the street, it quickly embroiled fellow soldiers, Rural Guards, and onlookers, whom US commanders disparaged as a "vagrant element" loitering constantly in and around the district's many cafés, saloons, and bordellos. These Cubans, "always armed with knives" and "revolvers," and "against constituted government in any form," alleged one American, goaded Rural Guards to attack the Yankees with "taunts of cowardice and vile epithets." The next night, as the city trembled "in a state of excitement," according to a Cuban newspaper, three more "collisions" occurred in the same area. Troops armed with sticks, iron bars, and walking canes injured several *rurales*.[74]

Though immersed in imperial sexual tensions of race and nation, Cuban and Yankee men translated the event through a shared patriarchal lens that nominally recognized Cuban women's power to instigate it. Col. Earl D. Thomas, commanding the city's garrison, blamed the trouble on Rural Guardsmen, who he claimed had "acquaintances among the demi-monde of the town," often "visited by soldiers," including an "abandoned woman of the town of no significance whatsoever." (This was "always the case," he regretted, "in personal clashes among soldiers and civilians.") Revealing how anti-Black racism figured in sovereignty's sexual politics, Thomas characterized the red-light district's "negro element" as "particularly violent, demonstrative, arrogant"—an "almost unbearable" multitude of "malicious-minded people." They made a "studied effort," he alleged, to "stir up trouble." Yet local officials insisted that arrogant Yankees provoked the violence. Pinar del Río's police chief maintained that he had serially complained to the alcalde and Thomas about his men's "misbehavior." The colonel, he insisted, failed to restrain them.[75]

As with road strikes in the region, panicked Americans associated racialized unrest, this time over sex, with rumors of Afro-Cuban rebellion. On the riots' heels, Gen. Bell and Gov. Charles Magoon received alarming intelligence reports that Black *pinareños* might be plotting another armed uprising. Sexual combat on city streets seemed to hint at the growing willingness of Pinar del Río's "clases de color" to challenge creole elites leading Cuba's Liberal and Conservative Parties. Nervous white US commanders blamed tensions over sex and sovereignty on Afro-Cubans as their protests for racial equity inspired efforts that soon coalesced in the Partido Independiente de Color. Col. James Parker, for one, blamed another vicious November 1907 street fight in downtown Pinar del Río on Black Cubans. Such men, he claimed, lingered in front of the town's theater and nearby cafés, harassing soldiers with epithets like "Malo Americano" and "puto," and elbowing them off sidewalks. Yet Parker also scorned as a "disgrace" white troops who prized masculine honor over professional decorum. Their "usefulness" for pacification was "ended," he wrote, if they did not "abstain from fighting the natives."[76]

Men's commentary about imperial sexual strife typically excluded the voices of Cuban women whose labor lay at its source. As with violence during the first occupation, Cuban men during the second generally narrated such incidents around their patriarchal duty to defend feminine and national honor. Yet the gender ideology of separate spheres dividing male-dominated public life from private spaces of female domesticity in the early republic tended to obscure and marginalize Cuban women's perspective and experience. Increasingly, Cuban men treated Cuba's women, including prostitutes, as passive objects over which they struggled. Not active citizens joining men in defending a sovereign nation, female Cubans were increasingly restricted to family and home, even as feminists agitated for women's civil equality. Elite Cuban men thus joined American men in papering over national tensions of sex when they shared a common patriarchal contempt for the island's most vulnerable women. Responding to the 1907 riots, one Pinar del Río newspaper insisted, rather disingenuously, that the "greatest harmony and brotherhood had existed" between male Cubans and Americans until "the rivalries of two or three women of the immoral life" rudely "interrupted" them.[77]

Still, Cuban men and US Army officers who blamed prostitutes for aggravating conflict hinted that sex workers were not just victims or bystanders. Instead, they left behind evidence that women had actively provoked and participated in these conflicts, thus exercising a degree of autonomy from men of both nations, even as they sometimes allied with Cuban men to secure sovereignty over their bodies and labor. In early February 1908, Capt. John W. Furlong, the occupation's chief of military intelligence, investigated a shooting fray between Cubans and American troops at Lajas, near Cienfuegos, that started inside a brothel. He discovered that prostitutes there had a regular Cuban clientele, some of whom were Afro-Cubans. Furlong concluded that a half-dozen white US soldiers—"degenerates," in his opinion, who "spend all their time and but little money" in bordellos—started the fight by trying to throw these Cuban men out of the establishment (likely as an attempt to impose the color line). Yet Furlong also stated that Cuban prostitutes who had been "determined to free their houses of the unprofitable Americans" actually planned the attack, perhaps not anticipating it would spiral out of control into a brawl and shoot-out sprawling throughout the red-light district. Similar abuses by occupiers frequently prompted sex workers—and women who soldiers presumed were prostitutes—to complain to Cuban police, municipal officials, and US commanders.[78]

By the second intervention's end, Cuba's women and men seemed less willing than they had been in 1898 to concede their national sovereignty and bodily autonomy to Yankee soldiers. That year, a new nation, exhausted by war, its economy in ruins, and vulnerable to a rising empire, but eager to benefit from Americans' modern culture, capital, and technology, negotiated the temporary US occupation that had followed separation from Spain. Now, ten years later, Cuban men and women of a neocolonial republic defended themselves against foreign soldiers who seemed to threaten not just their island's national independence but their control over their bodies, work, and sexuality. If a new empire's needs for martial manpower in the Philippines pushed American army officers to enhance their sexual-disciplinary power over enlisted men, their sovereignty over subaltern sex declined in tandem.

EPILOGUE

The Days of the Empire
Forgetting the Legacies of War's Work in the 1898 Era

In December 1913, months before a war erupted in Europe into which Gen. John J. Pershing eventually led US troops, he transferred authority over the Moro Province to American civilians and Filipinos they were incorporating into the colony's administration. The passage of power from occupying warriors to colonial bureaucrats symbolically ended an era, initiated in 1898, during which Pershing and fellow soldiers made their nation a new colonial power on a global scale in a world still dominated by Europeans and their empires. Yet the devolution of colonial state authority to Cuban and Filipino elites by 1913 also signified Americans' deep ambivalence about imperialism, especially following an acrimonious domestic debate over annexing the Philippines and controversies about how wars there had been fought.[1]

Policymakers in Washington responded by refraining from further annexations of foreign territories, which they knew would require assuming the international legal obligations, and political liabilities, of sovereignty over them. To project and protect Americans' growing commercial, financial, and strategic interests in the world, however, they intervened in and occupied weaker nation-states but formally left their sovereignty intact. This type of foreign rule was not new; Great Britain and other great powers had already devised indirect and informal kinds of imperial control, such as its protectorate in Egypt, that the United States imitated when it imposed the Platt Amendment on Cuba. For the intervened and occupied, however, these fictions of sovereignty failed to obscure who and what effectively controlled their countries. Yet American officials' newfound respect for other nations' sovereignty comported neatly with a Progressive Era foreign policy of liberal development that promoted their influence through political reform, investment and markets, and science and technology. Like US soldiers who rarely considered their use of tropical workforces as exploitation, American politicians, bureaucrats, and diplomats downplayed military action's coercive peoples dimensions. Instead, they emphasized how armed force taught less civilized peoples the benefits of industry, education, free trade, and prudent finance.[2]

Americans sanctified their newly de-territorialized empire of cosmopolitan capital and culture as a natural, organic, and liberating phenomenon, even as martial activity enabled its emergence and evolution. Since May 1898, when soldiers, sailors, and marines fired the first shots against Spain, Americans also occupied Puerto Rico, Hawai'i, Guam, and Samoa, securing them as coaling stations for a steamship navy meant to protect their nation's rising commerce. In 1900, US troops joined Europeans in suppressing the Boxers at Beijing, then left a garrison to ensure that China's doors stayed open to American exports. In 1904, the US Navy and US Marines, authorized by President Theodore Roosevelt's corollary to the Monroe Doctrine, occupied Santo Domingo and established a customs receivership at the behest of New York City bankers. The next year, the US Army took control of an isthmian strip in Panama to build a massive canal meant to enhance Americans' merchant shipping and naval capacities. Though usually narrated separately, these events for some US military personnel became episodes in careers as armed expansionists who mobilized and managed labor. To construct the Panama Canal, army engineers, some of whom had just employed thousands of Cubans and Filipinos on highways, supervised more than 60,000 workers.[3] Beyond bases, battleships, and canal zones, however, most Americans, if they noticed these interventions and occupations at all, perceived and remembered them as distant diplomatic crises that credited their nation as a uniquely anticolonial world power. The vast amount of work they required of US soldiers, much less foreigners, never registered in their consciousness.

From a global perspective, however, 1913 seemed to mark not rupture but continuity in Americans' militarized expansionism in an increasingly interconnected world, as the US government sent gunboats and installed garrisons in more countries and continents. In 1912, President William H. Taft, formerly the Philippines' governor and secretary of war, sent marines into Nicaragua for the second time, now to prevent nationalist insurgents' attacks on Americans, their property, and a friendly regime placing state finances in Yankees' hands. In 1915, New York bankers persuaded President Woodrow Wilson to dispatch marines to Haiti, to shore up a tottering state financed by their dollars. The next year, Wilson sent marines to occupy the Dominican Republic, partly to defend American lenders' interests in its sovereign debt. Simultaneously, Wilson intervened in Mexico's civil war, as rebels threatened American rail and mining companies. In 1914, the Democratic president sent marines into Veracruz; two years later, he ordered Gen. Pershing to invade northern Mexico to pursue Pancho Villa, after that revolutionary raided New Mexico while fighting a general whom Wilson backed. A growing chorus of

Latin Americans—including Cubans whose island in 1912 and 1917 again experienced minor US interventions, criticized this record as imperialism. Yet Wilson's insistence that his nation would fight in Europe to make the world safe for democracy subsumed Americans' interests in a rhetoric of national self-determination that seemed to undermine colonialism. That Wilson by 1916 granted Filipinos and Puerto Ricans limited self-government and citizenship, as some served in the US armed forces, seemed to validate this liberal idealism. Still, by 1919, when US troops joined British and French victors in occupying Germany's Rhineland, American rhetoric styling military occupation as the enlightened pursuit of national "reconstruction" veiled the coercive denial of sovereignty inherent to the phenomenon.[4]

Occupation, repackaged as reconstruction, shed its imperial swaddling clothes. Yet the politics of sovereignty innate to US wars and occupations in Cuba and the Philippines left an indelible colonial imprint on these islands' postwar and post-occupation histories, as well as American military culture itself. The work of empire and its effects lingered in imperial legacies of knowledge, infrastructure, and laboring bodies long after US soldiers departed Cuba and subdued insurgents in the Philippines.

The American army's organization of colonial paramilitary and police forces insinuated the cognitive work of local knowledge into strengthened insular central states. In Cuba, Rural Guards terrorized political opponents, workers, and labor organizers on behalf of Cuban political elites and foreign investors, and helped a new army crush Afro-Cubans' protests for racial equality. Filipinos by the thousands enlisted in new Philippine Scout cavalry regiments, incorporated into the regular US Army, and the Philippine Constabulary, controlled initially by American civilians at Manila. Similar to imperial armies recruited by Europeans in Asia and Africa, white US Army officers and veterans commanded Tagalogs, Ilocanos, and Moros in ethnolinguistically differentiated units. Americans established colonial armies and police not only to reduce empire's expense or preserve white men's health; employing subaltern troops obviated the racialized cultural barriers that frustrated military access to linguistic and geographic knowledge in the past. As one US Army colonel recognized in 1901, when endorsing congressional legislation founding the Philippine Scouts, "natives" who "know their country" and understood "the language and tricks of their people" could "secure information not attainable by white soldiers or white scouts."[5]

The challenges of pacifying a polyglot Philippine archipelago pushed Progressive Era American army officers to reduce their dependence on colonial intermediaries by assimilating their knowledge in new intelligence institutions. By late 1900, US commanders realized they would better exploit and weaponize Filipinos' linguistic, geographic, and cultural expertise against anticolonial insurgents if they internalized it. Directed by Generals Arthur MacArthur and Adna Chaffee, the army at Manila organized a Division of Military Information that started collecting, creating, and distributing topographical and route maps, and profiles of suspect individuals, to enhance operations and surveillance. Spotty recordkeeping and inconsistent efforts among junior officers forced American soldiers during the Pulahan and Moro Wars to continue to rely on local colonial guides and interpreters. If a few conscientious officers tried to impart lessons on how to manage such intermediaries, the War Department failed to integrate their practical knowledge into a professionalizing military culture. Not even reformers like John McAuley Palmer, whom fellow Mindanao veteran Gen. Leonard Wood tasked with devising plans to reorganize the army, required field units to retain linguists. Indeed, prior to World War I, an army focused on conventional warfare never codified into manuals or other doctrinal documents any of the techniques in counterinsurgency it devised since 1898. Only in the 1930s did the Marine Corps produce a colonial-style guide to "small wars."[6]

American soldiers' persistent reliance on civilian translators partly reflected an officer corps either unable or unwilling to train themselves or enlisted men in languages, even as successive interventions in Latin America suggested the wisdom of learning Spanish. Some US veterans of the 1898 era realized how formalizing language education would benefit their army. In late 1902, Gen. Chaffee, lamenting that officers in the archipelago foolishly never studied archipelagic dialects, predicted presciently they would eventually need soldiers who had. He urged Congress to provide $200 bounties to any officer or "intelligent enlisted man" who passed proficiency exams in one of the languages spoken at his station—essentially Ilocano, Pangasinan, Tagalo, Bicol, Visayan, and Moro—and a $100 bounty for passing a Spanish exam. Silence from Washington reflected Americans' disinterest in foreign tongues. Instead, civilian US colonial authorities continued to promote English instruction, believing the language could bridge vernaculars and unite Filipinos as a national people. By the 1930s, a third of the islands' population had become fluent, enabling English-speaking Filipinos to better assert control over a colony shifting toward autonomy and independence.[7]

Cuba's second occupation also suggested that the United States' new colonial army developed its spatial knowledge more than its linguistic capacities. By April 1907, American army engineers completed the map surveys of the island that their predecessors had left unfinished. With typical hubris,

Lt. Col. Robert Lee Bullard, serving as an intelligence officer due partly to his Spanish faculty, gloated prematurely that his army's cartographic knowledge would make Cubans think twice before launching another insurrection. Still, Bullard, before he went on to gather intelligence in revolutionary Mexico, shared his frustrations that fellow officers had not cultivated the language skills that US foreign policy trends implied they needed. "The carabao Spanish of the Manila coachman is not Spanish," Bullard bemoaned from Havana in 1907, and "will not serve in Cuba." Making soldiers effective linguists, he believed, was sure to negate the need for unwieldy, expensive, and untrustworthy interpreters.[8]

Knowledge of tropical labor receded even more as a military priority. Troops' evacuation from Cuba in 1902 and 1909 ended their commanders' curiosity regarding Cuban workers' efficiency, even as that question increasingly interested American investors. In the Philippines, however, civilian American bureaucrats sustained army and naval officers' earlier drive to scientifically enhance the efficiency of tropical labor. Officials including Gov. William Cameron Forbes revised the public school curriculum to emphasize the "racial uplift" model of industrial education. Yet as Filipino printers and other artisans at Manila organized unions, and workers walked out on the Benguet road, American colonizers discovered that Filipinos could be just as militant as Chinese. By 1924, even Philippine Scouts, risking charges of mutiny, struck to protest wage disparities between white and Filipino troops. If Gen. MacArthur maintained that Filipinos worked as hard as anyone else when paid fairly, they challenged Americans' racialization of subaltern colonial labor by acting collectively, just like workers in industrial metropoles.[9]

Infrastructure arguably represented the work of empire's most enduring legacy, as US military forces prizing mobility made enhancing overland transportation networks, often by coerced labor, a core feature of future interventions and occupations. Shortly after his marines invaded and occupied Haiti in 1915, Gen. Smedley Butler commenced an ambitious program to build modern highways designed to help suppress anti-American insurgents and facilitate peasants' access to markets. By reviving a moribund corvée to construct them, however, Butler angered Haitians who equated conscript labor for white marines with enslavement. Exacerbating warfare with "Caco" rebels, Butler's roadbuilding, accompanied by repression and disease in work camps, killed several thousand Haitians. After 1916, when US Marines simultaneously occupied the Dominican Republic next door, they employed thousands of Dominicans, and eventually Haitians, for road and bridge work under similar rubrics of counterinsurgency and economic development. As in Haiti, however, Americans' resort to an archaic corvée in the northern Cibao region spurred peasant resistance, though less bloody than the Gavillero rebellion in southeastern sugar zones. In Nicaragua by the late 1920s, US Marines fighting Augusto Sandino's nationalist guerrillas instituted "civic" programs to win popular support, including by building rural roads and schools. By the 1930s and 1940s, Latin Americans' and Asians' populist politics and rejection of colonialism amid recession and renewed world war ensured that the US military and local contractors would build roads, airports, and other infrastructure by voluntary means, establishing a pattern that lasted into the Cold War. During the Progressive era, American army officers and engineers returning to the states also celebrated colonial roadbuilding as a model for "good roads" at home. Among others, Gen. Hugh Scott by the early 1920s relished the pleasure of "serving my own people," overseeing $40 million worth of highway construction for his native New Jersey.[10]

Another legacy of the US empire of 1898 was found in Chinese migrants' and laborers' persistent marginalization. Though Chinese diplomats and nationals and Chinese Americans continued to protest exclusion in the Philippines, Cuba, and the United States, Sinophobic barriers remained. Employers' persistent calls to reopen the Philippine archipelago to Chinese labor emigrants, especially for plantation agriculture, failed to weaken the US colonial state's anti-Chinese wall. Though mobile Chinese merchants' rising wealth and control of foreign trade magnified interethnic tensions that manifested by the 1920s in Sinophobic riots and legislation, Chinese artisans who once dominated Manila gradually ceded occupational ground to Filipino craftsmen. By the Commonwealth era of the 1930s, American officials' tenuous alliance with Filipino economic nationalists nearly drove Chinese labor entirely from industries that US Army quartermasters had started to "Filipinize" during the war.[11]

The relational imperial racialization of Chinese and Filipino labor also played out in US military manpower policy, as Chinese men virtually disappeared from army and navy ranks enlisting a growing number of colonial subjects. Although Pershing's expeditions in northern Mexico and France used Chinese labor contingents, they generated little commentary compared to predecessors who served American soldiers in the Philippines. After 1902, white US naval officers, reflecting rising Sinophobia in the states and racialized fears of Japan's naval ascendancy, began discharging Chinese and Japanese mess attendants from Pacific warships. Tapping their nation's more open emigration and citizenship policies for Puerto Ricans and Filipinos, as well as domestic anti-Black racism, navy commanders used them to replace Asian and African American sailors. Chinese American recruits only returned to the US military in significant numbers during World War II, when the anti-Japanese alliance with republican China pushed President Franklin D. Roosevelt to finally end exclusion. Not even crucial Chinese labor for American soldiers and marines in US-occupied China during that conflict, and the civil war that followed, weakened strict quotas that severely limited Chinese migration to the states well into the 1960s.[12]

By contrast, colonial nation-building and Filipino nationalist agitation ensured that Filipinos became ever-more integrated in the United States' armed forces, even as Filipino migrants faced greater marginalization in North America. By World War I, recruitment policies welcoming Philippine "natives" to join the navy, combined with Supreme Court jurisprudence and the 1916 Jones Act's commitment to Filipino self-governance, spelled relative tolerance for Filipino emigrants on the mainland. By the late 1920s, Filipino naval veterans and families settling on the West Coast had been joined by some 60,000 Filipino migrants, most of whom found jobs in western agriculture by way of Alaska's fishing canneries and Hawai'i's sugar plantations. By 1934, rising anti-Filipino racism among white nativists, including trade unionists, exacerbated by the Great Depression, prompted Congress to finally promise the Philippines full independence, ten years in the future; World War II delayed it to 1946. Yet Filipinos still suffered limits on their nation's effective sovereignty, as their new government agreed to host US bases as a condition of trade treaties, and Filipinos faced new restrictions on their right to migrate to North America.[13]

The work of empire's body politics also reverberated in the continued efforts of US Army commanders, bureaucrats, politicians, and reformers to regulate and discipline the sexuality and labor of male military personnel and women at home and abroad. The need for healthy soldiers in war and peace continued to inflict on American enlisted men a sexual regime of medical policing which officers originally adapted from prostitution's regulation in colonial Cuba and the Philippines. Still, militarized attempts to suppress sexual disease barely reduced infection rates in the army. By the 1910s, VD rates in Philippine garrisons were double or higher than those in stateside posts; by 1914, one in five soldiers in the archipelago were infected. While new prophylactic and pharmaceutical techniques helped, medicalized sexual discipline in a newly global US military never became universal or consistent. American commanders in the tropics never exerted much control over off-post sexual economies that seemed to lure troops into unsafe encounters. Army surgeons-general briefly experimented with punitive methods; in 1912, the War Department tried stopping payments to troops while they received VD treatment.[14]

In the 1910s and 1920s, Progressive Era "military sanitarians," above all Col. L. Mervin Maus, crusaded to cleanse the ranks of the empire-fueled vices of alcohol and sex that seemed poised to racially and biologically degrade America's military manhood. Their efforts culminated in the high-water mark of military-libidinal discipline, and prohibition in general, during World War I. After social purity activists pushed Washington to criminalize prostitution near dry army camps, a majority of states by 1918 had passed laws requiring pelvic exams for prostitutes. As colonial-style regulation boomeranged in the metropole, American soldiers' and sailors' persistent stimulation of sex markets abroad continued to spark controversy and nationalist ire, perhaps nowhere more so than in the Philippines. By the Cold War, US military enclaves on Luzon, exerting less direct discipline on Filipinas, became part of a permanent regional militarized sex trade generating anti-imperialist sentiment, "mestizo" children, and tensions of race, sex, and nation for Americans and Asians alike.[15]

By the end of the Cold War, a US military of gargantuan size, global omnipresence, and high technology bore little resemblance to the miniscule army that war with Spain in 1898 thrust from North American frontiers into the strange and sultry tropics. Two world wars and, above all, a global conflict with the Soviet Union and international communism made it impossible for Americans to return to the republican limits and provincial sensibilities that constrained their military's size, power, and permanence for most of the nation's history. Yet the United States' war on Islamic terror in 2001 produced a labor politics that oddly echoed its imperial past. In Afghanistan and Iraq, an undermanned and underequipped neoliberal Department of Defense, ill-prepared for counterinsurgency, relied on private contractors to execute its missions. Recruiting and managing local and migrant workforces to aid field operations, logistics, and reconstruction, they organized a global army of workers. By 2008, defense contractors employed at least 260,000 civilians, nearly half of whom were "local" or "host-country" nationals, to support US warfare in the region. As many as 100,000 of these individuals, designated as "third-country nationals," hailed mostly from Africa and Asia. Including Filipinos, they provided domestic labor, engineering skill, and security, among other services. Critics accused contractors of exploiting and abusing this transnational workforce by confiscating their passports, paying less than promised, withholding wages and airfare, and subjecting them to long workdays and squalid living conditions. If colossal public works programs improved Iraqis' and Afghanis' everyday life, billions spent on roads and other infrastructure also enriched global American construction corporations and prompted watchdogs to allege extraordinary waste and corruption. As the US government withdrew troops from these nations, Washington often denied special immigration visas its officials had promised Afghanis and Iraqis, including interpreters, who had risked their lives for its armed forces. In all this, the muse of history exposed a new iteration of the work that had begun long ago, during an age that jaded American soldiers and veterans, in half jest, called the "days of the empire."[16]

Acknowledgments

Books, like empires, are made by multitudes. This project benefited immensely from the ideas, encouragement, criticism, and assistance of more people and institutions than could possibly be recognized here. Research was generously supported by Columbia University's Department of History and Graduate School of Arts and Sciences, the Andrew W. Mellon Foundation, the Howard and Natalie Shawn family, and the Doris G. Quinn Foundation. At New York University, the John W. Draper Interdisciplinary Master's Program in Humanities and Social Thought and Center for Latin American and Caribbean Studies funded travel to archives. For recognizing this work's potential, thanks go to Sven Beckert, Andreas Eckert, Jill Lane, Charles Maier, and Ana María Dopico, and Harvard University's Charles Warren Center for Studies in American History and the Weatherhead Initiative on Global History; re:work, or IGK Work and Human Life Cycle in Global History, at Humboldt University; the Society for Historians of American Foreign Relations; and the US Army Center of Military History. At critical junctures, academics and institutes in Cuba and the Philippines granted support essential for access to sources. I am especially grateful to the Third World Studies Center at the University of the Philippines Diliman and, in Havana, the Instituto de Historia and Instituto Cubano de Investigación Cultural "Juan Marinello." At these locations I benefited from guidance dispensed by scholars including Ricardo R. Jose, Benito J. Legarda Jr., Gustavo Placer Cervera, and Sergio Guerra Vilaboy. I am also grateful for the support of Bard College at Simon's Rock and colleagues there including Asma Abbas, David Baum, Leon Botstein, Wesley Brown, Chris Coggins, Brendan Matthews, Anne O'Dwyer, Francisca Oyogoa, Pat Sharpe, Carla Stephens, Larry Wallach, and John Weinstein.

The many staff at archives, libraries, and other repositories who enabled this research are too numerous to name here, but I am particularly grateful for the patient and perennial assistance of archivists at the Library of Congress and the National Archives. Despite fewer resources and my peculiar requests, professionals at archives and libraries in Cuba and the Philippines also made this book possible. At Havana, these included Migda Estevez, Martha Mariel Ferrol, Marcelo Santos, and Julio Vargas; at Cienfuegos, Iliana Alvarez Araujo, Yanet Casanova Valdes, Dadiana Despaigne Dorticos, Luis Raul Lanza Jimenez, Dayami Ochoa Sust, Felix Otero Molina, and Carmen Rosa Guillemi; at Pinar del Río, Ania Pampillo Cheda; and at Santiago de Cuba, Yenislaisy Abreu, Jacquelyn Jackson, Yoandra Ramirez Mustelier, and Milagros Villalón Salazar. Carrolee Bengelsdorf, Ariel Lambe, and Jana Lipman were trustworthy guides for Cuba, and Richard Chu, Paul Kramer, and Theresa Ventura for the Philippines. Assisting research from long distances were Jeffrey Bell, Joshua Fitzgerald, Marjorie Galelli, Zach Kopin, Robert Lease, and Bradley Mollmann.

Opportunities to share this research were granted by professional organizations, including the Association for Asian Studies, the Labor and Working-Class History Association, and the Philippine Studies Group. Academic entities sponsoring presentations of preliminary work included Birkbeck, University of London; the Centro Studi Americani and CISPEA in

Rome; the Freie Universität Berlin; Indiana University Bloomington; the International Institute of Social History at Amsterdam; the London School of Economics–Columbia University International and World History Research Seminar; and the University of Birmingham. For this, many thanks are due Roham Alvandi, Nathon Cardon, Ferdinando Fasce, Hillary Footit, Simon Jackson, Alexander Lichtenstein, Kelly Maddox, Michelle Moyd, Brigid O'Keefe, T. C. Sherman, Marcel van der Linden, Maurizio Vaudaugna, and Matthias Zachmann. This work was improved greatly by feedback, at these and other events, from Stefan Aune, Katie Bales, Daniel Bender, Eileen Boris, Matthew Casey, Patrick Chung, Michael Cullinane, Christopher Dietrich, Michael Donoghue, Elizabeth Esch, Rosa Ficek, Leon Fink, Harry Franqui-Rivera, Maria Fritsche, Joshua Gedacht, Cindy Hahamovitch, Timothy Keogh, Christopher Knowles, Amy Kohout, Nelson Lichtenstein, Diana Martinez, Al McCoy, Rebecca Tinio McKenna, April Merleaux, Karen Miller, James Parisot, David Prior, Lara Putnam, William Riddell, Roberto Saba, Quinn Slobodian, Vernadette Vicuña Gonzalez, Colleen Woods, and Micah Wright.

I have been exceedingly fortunate to learn so much from an extraordinary assemblage of scholars. This project originated at the University of Massachusetts at Amherst, inspired at an early stage by Chris Appy. Since then, History Department chairs Anne Broadbridge, Joye Bowman, and Brian Ogilvie, in addition to Andrew Donson, granted crucial access to books and seminars. I have also been lucky to have Richard Chu as an academic ambassador to all things Philippine. A true artisan of the historian's craft, Bruce Laurie skillfully made me a worker. He not only read much of this manuscript but over many years rescued me from all kinds of self-inflicted errors; I am forever grateful. Faculty at Columbia University who helped me envision this book included Elizabeth Blackmar, Victoria de Grazia, Barbara Fields, Mark Mazower, and Caterina Pizzigoni. Ira Katznelson and Alice Kessler-Harris inspired early iterations of the project, and Mae Ngai and Anders Stephanson pushed it over the finish line; Ada Ferrer and Paul Kramer also intervened and inspired at critical junctures. Eric Foner's erudition and encouragement modeled the scholarly rigor and professional excellence to which this historian only aspires but which I strive to impart to my own students; I hope this stands as some small tribute. At NYU, Fred Cooper, David Ludden, Robin Nagle, and Barbara Weinstein helped me transition this work from dissertation to book; I also had the privilege of discussing it with Marilyn Young before she passed, too soon. I owe special thanks to Chris Capozzola, who congenially supplied comment and counsel, and Julie Greene, whose intellect and enthusiasm always points me in the right direction—though never, it seems, to that other canal. At the University of North Carolina Press, Brandon Proia saw the manuscript's potential and passed the baton to Debbie Gershenowitz and her able stewardship and Alexis Dumain's technical wizardry; thanks also to Mary Ribesky, Jamie Thaman, and cartographer Gabriel Moss. Aiding revisions enormously were colleagues who read chapter drafts, including Oli Charbonneau, Holger Droessler, Zach Fredman, Rebecca Herman, Lauren Hirshberg, Jeongmin Kim, Ruth Lawlor, Jana Lipman, Adam Moore, A. J. Murphy, Kristin Oberiano, Roberto Saba, Stuart Schrader, Augustine Sedgewick, David Singerman, Quinn Slobodian, Christy Thornton, Simon Toner, Andy Urban, Patrick Vitale, and Kim Wagner.

In New York and beyond, I was blessed to enjoy conversation and criticism with a gregarious bunch of graduate students who provided energy and the will to persist; among others, cheers go to Jessica Adler, Toby Harper, Thai Jones, Nick Juravich, Ariel Mae

Lambe, Thomas Meaney, Rachel Newman, Keith Orejel, Victoria Phillips, Tim Shenk, Jude Webre, Stephen Wertheim, and Mason Williams. An extended community of family, friends, and good Samaritans furnished the logistics and infrastructure for research and writing. I am profoundly indebted to Cubans who welcomed me into their homes and clinicians at Viñales who saved my life, making my worst May Day the best ever. At Havana, I will never forget Raysa, Orlando, Ilya, Coci, Purita, and Alfredito (and Toni!), and at Pinar del Río, Dory, Osmani, Assaye, and Johan. Always hospitable in the states to a penurious and peripatetic young researcher was Paul Adler, Lance Baldwin and Erica Stewart, Pam Costain and Larry Weiss, Emily Pawley, Matthew Reiter, Michael Sherrard, and Andrew Younkins. Giancarlo Ambrosino and Morwin Schmookler cheered from the sidelines. Most important, family offered unfailing love and support, despite setbacks: my mother, Joan, who shepherded me the entire way; siblings Joshua, Joseph, and Jennifer and her family, Hans and Turner; Sarah; and Paula Costain. I am truly privileged to now have in my life Kate, not merely for endlessly reading drafts, and Gabrielle, Elizabeth, Diane, and George. Maturing in this book's shadow, Samuel and Alice will do bigger and better things. I always count on your rays of sunlight to dissipate the clouds—and deadlines.

Notes

Abbreviations

[1]AC	[First] Army Corps
[1]B	[First] Brigade
[1]D	[First] Division
[1]SB	[First] Separate Brigade
ACP	Army of Cuban Pacification
AG/AAG/AGO	Adjutant General/Assistant Adjutant General/Adjutant General's Office
AHPSDC	Archivo Histórico Provincial de Santiago de Cuba, Cuba
ANRC	Archivo Nacional de la República de Cuba, Havana, Cuba
ARGMP	*Annual Report of the Governor of the Moro Province*
ARPGC	*Annual Report of the Provisional Governor of Cuba*
ARWD	*Annual Report of the War Department*
BIA	Bureau of Insular Affairs, War Department
CG	Commanding General
CWS	*Correspondence Relating to the War with Spain*
DC	Division of Cuba/Department of Cuba
DM/DMJ	Department of Mindanao/Department of Mindanao and Jolo
DMSC	Department of Matanzas and Santa Clara
DNL	Department of Northern Luzon
DNP	Department of North Philippines
DP	Department of the Pacific
DPH	Division of the Philippines
DS/DSC/DSPP	Department of Santiago/Department of Santiago de Cuba/Department of Santiago and Puerto Principe
DSL	Department of Southern Luzon
E	Entry (in Record Group, NARA)
FGP	Fondo Gobierno Provincial
FRUS	*Papers Relating to the Foreign Relations of the United States*
GCM	General Courts Martial, Case Files
GO	General Order
GPO	Government Printing Office
HDP	Historical Data Papers
JJP	John J. Pershing Papers, Library of Congress, Washington, DC
LRB	Letter Received Book
LR/TR	Letter Received/Telegram Received
LSB	Letter Sent Book
LS/TS	Letter Sent/Telegram Sent

286 Notes to Introduction

LWP	Leonard Wood Papers, Library of Congress, Washington, DC
MG	Military Governor/Military Government (Philippines)
NARA	National Archives and Records Administration, United States
PC	Philippine Commission
PIR	Philippine Insurgent Records, Philippine National Archives, Manila
QM	Quartermaster
RG	Record Group
RLB	Robert L. Bullard Papers, Library of Congress, Washington, DC
RPC	*Report of the US Philippine Commission*
SAWS	Spanish-American War Survey, USAHEC, Carlisle, PA
SP	Secretaria de la Presidencia, Archivo Nacional de la República de Cuba, Havana
SW	Secretary of War
TS/TR	Telegram Sent/Telegram Received
USAHEC	US Army Heritage and Education Center, Carlisle, PA
USPC	US Philippine Commission
USVI	US Volunteer Infantry
WCF	William Cameron Forbes Papers, Harvard University, Cambridge, MA

Introduction

1. Bjork, *Prairie Imperialists*, chap. 2, 175, 181, 183–86; H. L. Scott to Mary Scott, Oct. 28, 1903, microfilm 17249, roll 2, Scott Papers, quoted in Bjork, *Prairie Imperialists*, 183; Scott, *Some Memories of a Soldier*, 4, 11, parts 2–5, passim; "Oct. 26 1909 Harvard," Writings, Speeches, 1907–09, box 81, Hugh Scott Papers, Library of Congress, Washington, DC.

2. "Delivered before the Society of Colonial Wars, N.Y. City, Nov. 17, 1908," Writings, Speeches, 1907–09; "Laurenceville Alumni Dinner, February 13, 1909," in Writings, Speeches, 1910; all box 81, Hugh Scott Papers, Library of Congress.

3. Tone, *War and Genocide in Cuba*, 223; Matthews, *New-Born Cuba*, 309; Wood to AG, War Department, May 6, 1899, vol. 6, box 2, E 1479, RG 395, NARA.

4. Bacardí y Moreau, *Cronicas*, vol. 10, 188–90; Nov. 1, 1899, and Nov. 23, 1899, in *Actas Capitulares*, vol. 1898–1899, Santiago de Cuba, APSDC; Lawton to AG, Washington, DC, Sept. 3, 1898, box 1, E 1479; H. C. Corbin to Lawton, Sept. 4, 1898, box 1, E 1487, both RG 395, NARA.

5. Couttie, *Hang the Dogs*, xii–xiv, 112–13, 118–33, 136–53; Linn, "The Struggle for Samar," 161–67; Linn, "'We Will Go Heavily Armed,'" 273–80; de Viana, "Eugenio Daza's Account," 54–59; Daza y Salazar, "Some Documents of the Philippine-American War in Samar," 168–69, 173–76.

6. Linn, "'We Will Go Heavily Armed,'" 273–74, 277, 280; Couttie, *Hang the Dogs*, 363–74; de Viana, "Eugenio Daza's Account," 57–63; Delmendo, *Star-Entangled Banner*, 168–98; Eu. Daza to Sr. Col., Oct. 6, 1901, PIR 820.5, Exhibit 1360, in Taylor, *Philippine Insurrection*, 5:704–5.

7. Burbank and Cooper, *Empires in World History*, 1, 7–8, 16–17, 28–32, 180–84, 219–35, 238–40, 249–50; Anghie, *Imperialism, Sovereignty, and the Making of International Law*; Kramer, "Power and Connection," 1349–50; Go, *Postcolonial Thought and Social Theory*, 2–5;

Stoler, *Duress*, chap. 5, esp. 177. On false distinctions between "empires" and "nations," see Kumar, *Visions of Empire*, chap. 1.

8. Kramer, *Blood of Government*, 7–10, 20, 43–52, 73–86; Ferrer, *Cuba*, esp. 16–17, 124–25; Downs, *Second American Revolution*.

9. Kramer, *Blood of Government*, 109–10, 162–66; L. A. Pérez, *Cuba between Empires*, 185–87, 275.

10. Greene, "Wages of Empire," 36.

11. Bender and Lipman, "Through the Looking Glass"; Montgomery, "Workers' Movements in the United States Confront Imperialism"; Poblete, *Islanders in the Empire*; De Leon, *Bundok*; Greene, *Canal Builders*; Lipman, *Guantánamo*; Greene, "Wages of Empire," 37–40; van der Linden, "Promises and Challenges of Global Labor History," 65; Seigel, *Violence Work*, 9–13; Riddell, *On the Waves of Empire*, 47–54.

12. Stoler and McGranahan, "Reconfiguring Imperial Terrains," 8–13; Stoler, *Duress*, 177–78, 189–99; Lefebvre, *Critique of Everyday Life*. For exceptions of colonial history as labor history in the Philippines, see Bankoff, "Wants, Wages, and Workers"; Bankoff, "Poblete's *Obreros*"; R. T. McKenna, *American Imperial Pastoral*, chap. 2. For different iterations of "military colonialism", see Pobutsky and Neri, "Patterns of Filipino Migration to Guam"; Shibusawa, "U.S. Empire and Racial Capitalist Modernity," 861–62; Manjapra, *Colonialism in Global Perspective*, 13. Few estimate the number of workers employed by US armies and occupations in Cuba and the Philippines between 1898 and 1913, in part because War Department reports and records do not include aggregate data. On Cuba during the first US intervention, see Hitchman, "Unfinished Business," 339; during its second US intervention, see Lockmiller, *Magoon in Cuba*, 101–2; and on the Philippines during the American War, see Linn, *Philippine War*, 127.

13. Millis, *Arms and Men*, 173–81; Cosmas, *An Army for Empire*, 1–4, 100, 105–8, 129, 295–314; Coffman, *Regulars*, 27–54; Skowronek, *Building a New American State*; Barr, *Progressive Army*, 100–22; Maier, *Among Empires*, 70–71; Linn, *Guardians of Empire*, 52–53; Wooster, *United States Army and the Making of America*; Katznelson, "Flexible Capacity"; Balogh, *Government Out of Sight*, 212–13; Novak, "Myth of the 'Weak' American State." Focused on the US Army, this study only tangentially addresses joint US Navy and Marine Corps operations. For their role in the wars of 1898, see V. Williams, "Naval Service in the Age of Empire"; Cosmas, "Marines in the Spanish-American War." The US Army occupied Cuba and the Philippines with far fewer troops than military scholars recommend for modern forces in terms of preferable solder-civilian ratios; see Goode, "A Historical Basis"; Healy, *United States in Cuba*, 58, 67–80; Trask, *War with Spain*, 145, 152, 155–56, 386–87; Tone, *War and Genocide in Cuba*, 210; Coffman, *Regulars*, 28, 34; Linn, *Philippine War*, 15, 42, 88–90, 213, 325; Linn, *Guardians of Empire*, chap. 2, 62; Capozzola, *Bound by War*, 45, 53.

14. Weigley, *American Way of War*; Downs, *After Appomattox*; Wooster, *Military and United States Indian Policy*, 11, 76–83; Greene, "Wages of Empire," 40–42; Bjork, *Prairie Imperialists*; Aune, *Indian Wars Everywhere*, chap. 2.

15. Healy, *United States in Cuba*, 81–84; L. A. Pérez, *Cuba between Empires*, xvi, 7, 19–20, 29–31; O. D. Corpuz, *Economic History of the Philippines*, 177–79, 186–88, 190–96; E. S. Rosenberg, *Financial Missionaries to the World*; Lumba, *Monetary Authorities*; Maurer, *Empire Trap*, 38–55; Akiboh, "Empire's Embezzlers."

16. L. A. Pérez, "Insurrection, Intervention, and the Transformation of Land Tenure Systems in Cuba"; L. A. Pérez, *Cuba and the United States*, 118–24; Golay, *Face of Empire*, 60–62; Merleaux, *Sugar and Civilization*, 42–43; Bankoff, "Poblete's *Obreros*"; Bankoff, "Wants, Wages, and Workers."

17. Go, *Postcolonial Thought and Social Theory*, 45–49, 59–63, chap. 4; Chakrabarty, *Provincializing Europe*; Greene, "Wages of Empire," 42–50; Preston and Rossinow, introduction, esp. 6–7; Andrews, *Killing for Coal*; Domínguez, "Response to Occupations by the United States"; May, "Resistance and Collaboration," 84–86; Paredes, "Origins of National Politics"; W. Johnson, "On Agency"; Cooper, "Conflict and Connection," 1532–35; Bender and Lipman, "Through the Looking Glass," 14–17; R. Herman, *Cooperating with the Colossus*, 4–6.

18. Van der Linden, *Workers of the World*, 17–37; Boris, *Making the Woman Worker*, 1–14; Prakash, "Colonialism, Capitalism and the Discourse of Freedom"; Fraser, "Expropriation and Exploitation in Racialized Capitalism"; Beckert, "Labor Regimes after Emancipation"; Bender and Lipman, "Through the Looking Glass," 10, 12; Greene, "Wages of Empire," 50–53; Harris, *God's Arbiters*.

19. Humphrey, "Sovereignty," 418, 420, 435; Fradera, "Reading Imperial Transitions"; Hansen and Stepputat, "Sovereignty Revisited"; Latham, "Social Sovereignty"; Onuf, "Sovereignty"; Evans et al., "Sovereignty," 1, 7; Karuka, *Empire's Tracks*, xii, chap. 1; Stoler and Cooper, "Between Metropole and Colony"; Anghie, *Imperialism, Sovereignty, and the Making of International Law*. For alternative concepts of subaltern sovereignty in the context of India's culture and history, see Berger, *Subaltern Sovereigns*, esp. 1–2; Banerjee, "Decolonization and Subaltern Sovereignty," 71–72.

20. B. R. Anderson, *Imagined Communities*; Guerra, *Myth of José Martí*. To recognize that some anticolonial elites embraced nationalist sovereignty by 1898 is not to imply any teleology of its inevitability; see Thomas, *Orientalists, Propagandists, and Ilustrados*, 8, 12–15.

21. Agoncillo, *Malolos*; Guerrero, *Luzon at War*; Rafael, *Motherless Tongues*, 21–42; Ileto, *Pasyon and Revolution*; Go, "*El cuerpo, razon at kapangyarihan*."

22. Sewell, "Marc Bloch and the Logic of Comparative History," 211–12; Levine, "Is Comparative History Possible?," esp. 331–33, 338–39; Seigel, "Beyond Compare," esp. 65; Hansen and Stepputat, "Sovereignty Revisited"; Howland and White, "Sovereignty and the Study of States," 2. Emphasis on formal state sovereignty's structuring effects on military-colonial labor relations here is not intended to reinforce any "artificial binary" between "formal" and "informal" empire, which, as historians note, "obscures the nature of working-class experience as well as the braided deployment of state, military, and corporate power and sovereignty." Bender and Lipman, "Through the Looking Glass," 5–6; Go, "Provinciality of American Empire," 82–85.

23. Kramer, "Power and Connection"; Hopkins, *American Empire*; Ballantyne and Burton, *Empires and the Reach of the Global*, esp. chap. 2; Hoganson and Sexton, introduction, 6–12; Kocka, "Comparison and Beyond," esp. 42–44; Scott, "Small-Scale Dynamics of Large-Scale Processes"; R. J. Scott, *Degrees of Freedom*, 4–6. Comparativist exceptions to typically "bilateral" histories of US empire include L. Thompson, "Imperial Republic"; Go, *American Empire and the Politics of Meaning*; Go, "Global Perspectives on the U.S. Colonial State in the Philippines," 20; McCoy, Scarano, and Johnson, "On the Tropic of Cancer," 3–33. For inter-imperial histories that focus on migration, see Poblete, *Islanders in the Empire*; Casey, *Empire's Guestworkers*; de Leon, *Bundok*.

24. Said, *Orientalism*; Cohn, *Colonialism and Its Forms of Knowledge*, esp. 3–56; Bayly, *Empire and Information*, 3–6; Brody, *Visualizing American Empire*, 97–103; J. C. Scott, *Seeing Like a State*, 1–6, 44–47; Bragge, Claas, and Roscoe, "On the Edge of Empire"; Kramer, *Blood of Government*, 220–26; McCoy, *Policing America's Empire*, 21–27; Ballantyne and Burton, *Empires and the Reach of the Global*, 79–84; Beckert, "From Tuskegee to Togo"; Zimmerman, *Alabama in Africa*; Droessler, *Coconut Colonialism*.

25. Rafael, *Contracting Colonialism*, ix–xi; Ngai, "'A Knowledge of the Barbarian Language,'" 5–32, esp. 6–7; Lawrance, Osborn, and Roberts, "African Intermediaries and the 'Bargain' of Collaboration," 3–33; Droessler, *Coconut Colonialism*, 170–77.

26. Guldi, *Roads to Power*; O'Connell, "Corps of Engineers and the Rise of Modern Management"; Tate, *Frontier Army in the Settlement of the West*, 52–64; Nye, *American Technological Sublime*; Adas, *Dominance by Design*, chap. 3; Karuka, *Empire's Tracks*, xiv, chap. 3; Ballantyne and Burton, *Empires and the Reach of the Global*, 79–90; Shamir, "Without Borders?"; B. Larkin, "Politics and Poetics of Infrastructure," 332–34.

27. Baron and Boris, "'The Body' as a Useful Category for Working-Class History"; Hansen and Stepputat, "Sovereignty Revisited," 297; Ballantyne and Burton, "Bodies, Empires, and World Histories"; Manjapra, *Colonialism in Global Perspective*, 200–202, 211–12; Roediger and Esch, *Production of Difference*; Greene, "Wages of Empire," 42–50; Stoler, *Duress*, chap. 9.

28. Cohen et al., "Body/Sex/Work Nexus," 12–15. The term "sex work" is employed here mostly for stylistic reasons as a synonym for prostitution, without entering the complex debate on these terms' politics and contested meanings; see Overall, "What's Wrong with Prostitution?"; Davidson, "Rights and Wrongs of Prostitution"; Berg, "Working for Love, Loving for Work," esp. 697–700.

29. Stoler, *Along the Archival Grain*, chap. 2.

Chapter One

1. Salman, *Embarrassment of Slavery*, 99–102; Abinales, *Orthodoxy and History*, 50–51; Driver, *Geography Militant*; Howland, "Field Service in Mindanao," 36–38, 42; ARWD 1905, vol. 3, 312; Philip Reade, diary, Aug. 13, 1904, Philip Reade Papers, Wisconsin Historical Society; LS 1043, H. van Orsdale to CO, Parang, Mindanao, Aug. 15, 1904, v. 4, E 3530; Jno. V. White to CO, Parang, Aug. 12, 1904, box 5; M. C. Kerth to AG, Dept. Mindanao, Dec. 26, 1904, box 7; both E 3534; all RG 395, NARA.

2. Gowing, *Mandate in Moroland*, 83, 151–54; Salman, *Embarrassment of Slavery*, 67, 112–15; Abinales, *Orthodoxy and History*, 47–56; ARWD 1902, Lt.-Gen., 497–98; ARWD 1905, vol. 3, 312; Tel., Van Orsdale to AG, Zamboanga, August 17, 1904, v. 4, E 3530; C. S. Frank to Adj., Cottabato, June 1, 1904; Frank to Adj., Cottabato, Dec. 21, 1904; both box 6; Kerth to AG, DM, Dec. 26, 1904, box 7; all E 3534; all RG 395, NARA. American officers in the Rio Grande criticized Moro guides for offering "limited information" they found "indefinite and often contradictory"; see C. M. Truitt to Adj., Cottabato, July 27, 1904; Kerth to Adj., Cotabato, Sept. 17, 1904; both box 5, E 3534, RG 395, NARA.

3. Hawkins, *Making Moros*, 35; Howland, "Field Service in Mindanao," 36–38, 42–44.

4. Hobbs, *Kris and Krag*, 137–42; H. S. Howland, "Field Service in Mindanao," 44–45; G. M. Best to AAG, DMJ, March 27, 1900, v. 2, E 3530; C. C. Smith to Van Orsdale, Sept. 2, 1904, box 5; White to McGunnegle, Dec. 12, 1904, box 7; both E 3534; all RG 395, NARA.

5. McCoy, *Policing America's Empire*; W. Anderson, *Colonial Pathologies*, esp. 184–93; Rafael, *White Love*, chap. 1; Rodríguez, *Right to Live in Health*, chaps. 1 and 2.

6. Hardin, *Trust and Trustworthiness*, esp. 1–27; Rafael, *Motherless Tongues*, 121–22; Tilly, *Trust and Rule*, esp. chaps. 1 and 2; Frevert, "Trust as Work"; Ataviado, *Philippine Revolution*, 2:85–86; T. L. Smith to Adj., Reina Regente, Aug. 3, 1904, box 5, E 3534, RG 395, NARA.

7. L. A. Pérez, *Colonial Reckoning*, esp. 70, 83–88, 94–95, 148–57; Quirino, "Spanish Colonial Army"; McCoy, *Policing America's Empire*, 30.

8. Dunlay, *Wolves for the Blue Soldiers*, chaps. 3–7, chap. 11; Utley, *Frontier Regulars*, 53–55, 196–98, 371–72, 377–92, 401; Smith, *View from Officers' Row*, chap. 8; McCoy, *Policing America's Empire*, 59–93; Bjork, *Prairie Imperialists*, chap. 2, 100–101; Capozzola, *Bound by War*, 34–41; Aune, *Indian Wars Everywhere*, 52–67; Wagner, *Service of Security and Information*, 227–28; H. L. Scott, *Some Memories of a Soldier*, 31–40.

9. Trask, *War with Spain in 1898*, 138, 174–75, 210, 235–28; L. A. Pérez, *War of 1898*, 81–107; Shafter, "Capture of Santiago de Cuba," 621; Matthew A. Batson, "Reconnaissance Work Performed by Me during the Santiago Campaign," box 1, Matthew A. Batson Papers, USAHEC.

10. Lisandro Pérez, *Sugar, Cigars, and Revolution*; L. A. Pérez, *Cuba in the American Imagination*, chap. 2; L. A. Pérez, *On Becoming Cuban*, 17–95; Guerra, *Myth of José Martí*, chap. 2; Ferrer, *Cuba*, 89, 91–94.

11. Trask, *War with Spain*, 212–13; Cosmas, *Army for Empire*, esp. 75–76.

12. L. A. Pérez, *Cuba between Empires*, 196; B. M. Miller, "Map-Mindedness in the Age of Empire," 24–26; L. A. Pérez, *Colonial Reckoning*, 67–68; Shafter, "Capture of Santiago de Cuba," 614; US Senate, *Conduct of the War Department*, 7:3200. In June 1898, the War Department, drawing on visits to Cuba and publications by Lt. Andrew S. Rowan and journalist Richard Harding Davis, printed a booklet, *Military Notes on Cuba*. The document lacked detailed maps of Oriente, however, and it is unclear how many copies were distributed to officers dispatched to Cuba; see Barnes, *Spanish-American War and the Philippine Insurrection*, 63, 88; War Dept., AGO, *Military Notes on Cuba*, Nov. 1898.

13. Trask, *War with Spain in 1898*, 204; Ferrer, *Freedom's Mirror*; Rynning, *Gun Notches*, 184; Miley, *In Cuba with Shafter*, 50, 53–54, 58; Funston, *Memories of Two Wars*, 5, 29–31, 63–66, 79; Shafter, "Capture of Santiago de Cuba," 615, 617; ARWD 1898, Maj.-Gen., 160; "R. H. Wilson's Part in the Spanish-American War," 11, 73, 90–91, box 1, Richard H. Wilson Papers, American Heritage Collection.

14. L. A. Pérez, *Cuba between Empires*, 199–205; L. A. Pérez, *War of 1898*, 82–86, 95; J. B. Atkins, *War in Cuba*, 108.

15. Bigelow, *Reminiscences*, 84; Roosevelt, *The Rough Riders*, 75; "R. H. Wilson's Part in the Spanish-American War," 26, 65–66, 68, box 1, Richard H. Wilson Papers.

16. Trask, *War with Spain*, 204, 209, 211–13; L. A. Pérez, *War of 1898*, 86–90; Muecke Bertel, *Patria y Libertad*; Gutierrez, *Oriente Heróica*, 66–67; Alger, *Spanish-American War*, 99–105; Collazo, *Los americanos en Cuba*, 144–49; Miley, *In Cuba with Shafter*, 55–56, 92, 105, 190–92, 203; Mingus and Melzer, "Letters Home," 31–32; Moss, *Memories of the Campaign of Santiago*, 23; Roosevelt, *The Rough Riders*, 86; Vivian, *The Fall of Santiago*, 101–4; Wheeler, *The Santiago Campaign, 1898*, 16; R. H. Davis, "Rough Riders' Fight at Las Guasimas," 262–64; Shafter, "Capture of Santiago de Cuba," 621; ARWD 1898, 162, 331–32; Calixto García to Máximo Gómez, July 15, 1898, reprinted in Torriente y Peraza,

Calixto García cooperó con las fuerzas armadas de los EE. UU. en 1898, 67–68; Wheeler to AG, 5AC, June 26, 1898, box 1, E 585, RG 395, NARA. Cuban historians who argue that Cuban scouts from Gen. Castillo's command initiated fighting at Las Guásimas include Abdala Pupo, *Intervención militar norteamericana*, 91–97.

17. L. A. Pérez, *Cuba between Empires*, 202–3; Trask, *War with Spain in 1898*, 175; L. A. Pérez, *War of 1898*, 81–107; T. W. Miller, *Theodore W. Miller*, 115; Post, *Little War of Private Post*, 126–28, 165; Gauvreau, *Reminiscences of the Spanish-American War*, 28–29; Kohr, *Around the World with Uncle Sam*, 66–69, quote on 69; Ward, *Springfield in the Spanish-American War*, 61; Society of Santiago de Cuba, *Santiago Campaign*, 8; S. Crane, *Wounds in the Rain*, 46–51, quote on 46; S. Crane, *War Dispatches*, 138, 161, 163.

18. L. A. Pérez, *Cuba between Empires*, 235–36; Trask, *War with Spain in 1898*, 311; Wagner, *Report of the Santiago Campaign*, 47, 61–63, 66–68; Miley, *In Cuba with Shafter*, 164, 172–73; Post, *Little War of Private Post*, 130; J. B. Atkins, *War in Cuba*, 107; ARWD 1898, 162, 173, 379; Wheeler to Shafter, July 1, 1898, box 1, E 535; H. W. Lawton to Demetrio Castillo, Aug. 19, 1898; Lawton to AG, US Army, Aug. 26, 1898; Lawton to AG, Washington, Sept. 10, 1898; all vol. 1, E 1479; R. G. Mendoza to AAG, DS, Oct. 1, 1898, box 2, E 1487; all RG 395, NARA; Lawton to AG, Sept. 11, 1898, box 1540, E 25, RG 94, NARA.

19. Trask, *War with Spain in 1898*, 311; Roff and Cucchiara, *From the Free Academy to CUNY*, 80; McCallum, *Leonard Wood*, 17–46; E. F. Atkins, *Sixty Years in Cuba*, 295–96; Holme, *Life of Leonard Wood*, 66; Bacardí, *Cronicas*, vol. 10, 172; "Cleaning up the City of Santiago," *New York Tribune*, Oct. 16, 1898; "Death List of a Day," *New York Times*, March 24, 1899; "Cleaning Up Santiago," *New York Sun*, May 14, 1899; *Chattanooga Times*, Dec. 3, 1899; A. E. Mestre to Wood, Oct. 16, 1898, box 26, LWP; Wheeler to AG, 5AC, June 26, 1898, box 1, E 585; S. G. Stark to Chief QM, Sept. 1, 1898, vol. 1, E 1479; J. W. Rooney to AG, Santiago, Sept. 24, 1898, in box 2, E 1487; all RG 395, NARA.

20. L. A. Pérez, *Cuba between Empires*, 287–89; L. A. Pérez, *On Becoming Cuban*, 149–50; Ferrer, *Insurgent Cuba*, 187; "Many Offices for Cubans," *New York Sun*, Oct. 3, 1898; Leonardo Ros to Demetrio Castillo Duany, April 29, 1899, exp. 18, caja 875, Penetracion Norte Americano, 1899; "Expediente que contiene los documentos que sirvieron de examen para los apsirantes a plazas de traductores en el Gobierno Interventor de EUA, Santiago de Cuba, Marzo 16–20 1899," exp. 21, caja 875, Intervencion Norte Americano, 1899; Emilio Bacardi to Demetrio Castillo Duany, March 4, 1899, exp. 27, caja 515, Ejercito Libertador, 1899; all FGP, APSDC; V. F. Cessio to Wilson, Feb. 8, 1899, box 2, E 1331; Wood to CO, Baracoa, Oct. 25, 1898, and T. S. Nylly, 1st endorsement (hereafter abbreviated end.), Oct. 28, 1898, box 3, E 1487; all RG 395, NARA.

21. L. A. Pérez, *Essays on Cuban History*, 21–22; Cohen, *Reconstruction of American Liberalism*, chap. 4; H. P. Williams, "The Outlook in Cuba," quotes on 830; Walter A. Donaldson to Wood, Nov. 15, 1898, box 3, E 1487; Remus B. Harrison to AG, 7AC, March 4, 1899, E 1387; Eduardo Diaz to James H. Wilson, March 8, 1899, box 3, E 1331; all RG 395, NARA.

22. L. A. Pérez, *Army Politics*, 8–16; Kramer, "Empire, Exceptions, and Anglo-Saxons"; Streets, *Martial Races*.

23. A. R. Millett, *Politics of Intervention*, 131; Healy, *United States in Cuba*, 58; L. Thompson, "Military Cartography and the Terrains of Visibility," 43–45; L. A. Pérez, *Colonial Reckoning*, 20–22; Pvt. St. Louis, *Forty Years After*, 34–35; Wood, "Memorandum," in Wood to McKinley, Oct. 27, 1899, box 27, LWP.

24. L. A. Pérez, *On Becoming Cuban*, 104–64, esp. 150–56; Iglesias Utset, *Cultural History of Cuba*, 64–69.

25. Gleeck, *American Institutions*, 19; Cosmas, *Army for Empire*, 25–26; Linn, "Intelligence and Low-Intensity Conflict," 90–91; Adas, *Dominance by Design*, 131; F. D. Millet, *Expedition to the Philippines*, 214; US Senate, *Affairs in the Philippine Islands*, pt. 2, 862.

26. Capozzola, *Bound by War*, 15; C. F. Baker, *History of the 30th Infantry*, 59, 73; Kohr, *Around the World*, 212–13; Rodney, *As a Cavalryman Remembers*, 53–54; Nielsen to Parents, Sisters, and Brothers, Dec. 9, 1898, in Nielsen, *Inside the Fighting First*, 75; Walter Cutter, diary, p. 57, 58, box 1, Walter Cutter Papers; "I Remember," p. 34, box 1, Michael J. Lenihan Papers; Richard Johnson, "My Life in the U.S. Army," 21–22, box 1, Richard Johnson Papers; Wilmer Blackett, questionnaire, folder 1, box 56, SAWS; all USAHEC. Montalvo capitalized on his service after the war when he returned to Cuba and secured a job in Havana's US Army-run public works department; see Feuer, *America at War*, 57–58, 64.

27. Linn, *Philippine War*, 14–15; T. M. Anderson, "Supply and Distribution," 205; F. D. Millet, *Expedition to the Philippines*, 59–60; O. K. Davis, *Our Conquests in the Pacific*, 152, 179–80, 225, 332; ARWD 1898, Maj.-Gen., 54, 60, 61–62; ARWD 1900, pt. 4, p. 7.

28. Aune, *Indian Wars Everywhere*, 57–65; Ganzhorn, *I've Killed Men*, 95–124, 127, 137–40; Funston, *Memories of Two Wars*, 172–73, 295–96, 315–16.

29. Majul, "Principales, Ilustrados, Intellectuals," 10–12; Rafael, *Promise of the Foreign*, 18–22; Kramer, *Blood of Government*, 61; Cullinane, *Ilustrado Politics*, 29–32; Rafael, *Motherless Tongues*, 44; Ileto, *Knowledge and Pacification*, 89–94. Filipino schoolteachers' bilingualism may have made them valuable to the Americans. At Carmen, near Tarlac, in November 1899, Lt. Col. James Parker, having learned Spanish at West Point, met a Filipino teacher "who spoke good Spanish" and guided his retreat to Aliaga; see Parker, *Old Army*, 218, 254.

30. Guerrero, *Luzon at War*; US Senate, *Affairs in the Philippine Islands*, pt. 1, 45–47; US Bureau of the Census, *Census of the Philippine Islands*, 1903, vol. 2, 77–79; Richard Johnson, "My Life in the U.S. Army," 21, 42; Peter Konrad, questionnaire; both SAWS.

31. Linn, *Philippine War*, 31, 200; RPC 1900, 106–7; "Soldier Teachers in the Philippines"; ARWD 1900, Lt.-Gen., pt. 2, 491–92; ARWD 1900, *Military Governor of the Philippines on Civil Affairs*, 221–39.

32. Gates, *Schoolbooks and Krags*, 138–39; May, *Social Engineering*, 78–79; ARWD 1900, Lt.-Gen., pt. 2, 491–92; ARWD 1900, *Military Governor of the Philippines on Civil Affairs*, 221–39; ARWD 1901, Lt.-Gen., pt. 2, 257–58.

33. May, *Social Engineering*, 83; Kramer, *Blood of Government*, 168–70, 201–4; Steinbock-Pratt, *Educating the Empire*, 29–34; Schueller, *Campaigns of Knowledge*, 45–49; Rafael, *Motherless Tongues*, 53–56; Racelis and Ick, *Bearers of Benevolence*, 80–98; Elliot, *Philippines*, 229; US Senate, *Affairs in the Philippine Islands*, pt. 1, 195–96, 201, 361, 701–2; RPC 1901, pt. 1, 87–88.

34. Buck, *Memories*, 84–86; Tel. 537, Grant to HQ, 1D, 8AC, Sept. 21, 1899, box 1, E 782; Frederick Funston to AG, 2D, 8AC, Jan. 24, 1900, vol. 1, E 2261; CO, San Fernando to HQ, 1D, DNL, May 15, 1900, LR 586 in LRB, HQ, 1D, DNL, box 13, Young Papers; TS 524, Smedberg to Ballance, April 4, 1900, vol. 1, E 2148; W. L. Buck to AG, 3D, DNL, Oct. 11, 1900, box 3, E 2215; all RG 395, NARA; H. L. Hawthorne to AG, DSL, April 4, 1900, vol. 6, 28th USVI Reg. Book, E 117, RG 94, NARA; USPC, *Taft Report*, 1901, 84; RPC 1901 pt. 1, 73, 80, 84–88.

35. Linn, *Philippine War*, 197–99; Lininger, *Best War at the Time*, 99; Rodney, *As a Cavalryman Remembers*, 116, 118; Miles, *Fallen Leaves*, 89; *ARWD* 1900, pt. 6, 237, 272, 274; David Kennybrook, questionnaire, folder 16, box 58; Johnson, "My Life in the Army," 42; both SAWS; Funston to AG, 2D, 8AC, Jan. 24, 1900, vol. 1, E 2261, RG 395, NARA.
36. Sullivan, *Exemplar of Americanism*, 10, 13–26, 35–36; Stanley, "'Voice of Worcester Is God,'" 121; F. D. Millet, *Expedition*, 53; USPC, *Reports*, 1900, vol. 2, 347–49; US Senate, *Affairs in the Philippine Islands*, pt. 2, p. 1898.
37. Kramer, *Blood of Government*, 182; Cullinane, *Ilustrado Politics*, 52–57, 63, 369n21; F. D. Millet, *Expedition*, 53; *ARWD* 1899, pt. 2, 260–61; USPC, *Reports*, 1900, vol. 2, 349–52, quote on 351; US Senate, *Affairs in the Philippine Islands*, pt. 2, p. 1898.
38. *RPC* 1900, vol. 2, 347–52; W. H. Taft to Elihu Root, Sept. 11, 1901, Taft Papers.
39. Agoncillo, *Malolos*, 104–6; Schumacher, *Propaganda Movement*, 156, 159, 176; Sullivan, *Exemplar of Americanism*, 62, 65–66, 71–72, 121–22; Senate of the Philippines, "Teodoro Sandico," https://legacy.senate.gov.ph/senators/former_senators/teodoro_Sandico.htm, accessed March 17, 2024; McCoy, *Policing America's Empire*, 67; LeRoy, *Americans in the Philippines*, 1:352–53; US Senate, *Affairs in the Philippine Islands*, pt. 1, 506, 510; T. Sandico to Sr. General Don Manuél Tinio, Exhibit 89, in Taylor, *Philippine Insurrection*, 1:501–2; F. Agoncillo to Aguinaldo, May 27, 1898, pp. 238–41; T. Sandico to Señor President, [Aug.?] 1898, PIR 416.3, Exhibit 183, pp. 306–7; A. Zialcita, "My Impressions," Aug. 31, 1898, PIR 4.11, Exhibit 220, pp. 330–1; T. Sandico to Señor President, August, 1898, Exhibit 222, pp. 332–33; T. Sandico to Sr. President and Friend Don Emilio Aguinaldo [Sept. 1898], PIR 458.9, Exhibit 223, pp. 333–4; T. Sandico to Señor Don Emilio Aguinaldo [Manila, Sept. 1898?], PIR 458.2, Exhibit 224, p. 335; Pipi to President R. G., n.d., PIR 849, Exhibit 397, p. 503; all in Taylor, *Philippine Insurrection*, vol. 3; A. Luna to the Field Officers of the Territorial Militia, Feb. 7, 1899, Exhibit 816, in Taylor, *Philippine Insurrection*, 4:546–51; Dean C. Worcester, July 9, 1899, vol. 16, box 1, Dean C. Worcester Papers, Bentley Historical Library. Years later, Dean Worcester claimed "our spies simply would not communicate results through interpreters"; see Worcester, *Philippines, Past and Present*, 1:320–21.
40. Linn, *Philippine War*, 104–9, 160–61; Kramer, "Empires, Exceptions, and Anglo-Saxons"; Jankowski, "History of the Chinese Collection," 253–54; Ramsden, "Diary of the British Consul at Santiago during Hostilities: Conclusion," 70; *ARWD* 1899, pt. 3, 36, 105, 150, 154, 164, 169, 209.
41. Stanley, "'Voice of Worcester Is God,'" 128–29; Linn, *Philippine War*, 119–20; *ARWD* 1899, pt. 2, 138, 141; *ARWD* 1900, pt. 3, 283, 313.
42. Manuel, *Felipe G. Calderon*, 4, 8, 28–29; Agoncillo, *Malolos*, 239–51, 523–26; Stanley, *Nation in the Making*, 53, 73–74; Cullinane, *Ilustrado Politics*, 55–57; Rafael, *White Love*, 71–72; Sullivan, *Exemplar of Americanism*, 75–78, 83; Worcester, "General Lawton's Work," 27–28; Worcester, *Philippines, Past and Present*, 1:321; Shay, *Civilian in Lawton's 1899 Philippine Campaign*, 116; *ARWD* 1899, pt. 2, 145–48; *RPC* 1900, vol. 1, 176–78; *RPC* 1900, pt. 2, 67–70, 136–46, quote on 143; William Bengough, "Home Rule in Luzon," folder 5, box 4, Henry W. Lawton Papers, Library of Congress; Dean C. Worcester, July 9, 1899, vol. 16, box 1, Worcester Papers. Joining Calderon was fellow *ilustrado* Benito Legarda, on a mission to resume contact with Trías, and Angel Fabie, a fluent Tagalog-speaking mestizo and former insurgent official at Mindoro, who told Schurman's commission that he wanted to promote English instruction as a "band of union." Fabie may be the informant who alerted the

Americans of Teodoro Sandico's plot at Manila the previous December; see Worcester, July 9, 1899, vol. 16, box 1, Worcester Papers.

43. Rafael, *White Love*, 69–75; "Affidavit of F. W. Carpenter, in re: M. K. Nelson, Interpreter," Feb. 13, 1901, box 1, E 2342; TS, Starr to Edwards, Dec. 5, 1899, box 1, E 774; both RG 395, NARA.

44. Bankoff, *Crime, Society, and the State*, 134–38; May, *Battle for Batangas*, 117–20; Ataviado, *Philippine Revolution*, 109–10; ARWD 1899, Maj.-Gen., pt. 3, 164, 248; ARWD 1900, pt. 4, 503; ARWD 1900, pt. 6, 369, 379–80, 416–17; Smiley to J. M. Bell, March 7, 1900, box 1, E 769; N. S. Schuyler to AG, DSL, March 31, 1901, E 2355; both RG 395, NARA.

45. C. J. Crane, *Experiences of a Colonel of Infantry*, 329–33, 356–57; Parker, *Old Army*, 323, 341–42; "Senor Ramon Rey," LR 691, HQ, 2D, 8AC, May 26, 1899, E 851, RG 395, NARA; Robert L. Bullard, "Autobiography," 37–42, box 9, RLB.

46. Ginsberg, "Chinese in the Philippine Revolution"; Apilado, "Nationalism and Discrimination"; May, *Battle for Batangas*, 199–200; Linn, *Philippine War*, 127; Linn, "Intelligence and Low-Intensity Conflict," 95; Owen, "Winding Down the War in Albay," 563–64; Felipe Buencamino, Feb. 14, 1899, PIR 215.4. For evidence of Chinese guides in other provinces, see "At Catbalogan and over the Hills," *Manila Times*, Feb. 16, 1900; "Captured," *Aparri News*, May 5, 1900; Frederick J. Podas, diary entry, Jan. 29, 1899, "Record of Service with 13th Minn. Vol. Inf.," folder 2, box 1, Frederick J. Podas Papers, USAHEC; Louis A. Craig to AG, 2B, 2D, 8AC, Nov. 24, 1899, box 3, E 851, RG 395, NARA.

47. Linn, *Philippine War*, 95, 105, 119–20; Brody, *Visualizing American Empire*, 97–103; Worcester, "General Lawton's Work," 25; ARWD 1900, pt. 3, 280–81, 307; Special Orders No. 62, HQ, US Forces, 1D, 8AC, Bacoor, Dec. 28, 1899, vol. 1, E 820; A. L. Ducat to Adj., April 24, 1900, LSB 1, Bacoor, E 2979; both RG 395, NARA.

48. Wassell, Smith, and Hamilton, *History of the Twenty-Second United States Infantry*, 47, 83, 107–8; Parker, *Old Army*, 261; ARWD 1899, Maj.-Gen., pt. 3, 235; ARWD 1900, pt. 3, 532; ARWD 1900, pt. 4, 258, 277–78.

49. US Senate, *Affairs in the Philippine Islands*, pt. 3, 2437; Seoane, *Beyond the Ranges*, 52–53; J. M. Bell to AAG, DSL, May 8, 1900, box 1, E 2330, RG 395, NARA. Published evidence of voluntary guide and interpreter service, and various methods for paying them, in the Ilocos include ARWD 1900, Lt.-Gen., pt. 4, 331, 334, 373–74, 379. Less often than men, Filipinas served as guides or interpreters; see Ileto, *Knowledge and Pacification*, 100–101; ARWD 1900, Lt.-Gen., pt. 6, 380; "Diary Account of Period L. S. Smith Was a Prisoner of Filipinos, 1899–1900," p. 6, Leland Smith Papers, USAHEC; Theo. J. Wint to Adj., Tanauan Column, Mount San Cristobal Exp., Nov. 27, 1901, box 1, E 2379, RG 395, NARA.

50. Linn, *U.S. Army and Counterinsurgency*, 23–24, 49–50, 57–58, 78; Linn, *Philippine War*, 173, 203–4, 211–14; Witt, *Lincoln's Code*, 173–81, 229–37, 338–53; Smiley, "Lawless Wars of Empire?"; Brundage, *Civilizing Torture*, 174–81; Ileto, "Colonial Wars in Southern Luzon," 110–13; Ileto, *Knowledge and Pacification*, 78–81; C. J. Crane, "Paragraphs 93, 97, and 88"; Blocksom, "Retrospect and Prospect of War"; ARWD 1900, Lt.-Gen., pt. 3, 60; US Senate, *Affairs in the Philippine Islands*, pt. 2, 985–89; pt. 3, 2860. MacArthur's orders and proclamation and GO 100's text appear in ARWD 1901, pt. 2, 90–93, and US Senate, *Affairs in the Philippine Islands*, pt. 2, 971–82.

51. Linn, *U.S. Army and Counterinsurgency*, 30–32; Kramer, *Blood of Government*, 208–20; Wernstedt and Spencer, *Philippine Island World*, 328.

52. Ochosa, *Tinio Brigade*, 88–89; Linn, *U.S. Army and Counterinsurgency*, 32; Linn, *Philippine War*, 157; Villamor, *Inedita cronica*, 20–36, 60; ARWD 1900, pt. 4, 162, 169, 172, 192, 195, 241–42, 282–84.

53. Ochosa, *Tinio Brigade*, 89; Linn, *U.S. Army and Counterinsurgency*, 33–34; Linn, *Philippine War*, 204–6; Villamor, *Inedita cronica*, 54, 80–82; Trafton, *We Thought We Could Whip Them*, 55; ARWD 1900, pt. 4, 244, 338–39; Brown, *Gentleman Soldier*, 142; "Ilocano Language, Vigan, Ilocos Sur, 1900," folder 8, box 1, Howard Papers; William H. Bowen, "A Visit to the Head Hunters," p. 7, box 2, Bowen Papers; LR 668, Arthur Thayer to Adj., Laoag, May 4, 1900; LR 586, CO, San Fernando to Young, May 15, 1900; both LRB, HQ, 1D, DNL, box 13; Young to William McKinley, July 4, 1900, box 3; all Young Papers; LR 325, D. L. Tate to Adj., 3rd Squadron, 3rd Cav., Jan. 31, 1900; Frederick Funston, 2nd ed., May 9, 1900, box 1, E 2269; LR 397, C. E. Meghar to Adj., San Fernando, July 1, 1900; both box 1, E 2157; all RG 395, NARA.

54. ARWD 1900, pt. 4, 334, 340, 373; Richard Johnson, "My Life in the Army," pp. 31, 35–36, SAWS; LR 708, George A. Dodd to Young, May 12, 1900, in LRB, HQ, 1D, DNL, box 13; Young Papers; E. Z. Steever to AG, NW Province of Luzon, Jan. 24, 1900, box 1; E. N. Coffey to Adj., 1st Batt., 33rd US Inf., March 7, 1900, box 2; both E 2157; Hugh Thomason to Adj., San Fernando de Union, April 16, 1900, box 1, E 2158; all RG 395, NARA.

55. Linn, *U.S. Army and Counterinsurgency*, 35, 46–48; Blocksom, "Retrospect and Prospect of War," 219–22; TR 9, Wheeler to AG, 2D, 8AC, Feb. 24, 1900, box 6, E 854; E. Wittenmeyer to AG, Nueva Caceres, July 10, 1901, box 1, E 2445; all RG 395, NARA. For examples in other provinces, see Ileto, "Colonial Wars in Southern Luzon," 114; Wagner to Lloyd Wheaton, April 13, 1900; TS 632, Wagner to Taggart, April 27, 1900; TS 696, Wagner to Lockett, April 30, 1900; TS, 701, Wagner to Porter, April 30, 1900; all TS, box 1, E 817; 3rd Dist. Hospital, Na. Caceres, July 8, 1900, LR 143, 3D, DSL, with D. C. Nolan, 2nd ed., and J. Lockett, 3rd end., both July 11, 1900, E 2420; all RG 395, NARA.

56. ARWD 1900, pt. 4, 331; ARWD 1901, pt. 5, 312; Paula Pardo to Sra. Ambrosia [Ambrosia Móxia], March 2, 1900, PIR 2035.3, Exhibit 1373, in Taylor, *Philippine Insurrection*, 5:733; LR 332½, Robert L. Howze to Young, Feb. 3, 1900, in LR, Office Military Governor of North-Western Luzon, folder 5, box 4, Young Papers; Jno. W. Bubb to AG, DNL, April 16, 1900, box 1, E 2215; AAAG, HQ, 1D, DNL to CO, South Ilocos, April 6, 1901, box 1, E 2164; Jno. A. Baldwin to AG, 4D, DNL, Tayug, Aug. 18, 1900, box 1, E 2269; all RG 395, NARA.

57. Parker, *Old Army*, 280; Ileto, "Orientalism and the Study of Philippine Politics"; Ileto, *Knowledge and Pacification*, 91; Go, *American Empire and the Politics of Meaning*, chap. 3; Mariano to Sr. Don Mena Crisólogo, Sept. 25, 1898, PIR 974.3, Exhibit 552, Taylor, *Philippine Insurrection*, vol. 5, addendum to vol. 3, 54–55; W. Smedberg to Louis F. Garrard, March 1, 1900, vol. 1, E 2148, RG 395, NARA.

58. Linn, *U.S. Army and Counterinsurgency*, 57–58, 167–68; Howard to Howze, Feb. 27, 1900; Smedberg to CO, May 19, 1900; Howard to Howze, June 6, 1900; Ballance to CO, Aug. 1, 1900; all vol. 1, E 4046; W. Smedberg to Louis F. Gerrard Jr., March 1, 1900, vol. 1, E 2148; Howze to Ballance, May 20, 1900; Howze to AAG, 1D, DNL, May 24, 1900; Howze to Ballance, Aug. 1, 1900; Howze to Ballance, August 2, 1900; all vol. 1, E 4043; Ballance to CO, Laoag, Aug. 1, 1900; Ballance to CO, Laoag, Aug. 29, 1900; both box 1, E 4055; Lloyd Wheaton to Sec, MG, Sept. 24, 1900, in LS vol. 3, box 1, E 2130; all RG 395, NARA. On the scandal's aftermath, see affidavits and Manuel Tinio to Swigert, May 1900; George K. Hunter to Taft, May 16, 1900;

Hunter to Taft, June 4, 1900; Alvord to Young, May 29, 1902, LRB; Taft to George W. Davis, Jan. 5, 1903; Elihu Root, May 28, 1903; all bulky file 56, box 282, E 13, RG 94, NARA.

59. Scott, *Ilocano Responses*, 101–2; Guerrero, *Luzon at War*, 134–35, 186, 205–35; Phelps Whitmarsh, "La Guardia de Honor," encl. to 1796, Office of the Military Governor, 1900, in "Correspondence re: conflict between Military and Civilian Authorities in the Province of Benguet," folder 2368–5, box 273, E 5, RG 350, NARA. For other guides and interpreters in northern Luzon accused of criminally abusing their position, see M. Vinuya to Gen. Smith, Dec. 4, 1900, Binmaley, box 3, E 2215; Escolastico de Guzman to CO, San Fernando de la Union, Feb. 22, 1902, and 2nd end., E. L. Steever, March 4, 1902, box 6, E 2635; both RG 395, NARA.

60. Scott, *Ilocano Responses*, 101–2; Linn, *U.S. Army and Counterinsurgency*, 42–45; Philip H. Stern to Adj., San Fernando, March 16, 1900; Stern to AG, Military Governor, NW Provinces, Luzon, March 18, 1900; both box 2, E 2157; Young to AG, Palacio, Manila, March 24, 1900, vol. 1, E 2148; John H. Parker to AG, 2D, DSL, April 26, 1900, box 1, E 2408; all RG 395, NARA.

61. Scott, *Ilocano Responses*, 102; Linn, *U.S. Army and Counterinsurgency*, 42–45; Lt. Col. 1st Chief, Proclamation, April 18, 1900, PIR 168.9, Exhibit 1055, in Taylor, *Philippine Insurrection*, 5:190–91; LR 1298, Ola W. Bell to Adj., San Fernando de Union, June 20, 1900, box 4, E 2158; John G. Ballance, 1st end., Jan. 25, 1901 on LR 172, P. W. Davidson to HQ, 1D, DNL, box 3, E 2167; J. F. Bell to AG, 1D, Vigan, April 4, 1901, E 5186; all RG 395, NARA.

62. Orton, *Up-to-Date History*, 40–41; "Anderson's Murderers to Be Hanged," *Aparri News*, March 30, 1901. Insurgents' orders targeting guides for the Americans in other Luzon provinces include Mariano Trías, Proclamation, Nov. 24, 1900, PIR 226.13, in Taylor, *Philippine Insurrection*, 5:278; Colonel-Politico-Military Chief of the Province, June 29, 1901, PIR 752.5, Exhibit 1164, in Taylor, *Philippine Insurrection*, 5:344; Miguel Malvar, "General Instructions and Dispositions," Aug. 28, 1901, box 1, E 2356, RG 395, NARA.

63. Linn, *U.S. Army and Counterinsurgency*, 49–50, 52; Linn, "Intelligence and Low-Intensity Conflict," 95; Tel., Young to AG, 8AC, Manila, Feb. 3, 1900, vol. 1, E 2148; Thomas Q. Ashburn to Adj., 33rd Infantry, Feb. 22, 1900, box 2, E 2157; D. Bright to COs, May 17, 1900, vol. 1, E 5617; Ballance, Circular, "Rules and Usages of Civilized Warfare," HQ, 1D, DNL, June 15, 1900, box 1, E 5583; all RG 395, NARA; LS 352, Tel., Kennon to AAG, 3B, 2D, 8AC, Mar. 13, 1900, LSB, vol. 1, 34th USVI, E 117, NARA 94; Manuel Tinio, March 20, 1900, PIR 353.6. John R. M. Taylor's history of the Philippine War translates this passage in Tinio's order as "misleading them from the right road"; see Exhibit 1050 in Taylor, *Philippine Insurrection*, 5:185.

64. Ochosa, *Tinio Brigade*, 17, 19, 140, 172, 215; Ileto, *Knowledge and Pacification*, 82–84; ARWD 1900, pt. 4, 285; ARWD 1901, pt. 3, 123–24; Marcelino Gadayan to Pedro Caballes, July 19, 1901, PIR 752.62; LS 201, S. B. M. Young to Loyd Wheaton, Jan. 17, 1901, in LS, private file, box 12, Young Papers; TS 486, Smedberg to CO, Narvacan, March 23, 1900, vol. 1, E 2148; W. O. Bennett to CO, 2nd Batt., 16th Inf., Tuguegarao, April 5, 1900, box 1, Entry 2204; both RG 395, NARA.

65. Scott, *Ilocano Responses*, 97–98; Linn, *U.S. Army and Counterinsurgency*, 39, 63–64, 76–79; Linn, *Philippine War*, 222; Funston, *Memories*, 315–16, 324–25, 338; Ganzhorn, *I've Killed Men*, 161; LR 483, C. J. Hollis to Howze, April 25, 1900, in LRB, HQ, 1D, DNL, box 13, Young Papers; Johnson, "My Life in the Army," 31–31, SAWS.

66. Trafton, *We Thought We Could Whip Them*, 91; Currier, *In the Early Days*, 47–49; Ballance to AG, DNL, April 11, 1901, box 4, E 2167, RG 395, NARA. Evidence of false guides, and Americans' torture and killing of them, in other provinces include Turnbull, "Reminiscences," 35; Norwood, *Fifty Thousand Miles*, 86; Carmony, Tannenbaum, and Johnson, "Three Years in the Orient," 274; John C. Brown, Oct. 30, 1900, diary entry, in J. C. Brown, *Gentleman Soldier*, 124; "A Brush with the Enemy," *Aparri News*, March 10, 1900; "Smart Work," *Aparri News*, April 21, 1900; "The Murders of Feagans and Gray Captured," *Aparri News*, April 13, 1901; J. M. Boyle to CO, Naic, Nov. 24, 1901, box 2, E 2354, RG 395, NARA.

67. Hart and Hart, "Juan Pusong"; Currier, *In the Early Days*, 47–49.

68. Linn, "Intelligence and Low-Intensity Conflict," 94; Ileto, "Toward a Local History of the Philippine-American War," 72–75; Kohout, *Taking the Field*, 144–54; Ataviado, *Philippine Revolution*, 2:93; Hoyt, *A Frontier Doctor*, 231, 234–36; ARWD 1902, vol. 9, 285–88; "Littell, Todd and Donald," 8–9, Todd Littell Papers, SAWS; Prudencio Batangan to Commandante Tinio, March 23, 1900, folder 98/99, PIR 99.7; Loyd Wheaton to AG, 1D, March 4, 1900, vol. 3, E 2403; John H. Parker to AG, DSL, May 24, 1900, box 1, E 2408; both RG 395, NARA.

69. Charles Hood to Adj., DNL, Aug. 23, 1900, vol. 3, E 2195; TR, McKain to HQ, 2D, DNL, Jan. 24, 1901; 2nd end., S. Whitall, Jan. 25, 1901; box 1, E 2201; all RG 395, NARA.

70. Funston, *Memories*, 217, 377–79, 384–95, 402–4; Funston to Adj., DNL, Aug. 18, 1900, vol. 3; Funston to Adj., DNL, June 26, 1901, vol. 6; both E 2261, RG 395, NARA.

71. Scott, *Ilocano Responses*, 94; Ochosa, *Tinio Brigade*, 215; RPC 1906, pt. 1, 207–11; Geo. K. Hunter to AG, DPH, Dec. 17, 1902, bulky file 56, folder 1, box 282, E 13, RG 94, NARA; Wm. S. McCaskey to Chief of Staff, 1D, DNL, March 25, 1901, vol. 1, E 4053; Epifiano de los Santos Cristobal to Civil Gov., Jan. 1903, F 2058, box 247, E 5; both RG 395, NARA. Col. Lyman W. V. Kennon, no stranger to alliances with controversial elites, endorsed Agbayani's candidacy; see Kennon to Chief Asst., 1D, DNL, Jan. 12, 1901, vol. 1, E 4053, RG 395, NARA.

72. Robert B. Stevens to AG, DNL, July 30, 1901; 1st end., Loyd Wheaton, July 31, 1901; both box 38, E 2133, RG 395, NARA.

Chapter Two

1. Millett, *Semper Fidelis*, 153, 160–63; Mitchell, *Rule of Experts*, 9; Said, *Orientalism*; Linn, "'We Will Go Heavily Armed,'" 273–78; Linn, *Philippine War*, 176, 215, 231–34, 306–15; Renda, *Taking Haiti*, 100–101; Walter, *Colonial Violence*, 121–23, 166–67; "General Waller of Marines Dead," *New York Times*, July 14, 1926; Littleton W. T. Waller, May 24, 1902 [hereafter "Waller Report"], 5–6, 22–23, folder "Samar Report," box 2, Waller Papers; Waller GCM Proceedings, 376, 436–38, box 3367, E 15, RG 153, NARA.

2. Driver, *Geography Militant*; Kramer, *Blood of Government*, 11–12; Kipling, "The White Man's Burden."

3. Waller GCM Proceedings, 85–86, 92–94, 111–13, 115, 122–24, 135, 169–70, 198–99, 203, 205, 209–13, 402; Waller Report.

4. Linn, "'We Will Go Heavily Armed,'" 283–85; Fabian, *Out of Our Minds*; Waller GCM Proceedings, 148, 156, 234–36, 246, 265, 269, 272–73; Waller Report, 70; "Jan. 1, 1902. Joaquin Cabañes (Presidente of Basey, Samar). To Major Edwin F. Glenn, 5th Inf'y," box 1, E 2574, RG 395, NARA.

298 Notes to Chapter Two

5. Kramer, *Blood of Government*, 88–90; Linn, "'We Will Go Heavily Armed,'" 284–87; Linn, "The Struggle for Samar," 161–67; Linn, *Echo of Battle*, 85–86; *ARWD* 1902, pt. 9, 440; Vicente Lukban to Mariano Trías, Feb. 25, 1901, PIR 882.8, Exhibit 1346, in Taylor, *Philippine Insurrection*, 5:681–85; Waller GCM Proceedings, 39, 41, 73–74, 86, 99, 104, 123, 135, 207, 234–37, 247, 303, 374–76; Edgar A. Macklin to Chief QM, 6SB, Jan. 14, 1901, vol. 1, E 3815; CO, Basey, Nov. 5, 1901, box 1, E 2574; Campbell King to AG, 6SB, Nov. 19, 1901, and W. E. Ayer, 1st end., Nov. 22, 1901, box 1, E 3818; all RG 395, NARA.

6. Millett, *Semper Fidelis*, 167–68, 172–74; Schmidt, *Maverick Marine*, 72, 75–81, 83–89, 94–95; Kramer, "Race-Making and Colonial Violence"; Einolf, *America in the Philippines*, 89–90, chap. 8, 157–58; Adams, *Exploits and Adventures*, 247–49; Waller GCM Proceedings, 1, 9, 4, 36, 118, 185, 269, 402–405; Chaffee to Henry Corbin, Jan. 31, 1902, folder 4, box 1, Corbin Papers.

7. Rafael, *White Love*, 23–24; Headrick, *Tools of Empire*, 116–18; Adas, *Machines as the Measure of Men*, 141–46, chap. 4; Adas, *Dominance by Design*, chaps. 2 and 3; Zimmerman, "'What Do You Really Want in German East Africa'"; Rockel, *Carriers of Culture*; Moyd, *Violent Intermediaries*, 119–30; Hull, *Absolute Destruction*, 159–60; Linn, *Echo of War*, 47–52, 62–64, 86–89; Zimmerman, *Alabama in Africa*; Beckert, "From Tuskugee to Togo"; Bousquet, *Scientific Way of Warfare*.

8. De la Fuente, "Two Dangers, One Solution"; Kramer, *Blood of Government*, 181, 313–18; Bender, *American Abyss*, 44–57; Roediger and Esch, *Production of Difference*, 121–35; Charbonneau, "Colonizing Workers."

9. Adas, *Dominance by Design*, 154–55, 165; de La Fuente, *Nation for All*, 39–45; Bender, *American Abyss*, chap. 2; Kramer, *Blood of Government*, esp. 312–22; Charbonneau, *Civilizational Imperatives*, 169–79.

10. Guridy, *Forging Diaspora*, chap. 1; Walther, "'The Same Blood as We in America'"; Charbonneau, "Teaching the World to Work"; Adas, *Dominance by Design*, 166, 176–77. US Army officers organizing public schools during the Philippine War were the first Americans to advocate technical labor instruction; see Gates, *Schoolbooks and Krags*, 137–38.

11. Haber, *Efficiency and Uplift*, esp. 1–3; Nelson, *Managers and Workers*, 56–62; Alexander, *Mantra of Efficiency*, 76–81.

12. Millis, *Arms and Men*, 137–41; Barr, *Progressive Army*, 13–20; Adler and Polsky, "Building the New American Nation," 106; Hope, *Scientific Way of War*, 107–27; Linn, *Echo of Battle*, 8–9, 19–20; J. P. Clark, *Preparing for War*, 3.

13. L. A. Pérez, *Slaves, Sugar, and Colonial Society*, 44–56, 60–64, 75–76, 89–90; L. A. Pérez, *Cuba between Empires*, 20–22; L. A. Pérez, *Cuba and the United States*, 18–23, 27–28; Dye, *Cuban Sugar in the Age of Mass Production*, 10–14; Ayala, *American Sugar Kingdom*, 56–58; R. J. Scott, *Degrees of Freedom*, 110–13; López, *Chinese Cubans*, 71–76; E. S. Rosenberg, *Transnational Currents*, chap. 4; Roedgier and Esch, *Production of Difference*; de la Fuente, "Two Problems, One Solution," 30–31, 37; Porter, *Industrial Cuba*, 83–84; E. F. Atkins, *Sixty Years in Cuba*, 36–40, 65, 74–76, 82–83, 87–89, 90–99, 101–4, 108–17, 138–39; Atkins to E. E. Greble, Jan. 19, 1900, vol. 2, Letterbooks, Atkins Family Papers, Massachusetts Historical Society. Of course, Cubans in the states observed labor there; José Martí, for one, studied Chinese laborers and white American workers' reaction to them; Martí, *Martí on the U.S.A.*, 175–77.

14. L. A. Pérez, *Army Politics in Cuba*, 6–16; L. A. Pérez, *Cuba between Empires*, chap. 18; Wintermute, *Public Health and the U.S. Military*, 1–2, 32–33, chap. 3; L. A. Pérez, *Colonial Reckoning*, 74–79, 134, 137–45.

15. Trask, *War with Spain*, 311–24; L. A. Pérez, *Cuba between Empires*, 196–97; *CWS*, vol. 1, 154, 157–63, 171–72, 174–77, 179–80, 185, 187, 200–201, 213, 231.

16. Trask, *War with Spain*, 206–7; Espinosa, *Epidemic Invasions*, 11–24, 31–33, 56–70.

17. Trask, *War with Spain*, 299–300, 305–6, 311, 324–35; Gillett, *Army Medical Department*, 149–60; Tone, *War and Genocide*, 209–17, 223; Polk, *Contagions of Empire*, 29–34; L. A. Pérez, *Cuba in the American Imagination*, 50–94.

18. McCallum, *Leonard Wood*, 7–46, 52–53, 58–59, 111–18; Mrozek, "Habit of Victory," 228–29; Aune, *Indian Wars Everywhere*, 52–53; Hoganson, *Fighting for American Manhood*, 118–19, 143–45, 151; Dubofksy, *State and Labor in Modern America*, 37–44; Wood, "Santiago since the Surrender," 515; *ARWD* 1899, *Report of Maj. Gen. J. R. Brooke on Civil Affairs in Cuba*, vol. 1, pt. 6, 367.

19. Lane, *Armed Progressive*; Gillette, "Military Occupation of Cuba"; Stromquist, *Reinventing "The People"*; Wood, "Existing Conditions and Needs in Cuba," 593; McKinley to Shafter, July 18, 1898, in *CWS*, vol. 1, 159–61. Some Cuban historians later praised Wood for instituting modern sanitary practices; see Rivero Muñiz, *El movimiento obrero durante la primera intervención*, 13–14.

20. Trask, *War with Spain*, 199–200; Alger, *Spanish-American War*, 122; Wood, "Santiago since the Surrender," 515–17; *ARWD* 1899, pt. 1, 301; US Senate, *Conduct of the War Department in the War with Spain*, 7:3600–3601; "Cleaning Up Santiago," *New York Sun*, May 14, 1899, 4; Wood to Louise, July 21, 1898, box 190, LWP.

21. L. A. Pérez, *On Becoming Cuban*, 22–23; Rotter, *Empire of the Senses*; Fleitas Salazar, *Medicina y sanidad en la historia de Santiago de Cuba*, 71; Wood, "Santiago since the Surrender," 515–17; Kennan, "Sanitary Regeneration of Santiago," 872; Wood to Louise Wood, July 21, 1898; Wood to Mother, July 30, 1898; both box 190, LWP. The wartime and postwar politics of urban public services in Santiago may have tracked that in Havana; see García, *Beyond the Walled City*, 179–80.

22. Hagedorn, *Leonard Wood*, 1:188–89; Melosi, *Garbage in the Cities*, 44–49; Davis, *Circus Age*, 11, 22, 57–59, chap. 6; Kantowicz, "Carter H. Harrison II," 16–19; Davenport, "Sanitation Revolution in Illinois"; Kennan, "Sanitary Regeneration of Santiago," 872; "Cleaning Up Santiago," *New York Sun*, May 14, 1899.

23. Melosi, *Garbage in the Cities*, 44–65; K. P. Murphy, *Political Manhood*, 73, 92–102; Porter, *Industrial Cuba*, 154–60; Hill, "Sanemiento de la Habana," 120; RDH, "Colonel Waring of the New York Street Sweeping Department ...," Sept. 6, 1929, box 13, Hagedorn Papers.

24. Wood, "Santiago since the Surrender," 517–19; Kennan, "Sanitary Regeneration of Santiago," 871–72; "Cleaning Up Santiago," *New York Sun*, May 14, 1899; RDH, Sept. 6, 1929, "Colonel Waring of the New York Street Sweeping Department ...," box 13, Hagedorn Papers.

25. Wood, "Santiago since the Surrender," 517–19; Kennan, "Sanitary Regeneration of Santiago," 871–72; "Cleaning Up Santiago," *New York Sun*, May 14, 1899; "Santiago under the American Occupation," *Chicago Daily Tribune*, Feb. 26, 1899; "Wood's Work," *Boston Globe*, Dec. 24, 1899, box 12; "Santiago de Cuba is the oldest community of white people ...," box 13; both Hagedorn Papers.

26. Wood, "Santiago since the Surrender," 517–19; "Clean Streets," *Times of Cuba*, Aug. 8, 1898; Wood to Louise, Aug. 4, 1898; Wood to Louise, Aug. 18, 1898; Wood to Louise, Aug. 14, 1898; all box 190, LWP.

27. Wood, "Santiago since the Surrender," 517–19; Kennan, "Sanitary Regeneration of Santiago," 873; Bangs, *Uncle Sam Trustee*, 131; "Report of Sanitary Commissioner George M. Barbour to Samuel H. Whiteside, Military Governor of the District of Santiago City," cited in Gillette, "Military Occupation of Cuba," 416; AGO #139813, Wood to Alger, Sept. 9, 1898, box 915, E 25, RG 94, NARA.

28. Wood, "Santiago since the Surrender," 517–18, 526; Bangs, *Uncle Sam Trustee*, 130–31; Kennan, "Sanitary Regeneration of Santiago," 873, 875; *ARWD* 1899, pt. 1, 301; *ARWD* 1899, *Report of Maj. Gen. J. R. Brooke on Civil Affairs in Cuba*, vol. 1, pt. 6, 22, 368; "The Street Cleaning Department," *Times of Cuba*, Aug. 15, 1898; AGO #139813, Wood to Alger, Sept. 9, 1898, box 915, E 25, RG 94, NARA.

29. "The Street Cleaning Department," *Times of Cuba*, Aug. 15, 1898; "Cubans Strike," *Boston Daily Globe*, Nov. 4, 1898; Wood to Louise, Aug. 14, 1898, box 190, LWP; W. H. Carter to CG, Santiago, Oct. 19, 1898, box 3, E 1487, RG 395, NARA.

30. L. A. Pérez, *Cuba between Empires*, 23; L. A. Pérez, *Lords of the Mountain*, 18–27; Montgomery, *Citizen Worker*, 83–89; John H. Beacom to Spanish-American Iron Co., Dec. 30, 1898, vol. 4, E 1479, RG 395, NARA.

31. Lewis, "General Wood at Santiago," 463–66; Kennan, "Sanitary Regeneration of Santiago," 874–76; Richard Harding Davis, *Boston Transcript*, Nov. 18, 1898, box 12; "Gen. Wood and His Work," *New York Evening Sun*, Dec. 23, 1899; Wood to Louise, Aug. 8, 1898; all box 13; all Hagedorn Papers; Wood, "Santiago since the Surrender," 520, 524; "Wood's Work," *Boston Globe*, Dec. 24, 1898; "Commit Nuisance," *Times of Cuba*, Aug. 1, 1898; "Trying to Clean Santiago," *New York Times*, Aug. 5, 1898; "Cleaning Up Santiago," *New York Sun*, May 14, 1899; "Santiago de Cuba is the oldest community of white people...", box 13, Hagedorn Papers; "Major Carr," box 1, E 1517; Henry Lawton to AG, US Army, Sept. 2, 1898; Lawton to Watson, Sept. 9, 1898; both vol. 1, E 1479; all RG 395, NARA. Wood and Barbour probably did not realize that Santiago residents may have associated street cleaning with unfree labor, as Spanish-era authorities had made prisoners sweep streets; see Lewis, "General Wood at Santiago," 463.

32. GO 11, Office Acting Civil Government, Santiago de Cuba, Oct. 20, 1898, box 294, LWP.

33. L. A. Pérez, *Cuba between Empires*, 323–324; L. A. Pérez, *Cuba in the American Imagination*, 105–74; Melosi, *Garbage in the Cities*, 53–55; Matthews, *New-Born Cuba*, 302; "Street Cleaners on Parade," *Chicago Daily Tribune*, Dec. 29, 1898; "Santiago under the American Occupation," *Chicago Daily Tribune*, Feb. 26, 1899; "Cleaning up Santiago," *New York Sun*, May 14, 1899.

34. W. Anderson, *Colonial Pathologies*, 49–50; Ileto, "Cholera and the Origins of the American Sanitary Order in the Philippines"; Hawkins, *Making Moros*, 45–46; Morley, *Cities and Nationhood*, 134–41; Charbonneau, *Civilizational Imperatives*, 123–25; *RPC*, 1903, pt. 2, 86–87; *ARGMP* 1905, 23; Barbour to H. S. Scott, Oct. 14, 1903, box 55, Scott Papers; Barbour to Wood, Nov. 27, 1903, box 33, LWP.

35. L. A. Pérez, *Cuba in the American Imagination*, 99–103; Go, "'Racism' and Colonialism"; Webber, *Twelve Months*, 139–40; *ARWD* 1899, Sec. War, Bureau Chiefs, vol. 1, pt. 2, 174–75.

36. Ferrer, *Insurgent Cuba*, 187–92; Goode, *The Eighth Illinois*, 127–28; Whipple, *Story of the Forty-Ninth*, 29, 33.

Notes to Chapter Two 301

37. L. A. Pérez, *Cuba between Empires*, 239, 292; de la Fuente, *Nation for All*, 39–45; US Department of War, *Annual Report of Colonel Samuel M. Whitside*, 153; Howard, "Cuban as a Labor Problem," 640; George Leroy Brown to AG, DMSC, Feb. 7, 1900; P. E. Betancourt to AG, DMSC, Feb. 12, 1900; both box 31, E 1331, RG 395, NARA.

38. L. A. Pérez, *Cuba under the Platt Amendment*, 80; de la Fuente, *A Nation for All*, 39–42, 46–47; de la Fuente, "Two Dangers, One Solution," 31; US Department of War, *Annual Report of Colonel Samuel M. Whitside*, 153; Wood, "Present Situation in Cuba," 639; US Senate, *Statements of Major-General Leonard Wood*, 18; "Cuban Frauds," *Los Angeles Times*, Jan. 1, 1899; "Building the Road," *Washington Evening Sun*, Jan. 7, 1899; AGO #144599, J. A. Porter to H. C. Corbin, Oct. 4, 1898, box 945, E 25, RG 94, NARA; John H. Beacom to Spanish-American Iron Co., Dec. 30, 1898, vol. 4, E 1479, RG 395, NARA.

39. Bangs, *Uncle Sam Trustee*, 163; US Department of War, *Annual Report of Colonel Samuel M. Whitside*, 153, 161; V. Clark, "Labor Conditions in Cuba," 665, 684–86, 706–8, 712, 778, 784; US Senate, *Statements of Major-General Leonard Wood*, 9; ARWD 1900, *Mil. Govt. Cuba, Civil Affairs*, vol. 2, pt. 3, 25, 159, 183; ARWD 1900, *Mil. Govt. Cuba, Civil Affairs*, vol. 2, pt. 4, p. 95; Wood to AG, DC, Feb. 13, 1899, vol. 4, E 1479, RG 395, NARA; Tel., Palma Soriano, March 8, 1900, box 70, E 4, RG 140, NARA.

40. Greene, "Entangled in Empires"; V. Clark, "Labor Conditions in Cuba," 686; US Senate, *Statements of Major-General Leonard Wood*, 9; F. J. Davies to Herman Hagedorn, Feb. 29, 1929, box 13, Hagedorn Papers.

41. Peck, *Reinventing Free Labor*, 197–204; Balboa Navarro, "Steeds, Cocks, and Guayaberas," 211–12; Bangs, *Uncle Sam Trustee*, 167–70; Kennan, "Cuban Character," 962–63; US Senate, *Statements of Major-General Leonard Wood*, 13; ARWD 1900, *Mil. Gov. Cuba, Civil Affairs*, vol. 2, pt. 3, 5; "Dinner for Gen. L. Wood," *New York Times*, Jan. 1, 1899; F. J. Davies, Feb. 16, 1929, box 13, Hagedorn Papers; W. W. Whitside to AG, Dist. of Santiago, July 1, 1901, box 196, RG 140, NARA.

42. Kramer, *Blood of Government*, 313–17; Adas, *Dominance by Design*, 154–55.

43. Adas, *Dominance by Design*, 165.

44. A. G. Corpuz, *Colonial Iron Horse*, 23–26; Linn, *Philippine War*, 29, 90–91, 100–101, 111–16, 120–21, 127, 141–43, 145–46, 152–53, 160–61; Bender, *American Abyss*, 51; Aune, *Indian Wars Everywhere*, chap. 2; Halsema, "Land Transportation in the Philippines," 69–70; Parker, "Some Random Notes," 317–19; ARWD 1900, *Lt.-Gen.*, pt. 4, 373–80; LS 207, Kennon to Chief of Staff, Manila, Dec. 20, 1899; LS 231, W. D. Newbill to D. C. Lyles, Dec. 26, 1899; both vol. 1, 34th USVI Regimental Book, E 117, RG 94, NARA.

45. W. H. Scott, *Discovery of the Igorots*, 155, 225, 235, 243–44, 258, 316; A. G. Corpuz, *Colonial Iron Horse*, 13; Linn, *Philippine War*, 157–58; Bankoff, "Wants, Wages, and Workers," 64; Trafton, *We Thought We Could Whip Them*, 53–54; ARWD 1900, *Lt.-Gen.*, pt. 4, 374–75; US Senate, *Affairs in the Philippine Islands*, pt. 2, 972; L.R. Hare to AG, 1D, DNL, May 24, 1900, vol. 13, Young Papers; CO, Namacpacan, La Union, to CO, Bangar, June 24, 1900 vol. 1, E 4555; Bomba to J. C. Chance, Dec. 1, 1900, vol. 1, E 3059; AAG, 2D, DNL, to CO, Laloc, Feb. 3, 1901, vol. 7, E 2195; all RG 395, NARA.

46. ARWD 1900, *Lt.-Gen.*, pt. 4, pp. 373–74, 378; L. R. Hare to AG, 1D, DNL, May 24, 1900, vol. 13, Young Papers; Styer to AG, 2D, 8AC, Jan. 5, 1900, box 5, E 854, RG 395, NARA.

47. Linn, *U.S. Army and Counterinsurgency*, 81–82; Bankoff, "'These Brothers of Ours,'" 1050, 1058–60; J. C. Scott, *Art of Not Being Governed*, 135–37, 143–46; ARWD 1900, *Lt.-Gen.*,

pt. 4, 369–70; William H. Bowen, "A Visit to the Head Hunters," p. 6, box 2, Bowen Papers; L. R. Hare to AG, 1D, DNL, May 24, 1900, vol. 13, Young Papers; LR 74, Bruno Madrid to Senor Coronel, May, 1900, 4D, DNL, with Kennon, 1st end., May 5, 1900, and Funston, 2nd end., May 1899, box 1, E 2269; Graves to AG, Vigan, [March] 23, 1901, box 1, E 2164; Petitions of Francisca Vega, et al., all 5th end., John Green Ballance, Jan. 8, 1901, vol. 3, E 2167; all RG 395, NARA. On Igorot cargadores before the war, and American soldiers' encounters and relations with them during it, see Linn, *Philippine War*, 126; W. H. Scott, *Discovery of the Igorots*, 2–3, 329–30, 240, 289; Fry, *History of the Mountain Province*, 4–13; J. C. Scott, *Art of Not Being Governed*, 135–37, 143–46; ARWD 1900, Lt.-Gen., pt. 4, pp. 372–80; Trafton, *We Thought We Could Whip Them*, 53–55.

48. Gowing, *Mandate in Moroland*, 31–34; Abinales, "American Colonial State," 7; Amoroso, "Inheriting the 'Moro Problem,'" 135–36.

49. Charbonneau, *Civilizational Imperatives*, 25–41, 169–72; Amoroso, "Inheriting the 'Moro Problem'"; Salman, *Embarrassment of Slavery*, 8, 27, 39.

50. Gowing, *Mandate in Moroland*, 5–6, 9; Abinales, "U.S. Army as an Occupying Force," 410; Beckett, "Defiant and the Compliant," 394–96; T. M. McKenna, *Muslim Rulers and Rebels*, 48–51, 63–64; Bernad, "Five Letters," 17; *Census of the Philippine Islands*, 1903, p. 402.

51. Beckett, "Defiant and the Compliant," 396–98; Abinales, *Making Mindanao*, 49–55; Ahmad, "Class and Colony in Mindanao," 9–11; Mastura, "American Presence in Mindanao," 40–41; T. M. McKenna, *Muslim Rulers and Rebels*, 70–72; Charbonneau, *Civilizational Imperatives*, 2; Horatio K. Bradford, "Military Information Regarding Cottabato," March 1904, p. 13, box 6, E 3534, RG 395, NARA.

52. Abinales, *Making Mindanao*, 48; Abinales, "U.S. Army as an Occupying Force," 413–14; Walther, *Sacred Interests*, 173–74; Charbonneau, "Colonizing Workers," 27; LR 43, Datto Piang, Oct. 14, 1901, Reg. LR and LS Relating to the Moro People, July 1901–May 1902, vol. 1, E 3545; both RG 395, NARA.

53. Mastura, "American Presence in Mindanao," 40–41; Kramer, *Blood of Government*, 200–201; Hawkins, *Making Moros*, 70, 75–85; Reade, diary, Aug. 31, 1904, Malabang, Mindanao, p. 2, folder "Philippine Islands," Biographical Papers, Reade Papers; J. C. Bates to Sec., Mil. Gov. in Philippine Islands, Dec. 22, 1899, box 2, Bates Papers.

54. Charbonneau, "Colonizing Workers," 27.

55. Mastura, "American Presence in Mindanao," 33; Beckett, "Defiant and the Compliant," 398–400; Ileto, *Magindanao*, 36–37, 63–64; Abinales, *Orthodoxy and History*, 46–49; T. M. McKenna, *Muslim Rulers and Rebels*, 5–7; Bernad, "Five Letters," 19–20, 22–23; ARWD 1903, vol. 3, 368; J. C. Bates to Chief of Staff, DP and 8AC, Dec. 17, 1899, box 2, Bates Papers.

56. Salman, *Embarrassment of Slavery*, 112; Marr, "Diasporic Intelligences in the American Philippine Empire," 79–80; Saleeby, *The History of Sulu*, 262; RPC 1901, pt. 2, 105–6; ARWD 1902, Lt.-Gen., 528; "Lloyd M. Brett," in Cullum, *Biographical Register*, vol. 4, p. 313; "Two Pictures of War," *Boston Daily Globe*, Aug. 21, 1898; J. C. Bates to Chief of Staff, DP and 8AC, Dec. 17, 1899; L. M. Brett to AG, Dist. Mindanao and Jolo, Dec. 16, 1899; Datto Piang to Datto Mandi, Dec. 3, 1899, attached to Horace M. Reeve to AG, Dist. Mindanao and Jolo, Dec. 17, 1899; all box 2, Bates Papers.

57. Gowing, *Mandate in Moroland*, 83–84; Abinales, *Making Mindanao*, 50–51; Walther, *Sacred Interests*, 169–70; Amoroso, "Inheriting the 'Moro Problem,'" 125; Reeve, "Opening of Mindanao and Jolo," 924; ARWD 1902, Lt.-Gen., 481–86, 497–98, 528; ARWD 1903, vol. 3,

Notes to Chapter Two 303

365–78; Taft to Root, April 3, 1901, v. 1901, box 167, Root Papers; Horatio K. Bradford, "Military Information Regarding Cottabato," March 1904, box 6, E 3534, RG 395, NARA.

58. *RPC* 1901, pt. 2, 105, 106, 108; Taft to Root, April 3, vol. 1901, 14, 15, box 167, Root Papers; Benjamin Stark, Feb. 24, 1902, box 1, E 3539; June 28, 1902, "Memorandum of Events in Connection with Civil Affairs (Moros), Cottabatto, Mindanao, P.I.," E 3546; both RG 395, NARA. Datus' requests to US commanders at Cotabato that they suppress Moros' gambling because they "lost their money" and then "did not work" implied these elites' motive to control male followers' wages; see "Memorandum of Events in Connection with Civil Affairs (Moros), Cottabatto, Mindanao, P.I.," Aug. 25, 1902, E 3546, RG 395, NARA.

59. Salman, *Embarrassment of Slavery*, 52–54; Mastura, "American Presence in Mindanao," 40; USPC, *AR*, 1901, pt. 2, 107.

60. Salman, *Embarrassment of Slavery*, 73–74, 76, 84–86, and Hagadorn to Adj., Aug 1, 1901, E 2105, RG 395, NARA, cited in Salman, *Embarrassment of Slavery*, p. 289, note 33; Scott, *Slave Emancipation in Cuba*, chap. 6; *ARWD* 1902, *Lt.-Gen.*, 526; *ARGMP*, 1904, p. 5; J. C. Bates to Sec., Mil. Gov. in Philippine Islands, Dec. 22, 1899, Box 2, Bates Papers; Major Lea Febiger, Official Diary, July 3, 1901 entry, E 3547; Datto Piang, July 7 and 9, 1901, Reg. LR and LS, Relating to the Moro People, July 1901–May 1902, vol. 1, E 3545; "Memorandum of Events in Connection with Civil Affairs (Moros), Cottabatto, Mindanao, P.I.," June 16, 1902, and Aug. 21, 1903 entries, E 3546; all RG 395, NARA.

61. Ileto, *Magindanao*, 46–53, 58–61; Salman, *Embarrassment of Slavery*, 65–66; *ARWD* 1902, *Lt.-Gen.*, 526, 528.

62. Walther, *Sacred Interests*, 203; Landor, *Gems of the East*, 331–49; *ARWD* 1900, vol. 3, 259; Bradford, "Military Information Regarding Cottabato," 10, March 1904, box 6, E 3534; H. M. Cooper to Adj., Cottabato, June 28, 1903, box 1, E 3539; both RG 395, NARA. Gen. William A. Kobbé noted that Cotabato's garrison by early 1900 fed Tirurays, "wretched" and near "starvation, in exchange for "nominal work on roads"; see *ARWD* 1900, vol. 3, 258.

63. Salman, *Embarrassment of Slavery*, 79–82, 94–97, and Davis, GO 12, March 4, 1902, file 5075–5, RG 350, NARA, cited in Salman, *Embarrassment of Slavery*, 79; *ARWD* 1902, vol. 9, 497, 561, 564, 565; *ARGMP* 1904, 16.

64. Gowing, *Mandate in Moroland*, 100, 112–17.

65. Amoroso, "Inheriting the 'Moro Problem,'" 137–41; Walther, *Sacred Interests*, 198–202.

66. Beckett, "The Defiant and the Compliant," 400–401, 407; Kramer, *Blood of Government*, 218; Salman, *Embarrassment of Slavery*, 100–101, 116–17; Abinales, *Orthodoxy and History*, 58–59; *ARWD* 1903, vol. 5; *RPC* 1903, pt. 1, 76–78, 481–82, 484; *ARGMP* 1904, 68. Wood's anti-vagrancy proposal may have inspired Mindanao's American planters to advocate vagrancy codes to induce Moro labor; see Walther, *Sacred Interests*, 229.

67. Beckett, "The Defiant and the Compliant," 400–401; Salman, *Embarrassment of Slavery*, 112–14; *ARGMP* 1904, 68; LR 167, Carl Reichmann to CO, Cottabato, Feb. 13, 1904, box 6, E 3534; Van Orsdale to AG, Dept. Zamboanga, Feb. 15, 1904, vol. 3, E 3530; both RG 395, NARA.

68. Salman, *Embarrassment of Slavery*, 114; Charbonneau, *Civilizational Imperatives*, 104; *ARGMP* 1904, 8–9; TS, Wood to Van Horn, May 12, 1904; TR, Van Orsdale to AG, DM, May 12, 1904; all Box 34, LWP; Wood to AG, Phil. Div., March 17, 1904; Van Orsdale, March 18, 1904; Van Orsdale to Datto Piang, April 15, 1904; Van Orsdale to AG, DM, July 28, 1904; all vol. 4, E 3530, RG 395, NARA.

69. Abinales, *Orthodoxy and History*, 154–59; Abinales, *Making Mindanao*, 21–22, 70–73; Hawkins, *Making Moros*, 85–100; Walther, *Sacred Interests*, 198–202; Charbonneau, *Civilizational Imperatives*, 41–47; Charbonneau, "Colonizing Workers," 39–42; Charbonneau, "'New West in Mindanao.'"

70. TR, White to CO, Cottabato, July 21, 1904, box 6, E 3534; Van Orsdale, end. to LR 2038, Aug. 4, 1904; TS 989, Van Orsdale to AG, DM, Aug. 4, 1904; both vol. 4, E 3530; all RG 395, NARA.

71. Abinales, *Making Mindanao*, 71–73; USPC, *Acts*, 1903, No. 926, Oct. 27, 1903, pp. 740–55; *ARGMP* 1904, pp. 20, 23–24.

72. Mastura, "American Presence in Mindanao," 36; Norwood, *Fifty Thousand Miles*, 85; *ARGMP* 1904, p. 12; TS 442, Van Orsdale to AG, DM, June 7, 1904; TS 854, Van Ordsale to AG, Zamboanga, July 10, 1904; LS 901, Van Orsdale to AG, DM, July 23, 1904; LS 961, Van Orsdale to AG, DM, July 31, 1904; all vol. 4, E 3530; LR 848, Datto Piang to CO, Cottabato, July 5, 1904; White to Van Orsdale, July 7, 1904; Jno. V. White to CO, Cottabato, Oct. 31, 1904; LR 3446, C.C. Smith to Adj., Cottabato, Dec. 24, 1904; all box 6; LR 1598, H. S. Harbord to Adj., Cottabato, July 10, 1905, box 7; all E 3534; all RG 395, NARA.

73. Philip Reade, diary entries, Sept. 14, Sept. 23, Sept. 26, Oct. 5, all 1904, Reade Papers; Waldo to Adj., Cottabato, Dec. 13, 1903; n.a. to CO, Cottabato, April 23, 1904; Leo A. Dewey to Adj., Cottabato, April 28, 1904, and 1st end., April 30, 1904; all box 5, E 3534, RG 395, NARA.

74. Adas, "From Avoidance to Confrontation," 218–19; Vellema, Borras, Jr., and Lara, Jr., "Agrarian Roots"; Charbonneau, "Colonizing Workers," 38; TR, Van Horn to CO, Cottabato, Dec. 14, 1904; TR, Crowley to Adj., Cottabato, Dec. 18, 1904; H. C. Bonnycastle to Adj., Cottabato, Dec. 21, 1904; Datto Piang to CO, Cottabato, Dec. 22, 1904; TR, Bonnycastle to Adj., Cottabato, Dec. 22, 1904; Smith to Adj., Cottabato, Dec. 23, 1904; TR, Crowley to Adj., Cottabato, Dec. 24, 1904; TR, J. R. White to Harbord, Dec. 26, 1904; TR, Bonnycastle to Adj., Cottabato, Dec. 27, 1904; TR, Crowley to Adj., Cottabato, Dec. 27, 1904; TR, Harper to Adj., Cottabato, Dec. 27, 1904; TR, W. S. Drysdale to McGunnegle, Dec. 30, 1904; all box 6; LR 145, M. C. Kerth to AG, DM, Dec. 26, 1904; TR, Crowley to Adj., Cottabato, Jan. 4, 1905; TR, Reade to CO, Cottabato, Jan. 4, 1905; TR, Poillon to Adj., Cottabato, Jan. 3, 1905; TR, Waldo to Adj., Cottabato, Jan. 13, 1905; Frost to Adj., Cottabato, Jan. 13, 1905; all box 7; all E 3534; all RG 395, NARA.

75. Abinales, "Progressive-Machine Conflict," 163–67; Charbonneau, *Civilizational Imperatives*, 170–77; Howland, "Field Service in Mindanao," 36.

76. Howland, "Field Service in Mindanao," 54–55, 61–62, 64–68.

77. J. C. Scott, *Domination and the Arts of Resistance*, xii; Howland, "Field Service in Mindanao," 62–64, 68.

78. Charbonneau, *Civilizational Imperatives*, 96–102; Howland, "Field Service in Mindanao," 61–62, 69–71.

79. Howland, "Field Service in Mindanao," 36–37, 71–73.

80. Charbonneau, *Civilizational Imperatives*, 104; Reade, "The Cargador in Mindanao"; Saleeby, *Moro Problem*, 23–24; Hobbs, *Kris and Krag*, 137–41; Reade diary, Sept. 2, 10, 1904 entries, Reade Papers; M. Gilheuser, March 17, 1907, box 47, Bliss Papers, LOFC; A. M. Shipp to John Howard, Oct. 28, 1905; Shipp to Howard, n.d.; Shipp to QM, Cotabato, Oct. 21, 1905; Certificates, Shipp, Cabacsalan, Oct. 26, 1905; Receipt for Piang, Shipp, Cudarangan, Oct. 28, 1905; H. B. Howland to Mil. Sec., DM, Nov. 7, 1905; all box 10, E 2108, RG 395, NARA.

81. Beckett, "The Defiant and the Compliant," 401; Abinales, *Orthodoxy and History*, 56–71; Salman, *Embarrassment of Slavery*, 117; T. M. McKenna, *Muslim Rulers and Rebels*, 87.

82. Abinales, *Making Mindanao*, 73–78; Abinales, "US Army as an Occupying Force," 413; Linn, *Guardians of Empire*, 44–45; Charbonneau, "'New West in Mindanao,'" 314–15; *ARWD* 1905, vol. 3, 304; TS, Williams to McCoy, Feb. 14, 1906, box 11, McCoy Papers; Waldo B. Williams to W. S. Scott, June 10, 1906; W. S. Scott to Bliss, June 22, 1906; G. T. Langhorne to Bliss, Malalag, June 22, 1906; all box 15; J. A. S. to CO, Malabang, Jan. 5, 1907, box 59, Bliss Papers, LOFC; Bliss, "Friends and Fellow Citizens," folder 5, box 43, Bliss Papers, USAHEC; M. C. Kerth to Adj., Cottabato, Sept. 2, 1904; William H. Wassell to AG, DM, Dec. 21, 1904; both box 5, E 3534; Edward Chynoweth to AG, DM, Oct. 4, 1904; LS 1285, F. Gaedecke to Cottabato, Nov. 9, 1904, 1st end. to LR 2807; both box 5, E 3530; LR 655, W. Harper to Adj., Cotabato, May 16, 1905, box 6, E 3534; all RG 395, NARA.

83. Cruikshank, *Samar: 1768–1898*, 145–50, 158–61, 187–201, 207–10; Adas, *Machines as the Measure of Men*, 204–10; Ileto, *Pasyon and Revolution*, 22–27; Linn, "'To Set All Law at Defiance,'" 556–60, 562–66, 573.

84. *ARWD* 1905, vol. 3, 296; "Additional Memorandum Supplementing Letter of Feb, 12, 1906," in Leonard Wood, Diary, Feb. 1, 1906–Dec. 31, 1906, box 3; Wood to CG, Dept. Visayas, June 8, 1906, Reel 3; both LWP; Alexander O. Mandee to CO, 5th Dist. of Samar, June 27, 1906; A. H. Bishop to Adj., CICFO, Tacloban, Leyte, June 11, 1907; both E 5212; H. E. Knight to Adj., Office in Charge Field Operations, Island of Samar, Jan. 2, 1907, E 5222; all RG 395, NARA.

85. Wise, "Field Notes from Samar," 3–5, 39–41; "Col. Hugh D. Wise, Officer 48 Years," *New York Times*, May 29, 1942; *ARWD* 1906, vol. 3, 267.

86. Rafael, *White Love*, 78–83, 81; Kramer, *Blood of Government*, 181, 318–21; Rice, *Dean Worcester's Fantasy Islands*, esp. 4–6, 63–78; Wise, "Field Notes from Samar," 7–10, 31, 34, 39–41.

87. Wise, "Field Notes from Samar," 30, 39–43, 50, 52.

88. Wise, "Field Notes from Samar," 25–28, 30, 39–41.

89. *ARWD* 1905, vol. 3, 288–93; *ARWD* 1906, vol. 3, 257–62; A. H. Bishop to Adj., CICFO, Tacloban, Leyte, June 11, 1907, E 5212; John M. True to QM, Camp Bumpus, Leyte, Oct. 6, 1906, E 3008; H. E. Knight to Adj., Officer in Charge Field Operations, Island of Samar, Jan. 2, 1907; H. E. Knight to Mil. Sec., Dept. Visayas, Jan. 25, 1907; both E 5222; B. L. Auttensultz to Adj., 4D, Dowa, Samar, Jan. 20, 1907, E 3002; all RG 395, NARA.

90. Cullum, *Biographical Register*, vol. 3, 235; *ARWD* 1906, vol. 3, 268–71; *ARWD* 1907, vol. 3, 265–71; Report of Operations, Frederick A. Smith to MS, DV 30 Sept. 1906, No. 6100–6106, E 2498; anonymous (Hugh D. Wise] to Frederick A. Smith, 15 Oct 1906, no. 51, E 2701; both RG 395, NARA, cited in Linn, "'To Set All Law at Defiance,'" 590n86, 581n87.

91. Linn, "'To Set All Law at Defiance,'" 573–74; Ileto, *Pasyon and Revolution*; "Albert Leopold Mills," in Cullum, *Biographical Register*, vol. 5, 292; *ARWD* 1907, vol. 3, 265–71.

Chapter Three

1. Lane, *Armed Progressive*, chap. 4; Cosmas, *Army for Empire*, 206–9; Trask, *War with Spain in 1898*, 215; Miley, *In Cuba with Shafter*, 79–80; Alger, *The Spanish-American War*, 120; S. Crane, *War Dispatches*, 155–56; Wheeler, *The Santiago Campaign, 1898*, 47; Sargent,

306 Notes to Chapter Three

Campaign of Santiago de Cuba, 2:10; Davis, "Rough Riders' Fight at Guasimas," 262–64; Society of Santiago, *Santiago Campaign*, 203; ARWD 1898, *Maj.-Gen.*, 160; US Senate, *Report of the Commission Appointed by the President*, 5:2059–60.

2. L. A. Pérez, *Cuba between Empires*, 199–205; Cosmas, *Army for Empire*, 188; S. Crane, *Wounds in the Rain*, 1, 12; J. B. Atkins, *The War in Cuba*, 289; Chadwick, *Relations of the United States and Spain*, 2: 69; LR 835, Wheeler to Shafter, July 3, 1898, folder 38; LR 844, Hunt J. Ford to AAG, 5AC, July 3, 1898, folder 39a; Humphrey to McClernand, Siboney, July 11, 1898, folder 43; all box 1, E 535, RG 395, NARA.

3. Nye, *American Technological Sublime*, 57–58, 62–64; Holley, *Highway Revolution*, 7–13; Adas, *Dominance by Design*, 170; Ballantyne and Burton, *Empires and the Reach of the Global*; Mitchell, *Rule of Experts*, 15.

4. R. J. Scott, *Slave Emancipation in Cuba*, 256–58; Hoernel, "Sugar and Social Change in Oriente," 220–21; L. A. Pérez, *Lords of the Mountain*, 12–18, 25–26, 76–83, 96–101; Ferrer, *Cuba: An American History*, 18–21; Chira, *Patchwork Freedoms*, esp. 248–49; US Department of War, *Military Notes on Cuba, 1898*, 417; US Department of War, *Military Notes on Cuba, 1909*, 535.

5. L. A. Pérez, *Cuba and the United States*, 70–71; L. A. Pérez, *On Becoming Cuban*, 9–13, 17–19, 115–25; L. A. Pérez, *Rice in the Time of Sugar*, 29–31; Zanetti and García, *Sugar and Railroads*, 64–65, 141–45; Chira, *Patchwork Freedoms*, 228; L. A. Pérez, *Colonial Reckoning*, 22–23, 42, 59–60, 67–68, 104–6; Porter, *Appendix to the Report*, 5, 129–30, 168, 173; "Tres disputados," Dec. 1892, Carreteras, exp. 5, caja 271; Ernesto Brooks to Gobernador Provincial, Nov. 6, 1894, Caminos, exp. 2, caja 215; Ayuntamento, Santiago de Cuba, July 9, 1894, Caminos, exp. 4, caja 215; all FGP, APSDC. For municipal officials' perspective on agriculture in Oriente in 1900, see "informes," box 101, E 3, RG 140, NARA.

6. L. A. Pérez, *Cuba between Empires*, 43; R. J. Scott, *Slave Emancipation in Cuba*, 256–58; L. A. Pérez, *Lords of the Mountain*, 4, 79–80, 85–89; Tone, *War and Genocide in Cuba*, 201–2; Wood, "Santiago since the Surrender," 517–22; ARWD 1899, pt. 6, *Report of Maj. Gen. J. R. Brooke*, 366–67 Wood to McKinley, Nov. 27, 1898, box 26, LWP; AGO #139813, Wood to Alger, Sept. 9, 1898, box 915, E 25, RG 94, NARA.

7. L. A. Pérez, *Lords of the Mountain*, 85–86; Tone, *War and Genocide in Cuba*, 201–2; L. A. Pérez, *Rice in the Time of Sugar*, chap. 1; Rodríguez, *Right to Live in Health*, 31–32; Wood, "Santiago since the Surrender," 517–22; Matthews, *New-Born Cuba*, 309; Barton, *Story of the Red Cross*, 156; Ramsden, "Diary of the British Consul," 587, 589; CWS, vol. 1, 185; "Clean Streets," *Times of Cuba*, Aug. 8, 1898; ARWD 1899, pt. 6, *Report of Maj. Gen. J.R. Brooke*, 366–67; US Senate, *Statements of Major-General Leonard Wood*, 20; AGO #139813, Wood to Alger, Sept. 9, 1898, box 915, E 25, RG 94, NARA.

8. Katz, *In the Shadow of the Poorhouse*, 68–83; L. A. Pérez, *On Becoming Cuban*, 107–9; de la Fuente, *Nation for All*, 40–42; Irwin, *Making the World Safe*, 3–8, 20–27; Rodríguez, *Right to Live in Health*, 30–35; Matthews, *New-Born Cuba*, 203; US Department of War, *Annual Report of Colonel Samuel M. Whitside*, 152; "The Situation," *Times of Cuba*, Aug. 4, 1898; "Work of Relief," *Los Angeles Times*, Sept. 10, 1898; "Cuban Frauds," *Los Angeles Times*, Jan. 1, 1899; Hanna to Lawrence F. Abbott, Nov. 8, 1928, box 6, Hagedorn Papers; AGO #139813, Wood to Alger, Sept. 9, 1898, box 915, E 25, RG 94, NARA; AG to Lawton, Sept. 9, 1898, box 2; H. C. Corbin to CG Sgo., Sept. 16, 1898, box 1; both E 1487; Wood to AG, War Department, May 6, 1899, vol. 6, box 2, E 1479; all RG 395, NARA. Relief workers at Santiago may have

wanted to compel "indigent" Cuban women to work for rations; "Allow No More Free Rations," *Atlanta Constitution*, Oct. 20, 1898.

9. Espinosa, *Epidemic Invasions*, 31–33; García, *Beyond the Walled City*, 8–15, 173–74, 177–82; Maurer, *Empire Trap*, 52–54, 80–85; US Senate, *Statements of Major-General Leonard Wood*, 10–11; Wood, "Santiago since the Surrender," 524; Kennan, "Sanitary Regeneration of Santiago," 871–72, 875, 877; ARWD 1899, pt. 1, 305; Antonio Vallejo, July 20, 1898, exp. 15, caja 1776, Obras Públicas, 1898, FGP, APSDC; R. G. Mendoza and Z. Ferrez to CG, Dept. of Santiago, Sept. 2, 1898, vol. 1; Wood to AG, US Army, Oct. 26, 1898, box 2; both E 1479, RG 395, NARA; AGO #139813, Wood to Alger, Sept. 9, 1898, box 915, E 25, RG 94, NARA.

10. Espinosa, *Epidemic Invasions*, 34–46, 74–84; García, *Beyond the Walled City*, 178–81; Wood, "Military Government of Cuba," 15–21; Kennan, "The Government of Santiago," 109–10; US Senate, *Establishment of Free Government in Cuba*, 22–23; ARWD 1899, *Report of Maj. Gen. J. R. Brooke*, 129; AGO #139813, Wood to Alger, Sept. 9, 1898, box 915, E 25, RG 94, NARA; Tel., Ord to Wilmer, Santiago, April 28, 1899, vol. 1, E 1484, RG 395, NARA.

11. R. J. Scott, *Degrees of Freedom*, 174–75; Kennan, "Friction in Cuba," 676; ARWD 1899, pt. 1, 302–306; AGO #139813, Wood to Alger, Sept. 9, 1898, box 915, E 25, RG 94, NARA; James H. McLeary to Adj., Dept. of Santiago, Dec. 18, 1898, box 3; Wood to Adj., DC, March 8, 1899; Wood to Chaffee, March 10, 1899: both vol. 2, E 1479, RG 395, NARA.

12. L. A. Pérez, *Cuba in the American Imagination*, 65–88; Wood, "Santiago since the Surrender," 526; "The Captured Cuban City," *New York Tribune*, Aug. 12, 1898; "Improvement of Santiago," *Washington Post*, Oct. 5, 1898; Wood to Louise Wood, Sept. 28, 1898; Frank R. McCoy, "Recall of General Lawton," Jan. 8, 1929; Brackett, "Lawton at Santiago," May 26, 1929; all box 13, Hagedorn Papers; Wood to Alger, Oct. 9, 1898, box 946, E 25, RG 94, NARA; J. W. Jacobs to AAG, Dept. of Santiago, Aug. 21, 1898, box 1, E 1487; Lawton to AG, US Army, Sept. 2, 1898; Lawton to M. I. Ludington, Sept. 6, 1898; Lawton to QM Gen., Sept. 6, 1898; TR 472, Ludington to Lawton, Sept. 7, 1898; Lawton to AG, Sept. 15, 1898; Lawton to AG, Washington, Sept. 16, 1898; all vol. 1, E 1479, RG 395, NARA.

13. Iglesias Utset, *Cultural History of Cuba*, 18–19; Brody, *Visualizing American Empire*, 149–50; Bacardí y Moreau, *Cronicas de Santiago de Cuba*, 172; Wood, "Existing Conditions and Needs in Cuba," 594–95; Kennan, "Friction in Cuba," 676; "'Wood Week' in Santiago," *New York Times*, Jan. 1, 1899; ARWD 1899, vol. 1, pt. 6, *Report of Maj.-Gen. J. R. Brooke*, 367; Hanna to Lawrence F. Abbott, Nov. 8, 1928, box 6; Frank McCoy, "Matthew E. Hanna," April 30, 1929, box 13; Herbert P. Williams, Feb. 14, 1899, box 12; all Hagedorn Papers; Wood to AG, DC, Feb. 13, 1899, vol. 4, E 1479; LR 447, DC, "Report of Civilian Employees, Hdqrs., Dept. Santiago & Pto. Principe," Dec. 31, 1899, box 24, E 1241; both RG 395, NARA.

14. Matthews, *New-Born Cuba*, 314; Kennan, "From Santiago to Havana," 202–3; "Gen. Wood at Santiago," *New York Times*, Oct. 6, 1898; US Senate, *Establishment of Free Government in Cuba*, 21; Herbert P. Williams, Feb. 14, 1899, box 12, Hagedorn Papers; James H. McLeary to Adj., DSC, Jan. 24, 1899, box 5, E 1479, RG 395, NARA.

15. L. A. Pérez, *Cuba between Empires*, 230–33, 235–47, 279; L. A. Pérez, *Lords of the Mountain*, 68–74, 129–51; Ferrer, *Insurgent Cuba*, 149–52.

16. Tone, *War and Genocide in Cuba*, 201–2; Helg, *Our Rightful Share*, 32–33; Lawton to Corbin, Aug. 16, 1898; Lawton to Corbin, Sept. 3, 1898; Lawton to AG, US Army, Sept. 3, 1898; Lawton, Sept. 6, 1898; Lawton to Cebreco, Sept., n.d., 1898; all vol. 1, E 1479; A.

Cebreco to Lawton, Sept. 3, 1898, box 1; AG to Lawton, Sept. 9, 1898, box 2; both E 1487; all RG 395, NARA.

17. Healy, *United States in Cuba*, 44–50; L. A. Pérez, *Cuba between Empires*, 234–35, 242–57; "Cuban Soldiers," *New York Times*, Sept. 6, 1898; "Collazo Warns Americans," *New York Tribune*, Sept. 29, 1898, trans. from *El Porvenir*, Sept. 29, 1898; "Improvement of Santiago," *Washington Post*, Oct. 5, 1898; "Gen. Wood on the Cubans," *New York Times*, June 24, 1899; J. W. Rooney to Adj., Santiago, Sept. 26, 1898, box 2; H. B. Osgood to AG, Dept. of Santiago, Oct. 15, 1898, box 3; both E 1487, RG 395, NARA.

18. Healy, *United States in Cuba*, 68–80; L. A. Pérez, "Pursuit of Pacification," 318–20; L. A. Pérez, *Essays on Cuban History*, 14–20; Wood to Sec. of War, May 6, 1899, file 384, box 73, E 5, RG 350, NARA.

19. L. A. Pérez, *Cuba between Empires*, 106–8, 135–37; L. A. Pérez, *Lords of the Mountain*, 84–85; Ferrer, *Insurgent Cuba*, 99–104; McGillivray, *Blazing Cane*, 46–51; Frymer, *Building an American Empire*, 57–59; Wood, *Opportunities in the Colonies*, 183; "Government of Santiago," *New York Times*, Oct. 2, 1898; "Americanizing Santiago," *New York Times*, Oct. 25, 1898; Wood to unknown, Nov. 1898, box 190, LWP; Wood to Alger, Oct. 9, box 946, E 25, RG 94, NARA; Wood to AG, DC, Oct. 31, 1899, box 11, E 3, RG 140, NARA.

20. Healy, *United States in Cuba*, 72–80; L. A. Pérez, "Pursuit of Pacification," 318–20; L. A. Pérez, *Essays on Cuban History*, 8–22; Matthews, *New-Born Cuba*, 314; Wood, "Existing Conditions and Needs in Cuba," 596; "Gen. Wood at Santiago," *New York Times*, Oct. 6, 1898; "Native Distaste for Work," *New York Tribune*, Jan. 25, 1899; "Cuban Soldiers on Their Dignity," *New York Tribune*, Jan. 30, 1899; Ignacio I. Aloma to Demetrio Castillo, Feb. 20, 1899, LR 87, Departamento de Santiago de Cuba, Gobierno Civil, exp. 23, caja 875, Intervencion Norteamericana, 1899, FGP, APSDC; Wood to Sec. of War, May 6, 1899, file 384, box 73, E 5, RG 350, NARA.

21. Zanetti and García, *Sugar and Railroads*, 64–68, 140, 203–204; Lichtenstein, *Twice the Work of Free Labor*; Wood, "Santiago since the Surrender," 522; "Conditions at Santiago," *New York Times*, Oct. 15, 1898; ARWD 1899, vol. 1, pt. 6, *Reports of Brig. Gen. Leonard Wood*, 822, 827–29; ARWD 1899, pt. 6, 829–30; ARWD 1900, *Civil Affairs of U.S. Military Government*, vol. 2, pt. 1, 142–43, 193; US Department of War, *Annual Report of Colonel Samuel M. Whitside*, 174; James H. McLeary to Adj., DSC, Dec. 19, 1898, box 3, E 1479, RG 395, NARA; Matthew E. Hanna to AG, Civil Dept., Dept. of Santiago & Puerto Principe, Sept. 30, 1899, box 203, LWP; Wood to AG, DC, Oct. 31, 1899, box 11, E 3, RG 140, NARA.

22. L. A. Pérez, *Cuba between Empires*, 279; L. A. Pérez, *Lords of the Mountain*, 91–95; ARWD 1899, pt. 1, 304–306; ARWD 1899, vol. 1, pt. 6, *Reports of Brig. Gen. Leonard Wood*, 822–35, 862; Baker, "General Leonard Wood," 376; Wood to AG, DC, March 6, 1899, box 6; Wood to AG, DC, Oct. 31, 1899, box 11; Alberto Sanchez et al. to Wood, Jan. 25, 1900, box 70; all E 3, RG 140, NARA.

23. Healy, *United States in Cuba*, 53–64, 88–97.

24. Healy, *United States in Cuba*, 51–52, 88–89, 93–94; ARWD 1899, vol. 1, pt. 6, *Report of Maj. Gen. J. R. Brooke*, 8, 13–14; Brooke to H. C. Corbin, May 24, 1899; Brooke to SW, Dec. 29, 1898; Brooke to CGs in Depts. of Division, Jan. 9, 1899; Brooke to H. C. Corbin, May 24, 1899; all reel 7, McKinley Papers.

25. Healy, *United States in Cuba*, 53–60; L. A. Pérez, *Essays on Cuban History*, 20–22; L. A. Pérez, *Cuba under the Platt Amendment*, 86–87; ARWD 1899, vol. 1, pt. 6, 368, 837.

26. L. A. Pérez, *Cuba between Empires*, 148, 208–10, 285–92; L. A. Pérez, *On Becoming Cuban*, 28–39.

27. Riera Hernandez, *Ejercito Libertador de Cuba*, 157–58; L. A. Pérez, *Cuba between Empires*, 196–97, 292; Meriño Fuentes, *Gobierno municipal y partidos políticos en Santiago de Cuba*, 27–29; L. A. Pérez, *On Becoming Cuban*, 38–39; L. A. Pérez, *Cuba and the United States*, 67–68; Wheeler, *Santiago Campaign*, 190; Ravelo y Asensio, *La ciudad de la historia y la Guerra del 95*, 238–40; Hagedorn, *Leonard Wood*, 199; Castellanos Garcia, *Historia en Santiago*, 87; Holme, *Life of Leonard Wood*, 74–75; Henry T. Allen, "Report of the Operations of Troop D, 2nd U.S. Cavalry, in the Santiago Campaign," 12, box 6, Correspondence, 1898, Allen Papers; AGO #111485, Tel., V. Albuerne to William McKinley, Aug. 6, 1898, box 779, E 25, RG 94, NARA.

28. Meriño Fuentes, *Gobierno municipal y partidos políticos en Santiago de Cuba*, 29; ARWD 1900, pt. 11, *Report of the Military Governor of Cuba on Civil Affairs*, vol. 1, pt. 1, 8; ARWD 1900, pt. 11, *Report of the Military Governor of Cuba on Civil Affairs*, vol. 1, pt. 2, 221; "Our Flag at Manzanillo," *The Sun*, Oct. 1898, in Scrapbook, Thomas S. Wylly Papers; Lawton to Demetrio Castillo, Aug. 19, 1898; Lawton to AG, Washington, DC, Sept. 10, 1898; both box 1, E 1479; LR 614, D. Castillo to Lawton, Santa Cruz, Sept. 9, 1898, box 1, E 1487; Kennon to Wood, Feb. 14, 1899, vol. 4, E 1479; all RG 395, NARA.

29. Buch López, *Historia de Santiago de Cuba*, 267, 279; Bacardi, *Emilio Bacardi*, 28, 48–54, 61–64, 71–81, 109–23, 133.

30. Meriño Fuentes, *Gobierno municipal y partidos políticos en Santiago de Cuba*, 24–27; Bacardi, *Emilio Bacardi*, 133–35, 140–41, 155–56; Bacardí y Moreau, *Crónicas*, 188–91, 194–96, 212; Emilio Bacardi, "Carta abierta a Sr. Alcalde Municipal," July 27, 1898," Archivo del Museo Historico Emilio Bacardi, and Emilio Bacardi to Leonard Wood, June 1901, AHPSDC, quoted by Gjelten, *Bacardi*, 78, 87; Wood to Bacardi, Aug. 3, 1899, exp. 34, caja 24, Archivo del Museo Histórico Emilio Bacardí; "Sesion del 28 de Febrero del 1899," Nov. 1, 1899, and Nov. 23, 1899, in Actas Capitulares, vol. 1898–1899, Santiago de Cuba; R. L. Hamilton to Alcalde, Santiago de Cuba, Jan. 18, 1900, exp. 1, caja 199, Calles, FGP; both APSDC. For insurgents' civil appointments by Wood and Castillo throughout Oriente in late 1898 and early 1899, see files in caja 515, FGP, APSDC; orden no. 742, June 9, 1898, Fondo Demetrio Castillo Duany, Archivo del Museo Histórico Emilio Bacardí.

31. Healy, *United States in Cuba*, 65–66; L. A. Pérez, *Cuba between Empires*, 257; Bacardí y Moreau, *Crónicas*, 198–99.

32. Chira, *Patchwork Freedoms*, 268; Zulueta Zulueta, "La Guerra de 1895," 105; Bacardi, *Emilio Bacardi*, 135; Bell, "Supreme Court of Santiago de Cuba"; "Santiago's Receipts Wanted," *New York Times*, Jan. 3, 1899; "God Save Cuba," *La Independencia*, Jan. 3, 1899; "Santiago Still Excited," *New York Sun*, Jan. 7, 1899; "The Cubans and Ourselves," *New York Times*, Jan. 24, 1899; "Building the Road," Jan. 7, 1899; Brooke; Jan. 4, 1899, box 12; all Hagedorn Papers; B. S. Willson to Wood to Brooke, Jan. 4, 1899; Chaffee to Wood, Jan. 10, 1899, vol. 5; both box 2, E 1479, RG 395, NARA.

33. Wood to Alger, Jan. 2, 1899; "Santiago Still Excited," *New York Sun*, Jan. 7, 1899; both box 12, Hagedorn Papers; V. V. Richards to CG, Santiago de Cuba, Jan. 5, 1899; Brooke to AG, Washington, DC, Jan. 5, 1899; Brooke to AG, US Army, Jan. 9, 1899; all box 1, E 1238, RG 395, NARA.

34. Zulueta Zulueta, "La Guerra de 1895," 108; US Senate, *Statements of Major-General Leonard Wood*, 25; "Customs Order Suspended," *New York Tribune*, Jan. 6, 1899; "Situation

at Santiago," *New York Times*, Jan. 9, 1899; "Comes Here by Order," *Washington Post*, Jan. 11, 1899; "Wood Here from Santiago," *New York Times*, Jan. 11, 1899; "Wood's Power Curtailed," *Washington Post*, Jan. 20, 1899; "Wood Obtains the Cash," *Washington Post*, Jan. 27, 1899; "Address at Union League Club," box 12, Hagedorn Papers; "Dictated by General Wood," Jan. 1900, folder 331, box 58, E 5, RG 350, NARA.

35. Kennan, "Friction in Cuba," 675; Roosevelt, "General Leonard Wood," 19–23; "Complaints from Santiago," *New York Tribune*, March 1, 1899; "Mutterings at Santiago," *Baltimore Sun*, March 3, 1899; "Work Ends at Santiago," *Chicago Daily Tribune*, March 4, 1899; "Out of Work in Santiago," *New York Tribune*, March 4, 1899; "Santiago Paper Displeased," *Atlanta Constitution*, March 6, 1899; "Discontent at Santiago," *New York Sun*, Feb. 27, 1899; "Gen. Leonard Wood, the military governor of the Province of Santiago, and Joaquin Castillo . . . ," Jan. 1899, box 12, Hagedorn Papers; Wood to AG, Havana, Cuba, March 6, 1899, box 6, E 3, RG 140, NARA; "Dictated by General Wood," Jan. 1900, folder 331, box 58, E 5, RG 350, NARA; Richards to CG, Santiago, Jan. 27, 1899, box 1, E 1238; Wood to M. E. Hanna, March 3, 1899; Wood to C. A. Allen, March 3, 1899; C. Richards to Wood, Feb. 28, 1899; Wood to Adj., DC, March 8, 1899; all vol. 5, E 1479; Chaffee to Brooke, March 8, 1899, box 9, E 1241; Chaffee to Wood, March 9, 1899, box 6, E 1487; all RG 395, NARA.

36. Healy, *United States in Cuba*, 98, 124; Meriño Fuentes, *Gobierno municipal y partidos políticos en Santiago de Cuba*, 29; Gjelten, *Bacardi*, 90; de la Fuente, *Nation for All*, 36–37; de la Fuente and Casey, "Race and the Suffrage Controversy"; Kramer, "Empire, Exceptions, and Anglo-Saxons"; Wood, "Existing Conditions and Needs in Cuba," 596; Wood, "Present Situation in Cuba," 639; Williams, "Outlook in Cuba," 831; "Santiago Crisis Over," *Washington Post*, March 10, 1899; "Cleaning up Santiago," *New York Sun*, May 14, 1899; "Wood in Pto Principe," *La Lucha*, Sept. 15, 1899; Wood to McKinley, April 27, 1899; Wood to AG, US Army, July 27, 1899; Roosevelt to Root, Sept. 4, 1899; Elihu Root to Wood, Jan. 27, 1900; Frank Steinhart to Herman Hagedorn, Dec. 28, 1928; all box 12, Hagedorn Papers; Hanna to Adj., Civil Dept., DSPP, Sept. 30, 1899, box 203, LWP; Wood to Root, Oct. 3, 1899, box 168, Root Papers; Wood to AG, DC, March 4, 1899; Wood to AG, DC, March 6, 1899; both box 6; Wood to Adj., DC, June 13, 1899, box 19; all E 3, RG 140, NARA; Brooke to SW, March 10, 1899, box 2; Brooke to SW, April 28, 1899, box 3; TS, Richards to Wood, July 26, 1899; TS, Chaffee to Wood, July 28; both box 4; all E 1238; Brooke to Wood, April 22, 1899, box 7, E 1487; Wood to AG, US Army, March 1, 1899, vol. 5; Wood to Adj., DC, March 8, 1899, both vol. 5, E 1479; TS, Chaffee to Wood, March 8, 1899, box 2, E 1238; Wood to Chaffee, March 10, 1899; Wood to Adj., DC, March 30, 1899; both vol. 5, E 1479; all RG 395, NARA; AGO #253383, J. C. Breckenridge to SW, July 14, 1899, box 1005; AGO #264599, H. C. Corbin, memorandum, Aug. 30, 1899, box 1754; both E 25, RG 94, NARA.

37. Healy, *United States in Cuba*, 98–125; Lane, *Armed Progressive*, 73–85; Wood, "Existing Conditions and Needs in Cuba," 594; Wood, "Military Government," 23–24; "Al gobierno interventor," *Revista de Agricultura*, Sept. 1, 1900; *ARWD 1900, Report of Military Governor on Civil Affairs*, vol. 1, pt. 1, 9–10, 129–31; *ARWD 1900, Civil Affairs of Military Government of Cuba*, vol. 1, pt. 2, 222; *ARWD 1900*, pt. 12, *Report of the Military Governor of Cuba on Civil Affairs*, vol. 2, pt. 3, 2–3; TS, Wood to S. M. Whitside, box 5, E 6, RG 140, NARA; Jose Miguel Gomez to James Wilson, June 4, 1899, box 9; E. St. J. Greble to CG, DMSC, Dec. 15, 1899, box 27; both E 1331, RG 395, NARA.

38. Hitchman, "Unfinished Business," 339; L. A. Pérez, *On Becoming Cuban*, 115–24; Cuevas Toraya, *500 años de construcciones en Cuba*, 159.

39. *ARWD* 1900, *Report of the Military Governor on Civil Affairs*, vol. 1, pt. 1, 129–31, 558–600; *ARWD* 1900, *Report of the Military Governor on Civil Affairs*, vol. 2, pt. 1, 189; Mercedes del Castillo y Bravo to Demetrio Castillo, March 24, 1900, LR 8–6, Obras Públicas, 1900, exp. 8, caja 271; Secretaría de Obras Públicas to Gobernador Civil, Oct. 30, 1902, Carreteras, 1902, exp. 10, caja 271; both FGP, APSDC.

40. Healy, *United States in Cuba*, 126–27; Montgomery, *Beyond Equality*, 312–23; L. A. Pérez, *Cuba between Empires*, 119, 130, 255–56, 292; L. A. Pérez, *Cuba under the Platt Amendment*, 80; Zanetti and García, *Sugar and Railroads*, 212–23; Rosenberg, *Financial Missionaries to the World*, 12–14; García, *Beyond the Walled City*, 178; V. Clark, "Labor Conditions in Cuba," 684, 749, 770, 776; Lacosta, "Opportunities in Cuba," 146–47; Marshall, "A Talk with General Wood," 672; *ARWD* 1900, *Report of the Military Governor on Civil Affairs*, vol. 1, pt. 1, 6, 74, 131; *ARWD* 1900, *Report of the Military Governor on Civil Affairs*, vol. 2, pt. 1, 22; *ARWD* 1900, *Report of the Military Governor on Civil Affairs*, vol. 2, pt. 3, 1–3; W. M. Black to AG, DC, Feb. 15, 1900, box 67; Villalon to Wood, March 7, 1900, box 83; both E 3, RG 140, NARA; TS, Wood to S. M. Whitside, April 3, 1900; Salvador Cisneros y Betancourt, "Appeal to the American People on Behalf of Cuba," Aug. 24, 1900, F 331, box 58, E 5, RG 350, NARA; Hugh Scott to Samuel Whitside, May 15, 1902, box 17, E 1487, RG 395, NARA.

41. L. A. Pérez, *Cuba between Empires*, 359; Hoernel, "Sugar and Social Change in Oriente," 228, 230; L. A. Pérez, *Lords of the Mountain*, 94–111, 129–140; L. A. Pérez, *Cuba and the United States*, 118–124; Dye, *Cuban Sugar in the Age of Mass Production*, 14–19; Olmstead, *Censo de la República de Cuba 1907*, 118.

42. L. A. Pérez, *Cuba between Empires*, 357–60; Hoernel, "Sugar and Social Change in Oriente," 229; L. A. Pérez, *Cuba under the Platt Amendment*, 58–86; L. A. Pérez, *Lords of the Mountain*, 68–74, 129–51; Hitchman, "U.S. Control over Sugar Production," 91; McGillivray, *Blazing Cane*, esp. 75–80; Ayala, *American Sugar Kingdom*, 200–21. Some Yankee sugar planters, including Edwin Atkins, promoted the reciprocity treaty by arguing that more trade would provide the Cuban state with revenues needed for sanitation and public works; see US Congress, *Reciprocity with Cuba*, 3.

43. L. A. Pérez, *Lords of the Mountain*, 136–39, 168, 170–71, 175–77; McGillivray, *Blazing Cane*, 89–108; de la Fuente and Casey, "Race and the Suffrage Controversy in Cuba," 229; "Distress Exists in Cuba," *New York Times*, Oct. 18, 1902; Matthew E. Hanna to Herbert G. Squiers, Sept. 30, 1902, 5, 7, in Theodore Roosevelt Papers; Cosby to Wood, Aug. 10, 1903, box 33, LWP; Latenlade & Co. to Gobernador Civil de Provincia de Santiago de Cuba, June 23, 1902, LR 3453, Gobierno Civil de Provincia de Santiago de Cuba, exp. 5, caja 217, Caminos; Bonet to Gobernador Civil, Santiago de Cuba, TR, June, 1902, exp. 9, caja 271, Carreteras, 1902; both FGP, APSDC; TR, Roca to Wood, March 16, 1900, box 83, E 3, RG 140, NARA. Jose Miguel Gomez, March 27, 1900, and 2nd end., F. P. Fremont, March 31, 1900, box 33, E 1331, RG 395, NARA.

44. Bankoff, "Wants, Wages, and Workers," 61–64; Wolters, "How Were Labourers Paid," 140, 153–57, 159–67; US Bureau of the Census, *Census of the Philippine Islands, 1903*, 2:865.

45. J. L. Phelan, *Hispanization of the Philippines*, 118–20, 126–27; J. Larkin, *Pampangans*, 30–40, 53, 57–63, 71–84, 91–93, 99–102; Bankoff, "Wants, Wages, and Workers," 64–66; Aguilar, *Clash of Spirits*, 70–71, 75–77.

46. Cushner, *Spain in the Philippines*, chap. 5; J. L. Phelan, *Hispanization of the Philippines*, 114–15, 124–27; J. Larkin, "Philippine History Reconsidered," 601–3; Abinales and Amoroso, *State and Society in the Philippines*, 89. The Schurman Commission narrated Spanish-era public works administration in *RPC* 1900, vol. 1, 53–55.

47. J. L. Phelan, *Hispanization of the Philippines*, 99, 115, 136–52; Sturtevant, *Popular Uprisings in the Philippines*, 35–41, 79–81; Ileto, *Pasyon and Revolution*, 67; B. R. Anderson, *Under Three Flags*, 57–58; A. G. Corpuz, *Colonial Iron Horse*, 25; Huetz de Lemps, "Provincial-Level Corruption in the Second Half of the Nineteenth Century," 219–20; Jagor, *Travels in the Philippines*, 110–11, 198–99; F. D. Millett, *Expedition to the Philippines*, 231–32; Foreman, *The Philippine Islands*, 224; "May 19th, 1893. Law for Organization and Government of Municipalities in the Philippines," Exhibit 1, in Taylor, *Philippine Insurrection*, 1:121–42, esp. 133, 137.

48. Kramer, *Blood of Government*, 98–102; O. K. Davis, *Our Conquests in the Pacific*, 321; *CWS*, vol. 2, 676–78; *ARWD* 1898, Maj-Gen., 40, 44, 49–50, 60–62.

49. Agoncillo, *Malolos*, 179–92, 195–97, 223–24, 228, 232–34; Guerrero, "Provincial and Municipal Elites of Luzon," 173–75; Cullinane, *Ilustrado Politics*, 14–35; Linn, *Philippine War*, 139–53; Lumba, *Monetary Authorities*, 33–39; *ARWD* 1899, pt. 2, 193–94; *ARWD* 1900, pt. 4, 13, 152, 192–93; *ARWD* 1900, pt. 6, 78, 81; Ambrosio Flores to the Inhabitants of the Province of Manila, Oct. 4, 1898, PIR 301.3, Exhibit 267, in Taylor, *Philippine Insurrection*, 3:378–79; S. B. M. Young to AG, DP and 8AC, Jan. 6, 1900, box 3, Young Papers.

50. Agoncillo, *Malolos*, 319–20; Guerrero, "Provincial and Municipal Elites of Luzon," 169–75; Kramer, *Blood of Government*, 114–15; Escalante, "Collapse of the Malolos Republic," 460–66; Felipe Buencamino, Order #34, Nov. 15, 1898; Obras Publicas to R. Canon, Sr. Jefe de Pangasinan, Order #40, Dec. 3, 1898; both folder 1, Circulars, Orders and Decrees, Public Works and Communications, Sec. of Interior; Secretario Interior to Jefes Provinciales, Order 50, Jan. 4, 1899; Gobierno Revolucionario, Secretario del Interior, Order 53, Jan. 7, 1899; all folder 1, Circulars, Orders and Decrees, Public Works and Communications, Sec. of Interior; all box I38, Philippine Revolutionary Papers, Philippine National Library; Emilio Aguinaldo, Jan. 5, 1899, Malolos, PIR 609.4, Exhibit 373, in Taylor, *Philippine Insurrection*, 3:485–86; Buencamino to the Provincial Chiefs, Oct. 21, 1898, PIR 224.2, Exhibit 504, in Taylor, *Philippine Insurrection*, 3:655. By late March 1899, Aguinaldo's government permitted Ilocos Sur's provincial council to compel the labor of male citizens who had not paid fines or taxes, or had been convicted of crimes; see PIR 385.8, Exhibit 795, in Taylor, *Philippine Insurrection*, 4:519–20.

51. Linn, *Philippine War*, 139–53; *ARWD* 1899, pt. 2, 193–94; *ARWD* 1900, pt. 4, 13, 152, 192–93; *ARWD* 1900, pt. 6, 78, 81; Ambrosio Flores to the Inhabitants of the Province of Manila, Oct. 4, 1898, PIR 301.3, Exhibit 267, in Taylor, *Philippine Insurrection*, 3:378–79; S. B. M. Young to AG, DP and 8AC, Jan. 6, 1900, box 3, Young Papers; Author unknown, Feb. 6, 1899, Dagupan, PIR 140.2; G. Bautista, Secretario de Guerra, Balanga, Bataan, April 5, 1899, PIR 140.3.

52. Agoncillo, *Malolos*, 207–212, 392–94; Guerrero, *Luzon at War*, 119–20; Escalante, "Collapse of the Malolos Republic," 463–66; Lumba, *Monetary Authorities*, 33–35; Secretario del Interior, Order 75, April 26, 1899, and Order 84, folder 1, Circulars, Orders and Decrees, Public Works and Communications; Circular, May 18, 1899, LR 1899; both Secretary of Interior, box I38, Philippine Revolutionary Papers, Philippine National Library; Juan Quesada to Sres Jefes locales del margen, April 24, 1899, PIR 201.5.

53. Ileto, "Food Crisis," 68–83; May, *A Past Recovered*, chap. 2; De Bevoise, *Agents of Apocalypse*, esp. 47–51, 57–63, 135–36, 156–63, 175–84; Veneracion, "State of Agriculture," 132–40; Ventura, "Medicalizing *Gutom*," 44–46.

54. M. Davis, *Late Victorian Holocausts*, 33–41; Linn, *Philippine War*, 93, 130–32; De Bevoise, *Agents of Apocalypse*, 63–66; ARWD 1899, vol. 1, pt. 2, 181. For a discussion of Filipino civilian mortality in south-central Luzon during the late 1890s and early 1900s, see Gates, "War-Related Deaths in the Philippines"; May, "The 'Zones' of Batangas"; May, *A Past Recovered*, chap. 4; May, *Battle for Batangas*, 280–84; De Bevoise, *Agents of Apocalypse*, 6–13.

55. Linn, *Philippine War*, 95, 101–2, 117–21; ARWD 1899, pt. 2, 228, 232; Faust, *Campaigning in the Philippines*, 239; Miles, *Fallen Leaves*, 87–88; Cullum, *Biographical Register*, vol. 4, 453; J. W. Pope, June 23, 1899, Diary, p. 458, box 1, Pope Papers; Calixto de Lara et al. to Capitan Gral. Jefe de Operaciones de los Americanos, June 30, 1899, box 1, E 777; TR 4, Grant to Edwards, Las Piñas, July 5, 1899; TS, Edwards to Grant, July 9, 1899; TS, Edwards to Grant, July 12, 1899; TR 39, Palace to Comdg. Gen., 1D; all box 3, E 773; LS 43, Grant to AG, 1D, 8AC, July 24, 1899; LS 67, C. W. Preston to CO, Bacoor, Aug. 27, 1899; LS 83, A. S. Daggett to AG, DP, Dec. 5, 1899; LS 88, H. G. Leonard to CO, Dec. 9, 1899; all vol. 1, E 812; LR 1738, CG to 1D, 8AC, July 25, 1899, vol. 4, E 776; all RG 395, NARA.

56. Carter, *Civilian in Lawton's 1899 Campaign*, 93–95; TR 31, Edwards to Grant, July 11, 1899; TS, Edwards to Grant, July 16, 1899; TR 39, HQ, 8AC to Lawton, July 31, 1899; TR, Hall to AG, 1D, 8AC, Calamba, July 31, 1899; TR 22, Grant to Edwards, July 26, 1899; TS, Starr to Hall, July 31, 1899; all box 3, E 773; LR 1658, Grant to AG, 1D, 8AC, July 17, 1899, box 1, E 777; all RG 395, NARA. Other Americans claimed rations dispensed as wages for roadwork went to insurgents; see George, *Our Army and Navy*, 265, 273.

57. W. H. Scott, *Ilocano Responses to American Aggression*, 140; Linn, *U.S. Army and Counterinsurgency*, 17–18, 37–38, 156; Linn, *Philippine War*, 192–93; May, *Battle for Batangas*, 192; Sastrón, *Filipinas*, 161; C. J. Crane, *Experiences of a Colonel of Infantry*, 356; *Manila American*, July 10, 1900; Lyman W. V. Kennon to Keller, Feb. 4, 1900, LSB 1, box 15, 34th USVI; Cornelius Gardener to AG, DSL, June 21, 1900, LSB 2, box 9, 30th USVI; C. J. Crane to Senor Valario, Lipa, July 4, 1900, vol. 2, box 12, 38th USVI; W. H. Butler to AAG, 2D, DNL, Aug. 8, 1900, in LSB 1, box 12, 49th USVI; all E 117, RG 94, NARA; Wenceslao Tares to Revolutionary Commanding Officer of Zambales, Jan. 20, 1901, PIR 163.5; "Laspinas, 1893. Relación de las polistas empleados en los trabajos comunales correspondiente al año actual," Las Piñas, Spanish Document Section 5035; "Provincia de Batangas, Villa de Lipa, Ano de 1897," Nov. 30, 1897, Spanish Document Section 4942; both Prestacion Personal, Philippine National Archives; "Tenientes, Tenientes," n.d., folder 5, Presidencia Local de Lipa, 1898, box P112, Batangas, Philippine Revolutionary Papers, Philippine National Library.

58. Ileto, *Pasyon and Revolution*, 3–11; Ileto, "Orientalism and the Study of Philippine Politics"; Ileto, "Colonial Wars in Southern Luzon." For histories of US soldiers' perceptions of public works' politics during the Philippine-American War, see Gates, *Schoolbooks and Krags*, 62, 139–40, 211, 239, 261, 271, 288; Linn, *U.S. Army and Counterinsurgency*, 51, 83, 84, 111, 154; Linn, *Philippine War*, 83, 127, 200–201, 206, 208, 213, 238, 248, 258, 261.

59. "History of Barrio Punta," p. 4; "History of Laguerta," p. 54; both Calamba, reel 30; "History and Cultural Life of the Barrio of Barraca," Bangar, La Union; reel 31, both HDP.

60. Ileto, *Knowledge and Pacification*, chaps. 6 and 7; Jose, "Labor Usage and Mobilization," 278–83; Arthur Wagner to CG, 1B, Calamba, March 8, 1900, in March 1899, TS, box 3,

E 774; Grant to AG, 1D, 8AC, July 17, 1899, box 1; William J. Birkhimer to AG, 1D, 8AC, Dasmarinas, March 16, 1900, vol. 2; both E 777, RG 395, NARA.

61. Guerrero, "Provincial and Municipal Elites of Luzon," 169–73; May, "Civic Ritual and Political Reality"; Linn, *Philippine War*, 129–30, 200–201; Go, "Chains of Empire"; "May 19th, 1893. Law for Organization and Government of Municipalities in the Philippines," Exhibit 1, in Taylor, *Philippine Insurrection*, 1:133, 136–37; LS 746, J. F. Bell to Mil. Sec., Manila, April 20, 1901, vol. 2, E 2167, RG 395, NARA. For GO 43 and 40, see US Senate, *Affairs in the Philippine Islands*, pt. 1, 111–28.

62. Linn, *U.S. Army and Counterinsurgency*, 30–34, 53–61; Linn, *Philippine War*, 200–201; McAlexander, *History of the Thirteenth Regiment*, 156–64, 159; Bisbee, *Through Four American Wars*, 266; Dorsey Green to Adj., Laoag, Sept. 10, 1901, and Nicholas Jornach to Gobierno de US, Ilocos Norte, Pueblo of Solsona, and 9th end., J. T. Monson, Nov. 30, 1901, and 12th end., Wm. S. McCarthy, Dec. 2, 1901, box 2, E 4047, RG 395, NARA. Significantly, US-era records of *polista* labor sometimes marked exact times at which men arrived at worksites and departed from them—possibly evidence that officious American commanders sought to rigorously impose clock time, calculating polista pay like hourly wages; see "Trabajadores en el Camine que dirige parar Baybay," box 1, E 2170, RG 395, NARA.

63. Linn, *U.S. Army and Counterinsurgency*, 33–37, 51; US Senate, *Affairs in the Philippine Islands*, pt. 2, 1513–14; C. P. Johnson to CO, 2D, DNL, Aparri, May 15, 1900, in LSB 1, box 12, E 117, 49th USVI, RG 94, NARA; Ballance to CO, Civil Sub-District, Laoag [Aug. 1900], box 1, E 4055; McKinley to W. J. Smedberg, Cabugao, Oct. 29, 1900; TR, William P. Duvall to AG, 1D, DNL, Nov. 3, 1900; both box 6, E 2158; LS 29, Ballance to CO, San Fernando, Jan. 4, 1901; LS 51, Ballance to CO, San Fernando, Jan. 8, 1901; both box 3, E 2167; TS, Bell to CO, Laoag, Nov. 20, 1901, vol. 1, E 2208; all RG 395, NARA.

64. US Senate, *Affairs in the Philippine Islands*, pt. 1, 711; J. M. Bell to Sec., Mil. Govt., DPH, June 23, 1900, vol. 1, E 2440; Udo Van Bosch to James Lockett, Sept. 16, 1900, box 2, E 2420; Horace L. Higgins to J. H. Smith, Nov. 26, 1900; Higgins to J. H. Smith, Jan. 18, 1901; Smith to Higgins, Jan. 22, 1901; R. Choa to Moore, Feb. 7, 1901; Higgins to E. H. Crowder, Feb. 9, 1901, and 5th end., Smith to AG, DNL, Feb. 25, 1901; all box 24, E 2133; "Act of Council Imposing Road Tax," March 28, 1901, box 2, E 2201; all RG 395, NARA.

65. W. H. Scott, *Ilocano Responses*, 10, 13, 116–78, 191; Foner, *Story of American Freedom*, 58–68, 115–30; Kramer, *Blood of Government*, 104, 190–91; "Municipal Council for Vigan," *Manila Times*, July 15, 1900; "Prova. de Yl. Sur, Cuidad de Vigan, Presupuesto de Ingresos y Gastos para 1898–99," folder 1; Mariano Acosta to Presidentes Locales, San Ildefonso, Santo Domingo, Magsingal, Dec. 3, 1898, folder 2; both box Pr35, Ilocos Sur, Provinces, Philippine Revolutionary Papers, Philippine National Library; LR 820, Rivero to AG, DNL, Nov. 6, 1900, box 2, E 2170; Ballance to CO, Civil Sub-District, Vigan, Nov. 9, 1900, box 1, E 5589; LS 198 to Alcalde, Vigan, Nov. 11, 1900, box 1, E 5586; all RG 395, NARA.

66. Linn, *U.S. Army and Counterinsurgency*, 113–14, 230; Kramer, *Blood of Government*, 196; Hawkins, *Making Moros*; Owen, "Abaca in Kabikolan," 194–98, 203; Owen, "Winding Down the War in Albay," 575–80; Parker, *Old Army*, 13, 215–21, 237–38, 353–57; James Parker to AAG, 3D, DSL, box 2, E 2420, RG 395, NARA.

67. Linn, *Philippine War*, 216–17; Lichtenstein, *Twice the Work of Free Labor*, 160–64; Plehn, "Municipal Government," 793; US Philippine Commission, *Reports of the Taft Philippine Commission*, 6–7; LR 86, C. A. Williams to AG, 3D, DNL, Dec. 31, 1900, box 4, E 2215;

Williams to Sec., USPC, Jan. 26, 1901, and end., Abernathy to AG, 3D, DNL, Jan. 31, 1901, and end., S. Mills, Feb. 6, 1901, box 23, E 2133; LS 18, Robert Abernathy to AG, 4B, 2D, 8AC, March 23, 1900, vol. 1, E 2225; LR 7879, Thomas Barry to J. F. Bell, April 8, 1901, box 30, E 2133; LS 746, Bell to Mil. Sec., MG, April 20, 1901, box 2, E 2167; all RG 395, NARA. In 1902, Taft similarly compared the polo to road taxes in the United States, where, he noted, labor was no longer compulsory; see US Senate, *Affairs in the Philippine Islands*, pt. 1, 143.

68. *ARWD* 1900, pt. 2, 445–46; *ARWD* 1900, pt. 3, 197; *CWS*, vol. 2, 1172–73; J. F. Bell to AG, 2D, 8AC, March 18, 1900, vol. 1, E 2206; George L. Anderson, 2nd end., to LR 12, HQ, DSL, vol. 2, E 770, RG 395, NARA; MacArthur to AG, Dept. of War, Aug. 11, 1900; W. W. Harts to Chief Engineer, DPH, April 21, 1903; both file 2146, box 254, E 5, RG 350, NARA.

69. Hendrickson, "Reluctant Expansionist," 410–11; Agoncillo, *Malolos*, 327–31; Golay, *Face of Empire*, 49–50; *RPC* 1900, vol. 1, 3–10, 63; *RPC* 1900, vol. 2, 15, 116–27. By December 1899, Schurman believed that roadbuilding was the Philippines' "first necessity when peace is restored." "Not even schools," he wrote, were "so important"; see Schurman, "Our Duty to the Philippines," 3467.

70. Agoncillo, *Malolos*, 424–26; May, *Battle for Batangas*, 222–24; Cullinane, "Bringing in the Brigands," 58–59; US Senate, *Affairs in the Philippine Islands*, pt. 3, 2408; Mariano Trías to My Dear Companions, March 1901, PIR 896.1, Exhibit 1148, in Taylor, *Philippine Insurrection*, 5:317.

71. May, *Social Engineering in the Philippines*, 7, 47, 49; Kramer, *Blood of Government*, 160–70; Adas, *Dominance by Design*, 144–47, 150, 154–55, 166–67; R. T. McKenna, *American Imperial Pastoral*, chap. 2; Morley, *Cities and Nationhood*, 31–40, 8–85, 141–44; US Philippine Commission, *Reports of the Taft Philippine Commission*, 71–72; *RPC* 1901, pt. 1, 9–10, 72–73, 245; *Filipinas ante Europa*, Nov. 10, 1900, cited in W. H. Scott, *Cracks in the Parchment Curtain*, 296–97.

72. Stanley, *Nation in the Making*, 98; McCoy, *Policing America's Empire*, 61–62, 96–97, 99–100; Harts, "William Wright Harts," 21, 24, William Wright Harts Papers, US Army Heritage and Education Center; US Senate, *Affairs in the Philippine Islands*, pt. 2, 878; *ARWD* 1901, pt. 5, 369–87; McArthur to AG, Washington, DC, Aug. 11, 1900; Harts to Chief Engineer, DPH, April 21, 1903, file 2146; both box 254, E 5, RG 350, NARA.

73. Bankoff, "Wants, Wages, and Workers," 61–66; B. R. Anderson, "Cacique Democracy," 10–13; V. Clark, "Labor Conditions in the Philippine Islands," 724–25.

74. V. Clark, "Labor Conditions in the Philippine Islands," 765–66, 768, 776; Kohr, *Around the World with Uncle Sam*, 190; US Senate, *Affairs in the Philippine Islands*, pt. 1, 645, 650; Harts, to AG, DNP, Jan. 27, 1902, box 3, E 2635, RG 395, NARA.

75. Gatewood, *"Smoked Yankees,"* 306–9; Harts, "Military Engineering and Civil Opportunities in the Philippines," 692–93; Harts, "William Wright Harts," 21, 24, William Wright Harts Papers; US Department of War, *Report of Lieutenant W. G. Caples*, 1–2, 8–9; US Senate, *Affairs in the Philippine Islands*, pt. 2, 1513–14; US Bureau of the Census, *Census of the Philippine Islands, 1903*, 31; *ARWD* 1901, pt. 5, 430–31; William Kelly to Harts, Jan. 22, 1901, box 10, E 2330; Florencio R. Caedo, R. D. Blanchard, and Chas. H. Kendall to Office of Provincial Governor, Batangas, Nov. 11, 1901, box 1, E 2066; Harts, to AG, DNP, Jan. 27, 1902, box 3; Harts to AG, DNP, Feb. 26, 1902; Harts to AG, DNP, March 28, 1902; Harts to April 28, 1902; all box 4; Harts to AG, DNP, May 1902, box 5; all E 2635; all RG 395, NARA. Some of these engineers experienced similar frustrations while supervising the Panama

Canal's construction; see Greene, *Canal Builders*, 144–47; Steese, "Corps of Engineers and the Isthmian Canal," 529.

76. Lumba, *Monetary Authorities*, 54–55, 79–87; V. Clark, "Labor Conditions in the Philippine Islands," 760–61; Rosenberg, "Filipinos as Workmen," 1024; Act #196, Aug. 12, 1901; Harts to Chief Engineer, DPH, April 21, 1903; both file 2146, box 254, E 5, RG 350, NARA.

77. May, *Social Engineering in the Philippines*, 49; Hutchcroft, "Colonial Masters," 286–88; Kramer, *Blood of Government*, 166–67, 170–74, 178–79, 192, 197–98; Adas, *Dominance by Design*, 154–55, 160, 180–81; Forbes, *The Philippine Islands*, 1:374.

78. Kramer, *Blood of Government*, 352–56; Harts, "William Wright Harts," 21–30, 41, 46–47, 63, Harts Papers.

79. Stanley, "William Cameron Forbes," 295–301; May, *Social Engineering*, 143–44; Golay, *Face of Empire*, 113–17; Golay, "Search for Revenues," 234–35; Hutchcroft, "Colonial Masters," 288; Go, *American Empire*, 122–25; Go, "Chains of Empire," 191–94; McCoy, "'An Anarchy of Families'"; Plehn, "Municipal Government," 793; US Senate, *Affairs in the Philippine Islands*, pt. 1, 23–25, 143, 170–71; US Department of War, *What Has Been Done in the Philippines*, 23; RPC 1907, pt. 2, 1017–18; Harts, "William Wright Harts," 24, Harts Papers. For 1901 municipal and provincial laws pertaining to taxation for roads, see USPC, *Public Laws and Resolutions*, 148–50, 171–72.

80. Bankoff, *Crime, Society, and the State*, 167–68; Linn, *U.S. Army and Counterinsurgency*, 81; McLennan, *Crisis of Imprisonment*, 149–88; Freeman, "Militarism, Empire, and Labor Relations," 105; Harts, "Military Engineering and Civil Opportunities in the Philippines," 692–93; Harts, "William Wright Harts," 21, Harts Papers; Harts to AG, DNP, Jan. 27, 1902, box 3, E 2635; Frank DeW. Ramsey to CG, DNP, July 23, 1902, box 1, E 2635, both RG 395, NARA; Harts to Chief Engineer, DPH, April 21, 1903, file 2146, box 254, E 5, RG 350, NARA.

81. Stanley, "William Cameron Forbes," 285–87; Stanley, *Nation in the Making*, 206–9; Golay, *Face of Empire*, 112–15; Forbes, *The Philippine Islands*, 1:368–69; US Senate, *Affairs in the Philippine Islands*, pt. 1, 190–92, 197, 202, 212, 458–59, 493–94, 496; US Senate, *Affairs in the Philippine Islands*, pt. 3, 2425; US Congress, *Philippine Tariff*, appendix; US Congress, *Public Hearings in the Philippine Islands*, 9; Forbes to Luke Wright, May 15, 1905, MS Am 1366, vol. 2; Forbes, Journal, Dec. 4, 1905, vol. 1; both WCF.

82. Kramer, *Blood of Government*, 316–17; Bankoff, *Crime, Society, and the State in the Nineteenth-Century Philippines*, 166–69, 177–78; Salman, "'Nothing without Labor,'" 116–18; Forbes, *The Philippine Islands*, 1:380–82, 384–85; ARGMP 1905, 19; RPC 1906 pt. 1, 19, 169–70; RPC 1906, pt. 3, 329; Forbes to Wood, Nov. 11, 1904, MS Am 1192.3, Additional Papers; Forbes to Theodore Roosevelt, Sept. 27, 1906, vol. 4, MS Am 1366; Forbes, Oct. 23 and Nov. 3, 1904, vol. 1; Forbes, Sept. 21, 1909, vol. 3; both Journals, First Series; "Bilibid prisoners on Benguet roads," Manila, P.I., Dec. 31, 1910, MS Am 1192.2, Philippine data: executive, 1909–1917, vol. 2; all WCF. In August 1903, Forbes's predecessor sent 200 convicts from Bilibid to the Benguet road, where US Army engineers struggled to secure labor without coercion; see Bankoff, "'These Brothers of Ours,'" 1053.

83. Kramer, *Blood of Government*, 165–66, 300–305; May, *Social Engineering*, 50; Thomas C. Welch, "Memorandum of the Chief of the Law Division concerning Voluntary Contributions," March 6, 1907, Dean Worcester Papers, cited by May, *Social Engineering*, 214n34; Act No. 1511, July 13, 1906, in *Acts of the U.S. Philippine Commission*, 285–89; RPC 1906, vol. 1, 158, 194–95, 416, 418–19; 474; Forbes, *The Philippine Islands*, 1:370–71; William Cameron Forbes,

Notes to Chapter Four 317

Journals, First Series, entry April 27, 1906; entry July 21, 1906; entry Aug. 29, 1906; entry Oct. 19, 1906; all vol. 2, WCF.

84. Cullinane, *Ilustrado Politics*, 5, 51, 68, 248, 270–71, 286–304; May, *Social Engineering*, 144–45; RPC 1907, vol. 2, 275–77; Forbes, *The Philippine Islands*, 1:370–72, 385. In 1907, William H. Taft, then secretary of war, explained popular Filipino resistance to a road tax as the legacy of the Spanish polo and its abuses; see RPC 1907, vol. 3, 265–66.

85. Golay, *Face of Empire*, 116; Stanley, *Nation in the Making*, 102–3; Act No. 1652, May 18, 1907, in *Acts of the U.S. Philippine Commission*, 1907, 164–66; RPC 1909, 61, 142–43; RPC 1910, 138–39; RPC 1911, 24, 108–9; RPC 1912, 149; RPC 1913, 178–79.

86. Hays, *Conservation and the Gospel of Efficiency*; May, *Social Engineering in the Philippines*, 145–46; Tyrell, *Crisis of the Wasteful Nation*, chap. 4; Adas, *Dominance by Design*, 169; Halsema, *E. J. Halsema*, 26; Halsema, "Land Transportation in the Philippines," 78–79; Forbes, *The Philippine Islands*, 1:376–77; Forbes, *The Philippine Islands*, 1:381, 383; Chamberlin, *The Philippine Problem, 1898–1913*, 133; ARWD 1900, pt. 12, *Report of the Military Governor of Cuba on Civil Affairs*, vol. 2, pt. 1, 11; ARWD 1903, 311–12; ARGMP 1905, 18, 19; ARGMP 1906, 17; RPC 1906, pt. 2, 170; RPC 1907, pt. 2, 276; Bureau of Public Works, Philippine Islands, *Capataz Manual of Road Work*; RPC 1909, 141; Harts to Chief Engineer, DPH, April 21, 1903, file 2146, box 254, E 5, RG 350, NARA; Forbes to J. W. Beardsley, Oct. 9, 1905; Forbes, "Address of the Honorable W. Cameron Forbes . . . Before the Assembly of District engineers," Nov. 6, 1906; J. F. Case to Forbes, April 15, 1909; all in MS Am 1192.3, Additional Papers; Forbes, Aug. 16, 1907, Journals, First Series, vol. 2, p. 281; Forbes, April 17, 1908, Journals, First Series, vol. 3, p. 79; all in WCF.

87. Fry, *History of the Mountain Province*, 76–85; Jenista, *White Apos*, 50–54, 135–45; Finin, *Making of the Igorot*, 57–59; Abinales, *Images of State Power*, 15; Kramer, *Blood of Government*, 208–20, 314–16; Lumba, *Monetary Authorities*, 77; Section 19, Act No. 1396, in *Acts of the Philippine Commission, 1905*, 178–80; RPC 1906, pt. 1, 212–13.

Chapter Four

1. A. R. Millett, *General*, 21–22, 32, 47–60, chaps. 5, 7–8; Zimmerman, *Alabama in Africa*, 38–40; Bullard, "Road Building among the Moros," 823–24.

2. A. R. Millet, *General*, 168–73, 194–98; Bjork, *Prairie Imperialists*, 144–47; Bullard, "Road Building among the Moros"; Bullard, "Autobiography," 71, box 9, RLB; Bullard, 2nd end., March 5, 1908, on M. Sobrado to Magoon, Feb. 28, 1908, exp. 36, caja 32, SP, ANRC.

3. This imperial division of public power is roughly analogous to contemporary states' delegation of sovereignty to privatized militaries; see Maogoto, "Subcontracting Sovereignty."

4. Saber, "Some Observations," 52; Gowing, *Mandate in Moroland*, 227; Funtecha, *American Military Occupation*, 2–4, 18; Hawkins, *Making Moros*, 15; Saber, "Lanao under American Rule," 194–97; Bullard, "Road Building among the Moros," 819; Bonsal, "Moros and Their Country"; ARWD 1902, Lt.-Gen., 493; ARWD 1903, vol. 3, 323, 328; Pershing to AG, Dept. Mindanao, May 15, 1903, folder 1; John J. Pershing, "Report of Census for District No. 54, Lake Lanao, Mindanao," May 15, 1903, folder 3, box 369; both JJP.

5. Mednick, "Encampment of the Lake," 42–46; Gowing, *Muslim Filipinos*, 44–55; Majul, *Muslims in the Philippines*, 337–39; Mednick, "Some Problems of Moro History and Political

Organization," 46–51; Saber, "Some Observations," 53; Landor, *Gems of the East*, 307; *ARWD* 1902, *Lt.-Gen.*, 493.

6. Saber, "Lanao under American Rule," 194–96; Saber, "Some Observations," 53; Charbonneau, *Civilizational Imperatives*, 189–90; Bullard, "Road Building among the Moros," 819; Saleeby, *Moro Problem*, 17; *ARWD* 1903, vol. 3, 328.

7. Funtecha, *American Military Occupation*, 5–10; Saber, "Lanao under American Rule," 197; *ARWD* 1902, *Lt.-Gen.*, 483–84, 503; *ARWD* 1903, vol. 3, *Dept. and Div. Commanders*, 392–98.

8. Saber, "Lanao under American Rule," 197; Bjork, *Prairie Imperialists*, 174–83; Charbonneau, *Civilizational Imperatives*, 36–41; *ARWD* 1900, pt. 3, 260, 268–70; *ARWD* 1901, pt. 4, 262–63.

9. Hawkins, *Making Moros*, chap. 3; Charbonneau, "Colonizing Workers."

10. Said, *Orientalism*; Funtecha, *American Military Occupation*, 18; Charbonneau, *Civilizational Imperatives*, 49–51; Bonsal, "Moros and Their Country"; Charles B. Hagadorn to AG, DMJ, April 17, 1901, box 6; Hagadorn to AG, DMJ, Aug. 1, 1901, box 9; both E 2105, RG 395, NARA. Oli Charbonneau helpfully characterizes this ideology as "labor missionizing"; email correspondence with author, May 4, 2023.

11. Abinales, *Making Mindanao*, 70–78; Hawkins, *Making Moros*, 32–37; Greene, *Canal Builders*, 88; Charbonneau, *Civilizational Imperatives*, 173–76; Charbonneau, "Colonizing Workers," 27; Charbonneau, "Permeable South"; *ARWD* 1899, vol. 1, pt. 6, 543–45; *ARWD* 1900, pt. 1, *Lt.-Gen.*, 291–92; *ARWD* 1902, *Lt.-Gen.*, vol. 9, 475, 482, 494, 515–16; Davis to Adna R. Chaffee, April 17, 1902, box 32, George W. Davis Papers.

12. Salman, *Embarrassment of Slavery*, 79; Walther, *Sacred Interests*, 163–68, 180–82; *ARWD* 1902, vol. 9, 494, 512–17, 561–65; USPC, *Report*, 1903, pt. 1, 492–93; *ARGMP* 1904, 6–7; Davis, GO 12, March 4, 1902, File 5075–5, RG 350, NARA, cited in Salman, *Embarrassment of Slavery*, 285n33.

13. Bjork, *Prairie Imperialists*, 92, 125–28, 236–51; Pershing, *My Life*, 14, 106–22, 149.

14. Saber, "Maranao Resistance," 277; Edgerton, *American Datu*, 5–6; Bjork, *Prairie Imperialists*, chap. 4, 150–52, 178; Pershing, *My Life*, 149–50.

15. Pershing, *My Life*, 150–54; John J. Pershing to AG, 7SB, Dec. 24, 1901; Pershing to AG, 7SB, Feb. 20, 1902; both Memoirs, file 2, box 369, JJP; Geo. Holden, "Road Report of Spanish Military Road from Iligan to Marahui on Lake Lanao," Jan. 1, 1903, box 1, E 3903, RG 395, NARA.

16. *ARWD* 1902, pt. 4, 556–57; *ARWD* 1903, vol. 3, 328; Pershing, "The Conquest of the Moros," Aug. 1908, p. 1, box 278, JJP. Proposing the army use Filipino convict labor, Pershing prefigured Americans' future techniques for procuring labor for Mindanao's roads and cutting construction costs; see Pershing to AG, 7SB, Dec. 24, 1901, JJP.

17. Funtecha, *American Military Occupation*, 12–24; Bullard, "Road Building among the Moros," 819–20; *ARWD* 1902, *Lt.-Gen.*, 481–92; *ARWD* 1903, vol. 3, *Lt.-Gen.*, 299, 319, 322–25; R. W. Hoyt to AG, Dept. Mindanao, Oct. 17, 1902; Hoyt to Fountain, Nov. 2, 1902; TS, Fountain to Peek, Cotabato, Nov. 3, 1902; Peek to AG, Zamboanga, Nov. 4, 1902; Peek to AG, Zamboanga, Nov. 6, 1902; Peek to Zamboanga, Nov. 8, 1902; all box 22, E 2105, RG 395, NARA.

18. Gatewood, *Black Americans*, 66–67, 79–80, 92–93; A. R. Millett, *General*, 47–60, chaps. 5–9; Zimmerman, *Alabama in Africa*, 38–40; Bjork, *Prairie Imperialists*, 139–43, 152–62, 194–96; Bullard, Diary Book #2, Pantar, March 11, 1903, box 1; Bullard, "Autobiography," 61–62;

Andrew J. Dougherty, "The Infantry Brings Civilization and Good Government to the Moros"; both box 9; all RLB; TS 120, Bullard to Adj., Wheaton's Brigade, March 21, 1900; Bullard to AG, 2D, DSL, April 29, 1900; both in LS, vol. 7, box 20, 39th USVI E 117, RG 94, NARA.

19. A. R. Millett, *General*, 169–71; W. Anderson, *Colonial Pathologies*, 76–81; Bankoff, "'These Brothers of Ours,'" 1050; Bullard, "Road Building among the Moros," 821–22; Bullard, "Preparing Our Moros for Government," 386–89; ARWD 1903, vol. 3, 301, 312; *U.S. Army and Navy Journal*, March 14, 1903.

20. Bullard, "Road Building among the Moros," 821–22; Bullard, "Preparing Our Moros for Government," 386–89; Bullard, "How I Became a Mohammadean Priest," box 7, RLB; Bullard to George T. Langhorne, Camp No. 1, Iligan-Lanao Military Road, Dec. 17, 1902, box 1, RLB; TR, Davis to Sumner, Nov. 25, 1902, E 2105; Morris C. Foote to AG, DPH, n.d., Iligan; Foote to Bullard, Feb. 2, 1903; both in TS and TR, 1902–3, box 1, E 2903; all RG 395, NARA.

21. Bullard, "Preparing Our Moros for Government," 386; Bullard, "Road Building among the Moros," 821–22; Noble to Sumner, Nov. 25, 1902; TR, Davis to Sumner, Nov. 25, 1902; Sumner to Davis, Nov. 26, 1902; G. B. to Davis, Nov. 29, 1902; Sumner to Davis, Dec. 27, 1902; Amai-Manibilang to General of Mind. and Comdg. Officers of Iligan, Nov. 6, 1902; all box 22, E 2105; TS, Sumner to Davis, Jan. 30, 1903, box 1, E 5572; Morris C. Foote to AG, DPH, n.d., Iligan; Foote to Bullard, Feb. 2, 1903; both in TS and TR, 1902–3, box 1, E 2903; all RG 395, NARA.

22. Smallman-Raynor and Cliff, "Philippines Insurrection and the 1902–4 Cholera Epidemic," 69–89, esp. 76; W. Anderson, *Colonial Pathologies*, 63–69; Saber, "Lanao under American Rule," 197; Charbonneau, *Civilizational Imperatives*, 57; ARWD 1903, vol. 3, 325, 328; Bullard, "Preparing Our Moros for Government," 387, 392; Bullard, "How I Became a Mohammadean Priest," box 9, RLB; "Writing from Mindanao...," *U.S. Army and Navy Journal*, March 14, 1903; Bullard, "Autobiography," 59–60; Dougherty, "The Infantry Brings Civilization and Good Government to the Moros"; both box 9; box 7; all RLB; Pershing, "Report of Census for District No. 54, Lake Lanao, Mindanao," May 15, 1903, box 269, JJP. Local oral tradition suggests that northern Lanao datus sent Bullard laborers because they wanted gold and silver coins for crafting jewelry and other metalwork; see Saber, "Lanao under American Rule," 197.

23. Mednick, "Encampment of the Lake," 25; Bullard, "Road Building among the Moros," 822; Bullard, "Preparing Our Moros for Government," 387–88, 392; Bullard, "How I Became a Mohammadean Priest"; Box 7; Bullard, "Autobiography," 59–60, Box 9; both RLB; TS, Sumner to Davis, Jan. 30, 1903, Box 1, E 5572; Bullard to Adj., Construction Force, Iligan, March 17, 1903, Pantar, Box 1, E 3908; both RG 395, NARA.

24. Bullard, "Road Building among the Moros," 822; Foote to Sumner, Jan. 29, 1903; Sumner to Foote, Feb. 1, 1903; Sumner to Foote, Feb. 2, 1903, Iligan, Mindanao, TS and TR, 1902–3, Box 1, E 2903; all RG 395, NARA.

25. Bullard, "Road Building among the Moros," 822; Foote to Bullard, Feb. 2, 1903; Sumner to Davis, Feb. 3, 1903; Foote to Sumner, Feb. 3, 1903; Foote to AG, Zamboanga, Feb. 3, 1903; Davis to Sumner, Feb. 4, 1903; Foote to AG, Zamboanga, Feb. 4, 1903; Foote to Sumner, Feb. 4, 1903; Sumner to Davis, Feb. 6, 1903; Sumner to Davis, Feb. 27, 1903; all in Iligan, Mindanao, TS and TR, 1902–3, Box 1, E 2903; Sumner to CO, Iligan, Feb. 27, 1903, Box 1, E 3903; "Report of Present and Absent Sick, in Major Bullard's Command," Camp #1, Construction Force, Iligan-Lanao Military Road, Feb. 23, 1903, Box 1, E 3908; all RG 395, NARA.

320 Notes to Chapter Four

26. Edgerton, *American Datu*, 82; Bullard, "Road Building among the Moros," 822–23; Bullard, "Preparing Our Moros for Government," 387–88.

27. Bullard to Adj., Construction Force, Iligan-Lake Lano Military Road, March 15, 1903; Bullard to C. A. Williams, Pantar, March 24, 1903; Bullard to Adj., Construction Force, Iligan, March 5, 15, 17, and 30; all box 1, E 3908; Bullard to Adj., Iligan, Aug. 17, 1903, box 1, E 3903; all RG 395, NARA.

28. Bullard, "Road-Building among the Moros," 823.

29. Bjork, *Prairie Imperialists*, 194–97; Charbonneau, *Civilizational Imperatives*, 96–102; Bullard, "Preparing Our Moros for Government," 388; Bullard, "Autobiography," 61–62, box 9, RLB; Bullard to AG, Zamboanga, Nov. 19, 1902, box 22, E 2105; Bullard to Adj., Construction Force, Iligan-Lanao Road, Feb. 22 and 25, 1903; Bullard to Adj., Pantar, March 15, 1903; Bullard to Adj., Construction Force, March 26, 1903; Henry F. McFeely to Adj., Camp #2, April 3, 1903; all box 1, E 3908; all RG 395, NARA.

30. Bullard, "Road Building among the Moros," 822, 824; Bullard, "Preparing Our Moros for Government," 388; Bullard, "Autobiography," 61–62, box 9, RLB; Bullard, GO #4, Jan. 29, 1903, Camp #1, box 1, E 3903, RG 395, NARA.

31. Bullard, "Road Building among the Moros," 819–23; Bullard, "Preparing Our Moros for Government," 387–88.

32. Mednick, "Encampment of the Lake," 36–38; Saber, "Lanao under American Rule," 197; Charbonneau, *Civilizational Imperatives*, 52, 66–67, 126–27, 176; Bullard, "Road Building among the Moros," 819–23; Bullard, "Preparing Our Moros for Government," 387–88; *ARWD* 1903, vol. 3, 312; *ARGMP* 1905, 32; Bullard, Diary Book #2, June 28, 1903, and Aug. 24, 1903, box 1, RLB; Bullard to C. A. Williams, April 4, 1903; F. P. Siviter, Camp at Pantar, June 19, 1903; both box 1, E 3903, RG 395, NARA. Palmer tried to promote capitalist culture in northern Lanao by establishing a model agricultural colony and market town, Dansalan, next to Marawi; see Charbonneau, *Civilizational Imperatives*, 127–28.

33. Charbonneau, *Civilizational Imperatives*, 15.

34. A. R. Millett, *General*, 173–83; Bullard, "Preparing Our Moros for Government," 389–94; "News of the Philippines," *U.S. Army and Navy Journal*, June 20, 1903; *ARGMP* 1904, 3, 6, 19–20.

35. Bjork, *Prairie Imperialists*, 194–97; Charbonneau, *Civilizational Imperatives*, 94, 112–13; *ARWD* 1903, *Lt.-Gen.*, 322–53; Davis to Bullard, July 3, 1903, in "Record of Robert L. Bullard," box 9, RLB; Pershing to AG, DPH, May 10, 1902, and attached, Ahmai-Manibilang to Pershing, April 26, 1902; Pershing to Ahmai-Manibilang, May 1, 1902; Ahmai-Manibilang to Pershing, May 6, 1902; Pershing to Ahmai-Manibilang, May 8, 1902; all box 278; Pershing, "Conquest of the Moros," 3 ; Pershing to "All Moros in the Laguna de Lanao," March 1, 1903, folder: Letters 40–77, box 318; all JJP; Pershing to AG, Zamboanga, Feb. 5, 1903, box 1, E 5572, RG 395, NARA.

36. Hawkins, *Making Moros*, 79–85; Charbonneau, *Civilizational Imperatives*, 49, 114–15; A Member of the Corps, "Telegraph Engineering in Moro Land"; *ARWD* 1901, pt. 4, 262–63; *ARWD* 1902, vol. 9, 497; *ARWD* 1903, *Lt.-Gen.*, 310–15; *ARWD* 1903, vol. 3, *Lt.-Gen.*, 311–12, 327; *RPC* 1905, pt. 3, 19; *ARGMP* 1905, 4, 16–19; *ARGMP* 1906, 16–17; Forbes to Wood, Nov. 11, 1904, MS Am 1192.3, Additional Papers, WCF.

37. Hawkins, *Making Moros*, 85–93; Abinales, *Making Mindanao*, 70–80; Charbonneau, *Civilizational Imperatives*, 62–65; Dacudao, *Abaca Frontier*, 75–79, 88–92, 165–68, 250–51; *ARGMP* 1905, 4–5; *ARGMP* 1906, 8–9; *ARGMP* 1913, 19.

38. Charbonneau, *Civilizational Imperatives*, 115, "Report on Military Situation: Moro Province and Department Philippines," Dec. 5, 1913, box 218, LWP.

39. Salman, *Embarrassment of Slavery*, 116–17; Abinales, "American Colonial State," 15; Charbonneau, *Civilizational Imperatives*, 16; ARGMP 1906, 61–62, 69–70.

40. Gowing, *Mandate in Moroland*, 234–42; S. K. Tan, *Filipino Muslim Armed Struggle*, 37; Morley, *Cities and Nationhood*, 119; Charbonneau, *Civilizational Imperatives*, 106, 119–20; Edgerton, *American Datu*, 224; ARGMP 1910, 15–16; ARGMP 1912, 8; ARGMP 1913, 25, 28.

41. L. A. Pérez, *Cuba under the Platt Amendment*, 70–82.

42. L. A. Pérez, *Cuba under the Platt Amendment*, 88–91; Guerra, *Myth of José Martí*, 156–64; de la Fuente, *Nation for All*, 28–31, 60–66; Ferrer, *Insurgent Cuba*, 195–202.

43. Diaz, *Memoria de Obras Públicas*, iv; Cuevas Toraya, *500 años de construcciones en Cuba*, 159; Olmstead, *Censo de la República de Cuba*, 71–73.

44. L. A. Pérez, *Cuba under the Platt Amendment*, 92–94; Guerra, *Myth of José Martí*, 159–60.

45. Lockmiller, *Magoon in Cuba*, 70–76, 84–85; A. R. Millett, *Politics of Intervention*, 59–63, 121–22.

46. ARPGC 1907, 40, 42–46.

47. Dye, *Cuban Sugar in the Age of Mass Production*, 93–95; Ayala, *American Sugar Kingdom*, 125; Bjork, *Prairie Imperialists*, 146; Tyrrell, *Crisis of the Wasteful Nation*; ARPGC 1907–1908, 15.

48. Davis, *Generals in Khaki*, 38–39; ARWD 1907, vol. 3, 335–36; Magoon, ARPGC 1907, 44, 89; Magoon, *Republic of Cuba*, 366; Black to Magoon, May 4, 1907, in folder 2112, box 252, E 5, RG 350, NARA.

49. Guerra, *Myth of José Martí*, 204–205; Yglesia Martinez, *Cuba*, 63–67; Magoon, *Republic of Cuba*, 368, 369; Magoon, ARPGC 1907, 35–36; ARPGC 1907–1908, 15.

50. L. A. Pérez, *On Becoming Cuban*, 220–38; Patrick, "Notes on Road Building in Cuba," 263; Magoon, *Republic of Cuba*, 368.

51. Guerra, *Myth of José Martí*, 204–5; Patrick, "Notes on Road Building in Cuba," 263–64; Magoon, *Republic of Cuba*, 366.

52. Stubbs, *Tobacco on the Periphery*, 15; Tone, *War and Genocide in Cuba*, 146, 149, 151, 158–63, 166–70, 212–15.

53. Lockmiller, "Agriculture in Cuba," 182–83; Stubbs, *Tobacco on the Periphery*, 22–32; Logan, "Conspirators, Pawns, and Patriots and Brothers," 10–11; Matthews, *New-Born Cuba*, 369–71; Magoon, ARPGC 1906–1907, 33; US Census Bureau, *Cuba: Population, History, Resources, 1907*, 249; Olmstead, *Censo de la Republica de Cuba*, 556; Porter, *Appendix to the Report on the Commercial and Industrial Conditions of the Island of Cuba*, 276.

54. Magoon, ARPGC 1907–1908, 9; Magoon, *Republic of Cuba*, 359–60, 369; Patrick, "Notes on Road Building," 263.

55. Patrick, "Notes on Road Building," 264–66; ARWD 1899, pt. 1, 271; Harts, "William Wright Harts," 24, Harts Papers; Markham to AG, ACP, n.d., box 1, LS and LR, Chief of Engineers, April to August 1907, E 992, ACP, RG 395, NARA.

56. Stubbs, *Tobacco on the Periphery*, 114; V. Clark, "Labor Conditions in Cuba," 697; Patrick to Edward M. Markham, April 23, 1907; Markham to Patrick, May 7, 1907; Patrick to Markham, May 7, 1907; Patrick to Markham, May 8, 1907; Markham to Patrick, May 8, 1907;

322 Notes to Chapter Four

Markham to Patrick, May 9, 1907; all box 1, LS and LR, Chief of Engineers, April to August 1907, E 992, ACP, RG 395, NARA.

57. Logan, "Conspirators, Pawns, Patriots, and Brothers," 15–16, 19; US Census Bureau, *Cuba*, 330; "Pinar del Rio, 8 of April 1907"; "Several members of this family..."; E. D. Thomas to Waltz; all box 1, E 1134; "Molino, Antonio Eugenio," box 12, E 1008; Tels., Patrick to Markham, May 8, 1907; Markham to Patrick, May 8, 1907; Markham to Patrick, May 12, 1907; all box 1, LS and LR, Chief of Engineers, April to August 1907, E 992; all RG 395, NARA; Jose Porta to Senor Alcalde Municipal, Nov. 17, 1907; James Parker to Chief of Police, Pinar del Río, Nov. 18, 1907; Alfredo Porta to Señor Gobernador Provincial, Dec. 31, 1907; all in exp. 18, caja 43, 2nd Intervencion documento 1907, FGP, Archivo Histórico Provincial de Pinar del Rio. On the April 1907 riot, see chap. 7, and E. D. Thomas to AG, March 25, 1907; Tel., W. A. Mann to Thomas, March 25, 1907; Thomas to AG, ACP, March 26, 1907; Thomas to AG, ACP, March 31, 1907; all case files 96, box 4, RG 199, NARA.

58. Patrick, "Notes on Road Building in Cuba," 281; Patrick to Markham, April 23, 1907; Downing to Patrick, Sept. 30, 1907; Patrick to Downing, Oct. 1, 1907; Downing to Patrick, Oct. 3, 1907; Youngberg to Patrick, Nov. 16, 1907; Patrick to Black, June 1, 1907; Patrick to Black, July 9, 1907, both in exp. 60, caja 33, Obras Publicas, SP, ANRC.

59. Guerra, *Myth of José Martí*, 207–20.

60. Logan, "Conspirators, Pawns, Patriots, and Brothers," 33–34; TR 35, Yndelecio Sobrado to Magoon, Sept. 8, 1907; Petition to Magoon, Sept. 22, 1907; TR 1, Jaime Mir, Presidente, Heulga, to Magoon, Sept. 24, 1907; Mir to Magoon, Sept. 25, 1907; T. S. Foltz to Mir, Sept. 25, 1907; TR 23, Sobrado to Magoon, Oct. 9, 1907; all in exp. 88, caja 107; Y. Sobrado to Magoon, Oct. 29, 1907; La Directiva, C/C, to Magoon, Nov, 5, 1907; Patrick to Black, Nov. 8, 1907; all in exp. 4, caja 114; all SP, ANRC.

61. Yglesia Martinez, *Cuba*, 335–37; *Diccionario enciclopédico de historia militar de Cuba*, 272; M. Sobrado to Magoon, Feb. 26, 1908; M. Sobrado to Magoon, Feb. 28, 1908; both in exp. 36, caja 32, SP, ANRC.

62. Stubbs, *Tobacco in the Periphery*, 23–26, 54; Olmstead, *Censo de la Republica de Cuba*, 308–309; Bullard to Magoon, March 5, 1908, exp. 36, caja 32, SP, ANRC.

63. Lockmiller, *Magoon in Cuba*, 145; L. A. Pérez, *Army Politics in Cuba*, 30; Magoon, memorandum, March 10, 1908, in exp. 36, caja 32; M. Sobrado to Magoon, April 3, 1908; Black to Magoon, April 14, 1908; Manuel Guintana to Black, April 20, 1908; all exp. 79, caja 96; all in SP, ANRC.

64. Logan, "Race and Politics in Western Cuba," 24; Herrera Fernandez, *Seis Alcaldes*, 7–9; US Census, *Cuba: Population, History, Resources* 1907, 171; "Igualmente se dio cuenta a la Camara...," folder 4, vol. 1908, Actas Capitulares, Provincial, Fondo Consejo Provincial, Archivo Histórico Provincial de Pinar del Rio; Magoon to Yndelecio Sobrado, March 25, 1908; Y. Sobrado to Magoon, March 25, 1908 (2 tels.); both in exp. 36, caja 32, SP, ANRC.

65. Magoon to William H. Taft, March 26, 1908, exp. 36, caja 32, SP, ANRC.

66. *Engineering World* 15, no. 9 (Nov. 1, 1919): 68; Dillon to Black, Oct. 26, 1908; Black to Magoon, Oct. 28, 1908; Black to J.A. Ryan, Oct. 27, 1908; all in exp. 36, caja 32, SP, ANRC.

67. De la Fuente, *Nation for All*, 68; Helg, *Our Rightful Share*, 118–19, 125–27, 142–45, 162–64; Logan, "Conspirators, Pawns, Patriots and Brothers," 24–28; Guerra, *Myth of José Martí*, 157, 178–82, 217, 239–40.

68. Lockmiller, *Magoon in Cuba*, 103; Magoon, *Government of Cuba*, 27; Wright, "Cart-Roads of Mr. Magoon," 645; DuPuy, "Road Building by the United States in Cuba," 136; Taft to Roosevelt, Jan. 13, 1908, in Magoon, *ARPGC* 1907, 5; Magoon, *ARPGC* 1907–1908, 15–16, 24, 87.

69. Magoon, *ARPGC* 1907–1908, 25–26; Luis Perez to José Miguel Gómez, San Juan y Martínez, July 5, 1908, exp. 43, caja 112, SP, ANRC.

70. Guerra, *Myth of José Martí*, 205; June 26, 1909; July 26, 1909; August 14, 1909; all folder 1909, vol. 5, Actas Capitulares, Provincia, Fondo Consejo Provincial, Archivo Histórico Provincial de Pinar del Río.

Chapter Five

1. Trask, *War with Spain in 1898*, 101–7, 386; Cosmas, *Army for Empire*, 181–83; Schwendinger, *Ocean of Bitter Dreams*, 169–93; Strobridge, "Chinese in the Spanish-American War and Beyond," 3–4; G. Murphy, *Shadowing the White Man's Burden*, 147–51; Sexton, "Steam Transport, Sovereignty, and Empire in North America," 638–43; Riddell, *On the Waves of Empire*, 13–14, 17–18, 27–29, 34–35, 43–46; *ARWD* 1899, pt. 2, 188; *Coast Seamen's Journal*, June 8 and 15, July 6 and 13, and Aug. 3, 1898.

2. Strobridge, "Chinese in the Spanish-American War and Beyond," 4; G. Murphy, *Shadowing the White Man's Burden*, 149; *ARWD* 1899, pt. 2, 189–91, 193–95, 220–21, 226; *ARWD* 1900, vol. 1, pt. 2, 1027, 1052; Funston, *Memories of Two Wars*, 309.

3. Devol, "Supply and Distribution," 214; *ARWD* 1899, pt. 2, 195.

4. Jung, *Coolies and Cane*, 4–6, chap. 1; McKeown, *Melancholy Order*, 47–49, chap. 3; Young, *Alien Nation*, 97–99; Ngai, *Chinese Question*, esp. chap. 4.

5. Daniels, *Guarding the Golden Door*, 18–20, 27–29; McKeown, *Melancholy Order*, 133–37; Riddell, *On the Waves of Empire*, 47–54.

6. Cosmas, *Army for Empire*, 111–13; Linn, *Philippine War*, 6–7, 9–12, 89–90, 100–101; Kramer, "Imperial Openings."

7. Wickberg, *Chinese in Philippine Life*, 4–36, chap. 2, 94–103, 106–11; A. S. Tan, *Chinese in the Philippines*, 51–55; Chu, *Chinese and Chinese Mestizos of Manila*, 58–65.

8. Wickberg, *Chinese in Philippine Life*, 61, 111–13, 212–14; McKeown, *Melancholy Order*, 77–82; McKeown, "Conceptualizing Chinese Diasporas," 313–17, 321–22; Chu, *Chinese and Chinese Mestizos of Manila*, 24–25, 38–42; Wilson, *Ambition and Identity*, 19–20, 60–74; Galang, "Living Carriers in the East," 83–85; Mencarini, "Philippine Chinese Labour Question," 167.

9. Wickberg, *Chinese in Philippine Life*, 111–13, 151, 170–75; Arensmeyer, "Chinese Coolie Labor Trade," 189–90, 195–96; Doeppers, "Destination, Selection, and Turnover," 396; Wilson, *Ambition and Identity*, 63–65, 67–74; Galang, "Living Carriers in the East," 80–82, 89–90; *Los Chinos en Filipinas*, 9–10.

10. Wickberg, *Chinese in Philippine Life*, 150, 159; Arensmeyer, "Chinese Coolie Labor Trade," 189; McKeown, *Melancholy Order*, 66–71; McKeown, "Social Life of Chinese Labor," esp. 62–67; Ngai, "Chinese Gold Miners," esp. 1083–86.

11. Wickberg, *Chinese in Philippine Life*, 150–54, 158–59, 169–70; Arensmeyer, "Chinese Coolie Labor Trade," 188–89; Doeppers, "Destination, Selection, and Turnover," 384–85; Chu, *Chinese and Chinese Mestizos of Manila*, 66–67, 75–78, 82–83; Wilson, *Ambition and*

324 Notes to Chapter Five

Identity, 61; Foreman, The Philippine Islands, 119n1; RPC 1900, vol. 1, 153; RPC 1900, vol. 2, 435–37.

12. Kramer, Blood of Government, 398–401; Baldoz, Third Asiatic Invasion, 74; Wong, Chinese in the Philippine Economy, 6; ARWD 1899, Lt.-Gen., pt. 2, 34. On Sept. 16, Otis telegrammed the War Department that he had applied US laws "for admission of Chinese and opium"; see CWS, vol. 2, 791. Otis's official orders, however, were dated Sept. 26, 1898; see Charles A. Whitter, "Admission of Chinese," Sept. 26, 1898, encl. 1, in John Hay to Wu Ting-Fang, Sept. 4, 1899, FRUS.

13. Jensen, Chinese in the Philippines, 45; Trask, War with Spain, 383–84; Alejandrino, History of the 1902 Chinese Exclusion Act; ARWD 1899, Maj.-Gen., pt. 2, 33–35; Tel., Otis to Asecwar, June 15, 1899; Alvey A. Adee to SW, Aug. 4, 1899; both box 69, folder 370, E 5, RG 350, NARA.

14. ARWD 1900, Lt.-Gen., pt. 2, 526; John Hay to Sec War, July 27, 1899; Alvey A. Adee to SW, Aug. 4, 1899; Wu to Hay, Sept. 12, 1899, FRUS; Tel., Otis to Agwar, Sept. 20, 1899; box 70, folder 370, E 5, RG 350, NARA.

15. Wilson, Ambition and Identity, 125–34; ARWD 1899, Maj.-Gen, pt. 2, 34; ARWD 1900, pt. 1, 524; Memorandum for the Asst. Sec. of State, "Chinese in the Philippine Islands. Chinese Consul at Manila, Etc.," Jan. 24, 1900; Otis, "Memorandum for the Military Governor"; all box 70, folder 370, E 5, RG 350, NARA.

16. Apilado, "Nationalism and Discrimination," 174–82; Foreman, The Philippine Islands, 420; ARWD 1899, Maj.-Gen, pt. 2, 33–35; Emilio Aguinaldo to Filipinos, May 24, 1898, Exhibit 7, in Taylor, Philippine Insurrection, 3:32–33; Decree, Oct. 30 1899, PIR 609.10, Exhibit 707, in Taylor, Philippine Insurrection, 4:189–91; "Mere Military Expedient," Washington Evening Star, Aug. 25, 1899; all box 69; "Memorandum for the Military Governor," all box 70, folder 370, E 5, RG 350, NARA.

17. Wu to Hay, Sept. 12, 1899, FRUS; John Hay to SW, July 27, 1899; Alvey A. Adee to SW, Aug. 4, 1899; all box 69; "Memorandum for the Military Governor," box 70; all folder 370, E 5, RG 350, NARA.

18. Wickberg, Chinese in the Philippines, 148, 152–53; Jensen, Chinese in the Philippines, 51–52; Cullinane, Ilustrado Politics, 52–54, 60–63; Agoncillo, Malolos, 232–34; ARWD 1899, Maj.-Gen., pt. 2, 33; US Senate, Affairs in the Philippine Islands, pt. 1, 834.

19. E. Lee, At America's Gates, 40–43, 49–50; Young, Alien Nation, 130–31; ARWD 1899, pt. 2, 15, 34–35, 300; RPC 1900, vol. 2, 221; "Memorandum for the Assistant Secretary, Chinese in the Philippine Islands," Jan. 24, 1900, box 70, folder 370, E 5, RG 350, NARA.

20. Lockmiller, Enoch H. Crowder, 66–80; Jensen, Chinese in the Philippines, 60, 71–74; E. Lee, At America's Gates, 2–4, 40–50, 194–207; Young, "Beyond Borders"; US Census Bureau, Census of the Philippine Islands, 1: 491; ARWD 1900, Lt.-Gen., pt. 2, 526; ARWD 1901, pt. 2, 237–39, 293–94; "Admission of Chinese," Sept. 26, 1898, in Hay to SW, Sept. 4, 1899, FRUS; Otis to SW, April 1, 1899, box 69; "Memorandum for the Assistant Secretary, Chinese in the Philippine Islands," Jan. 24, 1900; box 70; both folder 370, E 5, RG 350, NARA.

21. May, Social Engineering in the Philippines, 19; Chu, Chinese and Chinese Mestizos of Manila, 292–94; E. Lee, At America's Gates, 49–52; Detrick, First Regiment California U.S. Volunteers, 34; USPC, Schurman Report, 1900, vol. 2, 220; ARWD 1900, Report of the Military Government of the Philippine Islands, 13, 48–49; ARWD 1901, pt. 2, 237–39, 293–94; US Senate, Affairs in the Philippine Islands, pt. 2, 908; John Hay to SW, July 27, 1899; Wu Ting-Fang to John Hay, Sept. 12, 1899; both box 69, folder 370, E 5, RG 350, NARA.

22. Trask, *War with Spain in 1898*, 402–10; Schellings, "Advent of the Spanish-American War in Florida," 319–21; Wickberg, *Chinese in Philippine Life*, 108–11, 147–54; Alatas, *Myth of the Lazy Native*, 52–60, 98–110; F. D. Millett, *Expedition to the Philippines*, 80–81; Cullum, *Biographical Register*, 4:184; O. K. Davis, *Our Conquests in the Pacific*, 320–22; *ARWD* 1899, pt. 2, 189; *RPC* 1902, pt. 1, 161; J. W. Pope, diary, pp. 73, 244, box 1, James Worden Pope Papers, Merrill G. Burlingame Archives and Special Collections.

23. Bankoff, "Wants, Wages, and Workers," 69–70; *CWS*, vol. 2, 809; *ARWD* 1899, pt. 2, 195, 220–21; J. W. Pope, diary, 57–58, 63, 505, box 1, Pope Papers.

24. Chu, *Chinese and Chinese Mestizos of Manila*, 111, 128–36, 142; Wilson, *Ambition and Identity*, 110–19; *RPC*, 1900, vol. 2, 220.

25. Wickberg, *Chinese in the Philippines*, 179–82; Chu, *Chinese and Chinese Mestizos of Manila*, chap. 7; Wilson, *Ambition and Identity*, 84–87; *RPC* 1900, vol. 2, 220.

26. Wickberg, *Chinese in the Philippines*, 232; Ginsberg, "Chinese in the Philippine Revolution," 148–54; Chu, *Chinese and Chinese Mestizos of Manila*, 12, 78–81, 84–87; Wilson, *Ambition and Identity*, 119–25; *ARWD* 1899, pt. 2, 222–23; *RPC* 1900, vol. 2, 219–25.

27. Wickberg, *Chinese in the Philippines*, 123; Ginsberg, "Chinese in the Philippine Revolution," 155–56; Wilson, *Ambition and Identity*, 129–30; Doeppers, *Feeding Manila in Peace and War*, 74–75; Foreman, *The Philippine Islands*, 621; *ARWD* 1899, pt. 2, 195, 220–23; *RPC* 1900, vol. 2, 219–25.

28. Chu, *Chinese and Chinese Mestizos of Manila*, 282; Wilson, *Ambition and Identity*, 125–28; H. C. Corbin to Otis, Sept. 1, 1898; J. B. Moore to SW, Sept. 10, 1898; both *CWS*, vol. 2, 785, 789.

29. Wilson, *Ambition and Identity*, 128–36; *ARWD* 1900, Lt.-Gen., pt. 2, 520–26; G. D. Meiklejohn to Otis, Dec. 13, 1898, box 4, folder 29, E 5, RG 350, NARA.

30. Bankoff, "Wants, Wages, and Workers," 68; Bankoff, "'These Brothers of Ours,'" 1057; F. J. Herman, *Forty-Second Foot*, 123–27; *ARWD* 1899, pt. 2, 195.

31. *ARWD* 1899, pt. 2, 507; *RPC* 1900, vol. 1, 153; *RPC* 1900, pt. 2, 218–20.

32. Bender, *American Abyss*, 44–49, 55; W. Anderson, *Colonial Pathologies*, 31; Galang, "Living Carriers in the East," 72; Hoyt, *A Frontier Doctor*, 190; *ARWD* 1899, pt. 3, 566, 573, 577; Charles Greenleaf to AG, DP & 8AC, Jan. 30, 1899, box 339, E 26, RG 112, NARA.

33. Linn, *Philippine War*, 101–4; Kemp, "Field Work in the Philippines," 79–80; McManus, *Soldier's Life in the Philippines*, 29; *ARWD* 1899, Maj.-Gen., pt. 2, 195; *ARWD* 1899, pt. 3, 566.

34. Bowe, *With the 13th Minnesota in the Philippines*, 126, 128; Guy Howard to Adj., 21st US Inf., July 31, 1899; Howard to QM, 3B, 1D, 8AC, July 31, 1899; Howard to Chief QM, 1st South Dakota, Aug. 2, 1899; A. S. Bickham to Irwin, Sept. 8, 1899; all in box 1, E 834; Howard, 1st end., August 2, 1899, on Adj., 21st Inf., July 31, 1899, box 1, E 832; TS #7, Howard to Bickham, Aug. 6, 1899, box 2, E 817; all RG 395, NARA.

35. Wickberg, *Chinese in Philippine Life*, 37–38; Linn, *Philippine War*, 91, 104, 111–16; *ARWD* 1899, pt. 3, 78–79, 87, 106, 133–34; J. W. Pope, diary, 344, box 1, Pope Papers.

36. Linn, *Philippine War*, 116–20; Galang, "Living Carriers in the East," 77, 85–88; Hirrel, "Beginnings of the Quartermaster Graves Registration Service," 65.

37. Kemp, "Field Work in the Philippines," 78; *ARWD* 1899, pt. 3, 76, 87.

38. Bowe, *With the 13th Minnesota in the Philippines*, 126, 128; McManus, *Soldier's Life in the Philippines*, 29–30; Harold P. Howard, Diary, Aug. 6, 1899 entry, box 1, folder 10, Howard

Papers; LR 259, DP and 8AC, Feb. 15, 1900; LR 251, D. M. Carman to 1D, 8AC, Feb. 20, 1900; LR 394, March 9, 1900; LR 405, March 10, 1900; all box 1, E 797, RG 395, NARA.

39. Galang, "Living Carriers in the East," 82; F. J. Herman, *Forty-Second Foot*, 124–27.

40. Linn, *Philippine War*, 121–22; Galang, "Living Carriers in the East," 85; *ARWD* 1899, *Maj.-Gen.*, pt. 3, 573.

41. Linn, *Philippine War*, 122; Howard, end., July 18, 1899, on LR 1284, June 9, 1899; LR 1544, July 10, 1899; LR 2269, Aug. 27, 1899; all Chief QM, 1D, to HQ, 1D, 8AC, vol. 4, E 776, RG 395, NARA.

42. Kemp, "Field Work in the Philippines," 77; L. L. Seaman, "Native Troops for Our Colonial Possessions," 852–53; *ARWD* 1899, pt. 2, 195; *ARWD* 1899, pt. 3, 115, 573; Greenleaf to AG, DP & 8AC, Jan. 30, 1899, folder 339, Box 26, RG 112, NARA.

43. Miller, *Unwelcome Immigrant*, 25–26, 33–34, 44, 50, 109–10; Kramer, "Race-Making and Colonial Violence"; R. G. Lee, *Orientals*, 39; Hoyt, *A Frontier Doctor*, 195–96. Published allegations of Chinese laborers' cowardice under fire include A. C. Johnson, *Official History of the Operations of the First Colorado Infantry*, 15; H. C. Thompson, "War without Medals," 317; Sorley, *History of the Fourteenth United States Infantry*, 49; C. F. Baker, *History of the 30th Infantry*, 36–37; *ARWD* 1900, pt. 3, 278, 334, 359, 363.

44. Funston, *Memories of Two Wars*, 246–47; Steele, *Official History of the Operations of the Twentieth Kansas Infantry*, 20; F. J. Herman, *Forty-Second Foot*, 183; McManus, *Soldier's Life in the Philippines*, 29; Kemp, "Field Work in the Philippines," 78; L. L. Seaman, "Native Troops for Our Foreign Possessions," 853; "Chinese Immigration," *Manila American*, June 6, 1900; John Preder, "Buff's Men in a Trap," 14, folder 25, box 47, SAWS; MacQueen, "Campaigning with General Lawton," *National Magazine*, 364, folder 7, box 4, Henry Lawton Papers.

45. Wells, *War in the Philippines*, 71; "A Communication in Chinese," *Manila American*, Nov. 19, 1899; *ARWD* 1900, pt. 3, 100.

46. Hoganson, *Fighting for American Manhood*, 107–55; Jacobson, *Special Sorrows*, 177–216; Markey, *From Iowa to the Philippines*, 193, 220–21; Isselhard, *Filipino in Every-Day Life*, 39.

47. Ginsberg, "Chinese in the Philippine Revolution," 152–54; C. J. Crane, *Experiences of a Colonel of Infantry*, 317, 340; Kemp, "Field Work in the Philippines," 79; George Telfer to Lottie Telfer, Marilao, April 21, 1899, in Telfer, *Manila Envelopes*, 154; *ARWD* 1900, pt. 2, 355; TS 17, Peyton March to C. A. Devol, Aug. 10, 1899, box 1, E 846, RG 395, NARA.

48. Wickberg, *Chinese in Philippine Life*, 171–72; Chu, *Chinese and Chinese Mestizos of Manila*, 42; Galang, "Living Carriers in the East," 93, 101; Sawtelle to Hoyt, April 5 and April 10, 1899; Hoyt, June 4, 1899; both box 1, E 853; LR 1504, July 1899, HQ, 1D, 8AC, vol. 4, E 776; Erickson to Bickham, Dec. 21, 1899, box 1, E 809; LR 112, Jan. 25, 1900, 1D, 8AC, box 1, E 797; all RG 395, NARA; LS 6, Robert L. Bullard to Henderson, Dec. 20, 1899, vol. 19, 39th USVI, RB, E 117, RG 94, NARA.

49. S. C. Miller, *Unwelcome Immigrant*, 29–31; Wickberg, *Chinese in Philippine Life*, 49, 201; Wilson, *Ambition and Identity*, 78, 155; Foster, "Prohibiting Opium in the Philippines and the United States," 96–98; Wong, *Chinese in the Philippine Economy*, 25, 29–33; Chu, "Transnationalizing the History of the Chinese in the Philippines," 181–82; Galang, "Living Carriers in the East," 95–97; A. C. Johnson, *Official History of the Operations of the First Colorado Infantry*, 15; McManus, *Soldier's Life in the Philippines*, 26–28; *ARWD* 1901, pt. 5, 432;

RPC 1905, *Opium and the Traffic Therein*, 134–356; Muriel Bailey, "The Chinese and Their Ways in the Philippines," *Atlanta Constitution*, July 29, 1900.

50. Kemp, "Field Work in the Philippines," 78; "The Way of the Cunning 'Cheno,'" *Manila American*, Feb. 28, 1899; *ARWD* 1899, Maj.-Gen., pt. 2, 70; *ARWD* 1900, Lt.-Gen., pt. 3, 509; *ARWD* 1900, pt. 4, 452; William I. Johnston to Adj., Wheaton's Expeditionary Brigade, Jan. 27, 1900, LSB, 2nd Battalion, 46th USVI, E 117, RG 94, NARA.

51. "Career of D. M. Carman, Who Is Under Arrest at Manila," *San Francisco Chronicle*, Feb. 7, 1901; *ARWD* 1899, pt. 2, 80; *ARWD* 1901, Lt.-Gen., pt. 2, 288–89; *RPC* 1907, pt. 2, 1019.

52. Agoncillo, *Malolos*, 358; McCoy, *Policing America's Empire*, 66–82; "Seeks Heavy Damages for False Arrest," *San Francisco Chronicle*, Dec. 21, 1899; "Says the Charge Is True," *New York Tribune*, Feb. 9, 1901; "Accused of Aiding the Insurgents," *San Francisco Chronicle*, Feb. 7, 1901; "Arrested on the Eve of Flight," *San Francisco Chronicle*, Feb. 9, 1901; "In League with Insurgents," *Washington Post*, Feb. 21, 1901; "Carman's Release from Prison Granted by Military Governor," *Manila Times*, March 1, 1901; "D. M. Carman Denies Any Wrongdoing," *San Francisco Chronicle*, March 5, 1901; "D. M. Carman Back from the Philippines," *San Francisco Chronicle*, Aug. 13, 1901.

53. Bankoff, "Wants, Wages, and Workers," 69; Wilson, *Ambition and Identity*, 133; Linn, *Philippine War*, 142–48, 153; J. C. Brown, *Gentleman Soldier*, 87, 92–93, 120–21; "Taking Possession at Aparri," *Manila American*, April 1, 1900; *ARWD* 1900, pt. 2, 220–21; *ARWD* 1900, pt. 4, 110, 137, 395–97; John C. Oakes to C. O., Btln. of Engineers, 8AC, Dec. 2, 1899; Oakes to Adj., 1D, 8AC, Feb. 1, 1900; both in box 3, E 777, RG 395, NARA. In 1905, Taft told a US House of Representatives committee that "under the Chinese exclusion laws the Chinamen lawfully there were disposed to ask for higher wages and for greater privileges, because the Chinaman readily finds out his value in the market and what facts are with respect to that which he has to sell"; *RPC* 1907, pt. 2, 1008.

54. George Telfer to Lottie Telfer, Manila, Feb. 19, 1899, in Telfer, *Manila Envelopes*, 132; *ARWD* 1900, pt. 3, 100.

55. K. Adams, *Class and Race in the Frontier Army*, 57–64; Crozier, "Some Observations on the Pekin Relief Expedition," 230–31; E. B. Clark, *William L. Sibert*, 55; Kohr, *Around the World with Uncle Sam*, 215.

56. Chu, "Transnationalizing the History of the Chinese in the Philippines," 190–91; *ARWD* 1900, Bureau Reports, vol. 1, pt. 2, 667; *ARWD* 1901, pt. 3, 294–304; Todd Littell, questionnaire, SAWS; Shaffer, "Reminiscences of an Army Career," p. 29, Pearl M. Shaffer Papers; Wessells to Adj., Vigan, Feb. 7, 1900, box 1, E 2157; LR 233, DP and 8AC, Feb. 9, 1900, box 1, E 797; both RG 395, NARA.

57. May, *Social Engineering*, 89–93, 113–26; Kramer, *Blood of Government*, 312–14; Steinbock-Pratt, *Educating the Empire*, 16–17; Walther, "'Same Blood as We in America'"; US Census Bureau, *Census of the Philippine Islands*, 4:422–33.

58. Capozzola, *Bound by War*, 13–16; "Lazy Chinos Not Wanted," *Manila American*, Sept. 15, 1899; *ARWD* 1899, pt. 2, 33.

59. Hoganson, *Fighting for American Manhood*, 24–27; Roediger and Esch, *Production of Difference*, 129; Butt, *Both Sides of the Shield*, xiii, xvi, xvii; *ARWD* 1907, vol. 3, 322; "Biographical Note," in Finding Aid, Archibald Willingham Butt Letters, Manuscript, Archives, and Rare Book Library, Emory University, Atlanta, Georgia.

60. Murray, "Chinese-Filipino Wage Differentials in Early-Twentieth Century Manila," 779; *ARWD* 1901, pt. 2, 151–54; *RPC* 1902, pt. 1, 169–73.

61. Bankoff, "Wants, Wages, and Workers," 79–80; *ARWD* 1901, pt. 2, 151–54; *RPC* 1902, pt. 1, 169–76.

62. *ARWD* 1900, pt. 1, 268; *RPC* 1902, pt. 1, 159–63.

63. W. Anderson, *Colonial Pathologies*, 68; *RPC* 1902, pt. 1, 159–66, 257–58.

64. *RPC* 1907, pt. 2, 988–93.

65. *ARWD* 1901, pt. 2, 110–11, 294; US Senate, *Affairs in the Philippine Islands*, pt. 2, 906–7.

66. *RPC* 1900, vol. 2, 180, 206, 215–16, 252–55, 321; *ARWD* 1901, pt. 2, 110–11; Memorandum for the Asst. Sec., "Chinese in the Philippine Islands," Jan. 24, 1900, box 70, folder 370, E 5, RG 350, NARA.

67. Daniels, *Asian America*, 39–40; Alejandrino, *History of the 1902 Chinese Exclusion Act*, 12–17; *ARWD* 1901, pt. 2, 110–12, 294; US Senate, *Affairs in the Philippine Islands*, pt. 2, 906–7.

68. Cullinane, *Ilustrado Politics*, 5, 60–62, 66; Burns, "A New Pacific Border," 314–16; RPC, *Schurman Report*, 1900, vol. 2, 180; *ARWD* 1901, pt. 2, 238.

69. Martinez and Lowrie, "Transcolonial Influences on Everyday American Imperialism," 512, 525–26; Urban, *Brokering Servitude*, 188, 192–97; US Senate, *Affairs in the Philippines Islands*, pt. 1, 268; US Senate, *Chinese Exclusion*, Rept. 776, pt. 2, 492–501; J. W. Pope, diary, p. 216, box 1, Pope Papers.

70. Mojares, *Brains of the Nation*, 278–81; W. H. Scott, *Union Obrera Democratica*, 64; Linn, *Philippine War*, 213–15; Kramer, *Blood of Government*, 181; Bender, *American Abyss*, 57; Forbes, *The Philippine Islands*, 1:519; "Need the Chinese, Says Major Seaman," *New York Times*, March 24, 1907; US Senate, *Chinese Exclusion*, pt. 1, 496–99; US Census Bureau, *Census of the Philippines*, 4:427–31; *RPC* 1902, pt. 1, 21–24; *RPC* 1907, pt. 2, 1003; Taft to Root, Jan. 7, 1901, reel 3, WHT.

71. US Senate, *Chinese Exclusion*, Rep't 776, pt. 2, 496–505; US Senate, *Affairs in the Philippine Islands*, pt. 1, 165–268; US Senate, *Affairs in the Philippine Islands*, pt. 2, 906–9. In 1903, the Philippine Commission itself adopted the 1902 US exclusion renewal; see USPC, *Acts of the Philippine Commission*, 457–58.

72. Yun, *Coolie Speaks*, 216; Young, *Alien Nation*, 99,

73. Yun, *Coolie Speaks*, 13–38; Jung, *Coolies and Cane*, 81–89; Young, *Alien Nation*, 27–34, 64–76; López, *Chinese Cubans*, 18–39, 47–53.

74. Young, *Alien Nation*, 204–205; López, *Chinese Cubans*, 56–71; US Senate, *Report on the Census of Cuba*, 1899, 220, 472–75.

75. George D. Meiklejohn to John R. Brooke, Jan. 17, 1899; Brooke to Meiklejohn, Jan. 28, 1899; Tasker H. Bliss to Collector of Customs, At all Ports, Jan. 31, 1899; Meiklejohn to Gage, March 4, 1899; Tel., Meiklejohn to Bliss, March 2, 1899; Meiklejohn, Circ. No. 13, Division of Customs and Insular Affairs, WD, April 14, 1899; all box 23, folder 185, E 5, RG 350, NARA.

76. Young, *Alien Nation*, 157–59; Romero, "Transnational Chinese Immigrant Smuggling," 5–6; Gage to Meiklejohn, Tel., Bliss to Asecwar, May 1, 1899; Tel., Meiklejohn to Bliss, May 2, 1899; Meiklejohn, Circ. No. 13, Division of Customs and Insular Affairs, WD, April 14, 1900; all box 23, folder 185, E 5, RG 350, NARA.

77. *ARWD* 1899, *Report of Mil. Gov. of Cuba on Civil Affairs*, vol. 1, pt. 6, 386; "Immigration Regulations for the Island of Cuba," BCIA, WD, June 6, 1899, box 23, folder 185, E 5, RG 350, NARA.

78. Young, "Globalization and the Border Wall," 54–58; López, *Chinese Cubans*, 50, 86–87, 99, 102–4, 110–13; Hirota, *Expelling the Poor*, 2–3, 181; Bliss, Aug. 21, 1900, 2nd end. on Lyman Gage to SW, WD, Aug. 7, 1900, box 23, folder 185, E 5, RG 350, NARA; Bliss to H. C. Corbin, July 6, 1900, folder 25, box 8; John N. Clark to Commissioner-General of Immigration, July 31, 1900; both Bliss Papers.

79. López, "Gatekeeping in the Tropics"; Romero, "Transnational Chinese Immigrant Smuggling"; *ARWD* 1900, *Mil. Govt. Cuba Civil Affairs*, vol. 1, pt. 3, 161; Elias Chandler to Bliss, June 3, 1899; Chang Yin Tung to Bliss, June 6, 1900; Bliss to Collector of Customs, Ysabela la Sagua, June 6, 1899; W. T. Evans to Bliss, June 17, 1899; Chandler to Bliss, June 9, 1899; Bliss to Consul General of China [ca. June 1899]; John H. Clark to Commissioner General of Immigration, July 31, 1900; all folder 12, box 9; Bliss, 2nd end., June 7 1900, box 8, folder 37; all Bliss Papers; Bliss, June 7, 1901, 2nd end., on John A. Wright to Terence V. Powderly, May 20, 1901; Jos. Philippe Mora to Gentlemen and General, May 1899; Gage to SW, June 5, 1899; Hay to Root, April 12, 1900; all box 23, folder 185, E 5, RG 350, NARA.

80. Leonard Wood, Order No. 155, HQ, DC, May 1902, attached to Wu Tingfang, Letter No. 254, Aug. 20, 1902; Wu to Hay, April 29, 1902; Wu to Adee, Aug. 20, 1902; Adee to Wu, Sept. 12, 1902; all *FRUS*; Adee to Root, Aug. 28, 1902; all box 23, folder 185, E 5, RG 350, NARA. Wood's order permitted the return of Chinese merchants and laborers who could prove residency in Cuba prior to April 1899; see Wood, Order No. 155.

81. L. A. Pérez, *Cuba between Empires*, 351–65; Ayala, *American Sugar Kingdom*, 59–62; Merleaux, *Sugar and Civilization*, 28–41; W. W. Thompson, "Governors of the Moro Province," 110; Root to Wood, March 7, 1902; Wood to Root, March 30, 1902; Root to Wood, April 4, 1902; all box 31, LWP.

82. De la Fuente, *Nation for All*, 45–53, 99–102; López, "Gatekeeping in the Tropics," 49; Pappedemos, *Black Political Activism*, 101–3; Helg, *Our Rightful Share*, 134.

83. Yun, *Coolie Speaks*, 215–16; de la Fuente, *Nation for All*, 99–115; Young, *Alien Nation*, 205; Casey, *Empire's Guestworkers*, 8–9, 51–52, 56–57.

Chapter Six

1. Healy, *United States in Cuba*, 37–38, 53–54; R. J. Scott, "Race, Labor, and Citizenship," 690–92, 696, 700–708, 717–18; R. J. Scott, *Degrees of Freedom*, 17–20, 111–13, 135–50, 178–79; Iglesias Utset, *Cultural History of Cuba*, 52–53; E. F. Atkins, *Sixty Years in Cuba*, 294–302, 306–7; Bolton, *History of the Second Regiment Illinois Volunteer Infantry*, 122–27; "Nuestra Situacion," *Libertad*, Feb. 3, 1899; *ARWD* 1899, *Maj.-Gen.*, pt. 1, 132; C. G. Hampton to Companions, March 18, 1899, roll 1, Michigan Commandery Records, Military Order of the Loyal Legion of the United States, Bentley Historical Library, University of Michigan; Consejo municipal de Cienfuegos, Secretaría, Libros de actas de sesiones, June 17, 1899, vol. 43, Actas Capitulares, Fondo Ayuntamiento de Cienfuegos, Archivo Histórico Provincial de Cienfuegos; Atkins to Russell A. Alger, May 29, 1899, AGO #241639, and LR 5734, A. H. Bowman to AG, DMSC, June 20, 1899, both box 1565, E 25, RG 94, NARA.

2. Rousseau and Díaz de Villegas, *Memoria descriptiva*, 268; E. F. Atkins, *Sixty Years in Cuba*, 303; "Cuban Laborers and Working-Men Employed on the Government Works, in the Department of Matanzas and Santa Clara," box 1, E 1341; James H. Wilson to Miller, April 26, 1899, vol. 4, box 2, E 1323; W. H. Miller to AAG, DMSC, May 11, 1899, Affidavit,

Joaquin Oropresa y del Sol, May 16, 1899; J. H. Hysell to Cassaic, May 17, 1899; Frias to José Miguel Gómez, May 17, 1899; Orestres Ferrera to Wilson, May 18, 1899; Barker to C. E. Dempsey, May 18, 1899, all box 7; affidavits by C. L. Walsh, Eligio A. Brunet, P. Aldumin, E. S. Harrison, George L. Donald, C. H. Evans, and Luis Lewis, all May 27, 1899; Barker to J. H. Dorst, June 19, 1899; TR 5567, Bowman to DMSC, June 20, 1899, all box 12; A. H. Bowman to AG, DMSC, June 20, 1899, box 11; all E 1331; Walter B. Barker to C. E. Dempsey, May 18, 1899, box 15, E 1241; Cecil to Wilson, May 18, 1899, vol. 5, box 2, E 1323, all RG 395, NARA.

3. Healy, *United States in Cuba*, 78–79; Riera Hernandez, *Ejercito Libertador de Cuba*, 281; R. J. Scott, "Race, Labor, and Citizenship," 712; R. J. Scott, *Degrees of Freedom*, 97; Iglesias Utset, *Cultural History of Cuba*, 37–38; Rousseau and Díaz de Villegas, *Memoria descriptiva*, 268; "¿A que espera el General Wilson?" *La Patria*, June 27, 1899; "Investigaciones," *La Tribuna*, June 28, 1899; LS 1662, J. C. Bates to AG, DC, Havana, April 24, 1899, vol. 3, E 1462; C. Stevens to AG, DMSC, May 6, 1899, box 7, E 1331; "Exhibit A," in LR 4199, Civil File, DC, in LR 6286, HQ, DC, AGO #288561, box 17, E 1241; Tel., Frias to Wilson, June 24, 1899, in LR 5747, DMSC, June 26, 1899; Fenton to AG, Matanzas, June 24, 1899; Wilson to AG, DC, June 27, 1899, and Wilson, 5th end., June 28, 1899; Andrew Fuller to Wilson, July 3, 1899, all box 12; Wilson to AG, DC, June 27, 1899, box 11; all E 1331; A. H. Bowman to AG, DMSC, June 24, 1899, box 1, E 1351; Judge Advocate to AG, DMSC, July 3, 1899, box 1, E 1359, all RG 395, NARA; GO 25, HQ, DMSC, July 25, 1899, file 12107, box 2988, GCM, RG 153, NARA. In the Philippines, Catlin faced various accusations of misconduct, including killing a guide; see US Senate, *Affairs in the Philippine Islands*, pt. 3, 2234; AGO #421607, "Proceedings of a Board of Officers to Inquire into Allegations Made by Maj. Cornelius Gardener, 13th Infantry, in His Report of December 16, 1901," RG 94, NARA.

4. Caulfield, *In Defense of Honor*; Rousseau and Díaz de Villegas, *Memoria descriptiva*, 269; Barnet, *Biography*, 11, 182, 194–95, 197.

5. "Exhibit A," in LR 4199, Civil File, DC, in LR 6286, HQ, DC, AGO #288561, box 17, E 1241, RG 395, NARA.

6. Byers, *Sexual Economy of War*, 3–4; Vuic, "Girl in Every Port?" 88–90. Very little documentation exists for same-sex prostitution in either Cuba or the Philippines; see Byers, *Sexual Economy of War*, 78–84.

7. Stoner, *From the House to the Streets*, 13–15; Sippial, *Prostitution, Modernity, and the Making of the Cuban Republic*, chap. 5; Winkelmann, *Dangerous Intercourse*, 25; Greene, "Rethinking the Boundaries of Class," 98–99.

8. Stoner, *From the House to the Streets*, chap. 1; Camagay, *Working Women of Manila*, chap. 7; Dery, *History of the Inarticulate*, 133; McClintock, *Imperial Leather*, 353; Prados-Torreira, *Mambísas*, 5–8, 134; Rafael, *White Love*, 43–45, 48–50; Holt, *Colonizing Filipinos*, 74–80, 121–22; Roces, "Is the Suffragist an American Colonial Construct?," 25–29, 36–37; Reyes, *Love, Passion, and Patriotism*, 20–26, 54–59, 144–45, 240–42, 254–58; Sippial, *Prostitution, Modernity, and the Making of the Cuban Republic*, 6–9; Winkelmann, *Dangerous Intercourse*, 19–21; Emilio Aguinaldo to President of the Council of Secretaries, Oct. 23 1899, PIR 8.4, Exhibit 700, in Taylor, *Philippine Insurrection*, 4:177–78.

9. Stoner, *From the House to the Streets*, 23–33; Owen, "Masculinity and National Identity," 35–38; Sippial, *Prostitution, Modernity, and the Making of the Cuban Republic*, chap. 5; Roces, "Is the Suffragist an American Colonial Construct?," 27–33; Reyes, *Love, Passion, and Patriotism*, xxvii–xxix, chap. 6, 254–59; Winkelmann, *Dangerous Intercourse*, 106–16.

Notes to Chapter Six 331

10. W. Anderson, *Colonial Pathologies*, chap. 1; Holt, *Colonizing Filipinas*, 124; Wintermute, *Public Health and the U.S. Military*, 4, 122–25; Winkelmann, *Dangerous Intercourse*, 30–31; Bailey et al., introduction, 2.

11. Byers, *Sexual Economy of War*, 9–10, 32, 35; K. Adams, *Class and Race in the Frontier Army*, 98–101.

12. Pivar, "Military, Prostitution, and Colonial Peoples," 256–57; Sippial, *Prostitution, Modernity, and the Making of the Cuban Republic*, chaps. 1 and 2.

13. Stoner, *From the House to the Streets*, 23–33; Roces, "Reflections on Gender and Kinship"; Sippial, *Prostitution, Modernity, and the Making of the Cuban Republic*, chap. 5; Prados-Torreira, *Mambísas*, 125, 131–32; Edelmira Guerra, "Programa Revolucionario del club patriotico 'Esperanza del Valle,'" March 19, 1898, leg. 279, exp. 15, Fondo Donativos y Remisiones, ANRC, cited in Vinat de la Mata, "Dimensiones del amor tarifado," 182–83.

14. Lane, *Armed Progressive*, 64; Hard, *Banners in the Air*, 63–66; Hoganson, *Fighting for American Manhood*, 25–27, 51–54, 124–25; L. A. Pérez, *Cuba in the American Imagination*, 65–92; Wintermute, *Public Health and the U.S. Military*, 189; Lynk, *Black Troopers*, 120–24; *Times of Cuba*, Aug. 3, 5, 8, 12, 13, 17, 19, 1898; *Times of Santiago*, Aug. 15, 16, 17, 1898; "Colonel Ray's Immunes Arrive Safely in Cuba," *Atlanta Constitution*, Aug. 19, 1898, 1; Albert F. Gudatt Journal, Aug. 4, 1898 entry, Albert F. Gudatt Papers, Clements Library Special Collections, University of Michigan; V. G. Bell to Mother, Aug. 28, 1898; V. G. Bell to Mother, Sept. 17, 1898, Bell Collection; Tel., Shafter to Corbin, Aug. 16, 1898, AGO #241034; Tel., Shafter to Corbin, AGO#236515; Tel., Shafter to Corbin, Aug. 17, 1898; Tel., Corbin to Lawton, Aug. 21, 1898, all box 1939, E 25, RG 94, NARA.

15. Gatewood, *Black Americans*, 87–101, 123–34, 171–72; Lane, *Armed Progressive*, 64; Gatewood, "An Experiment in Color," 294–96, 298, 302–3, 306, 309–10; Blight, *Race and Reunion*, 347–54; Gilmore, *Gender and Jim Crow*, 61–77; R. J. Scott, *Degrees of Freedom*, 167–78; Ferrer, *Insurgent Cuba*, 187–92; Helg, "Black Men, Racial Stereotyping, and Violence," 576, 578, 582–83, 591; Coston, *Spanish-American War Volunteer*, 10; Goode, *The Eighth Illinois*, 140–41, 145, 157–58, 161–62, 167–68, 171, 188, 202, 217–18; McCard, *History of the Eighth Illinois*, 92; Steward, *Colored Regulars*, 287.

16. Sippial, *Prostitution, Modernity, and the Making of the Cuban Republic*, 33–43; Byers, *Sexual Economy of War*, 63; Bacardí, *Cronicas*, 192; ARWD 1899, Maj.-Gen., pt. 1, 208; H. H. Sargent to AG, Dept. of Santiago, Dec. 1, 1898, vol. 5, Regimental Books, 5th USVI, E 116, RG 94, NARA; Reyes Olivera to John R. Brooke, June 9, 1899; William E. Dougherty to AAG, Dept. of Havana and Pinar del Rio, May 30, 1899; E. E. Benjamin to Francisco Oberto, July 18, 1899; E. E. Benjamin to IG, Dept. of Havana and Pinar del Rio, July 26, 1899, all box 1, E 1410, RG 395, NARA; H. L. Scott to CG, Dept. of Havana and Pinar del Rio, June 19, 1900, box 6, E 6, RG 140, NARA.

17. Gatewood, *"Smoked Yankees,"* 194–96; Kessler-Harris, *Out to Work*, 49–53; Vinat de la Mata, *Las cubanas en la posguerra*, 22–23, 41–42; Prados-Torreira, *Mambísas*, 109; US Department of War, *Report on the Census of Cuba, 1899*, 223, 225, 330, 404–405, 434, 436–37, 471, 480; *Censo de la República de Cuba*, 1907, 548; V. Clark, "Labor Conditions in Cuba," 689, 691, 715.

18. Hicks, *Hierarchies at Home*, 3–16, chap. 2.

19. Butler, *Daughters of Joy, Sisters of Misery*, 139–45; R. J. Scott, "Race, Labor, and Citizenship," 724; K. Adams, *Class and Race in the Frontier Army*, 99; Prados-Torreira, *Mambísas*, 122; Alfonso, *La prostitución en Cuba*, 29–30; Albert F. Gudatt Journal, Sept. 23, 1898 entry,

332 Notes to Chapter Six

Albert F. Gudatt Papers, Clements Library Special Collections, University of Michigan; W. L. Scott to AG, DS, Sept. 15, 1898, box 1, E 1487, RG 395, NARA; Circular #22, HQ, 5th USVI, Oct. 26, 1898, vol. 3, Regimental Orders and Circulars, 5th USVI, E 116, RG 94, NARA.

20. Sippial, *Prostitution, Modernity, and the Making of the Cuban Republic*, 57, 63, 73; Alfonso, *La prostitución en Cuba*, 16–17; *Reglamento para el régimen de la prostitución*; Pepper, *To-Morrow in Cuba*, 282; ARWD 1899, Maj.-Gen., pt. 1, 217–18, 223–24, 249; William L. Kneedler to AAG, Dept. of Pinar del Rio, March 4, 1899, box 1, E 1380, RG 395, NARA; William Ludlow to M. R. Suarez, April 8, 1900, box 231, E 3, RG 140, NARA.

21. United States Department of War, *Annual Report of Colonel Samuel M. Whitside*, 100–101; Alfonso, *La prostitución*, 20–25; Orden Publico Numero 4637, Oct. 22, 1896; Luis Algarzon to Sr. Gobernador Civil de la Provincia, Nov. 26, 1900; "Sinopsis de informacion necessaria de Comision de Higiene Especial," Stgo. de Cuba, Nov. 1902, all exp. 12, leg. 2226, Prostitución, FGP, AHPSDC.

22. L. A. Pérez, *Lords of the Mountain*, 75–78, 169–70; "Sinopsis de informacion necessaria de Comision de Higiene Especial," Stgo. de Cuba, Nov. 1902, exp. 12, leg. 2226, Prostitución, FGP, AHPSDC; Frank R. McCoy to Emilio Bacardi, n.d. [Nov. 1901], vol. 1, E 1493, RG 395, NARA.

23. Sippial, *Prostitution, Modernity, and the Making of the Cuban Republic*, 60, 62, 68, 100–102, 121, 136; J. H. Dorst to AG, DMSC, July 20, 1899, box 16, E 1331, RG 395, NARA.

24. B. Silbey, AAG, DC to Civil Gov., Province of Santiago, Jan. 23, 1901; M. A. Tirada to Sr. Gobor. de la provincia de Santiago de Cuba, Feb. 4, 1901; "Sinopsis e informacion necessaria a la Comision de Higene Especial ... Ayuntamento Manzanillo," Oct. 31, 1902, all exp. 12, leg. 2226, Prostitución, FGP, AHPSDC; J. H. Dorst to AG, DMSC, July 17, 1899; J. H. Dorst to AG, DMSC, July 21, 1899; Frank J. Ives to AG, DMSC, Aug. 26, 1899, all box 16; Frank J. Ives, July 1, 1900, 2nd end., on W. W. Benham to AG, DMSC, June 18, 1900, box 40, all E 1331; L. C. Carr to Chief Surgeon, DSPP, Jan. 16, 1900, box 12, E 1487, all RG 395, NARA.

25. Stoner, *From the House to the Streets*, 23–33; Sippial, *Prostitution, Modernity, and the Making of the Cuban Republic*, chap. 5; Consejo municipal de Cienfuegos, Secretaría, *Libros de actas de sesiones*, March 9, 1899, vol. 43, Actas Capitulares, Fondo Ayuntamiento de Cienfuegos, Archivo Histórico Provincial de Cienfuegos; Louis M. Schafer, file 26894, box 3296, GCM, RG 153, NARA; A. G. Hennissee to AG, DMSC, June 28, 1899, box 40, E 1331; Judge Advocate to AG, DMSC, Sept. 21, 1899, box 1, E 1359; Frank Ives to AG, DMSC, Sept. 28, 1899; Hermon Donn, box 1, E 1361, all RG 395, NARA.

26. L. A. Pérez, *Essays on Cuban History*, 21; H. L. Scott, *Some Memories of a Soldier*, 248–51; E. F. Atkins, *Sixty Years in Cuba*, 314–17; Judge Advocate to AG, DMSC, Sept. 21, 1899, box 1, E 1359; H. C. Carbaugh to AG, DMSC, Sept. 21, 1899; Frank J. Ives to AG, DMSC, Sept. 28, 1899; J. H. Hernandez to Sr. E. S. y Greble, Oct. 14, 1899; Fred J. Foltz to AG, DMSC, Oct. 24, 1899, all box 21; "Statement of Private George W. Van Wyck, Company G., 10th U.S. Infantry," n.d. [ca. Feb. 1900], box 1, E 1363; Walter Barker to Greble, Feb. 21, 1900; Frias to James Wilson, Feb. 23, 1900; Frias to Wilson, Feb. 26, 1900; A. H. Bowman, March 9, 1900, all box 31; Anon. to Wilson, June 6, 1900, and 3rd end., A. H. Bowman, July 14, 1900, box 38; all E 1331, RG 395, NARA; Aug. 18, 1899 session, Actas, 2nd Semestre, 1899, vol. 44, Actas Capitulares, Fondo Ayuntamiento de Cienfuegos, Archivo Histórico Provincial de Cienfuegos; Jose A. Frias to J. R. Kean, Sept. 16, 1901; LR 2362, CD, DC, W. H. Barker, Sept. 23, 1901, both

box 176; Edwin Atkins to Leonard Wood, Feb. 21, 1900; Castano Gaciedo et al. to Wood, Feb. 21, 1900, both box 61; Charles A. P. Hatfield to AG, DC, June 14, 1900, box 98, all E 3, RG 140, NARA.

27. Coffman, *Old Army*, 389; Harrison, *City of Canvas*, 34; Byers, *Sexual Economy of War*, 38–39; US Department of War, *Annual Report of Colonel Samuel M. Whitside*, 100–101; J. H. Dorst to AG, DMSC, July 20, 1899, box 16; Ives to AG, DMSC, March 8, 1900, box 34; Frank Ives to AG, DMSC, May 10, 1900; Artemis Ward to CG, DMSC, May 26, 1900, both box 39; F. P. Fremont to AG, DMSC, June 30, 1900; Chief Surgeon to AG, DMSC, June 30, 1900, both box 40; all E 1331, RG 395, NARA.

28. *ARWD* 1900, vol. 1, pt. 2, 684, 789–90; *ARWD* 1903, vol. 2, 161–62.

29. De Bevoise, *Agents of Apocalypse*, 69–70, 74–76, 84; Bankoff, *Crime, Society, and the State*, 41–44; Camagay, "Prostitution in Nineteenth Century Manila," 248–49; Doeppers, "Migrants in Urban Labor Markets," 255–58; V. Clark, "Labor Conditions in the Philippine Islands," 836–37.

30. De Bevoise, *Agents of Apocalypse*, 76; Bankoff, *Crime, Society, and the State*, 44; Camagay, *Working Women of Manila*, 109–11; Camagay, "Prostitution in Nineteenth Century Manila," 249–51; Dery, *History of the Inarticulate*, 134; Galang, "Living Carriers in the East," 99–100.

31. Camagay, *Working Women of Manila*, 115–16; Bankoff, *Crime, Society, and the State*, 26–27, 41–44; Camagay, "Prostitution in Nineteenth Century Manila," 241–48; De Bevoise, *Agents of Apocalypse*, 76–81.

32. Camagay, *Working Women of Manila*, 115–16; De Bevoise, *Agents of Apocalypse*, 78–84; Camagay, "Prostitution in Nineteenth Century Manila," 254–55; Dery, *History of the Inarticulate*, 135–37, 140–41.

33. De Bevoise, *Agents of Apocalypse*, 69–74; Dery, "Prostitution in Colonial Manila," 483, 488; Camagay, *Working Women of Manila*, 99; Kramer, "Darkness That Enters the Home," 373; Winkelmann, *Dangerous Intercourse*, 29–30; *ARWD* 1898, *Maj.-Gen.*, 54–55; Emiliano R. de Dios to Señor President of the Philippine Revolutionary Government, Aug. 7, 1898, and Emilio Aguinaldo and Leandro Ibarra, decree, Aug. 13, 1898, both Exhibit 96, PIR 312.1, in Taylor, *Philippine Insurrection*, 3:194–95.

34. Trask, *War with Spain*, 384; Hoganson, *Fighting for American Manhood*; Linn, *Philippine War*, 33; De Bevoise, *Agents of Apocalypse*, 85–86; Kramer, *Blood of Government*, 103; Marasigan, "'Between the Devil and the Deep Sea,'" 57–58; Winkelmann, *Dangerous Intercourse*, 42–43; Sheridan, *Filipino Martyrs*, 103–6; Taggart, "California Soldiers in the Philippines," 298–300, 51; Martin, "The Saloon in Manila," 1537–39; US House, *Sale of Beer and Light Wines in Post Exchanges*, 394–498; Davis, *Report on the Military Government of the City of Manila*, 37–39; *ARWD* 1899, vol. 1, pt. 2, 455–56, 459; Emilio Aguinaldo, Sept. 13, 1899, Exhibit 1, in Taylor, *Philippine Insurrection*, 3:23; "Countrymen," Feb. 24, 1899, PIR 17.6, Exhibit 839, in Taylor, *Philippine Insurrection*, 4:595; GO 14, HQ, 1D, 8AC, Nov. 1, 1899, vol. 28, E 783, RG 395, NARA.

35. Rafael, *Motherless Tongues*, 58–59; Davis, *Military Government*, 38–39, 261–62, 265; Circular 6, HQ, 1D, 8AC, Nov. 10, 1898, vol. 1, E 786, RG 395, NARA; Hughes to AG, US Army, Feb. 7, 1902, AGO #343790, box 2307, E 24, RG 94, NARA.

36. Byers, *Sexual Economy of War*, 61; McCoy, *Policing America's Empire*, 70–71; Davis, *Military Government*, 261–62; Hughes to AG, US Army, Feb. 7, 1902, AGO #343790, box 2307, E 24, RG 94, NARA.

37. De Bevoise, *Agents of Apocalypse*, 74–75; Terami-Wadi, "Karayuki-san of Manila," 289, 296–99; Kramer, "Darkness That Enters the Home," 371, 375–76; E. Lee, *At America's Gates*, 30; Davis, *Military Government*, 38, 264–68.

38. De Bevoise, *Agents of Apocalypse*, 74–75; Kramer, "Darkness That Enters the Home," 373–75, 380–90; Doeppers, "Migrants in Urban Labor Markets," 257; Davis, *Military Government*, 275–76; Willis, *Our Philippine Problem*, 256–61; "Must Move Out," *Manila Freedom*, Aug. 31, 1900; A. Lester Hazlett, "A View of the Moral Conditions Existing in the Philippines," March 17, 1902, AGO #343790, E 25, RG 94, NARA.

39. Pivar, "Military, Prostitution, and Colonial Peoples," 257–60; Kramer, "Darkness That Enters the Home," 380–89; Winkelmann, *Dangerous Intercourse*, 34; A. Lester Hazlett, "A View of the Moral Conditions Existing in the Philippines," March 17, 1902, AGO #343790, E 25, RG 94, NARA.

40. Linn, *Philippine War*, 216–17; Tel., Taft to Root, Jan. 19, 1901, quoted in "Moral Conditions in the Philippines," box 2909, E 25, RG 94, NARA; MacArthur to AG, US Army, Feb. 4, 1901, box 246, E 5, RG 350, NARA.

41. "Immoral Women Refused Admission," *Manila American*, Oct. 20, 1899; "Police Raid a House of Ill-Repute," *Manila American*, Nov. 17, 1899; "Three More Deported," *Manila Freedom*, June 9, 1900; "Forced to Shame," *Manila Freedom*, June 23, 1900; "Girl's Life Ruined," *Manila Freedom*, July 12, 1900; Hazlett, "View of the Moral Conditions Existing in the Philippines"; USPC, *Schurman Report*, 1900, vol. 1, 262; Hughes to AG, US Army, Feb. 7, 1902, box 2307, E 25, RG 94, NARA.

42. Gatewood, *"Smoked Yankees,"* 253; S. C. Miller, *"Benevolent Assimilation,"* 187–88; Feuer, *America at War*, 28–29; Linn, *Philippine War*, 123–25, 128; May, *A Past Recovered*, 146–47; Kramer, *Blood of Government*, 148–49; Roces, "Reflections on Gender and Kinship," 32–37; Rafael, *White Love*, 48–51; Winkelmann, *Dangerous Intercourse*, 23–25; Trafton, *We Thought We Could Whip Them*, 22–23; Johnson, "My Life in the U.S. Army," 29, SAWS; Anon. to Countrymen, Feb. 24, 1899, PIR 17.6, Exhibit 839, in Taylor, *Philippine Insurrection*, 4:595–96.

43. Rotundo, *American Manhood*, 120–21; Byers, *Sexual Economy of War*, 47–48; Mrozek, "Habit of Victory," 225–26, 234; Thomas M. Anderson, Oct. 4, 1898, HQ, 1D, 8AC, end. on LR 143, vol. 1, E 770; Edgar J. Mason to AG, 3B, Feb. 5, 1903; "Statement of Private James P. Hurley"; "Statement of Private Rudolph Stiepan," both box 1, E 3015; all RG 395, NARA.

44. Linderman, *Mirror of War*, 64–69; Winkelmann, *Dangerous Intercourse*, 138–50; ARWD 1900, *Mil. Govt. Phil. Civ. Affairs*, 156–57; ARWD 1901, Lt.-Gen., pt. 2, 245–47; J. W. Corcoran to CO, Troop A, 13th Cav., June 2, 1903, box 2, E 3287, RG 395, NARA.

45. "History and Cultural Life of Buraboc," p. 2, reel 3, HDP; Campbell, T. R. J., March 9, 1900, LR 49, Office of Mil. Gov., Albay & Catanduanes, box 3077, GCM, RG 153, NARA. For punishment of an officer who repeatedly exploited legalized prostitution, see P. Davison to Adj., 22nd Inf., Feb. 14, 1900; Sisenando P. Pineda, Presidente del pueblo de Santo Simon to General Otis, Jan. 22, 1900; "Sr. Commandante of the detachment at San Luis"; Harry R. Campbell, Feb. 2, 1900; Harry J. Brown, Feb. 2, 1900; affidavits of Frank Johnson, William J. Ryan, Thomas Blackford, all Feb. 12, 1900; John Luick to AG, 2D, 8AC, Feb. 12, 1900, all box 3286; affidavits of Foley A. Johnson, Edward Morrill, Charles G. Holmes, Gust Anderson, Eugene Baldwin, all Feb. 12, 1900; R. A. Brown to AG, 2D, 8AC, March 7, 1900; "Statements of Natives of San Simon," March 3, 1900; Charge and Specification, 1st Lt. Harry R. Campbell, Feb. 10, 1904, all box 773, E 25, RG 94, NARA.

46. Butler, *Daughters of Joy, Sisters of Misery*, 111–12; McClintock, "Screwing the System," 76–79; Bankoff, "Households of Ill-Repute," 41; Byers, *Sexual Economy of War*, 47–48; *ARWD* 1900, *Lt.-Gen.*, pt. 5, 10–11, 15; Campbell, T. R. J., March 9, 1900, LR 49, Office of Mil. Gov., Albay & Catanduanes, box 3077, GCM, RG 153, NARA.

47. W. Anderson, *Colonial Pathologies*, 64–65; Reyes, *Love, Passion, and Patriotism*, 230; Andaya, "Gender, Warfare, and Patriotism," 4–6; Winkelmann, *Dangerous Intercourse*, 22, 24; Rodney, *As a Cavalryman Remembers*, 60–62, 135–36; F. J. Herman, *Forty-Second Foot*, 85–86; Lucian, *A Soldier's Letter*, 27; MacClintock, "Around the Island of Cebu," 438; Wise, "Notes on Field Service," 27; "Foul Murder in Panay," *Manila Times*, March 3, 1901; R. H. Van Deman to Division Commander, n.d., 1901, folder 1303, roll 80, PIR; Hilaria Ro. Reyes de Aguinaldo, "A Lament," Oct. 5, 1899, PIR 347.3, Exhibit 699, in Taylor, *Philippine Insurrection*, 4:174; 1st end., LR 165, H. N. Ripley, Oct. 18, 1900, vol. 1, E 5586; F. Marcelino, M. Rafuel, and M. Agueva to CO, Vigan, Nov. 8, 1900, box 1, E 5589; R. Williams, June 4, 1903, 1st end., J. W. Corcoran to CO, Troop A, 13th Cav., June 2, 1903, box 2, E 3287, all RG 395, NARA.

48. Camagay, *Working Women of Manila*, 23–24, 37; Seoane, *Beyond the Ranges*, 54; Harper, *Just Outside of Manila*, 46; H. Phelan, "Sanitary Service in Surigao," 16; Johnson, "My Life in the U.S. Army," 21–23; G. E. Seaman, "Some Observations," 188.

49. McClintock, *Imperial Leather*, 21–24; Balce, "Filipina's Breast," 91; Walsh, *Tin Pan Alley and the Philippines*, 118–19; Winkelmann, *Dangerous Intercourse*, 33, 39; Haslam, *Forty Truths*, 90–94; Clements, "Medical Survey of the Town of Taytay," 250–51; G. E. Seaman, "Some Observations," 188; Johnson, "My Life in the U.S. Army," 136; "I Remember," 34–35, box 1, Michael J. Lenihan Papers, both USAHEC; C. Formas, Presidente of Aparri, to Senor Commandante Militar de las fuerzas de los E.U. estadcedar en este pueblo," Dec. 29, 1900, box 1, E 2842; Antonia Vallejo to Señor Coronel, Jan. 4, 1901, box 2, E 5589, both RG 395, NARA.

50. Gatewood, *"Smoked Yankees,"* 262–63, 309–10; Winkelmann, *Dangerous Intercourse*, 39–42; US Senate, *Sale of Intoxicating Liquors*, 49; Magdalena Abayax to E. Huggins, Sept. 20, 1901, box 2, E 4047, RG 395, NARA.

51. May, *Battle for Batangas*, 155; Rafael, *White Love*, 54; Stoler, *Carnal Knowledge and Imperial Power*, 46–51; Greene, "Wages of Empire," 36; Johnson, "My Life in the U.S. Army," 59–60; SAWS; Pefley, questionnaire, SAWS, USAHEC; A. Lester Hazlett, "A View of the Moral Conditions Existing in the Philippines," box 2307, E 25, RG 94, NARA.

52. Doeppers, "Migration to Manila," 145, 149–50; Owen, "Masculinity and National Identity," 35–36; Blanc-Szanton, "Collision of Cultures," 369–70; Reyes, *Love, Passion, and Patriotism*, 117, 121–28; Winkelmann, *Dangerous Intercourse*, 6–7, 10, 52–53, 61, 90, 105–6, 177, 190–91, 197–98; Sawyer, *Inhabitants of the Philippines*, 204–5; Willis, *Our Philippine Problem*, 261; Fee, *Woman's Impressions*, 127; Johnson, "My Life in the U.S. Army," 28–31, 66.

53. US House, *Sale of Beer and Light Wines*, 447–48.

54. Blanc-Szanton, "Collision of Cultures," 352–53; Winkelmann, *Dangerous Intercourse*, 10, 227; Blunt, *Army Officer's Philippine Studies*, 21; Johnson, "My Life in the U.S. Army," 28–31.

55. Schumacher, "Recent Perspectives on the Revolution," 476–77; Johnson, "My Life in the U.S. Army," 28–31; US Census Bureau, *Census of the Philippine Islands*, 3:228, 328.

56. W. Anderson, *Colonial Pathologies*, 40–41, 134–41; "On Filipino Marriages," *Army and Navy Journal*, Feb. 18, 1905; Johnson, "My Life in the U.S. Army," 59–60, 66, 134, 141–42.

57. Bisbee, *Through Four American Wars*, 264–65; Sotero Botallones to CO, Calamba, Nov. 14, 1901, box 1, E 3287, RG 395, NARA.

58. Linn, *Guardians of Empire*, 60, 62–63; Dery, *History of the Inarticulate*, 134; Winkelmann, "Rethinking the Sexual Geography of American Empire in the Philippines," 44–45; Blunt, *Army Officer's Philippine Studies*, 17–19; Johnson, "My Life in the U.S. Army," 138, 142–43; Bryce Disque to Adj. 2B, Oct. 23, 1902, box 1, E 4967, RG 395, NARA.

59. Winkelmann, *Dangerous Intercourse*, 84, 149, 194–96; Capozzola, *Bound by War*, 84; "Secretary Taft's Recommendations for the Army in the Philippines," *Manila Times*, Feb. 24, 1908, cited by Winkelmann, *Dangerous Intercourse*, 239n40; Blunt, *Army Officer's Philippine Studies*, 17; Devins, *American Observer in the Philippines*, 127–28; LS 131, Van Orsdale to AG, Dept. Mindanao, Feb. 17, 1904, vol. 3, E 3530, RG 395, NARA.

60. Gatewood, *"Smoked Yankees,"* 315; Rotundo, *American Manhood*, 140–41; Winkelmann, *Dangerous Intercourse*, 11–12; Johnson, "My Life in the U.S. Army," 60, 66, 142–43.

61. Gatewood, *"Smoked Yankees,"* 243; Helg, "Black Men, Racial Stereotyping, and Violence," 577–78; Marasigan, "'Between the Devil and the Blue Sea,'" 1–2, 75–76; Molnar, *American Mestizos*, chap. 1; Morey, *Fagan*, 176, 215; Greene, "Wages of Empire," 36; Winkelmann, *Dangerous Intercourse*, 9, 59–60, 84–85, 129–31, 196–99; Bonsal, "Negro Soldier in War and Peace," 325–26; Steward, "Two Years in Luzon," 1, 9; Parker, *Old Army*, 238; Taft to Root, April 27, 1901, box 167, Root Papers; A. Lester Hazlett, "A View of the Moral Conditions Existing in the Philippines," box 2307; "Soldiers Allowed to Live with Women," *Canton Morning News*, May 3, 1909, in Stewart A. Romig to Sec. War, May 3, 1909, box 5771; both E 25, RG 94, NARA. Taft's ban on Black soldiers in the Philippines continued until 1907, when, despite his wishes that they be restricted to the Moro Province, Leonard Wood deployed them there and on Samar to fight Pulahanes; see Linn, *Guardians of Empire*, 60–61.

62. Kramer, "Darkness That Enters the Home," 393; Davis, *Military Government*, 262–63, 268–69.

63. Kramer, "Darkness That Enters the Home," 389–91; Wintermute, *Public Health and the U.S. Military*, 212–16; Byers, *Sexual Economy of War*, 65–69; ARWD 1899, *Reports of Chiefs of Bureaus*, 450; ARWD 1899, vol. 1, pt. 2, 488; LR 65, Harry Smusk to CO, Calamba, Feb. 17, 1901, and 1st end., Herman Hall, Feb. 18, 1901; C. P. Terrett to AG, 2D, DSL, Feb. 18, 1901; J. F. Stretch to J. W. McHarg, March 19, 1901; Porter V. Ballou to Chief Surgeon, DSL, June 30, 1901; 1st end., L. M. Maus, July 3, 1901, and 2nd end., L. Suplineen, July 6, 1901, all box 1, E 3287, RG 395, NARA.

64. ARWD 1901, vol. 1, pt. 2, 709–10; LS 29, AGO #416181, Wilbur Crafts to Theodore Roosevelt, Jan. 14, 1902, box 2909, E 25, RG 94, NARA; James Partello to Marcel Gustrat, Feb. 27, 1902, vol. 1, E 3623, RG 395, NARA.

65. Kramer, "Darkness That Enters the Home," 389–95; Theodore Roosevelt, March 18, 1902, Circ. No. 10, US Army HQ, reprinted in GO 6, HQ, DP, Jan. 31, 1905, AGO #427646, box 2984, E 25, RG 94, NARA.

66. Kramer, "Darkness That Enters the Home," 389–95; Byers, *Sexual Economy of War*, 2, 62–63; Root to Wright, Feb. 18, 1902, file 2039, box 246, E 5, RG 350, NARA.

67. Winkelmann, *Dangerous Intercourse*, 70–74; US Senate, *Affairs of Philippine Islands*, vol. 2, 1746–50, 1854–85, 1873; Clarence R. Edwards to Margaret Dye Ellis, April 3, 1902, box 246, E 5, RG 350, NARA.

68. Ordinance 27, Municipal Board of the City of Manila, March 18, 1902; *RPC* 1903, pt. 1, 37; *RPC* 1905, pt. 2, 19; A. Lester Hazlett, "A View of the Moral Conditions Existing in the Philippines," box 2307; Act #709, Philippine Commission, March 28, 1903, box 2415, both E 25, RG 94, NARA; E. C. Carter, 2nd end., Jan. 10, 1905, on "A Horrible Story," box 246, E 5, RG 350, NARA.

69. Wintermute, *Public Health and the U.S. Military*, 212–16; Mervin Maus File, AGO #746ACP, box 765, E 25, RG 94, NARA.

70. Maus, "Venereal Diseases in the United States Army," 132, 135, 137–38.

71. Wintermute, *Public Health and the U.S. Military*, 209–11; *ARWD* 1901, *Lt.-Gen.*, pt. 2, 192–93; *ARWD* 1901, vol. 1, pt. 2, 670–71; *ARWD* 1902, *Sec. War and Chiefs of Bureaus*, 622; *ARWD* 1911, vol. 1, 486–87; H. C. Corbin to Mil. Sec., War Dept., Feb. 6, 1905; GO 6, HQ, PD, Jan. 31, 1905; GO 185, WD, Nov. 2, 1905, all in AGO #427646, box 2984, E 25, RG 94, NARA.

72. Schwartz, *Pleasure Island*, 24–25; *ARWD* 1901, *Lt.-Gen.*, pt. 2, 264; J. F. Bell, "Memorandum for the Provisional Governor," Oct. 24, 1906; Paul B. Malone to Judge of the 1st Instance, Jan. 11, 1907; Malone to Arturo Nespereira, Jan. 12, 1907, both box 1, E 1014; Circ. 4, HQ, ACP, Jan. 11, 1907; John H. Stone to Adj., Matanzas, Cuba, June 12, 1907, both box 4, E 974; all RG 395, NARA.

73. LR 646, Camp Camaguey, May 2, 1908, box 1, E 1054, RG 395, NARA.

74. Thomas to AG, ACP, March 31, 1907; E. D. Thomas to AG, March 25, 1907; Thomas to AG, ACP, March 26, 1907; Tel., W. A. Mann to Thomas, March 25, 1907; all case files 96, box 4, E 5, RG 199, NARA.

75. Gregorio Llano y Raymat, March 25, 1907, box 1, E 1134, NARA 395; E. D. Thomas to AG, March 25, 1907; affidavits, Robert E. Cotti, John D. Costello, and Bert Ashby, all March 31, 1907; all case files 96, box 4, RG 199, NARA.

76. Logan, "Conspirators, Pawns, and Patriots and Brothers," 19; "Pinar del Rio, 8 of April 1907," box 1, E 1134; "Tumulto en Pinar del Rio," *El Mundo*, Nov. 18, 1907; Tel., Parker to AG, Marianao, Nov. 17, 1907; GO 51, PDR, Nov. 17, 1907; James Parker to Chief of Police, PDR, Nov. 18, 1907; Parker to Waltz, Nov. 19, 1907, all box 40, E 977; all RG 395, NARA.

77. Stoner, *From the House to the Streets*; Logan, "Conspirators, Pawns, and Patriots and Brothers," 16; "Noticias de Pinar del Rio," box 22, E 977; "Subject-Chief of Police Havana," Feb. 4, 1907, Office of the Provost Marshal, HQ, ACP; Paul B. Malone to CO, USS *Columbia*, Feb. 18, 1907; Malone to Judge, Court of First Instance, Marianao, Cuba, Feb. 25, 1907; "Translation of Capt. Paul B. Malone," Office of the Provost Marshal, HQ, ACP, March 5, 1907, all box 2, E 1014; all RG 395, NARA.

78. Furlong, memo for Chief of Staff, Feb. 17, 1908, folder 225, box 10, E 5, RG 199, NARA.

Epilogue

1. Gowing, *Mandate in Moroland*, 260; Abinales, "American Colonial State"; Kramer, *Blood of Government*, 345–46.

2. Rosenberg, *Spreading the American Dream*; Benton and Clulow, "Long, Strange History of Protection."

3. Millett, *Semper Fidelis*, 155–63, 212–13; Greene, *Canal Builders*, 19, 88; Maurer, *Empire Trap*, 60–75; Droessler, *Coconut Colonialism*, 8, 11.

4. Millett, *Semper Fidelis*, 168; Kramer, *Blood of Government*, 352–56; Maurer, *Empire Trap*, 99–102, 108, 112–13, 119–22, 137–40; Hopkins, *American Empire*, 450–52, 546; Ekbladh, *Great American Mission*, 16–18.

5. L. A. Pérez, *Army Politics in Cuba*, 10–20; Linn, *U.S. Army and Counterinsurgency*, 77, 81–82; Linn, *Philippine-American War*, 128, 215–16, 260; Kramer, *Blood of Government*, 318–19; Linn, *Guardians of Empire*, 19; Capozzola, *Bound by War*, chaps. 1–2; *ARWD* 1902, vol. 9, 203; Parker, "Some Random Notes on Fighting in the Philippines," 337–39; Powell, "Utilization of Native Troops in Our Foreign Possessions," 36.

6. Linn, "Intelligence and Low-Intensity Conflict in the Philippine War," 100–103; Bickel, *Mars Learning*, 213–19; McCoy, *Policing America's Empire*, 26–29, 76–82; Linn, *Guardians of Empire*, 30–34, 47; Charbonneau, *Civilizational Imperatives*, 180–81; Howland, "Field Service in Mindanao"; Wise, "Notes on Field Service in Samar," 28–29; Palmer, *America in Arms*, 135–48; *ARWD* 1912, 69–153.

7. Kramer, *Blood of Government*, 203–204; Rafael, *Motherless Tongues*, 44–45; *ARWD* 1902, vol. 9, 205.

8. Millet, *Politics of Intervention*, 131–32; Parker, *Old Army*, 400; Millet, *General*, 195; Bullard, "Preparing Our Moros for Government," 388; Bullard, "Military Pacification," 15–16; Bullard, "The Army in Cuba," 153.

9. May, *Social Engineering in the Philippines*, 89–93, 113–26; Bankoff, "Wants, Wages, and Workers," 73–76; Bankoff, "'These Brothers of Ours,'" 1050–52; Capozzola, "Secret Soldiers' Union."

10. Calder, *Impact of Intervention*, 49–54; San Miguel and Berryman, "Peasant Resistance to State Demands in the Cibao," 44–48; Renda, *Taking Haiti*, 32–33, 139–51; Gobat, *Confronting the American Dream*, 216–17; Herman, *Cooperating with the Colossus*, chap. 3; Heefner, "Building the Bases of Empire"; Cosby, "Work of the Army in the Construction and Maintenance of Roads"; Scott, *Some Memories of a Soldier*, 627–28.

11. Jensen, *Chinese in the Philippines*, 32, 36; Kramer, *Blood of Government*, 349–50; Alejandrino, *History of the 1902 Chinese Exclusion Act*, 40–44; Chu, *Chinese and Chinese Mestizos of Manila*, 295, 297, 322–30; Wong, *Chinese in the Philippine Economy*, 50–51, 59–73.

12. Daniels, *Guarding the Golden Door*, 39, 94, 150; Harrod, *Manning the New Navy*, 34–36; Reckner, "'Men behind the Guns,'" 95–107; Baldoz, *Third Asiatic Invasion*, 46, 248n2; Espiritu, *Home Bound*, 28; Urban, "Asylum in the Midst of Chinese Exclusion"; Fredman, *Tormented Alliance*.

13. Baldoz, *Third Asiatic Invasion*, 32–33, 49–69; Kramer, *Blood of Government*, 397–98, 406–18, 423–28; Capozzola, *Bound by War*, 219–20; de Leon, *Bundok*, chaps. 5 and 6.

14. Wintermute, *Public Health and the U.S. Military*, 205–12; Byers, *Sexual Economy of War*, 59, 71–78.

15. Wintermute, *Public Health and the U.S. Military*, 212–18; Byers, *Sexual Economy of War*, 11–12, 97–99; Molnar, *American Mestizos*, chap. 7; Capozzola, *Bound by War*, 304–6; Lipman, *Guantánamo*, 109–17; Vuic, "Girl in Every Port?," 98–104.

16. Wooster, *United States Army and the Making of America*, 1–3, 279; Rafael, *Motherless Tongues*, 115–9; Moore, *Empire's Labor*, 1–4, 29–34, 46–48, 91–98; Norwood, *Fifty Thousand Miles*, 31–32.

Bibliography

Primary Sources

ARCHIVES

Cuba
   Archivo del Museo Histórico Emilio Bacardí, Santiago de Cuba
      Fondo Demetrio Castillo Duany
   Archivo Histórico Provincial de Cienfuegos
   Archivo Histórico Provincial de Pinar del Río, Pinar del Río
      Fondo Consejo Provincial
      Fondo Gobierno Provincial
   Archivo Nacional de la República de Cuba, Havana
      Fondo Secretaria de la Presidencia
         Obras Públicas
   Archivo Provincial de Santiago de Cuba, Santiago de Cuba
      Actas Capitulares
      Fondo Gobierno Provincial
Philippines
   Philippine National Archives, Manila
      Prestación Personal
      Spanish Document Section
   Philippines National Library, Manila
      Historical Data Papers
      Philippine Revolutionary Papers
United States
   California
      Bancroft Library, University of California, Berkeley
         David P. Barrow Papers
         Oscar F. Long Papers
      California Museum of Photography, University of California, Riverside
         Keystone-Mast Collection
   Georgia
      Manuscript, Archives, and Rare Book Library, Emory University, Atlanta
         Archibald Willingham Butt Letters
   Louisiana
      Jackson Barracks Museum, Louisiana National Guard Archives, New Orleans
         V. G. Bell Collection
   Maryland
      National Archives and Records Administration, College Park
         Record Group 111-SC: Prints Relating to the Spanish-American War

340 Bibliography

      Record Group 140: Records of the Military Government of Cuba
      Record Group 350: Records of the Bureau of Insular Affairs
      Record Group 350-P: Photographs of the Philippine Islands, 1898,
         Bureau of Insular Affairs Prints
Massachusetts
   Houghton Library, Harvard University, Cambridge
      William Cameron Forbes Papers
   Massachusetts Historical Society, Boston
      Atkins Family Papers
Michigan
   Clements Library Special Collections, University of Michigan, Ann Arbor
      Albert F. Gudatt Papers
   Bentley Historical Library, University of Michigan, Ann Arbor
      Dean C. Worcester Papers
      Military Order of the Loyal Legion of the United States, Michigan Commandery
         Records
Montana
   Merrill G. Burlingame Archives and Special Collections, Montana State University,
      Bozeman
      James Worden Pope Papers
North Carolina
   Duke University, Special Collections Library, Raleigh
      George Percival Scriven Papers
Pennsylvania
   US Army Heritage and Education Center, Carlisle
      Frederick J. Podas Papers
      George W. Davis Papers
      John M. Heller Papers
      Julius A. Penn Photographs
      Matthew A. Batson Papers
      Michael J. Lenihan Papers
      Pearl M. Shaffer Papers
      Samuel B. M. Young Papers
      Spanish-American War Survey
      Tasker H. Bliss Papers
      Thomas S. Wylly Papers
      Walter R. Cutter Papers
      William Dinwiddie Papers
      William H. Bowen Papers
      William Wright Harts Papers
Virginia
   MacArthur Memorial Archives and Library, Norfolk
      Harold Palmer Howard Papers
   Marine Corps History Division, Archives Branch, Quantico
      Littleton W. T. Waller Papers

Washington, DC
  Library of Congress
    Elihu Root Papers
    Frank R. McCoy Papers
    Henry T. Allen Papers
    Henry W. Lawton Papers
    Hermann Hagedorn Papers
    Hugh Scott Papers
    John J. Pershing Papers
    Leonard Wood Papers
    Robert L. Bullard Papers
    Tasker Bliss Papers
    Theodore Roosevelt Papers
    William Howard Taft Papers
    William T. McKinley Papers
  National Archives and Records Administration
    Philippine Insurgent Records, microfilm
    Record Group 92: Records of the Office of the Quartermaster General, Army
    Record Group 94: Records of the Adjutant General's Office, Army
    Record Group 112: Records of the Office of the Surgeon General, Army
    Record Group 153: Records of the Judge Advocate General, Army
    Record Group 199: Records of the Provisional Government of Cuba
    Record Group 395: Records of US Army Overseas Operations and Commands, 1898–1942
Wisconsin
  Wisconsin Historical Society, ARC Stout, Madison
    Philip Reade Papers
Wyoming
  American Heritage Collection, University of Wyoming, Laramie
    Richard H. Wilson Papers

NEWSPAPERS AND PERIODICALS

Aparri News
Atlanta Constitution
Baltimore Sun
Chattanooga Times
Chicago Daily Tribune
Coast Seamen's Journal
El Cubano (Santiago de Cuba)
El Mundo (Pinar del Río)
El Porvenir (Santiago de Cuba)
La Higiene (Havana)
La Lucha (Havana)
La Patria (Sagua la Grande)
La Tribuna (Cienfuegos)
Libertad (Cienfuegos)
Los Angeles Times
Manila American
Manila Freedom
Manila Times
New York Sun
New York Times
New York Tribune
Revista de Agricultura (Havana)

342 Bibliography

San Francisco Chronicle
Times of Cuba (Santiago de Cuba)
United States Army and Navy Journal

Washington Evening Sun
Washington Post

CUBAN GOVERNMENT PUBLICATIONS

Alfonso, Ramon M. *La prostitución en Cuba y especialmente en la Habana*. Havana: P. Fernández y Cía, 1902.
Diaz, Manuel L. *Memoria de Obras Públicas correspendiente al periodo de 20 de Mayo de 1902 a 30 de Junio de 1903*. Havana: Rambla y Bouza, 1904.
Magoon, Charles E. *Republic of Cuba: Report of Provisional Administration, from October 13th, 1906 to December 1, 1907*. Havana: Rambla and Bouza, 1908.
Olmstead, Victor H. *Censo de la República de Cuba bajo la Administración Provisional de los Estados Unidos, 1907*. Washington, DC: Oficino del Censo, de los Estados Unidos, 1908.
Reglamento para el régimen de la prostitución en la ciudad de la Habana, 1899. Havana: Imprenta del "Aviador Commercial," 1899.

US GOVERNMENT PUBLICATIONS

Davis, George W. *Report on the Military Government of the City of Manila, P.I., from 1898 to 1901*. Manila: Headquarters, Division of the Philippines, 1901.
Magoon, Charles E. *Government of Cuba*, 61st Cong., 1st Sess., Doc. No. 80. Washington, DC: GPO, 1909.
Porter, Robert P. *Appendix to the Report on the Commercial and Industrial Conditions of the Island of Cuba*. Washington, DC: GPO, 1899.
———. *Report on the Commercial and Industrial Condition of the Island of Cuba*. Washington, DC: GPO, 1898.
United States. *Correspondence Relating to the War with Spain, Including the Insurrection in the Philippine Islands and the China Relief Expedition*. 2 vols. Washington, DC: GPO, 1901.
United States. House of Representatives.
———. *Reciprocity with Cuba*, 57th Cong., 1st Sess., Doc. No. 535. Washington, DC: GPO, 1902.
———. *Sale of Beer and Light Wines in Post Exchanges*. 57th Cong., 2nd Sess., Doc. No. 252. Washington, DC: GPO, 1903.
United States Bureau of Public Works. *Capataz Manual of Road Work*. Manila: Bureau of Public Works, 1909.
United States Census Bureau. *Census of the Philippine Islands, 1903*. 5 vols. Washington, DC: GPO, 1903.
———. *Cuba: Population, History, Resources, 1907*. Washington: United States Bureau of the Census, 1909.
United States Congress. "Municipal Government in the Philippine Islands." 56th Cong., 1st Sess., Doc. No. 659. Washington, DC: GPO, 1900.
———. *Philippine Tariff*, 59th Cong., 1st Sess., 1905. Washington, DC: GPO, 1906.
———. *Public Hearings in the Philippine Islands Upon the Proposed Reduction of the Tariff upon Philippine Sugar and Tobacco*. Manila: Bureau of Public Printing, 1905.

United States Department of State. *Papers Relating to the Foreign Relations of the United States.* 1898–1902. Washington, DC: GPO, 1898–1902.
United States Department of War. *Annual Report of Charles E. Magoon, Provisional Governor of Cuba, to the Secretary of War, 1907.* Washington, DC: GPO, 1908.
———. *Annual Report of Colonel Samuel M. Whitside, 10th U.S. Cavalry, Commanding Department of Santiago and Puerto Principe, 1900.* Adjutant General's Office: Santiago, August 1900.
———. *Annual Report of the War Department.* Washington, DC: GPO, 1898–1913.
———. *Informe sobre el censo de Cuba, 1899.* Washington, DC: GPO, 1900.
———. *Military Notes on Cuba, November 1898.* Washington, DC: GPO, 1898.
———. *Military Notes on Cuba, 1909.* Washington, DC: GPO, 1909.
———. *Report of Lieutenant W. G. Caples, Corps of Engineers, U.S. Army, Upon the Construction of the Calamba-Batangas Road, Luzon, P.I.* Washington: Press of the Engineer School of Application, Washington Barracks, 1903.
———. *Report of the Philippine Commission to the President.* 2 vols. Washington, DC: GPO, 1900.
———. *Report of the Provisional Governor of Cuba, from December 1, 1907 to December 1, 1908.* Washington, DC: GPO, 1909.
———. *Report on the Census of Cuba, 1899.* Washington, DC: GPO, 1900.
United States Philippine Commission. *Acts of the Philippine Commission.* Washington, DC: GPO, 1903–1907.
———. *Public Laws and Resolutions.* Washington, DC: GPO, 1901.
———. *Report of the Philippine Commission to the President.* 2 vols. Washington, DC: GPO, 1900.
———. *Reports of the United States Philippine Commission.* Washington, DC: GPO, 1900–1913.
United States, Philippine Islands. *Annual Report of the Governor of the Province of Moro.* 1904–1913. Washington, DC: GPO, 1904.
United States Senate. *Affairs in the Philippine Islands.* Parts 1–3. Washington, DC: GPO, 1902.
———. *Chinese Exclusion*, 57th Cong., 1st Sess., Rep't 776, pt. 1. Washington, DC: GPO, 1902.
———. *The Establishment of Free Government in Cuba*, 58th Cong., 2nd Sess., Doc. 312. Washington, DC: GPO, 1904.
———. *Issuance of Certain Military Orders in the Philippines*, 57th Cong., 1st Sess., Doc. No. 347. Washington, DC: GPO, 1902.
———. *Report of the Commission Appointed by the President to Investigate the Conduct of the War Department in the War with Spain*, 56th Cong., 1st Sess., Doc. No. 221. Washington, DC: GPO, 1900. 8 vols.
———. *Sale of Intoxicating Liquors at the Army Canteens. Hearings Before the Committee on Military Affairs, United States Senate. December 7, 8, 11, 12, 13, and 14.* Washington, DC: GPO, 1900.
———. *Statements of Major-General Leonard Wood, U.S.V., Department of Santiago, Cuba, Made January 18 and 19, 1899.* Washington, DC: GPO, 1899.
United States Senate, Committee on Relations with Cuba. *Statement of the Secretary of War of Expenditures Made under the Heading of "Agriculture, Industry, Commerce, and Public Works" in the Island of Cuba, from January 1, 1899, to April 30, 1899, as Audited.* Washington, DC: GPO, 1900.

BOOKS

Adams, William L. *The Exploits and Adventures of a Soldier Ashore and Afloat*. Philadelphia: J. B. Lippincott, 1911.
Alfonso, Ramon M. *La reglamentacion de la prostitucion en Cuba*. Habana: Imprenta el siglo XX, 1912.
Alger, Russell A. *The Spanish-American War*. New York: Harper & Bros., 1901.
Ataviado, Elias M. *The Philippine Revolution in the Bicol Region*. 2 vols. Quezon City: New Day, 2011.
Atkins, Edwin F. *Sixty Years in Cuba*. Cambridge, MA: Arno Press, 1926.
Atkins, John Black. *The War in Cuba: The Experience of an Englishman with the United States Army*. London: Smith, Elder, 1899.
Bacardí y Moreau, Emilio. *Crónicas de Santiago de Cuba*. Vol. 10., 2nd ed. Madrid: Gráf Breogán, 1973.
Baker, Charles F. *A History of the 30th Infantry, U.S. Volunteers, in the Philippine Insurrection, 1899–1901*. Clarkston, WA: Clarkston Herald, 1934.
Bangs, John Kendrick. *Uncle Sam Trustee*. New York: Riggs, 1902.
Barton, Clara. *A Story of the Red Cross: Glimpses of Field Work*. New York: D. Appleton, 1918.
Bigelow, John, Jr. *Reminiscences of the Santiago Campaign*. New York: Harper & Bros., 1899.
Bisbee, William H. *Through Four American Wars*. Boston: Meador, 1931.
Blunt, J. Y. Mason. *An Army Officer's Philippine Studies*. Manila: University Press, 1912.
Bolton, H. W. *History of the Second Regiment Illinois Volunteer Infantry from Organization to Muster-Out*. Chicago: R. R. Donnelly & Sons, 1899.
Bowe, John. *With the 13th Minnesota in the Philippines*. Minneapolis: A.B. Farnham, 1905.
Brown, Fred R. *History of the Ninth U.S. Infantry, 1799–1909*. Chicago: R. R. Donnelley & Sons, 1909.
Brown, John Clifford. *Gentleman Soldier: John Clifford Brown and the Philippine-American War*. Edited by Joseph P. McCallus. College Station: Texas A&M University Press, 2004.
Buck, Beaumont B. *Memories of Peace and War*. San Antonio, TX: Naylor, 1935.
Butt, Archibald W. *Both Sides of the Shield*. Philadelphia: J. B. Lippincott, 1912.
Carter, Robert D. *A Civilian in Lawton's 1899 Philippine Campaign: The Letters of Robert D. Carter*. Edited by Michael E. Shay. St. Louis: University of Missouri Press, 2013.
Chadwick, French Ensor. *The Relations of the United States and Spain: The Spanish-American War*. 2 vols. New York: Charles Scribner's Sons, 1911.
Chamberlin, Frederick. *The Philippine Problem, 1898–1913*. Boston: Little, Brown, 1913.
Clark, Edward B. *William L. Sibert: The Army Engineer*. Philadelphia: Dorrance, 1930.
Collazo, Enrique. *Los americanos en Cuba*. Havana: Editorial de Ciencias Sociales, 1972; 1st ed., 1905.
Coston, W. Hilary. *The Spanish-American War Volunteer*. Middletown, PA: Author, 1899.
Crane, Charles Judson. *The Experiences of a Colonel of Infantry*. New York: Knickerbocker Press, 1923.
Crane, Stephen. *The War Dispatches of Stephen Crane*. Edited by R. W. Stallman and E. R. Hagemann. New York: New York University Press, 1964.

———. *Wounds in the Rain: A Collection of Stories Relating to the Spanish-American War of 1898.* London: Methuen, 1900.
Cullum, George. *Biographical Register of the Officers and Graduates of the U.S. Military Academy at West Point, New York, since Its Establishment in 1802.* 8 vols. 3rd ed., rev. and exp. Boston: Houghton, Mifflin, 1891.
———. *Supplement.* Vol. 5. Edited by Charles Braden. Saginaw, MI: Seeman & Peters, 1910.
Currier, Charles Elliot. *In the Early Days; Philippine Sketches.* New York: Broadway, 1914.
Davis, Oscar King. *Our Conquests in the Pacific.* New York: Frederick A. Stokes, 1898.
Detrick, Charles R. *History of the Operations of the First Regiment California U.S. Volunteer Infantry in the Campaign in the Philippine Islands.* N.p., 1899.
Devins, John Bancroft. *An American Observer in the Philippines: Or, Life in Our New Possessions.* Boston: American Tract Society, 1905.
El archipiélago Filipino. Washington: Imprenta del gobierno, 1900.
Elliot, Charles Burke. *The Philippines, to the End of the Commission Government.* Indianapolis: Bobbs-Merrill, 1917.
Faust, Karl Irving. *Campaigning in the Philippines.* San Francisco: Hicks-Judd, 1899.
Fee, Mary H. *A Woman's Impressions of the Philippines.* Chicago: A. C. McClurg, 1912.
Forbes, William Cameron. *The Philippine Islands.* 2 vols. Boston: Houghton Mifflin, 1928.
Foreman, John. *The Philippine Islands.* Shanghai: Kelly & Walsh, 1906.
Funston, Frederick. *Memories of Two Wars: Cuban and Philippine Experiences.* New York: C. Scribner's Sons, 1911.
Ganzhorn, Jack. *I've Killed Men: An Epic of Early Arizona.* London: Robert Hale, 1940.
Gauvreau, Charles F. *Reminiscences of the Spanish-American War in Cuba and the Philippines.* Rouses Point, NY: The Authors, 1915.
George, Jesse. *Our Army and Navy in the Orient.* Manila: Chofré, 1899.
Goode, W. T. *The Eighth Illinois.* Chicago: Blakely, 1899.
Gutierrez, Rafael. *Oriente Heróica.* Santiago, Cuba: Tipografia el Nuevo Mundo, 1915.
Hagedorn, Hermann. *Leonard Wood: A Biography.* 2 vols. New York: Harper & Bros., 1931.
Hard, Curtis V. *Banners in the Air: The Eighth Ohio Volunteers and the Spanish-American War.* Edited by Robert H. Ferrell. Kent, OH: Kent State University Press, 1988.
Haslam, Andrew J. *Forty Truths and Other Truths.* Manila: Philippines Publishing, 1900.
Hemment, John C. *Cannon and Camera.* New York: D. Appleton, 1898.
Herman, Frederick J. *The Forty-Second Foot: A History of the Forty-Second Regiment of Infantry United States Volunteers.* Kansas City: n.p., 1942.
Hobbs, Horace. *Kris and Krag: Adventures among the Moros of the Southern Philippine Islands.* S.I.: Hobbs, 1962.
Holme, John G. *The Life of Leonard Wood.* New York: Doubleday Page, 1920.
Hoyt, Henry F. *A Frontier Doctor.* Boston: Houghton Mifflin, 1929.
Hyatt, Pulaski F., and John T. Hyatt. *Cuba: Its Resources and Opportunities.* New York: J. S. Ogilvie, 1898.
Isselhard, Jacob. *The Filipino in Every-Day Life: An Interesting and Instructive Narrative of the Personal Observations of an American Soldier during the Late Philippine Insurrection.* Chicago: author, 1904.
Jagor, Fedor. *Travels in the Philippines.* London: Chapman and Hall, 1875.

Johnson, Arthur C. *Official History of the Operations of the First Colorado Infantry, U.S.V., in the Campaign in the Philippine Islands.* San Francisco: n.p., 1899.

Kennan, George. *Campaigning in Cuba.* New York: Century, 1899.

Kohr, Herbert O. *Around the World with Uncle Sam; or, Six Years in the United States Army.* Akron, OH: Commercial Print Co., 1907.

Lacosta, Perfecto. "Opportunities in Cuba." In *Opportunities in the Colonies and Cuba.* New York: Lewis, Scribner, 1902.

Landor, A. Henry Savage. *The Gems of the East: Sixteen Thousand Miles of Research Travel among Wild and Tame Tribes of Enchanting Islands.* New York: Harper & Brothers, 1904.

LeRoy, James A. *The Americans in the Philippines.* 2 vols. Boston: Houghton Mifflin, 1914.

Lininger, Clarence. *The Best War at the Time.* New York: Robert Speller & Sons, 1964.

Los Chinos en Filipinas; males que se experimentan actualmente y peligros de esa ceciente inmigración. Manila: Establecimiento tipográfico de "La Oceania Española," 1886.

Lynk, Miles V. *The Black Troopers, or the Daring Heroism of the Negro Soldiers in the Spanish-American War.* Jackson, Tennessee: M. V. Lynk Publishing, 1899.

Markey, Joseph I. *From Iowa to the Philippines: A History of Company M, Fifty-First Iowa Volunteers.* Red Oak, IA: T.D. Murphy Co., 1900.

Martí, José. *Martí on the U.S.A.,* transl. Luis A. Baralt. Carbondale: Southern Illinois University Press, 1966.

Matthews, Franklin. *New-Born Cuba.* New York: Harper & Bros., 1899.

McAlexander, Ulysses G. *History of the Thirteenth Regiment, United States Infantry, Compiled from Regimental Records and Other Sources.* Regimental Press, Thirteenth Infantry, F.D. Gunn, 1905.

McCard, Harry Stanton. *History of the Eighth Illinois United States Volunteers.* Chicago: E. F. Harman, 1899.

McManus, Joseph Forde Anthony. *Soldier Life in the Philippines.* Milwaukee: Riverside Printing Company, n.d. [ca. 1900].

Miles, Perry L. *Fallen Leaves: Memories of an Old Soldier.* Berkeley: Wuerth, 1961.

Miley, John D. *In Cuba with Shafter.* New York: C. Scribner's Sons, 1899.

Miller, Theodore Westwood. *Theodore W. Miller, Rough Rider: His Diary as a Soldier Together with the Story of His Life.* Akron, OH: Privately printed, 1899.

Millett, Frank Davis. *The Expedition to the Philippines.* New York: Harper and Brothers, 1899.

Moss, James Alfred. *Memories of the Campaign of Santiago. June 6, 1898–Aug. 18, 1898.* San Francisco: Press of the Mysell-Rollins Company, 1899.

Muecke Bertel, Carlos. *Patria y Libertad; en defensa del ejército libertador de Cuba como aliado de los americanos en 1898.* Camagüey, Cuba: Ramentol & Boan, 1928.

Nielsen, Thomas Solevad, ed. *Inside the Fighting First: Papers of a Nebraska Private in the Philippine War.* Blair, NE: Lur, 2001.

Norwood, John Wall. *Fifty Thousand Miles with Uncle Sam's Army.* Waynesville, NC: Enterprise, 1912.

Noyes, Theodore W. *Oriental America and Its Problems.* Washington, DC: Press of Judd & Detweiler, 1903.

Orton, Arthur W. *An Up-to-Date History of the 39th U.S. Vol. Inf. ("Bullard's Indians").* 39th US Volunteer Infantry Association, 1949.

Parker, James. *The Old Army: Memories, 1872–1918.* Philadelphia: Dorrance, 1929.

Pepper, Charles. *To-Morrow in Cuba*. New York: Young People's Missionary Movement of the United States and Canada, 1910.
Pershing, John J. *My Life before the World War, 1866–1917: A Memoir*. Lexington: University Press of Kentucky, 2013.
Porter, Robert P. *Industrial Cuba*. New York: G. P. Putnam, 1899.
Post, Charles Johnson. *The Little War of Private Post: The Spanish-American War Seen Up Close*. Lincoln, NE: University of Nebraska Press, 1999.
Rodney, George Brydges. *As a Cavalryman Remembers*. Caldwell, ID: Caxton Printers, 1944.
Roosevelt, Theodore. *The Rough Riders*. New York: Scribner, 1902.
Rousseau, Pablo L., and Pablo Díaz de Villegas. *Memoria descriptiva, histórica y biográfica de Cienfuegos y las fiestas del premer centenario de la fundación de esta ciudad, 1819–1919*. Habana: Establecimiento Tipogràfico "el siglo xx," 1920.
Rynning, Thomas H. *Gun Notches: The Life of a Cowboy-Soldier*. New York: Frederick A. Stokes Co., 1931.
Saleeby, Najeeb. *The History of Sulu*. Manila: Bureau of Printing, 1908.
———. *The Moro Problem: An Academic Discussion of the History and Solution of the Problem of the Government of the Moros of the Philippine Islands*. Manila: n.p., 1913.
Sargent, Herbert H. *The Campaign of Santiago de Cuba*. 3 vols. Chicago: A. C. McClurg, 1907.
Sastrón, Manuel. *Filipinas; pequeños estudios; Batangas y su provincia*. Malabong: n.p., 1895.
Sawyer, Frederic H. *The Inhabitants of the Philippines*. New York: Charles Scribner's Sons, 1900.
Scheidnagel, Manuel d. *Distrito de Benguet. Memoria descriptiva y económica, acompañada del primer plan-cróquis del mismo*. Madrid: Imprenta de la Direccion General de Infanterio, 1898.
Scott, Hugh L. *Some Memories of a Soldier*. New York: Century, 1928.
Seoane, Consuelo Andrew. *Beyond the Ranges*. New York: Robert Speller, 1960.
Sheridan, Richard Brinsley. *The Filipino Martyrs: A Story of the Crime of February 4, 1899*. London: John Lane; The Bodley Head, 1900.
Society of Santiago de Cuba. *The Santiago Campaign: Reminiscences of the Operations for the Capture of Santiago de Cuba in the Spanish-American War, June and July, 1898*. Richmond, VA: Williams Printing, 1927.
Sorley, Lewis S. *History of the Fourteenth United States Infantry, from January, 1890 to December, 1908*. Chicago: R. H. Donnelley & Sons, 1909.
Steele, J. M. *Official History of the Operations of the Twentieth Kansas Infantry, U.S.V., in the Campaign in the Philippine Islands*. San Francisco: n.p., 1899.
Steward, Theophilus G. *The Colored Regulars in the United States Army*. Philadelphia: A.M.E. Book Concern, 1904.
St. Louis, Private/Private Alfred C. Petty. *Forty Years Later*. Boston: Chapman & Grimes, 1939.
Taylor, John R. M., comp. *The Philippine Insurrection against the United States: A Compilation of Documents*. 5 vols. Pasay City, Philippines: Eugenio Lopez Foundation, 1971.
Telfer, George. *Manila Envelopes: Oregon Volunteer Lt. George F. Telfer's Spanish-American War Letters*. Edited by Sara Bunnett. Portland: Oregon Historical Society Press, 1987.
Trafton, William Oliver. *We Thought We Could Whip Them in Two Weeks*. Edited by William Henry Scott. Quezon City: New Day, 1990.

Villamor, Juan. *Inedita cronica de la guerra americano-filipina en el norte de Luzon, 1899–1901.* Manila: Imprenta Juan Fajardo, 1924.

Vivian, Thomas J. *The Fall of Santiago.* New York: R. F. Fenno, 1898.

Wagner, Arthur L. *Report of the Santiago Campaign, 1898.* Kansas City, MO: Franklin Hudson, 1906.

———. *The Service of Security and Information.* Washington, DC: James J. Chapman, 1893.

Ward, Walter W. *Springfield in the Spanish-American War.* Easthampton, MA: Enterprise Printing, 1899.

Wassell, W. H., O. M. Smith, and R. L. Hamilton. *A History of the Twenty-Second United States Infantry.* Manila: Press of E. C. McCullough, 1904.

Webber, Harry. E. *Twelve Months with the Eighth Massachusetts Infantry in the Service of the United States.* Salem, MA, 1908.

Wells, Harry L. *The War in the Philippines.* San Francisco: Sunset Photo-engravers, 1899.

Wheeler, Joseph. *The Santiago Campaign, 1898.* Boston: Lamson, Wolffe, 1898.

Whipple, J. E. *The Story of the Forty-Ninth.* Vinton, IA: 1903.

Wilcox, Marrion. *Harper's History of the War in the Philippines.* New York: Harper & Bros., 1900.

Willis, Henry Parker. *Our Philippine Problem: A Study of American Colonial Policy.* New York: H. Holt, 1905.

Wood, Leonard. *Opportunities in the Colonies and Cuba.* New York: Lewis, Scribner, 1902.

Worcester, Dean C. *The Philippines, Past and Present.* 2 vols. New York: MacMillan, 1914.

JOURNAL ARTICLES

A Member of the Corps. "Telegraph Engineering in Moro Land." *Engineering Magazine* 24 (October 1902–March 1903): 209–14.

Anderson, Thomas M. "Supply and Distribution. I. Eighteen Hundred and Ninety Eight." *Journal of the Military Service Institution* 29, no. 113 (September 1901): 198–208.

Baker, Ray Stannard. "General Leonard Wood: A Character Sketch." *McClure's Magazine* 14, no. 4 (February 1900): 368–79.

Bateman, Cephas C. "Military Road Making in Mindanao." *Journal of the Military Service Institution* 33, no. 125 (September–October 1903): 191–99.

Bell, Clark. "The Supreme Court of Santiago de Cuba." *Medico-Legal Journal* 16, no. 4 (1899): 507–14.

Bernad, Miguel A., S.J. "Five Letters Describing the Exploration of the Pulangi or Rio Grande de Mindanao: 1890." *Philippine Historical Review* 1, no. 2 (1966): 17–62.

Betts, Arlington. "Memoirs of Captain A.U. Betts." *Bulletin of the American Historical Collection* 24 (1973): 3–107.

Blocksom, Augustus P. "A Retrospect and Prospect of War." *Journal of the Military Service Institution of the United States* 35, no. 131 (September–October 1904): 215–26.

Bonsal, Stephen. "The Moros and Their Country." *Outlook* 71, no. 2 (May 10, 1902): 115–19.

———. "The Negro Soldier in War and Peace." *North American Review* 185, no. 616 (June 7, 1907): 321–27.

Bullard, Robert L. "The Army in Cuba." *Journal of the Military Service Institution* 441, no. 149 (September 1907): 152–57.

———. "Military Pacification." *Journal of the Military Service Institution* 46, no. 163 (January–February 1910): 1–24.

———. "Preparing Our Moros for Government." *Atlantic Monthly* 97 (March 1906): 385–94.

———. "Road Building among the Moros." *Atlantic Monthly* 92 (December 1903): 818–26.

Carmony, Donald F., Karen Tannenbaum, and Bess Sellers Johnson. "Three Years in the Orient: The Diary of William R. Johnson, 1898–1902." *Indiana Magazine of History* 63, no. 4 (December 1967): 263–98.

Clark, Victor. "Labor Conditions in Cuba." *Bulletin of the Department of Labor* 41 (July 1902): 663–793.

———. "Labor Conditions in the Philippine Islands." *Bulletin of the Bureau of Labor* 58 (May 1905): 721–905.

Clements, Paul. "Medical Survey of the Town of Taytay." *Philippine Journal of Science* 4, no. 4 (August 1909): 247–55.

Cosby, Spencer. "Work of the Army in the Construction and Maintenance of Roads." *Southern Good Roads* 7, no. 1 (January 1913): 10–15.

Crane, Charles Judson. "Paragraphs 93, 97, and 88, of General Orders 100." *Journal of the Military Service Institution of the United States* 32 (March 1903): 254–58.

Crozier, William. "Some Observations on the Pekin Relief Expedition." *North American Review* 172, no. 2 (February 1, 1901): 225–40.

Davis, Richard Harding. "The Rough Riders' Fight at Guasimas." *Scribner's Magazine* 24, no. 3 (September 1898): 259–73.

Denison, Edgar. "Transportation in Cuba." *World To-Day* 11, no. 4 (October 1906): 1071–76.

Devol, Carroll A. "Supply and Distribution, II. Nineteen Hundred and One." *Journal of the Military Service Institution of the United States* 29, no. 113 (September 1901): 208–15.

DuPuy, William A. "Road Building by the United States in Cuba." *Scientific American* 100, no. 7 (February 13, 1909): 136–38.

Harts, William Wright. "Military Engineering and Civil Opportunities in the Philippines." *Engineering Magazine* 25 (August 1903): 688–98.

Hill, G. R. "Sanemiento de la Habana." *La Higiene* 1, no. 10 (April 10, 1900): 129–31.

Howard, William Willard. "The Cuban as a Labor Problem." *Century Magazine* 58 (August 1899): 640–41.

Howland, H. S. "Field Service in Mindanao." *Journal of the U.S. Infantry Association* 2, no. 2 (October 1905): 36–79.

Kemp, Franklin M. "Field Work in the Philippines." In *Proceedings of the Ninth Annual Meeting of the Association of Military Surgeons of the United States Held at New York City, May 31, June 1 and 2, 1900*. Chicago: R. R. Donnelley & Sons, 1901.

Kennan, George. "Cuban Character." *Outlook* 63, no. 17 (December 23, 1899): 959–65.

———. "Friction in Cuba: A Special Letter from George Kennan on General Wood's Work." *Outlook* 61, no. 12 (March 25, 1899): 675–78.

———. "The Regeneration of Cuba." Pt. 4, "The Sanitary Regeneration of Santiago." *Outlook* 61, no. 15 (April 15, 1899): 871–77.

———. "The Regeneration of Cuba." Pt. 6, "The Government of Santiago." *Outlook* 62, no. 2 (May 13, 1899): 109–15.

———. "The Regeneration of Cuba." Pt. 7, "From Santiago to Havana." *Outlook* 62, no. 4 (May 27, 1899): 202–9.

Kipling, Rudyard. "The White Man's Burden." *McClure's Magazine* 12, no. 2 (February 1899): 240–41.

Lewis, Henry H. "General Wood at Santiago: Americanizing a Cuban City." *McClure's Magazine* 12, no. 5 (March 1899): 460–69.

MacClintock, Samuel. "Around the Island of Cebu on Horseback." *American Journal of Sociology* 8, no. 4 (January 1903): 433–41.

MacQueen, Peter. "Campaigning with General Lawton." *National Magazine* 10, no. 4 (July 1899): 361–64.

Marshall, Edward. "A Talk with General Wood." *Outlook* 68, no. 12 (July 20, 1901): 669–73.

Martin, Harold. "The Saloon in Manila." *The Independent* 52 (June 28, 1900): 1537–40.

Maus, L. Mervin "Venereal Diseases in the United States Army—Their Prevention and Treatment." *Military Surgeon* 27 (1910): 130–48.

Mencarini, Juan. "The Philippine Chinese Labour Question." *Journal of the China Branch of the Royal Asiatic Society* 33 (1899–1900): 157–89.

Munro, J. N. "The Philippine Native Scouts." *Journal of the U.S. Infantry Association* 2, no. 1 (July 1905): 178–90.

Page, Arthur W. "The Building of the Benguet Road." *The World's Work* 17, no. 3 (January 1909): 11135–45.

Parker, James. "Some Random Notes on Fighting in the Philippines." *Journal of the Military Service Institution* 27, no. 108 (November 1900): 317–40.

Patrick, Mason M. "Notes on Road Building in Cuba." *Professional Memoirs, Corps of Engineers, United States Army* 2, no. 7 (July–September 1910): 263–84.

Phelan, Henry du Rest. "Sanitary Service in Surigao, a Filipino Town on the Island of Mindanao." *Journal of the American Military Surgeon* 14 (1904): 1–18.

Plehn, Carl C. "Municipal Government in the Philippine Islands." *Municipal Affairs* 5 (December 1901): 793–801.

Powell, James W. "The Utilization of Native Troops in Our Foreign Possessions." *Journal of the Military Service Institution of the United States* 30, no. 115 (January 1902): 23–41.

Ramsden, Frederick W. "Diary of the British Consul at Santiago during Hostilities." *McClure's Magazine* 11 (October 1898): 580–90.

———. "Diary of the British Consul at Santiago during Hostilities: Conclusion." *McClure's Magazine* 12 (November 1898): 62–70.

Reeve, Horace. "Opening of Mindanao and Jolo." *Independent* 52 (April 19, 1900): 922–25.

Roosevelt, Theodore. "General Leonard Wood: A Model American Military Administrator." *Outlook* 61, no. 1 (January 7, 1899): 19–23.

Rosenberg, Edward. "Filipinos as Workmen." *American Federationist* 10, no. 10 (October 1903): 1021–31.

Schmeling, B. Von. "Maintenance of First-Class Roads in the Philippines." Bureau of Public Works, *Quarterly Bulletin* 1, no. 4 (January 1, 1913): 14–19.

Schurman, Jacob G. "Our Duty to the Philippines." *The Independent* 51, no. 2665 (December 1899): 3464–67.

Seaman, Gilbert E. "Some Observations of a Medical Officer in the Philippines." *Milwaukee Medical Journal* 10, no. 7 (July 1902): 181–89.

Seaman, Louis Livingston. "Native Troops for Our Colonial Possessions." *North American Review* 171, no. 529 (December 1900): 847–60.
Shafter, William R. "The Capture of Santiago de Cuba." *Century Magazine* 57 (1899): 612–30.
"Soldier Teachers in the Philippines." *Harper's Weekly* 46 (January 18, 1902): 76.
Steese, James Gordon. "The Corps of Engineers and the Isthmian Canal." *Professional Memoirs, Corps of Engineers, United States Army and Engineer Department at Large* 4, no. 16 (July–August 1912): 523–29.
Steward, Theophilus G. "Two Years in Luzon." Pt. 1. *Colored American Magazine* 4, no. 1 (November 1901): 4–10.
Strong, Richard P. "Medical Survey of the Town of Taytay." *Philippine Journal of Science* 4B, no. 4 (August 1909): 207–99.
Thompson, H. C. "War without Medals." *Oregon Historical Quarterly* 59, no. 4 (December 1958): 293–325.
Turnbull, Winfred. "Reminiscences of an Army Surgeon in Cuba and the Philippines." *Bulletin of the American Historical Collection* 2, no 2 (April 1974): 31–49.
Ward, John W. "The Use of Native Troops in Our New Possessions." *Journal of the Military Service Institution of the United States* 31, no. 120 (November 1902): 793–805.
White, Herbert A. "The Pacification of Batangas." *International Quarterly* 7 (1903): 432–44.
Williams, Herbert P. "The Outlook in Cuba." *Atlantic Monthly* 83 (June 1899): 827–36.
Wise, Hugh D. "Notes on Field Service in Samar." *Journal of the United States Infantry Association* 4, no. 1 (July 1907): 3–58.
Wood, Leonard. "The Existing Conditions and Needs in Cuba." *North American Review* 168, no. 510 (May 1899): 593–601.
———. "The Military Government of Cuba." *Annals of the American Academy of Political and Social Science* 21, no. 2 (March 1903): 1–30.
———. "The Present Situation in Cuba." *Century Magazine* 58 (August 1899): 639–40.
———. "Santiago since the Surrender." *Scribner's* 25, no. 5 (May 1899): 515–27.
Worcester, Dean C. "General Lawton's Work in the Philippines." *McClure's Magazine* 15, no. 1 (May 1900): 19–31.
Wright, Irene. "The Cart-Roads of Mr. Magoon." *World To-Day* 16, no. 6 (June 1909): 641–48.

Secondary Sources

BOOKS

Abdala Pupo, Oscar Luis. *Intervención militar norteamericana en la contienda independetista Cubana: 1898*. Santiago de Cuba: Editorial Oriente, 1998.
Abinales, Patricio N. *Images of State Power: Essays on Philippine Politics from the Margins.* Diliman, Quezon City: University of the Philippines Press, 1998.
———. *Making Mindanao: Cotabato and Davao in the Formation of the Philippine Nation-State.* Quezon City: Ateneo de Manila University Press, 2000.
———. *Orthodoxy and History in the Muslim-Mindanao Narrative.* Quezon City: Ateneo de Manila University Press, 2010.
Abinales, Patricio N., and Donna J. Amoroso. *State and Society in the Philippines.* New York: Rowman & Littlefield, 2005.
Adams, Kevin. *Class and Race in the Frontier Army: Military Life in the West, 1870–1890.* Norman: University of Oklahoma Press, 2009.

Adas, Michael. *Dominance by Design: Technological Imperatives and America's Civilizing Mission.* Cambridge, MA: Belknap Press of Harvard University Press, 2006.

———. *Machines as the Measure of Men: Science, Technology, and Ideologies of Western Dominance.* Ithaca, NY: Cornell University Press, 1989.

Agoncillo, Teodoro A. *Malolos: The Crisis of the Republic.* Quezon City: University of the Philippines, 1960.

Aguilar, Filomeno V., Jr. *Clash of Spirits: The History of Power and Sugar Planter Hegemony on a Visayan Island.* Honolulu: University of Hawai'i Press, 1998.

Alatas, Syed Hussein. *The Myth of the Lazy Native: A Study of the Image of the Malays, Filipinos and Javanese from the 16th to the 20th Century and Its Function in the Ideology of Colonial Capitalism.* London: Frank Cass, 1977.

Alejandrino, Clark L. *A History of the 1902 Chinese Exclusion Act: American Colonial Transmission and Deterioration of Filipino-Chinese Relations.* Manila: Kaisa Para Sa Kuanlaran, 2003.

Alexander, Jennifer Karns. *The Mantra of Efficiency: From Waterwheel to Social Control.* Baltimore: Johns Hopkins University Press, 2008.

Anderson, Benedict R. *Imagined Communities: Reflections on the Origins and Spread of Nationalism.* London: Verso, 2016.

———. *Under Three Flags: Anarchism and the Colonial Imagination.* New York: Verso Press, 2005.

Anderson, Warwick. *Colonial Pathologies: American Tropical Medicine, Race, and Hygiene in the Philippines.* Durham, NC: Duke University Press, 2006.

Andrews, Thomas G. *Killing for Coal: America's Deadliest Labor War.* Cambridge, MA: Harvard University Press, 2010.

Anghie, Antony. *Imperialism, Sovereignty, and the Making of International Law.* New York: Cambridge University Press, 2007.

Aune, Stefan. *Indian Wars Everywhere: Colonial Violence and the Shadow Doctrines of Empire.* Berkeley: University of California Press, 2023.

Ayala, César J. *American Sugar Kingdom: The Plantation Economy of the Spanish Caribbean, 1898–1934.* Chapel Hill: University of North Carolina Press, 1999.

Bacardi, Amalia. *Emilio Bacardi en su tiempo.* Madrid: Edición del autor, 1986.

Baldoz, Rick. *The Third Asiatic Invasion: Empire and Migration in Filipino America, 1898–1946.* New York: New York University Press, 2011.

Ballantyne, Tony, and Antoinette Burton. *Empires and the Reach of the Global, 1870–1945.* Cambridge, MA: Belknap Press of Harvard University Press, 2012.

Balogh, Brian. *A Government Out of Sight: The Mystery of National Authority in Nineteenth-Century America.* New York: Cambridge University Press, 2009.

Bankoff, Greg. *Crime, Society, and the State in the Nineteenth-Century Philippines.* Quezon City: Ateneo de Manila University Press, 1996.

Barnes, Mark R. *The Spanish-American War and the Philippine Insurrection, 1898–1902: An Annotated Bibliography.* London: Routledge, 2001.

Barnet, Miguel. *Biography of a Runaway Slave.* Translated by Nick Hill. Willamantic, CT: Curbstone Press, 1994.

Barr, Ronald J. *The Progressive Army: U.S. Army Command and Administration, 1870–1914.* New York: St. Martin's Press, 1998.

Bayly, C. A. *Empire and Information: Intelligence Gathering and Social Communication in India, 1780–1870*. New York: Cambridge University Press, 1996.
Beaver, Daniel. *Modernizing the American War Department: Change and Continuity in a Turbulent Era, 1885–1920*. Kent State, OH: Kent State University Press, 2014.
Bender, Daniel E. *American Abyss: Savagery and Civilization in the Age of Industry*. Ithaca, NY: Cornell University Press, 2009.
Berger, Peter. *Subaltern Sovereigns: Rituals of Rule and Regeneration in Highland Odisha, India*. Boston: De Gruyter, 2023.
Bickel, Keith B. *Mars Learning: The Marine Corps' Development of Small Wars Doctrine, 1915–1940*. Boulder, CO: Westview Press, 2001.
Bjork, Katharine. *Prairie Imperialists: The Indian Country Origins of American Empire*. Philadelphia: University of Pennsylvania Press, 2019.
Blight, David W. *Race and Reunion: The Civil War in American Memory*. Cambridge, MA: Belknap Press of Harvard University Press, 2001.
Boris, Eileen. *Making the Woman Worker: Precarious Labor and the Fight for Global Standards, 1919–2019*. New York: Oxford University Press, 2019.
Bousquet, Antoine. *The Scientific Way of Warfare: Order and Chaos on the Battlefields of Modernity*. New York: Columbia University Press, 2009.
Brody, David. *Visualizing American Empire: Orientalism and Imperialism in the Philippines*. Chicago: University of Chicago Press, 2010.
Brundage, W. Fitzhugh. *Civilizing Torture: An American Tradition*. Cambridge, MA: Harvard University Press, 2018.
Buch López, Ernesto. *Historia de Santiago de Cuba*. Havana: Editorial Lex, 1947.
Burbank, Jane, and Frederick Cooper. *Empires in World History: Power and the Politics of Difference*. Princeton, NJ: Princeton University Press, 2010.
Butler, Anne M. *Daughters of Joy, Sisters of Misery: Prostitutes in the American West, 1865–90*. Urbana: University of Illinois Press, 1985.
Byers, Andrew. *The Sexual Economy of War: Discipline and Desire in the U.S. Army*. Ithaca, NY: Cornell University Press, 2019.
Calder, Bruce J. *The Impact of Intervention: The Dominican Republic during the U.S. Occupation of 1916–1924*. Austin: University of Texas Press, 1984.
Camagay, Maria Luisa T. *Working Women of Manila in the Late 19th Century*. Manila: University of the Philippines Press and the University Center for Women's Studies, 1995.
Capozzola, Christopher. *Bound by War: How the United States and the Philippines Built the First American Century*. New York: Basic Books, 2020.
Casey, Matthew. *Empire's Guestworkers: Haitian Migrants in Cuba during the Age of the U.S. Occupation*. New York: Cambridge University Press, 2017.
Castellanos Garcia, Gerardo. *Historia en Santiago (Reflejos de un Congreso)*. La Habana: Im. Alfa, 1946.
Caulfield, Sueann. *In Defense of Honor: Sexual Morality, Modernity, and Nation in Early-Twentieth-Century Brazil*. Durham, NC: Duke University Press, 2000.
Chakrabarty, Dipesh. *Provincializing Europe: Postcolonial Thought and Historical Difference*. Princeton, NJ: Princeton University Press, 2008.
Charbonneau, Oliver. *Civilizational Imperatives: Americans, Moros, and the Colonial World*. Ithaca, NY: Cornell University Press, 2020.

Chira, Adriana. *Patchwork Freedoms: Law, Slavery, and Race Beyond Cuba's Plantations.* New York: Cambridge University Press, 2022.
Chu, Richard T. *Chinese and Chinese Mestizos of Manila: Family, Identity, and Culture, 1860s–1930s.* Boston: Koningklijke Brill NV, 2010.
Clark, J. P. *Preparing for War: The Emergence of the Modern U.S. Army, 1815–1917.* Cambridge, MA: Harvard University Press, 2017.
Coates, Benjamin Allen. *Legalist Empire: International Law and American Foreign Relations in the Early Twentieth Century.* New York: Oxford University Press, 2016.
Coffman, Edward M. *The Old Army: A Portrait of the American Army in Peacetime, 1784–1898.* New York: Oxford University Press, 1986.
———. *The Regulars: The American Army, 1898–1941.* Cambridge, MA: Belknap Press of Harvard University Press, 2004.
Cohen, Nancy L. *The Reconstruction of American Liberalism, 1865–1914.* Chapel Hill: University of North Carolina Press, 2002.
Cohn, Bernard S. *Colonialism and Its Forms of Knowledge: The British in India.* Princeton, NJ: Princeton University Press, 1996.
Colby, Jason. *The Business of Empire: United Fruit, Race, and U.S. Expansion in Central America.* Ithaca, NY: Cornell University Press, 2011.
Corpuz, Arturo G. *The Colonial Iron Horse: Railroads and Regional Development in the Philippines, 1875–1935.* Quezon City: University of the Philippines Press, 1999.
Corpuz, Onofre D. *An Economic History of the Philippines.* Quezon City: University of the Philippines Press, 1997.
Cosmas, Graham A. *An Army for Empire: The United States Army in the Spanish-American War.* Columbia: University of Missouri Press, 1971.
Couttie, Bob. *Hang the Dogs: The True Tragic History of the Balangiga Massacre.* Manila: New Day, 2004.
Cruikshank, Bruce. *Samar: 1768–1898.* Makati: Makati Historical Conservation Society, 1985.
Cuevas Toraya, Juan de las. *500 años de construcciones en Cuba.* Havana: Chavin, 2001.
Cullinane, Michael. *Ilustrado Politics: Filipino Elite Responses to American Rule, 1898–1908.* Quezon City: Ateneo de Manila University Press, 2003.
Cushner, Nicholas P. *Spain in the Philippines: From Conquest to Revolution.* Quezon City: Ateneo de Manila University Press, 1971.
Dacudao, Patricia Irene. *Abaca Frontier: The Socioeconomic and Cultural Transformation of Davao, 1898–1941.* Quezon City: Ateneo de Manila University Press, 2003.
Daniels, Roger. *Asian America: Chinese and Japanese in the United States since 1850.* Seattle: University of Washington Press, 1988.
———. *Guarding the Golden Door: American Immigration Policy and Immigrants since 1882.* New York: Hill and Wang, 2004.
Davis, Henry Blaine, Jr. *Generals in Khaki.* Raleigh, NC: Pentland Press, 1998.
Davis, Janet M. *The Circus Age: Culture and Society under the American Big Top.* Chapel Hill: University of North Carolina Press, 2002.
Davis, Mike. *Late Victorian Holocausts: El Niño Famines and the Making of the Third World.* New York: Verso, 2017.

De Bevoise, Ken. *Agents of Apocalypse: Epidemic Disease in the Colonial Philippines.* Princeton, NJ: Princeton University Press, 1995.

De la Fuente, Alejandro. *A Nation for All: Race, Inequality, and Politics in Twentieth-Century Cuba.* Chapel Hill: University of North Carolina Press, 2001.

De Leon, Adrian. *Bundok: A Hinterland History of Filipino America.* Chapel Hill: University of North Carolina Press, 2023.

Delmendo, Sharon. *Star-Entangled Banner: One Hundred Years of America in the Philippines.* New Brunswick, NJ: Rutgers University Press, 2004.

Dery, Luis Camara. *A History of the Inarticulate: Local History, Prostitution, and Other Views from the Bottom.* Quezon City: New Day, 2001.

Diccionario enciclopédico de historia militar de Cuba. Primera Parte (1510–1898). Tomo 1, Biografías. Havana: Casa Editorial Verde Olivo, 2014.

Doeppers, Daniel F. *Feeding Manila in Peace and War, 1850–1945.* Madison: University of Wisconsin Press, 2016.

Downs, Gregory P. *After Appomattox: Military Occupation and the Ends of War.* Cambridge, MA: Harvard University Press, 2015.

———. *The Second American Revolution: The Civil War-Era Struggle over Cuba and the Rebirth of the American Republic.* Chapel Hill: University of North Carolina Press, 2019.

Driver, Felix. *Geography Militant: Cultures of Exploration and Empire.* Malden, MA: Blackwell, 2001.

Droessler, Holger. *Coconut Colonialism: Workers and the Globalization of Samoa.* Cambridge, MA: Harvard University Press, 2022.

Dubofksy, Melvyn. *The State and Labor in Modern America.* Chapel Hill: University of North Carolina Press, 1994.

Dunlay, Thomas W. *Wolves for the Blue Soldiers: Indian Scouts and Auxiliaries with the United States Army, 1860–90.* Lincoln: University of Nebraska Press, 1982.

Dye, Alan. *Cuban Sugar in the Age of Mass Production: Technology and the Economics of the Sugar Central, 1899–1929.* Stanford, CA: Stanford University Press, 1998.

Edgerton, Ronald K. *American Datu: John J. Pershing and Counterinsurgency Warfare in the Muslim Philippines, 1899–1913.* Lexington: University Press of Kentucky, 2020.

Einolf, Christopher J. *America in the Philippines, 1898–1902: The First Torture Scandal.* New York: Palgrave Macmillan, 2014.

Ekbladh, David. *The Great American Mission: Modernization and the Construction of an American World Order.* Princeton, NJ: Princeton University Press, 2010.

Ellinghaus, Katherine. *Taking Assimilation to Heart: Marriages of White Women and Indigenous Men in the United States and Australia, 1887–1937.* Lincoln: University of Nebraska Press, 2009.

Espinosa, Mariola. *Epidemic Invasions: Yellow Fever and the Limits of Cuban Independence, 1878–1930.* Chicago: University of Chicago Press, 2009.

Espiritu, Yen Le. *Home Bound: Filipino American Lives across Cultures, Communities, and Countries.* Berkeley: University of California Press, 2003.

Fabian, Johannes. *Out of Our Minds: Reason and Madness in the Exploration of Central Africa.* Berkeley: University of California Press, 2000.

Ferrer, Ada. *Cuba: An American History.* New York: Scribner, 2021.

———. *Freedom's Mirror: Cuba and Haiti in the Age of Revolution.* New York: Cambridge University Press, 2014.

———. *Insurgent Cuba: Race, Nation, and Revolution, 1868–1898.* Chapel Hill: University of North Carolina Press, 1999.

Feuer, A. B. *America at War: The Philippines, 1898–1913.* Westport, CT: Praeger, 2002.

Finin, Gerard A. *The Making of the Igorot: Contours of Cordillera Consciousness.* Quezon City: Ateneo de Manila University Press, 2005.

Flake, Dennis. *Loyal Macabebe: How the Americans Used the Macabebe Scouts in the Annexation of the Philippines.* Angeles City, Philippines: Holy Angel University Press, 2009.

Fleitas Salazar, Carlos Rafael. *Medicina y sanidad en la historia de Santiago de Cuba, 1515–1898.* Santiago de Cuba: Ediciones Santiago, 2003.

Foner, Eric. *Reconstruction: America's Unfinished Revolution, 1863–1877.* New York: Harper & Row, 1988.

———. *The Story of American Freedom.* New York: W. W. Norton, 1998.

Fredman, Zach. *The Tormented Alliance: American Servicemen and the Occupation of China, 1941–1949.* Chapel Hill: University of North Carolina Press, 2022.

Fry, Howard T. *A History of the Mountain Province.* Quezon City: New Day, 1983.

Frymer, Paul. *Building an American Empire: The Era of Territorial and Political Expansion.* Princeton, NJ: Princeton University Press, 2017.

Funtecha, Henry Florida. *American Military Occupation of the Lake Lanao Region, 1901–1913: An Historical Study.* Marawi City: University Research Center, Mindanao State University, 1979.

Galloway, Patton Gardenier. *Joseph Patton and Cornelius Gardener: Two Men, Three Wars.* Self-published, Lulu.com, 2015.

García, Guadalupe. *Beyond the Walled City: Colonial Exclusion in Havana.* Berkeley: University of California Press, 2016.

Gates, John Morgan. *Schoolbooks and Krags: The United States Army in the Philippines, 1898–1902.* Westport, CT: Greenwood Press, 1973.

Gatewood, Willard B., Jr. *Black Americans and the White Man's Burden, 1898–1903.* Urbana: University of Illinois Press, 1975.

———. *"Smoked Yankees" and the Struggle for Empire: Letters from Negro Soldiers, 1898–1902.* Urbana: University of Illinois Press, 1971.

Gillett, Mary C. *The Army Medical Department, 1865–1917.* Washington, DC: Center of Military History, United States Army, 1995.

Gilmore, Glenda Elizabeth. *Gender and Jim Crow: Women and the Politics of White Supremacy in North Carolina, 1896–1920.* Chapel Hill: University of North Carolina Press, 1996.

Gjelten, Tom. *Bacardi and the Long Fight for Cuba.* New York: Viking Press, 2008.

Gleeck, Lewis E., Jr. *American Institutions in the Philippines (1898–1941).* Manila: Historical Conservation Society, 1976.

Go, Julian. *American Empire and the Politics of Meaning: Elite Political Cultures in the Philippines and Puerto Rico during U.S. Colonialism.* Durham, NC: Duke University Press, 2008.

———. *Postcolonial Thought and Social Theory.* New York: Oxford University Press, 2016.

Gobat, Michael. *Confronting the American Dream: Nicaragua under U.S. Imperial Rule*. Durham, NC: Duke University Press, 2005.

Golay, Frank H. *Face of Empire: United States-Philippine Relations, 1898–1946*. Madison: University of Wisconsin Press, 1998.

Gowing, Peter Gordon. *Mandate in Moroland: The American Government of Muslim Filipinos, 1899–1920*. Quezon City: University of the Philippines, 1997.

———. *Muslim Filipinos–Heritage and Horizon*. Quezon City: New Day, 1979.

Greene, Julie. *The Canal Builders: Making America's Empire at the Panama Canal*. New York: Penguin Press, 2009.

Guerra, Lillian. *The Myth of José Martí: Conflicting Nationalisms in Early Twentieth-Century Cuba*. Chapel Hill: University of North Carolina Press, 2005.

Guerrero, Milagros Camayon. *Luzon at War: Contradictions in Philippine Society, 1898–1902*. Pasig City, Philippines: Anvil, 2016.

Guldi, Jo. *Roads to Power: Britain Invents the Infrastructure State*. Cambridge, MA: Harvard University Press, 2012.

Guridy, Frank. *Forging Diaspora: Afro-Cubans and African Americans in a World of Empire and Jim Crow*. Chapel Hill: University of North Carolina Press, 2010.

Gyory, Andrew. *Closing the Gate: Race, Politics, and the Chinese Exclusion Act*. Chapel Hill: University of North Carolina Press, 1998.

Haber, Samuel. *Efficiency and Uplift: Scientific Management in the Progressive Era, 1890–1920*. Chicago: University of Chicago Press, 1964.

Halsema, James J. *E. J. Halsema, Colonial Engineer: A Biography*. Quezon City: New Day Publishers, 1991.

Hardin, Russell. *Trust and Trustworthiness*. New York: Russell Sage Foundation, 2002.

Hardt, Michael, and Antonio Negri. *Assembly*. New York: Oxford University Press, 2017.

Harper, Frank, ed. *Just Outside of Manila: Letters from Members of the First Colorado Regiment in the Spanish-American and Philippine-American Wars*. Denver: Colorado Historical Society, 1992.

Harris, Susan K. *God's Arbiters: Americans and the Philippines, 1898–1902*. New York: Oxford University Press, 2011.

Harrison, Noel Garraux. *Harrison City of Canvas: Camp Russell A. Alger and the Spanish-American War*. Falls Church, VA: Falls Church Historical Commission, 1988.

Harrod, Frederick S. *Manning the New Navy: The Development of a Modern Naval Enlisted Force, 1899–1940*. Westport, CT: Greenwood Press, 1978.

Hawkins, Michael C. *Making Moros: Imperial Historicism and American Military Rule in the Philippines' Muslim South*. DeKalb: Northern Illinois University Press, 2013.

Headrick, Daniel R. *The Tools of Empire: Technology and European Imperialism in the Nineteenth Century*. New York: Oxford University Press, 1981.

Healy, David F. *The United States in Cuba, 1898–1902: Generals, Politicians, and the Search for Policy*. Madison: University of Wisconsin Press, 1963.

Helg, Aline. *Our Rightful Share: The Afro-Cuban Struggle for Equality, 1886–1912*. Chapel Hill: University of North Carolina Press, 1995.

Herman, Rebecca. *Cooperating with the Colossus: A Social and Political History of US Military Bases in World War II Latin America*. Berkeley: University of California Press, 2022.

Herrera Fernandez, Manuel. *Seis Alcaldes*. Pinar del Río: Municipio de Pinar del Río, 1956.

Hicks, Anasa. *Hierarchies at Home: Domestic Service in Cuba from Abolition to Revolution*. New York: Cambridge University Press, 2022.

Hirota, Hidetaka. *Expelling the Poor: Atlantic Seaboard States and the Nineteenth-Century Origins of American Immigration Policy*. New York: Oxford University Press, 2017.

Hirschfield, Katherine. *Health, Politics, and Revolution in Cuba since 1898*. New Brunswick, NJ: Transaction, 2007.

Hofstadter, Richard. *Social Darwinism in American Thought*. Boston: Beacon Press, 1944.

Hoganson, Kristin L. *Fighting for American Manhood: How Gender Politics Provoked the Spanish-American War and Philippine-American Wars*. New Haven, CT: Yale University Press, 1998.

Holley, I. B. *The Highway Revolution, 1895–1925: How the United States Got Out of the Mud*. Durham, NC: Carolina Academic Press, 2008.

Holt, Elizabeth Mary. *Colonizing Filipinas: Nineteenth-Century Representations of the Philippines in Western Historiography*. Quezon City: Ateneo de Manila University Press, 2002.

Hope, Ian C. *A Scientific Way of War: Antebellum Military Science, West Point, and the Origins of American Military Thought*. Lincoln: University of Nebraska Press, 2005.

Hopkins, A. G. *American Empire: A Global History*. Princeton, NJ: Princeton University Press, 2018.

Hull, Isabel V. *Absolute Destruction: Military Culture and the Practices of War in Imperial Germany*. Ithaca, NY: Cornell University Press, 2005.

Iglesias Utset, Marial. *A Cultural History of Cuba during the U.S. Occupation, 1898–1902*. Chapel Hill: University of North Carolina Press, 2011.

Ileto, Reynaldo Clemeña. *Knowledge and Pacification: On the U.S. Conquest and the Writing of Philippine History*. Quezon City: Ateneo de Manila University Press, 2017.

———. *Magindanao, 1860–1888: The Career of Dato Uto of Buayan*. Ithaca, NY: Cornell University Press, 1971.

———. *Pasyon and Revolution: Popular Movements in the Philippines, 1840–1910*. Quezon City: Ateneo de Manila University Press, 2003. First published 1979.

Irwin, Julia F. *Making the World Safe: The American Red Cross and a Nation's Humanitarian Awakening*. New York: Oxford University Press, 2013.

Jacobson, Matthew Frye. *Special Sorrows: The Diasporic Imagination of Irish, Polish, and Jewish Immigrants in the United States*. Berkeley: University of California Press, 2002.

Jenista, Frank L. *The White Apos: American Governors on the Cordillera Central*. Quezon City: New Day, 1987.

Jensen, Irene Khin Khin Myint. *The Chinese in the Philippines during the American Regime: 1898–1946*. San Francisco: R and E Research Associates, 1975.

Jung, Moon-Ho. *Coolies and Cane: Race, Labor, and Sugar in the Age of Emancipation*. Baltimore: Johns Hopkins University Press, 2006.

Karuka, Manu. *Empire's Tracks: Indigenous Nations, Chinese Workers, and the Transcontinental Railroad*. Oakland: University of California Press, 2019.

Katz, Michael B. *In the Shadow of the Poorhouse: A Social History of Welfare in America*. New York: Basic Books, 1996.

Kessler-Harris, Alice. *Out to Work: A History of Wage-Earning Women in the United States.* New York: Oxford University Press, 2003.
Kohout, Amy. *Taking the Field: Soldiers, Empire, and Nature on American Frontiers.* Lincoln: University of Nebraska Press, 2023.
Kramer, Paul A. *The Blood of Government: Race, Empire, the United States, and the Philippines.* Chapel Hill: University of North Carolina Press, 2006.
Kumar, Krishan. *Visions of Empire: How Five Imperial Regimes Shaped the World.* Princeton, NJ: Princeton University Press, 2017.
Lane, Jack C. *Armed Progressive: General Leonard Wood.* San Rafael, CA: Presidio Press, 1978.
Larkin, John. *The Pampangans: Colonial Society in a Philippine Province.* Berkeley: University of California Press, 1972.
Lee, Erika. *At America's Gates: Chinese Immigration during the Exclusion Era, 1882–1943.* Chapel Hill: University of North Carolina Press, 2003.
Lee, Robert G. *Orientals: Asian Americans in Popular Culture.* Philadelphia: Temple University Press, 1999.
Lefebvre, Henri. *Critique of Everyday Life.* New York: Verso, 1991.
Lichtenstein, Alex. *Twice the Work of Free Labor: The Political Economy of Convict Labor in the New South.* London: Verso, 1996.
Linderman, Gerald F. *The Mirror of War: American Society and the Spanish-American War.* Ann Arbor: University of Michigan Press, 1974.
Linn, Brian McAllister. *The Echo of Battle: The Army's Way of War.* Cambridge, MA: Harvard University Press, 2007.
———. *Guardians of Empire: The U.S. Army and the Pacific, 1902–1940.* Chapel Hill: University of North Carolina Press, 1997.
———. *The Philippine War, 1899–1902.* Lawrence: University Press of Kansas, 2000.
———. *The U.S. Army and Counterinsurgency in the Philippine War, 1899–1902.* Chapel Hill: University of North Carolina Press, 2000.
Lipman, Jana K. *Guantánamo: A Working-Class History between Empire and Revolution.* Berkeley: University of California Press, 2009.
Lockmiller, David A. *Enoch H. Crowder: Soldier, Lawyer, and Statesman.* Columbia: University of Missouri Press, 1955.
———. *Magoon in Cuba: A History of the Second Intervention, 1906–1909.* Chapel Hill: University of North Carolina Press, 1938.
López, Kathleen. *Chinese Cubans: A Transnational History.* Chapel Hill: University of North Carolina Press, 2013.
Lucian, Justin. *A Soldier's Letter: April 19, 1900, Lipa, Batangas, Philippines.* Manila: De La Salle University Press, 1995.
Lumba, Allan E. S. *Monetary Authorities: Capitalism and Decolonization in the American Colonial Philippines.* Durham, NC: Duke University Press, 2022.
Maier, Charles. *Among Empires: American Ascendancy and Its Predecessors.* Cambridge, MA: Harvard University Press, 2006.
Manjapra, Kris. *Colonialism in Global Perspective.* Cambridge, MA: Cambridge University Press, 2020.
Manuel, E. Arsenio. *Felipe G. Calderon: A Biographical Portrait.* Manila: Bookman, 1954.

Martinez Ortiz, Rafael. *Cuba: Los primeros años de independencia.* 2 vols. 2d ed. Paris: Imprimerie Artistique "Lux," 1921.

Maurer, Noel. *The Empire Trap: The Rise and Fall of U.S. Intervention to Protect American Property Overseas, 1893–2013.* Princeton, NJ: Princeton University Press, 2013.

May, Glenn Anthony. *Battle for Batangas: A Philippine Province at War.* New Haven, CT: Yale University Press, 1991.

———. *A Past Recovered.* Quezon City, Philippines: New Day, 1987.

———. *Social Engineering in the Philippines: The Aims, Execution, and Impact of American Colonial Policy, 1900–1913.* Westport, CT: Greenwood Press, 1980.

McCallum, Jack. *Leonard Wood: Rough Rider, Surgeon, Architect of American Imperialism.* New York: New York University Press, 2006.

McClintock, Anne. *Imperial Leather: Race, Gender and Sexuality in the Colonial Contest.* New York: Routledge, 1995.

McCoy, Alfred W. *Policing America's Empire: The United States, the Philippines, and the Rise of the Surveillance State.* Madison: University of Wisconsin Press, 2009.

McGillivray, Gillian. *Blazing Cane: Sugar Communities, Class, and State Formation in Cuba, 1868–1959.* Durham, NC: Duke University Press, 2009.

McKenna, Rebecca Tinio. *American Imperial Pastoral: The Architecture of US Colonialism in the Philippines.* Chicago: University of Chicago Press, 2017.

McKenna, Thomas M. *Muslim Rulers and Rebels: Everyday Politics and Armed Separatism in the Southern Philippines.* Berkeley: University of California Press, 1998.

McKeown, Adam M. *Melancholy Order: Asian Migration and the Globalization of Borders.* New York: Columbia University Press, 2008.

McLennan, Rebecca M. *The Crisis of Imprisonment: Protest, Politics, and the Making of the American Penal State, 1776–1941.* New York: Cambridge University Press, 2008.

Melosi, Martin V. *Garbage in the Cities: Refuse, Reform, and the Environment.* Rev. ed. Pittsburgh: University of Pittsburgh, 2005.

Meriño Fuentes, María de los Ángeles. *Gobierno municipal y partidos políticos en Santiago de Cuba (1898–1912).* Santiago de Cuba: Ediciones Santiago, 2001.

Merleaux, April. *Sugar and Civilization: American Empire and the Cultural Politics of Sweetness.* Chapel Hill: University of North Carolina Press, 2015.

Miller, Stuart Creighton. *"Benevolent Assimilation": The American Conquest of the Philippines, 1899–1903.* New Haven, CT: Yale University Press, 1982.

———. *The Unwelcome Immigrant: The American Image of the Chinese, 1785–1882.* Berkeley: University of California Press, 1969.

Millett, Allan R. *The General: Robert L. Bullard and Officership in the U.S. Army, 1881–1925.* Westport, CT: Greenwood Press, 1975.

———. *The Politics of Intervention: The Military Occupation of Cuba, 1906–1909.* Columbus: University of Ohio Press, 1968.

———. *Semper Fidelis: The History of the United States Marine Corps.* New York: Macmillan, 1980.

Millis, Walter. *Arms and Men: A Study in American Military History.* New York: Capricorn Books, 1956.

Mitchell, Timothy. *Rule of Experts: Egypt, Techno-Politics, Modernity.* Berkeley: University of California Press, 2002.

Mojares, Resil B. *Brains of the Nation: Pedro Paterno, T.H. Pardo de Tavera, Isabelo de los Reyes and the Production of Modern Knowledge*. Quezon City: Ateneo de Manila University Press, 2006.

Molnar, Nicholas Trajano. *American Mestizos, the Philippines, and the Malleability of Race, 1898–1961*. Columbia: University of Missouri Press, 2017.

Montgomery, David. *Beyond Equality: Labor and the Radical Republicans, 1862–1872*. Urbana: University of Illinois Press, 1981.

———. *Citizen Worker: The Experience of Workers in the United States with Democracy and the Free Market during the Nineteenth Century*. New York: Cambridge University Press, 1993.

Moore, Adam. *Empire's Labor: The Global Army That Supports U.S. Wars*. Ithaca, NY: Cornell University Press, 2019.

Morey, Michael. *Fagan: An African American Renegade in the Philippine-American War*. Madison: University of Wisconsin Press, 2019.

Morley, Ian. *Cities and Nationhood: American Imperialism and Urban Design in the Philippines, 1898–1916*. Honolulu: University of Hawai'i Press, 2018.

Moyd, Michelle R. *Violent Intermediaries: African Soldiers, Conquest, and Everyday Colonialism in German East Africa*. Athens: Ohio University Press, 2014.

Murphy, Gretchen. *Shadowing the White Man's Burden: U.S. Imperialism and the Problem of the Color Line*. New York: New York University Press, 2010.

Murphy, Kevin P. *Political Manhood: Red Bloods, Mollycoddles, and the Politics of Progressive Era Reform*. New York: Columbia University Press, 2008.

Nelson, Daniel. *Managers and Workers: Origins of the New Factory System in the United States, 1880–1920*. Madison: University of Wisconsin Press, 1975.

Ngai, Mae M. *The Chinese Question: The Gold Rushes and Global Politics*. New York: W. W. Norton, 2021.

———. *Impossible Subjects: Illegal Aliens and the Making of Modern America*. Princeton, NJ: Princeton University Press, 2004.

Nye, David E. *American Technological Sublime*. Cambridge, MA: MIT Press, 1994.

Ochosa, Orlino A. *The Tinio Brigade: Anti-American Resistance in the Ilocos Provinces, 1899–1901*. Quezon City: New Day, 1989.

Palmer, John McAuley. *America in Arms: The Experience of the United States with Military Organization*. New York: Arno Press, 1979.

Pappademos, Melina. *Black Political Activism and the Cuban Republic*. Chapel Hill: University of North Carolina Press, 2011.

Peck, Gunther. *Reinventing Free Labor: Padrones and Immigrant Workers in the North American West, 1880–1930*. New York: Cambridge University Press, 2000.

Pérez, Lisandro. *Sugar, Cigars, and Revolution: The Making of Cuban New York*. New York: New York University Press, 2018.

Pérez, Louis A., Jr. *Army Politics in Cuba, 1898–1958*. Pittsburgh: University of Pittsburgh Press, 1976.

———. *Colonial Reckoning: Race and Revolution in Nineteenth-Century Cuba*. Durham, NC: Duke University Press, 2023.

———. *Cuba and the United States: Ties of Singular Intimacy*. Athens: University of Georgia Press, 2003.

———. *Cuba between Empires, 1878–1902*. Pittsburgh: University of Pittsburgh Press, 1983.
———. *Cuba in the American Imagination: Metaphor and the Imperial Ethos*. Chapel Hill: University of North Carolina Press, 2008.
———. *Cuba under the Platt Amendment, 1902–1934*. Pittsburgh: University of Pittsburgh Press, 1986.
———. *Essays on Cuban History: Historiography and Research*. Gainesville: University of Florida Press, 1995.
———. *Lords of the Mountain: Social Banditry and Peasant Protest in Cuba, 1878–1918*. Pittsburgh: University of Pittsburgh Press, 1989.
———. *On Becoming Cuban: Identity, Nation, and Culture*. Chapel Hill: University of North Carolina Press, 1999.
———. *Slaves, Sugar, and Colonial Society: Travel Accounts of Cuba, 1801–1899*. Wilmington, DE: Scholarly Resources, 1992.
———. *The War of 1898: The United States and Cuba in History and Historiography*. Chapel Hill: University of North Carolina Press, 1998.
Phelan, John Leddy. *The Hispanization of the Philippines: Spanish Aims and Filipino Responses, 1565–1700*. Madison: University of Wisconsin Press, 1967.
Poblete, JoAnna. *Islanders in the Empire: Filipino and Puerto Rican Laborers in Hawai'i*. Urbana: University of Illinois Press, 2014.
Polk, Khary Oronde. *Contagions of Empire: Scientific Racism, Sexuality, and Black Military Workers Abroad, 1898–1948*. Chapel Hill: University of North Carolina Press, 2020.
Prados-Torreira, Teresa. *Mambísas: Rebel Women in Nineteenth-Century Cuba*. Gainesville: University Press of Florida, 2005.
Quirino, Carlos. *Amang: The Life and Times of Eulogio Rodriguez, Sr.* Quezon City: New Day, 1983.
Racelis, Mary, and Judy Celine A. Ick, eds. *Bearers of Benevolence: The Thomasites and Public Education in the Philippines*. Pasig City, Philippines: Anvil, 2001.
Rafael, Vicente L. *Contracting Colonialism: Translation and Christian Conversion in Tagalog Society under Early Spanish Rule*. Ithaca, NY: Cornell University Press, 1988.
———. *Motherless Tongues: The Insurgency of Language amid Wars of Translation*. Durham, NC: Duke University Press, 2016.
———. *The Promise of the Foreign: Nationalism and the Technics of Translation in the Spanish Philippines*. Durham, NC: Duke University Press, 2005.
———. *White Love and Other Events in Filipino History*. Durham, NC: Duke University Press, 2000.
Renda, Mary A. *Taking Haiti: Military Occupation and the Culture of U.S. Imperialism, 1915–1940*. Chapel Hill: University of North Carolina Press, 2001.
Reyes, Raquel A. G. *Love, Passion, and Patriotism: Sexuality and the Philippine Propaganda Movement, 1882–1892*. Singapore: NUS Press, 2008.
Rice, Mark. *Dean Worcester's Fantasy Islands: Photography, Film, and the Colonial Philippines*. Ann Arbor: University of Michigan, 2014.
Riddell, William D. *On the Waves of Empire: U.S. Imperialism and Merchant Sailors, 1872–1924*. Urbana: University of Illinois Press, 2023.
Riera Hernandez, Mario. *Ejercito Libertador de Cuba, 1895–1898*. Miami: Mario Riera Hernandez, 1985.

Rivero Muñiz, José. *El movimiento obrero durante la primera intervención: apuntes para la historia del proletariado en Cuba*. Direccion de Publicaciones, Universidad Central de las Villas, 1961.

Rockel, Stephen J. *Carriers of Culture: Labor on the Road in Nineteenth-Century East Africa*. Portsmouth, NH: Heinemann, 2006.

Rodríguez, Daniel A. *The Right to Live in Health: Medical Politics in Postindependence Havana*. Chapel Hill: University of North Carolina Press, 2020.

Roediger, David R., and Elizabeth D. Esch. *The Production of Difference: Race and the Management of Labor in U.S. History*. New York: Oxford University Press, 2012.

Roff, Sandra, and Anthony M. Cucchiara. *From the Free Academy to CUNY: Illustrating Public Higher Education in NYC, 1847–1997*. New York: Fordham University Press, 2000.

Rosenberg, Emily S. *Financial Missionaries to the World: The Politics and Culture of Dollar Diplomacy, 1900–1930*. Durham, NC: Duke University Press, 2003.

———. *Spreading the American Dream: American Economic and Cultural Expansion, 1890–1945*. New York: Hill & Wang, 1982.

———. *Transnational Currents in a Shrinking World, 1870–1945*. Cambridge, MA: Harvard University Press, 2012.

Rotter, Andrew J. *Empire of the Senses: Bodily Encounters in Imperial India and the Philippines*. New York: Oxford University Press, 2019.

Rotundo, Anthony. *American Manhood: Transformations in Masculinity from the Revolution to the Modern Era*. New York: Basic Books, 1993.

Said, Edward. *Orientalism*. New York: Vintage Books, 1979.

Salman, Michael. *The Embarrassment of Slavery: Controversies over Bondage and Nationalism in the American Colonial Philippines*. Berkeley: University of California Press, 2001.

Saxton, Alexander. *The Indispensable Enemy: Labor and the Anti-Chinese Movement in California*. Berkeley: University of California Press, 1971.

Schmidt, Hans. *Maverick Marine: General Smedley D. Butler and the Contradictions of American Military History*. Lexington: University Press of Kentucky, 1987.

Schueller, Malini Johar. *Campaigns of Knowledge: U.S. Pedagogies of Colonialism and Occupation in the Philippines and Japan*. Philadelphia: Temple University Press, 2019.

Schumacher, John N. *The Propaganda Movement, 1880–1895: The Creators of a Filipino Consciousness, the Makers of the Revolution*. Manila: Solidaridad, 1975.

Schwartz, Rosalie. *Pleasure Island: Tourism and Temptation in Cuba*. Lincoln: University of Nebraska Press, 1997.

Schwendinger, Robert J. *Ocean of Bitter Dreams: Maritime Relations between the United States and China, 1850–1915*. Tucson, AZ: Westernlore, 1988.

Scott, James C. *The Art of Not Being Governed: An Anarchist History of Upland Southeast Asia*. New Haven, CT: Yale University Press, 2009.

———. *Domination and the Arts of Resistance: Hidden Transcripts*. New Haven, CT: Yale University Press, 1990.

———. *Seeing Like a State: How Certain Schemes to Improve the Human Condition Have Failed*. New Haven, CT: Yale University Press, 1998.

Scott, Rebecca J. *Degrees of Freedom: Louisiana and Cuba after Slavery*. Cambridge, MA: Harvard University Press, 2005.

———. *Slave Emancipation in Cuba: The Transition to Free Labor, 1860–1899*. Princeton, NJ: Princeton University Press, 1985.
Scott, William Henry. *Cracks in the Parchment Curtain and Other Essays in Philippine History*. Quezon City: New Day, 1982.
———. *The Discovery of the Igorots: Spanish Contacts with the Pagans of Northern Luzon*. Quezon City: New Day, 1974.
———. *Ilocano Responses to American Aggression, 1900–1901*. Quezon City: New Day, 1986.
———. *The Union Obrera Democratica: First Filipino Labor Union*. Quezon City: New Day, 1992.
Seigel, Micol. *Violence Work: State Power and the Limits of the Police*. Durham, NC: Duke University Press, 2018.
Sippial, Tiffany A. *Prostitution, Modernity, and the Making of the Cuban Republic, 1840–1920*. Chapel Hill: University of North Carolina Press, 2013.
Skowronek, Stephen. *Building a New American State: The Expansion of National Administrative Capacities, 1877–1920*. New York: Cambridge University Press, 1982.
Smith, Sherry L. *The View from Officers' Row: Army Perceptions of Western Indians*. Tucson: University of Arizona Press, 1990.
Snyder, Timothy. *On Freedom*. New York: Penguin Random House, 2024.
Stanley, Peter. *A Nation in the Making: The Philippines and the United States, 1899–1921*. Cambridge, MA: Harvard University Press, 1974.
Steinbock-Pratt, Sarah. *Educating the Empire: American Teachers and Contested Colonization in the Philippines*. New York: Cambridge University Press, 2019.
Stephanson, Anders. *Manifest Destiny: American Expansion and the Empire of Right*. New York: Hill & Wang, 1995.
Stoler, Ana Laura. *Along the Archival Grain: Epistemic Anxieties and Colonial Common Sense*. Princeton, NJ: Princeton University Press, 2009.
———. *Carnal Knowledge and Imperial Power: Race and the Intimate in Colonial Rule*. Berkeley: University of California, 2002.
———. *Duress: Imperial Durabilities in Our Times*. Durham, NC: Duke University Press, 2016.
Stoner, K. Lynn. *From the House to the Streets: The Cuban Woman's Movement for Legal Reform, 1898–1940*. Durham, NC: Duke University Press, 1991.
Streets, Heather. *Martial Races: The Military, Race, and Masculinity in British Imperial Culture, 1857–1914*. New York: Manchester University Press, 2004.
Stromquist, Shelton. *Reinventing "The People": The Progressive Movement, the Class Problem, and the Origins of Modern Liberalism*. Urbana: University of Illinois Press, 2006.
Stubbs, Jean. *Tobacco on the Periphery: A Case Study in Cuban Labour History, 1860–1958*. New York: Cambridge University Press, 1985.
Sturtevant, David. *Popular Uprisings in the Philippines, 1840–1940*. Ithaca, NY: Cornell University Press, 1976.
Sullivan, Rodney J. *Exemplar of Americanism: The Philippine Career of Dean C. Worcester*. Ann Arbor: University of Michigan Center for South and Southeast Asian Studies, 1991.
Tan, Antonio S. *The Chinese in the Philippines, 1898–1935: A Study of Their National Awakening*. Quezon City: R. P. Garcia, 1972.
Tan, Samuel K. *The Filipino Muslim Armed Struggle, 1900–1972*. Manila: Filipinas Foundation, 1977.

Tate, Michael L. *The Frontier Army in the Settlement of the West.* Norman: University of Oklahoma Press, 1999.
Thomas, Megan C. *Orientalists, Propagandists, and Ilustrados: Filipino Scholarship and the End of Spanish Colonialism.* Minneapolis: University of Minnesota Press, 2012.
Tilly, Charles. *Trust and Rule.* New York: Cambridge University Press, 2005.
Tone, John Lawrence. *War and Genocide in Cuba, 1895–1898.* Chapel Hill: University of North Carolina, 2006.
Torriente y Peraza, Cosme de la. *Calixto García cooperó con las fuerzas armadas de los EE. UU. en 1898, cumpliendo órdenes del gobierno cubano.* Havana: Imprenta "El Siglo XX," 1952.
Trask, David F. *The War with Spain in 1898.* New York: Macmillan, 1981.
Tsai, Shih-shan Henry. *China and the Overseas Chinese in the United States, 1868–1911.* Fayetteville: University of Arkansas Press, 1983.
Tyrrell, Ian. *Crisis of the Wasteful Nation: Empire and Conservation in Theodore Roosevelt's America.* Chicago: University of Chicago Press, 2015.
———. *Reforming the World: The Creation of America's Moral Empire.* Princeton, NJ: Princeton University Press, 2010.
Urban, Andrew. *Brokering Servitude: Migration and the Politics of Domestic Labor during the Long Nineteenth Century.* New York: New York University Press, 2018.
Utley, Robert M. *Frontier Regulars: The United States Army and the Indian, 1866–1891.* New York: Macmillan, 1974.
Utset, Marial Iglesias. *A Cultural History of Cuba during the U.S. Occupation, 1898–1902.* Chapel Hill: University of North Carolina Press, 2011.
Van der Linden, Marcel. *Workers of the World: Essays toward a Global Labor History.* Leiden, Netherlands: Brill, 2008.
Vicuña Gonzalez, Vernadette. *Securing Paradise: Tourism and Militarism in Hawai'i and the Philippines.* Durham, NC: Duke University Press, 2013.
Vinat de la Mata, Raquel. *Las cubanas en la posguerra (1898–1902): Acercamiento a la reconsctrucción de una etapa olvidada.* Havana: Editora Politica, 2001.
Walsh, Thomas P. *Tin Pan Alley and the Philippines: American Songs of War and Love, 1898–1946, a Resource Guide.* Lanham, MD: Scarecrow Press, 2013.
Walter, Dierk. *Colonial Violence: European Empires and the Use of Force.* New York: Oxford University Press, 2017.
Walther, Karine V. *Sacred Interests: The United States and the Islamic World, 1821–1921.* Chapel Hill: University of North Carolina Press, 2015.
Weigley, Russell F. *The American Way of War: A History of United States Military Strategy and Policy.* Bloomington: Indiana University Press, 1973.
Wernstedt, Frederick L., and J. E. Spencer. *The Philippine Island World: A Physical, Cultural, and Regional Geography.* Berkeley: University of California Press, 1967.
Wickberg, Edgar. *The Chinese in Philippine Life: 1850–1898.* New Haven, CT: Yale University Press, 1965.
Wilson, Andrew R. *Ambition and Identity: Chinese Merchant Elites in Colonial Manila, 1880–1916.* Honolulu: University of Hawai'i Press, 2004.
Winkelmann, Tessa. *Dangerous Intercourse: Gender and Interracial Intercourse in the American Colonial Philippines, 1989–1946.* Ithaca, NY: Cornell University Press, 2023.

Wintermute, Bobby. *Public Health and the U.S. Military: A History of the Army Medical Department, 1818–1917*. New York: Routledge, 2011.
Witt, John Fabian. *Lincoln's Code: The Laws of War in American History*. New York: Free Press, 2012.
Wong Kwok-Chu. *The Chinese in the Philippine Economy, 1898–1941*. Quezon City: Ateneo de Manila University Press, 1999.
Wooster, Robert Allen. *The Military and United States Indian Policy, 1865–1903*. New Haven, CT: Yale University Press, 1988.
———. *The United States Army and the Making of America: From Confederation to Empire, 1775–1903*. Lawrence: University Press of Kansas, 2021.
Yglesia Martinez, Teresita. *Cuba: Primera republica, segunda ocupación*. Havana: Editorial de Ciencias Sociales, 1977.
Young, Elliot. *Alien Nation: Chinese Migration in the Americas from the Coolie Era through World War II*. Chapel Hill: University of North Carolina Press, 2014.
Yun, Lisa. *The Coolie Speaks: Chinese Indentured Laborers and African Slaves in Cuba*. Philadelphia: Temple University Press, 2008.
Zanetti, Oscar, and Alejandro García. *Sugar and Railroads: A Cuban History, 1837–1959*. Chapel Hill: University of North Carolina Press, 1998.
Zimmerman, Andrew. *Alabama in Africa: Booker T. Washington, the German Empire, and the Globalization of the New South*. Princeton, NJ: Princeton University Press, 2010.

JOURNAL ARTICLES AND ESSAYS

Abinales, Patricio N. "An American Colonial State: Authority and Structure in Southern Mindanao." In *Images of State Power: Essays on Philippine Politics from the Margins*, 1–62. Diliman, Quezon City: University of the Philippines Press, 1998.
———. "Progressive-Machine Conflict in Early-Twentieth Century U.S. Politics and Colonial-State Building in the Philippines." In *The American Colonial State in the Philippines: Global Perspectives*, edited by Julian Go and Anne L. Foster, 148–81. Durham, NC: Duke University Press, 2003.
———. "The U.S. Army as an Occupying Force in Muslim Mindanao, 1899–1913." In *Colonial Crucible: Empire in the Making of the Modern American State*, edited by Alfred W. McCoy and Francisco A. Scarano, 410–20. Madison: University of Wisconsin Press, 2009.
Adas, Michael. "From Avoidance to Confrontation: Peasant Protest in Precolonial and Colonial Southeast Asia." *Comparative Studies in Society and History* 23, no. 2 (April 1981): 217–47.
Adler, William D., and Andrew J. Polsky. "Building the New American Nation: Economic Development, Public Goods, and the Early U.S. Army." *Political Science Quarterly* 125, no. 1 (Spring 2010): 87–110.
———. "The State in a Blue Uniform." *Polity* 40, no. 3 (July 2008): 348–54.
Ahmad, Aijaz. "Class and Colony in Mindanao." In *Rebels, Warlords, and Ulama: A Reader on Muslim Separatism and the War in Southern Philippines*, edited by Eric Gutierrez, Gaerlan, and Stankovitch, 1–20. Quezon City: Institute for Popular Democracy, 1999.

Akiboh, Alvita. "Empire's Embezzlers: Fraud and Scandal in U.S.-Occupied Cuba, 1900–1902." *Modern American History* 6 (2023): 301–21.

Amoroso, Donna J. "Inheriting the 'Moro Problem': Muslim Authority and Colonial Rule in British Malaya and the Philippines." In *The American Colonial State in the Philippines: Global Perspectives*, edited by Julian Go and Anne L. Foster, 118–47. Durham: Duke University Press, 2003.

Andaya, Barbara Watson. "Gender, Warfare, and Patriotism in Southeast Asia and the Philippine Revolution." In *The Philippine Revolution of 1896: Ordinary Lives in Extraordinary Times*, edited by Florentino Rodao and Felice Noelle Rodriguez, 1–30. Quezon City: Ateneo de Manila University Press, 2002.

Anderson, Benedict R. "Cacique Democracy in the Philippines: Origins and Dreams." In *Discrepant Histories: Translocal Essays on Filipino Cultures*, edited by Vicente L. Rafael, 3–47. Philadelphia: Temple University Press, 1995.

Apilado, Digna P. "Nationalism and Discrimination: Policies of the Revolutionary Government of 1898 toward the Chinese in the Philippines." In *Imperios y naciones en el Pacífico*, vol. 2, *colonialismo e identidad nacional en Filipinas y Micronesia*, edited by María Dolores Elizalde, Josep M. Fradera, and Luis Alonzo. Spain: Consejo Superior de Investigaciones Científicas, 2001.

Arensmeyer, Elliot C. "The Chinese Coolie Labor Trade and the Philippines: An Inquiry." *Philippine Studies* 28 (1980): 187–98.

Bailey, Beth, Alesha E. Doan, Shannon Portillo, and Kara Dixon Vuic. Introduction to *Managing Sex in the U.S. Military: Gender, Identity, and Behavior*, 1–15. Edited by Beth Bailey, Alesha E. Doan, Shannon Portillo, and Kara Dixon Vuic. Lincoln: University of Nebraska Press, 2022.

Balboa Navarro, Imilcy. "Steeds, Cocks, and Guayaberas: The Social Impact of Agrarian Reorganization in the Republic." In *State of Ambiguity: Civic Life and Culture in Cuba's First Republic*, edited by Steven Palmer, José Antonio Piqueras, and Amparo Sánchez Cobos, 208–30. Durham, NC: Duke University Press, 2014.

Balce, Nerissa. "The Filipina's Breast: Savagery, Docility, and the Erotics of the American Empire." *Social Text* 24, no. 2 (Summer 2006): 89–110.

Ballantyne, Tony, and Antoinette Burton. "Bodies, Empires, and World Histories." In *Bodies in Contact: Rethinking Colonial Encounters in World History*, edited by Tony Ballantyne and Antoinette Burton, 1–15. Durham, NC: Duke University Press, 2005.

Banerjee, Milinda. "Decolonization and Subaltern Sovereignty: India and the Tokyo Trial." In *War Crimes Trials in the Wake of Decolonization and Cold War in Asia, 1945–1956: Justice in Time of Turmoil*, edited by Kerstin von Lingen, 69–92. London: Palgrave Macmillan, 2016.

Bankoff, Greg. "Households of Ill-Repute: Rape, Prostitution, and Marriage in the Nineteenth Century Philippines." *Pilipinas* 17 (Fall 1991): 35–49.

———. "'These Brothers of Ours': Poblete's *Obreros* and the Road to Baguio, 1903–1905." *Journal of Social History* 38, no. 4 (Summer 2005): 1047–72.

———. "Wants, Wages, and Workers: Laboring in the American Philippines, 1899–1908." *Pacific Historical Review* 74, no. 1 (February 2005): 59–86.

Baron, Ava, and Eileen Boris. "'The Body' as a Useful Category for Working-Class History." *Labor: Studies in Working-Class History of the Americas* 4, no. 2 (2007): 23–43.

Beckert, Sven. "From Tuskugee to Togo: The Problem of Freedom in the Empire of Cotton." *Journal of American History* 92, no. 2 (September 2005): 498–526.

———. "Labor Regimes after Emancipation: The Case of Cotton." In *Labour History Beyond Borders: Concepts and Explorations*, edited by Marcel van der Linden, 139–53. Vienna: Akademische Velragsangstalt, 2010.

Beckett, Jeremy. "The Defiant and the Compliant: The Datus of Magindanao under Colonial Rule." In *Philippine Social History: Global Trade and Local Transformations*, edited by Alfred W. McCoy and Ed. C. de Jesus, 390–414. Quezon City: Ateneo de Manila University Press, 1982.

Bender, Daniel E., and Jana Lipman. "Through the Looking Glass: U.S. Empire through the Lens of Labor History." In *Making the Empire Work: Labor and United States Imperialism*, edited by Daniel Bender and Jana Lipman, 1–32. New York: New York University Press, 2015.

Benton, Lauren, and Adam Clulow. "The Long, Strange History of Protection." In *Protection and Empire: A Global History*, edited by Lauren Benton, Adam Clulow, and Bain Attwood, 1–9. New York: Cambridge University Press, 2018.

Berg, Heather. "Working for Love, Loving for Work: Discourses of Labor in Feminist Sex-Work Activism." *Feminist Studies* 40, no. 3 (2014): 693–721.

Blanc-Szanton, Catherine. "Collision of Cultures: Historical Reformulations of Gender in the Lowland Visayas, Philippines." In *Power and Difference: Gender in Island Southeast Asia*, edited by Jane Monnig Atkinson and Shelley Errington, 345–83. Stanford, CA: Stanford University Press, 1990.

Bragge, Lawrence, Ulrike Claas, and Paul Roscoe. "On the Edge of Empire: Military Brokers in the Sepik 'Tribal Zone.'" *American Ethnologist* 33, no. 1 (February 2006): 100–113.

Brown, Carolyn, and Marcel van der Linden. "Shifting Boundaries between Free and Unfree Labor." *International Labor and Working-Class History* 78 (Fall 2010): 4–11.

Burns, Adam D. "A New Pacific Border: William H. Taft, the Philippines, and Chinese Immigration, 1898–1903." *Comparative American Studies* 9, no. 4 (December 2011): 309–24.

Camagay, Maria Luisa T. "Prostitution in Nineteenth Century Manila." *Philippine Studies* 36, no. 2 (1988): 241–55.

Capozzola, Christopher. "The Secret Soldiers' Union: Labor and Soldier Politics in the Philippine Scout Mutiny of 1924." In *Making the Empire Work: Labor and United States Imperialism*, edited by Daniel Bender and Jana Lipman, 85–103. New York: New York University Press, 2015.

Charbonneau, Oli. "Colonizing Workers: Labor, Race, and U.S. Military Governance in the Southern Philippines." *Modern American History* 4 (2021): 25–47.

———. "'A New West in Mindanao': Settler Fantasies on the U.S. Imperial Fringe." *Journal of the Gilded Age and Progressive Era* 18, no. 3 (2019): 304–23.

———. "The Permeable South: Imperial Interactivities in the Islamic Philippines, 1899–1930s." In *Crossing Empires: Taking U.S. History into Transimperial Terrain*, edited by Kristin L. Hoganson and Jay Sexton, 183–202. Durham, NC: Duke University Press, 2020.

———. "Teaching the World to Work: Industrial Education as U.S. Imperial Tradition." *Diplomatic History* 47, no. 3 (June 2023): 369–90.

Chu, Richard T. "The 'Chinaman' Question: A Conundrum in US Imperial Policy in the Pacific." *Kritika Kultura* 7 (2006): 5–23.

———. "Transnationalizing the History of the Chinese in the Philippines." In *Filipino Studies: Palimpsests of Nation and Diaspora*, edited by Martin F. Manalansan IV, and Augusto F. Espiritu, 179–96. New York: New York University, 2016.

Cohen, Rachel Lara, Kate Hardy, Teela Sanders, and Carol Wolkowitz. "The Body/Sex/Work Nexus: A Critical Perspective on Body Work and Sex Work." In *Body/Sex/Work: Intimate, Sexualised and Embodied Work*, edited by Rachel Lara Cohen, Kate Hardy, Teela Sanders, and Carol Wolkowitz, 3–27. Basingstoke, England: Palgrave MacMillan, 2013.

Cooper, Frederick. "Conflict and Connection: Rethinking Colonial African History." *American Historical Review* 99, no. 5 (December 1994): 1516–45.

Cosmas, Graham A. "Joint Operations in the Spanish-American War." In *Crucible of Empire: The Spanish-American War and Its Aftermath*, edited by James C. Bradford, 102–26. Annapolis: US Naval Institute Press, 1993.

Cullinane, Michael. "Bringing in the Brigands: The Politics of Pacification in the Colonial Philippines, 1902–1907." *Philippine Studies* 57, no. 1 (March 2009): 49–76.

Davenport, F. Garvin. "The Sanitation Revolution in Illinois, 1870–1900." *Journal of the Illinois State Historical Society* 66, no. 3 (Autumn 1973): 306–26.

Davidson, Julia O'Connell. "The Rights and Wrongs of Prostitution." *Hypatia* 17, no. 2 (Spring 2022): 84–98.

Daza y Salazar, E[ugenio]. "Some Documents of the Philippine-American War in Samar." *Leyte-Samar Studies* 17 (1983): 165–87.

De la Fuente, Alejandro. "Two Dangers, One Solution: Immigration, Race, and Labor in Cuba, 1900–1930." *International Labor and Working-Class History* 51 (Spring 1997): 30–49.

De la Fuente, Alejandro, and Matthew Casey. "Race and the Suffrage Controversy in Cuba, 1898–1901." In *Colonial Crucible: Empire in the Making of the Modern American State*, edited by Alfred W. McCoy and Francisco A. Scarano, 220–29. Madison: University of Wisconsin Press, 2009.

Dery, Luis Camara. "Prostitution in Colonial Manila." *Philippine Studies* 39, no. 4 (1991): 475–89.

De Viana, Augusto V. "Eugenio Daza's Account of the American Occupation of Balangiga on September 28, 1901: The Balangiga Massacre." *Unitas* 76, no. 1 (March 2003): 53–64.

Doeppers, Daniel F. "Destination, Selection, and Turnover among Chinese Migrants in Philippine Cities in the Nineteenth Century." *Journal of Historical Geography* 12, no. 4 (1986): 381–401.

———. "Migrants in Urban Labor Markets: The Social Stratification of Tondo and Sampaloc in the 1890s." In *Population and History: The Demographic Origins of the Modern Philippines*, edited by Daniel F. Doeppers and Peter Xenos, 253–63. Madison: University of Wisconsin, Center for Southeast Asian Studies, 1998.

———. "Migration to Manila: Changing Gender Representation, Migration Field, and Urban Structure." In Doeppers and Xenos, *Population and History*, 139–79.

Domínguez, Jorge I. "Response to Occupations by the United States: Caliban's Dilemma." *Pacific Historical Review* 48, no. 4 (November 1979): 591–605.

Elizalde, María Dolores, Josep M. Fradera, and Luis Alonso. *Imperios y naciones en el Pacífico*. Madrid: Consejo Superior de Investigaciones Cientificas, 2001.

Escalante, Rene. "The Collapse of the Malolos Republic." *Philippine Studies* 46, no. 4 (Fourth Quarter 1998): 452–76.

Evans, Julie, Ann Genovese, Alexander Reilly, and Patrick Wolfe. "Sovereignty: Frontiers of Possibility." In *Sovereignty: Frontiers of Possibility*, edited by Julie Evans, Ann Genovese, Alexander Reilly, and Patrick Wolfe, 1–16. Honolulu: University of Hawai'i Press, 2013.

Foster, Anne. "Prohibiting Opium in the Philippines and the United States: The Creation of an Interventionist State." In *Colonial Crucible: Empire in the Making of the Modern State*, edited by Alfred W. McCoy and Francisco A. Scarano, 95–105. Madison: University of Wisconsin Press, 2009.

Fradera, Josep M. "Reading Imperial Transitions: Spanish Contraction, British Expansion, and American Irruption." In *Colonial Crucible: Empire in the Making of the Modern State*, edited by Alfred W. McCoy and Francisco A. Scarano, 34–62. Madison: University of Wisconsin Press, 2009.

Fraser, Nancy. "Expropriation and Exploitation in Racialized Capitalism: A Reply to Michael Dawson." *Critical Historical Studies* 3, no. 1 (Spring 2016): 163–78.

Freeman, Joshua B. "Militarism, Empire, and Labor Relations: The Case of Brice P. Disque." *International Labor and Working-Class History* 80 (Fall 2011): 103–20.

Frevert, Ute. "Trust as Work." In *Work in a Modern Society: The German Historical Experience in Comparative Perspective*, edited by Jürgen Kocka, 93–108. New York: Berghahn Books, 2010.

Galang, Jely A. "Living Carriers in the East: Chinese Cargadores in Nineteenth-Century Manila." *Philippine Studies* 69, no. 1 (2021): 71–108.

Gates, John Morgan. "Indians and Insurrectos: The US Army's Experience with Insurgency." *The U.S. Army War College Quarterly: Parameters* 13, no. 1 (1983): 59–68.

———. "War-Related Deaths in the Philippines, 1898–1902." *Pacific Historical Review* 53, no. 3 (August 1984): 367–78.

Gatewood, Willard B., Jr. "An Experiment in Color: The Eighth Illinois Volunteers, 1898–1899." *Journal of Illinois State Historical Society* 65, no. 3 (Autumn 1972): 293–312.

Gillette, Howard, Jr. "The Military Occupation of Cuba, 1899–1902: Workshop for American Progressivism." *American Quarterly* 25, no. 4 (October 1973): 410–25.

Ginsberg, Philip. "The Chinese in the Philippine Revolution." *Asian Studies* 8, no. 1 (1970): 143–59.

Go, Julian. "Chains of Empire, Projects of State: Colonial State-Building in Puerto Rico and the Philippines." *Comparative Studies in Society and History* 42, no. 2 (2000): 332–62.

———. "*El cuerpo, razon at kapangyarihan*/The Body, Reason and Power: Filipino Elite Cosmologies of State under American Colonial Rule, 1890s–1920s." *Asian Studies* 34, no. 1 (1998): 146–93.

———. "Global Perspectives on the U.S. Colonial State in the Philippines." In *The American Colonial State in the Philippines: Global Perspectives*, edited by Julian Go and Anne L. Foster, 1–42. Durham, NC: Duke University Press, 2003.

———. "The Provinciality of American Empire: 'Liberal Exceptionalism' and U.S. Colonial Rule, 1898–1912." *Comparative Studies in Society and History* 49, no. 1 (2007): 74–108.

———. "'Racism' and Colonialism": Meanings of Difference and Ruling Practices in America's Pacific Empire." *Qualitative Sociology* 27, no. 1 (March 2004): 35–58.
Go, Julian, and Anne L. Foster, eds. *The American Colonial State in the Philippines: Global Perspectives*. Durham, NC: Duke University Press, 2003.
Goode, Steven M. "A Historical Basis for Force Requirements in Counterinsurgency." *Parameters* 39, no. 4 (Winter 2009–2010): 45–57.
Greene, Julie. "Entangled in Empires: British Antillean Migrations in the World of the Panama Canal." In *Crossing Empires: Taking U.S. History into Transimperial Terrain*, edited by Kristin L. Hoganson and Jay Sexton, 222–40. Durham, NC: Duke University Press, 2020.
———. "Rethinking the Boundaries of Class: Labor History and Theories of Class and Capitalism." *Labor: Studies in Working-Class History* 18, no. 2 (May 2021): 92–112.
———. "The Wages of Empire: Capitalism, Expansionism, and Working-Class Formation." In *Making the Empire Work: Labor and United States Imperialism*, edited by Jana Lipman and Daniel Bender, 35–58. New York: New York University Press, 2015.
Guerrero, Milagros Camayon. "The Provincial and Municipal Elites of Luzon during the Revolution, 1898–1902." In *Philippine Social History: Global Trade and Local Transformation*, edited by Alfred W. McCoy and Ed. C de Jesus, 155–90. Honolulu: University Press of Hawai'i Press, 1982.
Halsema, James J. "Land Transportation in the Philippines (I)." *Bulletin of the American Historical Collection* 33, no. 2 (April–June 2005): 69–81.
Hansen, Thomas Blom, and Finn Stepputat. "Sovereignty Revisited." *Annual Review of Anthropology* 35 (2006): 295–315.
Hart, Donn V., and Harriet Hart. "Juan Pusong, the Filipino Trickster Revisited." *Asian Studies* 12, nos. 2–3 (1974): 129–62.
Heefner, Gretchen. "Building the Bases of Empire: The US Army Corps of Engineers and Military Construction during the Early Cold War." In *The Military and the Market*, edited by Jennifer Mittelstadt and Mark R. Wilson, 105–19. Philadelphia: University of Pennsylvania Press, 2022.
Helg, Aline. "Black Men, Racial Stereotyping, and Violence in the U.S. South and Cuba." *Comparative Studies in Society and History* 42, no. 3 (July 2000): 576–604.
Hendrickson, Kenneth E. "Reluctant Expansionist—Jacob Gould Schurman and the Philippine Question." *Pacific Historical Review* 36, no. 4 (November 1967): 405–21.
Hirrel, Leo P. "The Beginnings of the Quartermasters Graves Registration Service." *Army Sustainment* 46 (July–August 2014): 64–67.
Hitchman, James J. "Unfinished Business: Public Works in Cuba, 1898–1902." *The Americas* 31, no. 3 (January 1975): 335–59.
———. "U.S. Control Over Cuban Sugar Production, 1898–1902." *Journal of Interamerican Studies and World Affairs* 12, no. 1 (January 1970): 90–106.
Hoernel, Robert B. "Sugar and Social Change in Oriente, Cuba, 1898–1946." *Journal of Latin American Studies* 8, no. 2 (November 1976): 215–49.
Hoganson, Kristin L., and Jay Sexton. Introduction to *Crossing Empires: Taking U.S. History into Transimperial Terrain*, 1–22. Edited by Kristin L. Hoganson and Jay Sexton. Durham, NC: Duke University Press, 2020.
Holli, Melvin G., ed. "A View of the American Campaign against Filipino Insurgents: 1900." *Philippine Studies* 17, no. 1 (January 1969): 97–111.

Howland, Douglas, and Luise White. "Sovereignty and the Study of States." In *The State of Sovereignty: Territories, Laws, Populations*, edited by Douglas Howland and Luise S. White, 1–18. Bloomington: Indiana University Press, 2009.

Huetz de Lemps, Xavier. "Provincial-Level Corruption in the Second Half of the Nineteenth Century." In *The Philippine Revolution of 1896: Ordinary Lives in Extraordinary Times*, edited by Florentino Rodao and Felice Noelle Rodriguez, 217–230. Quezon City: Ateneo de Manila University Press, 2001.

Humphrey, Caroline. "Sovereignty." In *A Companion to the Anthropology of Politics*, edited by David Nugent and Joan Vincent, 418–36. Malden, MA: Blackwell, 2004.

Hutchcroft, Paul D. "Colonial Masters, National Politicos, and Provincial Lords: Central Authority and Local Autonomy in the American Philippines, 1900–1913." *Journal of Asian Studies* 59, no. 2 (May 2000): 277–306.

Ileto, Reynaldo Clemeña. "Cholera and the Origins of the American Sanitary Order in the Philippines." In *Imperial Medicine and Indigenous Societies*, edited by David Arnold, 125–48. New York: Manchester University Press, 1988.

———. "Colonial Wars in Southern Luzon: Remembering and Forgetting." *Hitotsubashi Journal of Social Studies* 33 (2001): 103–18.

———. "Food Crisis and the Philippine Revolution: Southwestern Luzon, 1896–1902." *Journal of History* 30, nos. 1–2 (January–December 1985): 68–83.

———. "Orientalism and the Study of Philippine Politics." *Philippine Political Science Journal* 22, no. 45 (2001): 1–32.

———. "Toward a Local History of the Philippine-American War: The Case of Tiaong, Tayabas (Quezon) Province, 1901–1902." *Journal of History* 27, nos. 1–2 (1982): 67–79.

Jackson, Justin F. "'The Right Kind of Men': Flexible Capacity, Chinese Exclusion, and the Imperial Origins of Maritime Labor Reform in the United States, 1898–1905." *Labor: Working-Class Studies in the Americas* 10, no. 4 (Winter 2014): 39–60.

Jankowski, Lyce. "History of the Chinese Collection at the American Numismatic Society." *American Journal of Numismatics*, 2nd ser. 30 (2018): 251–92.

Johnson, Walter. "On Agency." *Journal of Social History* 37, no. 1 (Fall 2003): 113–24.

Jose, Ricardo T. "Labor Usage and Mobilization during the Japanese Occupation of the Philippines, 1942–45." In *Asian Labor in the Wartime Japanese Empire*, edited by Paul H. Kratoska, 267–84. Armonk, NY: M.E. Sharpe, 2005.

Kantowicz, Edward R. "Carter H. Harrison II: The Politics of Balance." In *The Mayors: The Chicago Political Tradition*, edited by Paul M. Green and Melvin G. Holli, 16–32. Carbondale: Southern Illinois University Press, 2013.

Katznelson, Ira. "Flexible Capacity: The Military and Early American Statebuilding." In *Shaped by War and Trade*, edited by Ira Katznelson and Martin Shefter, 82–110. Princeton, NJ: Princeton University Press, 2002.

Kocka, Jürgen. "Comparison and Beyond." *History and Theory* 42, no. 1 (February 2003): 39–44.

Kramer, Paul A. "The Darkness That Enters the Home: The Politics of Prostitution during the Philippine-American War. In *Haunted by Empire: Geographies of Intimacy in North American History*, edited by Ann Laura Stoler, 366–404. Durham, NC: Duke University Press, 2006.

———. "Empire, Exceptions, and Anglo-Saxons: Race and Rule between the British and United States Empires, 1880–1910." *Journal of American History* 88, no. 4 (March 2002): 1315–53.

———. "Imperial Openings: Civilization, Exemption, and the Geopolitics of Mobility in the History of Chinese Exclusion, 1868–1910." *Journal of the Gilded Age and Progressive Era* 14 (2015): 317–47.

———. "Power and Connection: Imperial Histories of the United States in the World." *American Historical Review* 116, no. 5 (December 2011): 1348–91.

———. "Race-Making and Colonial Violence in the U.S. Empire: The Philippine-American War as Race War." *Diplomatic History* 30, no. 2 (April 2006): 169–210.

Larkin, Brian. "The Politics and Poetics of Infrastructure." *Annual Review of Anthropology* 42 (2013): 327–43.

Larkin, John. "Philippine History Reconsidered: A Socioeconomic Perspective." *American Historical Review* 87, no. 3 (June 1982): 595–628.

Latham, Robert. "Social Sovereignty." *Theory, Culture, and Society* 17, no. 4 (August 2000): 1–18.

Lawrance, Benjamin N., Emily Lynn Osborn, and Richard L. Roberts. "African Intermediaries and the 'Bargain' of Collaboration." In *Intermediaries, Interpreters, and Clerks: African Employees in the Making of Colonial Africa*, edited by Benjamin N. Lawrance, Emily Lynn Osborn, and Richard L. Roberts, 3–34. Madison: University of Wisconsin Press 2006.

Levine, Philippa. "Is Comparative History Possible?" *History and Theory* 53, no. 3 (October 2014): 331–47.

Linn, Brian McAllister. "Intelligence and Low-Intensity Conflict in the Philippine War, 1899–1902." *Intelligence and National Security* 6, no. 1 (1991): 90–114.

———. "Provincial Pacification in the Philippines, 1900–1901: The First District Department of Northern Luzon." *Military Affairs* 51, no. 2 (April 1987): 62–66.

———. "The Struggle for Samar." In *Crucible of Empire: The Spanish-American War and Its Aftermath*, edited by James C. Bradford, 158–82. Annapolis, MD: US Naval Institute Press, 1993.

———. "'To Set All Law at Defiance': The Pulahan Revolt on Samar and U.S. Pacification." In *The Philippine Revolution and Beyond: Papers from the International Conference on the Centennial of the 1896 Philippine Revolution*, vol. 1, edited by Elmer A. Ordoñez, 556–81. Manila: Philippine Centennial Commission; National Commission for Culture and the Arts, 1998.

———. "'We Will Go Heavily Armed': The Marines' Small War on Samar, 1901." In *New Interpretations of Naval History: Selected Papers from the Ninth Naval History Symposium*, edited by W. R. Roberts and Jack Sweetman, 273–92. Annapolis, MD: Naval Institute Press, 1991.

Lockmiller, David A. "Agriculture in Cuba during the Second United States Intervention, 1906–1909." *Agricultural History* 11, no. 3 (July 1937): 181–88.

Logan, Enid Lynette. "Conspirators, Pawns, and Patriots and Brothers: Race and Politics in Western Cuba, 1907–1909." In *Political Power and Social Theory* 14, edited by Diane E. Davis, 3–51. New York: JAI, 2000.

López, Kathleen. "Gatekeeping in the Tropics: US Immigration Policy and the Cuban Connection." In *A Nation of Immigrants Reconsidered: US Society in an Age of Restriction, 1924–1965*, edited by Maddalena Marinari, Madeline Y. Hsu, and María Cristina García, 45–64. Urbana-Champaign: University of Illinois Press, 2019.

Majul, Cesar Adib. "*Principales, Ilustrados*, Intellectuals and the Original Concept of a Filipino National Community." *Asian Studies* 15 (1977): 1–20.

Maogoto, Jackson Nyamuya. "Subcontracting Sovereignty: Commodification of Military Force and Fragmentation of State Authority." *Brown Journal of World Affairs* 13, no. 1 (Fall/Winter 2006): 147–60.

Marr, Timothy. "Diasporic Intelligences in the American Philippine Empire: The Transnational Career of Dr. Najeeb Mitry Saleeby." *Mashriq and Mahjar* 2, no. (2014): 78–106.

Martínez, Julia, and Claire Lowrie. "Transcolonial Influences on Everyday American Imperialism: The Politics of Chinese Domestic Servants in the Philippines." *Pacific Historical Review* 81, no. 4 (November 2012): 511–36.

Mastura, Michael. "American Presence in Mindanao: The Eventful Years in Cotabato." *Mindanao Journal* 8, nos. 1–4 (1981–1982): 31–53.

May, Glenn Anthony. "Civic Ritual and Political Reality: Municipal Elections in the Late Nineteenth Century." In *Philippine Colonial Democracy*, edited by Ruby R. Paredes, 13–40. New Haven, CT: Yale University Press, 1988.

———. "Resistance and Collaboration in the Philippine-American War: The Case of Batangas." *Journal of Southeast Asian Studies* 15, no. 1 (March 1984): 69–90.

———. "The 'Zones' of Batangas." *Philippine Studies* 29, no. 1 (1981): 89–103.

McClintock, Anne. "Screwing the System: Sexwork, Race, and the Law." *boundary* 19, no. 2 (Summer 1992): 70–95.

McCoy, Alfred W. "'An Anarchy of Families': The Historiography of State and Family in the Philippines." In *An Anarchy of Families: State and Family in the Philippines*, edited by Alfred W. McCoy, 1–31. Madison: University of Wisconsin Press, 2009.

———. "The Philippine Oligarchy at the Turn of the Twenty-First Century." In *An Anarchy of Families: State and Family in the Philippines*, edited by Alfred W. McCoy, xi–xxx. Madison: University of Wisconsin Press, 2009.

McCoy, Alfred W., Francisco Scarano, and Courtney Johnson. "On the Tropic of Cancer: Transitions and Transformations in the US Imperial State." In *Colonial Crucible: Empire in the Making of the Modern American State*, edited by Alfred W. McCoy and Francisco Scarano, 3–33. Madison: University of Wisconsin Press, 2009.

McKeown, Adam M. "Conceptualizing Chinese Diasporas, 1842 to 1949." *Journal of Asian Studies* 58, no. 2 (May 1999): 306–37.

———. "The Social Life of Chinese Labor." In *Chinese Circulations: Capital, Commodities, and Networks in Southeast Asia*, edited by Eric Tagliacozzo and Wen-chin Chang, 62–83. Durham, NC: Duke University Press, 2011.

Mednick, Melvin. "Some Problems of Moro History and Political Organization." *Philippine Sociological Review* 5, no. 1 (January 1957): 39–52.

Miller, Bonnie M. "Map-Mindedness in the Age of Empire: The Role of Maps in Shaping US Imperial Interests in Cuba, Puerto Rico, and the Philippines, 1898–1904." In *Imperial*

Islands: Art, Architecture, and Visual Experience in the US Insular Empire after 1898, edited by Joseph R. Hartman, 17–42. Honolulu: University of Hawai'i Press, 2022.

Mingus, Phyllis A., and Richard Melzer. "Letters Home: The Personal Observations of the New Mexico Rough Riders in the Spanish-American War." *El Palacio: Magazine of the Museum of New Mexico* 91, no. 2 (Fall 1985): 26–35.

Montgomery, David. "Workers' Movements in the United States Confront Imperialism: The Progressive Era Experience." *Journal of the Gilded Age and Progressive Era* 7, no. 1 (January 2008): 7–42.

Mrozek, Donald J. "The Habit of Victory: The American Military and the Cult of Manliness." In *Manliness and Morality: Middle-Class Masculinity in Britain and America, 1800–1940*, edited by J. A. Mangan and James Walvin, 220–41. New York: St. Martin's Press, 1987.

Murolo, Priscilla. "Wars of Civilization: The US Army Contemplates Wounded Knee, the Pullman Strike, and the Philippine Insurrection." *International Labor and Working-Class History* 80, no. 1 (Fall 2017): 77–102.

Murray, John E. "Chinese-Filipino Wage Differentials in Early-Twentieth Century Manila." *Journal of Economic History* 62, no. 3 (September 2002): 773–91.

Ngai, Mae M. "Chinese Gold Miners and the 'Chinese Question' in Nineteenth-Century California and Victoria." *Journal of American History* 101, no. 4 (March 2015): 1082–1105.

———. "'A Knowledge of the Barbarian Language': Chinese Interpreters in Late-Nineteenth Century America." *Journal of Ethnic History* 30, no. 2 (Winter 2011): 5–32.

Novak, William J. "The Myth of the 'Weak' American State." *American Historical Review* 113, no. 3 (June 2008): 752–72.

O'Connell, Charles F., Jr. "The Corps of Engineers and the Rise of Modern Management, 1827–1856." In *Military Enterprise and Technological Change: Perspectives on the American Experience*, edited by Merritt Roe Smith, 87–116. Cambridge, MA: MIT Press, 1985.

Onuf, Nicholas Greenwood. "Sovereignty: Outline of a Conceptual History." *Alternatives: Global, Local, Political* 16, no. 4 (Fall 1991): 425–46.

Overall, Christine. "What's Wrong with Prostitution?: Evaluating Sex Work." *SIGNS* 17, no. 4 (1992): 705–24.

Owen, Norman G. "Abaca in Kabikolan: Prosperity without Progress." In *Philippine Social History: Global Trade and Local Transformations*, edited by Alfred McCoy and Ed. C. de Jesus, 191–216. Honolulu: University of Hawai'i Press, 1982.

———. "Masculinity and National Identity in the 19th Century Philippines." *Illes i imperis* 3 (January 1999): 23–47.

———. "Philippine Society and American Colonialism." In *Compadre Colonialism: Studies on the Philippines under American Rule*, edited by Norman G. Owen, 1–12. Ann Arbor: University of Michigan Center for South and Southeast Asian Studies, 1971.

———. "Winding Down the War in Albay, 1900–1903." *Pacific Historical Review* 48, no. 4 (November 1979): 557–89.

Paredes, Ruby. "The Origins of National Politics: Taft and the Partido Federal." In *Philippine Colonial Democracy*, edited by Ruby R. Paredes, 41–69. New Haven, CT: Yale University Press, 1988.

Pérez, Louis A., Jr. "Insurrection, Intervention, and the Transformation of the Land Tenure Systems in Cuba, 1895–1902." *Hispanic American Historical Review* 65, no. 2 (May 1985): 229–54.

———. "Politics, Peasants, and People of Color: The 1912 'Race War' in Cuba Reconsidered." *Hispanic American Historical Review* 66, no. 3 (August 1986): 509–39.

———. "The Pursuit of Pacification: Banditry and the United States' Occupation of Cuba, 1899–1902." *Journal of Latin American Studies* 18, no. 2 (November 1986): 313–32.

Pivar, David J. "The Military, Prostitution, and Colonial Peoples: India and the Philippines, 1885–1917." *Journal of Sex Research* 17, no. 3 (August 1981): 256–69.

Pobutsky, Ann M., and Enrico I. Neri. "Patterns of Filipino Migration to Guam: United States Military Colonialism and Its Aftermath." *Philippine Studies: Historical and Ethnographic Viewpoints* 66, no. 1 (March 2018): 77–94.

Prakash, Gyan. "Colonialism, Capitalism and the Discourse of Freedom." *International Review of Social History* 41, Supplement 4 (1996): 9–25.

Preston, Andrew, and Doug Rossinow. "America within the World." In *Outside In: The Transnational Circuitry of US History*, edited by Andrew Preston and Doug Rossinow, 1–18. New York: Oxford University Press, 2017.

Quirino, Carlos. "The Spanish Colonial Army: 1878–98." *Philippine Studies* 36, no. 3 (3rd Quarter, 1988): 381–86.

Reade, Philip. "The Cargador in Mindanao." *Journal of the Military Service Institution* 37, no. 136 (July–August 1905): 114–20.

Reckner, James R. "'The Men behind the Guns': The Impact of the War with Spain on the Navy Enlisted Force." In *Theodore Roosevelt, the U.S. Navy, and the Spanish-American War*, edited by Edward J. Marolda, 95–108. New York: Palgrave, 2001.

Roces, Mina. "Is the Suffragist an American Colonial Construct? Defining 'The Filipino Woman' in the Colonial Philippines." In *Woman's Suffrage in Asia: Gender, Nationalism, and Democracy*, edited by Louise Edwards and Mina Roces, 24–58. London: Taylor and Francis, 2004.

———. "Reflections on Gender and Kinship in the Philippine Revolution, 1896–1898." In *The Philippine Revolution of 1896: Ordinary Lives in Extraordinary Times*, edited by Florentino Rodao and Felice Noelle Rodriguez, 379–90. Quezon City: Ateneo de Manila University Press, 2002.

Romero, Robert Chao. "Transnational Chinese Immigrant Smuggling to the United States via Mexico and Cuba, 1882–1916." *Amerasia Journal* 30, no. 3 (2004): 1–16.

Saber, Mamitua. "Lanao under American Rule." *Mindanao Journal* 8, no. 1–4 (1981–1982): 193–201.

———. "Maranao Resistance to Foreign Invasions." *Philippine Sociological Review* 27, no. 4 (October 1979): 273–82.

———. "Some Observations on Maranao Social and Cultural Transition." *Philippine Sociological Review* 11, no. 1/2 (January–April 1963): 1–56.

Salman, Michael. "'Nothing without Labor': Penology, Discipline, and Independence in the Philippines under United States Colonial Rule, 1898–1914." In *Discrepant Histories: Translocal Essays on Filipino Cultures*, edited by Vicente L. Rafael, 113–29. Philadelphia: Temple University Press, 1995.

San Miguel, Pedro L., and Phillip Berryman. "Peasant Resistance to State Demands in the Cibao during the U.S. Occupation." *Latin American Perspectives* 22, no. 3 (Summer 1995): 41–62.

Schellings, William J. "The Advent of the Spanish-American War in Florida, 1898." *Florida Historical Quarterly* 39, no. 4 (April 1961): 311–29.

Schumacher, John N. "Recent Perspectives on the Revolution." *Philippine Studies* 30, no. 4 (Fourth Quarter, 1982): 445–92.

Scott, Rebecca J. "Race, Labor and Citizenship in Cuba: A View from the Sugar District of Cienfuegos, 1886–1909." *Hispanic American Historical Review* 78, no. 4 (November 1998): 687–728.

Seigel, Micol. "Beyond Compare: Comparative Method after the Transnational Turn." *Radical History Review* 91 (Winter 2005): 62–90.

Sewell, William. "Marc Bloch and the Logic of Comparative History." *History and Theory* 6, no. 2 (1967): 208–18.

Sexton, Jay. "Steam Transport, Sovereignty, and Empire in North America, circa 1850–1885." *Journal of the Civil War Era* 7, no. 4 (December 2017): 620–47.

Shamir, Ronen. "Without Borders? Notes on Globalization as a Mobility Regime." *Sociological Theory* 23, no. 2 (June 2005): 197–217.

Shibusawa, Naoko. "U.S. Empire and Racial Capitalist Modernity." *Diplomatic History* 45, no. 1 (2021): 855–84.

Smallman-Raynor, Matthew, and Andrew D. Cliff. "The Philippines Insurrection and the 1902–4 Cholera Epidemic: Part 1: Epidemiological Diffusion Processes in War." *Journal of Historical Geography* 24, no. 1 (January 1998): 69–89.

Smiley, Will. "Lawless Wars of Empire?: The International Law of War in the Philippines, 1898–1903." *Law and History Review* 36, no. 3 (August 2018): 511–50.

Stanley, Peter. "'The Voice of Worcester Is God': How One American Found Fulfillment in the Philippines." In *Reappraising an Empire: New Perspectives on Philippine-American History*, edited by Peter W. Stanley, 117–41. Cambridge, MA: Harvard University Press, 1984.

———. "William Cameron Forbes: Proconsul in the Philippines." *Pacific Historical Review* 35, no. 3 (August 1966): 285–301.

Stoler, Ana Laura, and Frederick Cooper. "Between Metropole and Colony: Rethinking a Research Agenda." In *Tensions of Empire: Colonial Cultures in a Bourgeois World*, edited by Ana Laura Stoler and Frederick Cooper, 1–56. Berkeley: University of California Press, 1997.

Stoler, Ana Laura, and Carole McGranahan. "Reconfiguring Imperial Terrains." In *Imperial Formations*, edited by Ann Laura Stoler, Carole McGranahan, and Peter C. Perdue, 3–43. Santa Fe, NM: School for Advanced Research Press, 2007.

Strobridge, William F. "Chinese in the Spanish-American War and Beyond." In *The Chinese American Experience: Papers from the Second National Conference on Chinese American Studies*, edited by Genny Linn, 3–5. San Francisco: Chinese Historical Society, 1980.

Taggart, Harold F., ed. "California Soldiers in the Philippines: From the Correspondence of Howard Middleton, 1898–1899." *California Historical Society Quarterly* 30, no. 4 (December 1951): 289–304.

———. "California Soldiers in the Philippines: From the Correspondence of Howard Middleton, 1898–1899 (continued)." *California Historical Society Quarterly* 31, no. 1 (March 1952): 49–67.

Terami-Wada, Motoe. "Kariyuki-san of Manila: 1890–1920." *Philippine Studies* 34 (1986): 287–316.

Thompson, Lanny. "The Imperial Republic: A Comparison of Insular Territories under U.S. Dominion after 1898." *Pacific Historical Review* 71, no. 4 (November 2002): 535–75.

———. "Military Cartography and the Terrains of Visibility: The Field Books of Lt. William H. Armstrong, Puerto Rico, 1898–1912." In *Imperial Islands: Art, Architecture, and Visual Experience in the US Insular Empire after 1898*, edited by Joseph R. Hartman, 43–61. Honolulu: University of Hawaiʻi Press, 2022.

Urban, Andrew. "Asylum in the Midst of Chinese Exclusion: Pershing's Punitive Expedition and the Columbus Refugees from Mexico, 1916–1921." *The Journal of Policy History* 23, no. 2 (2011): 204–29.

Van der Linden, Marcel. "The Promises and Challenges of Global Labor History." *International Labor and Working-Class History* 82 (Fall 2012): 57–76.

Vellema, Sietze, Saturnino M. Borras, Jr., and Francisco Lara, Jr. "The Agrarian Roots of Contemporary Violent Conflict in Mindanao, Southern Philippines." *Journal of Agrarian Change* 11, no. 3 (July 2011): 298–320.

Veneracion, Jaime B. "State of Agriculture during the Philippine-American War." *Kasaysayan: Journal of the National Historical Institute* 1, no. 3 (September 2001): 132–40.

Ventura, Theresa. "Medicalizing *Gutom*: Hunger, Diet, and Beriberi during the American Period." *Philippine Studies: Historical and Ethnographic Viewpoints* 63, no. 1 (March 2015): 39–69.

Vinat de la Mata, Raquel. "Dimensiones del amor tarifado: La prostitución entre 1899 y 1902." In *La sociedad cubana en los albores de la Republica*, 179–205. La Habana: Editorial de Ciencias Sociales, 2002.

Vuic, Kara Dixon. "A Girl in Every Port? The US Military and Prostitution in the Twentieth Century." In *The Military and the Market*, edited by Jennifer Mittelstadt and Mark R. Wilson, 87–104. Philadelphia: University of Pennsylvania Press, 2022.

Walther, Karine V. "'The Same Blood as We in America': Industrial Schooling and American Empire." In *Religion and U.S. Empire: Critical New Histories*, edited by Tisa Wenger and Sylvester Johnson, 151–78. New York: New York University Press, 2002.

Williams, Vernon. "Naval Service in the Age of Empire." In *Crucible of Empire: The Spanish-American War and Its Aftermath*, edited by James C. Bradford, 183–204. Annapolis, MD: US Naval Institute Press, 1993.

Winkelmann, Tessa. "Rethinking the Sexual Geography of American Empire in the Philippines: Interracial Intimacies in Mindanao and the Cordilleras, 1898–1921." In *Gendering the Trans-Pacific World*, edited by Catherine Ceniza Choy and Judy Tzu-Chun Wu, 39–76. Leiden: Brill, 2017.

Wolters, Willem G. "How Were Labourers Paid in the Philippine Islands during the Nineteenth Century?" In *Wages and Currency: Global Comparisons from Antiquity to the Twentieth Century*, edited by Jan Lucassen, 139–67. New York: Peter Lang, 2007.

Young, Elliot. "Beyond Borders: Remote Control and the Continuing Legacy of Racism in Immigration Restriction." In *A Nation of Immigrants Reconsidered: US Society in an Age of Restriction, 1924–1965*, edited by Maddalena Marinari, Madeline Y. Hsu, and María Cristina García, 25–44. Urbana-Champaign: University of Illinois Press, 2019.

———. "Globalization and the Border Wall: Transnational Policing Regimes in North America, 1890s to the Present." In *Deportation in the Americas: Histories of Exclusion and Resistance*, edited by Kenyon Zimmer and Cristina Salinas, 50–69. College Station, TX: Texas A&M University Press, 2018.

Zimmerman, Andrew. "'What Do You Really Want in German East Africa, Herr Professor?': Counterinsurgency and the Science Effect in Colonial Tanzania." *Comparative Studies in Society and History* 48, no. 2 (2006): 419–61.

Zulueta Zulueta, Rolando. "La Guerra de 1895 en el Departamento Oriental." In *Guerra de Independencia, 1895–1898*, 81–159. Havana: Editorial de Ciencias Sociales, 1998.

DISSERTATIONS

Marasigan, Cynthia L. "'Between the Devil and the Deep Sea': Ambivalence, Violence, and African-American Soldiers in the Philippine-American War." PhD diss., University of Michigan, 2010.

Mednick, Melvin. "Encampment of the Lake: The Social Organization of a Moslem-Philippine (Moro) People." PhD diss., University of Chicago, 1965.

Thompson, Wayne W. "Governors of the Moro Province: Wood, Bliss, and Pershing in the Southern Philippines, 1903–1913." Phd diss., University of California, San Diego 1975.

Index

Italic page numbers refer to illustrations. Place names in the Philippines are identified by island.

Abernathy, Robert S., 141
Abra province (Luzon), 51, 53, 57–58, 59
Acosta, Mariano, 55
Afghanistan, US war in, 278; Afghanis working for US military, 279
African American servicemen, 69, 78, 161, 239, 260–61, 277, 336n61
Afro-Cubans, 75, 111; in Pinar del Río province, 182, 267; racism against, 26, 30, 76–77, 182, 188, 240–41, 267. *See also* Partido Independiente de Color
Agbayani, Aguedo, 55–56, 61
agriculture (Cuba), 27, 111–12, 128; and employment, 179; and road systems, 127, 176–77; sugar industry, 67–68, 128; tobacco industry, 178–79; wage labor and workforce, 175, 176
agriculture (Philippines), 130–31, 135; Chinese labor, 196, 276; and corvée in Philippines, 131–32; and enforced labor, 171
Aguinaldo, Emilio: and abolishment of polo, 133; capture of (1901), 58, 60–61; and Chinese exclusion, 200; exile in Hong Kong, 44; and insurgent army, 49, 81, 134; as mestizo landowner, 132–33; nationalism of, 14; organizing of Malolos republic by, 132–33; regulation of sex work by, 247; and siege of Manila, 198. *See also* Philippine army; Philippine government; Philippine-American War
Aguinaldo, Hilaria, 253
Alandug, Datu, 163–65
Albay province (Luzon): forced labor in, 140–41, 148; sexual labor and violence in, 252; war in, 49

alcohol, US regulation of: in Cuba, 239, 241; in Philippines, 247, 264
Aleshire, James B., 221–22
Alger, Russell, 115, 124, 126
Ali, Datu, 23, 85, 88, 93, 95, 98
American Federation of Labor, 146
"amigo guides." *See* guides
Anderson, Thomas, 43, 132, 203, 247–48, 251
anti-Chinese attitudes and politics. *See* Chinese exclusion; Sinophobia
anticolonialism: nationalist projects, 13–14, 236, 288n20; Philippines, 40, 56, 140, 251, 274; US intervention in revolutions, 5. *See also* Propaganda movement
anti-imperialism: Cuban, 235; Filipino, 278; infantile, 97; Latin American, 272–73; in US Congress, 11, 231
anti-monopoly movement: in Cuba, 119, 176; in Philippines, 94; in United States, 11, 70
antislavery movement: in Cuba, 123; in Philippines, 23, 89–91, 98, 100, 158–59, 171
anti-vagrancy laws. *See* vagrancy
Apache Wars. *See* Native Americans
Arellano, Cayetano, 46
Arguelles, Manuel, 142–43
"armed progressives," 70, 104; *See also* Progressive Era; progressivism; US Army; Wood, Leonard
Ashburn, Thomas, 58
Atkins, Edwin, 68, 227, 233–34, 241, 243–44, 311n42. *See also* Cienfuegos (Cuba)
Atkinson, Fred, 219. *See also* education, industrial
Atlantic Monthly (periodical), 163, 164, 167

Bacardí y Moreau, Emilio, 2, 9, 122–23, *124*, 125, 242. *See also* Santiago (Cuba).
Bacolod (Mindanao): sultan of, 160; opposition to roadbuilding in, 165
Bacoor (Luzon), 46, 49, 135, 136
Baguio (Luzon), 144
Balangiga (Samar), 64; battle of (1901), 3, 63, 64–65
Bandera, Quintín, 126, 178–79
Barber Asphalt Company, 113
Barbour, George M., 72–77, *124*, 126, 129, 239. *See also* Santiago (Cuba).
Barton, Clara, 113. *See also* Red Cross; "scientific charity"
Basey (Samar), 64, 65
Batangas province (Luzon), 46; counterinsurgency in, 48, 49, 57, 135, 161; queridas in, 258; roadbuilding in, 145–46; sexual violence in, 251
Bates, John, 83–84, 88. *See also* Kiram-Bates Treaty
Batson, Matthew, 26, 219
Bayan (Mindanao), battle of (1902), 160–61
Bell, James Franklin, 176, 266, 267
Benguet province (Luzon), 51; counterinsurgency in, 57
Benguet Road, 144, 162, 169; forced labor, 142, 316n82; strike, 275
Betancourt, Pedro, 78
Beveridge, Albert, 226
Bikol language, 40
Bilibid Prison (Manila), 148, 171, 316n82
Black, William Murray, 127, 177, 179–80, 181, 186, 187–88
Blackett, Wilmer, 38
Blanco, Ramón, 156, 159
Bliss, Tasker H.: government of Moro Province, 170–71, 172; regulation of migration in Cuba, 228–30
Boer War. *See* Britain
Bolton, Edward C., 99–100
Bourns, Frank S., 43–44, 45, 248. *See also* interpreters and translators
Bowe, John, 211
Boxer Rebellion (1901), 63, 213, 272

Brett, Lloyd M., 88
Britain: Boer War (South Africa), 220; consul in Philippines, 45, 48, 206; consul in Santiago, 45; Contagious Disease Acts, 237; empire in Egypt, 63, 92, 271; imperial rule, 271; indentured labor, 194; and India, 92, 158; and Jamaica, 79, 176, 242; and repeal of Contagious Disease Acts, 249–50
British Army: occupation of Germany, after World War I, 273; and regulation of sex work, 250; use of "native" soldiers, 35, 213
Brooke, John R., 34, 120–26, 228–29. *See also* Cuba, US occupation (Military Government, 1899–1902)
Brown, George, 78
Brown, Ira, 249
Buchanan, James, 104
Buencamino, Felipe, 49, 133, 143
Bulacan province (Luzon), 62
Bullard, Robert Lee, 26, 48; in Cuba, 185–86, 275; government of Lanao, 169–70; and Iligan-Marawi road, 161–69, *166*, 319n22; management of subaltern labor, 152–53, 214
Butler, Smedley, 275
Butt, Archibald W., 220–21, 225–26. *See also* Chinese labor; Filipino labor

cabecillas. See Chinese, in Philippines
Cailles, Juan, 149
Caiñas, Jose Antonio, 182, 186
Calamba (Luzon), 135–36; memory of US roadbuilding, 137; queridas near, 259; and VD investigations, 101, 262–63
Calderon, Felipe, 46–47, 47, 256, 293n42
Calumpit (Luzon), 211, 218
camineros, 150, *151*, 171, 172. *See also* roadbuilding and public works
Campbell, Thomas, 252
Caney, El (Cuba): battle at, 26, 30, 31; roads and roadbuilding at, 109, 115; US occupation of, 121
capitalism: and civilizing mission, 16, 65–66, 81, 83, 157, 158, 160, 164, 171, 219,

254, 320n32; colonial, 140, 224; consumer culture, 35–36; in Cuba, 114; and imperialism, 6, 9; industrial, 12, 67, 220; and modernity, 12–13, 35–36, 93–94, 164, 269; and Moro culture, 85–87; and Moro society, 89, 157; neocolonial, 128–29, 173–74, 176; scientific, 89, 104; trade and trade policy, 9, 11, 128, 174, 196, 231, 271, 277, 311n42; transformation and transition, under US occupation, 3–4, 11, 129–30; and wage labor, 81, 93. *See also* infrastructure; "scientific management"; Taylor, Frederick Winslow

Caples, William, 145–46

cargadores (porters): cargador policies and wage labor, 89, 93–95; cargador-soldier ratios, 96, 100; cargador system, 81–84; Chinese, 210; coercion of, 53; "Corps of Cargadores," 101–2; General Order 100, 82; harsh treatment of, 64–65; militarization of, 81, 83–84, 87; Moro, 88, 91, 154; Moro assertions of sovereignty, 96–100, 99, *100*; science of, 96–98, 100–105, *103*; Waller expedition, 63–64. *See also* efficiency; forced labor; labor

Carman, Dickerson M., 217

Carr, Lawrence C., 242

Carter, Edward C., 264

Carter, Robert D., 136

Carter, William H., 101

cartography. *See* maps

Casino Chung Wah (Havana), 229

Castilian. *See* language

Castillo Duany, Demetrio, 30–31, 33, 121–22, *124, 125*, 126, 175, 291n16, 309n30. *See also* infrastructure; Oriente; roadbuilding and public works

Castillo Duany, Joaquín, 28, 30, 31–32, *124, 125*, 126

Catholic Church: and colonial rule in Philippines, 39–40, 130–31; La Guardia de Honor sect, 56; opposition to slavery, 90

Catlin, George DeGrasse, 234, 330n3

cavalry and cavalrymen. *See* US Army Cavalry

Cavite province (Luzon), 36, 38–39, 43, 46–47, 47, 49; food-for-work policies at, 135–37; mutiny against forced labor (1872), 131–32

Cebreco, Agustín, 117

cedula tax (Philippines), 92, 147, 149–50, 170, 197, 198, 201–2

Chaffee, Adna, 62, 64, 65, 265–66, 274

Charbonneau, Oli, 87

Chen Gang, 206

Chen Qianshan (Don Carlos Palanca), 199, 200–201, 204–6, 208, 216–17

China (Pacific Mail steamship), 193

China (Qing empire): consuls at Havana, 206, 229; consuls at Manila, 206, 214; diplomatic protection, 194, 199, 203, 205–6, 230–31, 232, 276; US consuls in, 202

Chinese exclusion, 18, 193, 195–96, 198, 201–3, 226, 276–77; in Cuba, 226–32; Cubans' support for, 231–32; Filipinos' support for, 198, 200; and "Otis order," 198–201; in Philippines, 198–203, 222–26, 327n53

Chinese labor, 18; and accusations of criminality, 216–17, 219; in North America, 194–95; for US military in Pacific, 193–96

Chinese labor (Cuba), 227–28; Chinese merchant brokers, 229, 230–31, 232; documentation of migrants, 228–29; indentured migration, 227–28; Spanish policy, 227

Chinese labor (Philippines), 198; Chinese merchant brokers (*cabecillas*), 196, 197–98, 204–5, 206, 216; Chinese mestizos, 48–49; collective action, 217–18, 219–20, 222, 327n53; contract, 203–4, 205, 206–22, *208*; documentation of migrants, 201–3; experiments in, 207–8; Filipinos vs. Chinese labor, 196, 203–4, 221–25, 223; and imperial wage, 218–19; indentured migration, 196–98; Orientalist stereotypes, 198, 213–17; Qing treaty on migration, 196; racialized control, 208–12; sovereignty over, 198–202, 209–12; Spanish policy, 196, 197, 198, 200, 201, 210

Chinese Restriction Act (1882), 193, 229
Chira, Adriana, 123
cholera, 163, 222
Cienfuegos, Cuba, 16, 68, 233–35, 243–44, 268; elections, 244
Circular No. 13 (Bureau of Insular Affairs), 228. *See also* Chinese exclusion
Círculo de Hacendados y Agricultores, 126
Cisneros Betancourt, Salvador, 127
Clark, Victor, 79, 144–45
Clavell, Carlos Gonzalo, 31–32
Club Moncada, 122, 123
Cobre, El (Cuba): rations for camps at, 117; roadbuilding at, 115
coercion. *See* forced labor
Cold War, 276, 278
Collazo, Enrique, 117, 118
colonialism: Americans' comparisons of colonialisms, 1–2, 143, 162, 176; comparisons of, 84, 92, 256–57; economic development, 11; "food-for-work" policies, 135; and historiography, 9, 15, 18, 137; "military colonialism," 9–11; and "scientific charity," 112–13, 136. *See also* neocolonialism
Comité de Veteranos de Color, 188
common-law marriage, 239, 256–61. *See also* sex work and sexual economy
Constitutional Army, Cuba (August Revolt, 1906), 175
"contagionist" concepts of disease, 69. *See also* public health; sanitation; science
Contagious Diseases Acts, 237; repeal of, 249–50
Cooper, H. M., 91
Corbin, Henry, 148, 265
Corps of Engineers. *See* US Army, Corps of Engineers
corvée (labor tax, Philippines), 82, 131–32, 139, 141–42, 172; abolishment of by Aguinaldo, 133; American efforts to restore, 147–49; casual persistence of, 147, 150–51; Philippine Commission ban of, 101, 142. *See also* forced labor; *polo y servicio*

Cotabato port (Philippines): 84, 85, 88, 90, 94, 303n58, 303n62
Cotabato region (Philippines), 84–85, 88, 92–93, 99
Couden, Albert R., 222
counterinsurgency (Philippines), 25, 36, 39, 40, 42, 45, 47, 219; and food policy, 135–36; and forced labor, 3, 64, 81, 95, 103–4, 129, 139; legitimatization of, 224; manuals, 274; political economy of, 48, 50, 59; *reconcentratión* policies, 70, 112, 178–79, 238; roadbuilding for, 144; sexual economy, 245; sexual sovereignty's effect on, 250–51
Crane, Stephen, 32, 109
Crowder, Enoch, 202–3, 225
Cuba: American influence in, 5, 27, 33–34, 35–36; anti-Americanism in, 119, 121, 244; anti-imperialism in, 273; civilian deaths in, 70; class and social divisions in, 11, 14, 27, 30, 126; Cuban elites, 35, 75, 78, 121, 174; *cubanidad*, 14; economy of, 2, 11, 13, 14, 27, 36, 111–12, 128–29, 173–74, 176–77, 190; foreign investment in, 11, 27, 67–68, 173–74, 176, 177–78, 179, 273; land tenure in, 11, 173–74; maps of, 7, 29, *180*; migration, 27, 75, 79, 179, 231–32; mythic perceptions of, 27; patronage, clientage, and political culture and networks, 80, 121, 123, 128–29, 174–75, 177–78, 184, 189–90; capacity for self-rule and sovereignty, 12, 34, 66, 76–77, 80; Spanish rule of, 5, 11, 25, 71, 118, 126, 175, 246; terrain and transportation, 110. *See also* Cienfuegos, Cuba; Cuban government; Cuban labor; Oriente province, Cuba; Pinar del Río province, Cuba
Cuba, government: constitutional convention (1901), 6, 126; elections, 174, 175, 177, 186–87; immigration politics and policy, 230–32; and Platt Amendment (1901), 6, 114, 173, 175, 230, 271; prohibition of vouchers, 80; roadbuilding and public works, 128–29, 175, 177–78, 189–90; Rural Guard, 68, 175,

273. *See also* Estrada Palma, Tomás; Miguel Gómez, José; Partido Revolucionario Cubano
Cuba, Liberation Army: 2, 26, 30, 31, 68; demobilization and dissolution of, 33, 116–19, 125; scouts, 30–32, *31*; veterans, 175, 188
Cuba, US interventions of 1913 and 1917, 273
Cuba, US occupation in (Military Government, 1899–1902), 9; and Cuban support for, 2, 123, *124*, 126, 299n19; economic policy, 128; elite cooperation with, 32–33, 121–23; fiscal policy and disputes, 123–26; immigration policy, 226, 228–29, 230; language in, 33–34; roadbuilding and public works during, 126–27; Rural Guard, 68, 234; sanitation during, 76–77, 113–14. *See also* Brooke, John R.; Wood, Leonard
Cuba, US occupation in (Provisional Government, 1906–9), 9, 175–76; economic policy, 176–77; elite cooperation with, 177–78; roadbuilding and public works during, 177; Rural Guards, 182, 187, 266–67; support for, 177–78, 189. *See also* Magoon, Charles E.
Cuban labor, 68, 69; American labor and, 79; collective action, 79; pay practices, 80; as performance, 77–78; productivity of, 67–68, 77–78; rationalization of, 80; science of, 79; skilled, 79; Spanish labor and, 79; strikes, 75, 117, 152, 181–82, 183–84, 233; theories of, 78–79; unions, 233
Cuban Land and Leaf Tobacco Company, 186
Cuban Revolutionary Party, 5, 27, 116, 122, 174
Cuban War for Independence (1895–98), 5, 25, 69, 122, 233

Daiquirí (Cuba): Cuban operations at, 31, 32; US operations at, 109
datus. *See* names of individual datus
Davis, George W., 91, 157–59, 160–62, 165
Davis, Oscar, 38–39
Davis, Richard Harding, 32, 290n12,
Daza, Eugenio, 3, 13
de los Reyes, Isabelo, 144, 226, 253
Dewey, George, 44, 193
Dillon, Theodore H., 187
Dios-Dios movement (Samar), 100
disease. *See* venereal disease; yellow fever
Dodd, George A., 54
domésticas (Cuba), 240–41. *See also* sex work and sexual economy in Cuba
Dominican Republic, 272, 275–76
Dorst, Joseph H., 243
Duvall, William, 56–57, 58, 59, 139–40

economy. *See* agriculture; capitalism; Cuba; infrastructure; labor; Philippines
education and schools: compared to roadbuilding, 144, 315n69; "industrial education" in Philippines, 171, 219–22, 225–26, 275; Spanish (Philippines), 39–40; US policy in Philippines, 40–42, 171, 219, 222, 225–26, 275
Edwards, Clarence, 264
efficiency, 16; cult of, 67–68, 183; military, 35, 66, 80, 218, 247, 262–63, 266; US demands for, 94, 95–96, 101, *103*, 145, 167, 176, 183, 211–12, 218, 219, 221
El Cubano (newspaper), 123
El Filibusterismo (Rizal), 204
El Porvenir (newspaper), 125
empire and empires: Americans' ambivalence about, 271, 273, 279; Americans' comparisons of, 1, 76, 158, 213; ancient Roman, 4, 17; comparative history of, 64, 92, 271, 288n23; criticism of, 12–13; de-territorialization of United States, 271–73; empires vs. nations, 4; European, 214; nostalgia for, 279; origins of, 4; resistance to, 231, 235, 261, 278; revisionist narratives of, 27, 30–31; US approaches to, 4–5, 15, 16–17, 153, 194. *See* Britain; colonialism; Ottoman empire; Spain
enslaved people. *See* slavery
Esparanza del Valle (Cuban women's separatist club), 238

Esquerra y Rodríguez, Higinio, 234
Estenoz, Evaristo, 188
Estrada Palma, Tomás, 129, 174–75, 177, 178
Europe, 1, 4, 11, 12, 66, 67, 232; Eurocentrism in historiography, 13–14; Europeans' colonial warfare, 66, 213; and historicism, 12, 87, 141; immigration from, 246, 249; World War I, 271, 273
Ewers, Ezra P., 124

Febiger, Lea, 90
Fegan, David, 261
Fenton, Eben B., 234
Ferrer, Ada, 77–78
Filipino elites: corruption of, 134; facilitate forced labor, 139–40; in Malolos republic, 132–33; in US colonial state, 148–49
Filipino labor, 77, 147, 221–25, 223; forced, 82–83, 132–33, 133–34, 136–41, 145–46, 150–51; memory of, 137–38; and US policy, 134–40, 141–42, 148–49, 150
Finlay, Carlos J., 69
Finley, John, 171
Florida: cigar manufacturing in, 178; as destination for Cuban immigrants and exiles, 27; Tampa, 28
food. *See* Cuba; forced labor; Philippines
Foraker Act, 113, 127. *See also* anti-monopoly movements
Forbes, William Cameron, 148–51, 171, 172, 275
forced labor: 12–13; and cash wages, 74–75, 113, 134, 136, 138, 145–47, 157; and counterinsurgency and pacification, 2, 3, 64, 65, 116–19; criticism of and opposition to, 114–15, 140–42; in Cuba, 2, 11, 73–74; "dignity of work," 144–45; Filipino memory of, 137–38; "food for work," 74–75, 112, 134–36; in Philippines, 82–83, 132–33, 133–34, 136–41, 145–46, 150–51; records of, 119, 139, 314n62; for sanitation (Cuba), 70–73, 113–14; use of prisoners for, 24, 54, 59–60, 65, 119, 147, 148, 171; US policy in Philippines,
139–40, 141–42, 148–89, 150. *See also* colonialism; labor; slavery
Foreman, John, 200
Funston, Frederick, 28, 39, 58–59, 62, 83; Aguinaldo's capture, 60–61
Furlong, John W., 268

Galang, Jely, 210
gallego immigrants, 75, 232
Gallman, Jefferson Davis, 150
Ganzhorn, Jack, 39
García, Calixto, 28, 30–32, 109, 116–18
Gauvreau, Charles, 32
gender ideology and hierarchy, 4, 17–18; public vs. private space, 268; in United States, Cuba, and Philippines, 235–36. *See also* masculinity; sex work and sexual economy
General Order 40 (Philippines, 1900), 138–39
General Order 43 (Philippines, 1899), 138
General Order 100 (US Army) (Lieber Code), 51, 58, 59, 82, 294n50
General Order 101 (US Army), 261–63
Germany, 273
germ theory, 72–73. *See also* public health
Geronimo (Goyahkla), 70, 161
Giberga, E. A., 181–83
Go, Julian, 12
Gómez, José Miguel, 174, 175, 186, 188, 189–90, 232, 233–34, 244
Gómez, Máximo, 28, 35, 118–19, 126, 233, 235
Goyahkla (Geronimo), 70, 161
Grant, F. H., 222
Grant, Frederick D., 47
Graves, Ernest, 184
Greene, Francis V., 43, 113, 150
Greene, Julie, 6
Greene, Warwick, 150
Greenleaf, Charles, 208
Gremio de Chinos (Manila), 204–5
Grito de Baire, 233
Guam, 6, 272
Guane, Cuba, 184–85, *185*, 187
Guantánamo (Cuba), 9; roadbuilding at, 115
Guardia Civil (Philippines), 25–26

Guerra, Edelmira, 238
Guerra, Faustino "Pino," 186
Guerra y Sánchez, Ramiro, 176
guides. *See* guides in Cuba; guides in Philippines; intermediaries, military-colonial
guides in Cuba: insurgents as, 26, 28, 31–32; *prácticos*, 25, 32
guides in Philippines: accusations of abuse, 296n59; "amigo," 50; coercion and torture of, 51, 54, 59, 297n66; false, 59–60; in Moro Wars, 23–24, 88, 91, 274; in Philippine-American War, 45, 48–51, 53–55, 57–58, 59–61; in Pulahan War, 274; retaliation against, 49, 53, 55, 57–58

Hagadorn, Charles B., 157
Haiti, 272, 275–76; and Haitian Revolution, 4, 30
Hamilton, Robert, 79
Hanna, Matthew, 115, 124–25, 129
Harts, William Wright, 146–48, 150, 181
Havana (Cuba), 15; Chinese migrant labor in, 227–30, 232, 241; fair labor practices in, 80; public works in, 72, 113; road building concentrated in, 127; scientific charity in, 113; sexual economy at, 237–38, 240–42, 243, 266; and skilled Cuban labor for, 79; strikes at, 181; sugar industry near, 110; US intervention (1906) in, 175–76; William Ludlow, 126
Havard, Valery, 245
Hawaiʻi, 10, 231, 272, 277
Hawkins, Michael, 87
Hay, John, 200
Herman, Frederick J., 206–7, 211
highways. *See* roads; roadbuilding and public works
Howard, Guy, 210, 212
Howard, Harold P., 53, 211
Howard, Oliver Otis, 210
Howland, Harry S., 23–25, 50, 96–98
Howze, Robert Lee, 54, 55–56, 62
Hoyt, Henry F., 207–9, 213, 250

Hughes, Robert P., 45, 248
hygiene. *See* public health

Igorot people, 51–53, 150; porterage, 53, 83, 302n47; road labor, 150
Ileto, Reynaldo, 137–38
Iligan (Mindanao), 153–54, 156, 159, 171
Iligan-Marawi Road, 155, 159–60, 161–62, 168, 169, 170–71, 219; Spanish builders of, 156
Ilocano dialect, 40, 51, 53, 61, 274; language primer for US Army, 53
Ilocano people, 51–53
Ilocos Norte province (Luzon), 54, 56, 58, 61
Ilocos region, 51, 58; counterinsurgency, 53–60; occupation of, 57–58
Ilocos Sur province (Luzon), 53, 56, 57, 59, 312n50
ilustrados ("enlightened ones"), 5, 14, 133; attitudes toward Chinese, 198, 201; as interpreters and translators, 46
imperialism, 12; American ambivalence, 271; and capitalism, 6–9; of "good housekeeping," 256; sanitary, 74. *See also* colonialism; empire and empires
indentured labor, 90, 196, 227. *See also* Chinese labor
"Indian Scouts." *See* Native Americans
industrialization. *See* United States
infrastructure state: 17, 109–10; in Cuba, 129–30, 172–73, 176–77, 184–85, 188–89, 189–90; legacy of, 275–76; Manila-Dagupan railway, 81, 140, 218; military use of, 118, 128, 129–30, 144, 159, 170, 171; in Philippines, 129–30, 170–71, 172; and reform, 127–28, 143–44; in War on Terror, 278–79. *See also* forced labor; labor; roadbuilding and public works
Insular Cases (US Supreme Court), 6
intermediaries, military-colonial, 23–25; payment of, 50, 55, 294n49; in Philippines, 25–26; political economy of counterinsurgency, 25, 62; reduced dependence on, 273–74; Spaniards as (Philippines), 24, 48, 61; Spanish use of (Cuba), 25; and status, 56–57, 61–62; and trust in, 50,

intermediaries (cont.)
59, 60–61; versatility of, 53. *See also* guides; interpreters and translators; Native America

interpreters and translators (Cuba): Cuban elite, 28–29; enabling of occupation, 32–33; frustration with, 34; little need for, 34–36; and politics of sovereignty, 34

interpreters and translators (Philippines): American, 39, 43–44; enabling of occupation, 46–47; Filipino elite, 40, 42, 46–47, 47, 55–56; frustration with, 38–39, 42–43, 45, 47–48; as insurgent assets, 44–45, 58; need for, 32–33, 38–39, 42, 45, 47–48, 50, 54; and politics of sovereignty, 38–39. *See also* guides; intermediaries, military-colonial; language; local knowledge

Iraq and Iraqis, 278–79

Islam: Moro people (Philippines), 83–87, 92, 162; Muslim populations, 83–84; ritual suicide, 167; stereotypes of, 158; Sulu Archipelago, 83–84

Isselhard, Jacob, 215

Ives, Frank, 244

Johnson, Anson Burlingame, 202

Johnson, Richard, 59, 253, 257–60

Johnston, William T., 57, 59

Kaemmerling, Gustave, 222

Katipunan (nationalist society), 5, 56; Katipuneros revolt (1896), 14, 26, 48, 156, 198, 246

Kemp, Franklin M., 208–9, 210–11, 213

Kennan, George, 73

Kennon, Lyman W. V., 83, 162, 297n71

kinship and communal networks: of Chinese immigrants, 196, 229; of Maranao society, 154; of Moro society, 87; in Philippines, 58, 130–31, 137

Kipling, Rudyard, 63

Kiram, Jamalul II (Sultan of Sulu), 83, 84. *See also* Kiram-Bates Treaty

Kiram-Bates Treaty, 83–84, 89–90, 92, 156, 158, 169

Kobbé, William A., 156–57, 158–59, 252, 303n62

Kohr, Herbert, 32

Konrad, Peter, 40

labor and laborers: civilian (Cuba), 69, 71–74; cognitive labor, 16, 25, 38–39, 53–54; Cuban labor and scientific racism, 78–79; estimated number of, 287n12; "free" vs. "unfree," 13, 65, 197–98; Filipino vs. Chinese, 221–25, 223; gendered aspects of, 235–36; of imperial sovereignty, 6, 9, 12–13; "military labor" 12; public health (Philippines), 77; racialized, 68, 221–22; receding knowledge of, 275; subaltern, 65–67, 77, 81, 96; "working class," 12. *See also* cargador (porter) system; Chinese labor; corvée (labor tax); Cuban labor; Filipino labor; forced labor

Lacosta, Perfecto, 127

Lacuna, Urbano, 61

La Guardia de Honor, 56–57

Laguna province (Philippines), 135, 136–38, 145, 149, 253, 259, 262; *La Independencia* (newspaper), 123

Lambier, Nicodemus, 24

Lanao region (Mindanao), 23, 153–54; governors of, 169–70; map of, 155. *See also* Iligan-Marawi road; Maranao people; Mindanao; Moro people; Moro Province

land titles, 94, 128

language: and Americans in Cuba, 36, 275; English fluency of Cubans, 28, 32–34, 35–36; English fluency of Filipinos, 41–42; Filipino dialects, 24, 43; and Filipino elites, 39–40; linguistic colonization, 34–36, 41–42; linguistic complexity, 36, 39–40, 43, 273–75; in occupied Cuba, 33–34; pidgins, 38, 275; Spanish, 36, 39–40

Laoag (Philippines), 54, 55, 62

Las Guásimas (Cuba), battle of, 32, 33, 290n16
La Solidaridad (newspaper), 44
Las Piñas (Luzon), 43, 46, 47, 135–36
La Union province (Luzon), 51, 57
lavenderas (Cuba), 114, 240–41, 252, 254–55
lavenderas (Philippines), 253–56
Lawton, Henry W., 47; and Chinese labor, 209–11, 212; death of, 48; and Castillo Duany, 122; food-for-work policy in Cuba, 117–18; food-for-work policy in Philippines, 135–37; frontier myth, 82; government of Santiago with Wood, 70, 76; "Indian fighting," 26; and interpreters, 32–33, 39, 45, 47–48; and labor policies, 114–15, 117; municipal government in Philippines, 46–47; use of guide, 49–50
Legarda, Benito, 149, 201, 225, 293n42
Legazpi (Luzon): sexual economy and violence at, 252, 257
Lemus, Rienzi B., 254–56, 260–61
Liberal Party, Cuba, 122, 174–75, 186, 189–90
Liberation Army, Cuban; *See* Cuba, Liberation Army
Lieber, Francis, 51
Lieber Code (GO 100), 51, 58, 59, 82, 294n50
Liga Agraria, Cuba, 189
Li Rongyao, 206
local knowledge, 16, 24–25; as capital, 61–62; of Filipino elites, 55; forced extraction of Philippines, 24, 50–51, 54; military value of in Philippines, 54; need for, 27–28, 30–33, 36, 42–43; of paramilitary and police units, 273. *See also* guides; intermediaries, military-colonial; language; maps; interpreters and translators in Cuba; interpreters and translators in Philippines
Lombillo Clark, Diego, 178
Ludlow, William, 126
Lumad people, 85

Luna, Antonio, 45, 142–43, 209
Luzon, Philippines, 15; cargador (porter) system, 81–84; maps of, 37, 52

Mabini, Apolinario, 14, 143
Macabebe people: as laborers, 218, 219; military recruitment of, 26; as scouts, 61
MacArthur, Arthur, Jr.: and Chinese immigration in Philippines, 199–200; and Chinese labor, 207–8, 208; and Division of Military Information, 274; ignorance of Philippines, 36; and roadbuilding, 142, 144; on schools in Philippines, 41; and sexual regulations, 250, 263; venereal disease (VD), 261–63; "yellow peril" discourse, 222–25
MacArthur, Walter, 193. *See also* Sailors' Union of the Pacific
Maceo, Antonio, 121, 122, 123, 178–79, 240
Madrid, Francisco, 83
Magoon, Charles E., 176–79, 183–86, 187–89, 190, 267
Maguindanao (Moro) people, 84–85; resistance to Spanish, 93; slavery, 89–91; wage labor, 90–91
Malabang (Mindanao), 90, 95, 98, 99, 100, 157, 160, 161, 170
malaria, 68, 69, 71
Malolos republic. *See* Philippine government
Malvar, Miguel, 48
Manabilang, Amai, 159, 160, 163
Mandi, Datu 88
Manila (Luzon), 15; Americans at, 47, 225; Board of Health, 44; Chamber of Commerce, 225; Chinese, public works employment, 198; courts, 46; deportations, 199; education, 39, 40–41, 226; *ilustrados* at, 133; industries, 217; intelligence and counter-intelligence in, 44–45; labor, 193, 198, 210, 214; occupation, 39, 40, 132; and regulation, 247–50, 263–65; sanitation, 77; sexual economy, 245–46; unions, 275; wage labor, 130
Manila American (newspaper), 218

Manila, battle of, 36, 38–39, 81
Manila Bay, battle of, 193
Manila-Dagupan railway, 81, 140, 218. *See also* infrastructure state
Manzanillo (Cuba): clandestine prostitution at, 243; public works at, 115
maps: in Cuba, 274–75; of Cuba, 7, 29, *180*; lack of in Philippines, 50; making, 35, 49, 274; of Philippines, *8*, *37*, *52*, *86*, *155*; used in Philippines, 49; useless, 28, 54
Maranao people, 153–56; cholera epidemic, 163; labor brokers, 162–69, *166*; political and social organization, 154–56; resistance of Spanish, 156; wage labor, 161–71, *168*
Marawi (Mindanao). *See* Iligan-Marawi Road
Markey, Joseph, 215
Markham, Edward M., 181–83
Martí, José, 5, 14, 27, 122
masculinity, 18; and Gilded Age reform, 72; imperial crises of, 238, 247; "machismo," 233, 235, 267–68; masculine honor, 215, 251; "strenuous life" ideal, 70, 263
Matanzas province (Cuba): roads for sugar industry, 175; sexual economy at, 242, 244; social Darwinism at, 78
Maura Law (1893), 46, 132, 139, 142
Maus, Louis Mervin, 262–63, 264–65, 278
McCaskey, William, 62
McKinley, William: and colonial army for Cuba, 34–35; correspondence with Atkins, 233; and First Philippine Commission, 44; imperial approach of, 5; occupation of Manila, 132; occupation of Oriente, 68, 70–71; and relief policy in Cuba, 112; Thirteenth Amendment, 84; and visitors from Cuba, 33, 125; works with Wood, 125–26
McLeary, James H., 123
McManus, Joseph, 213–14
Meiklejohn, George de Rue, 228–29
Mendoza, Ramón G., 32–33
Merritt, Wesley, 132,
Mestre, Aurelius E., 33

Mexico, 230, 242, 272, 275, 276
Miguel Gómez, José, 188–90, 232, 233–34, 244
Miles, Nelson, 162
Miles, Perry, 43
"military colonialism." *See* colonialism.
Military Information Division (MID), US War Dept., 27, 36
"military labor." *See* labor
"military sanitarians." *See* Progressive Era
millenarian sects, 14, 56, 100. *See also* Guardia de Honor; Pulahan War
Miller, Crosby P., 214, 218–19
Mills, Albert L., 104–5
Mindanao island (Philippines), 16, 23–24, 84–85; agriculture, 171; map of, *86*; planters, 94. *See also* Cotabato region; Lanao region
Mir, Jaime, 184
missionaries, 67; educational, 41–42; Jesuit, 87; military-colonial labor, 157, 158; Muslim, 154
Moderate Party, Cuba, 174, 175, 177
Molina, Gonzalez, 182
Monroe Doctrine, 272
Montalvo, Evaristo de, 38, 292n26
Montejo, Esteban, 234–35
Moro people: culture of, 77; dialects of, 24, 161, 168; modernization of, 157, 320n32; politics and society of, 85–86; resistance, 170, 172; slavery, 84, 85–87, 89–90, 158–59; sovereignty vs. antislavery, 83–86; stereotypes of, 156–57; war, 160–61, 172. *See also* Ali, Datu; datus; Islam; Kiram, Jamalul; Kiram-Bates Treaty; Maguindanao; Maranao; Piang, Datu
Moro elites. *See* names of individual datus
Moro labor: defiance of and brokers, 95–96; mission to promote wage labor, 90–91, 93–95, 157–60, 162–69; strikes, 95, 165; as workers, 152–53
Moro Province, 91–92; antislavery policy, 92; civilian rule, 172, 271; corvee, 172; firearms policy, 172; military rule, 169; Moro Exchanges, 171; tax policy, 92

Mountain province (Luzon), 51, 150
Muslim populations. *See* Islam

Naguilian (Luzon), 57, 59, 258
nationalism, 4–6, 13–14, 25, 195–96, 236; in Cuba, 2, 33–34, 116, 121, 122–23, 125–26, 174, 177, 184, 195–96, 231–32, 238; in Philippines, 13–14, 36, 39, 40, 48–49, 51, 100, 129, 132, 133–34, 143, 144, 149, 152, 200, 203, 215, 226, 247–48, 251, 253, 256, 257–58, 276, 277, 278
Native Americans: Apache Wars, 33, 70; common-law marriage, 256; compared to Moros, 156–57; "Indian fighting," 10, 82, 161; "Indian Scouts," 26; war in US West, 10
Natividad, Joaquin, 58–59, 61–62
Nelson, M. K., 48
neocolonialism, 12; Cuban capitalism, 26–27, 128–29, 173; Cuban public works, 113, 127, 184; Cuban state formation, 33, 35, 123, 189–90; and scientific racism, 73–74. *See also* colonialism
New Orleans, 228, 230
New York: Cuban immigrants and exiles, in, 27, 28, 33; public health, 72
Nicaragua, 272, 276
North American Review (periodical), 213
Nueva Ecija province (Luzon), 39, 56, 58, 61–62, 218

Oakes, James C., 218
occupation, 3, 6, 9, 12; number of US troops for Cuba and Philippines, 287n13; as "reconstruction," 273
Olmstead, Frederick Law, 72
opium, 216; in China, 196; monopoly in Philippines, 216; in US mainland, 216
Order No. 155 (Leonard Wood), 226, 230, 231, 329n80
Orientalism, 63, 90, 97, 102, 140–41, 145, 157, 162, 170, 213–14
Oriente province (Cuba), 16, 110–11; Afro-Cubans in, 111; economy in, 111–12; infrastructural development's impact, 119–20, 128–29; roadbuilding and roads in, 109, 118–19; sex work and sexual economy, 238–41, 242; terrain and transportation, 110–11; US occupation of, 2, 32–34, 70–71
Osgood, Henry B., 117–18
Otis, Elwell S., austerity of, 81, 135; Chinese exclusion, 198–202; and Chinese labor, 206, 212, 216, 219; on common-law marriage, 256; General Orders 43 and 40, 138–39; on insurgency, 45; and interpreters and guides, 54–55; municipal government, 46–47; as Philippines' governor, 43–44; and roadbuilding, 142
"Otis order." *See* Chinese exclusion
Ottoman empire, 76, 154, 158

Pacific Mail Steamship Company, 193, 229
"pail conservancy system." *See* sanitation
Palma Soriano (Cuba), 79, 129
Palmer, John McAuley, 169, 274, 320n32
Panama Canal Zone, 9, 10, 79, 158, 176, 272, 315n75
Pangasinan dialect, 61
Pangasinan province (Luzon), 50, 56
Pardo de Tavera, Trinidad H., 44, 149, 201
Parker, James, 140–41, 261, 267, 292n29
Partido Federal (Philippines), 44, 44, 45, 61, 143, 149, 201, 226
Partido Independiente de Color (Cuba), 188, 232, 273
Partido Nacional Cubano, 126
Partido Nacional Progresista (Philippines), 149
Partido Regionalista Vueltabajero, (Pinar del Río, Cuba), 186–87
Partido Republicano Federal Democrático (Oriente, Cuba), 126
Partido Revolucionario Cubano, 5, 27, 116, 122, 174
Patajo, Crispulo, 56–57. *See also* Guardia de Honor
Paterno, Pedro, 143
Patrick, Mason M., 181–83

patronato system (Cuba), 90
Pershing, John J., 26, 154, 159–60, 172, 176, 260, 271, 272, 276, 318n16
Philippine-American War, 9, 39
Philippine Commission; *See* US Philippine Commission (First, Schurman); US Philippine Commission (Second, Taft)
Philippine Constabulary, 26, 273
Philippines: class and social divisions of, 14, 41, 44, 55–56, 85, 134; economy of, 130; Filipino elites, 11, 14, 39–40, 42, 55, 85, 132–33; folklore: 60, 253; food crisis in, 134–35; *indio* elite or *principalía*, 5, 14, 39, 130–31, 139; Katipunan revolt (1896), 14, 26; linguistic colonization, 36, 38; linguistic complexity, 36, 39–40, 43, 273–74; maps of, *8, 37, 52, 86, 155*; national identity, 14, 198; patronage and clientage, 55, 89, 143, 167; propaganda movement, 14, 132–33; under Spanish rule, 130–31. *See also* Cotabato region, Philippines; Ilocos region; Lanao region; Luzon; Mindanao; Samar
Philippines, government, 14; Chinese policy, 49, 200; constitution, 46; diplomacy, 142–3; forced labor, 312n50; internal tensions, 143; labor control, 132–33; organization, 132–33; *polo y servicio*, 133; revenue, 134; tax policy, 134, 216
Philippines, labor: complexity of, 80–81; migration to US mainland, 277; for War on Terror, 278. *See also* cargador (porter) system
Philippines, Liberation Army, 49; labor coercion, 53; requisitions, 134; retaliation of, 57–58; Tagalogs in, 53; veterans, 3
Philippines, US occupation (Luzon and Visayas, 1898–1902; Mindanao-Sulu, 1899–1913), 36, 39, 205; civilians, 254–59; municipal government, 46–47, *46*, 53, 138–39; schools, 40–41; US acquisition (1898–99), 5–6, 205. *See also* Manila; Moro Province
Philippine Scouts, 26, 169, 273, 275

Piang, Datu, 23–24, 85, 87–88, 89, 90, 91, 93, 94, 95–96, 99
pidgins. *See* language
Pierce, Charles C., 210
Pinar del Río province (Cuba), 178–79; demographics of, 182; elections (1908), 186; map, *180*; roadbuilding in, 179–81, 183–84, 186–90
Pinar del Rio (city), Cuba, 182, 266–67
Platt Amendment, 6, 77, 114, 173, 174, 175, 230, 271
polo y servicio, 82, 131–32, 137–42; Filipino opposition to, 133, 140, 149; persistence of, 150; Philippine Commission ban, 145, 147; and road tax in United States, 141, 314n67, 317n84. *See also* corvée (labor tax); forced labor; infrastructure
Pope, James Worden, 194, 203–4, 212, 225
porters. *See* cargador (porter) system
prácticos (Cuban guides). *See* guides in Cuba
principalía (Philippines), 39, 40, 130–31, 139
prisoners and convict labor, 13, 92, 111, 119, 141, 147, 148, 171, 316n82, 318n16
Progressive Era, 65–66
progressivism and progressives, 16, 65–66, 276; American, 70–71, 72, 73, 79, 92, 94, 98, 104, 114, 120–21, 137, 178, 244, 249; anti-partisan, 121, 178; "armed progressives," 70, 104; colonialism, 143–44; and conservation, 150, 176; economic growth, 120–21, 176–77, 189; foreign policy, 271; ideals, 34; "military sanitarians," 278; sexual regulation, 244, 249, 263, 265; social Darwinism, 244; social science, 79; urban reform, 69, 71–72; women, 236
Propaganda movement (Philippines), 14, 44, 132–33, 198, 256. *See also* nationalism
prostitution. *See* sex work and sexual economies
Provisional Government (Cuba). *See* US, Provisional Government
public health: "contagionist" concepts of disease, 69; and hygiene, 69–71;

in Manila, 77. *See also* sanitation; venereal disease (VD)
Puerto Rico, 6, 10, 272; immigration in, 228; roadbuilding in, 157–58; servicemen, 273, 276
Pulahan War (Samar, 1905–7), 100–101, 103, 104, 253, 274

queridas (common-law wives, Philippines), 256–61
Quezon, Manuel, 149

race and racism, 17–18; African Americans, 152, 159; African American troops, 161, 239, 260–61; Afro-Cubans, 26, 30, 68, 76–77, 182, 188, 240–41; cargador (porter) system, 101–3, *103*; against Chinese people, 194–95, 198–99, 226–27, 276–77; Chinese exclusion debate (1902), 226–27; and climatic theory of labor, 69–70, 158, 207; as colonial rationale, 63; Cubans, 75; and Filipino labor, 144–46; and forced labor, 65, 73–74, 77; and industrial rationality, 168–69; Moro labor, 157, 160; Native Americans, 156–57, 159; paternalism, 52, 68, 161; progressivism, 220; public health in Cuba, 71–72; scientific, 12, 73, 78–79; in sexual economy in Cuba, 238–39; in sexual economy in Philippines, 251, 254, 26–61; social Darwinism, 244; and stereotypes, 68, 78, 112; "yellow peril," 222–24
Rafael, Vicente, 38
Ramsden, Henry A., 45, 47
rations and rationing. *See* forced labor
Reade, Philip, 98, 99, *100*
reconcentratión policies, 70, 112, 178–79, 238
Red Cross: American, 74, 112; Philippine, 253
Remates (Cuba), 185–86, *187*
Riego de Dios, Emiliano, 247
rinderpest, 135, 163, 164
Rio Grande de Mindanao (Pulangi) River, 23–24, 84
Rivero, Jose, 140
Rizal, José, 5, 204

roadbuilding and public works: in Cuba, 109–10, *116*, 118–21, 126–29, 176–90, *185*; economic impact of in Cuba, 171; economic impact of in Philippines, 149–50, 171; "Good Roads" in United States, 109, 141, 276; military-colonial, 17; in Philippines, 131–32, *133*, 136, 137–38, 139–51, 152–53, 156, 157–58, 159–72
Rodney, George, 253
Roosevelt, Franklin D., 277
Roosevelt, Theodore, 113; corollary, Monroe Doctrine, 272; and declaration of victory in Philippines, 9; intervention in Cuba in 1906, 175–76; issues GO 101 (1901), 263; and labor policy, 183; as progressive, 263; and Rough Riders, 30–32, 70; and Wood, 125, 126
Root, Elihu, 10, 35, 89, 126, 231, 250, 263–65
Roque, Roman, 61–62
Rough Riders, 30–32, 70. *See also* US Army, Cavalry, 1st Volunteers; Roosevelt, Theodore; Wood, Leonard
Rural Guards (Cuba), 34, 267, 273

Sailors' Union of the Pacific (SUP), 193
Saleeby, Najeeb, 88, 92
Salman, Michael, 93
Samar island (Philippines), 3, 15; Waller expedition (1901), 63–65. *See also* Pulahan War
Samoa, 272
Sandico, Teodoro, 44–45, 62, 133, 293n42
Sandino, Augusto, 276
San Isidro (Luzon), 39, 61
sanitation: in Cuba, 68–74, 75–76, 113–14; in Philippines, 77, 88; as war, 73, 77. *See also* public health
San Juan Hill (Cuba), battle of, 30, 32, 33
San Juan y Martínez (Cuba), 184, 188
San Luis (Cuba): antimonopoly roadbuilding in, 119; Maceo's family, domestic labor, 240; protest against forced labor at, 119
Santa Clara province (Cuba): roads for sugar industry, 175; sexual economy in, 242, 243, 244

Santa Cruz de la Sur Assembly (Cuba), 33, 117
Santiago, Cuba, 2, 68, 116–17; elections in, 121, 122, 123; health codes in, 75–76; infrastructural reform in, 113–16, *116*; map of, *29*; occupation of, 28; sanitation in, 69–72, 76–77; sexual economy of, 239, 241, 242
Santo Domingo. *See* Dominican Republic
Sargent, Herbert, 241
Savage-Landor, Arnold Henry, 91
Sawtelle, Charles G., Jr., 207, 212, 216
schools. *See* education
Schurman, Jacob, 44, 142–43, 205, 224, 250, 293n42, 315n69. *See also* US Philippine Commission (First)
science, 16–17, 66, 77, 81, 92, 163, 247, 271. *See also* capitalism; disease; efficiency; labor; progressivism; race and racism
"scientific charity." *See* forced labor
"scientific management": military-colonial, 67, 70–71. *See also* efficiency; Taylor, Frederick Winslow
"scientific way of war," 67. *See also* efficiency
Scott, Hugh Lenox, 1–2, 10, 12, 26, 243–44, 276
Seaman, Gilbert, 254
Seaman, Louis Livingston, 213–14, 226
Segovia, Lazaro, 61
self-rule, 76–78, 80, 121, 126, 133, 273, 277
sexually-transmitted disease. *See* venereal disease (VD)
sexual violence: in Cuba, 238–39, 266; in Philippines, 250–53, 268
sex work and sexual economy: 18, 235–37; prostitution, attitudes toward, 236; terminology, 289n28; *See also* British Contagious Disease Acts; venereal disease
sex work and sexual economy in Cuba: Afro-Cuban women, 240–41; clandestine, 242–43, 266; Cuban officials, 243–44; demography of, 242; *lavenderas*, 254–55; and Pinar del Río, 266–67; prohibitions, 241; regulations and focus on women, 237–38, 244–45; sexual chaos in Cuba, 238–39; sex work vs. domestic work, 239–41, 242; spatial regulation, 238, 239, 242, 266; "Special Hygiene" rules, 237–38, 241–45, 266; unrest at Cienfuegos, 233–35, 243, 268; US enlisted men, 244–45, 266; women's labor, 239–41
sex work and sexual economy in Philippines: clandestine, 248–49; demography, 245–46, 28–49; Filipino officials, 247, 251–52; *lavenderas*, 253–56; legal manipulation of, 252; politics of, 263–64; prohibitions, 248; "Public Hygiene" rules, 246–47; *queridas* (common-law wives), 256–61; and race and racism, 261; regulation and focus on women, 244–45, 247, 248–50; repression of, 264; sexual chaos, 247–48; "social purity" reformers, 249–50, 263, 264, 265; spatial regulation of, 249; *tenderas*, 253–54, 255; US enlisted men, 261–63, 264, 265–66; women's labor, 245–46
Shafter, William, 28, 30, 31, 33, 68–70, 109, 238–39, 247; and interpreter, 32; occupation of Santiago, 68
Sibert, William I., 218
Siboney (Cuba): Cuba operations, intermediaries, at, 31, 32
Sinophobia, 195, 198, 226–27, 276–77. *See also* Chinese exclusion; race and racism
Sitangkai island (Sulu Archipelago), 77
slavery, 12; abolition of in Cuba, 227; in Cuba, 5, 68, 75, 76, 123, 227; debt bondage, 89–91, 92–93; debt bondage vs. chattel slavery, 90, 154; Filipinos invoke, 140; gradual emancipation from, 89–90; in Haiti, 30; and military-colonial labor, 12–13; in Moro, 83–84; nostalgia for, 68; in Philippines, 2, 84, 89–91, 100, 140, 158–59; post-slavery labor markets, 75; runaway slaves in Philippines, 158–59; transitional indenture systems, 90; in United States, 5, 66, 239, 240
Smith, Jacob Hurd, 63, 64, 65
Smith, James F., 41, 202–3, 224

Sobrado, Indalecio, 184–85, 187
social Darwinism, 112, 226, 244, 250. *See also* science
social evolution, 78–79. *See also* social Darwinism
"social reproduction," 235. *See also* gender ideology and hierarchies; sex work and sexual economy
"social sovereignty." *See* sovereignty
sovereignty: in Cuba, 173, 187, 190; divided, 153; empire and military power, 6, 9; as negotiated state, 15; in Philippines, 163–64; "popular sovereignty," 4; social dimensions of, 14–15; "social sovereignty," 13; "subaltern sovereignty," 13; "subcontracted sovereignty," 17, 153, 317n3; "territorial sovereignty," 4; theories of, 13–14, 288n22
Spain: anticolonial revolutions against, 5; cession of Philippines (1898), 5–6; in Cotabato region, 87–88; *gallego* emigrants to Cuba, 75, 232; migrant work in Cuba, 79; Spaniards in Philippines, 48, 61, 90; Spanish army engineers' use of convicts, 147; trade policies, 11
Spanish language. *See* language
Spanish-American War, 9–10, 27–33
"Special Hygiene." *See* sex work and sexual economy
Steere, Joseph B., 43, 45
Steward, Theophilus G., 261
Strong, William, 72
"subaltern sovereignty." *See* sovereignty
"subaltern standpoint," 12
"subcontracted sovereignty." *See* sovereignty
sugar industry, 128, 231; enslaved and indentured labor, 5; plantations, 111–12
Sulu Archipelago (Philippines), 83–84; map of, 86
Sumner, Samuel S., 162, 164–65

Taft, William H.: and ban of Black soldiers from Philippines, 261, 336n61; on Chinese vs. Filipino labor, 225–26; on common-law marriages with Filipinas, 260; and Philippine Commission, 40, 91, 219–20; and prostitution regulation, 250; on public works in Cuba, 188; and roadbuilding in Philippines, 141–42, 143–44; on road tax in United States, 315n67; as Secretary of War, 175; US-Filipino relations, 55–56; as US president, 272; on US sovereignty in Philippines, 89
Taglaog language and dialects, 40, 42–46, 61
Tañgadan Pass, battle of, 53.
Taylor, Frederick Winslow, 67
Taylorism, 66, 67, 73, 220
Telfer, George, 218
Teller Amendment (1898), 5, 27
temperance movement, 250. *See also* alcohol
Ten Years' War, 5, 25, 111, 122, 123, 174, 237
Thayer, Arthur, 257
Thomas, Earl D., 267
"Thomasites," 41–42. *See also* education
Tinio, Manuel, 53, 55–56, 57–58, 296n63
tobacco industry: cigar workers' strike, 181, 183; Cuban Land and Leaf Tobacco Company, 185–86; in Pinar del Río province, 178, 179
Todd, Albert, 41
Toral, José, 33
Torres, Tomas (Filipino guide), 49–50
Torres, Tomas (Spaniard), 24
torture: General Order 100, 51, 58; prohibition of, 59
Trafton, William Oliver, 59–60
translation. *See* interpreters and translators
Trías, Mariano, 46, 49, 143, 293n42
Triscornia immigration station (Havana), 229
trust and distrust: forged correspondence, 61. *See also* intermediaries, military-colonial
Turner, Frederick Jackson, 120

United States: acquisition of Philippines (1898), 5–6, 205; Cuban migration to, 27; and empire, 6; frontier myths, 81–82;

United States (cont.)
  industrialization of, 27, 67; military interventions, 272–73
US Army: African American troops, 161, 239, 260–61; courts in Philippines, 42; history of, 10; Civil War-era doctrine of "military necessity," 51; discipline and behavior in, 250–53; language training in, 274; Division of Military Information, Manila, 274; enlisted men as "subalterns," 18; Filipino intelligence assets, 44, 50; "immune" regiments, 69–71, 239; progressive reform, 1, 10, 16–17, 63, 66, 273, 276; and regulation of sex, 237, 239, 241–45, 276–77; sanitation, 68
US Army cavalry: 31–32, 50, 51, 159, 182, 208, 259; First Volunteer ("Rough Riders"), 70, 109; Philippine Scouts, 57, 98, 101, 169, 273
US Army corps and divisions: Fifth Corps, 28–30, 68, 69–70, 109, 238–39; Eighth Corps, First Division, 39, 45, 46, 47, 49, 81–82, 135–37, 209–11, 212, 217–18; and Second Division, 207–8
US Army Corps of Engineers, 17, 89, 113, 213; and economic development in United States, 67, 276; map surveys of Cuba, 35, 274; map surveys of Philippines, 49; and Panama Canal, 272, 315n75; public works in Cuba, 113, 126, 127, 177, 179–83, 183–84, 187–89; public works in Philippines, 89, 141, 144, 145–47, 150, 157, 161, 217–19; sanitation, 72
US Army infantry, regular: Ninth, 3; Sixteenth, 255; Twenty-Third, 23, 99, 100; Twenty-Fifth, 261; Twenty-Eighth, 162, 165
US Army infantry volunteers, 39; Third Alabama, 161; Eighth Illinois, 78; Thirty-Ninth US, 161
US Army quartermasters: in Cuba, 33, 109, 114, 233–34; in Philippines, 38, 81, 132, 136, 204, 206, 207, 209, 210, 212, 220–25, 276
US Army Signal Corps, 144
US Army Transport Service, 221, 223
US Army Utah Artillery, 38

US Bureau of Labor, 79, 144
US Congress: anti-monopoly, 94, 231; army legislation, 273, 274; ban on franchises in Cuba (Foraker Act), 11, 113; Chinese exclusion, 195, 198–99, 200, 226, 231; delegations in Cuba, 76; funds bounties for Cuban soldiers, 118; funds roadbuilding in Cuba, 177; Teller Amendment, funds war with Spain, 5; investigation of wars, 10, 250; opium laws, 216; organic laws, island territories, 6; Platt Amendment, 6; Philippines' independence, 277; prostitution, 263; sugar treaty with Cuba, 231. *See also* Beveridge, Albert
US Constitution: Bill of Rights, 76, 125; Thirteenth Amendment, 84
US, Interior, Department of, Indian Bureau, 10
US Marine Corps, 3, 63–65, 272, 274, 275–76, 277, 287n13
US Military Academy, West Point, New York, 1, 51, 67, 292n29
US Military government (Cuba, 1899–1902), 9; immigration policy, 229; installed, 120; organization of, 120–21; prostitution regulation, 241–42; public works spending, 126–27; roadbuilding record of, 175, 190; veterans of, 177
US Navy, 63, 65, 112, 193, 222, 247, 272, 276–77, 287n13
US Philippine Commission (First), 44; anti-Chinese attitudes, 205, 224; on English learning, 293n42; prohibition, 250; roadbuilding and public works, 142–43, 312n46; reform promises, 46, 142
US Philippine Commission (Second): authority of, 141; and ban of corvée, 101, 142; delegation of local authority, 146; Public Works, Bureau of, 146, 149, 150, 151; Education, Bureau of, 41; educational and language policies of, 40, 41–42; and Filipino wage labor, 219, 222, 225–26; governance of non-Christians, 150; funds for army translators, 62; and Moro Province organization, 91, 169; and

Mountain Province organization, 51; provincial organization, 91; public works and roadbuilding, 142, 143–44, 147–49, 172; reformist rhetoric, 140; road tax laws, 316n79; US sovereignty, support for, 143; war crimes of, 62. *See* Taft, William H.

US Provisional Government (Cuba, 1906–9), 9; organization of, 175–76; Public Works, Bureau of, 176, 179; roadbuilding and public works, 172–73, 179–81, 188–89. *See also* Magoon, Charles E.; Roosevelt, Theodore; Taft, William H.

US State, Department, 199, 200, 206

US Treasury, Department of, 193, 223

U.S War, Department: anti-contract labor policy (Cuba, 1899), 229; and Circular No. 13 (1899), 228; Insular Affairs, Bureau of/Division of Customs, 159, 228, 264; Military Information Division (MID), 27; reform, 10, 67

Uto, Datu, 87

vagrancy laws and forced labor, 75, 146, 171, 246, 264, 303n66

Van Horne, William C., 127

venereal disease (VD), 237, 238, 241–43; infection rates in Philippines, 246–48, 265, 277; in military, 265–66, 277–78; prevention and reduction efforts, 245, 261–66; resistance to anti-venereal efforts, 262–63

Vigan (Luzon), 53, 55, 140

Villa, Pancho, 272–73

Villalón, José Ramón, 127

Villamor, Blas, 53

Villamor, Juan, 53, 57–58

Viñales (Cuba), 181

Viñales Road (Cuba), 181–83

violence, sexual. *See* sexual violence

Visayan archipelago, 3

Visayan language, 40

vocational education. *See* "education, industrial"

wage labor. *See* labor

Wagner, Arthur, 26, 32

Waller, Littleton W. T., 101, 102; "Waller expedition" (Samar), 63–65, 80, 81

Waring, George E., Jr., 72–73

"War on Terror," US, 278–79

Washington, Booker T., 219

welfare and government aid, 112–13. *See also* scientific charity; forced labor

Wells, Harry L., 214, 215

West Point Military Academy. *See* US Military Academy, West Point, New York

Weyler, Valeriano, 70, 156, 178

Wheeler, Joseph, 31, 33, 109

"White Man's burden," 1, 63. *See also* Kipling, Rudyard; race and racism

Williams, Alexander, 64, 65

Williams, Charles A., 104, 141–42

Williams, Herbert P., 34

Williams, Oscar F., 224

Wilson, Andrew, 199

Wilson, James, 234, 243

Wilson, Richard, 28–30

Wilson, Woodrow, 146, 272–73

Wise, Hugh D., 101–4, 25

Wood, Leonard, 33–35, 124; on army linguists, 274; Bill of Rights, 76; and Brooke, 120–26; and brothels and sanitation, 239; cargador policy, 93–96, 101–2; Chinese exclusion, 226–27, 230–32; and Cuban governor, 126–27; "developmentalist fantasy," for Mindanao and Oriente, 93–94, 120; economic regulation in Cuba, 76; on Indian Scouts, 26; infrastructural reform, 113, 114–15, 127–28; interpreters, 32–33; labor policy as counterinsurgency, 93–95, 118–19; labor policy disrupts counterinsurgency, 95–96; language policy in Cuba, 33–35; Liberation Army's dissolution, 118–19; Moro Province, governor of, 77, 92–93, 171; on Moro wage labor, 158; Order No. 155 (Cuba), 230, 231; Oriente food monopoly, 74, 117; as progressive, 94; public health in Cuba, 70–72; public works and policy reform, 120–25, 170; public works,

Wood (cont.)
  political economy of, 114, 115; public works scheme with Cuban elite, 121–23, 309n30; and Rural Guard organization, 34; sanitation efforts in Cuba, 112; sanitation efforts in Santiago, 73–75; and Santiago occupation, 70–77, 112; Santiago and Oriente, governor of, 79–80; scientific racism, theories of, 79–80; strikes in Cuba, 75; sex work, regulation of in Santiago, 239
Worcester, Dean, 43, 45, 46–47, 47, 143, 293n39
working class. *See* labor
World War I, 271–73, 277, 278

World War II, 277
Wright, Irene, 189
Wu Tingfang, 200–201

yellow fever, 68, 69, 71, 114. *See also* public health; sanitation
Young, Samuel B. M., 31, 50, 51, 53–56, 58–59, 61, 139–40

Zambales province (Luzon), 56, 254, 261
Zamboanga (Mindanao), 77, 88, 92, 94, 96, 156, 159, 260
Zapote Bridge, battle of, 49–50
Zayas, Alfredo de, 186, 187–88
Zongli Yamen, 205. *See also* Chinese exclusion